THE OFFICIAL®

2015 BLACKBOOK PRICE GUIDE TO UNITED STATES POSTAGE STAMPS

THE OFFICIAL®

2015 BLACKBOOK PRICE GUIDE TO UNITED STATES POSTAGE STAMPS

THIRTY-SEVENTH EDITION

BY MARC HUDGEONS, N.L.G., TOM HUDGEONS JR., AND TOM HUDGEONS SR.

HOUSE OF COLLECTIBLES
Random House Reference • New York

Copyright © 2014 by Random House LLC

All rights reserved. Published in the United States by House of Collectibles, an imprint of Random House LLC, New York, a Penguin Random House Company, and in Canada by Random House of Canada Limited, Toronto.

House of Collectibles and colophon are registered trademarks of Random House LLC

RANDOM HOUSE is a registered trademark of Random House LLC.

Please address inquiries about electronic licensing of any products for use on a network, in software, or on CD-ROM to the Subsidiary Rights Department, Random House Audio Publishing Group, fax 212-572-6003.

This book is available for special discounts for bulk purchases for sales promotions or premiums. Special editions, including personalized covers, excerpts of existing books, and corporate imprints, can be created in large quantities for special needs. For more information, write to Random House LLC, Special Markets/Premium Sales, 1745 Broadway, MD 3-1, New York, NY 10019 or e-mail specialmarkets@randomhouse.com.

Visit the Random House Web site:
www.randomhouse.com

ISBN: 978-0-375-72362-9

ISSN: 0195-3559

Printed in the United States of America

10 9 8 7 6 5 4 3 2 1

Thirty-Seventh Edition: June 2014

TABLE OF CONTENTS

OFFICIAL BOARD OF CONTRIBUTORS

We would like to thank the following contributors for sharing their professional expertise and experiences in the field of United States Stamp collecting with our readers.

Jessica Armstrong of Mystic Stamp Company, Camden, NY for providing the color photographs of General Issue stamps.

George Amick of **Linn's Stamp News in** Sidney, OH for his article "Linn's Look at New Stamp Issues." George is a longtime freelance contributor to *Linn's Stamp News* who writes *Linn's United States Stamps Yearbook* each year. *Linn's Stamp News* is the world's largest newspaper devoted to stamp collecting.

Scott Barman for his article "Using Technology to Enhance Your Collecting Experience." Scott is a collector and author of the Coin Collectors Blog (coinsblog.ws). He is also President of the Montgomery County Coin Club (montgomerycoinclub .org) and President of the Maryland State Numismatic Society (mdstatenumisassn.org). After more than 30 years in the computer and information security industry, Scott recently started Having-Fun Collectibles to serve collectors in more than just numismatics because collecting should be fun.

Alex Bereson at the United Nations Philatelists, San Francisco, CA for his pricing information.

Lloyd de Vries, President of **The American First Day Cover Society (AFDCS)** in Tucson, AZ for information on the AFDCS as well as United States chapter listings.

Bob Dumaine, founder of the National Duck Stamp Collectors Society for his articles "Federal Duck Stamps" and "Federal Migratory Bird Hunting Stamps" including pricing information. Bob is the owner of Sam Houston Philatelics and Sam Houston Duck Company in Houston, TX. Dumaine is co-author of *The Duck Stamp Story,* which has been widely praised as the most complete work on the history of the duck stamp program, and the stamps themselves. *The Specialized Duck Stamp Catalogue,* published by Sam Houston Duck Company, has been praised for setting the industry standard for duck stamp information and prices, and has won many awards. Bob wrote a monthly duck stamp column in Linn's Stamp News for over fourteen years, and has been published in many other art and philatelic journals. He assists the National Postal Museum, Smithsonian Institution, in research and preparation of material for their duck stamp gallery. In 2012, Bob was added to the American Stamp Dealers Association Hall of Fame.

Marshall F. (Marty) Emery, Manager Public Relations & Internet Affairs, **Smithsonian Institution,** for the section entitled "National Postal Museum."

Judy Johnson, Membership Administration Manager of **The American Philatelic Society,** Bellefonte, PA for their directory listings.

Michael Schreiber and Donna Houseman at Linn's Stamp News in Sidney, OH for their article.

Kelly L. Spinks at the United States Postal Service, Washington, DC for permission to reproduce the photography of U.S. stamps. *The designs for the stamps issued from 1978 to date are copyrighted by The U.S. Postal Service and are used with the permission of the U.S. Postal Service.*

Donald Sundman, President of **Mystic Stamp Company**, Camden, NY for his article "2012 Market Review." In addition to heading America's Leading Stamp Dealer, Donald serves on the Philatelic Foundation's Board of Trustees and is actively involved with the American Philatelic Society. Sundman serves as Chairman of the National Postal Museum's Council of Philatelists and co-sponsors its Maynard Sundman Philatelic Lecture series. Sundman has also created the "Shaping the Future of Philately" commission, which has created several initiatives to promote the hobby and increase the number of collectors.

2015
BLACKBOOK
PRICE GUIDE TO
UNITED STATES
POSTAGE
STAMPS

LINN'S LOOK AT THE NEW STAMP ISSUES

by George Amick

In 2013, the United States Postal Service issued 158 varieties of stamps and postal stationery that qualified for listings in the Scott catalogs, 30 fewer than were issued the year before. The cost of collecting one of each also was lower: $103.79 this year, compared to $140.18 in 2012.

As usual, the largest category was commemoratives, with 73. There were 63 definitives, many of them denominated to reflect new mail rates that took effect last Jan. 27, and 16 special stamps. The commemoratives and specials were forever stamps, with one exception.

The exception was also the year's most unusual issue: a pane of six stamps reproducing philately's most famous printing error, the 24¢ airmail stamp of 1918 with a blue Jenny biplane flying upside down in a red frame. The stamps were printed by intaglio using the 95-year-old original dies, but their denomination was changed to $2.

After the stamps went on sale, the USPS revealed it had created a mini-lottery by randomly planting 100 panes with the planes flying right side up among the 2.2 million normal panes. To prevent cherry-picking, the panes are sold in shrink-wrapped packages that conceal the contents, and only intact packages can be returned.

The Scott catalog editors noted the existence of the manufactured rarity in a footnote but didn't assign it a number because of the company's policy against listing varieties that are intentionally created in small quantities. For the same reason, *Linn's* isn't including the "inverted invert" as a collectible variety in its annual count.

The Postal Service surprised collectors—not to mention the first-day cover industry—by waiting until very late to disclose details of its largest multiple issue of the year. This was a five-panel booklet of 20 different commemoratives depicting stills from the Warner Brothers films that were based on the Harry Potter novels by Great Britain's J.K. Rowling.

Plans for a Harry Potter issue were first reported in May, but officials waited until less than a week before the Nov. 19 issue date to disclose the number of varieties, the fact that they would be the first-ever U.S. stamps to clearly and intentionally show photographs of living people, and other essential facts.

The agency doubled down on a practice it introduced last year of offering selected commemoratives and special stamps in uncut press sheets with a choice of sheets that were die-cut or imperforate. In 2013, the offer was extended to all new commemoratives, most of the special stamps, and a few definitives.

The Scott catalog took note of the press sheets and imperforate stamps and assigned values to various position blocks and pairs. Again, however, because the imperfs were created in limited numbers for sale to collectors, they weren't given separate catalog listings and aren't included in *Linn's* tally of collectible varieties.

An innovation this year was the global forever stamp, which always will be valid for an amount equal to the prevailing 1-ounce letter rate to foreign addresses. Two were issued, both circular in shape—the stamp will "always be round," the USPS explained—and sold for this year's $1.10 rate.

The first example, a definitive, bears a computer-generated image of Earth, while the second, created for Christmas holiday mailings, depicts an evergreen wreath.

The debut of global forever stamps was accompanied by the introduction of a uniform rate for 1-ounce letters to any country in the world, including Canada and Mexico, which for decades had been carried for a lower rate. These changes made international airmail stamps unnecessary and led to the demise of the popular Scenic Landscape series of pictorial airmail stamps, which ran from 1999 to 2012 and comprised 18 major varieties.

Except for the late-blooming Harry Potter stamps, the USPS depicted only real people on its 2013 commemoratives, in contrast to its frequent practice in recent years of featuring fictitious characters from films and comic strips. The Harry Potter issue also is one of several examples this year of multiple varieties on a single pane.

Another example is the Made in America set, which reproduces 12 black-and-white photographs depicting early 20th century industrial workers. The USPS produced the pane in five different versions, each with a different selvage photograph. Modern Art in America 1913–1931, another 12-stamp pane, celebrates the centennial of the opening of the Armory Show, a modern art exhibition in New York City. The artists represented on the pane include Stuart Davis, Georgia O'Keeffe, Man Ray and Marcel Duchamp, all of whom previously were showcased on U.S. stamps.

Ten forever definitives depicting photographs of flower seed packets from 1910 to 1920 were issued in a convertible booklet of 20. Five Lighthouses stamps with artwork by Howard Koslow, the sixth such set since 1990, depict structures in the five New England states that touch the Atlantic.

Another five stamps feature muscle cars—a Dodge Charger, a Pontiac GTO, a Ford Mustang, a Chevrolet Chevelle and a Plymouth Hemi—as part of the America on the Move series that earlier had included five sporty cars of the 1950s in 2005, and five fins-and-chrome cars of the 1950s in 2008. So strong was the demand for the new stamps that the Postal Service ordered a rare two additional print runs.

Four stamps with designs that combine to create one continuous floral pattern celebrate the 500th anniversary of the first Spanish expedition to the peninsula that explorer Juan Ponce de Leon named "La Florida." The plants are hibiscus, cannas, morning glories, and passion flowers.

The Medal of Honor: World War II issue consists of two varieties depicting the Medal of Honor for the Army and its equivalent for the Navy. These stamps are sold in a folded pane of 20 that the Postal Service calls a "prestige folio." Two stamps are on what serves as the front cover of the folder, with 18 on the reverse. Inside are the names of the 464 U.S. service personnel who received the medal for actions in WWII, as well as photos of 12 of the last living recipients. However, four of those pictured died before the stamps were issued: Sen. Daniel K. Inouye, Vernon McGarity, Nicholas Oresko, and John D. Hawk. Hawk died Nov. 4, one week before the Veterans Day first-day ceremony.

The Music Icons series made its debut with single stamps honoring Tejano musician Lydia Mendoza, country star Johnny Cash, and pianist-singer-songwriter Ray Charles. The stamps and stamp panes of 16 are designed to look like the sleeves of 45 rpm records, and post office clerks were instructed to sell the stamps only in full panes.

The new series recalls the earlier Legends of American Music, which comprises 93 varieties and 80 designs in 14 musical categories issued between 1993 and 1999.

Civil rights for African Americans is the subject of three single commemoratives. The first was issued Jan. 1, a federal holiday, to mark the sesquicentennial of President Abraham Lincoln's Emancipation Proclamation in the midst of the Civil War. In February, the USPS noted the 100th birth anniversary of Rosa Parks, who was a Montgomery, Ala., seamstress when her arrest in 1955 for refusing to give her seat on a bus to a white man sparked a citywide bus boycott led by the Rev. Martin Luther King Jr. Parks had been considered a sure bet for stamp honors since her death in 2005.

A stamp in August with an illustration of sign-carrying marchers celebrated the 50th anniversary of the March on Washington for Jobs and Freedom, at which King delivered his famous "I Have a Dream" speech.

Ongoing series that were augmented in 2013 were Black Heritage, honoring tennis star Althea Gibson; the Civil War sesquicentennial, with two varieties marking the Battle of Gettysburg and the Battle of Vicksburg on a double-sided pane of 12; the 200th anniversary of the War of 1812, reproducing an 1873 painting of the Battle of Lake Erie; and Lunar New Year, observing the Year of the Snake. Another single commemorative marked the 150th anniversary of West Virginia statehood.

Among the definitives, the traditional American Flag design was represented by a block of four forever stamps depicting Old Glory in each of the four seasons and produced by three printers in coils of 100 and convertible booklets of 10 and 20. To cover the 1-ounce first-class rate, the USPS also issued denominated 46¢ stamps, primarily for use by business mailers, that depict a stylized patriotic star in a coil of 10,000, and four flowers resembling kaleidoscope images in coils of 3,000 and 10,000.

The third stamp in the Postal Service's Butterfly definitive series bears a 66¢ denomination and shows a computer illustration of a spicebush swallowtail butterfly. The square stamps in the series cover the special rate for nonmachinable (square or odd-shaped) envelopes, which this year was also the rate for 2-ounce first-class letters.

A pair of tufted puffins appear on an 86¢ definitive for the 3-ounce first-class rate. Later in the year, a change in ink colors on the stamp created a separate collectible variety.

Four different 33¢ stamps for the postcard rate, each picturing a different variety of apple, were produced in panes and coils of 100.

A $5.60 stamp for Priority Mail shows the Arlington Green covered bridge in Vermont, while a $19.95 stamp for Express Mail, now officially known as Priority Mail Express, depicts New York City's 100-year-old Grand Central Terminal. The latter set a new high mark for face value on a regular-mail stamp, something that happens each time a stamp is issued to accompany a new rate for this next-day service.

A strip of five nondenominated coil stamps depicting magnified photos of snowflakes was made for use by bulk mailers. The photos were created by scientist Kenneth G. Libbrecht, who also had made the photos for the four 39¢ Holiday Snowflakes stamps of 2006. The year's only stamp with moisture-activated gum is a 1¢ coil stamp displaying the same Bobcat design that appeared on a self-adhesive coil stamp the year before.

Among the 2013 special stamps, a forever Love stamp shows a heart embossed in sealing wax affixed to the back of an envelope. Stylized bouquets are depicted on companion stamps, a forever stamp that the USPS dubbed "Where Dreams Blossom" and a 66¢ 2-ounce-rate stamp that bears the words "Yes" and "I Do" embedded in the design, the primary purpose of which was to send wedding invitations accompanied by stamped return envelopes. An additional 66¢ stamp for wedding invitations bears the familiar wedding cake image that previously appeared on stamps in 2009, 2011, and 2012.

The year also saw new stamps for the holidays of Eid, Hanukkah, and Kwanzaa. The calligraphic design of the new Eid Greetings stamp is nearly identical to that of the 2011 version, but with a green instead of red background; the Hanukkah stamp features a photo of glowing candles on a forged-iron menorah, and the Kwanzaa stamp shows a stylized man, woman, and child dressed in African-inspired clothing. The traditional Christmas stamp reproduces the Virgin and Child from a 1531 oil painting by Flemish artist Jan Gossaert, in a design format that the USPS has used for these stamps since 1986.

The year saw only six postal stationery items: a forever postal card and double-reply card depicting a golden deer; two forever stamped envelopes that feature the image of a bank swallow in different sizes; an envelope showing an eagle, shield, and two American flags from a folk art plaque; and a

Priority Mail envelope with a stamped imprint reproducing the $5.60 Arlington Green Bridge self-adhesive stamp. For the first time since 1991, no picture postal cards were issued.

The USPS took a long step toward ending its use of Official stamps by announcing that it no longer would sell them and that federal offices could continue to use their existing supplies until they were exhausted. Modern Official stamps were issued between 1983 and 2009.

The total number of stamp varieties in 2013 would have been larger by 15 if the USPS had followed through on plans to issue a pane of "Just Move" social-awareness commemoratives urging children to become more active. The entire press run of the stamps was slated for possible shredding after the President's Council on Fitness, Sports and Nutrition objected to three designs that show children doing recreational stunts the council members considered unsafe.

Several other previously announced issues for 2013 also were postponed, including a Legends of Hollywood stamp honoring actress Ingrid Bergman, a set of five depicting writers of science fiction, a set of ten 2-ounce-rate stamps celebrating the art of basketmakers of the late 19th and early 20th centuries, and a 20¢ extra-ounce-rate stamp showing a hummingbird.

SCOTT
NATIONAL
ALBUM SERIES

The National series offers a panoramic view of our country's heritage through postage stamps. It is the most complete and comprehensive U.S. album series you can buy. There are spaces for every major U.S. stamp listed in the Scott Catalogue, including Special Printings, Newspaper stamps and more.

- Pages printed on one side.
- All spaces identified by Scott numbers.
- All major variety of stamps are either illustrated or described.
- Chemically neutral paper protects stamps.

Item			Retail	AA*
100NTL1	1845-1934	108 Pgs.	$64.99	$51.99
100NTL2	1935-1976	108 Pgs.	$64.99	$51.99
100NTL3	1977-1993	114 Pgs.	$64.99	$51.99
100NTL4	1994-1999	96 Pgs.	$64.99	$51.99
100NTL5	2000-2005	126 Pgs.	$64.99	$51.99
100NTL6	2006-2009	84 Pgs.	$55.00	$43.99
100S010	2010	14 Pgs.	$14.99	$11.99
100S011	2011	17 Pgs.	$15.99	$12.99

Binders, labels and slipcases sold separately.

For ordering information call 1-800-572-6885
Shop online at www.amosadvantage.com

*AA prices apply to paid subscribers to Amos Hobby titles, or orders placed online.

2014 MARKET REVIEW

by Donald J. Sundman

The market for classic U.S. stamps remained strong in 2013, continuing a trend we've seen for quite some time. Demand for rarities, graded stamps, and quality items was especially high as reflected in the prices realized at several auctions. Essays, proofs, and historic covers in premium condition also sold for prices well in excess of their catalog values. Even some common classic stamps are becoming more difficult to buy in quantity as many are locked in permanent collections.

This suggests "Baby Boomers" have returned to stamp collecting and are eager to use their disposable income to build outstanding collections. It also signals the continued good financial health of our hobby.

Also continuing was strong demand for all Asian stamps. Stamp collecting is enormously popular in Asia–it's estimated that two-thirds of all stamp collectors are from the Far East. China is one of the most active stamp-collecting nations. The hobby was banned under Mao until 1976. Today, affluent Chinese are eager to buy back their national heritage in the form of postage stamps.

Several rare items made headlines in 2013. In June, the legendary Dawson Hawaii Missionary cover sold for $2.24 million, placing it in seventh place in the list of record auction prices. An unused China 1897 Red Revenue stamp (Scott #83) with $1-on-3¢ surcharge was auctioned for $890,000 in Hong Kong. Earlier in the year, an 1868 Canada 2¢ green Large Queen stamp was found, bringing the total known to just three examples. And the collecting world was surprised to learn that two of the 1869 Pictorial inverts, stolen from the Benjamin K. Miller collection in 1977, had been recovered.

In September, the National Postal Museum celebrated the grand opening of the William H. Gross Stamp Gallery. The 12,000-square-foot area showcases more than 20,000 postal artifacts cleverly displayed in pullout frames for a fun and educational visit. Interactive exhibits let visitors discover the untold stories of rare stamps that have never before been on public display. The gallery is destined to become a mecca for stamp collectors from around the world, and I urge you to visit at your first opportunity.

The U.S. Postal Service generated a lot of buzz for collectors again in 2013. A souvenir sheet of six $2 stamps picturing the Jenny Invert was issued in September. Released to coincide with the opening of the Gross Stamp Gallery, the commemorative stamps were printed using the same plates used to create the original 1918 stamps. The choice of the stamp subject was appropriate, as William Gross owns four of the six known blocks of four Jenny Inverts and has loaned one of them to the National Postal Museum.

Without explaining their reasoning, the U.S.P.S. sold the 2013 Jenny Inverts to customers in sealed packaging that hid the stamp sheet. Shortly after the First Day of Issue ceremony, it was learned 100 sheets of the new Jenny Invert stamps were purposely created with the "Upside-Down Plane" flying right-side up. The sheets were distributed randomly, with the packaging disguising the sheets, apparently to build interest by recreating the thrill of the original Jenny Invert discovery. Almost immediately, offers to buy the "Unvert" sheet appeared in the philatelic media. It will be interesting to see how many of the 100 sheets reach collectors' hands, and what prices are paid for these modern rarities.

Late in the year, the U.S.P.S. confirmed rumors of a commemorative issue honoring Harry Potter. Many praised the set of 20 stamps as a positive move that would encourage youngsters to collect. Others listed a number of faults, which included the depiction of a living person, the lack of an American subject, a confusing distribution process, and gross commercialization. The Harry Potter stamps may have also been a factor in the apparent falling out between the U.S.P.S. and the Citizens' Stamp Advisory Committee, which could have a major impact on future commemorative issues.

As we look forward to 2014, it will be interesting to see how the story unfolds. The U.S. Postal Service continues to look for new ways to boost sales and limit expenses. Some post offices closed, but 2013 didn't see the sweeping closures many had predicted. The notion of eliminating certain delivery days or home delivery continues to be discussed.

Regardless of developments with modern issues and new strategies to help keep the Postal Service afloat, the classic stamp market remained strong last year and I predict it will again in 2014.

USING TECHNOLOGY TO ENHANCE YOUR COLLECTING EXPERIENCE

By Scott Barman

When I started collecting coins in the early 1970s, it was still possible to find silver coins and other older coins in pocket change. In fact, it was after being paid several Indian Head cents for delivering newspapers that made me interested in collecting coins. After gathering coins from collecting payments for delivering newspapers, I started to look through my father's pocket change, looking for coins to insert into my folders.

Collecting today has advanced far beyond the way I started. To find out more about those Indian Head cents I bought a reference book. To buy or sell coins, I had to travel to a dealer. While there is nothing wrong with dealers, I did not have one in my neighborhood and that made it a difficult proposition. Today, someone can go online and use their favorite search engine to find information about the coin they found or the coin someone wants to sell them.

Prior to the arrival of the World Wide Web, those of us with access to what was then called the ARPAnet could access simple e-mail lists and a bulletin board-like system called Usenet. Usenet was a distributed messaging system similar to today's online forums except that the articles were distributed to each computer with access. When it was conceived in 1979, computing power and the architecture of the Internet made it easier to distribute the articles in bulk, sometimes overnight, rather than accessing them across the network as we do today.

Among the first technology breakthroughs that helped collectors were the invention of the simple database and spreadsheet programs. Collectors would use these programs to create databases and spreadsheets to track their collection. These would become the basis for inventory programs that would see their popularity rise in the late part of the last century.

Newcomers to the technologies of the Internet and mobile computing might look at these beginnings as ancient times, but it set the tone for the future of adding technology to enhance the collecting experience. The first breakthrough in expanding the information available was the invention of the World Wide Web.

Sir Tim Berners-Lee and Belgian computer scientist Robert Cailliau, while working at CERN, The European Organization for Nuclear Research, invented the concept of the Web. Using the power of technology offered by the Internet, the Web has brought a new way of delivering information from those who have it to those who want it.

In the computing industry, we look at the growth in the capability of technology in the terms of "Moore's Law." Named for Intel Corporation co-founder Gordon E. Moore, Moore's Law says that the capabilities of technology double every two years. While Moore was talking about the growth of the microprocessors that are the brains behind the computers, there has been a growth in the capabilities of the computers that make them wonderful tools to enhance your collecting experience.

Online Price Guides

The perpetual question from collectors, investors, and those with passing interest is "What is it and what does the stamp cost?" While paper books are wonderful references and can be more convenient than electronic alternatives, books have the problem with being static from one year to another. To answer the collecting public's desire for more information, one of the first online services for collectors are online price guides.

Price guides are as varied as their publishers but most are based on the Scott catalog. The choice to use a paper or online resource is a matter of personal preference.

News and Blogs

Finding Philatelic news and information used to be limited to the weekly and monthly publications sent to us via the postal service. Collectors were tied to publishing schedules, causing news to travel slowly. With the ease of producing a well-designed website and hiring writers to look for stories that would be of interest to collectors, there are now websites dedicated to delivering stamp community news.

There are some excellent resources available, two websites have proven to be invaluable to stamp collectors:

- The American Philatelic Society (stamps.org)
- Linn's Stamp News (linns.com)

While these sites offer e-mail support to their subscribers, others provide various ways for readers to keep up to date with new articles. Some offer a daily e-mail notice while others offer RSS (Rich Site Summary or Really Simple Syndication) feeds. An RSS feed is a special file accessed from the Web that will tell you when new information is available.

As RSS feeds proliferate and their function has expanded, Web browsers have been either dropping support for reading RSS feeds (like Apple's

Safari) or have not added new enhancements (Microsoft's Internet Explorer and Mozilla Firefox) making it difficult to keep up with the news. Two good stand-alone replacements to use at your computer are SharpReader for Windows (sharpreader.net) and NetNewsWire for the Mac (netnewswireapp .com). Both programs have won many industry awards.

Last year, the popular Google shut down its Reader service that provided web-based access to subscribe to RSS feeds. Reader also had the advantage of being a central repository that allowed other programs to repackage the feeds so the user can read them in more friendly formats. Since the shutdown of the Reader service, there have been others who have stepped into the void. Here is a sample of services that you can choose from:

Web-only Resources

- AOL Reader (reader.aol.com) is a web-based service that was started shortly before Google announced the end of the Reader service, but has gained a following for having a plain, no-nonsense but solid working interface that has satisfied some of the people who have switched to their service.
- The Old Reader (theoldreader.com) is a web-based service that looks and acts like Google's old Reader service. The author of the service makes it clear that this was not an accident.

Web and Mobile App

- Feedly (feedly.com) is a web-based service that is nearly a drop-in replacement for Reader. Feedly has its own apps for iOS devices (iPhone and iPad), Android, and Kindle Fire but interfaces with many other apps to use its data. See www.feedly.com/apps.html for the list of apps that can read Feedly saved feeds.
- FeedBin (feedbin.me) is a paid service that also has support for many mobile apps. The advantage of using a paid service over a free service is that the paid service comes with support and without advertisements.
- NetVibes (netvibes.com) is an all-inclusive dashboard to manage your web-based reading. It is free for users but has paid accounts for businesses to monitor trends on the Web. Being a paid service, NetVibes also creates its own "apps" that help cultivate news and information from the Internet and deliver it to your NetVibes account.
- Reeder 2 (reederapp.com) is a no-frills reading app for iOS (iPhone and iPad) that integrates with other services. Reeder started as an iOS interface with Google Reader but had to evolve when Reader was discontinued. Reeder is a paid app with a different version for the iPhone and iPad.

Mashup Services

Mashup services combine information from multiple resources to provide a single interface as if it came from a single resource. Mashup services are usually free to the user but rely on advertising for revenues.

- •Digg Reader (digg.com/reader) is a new service from the long-time mashup system Digg. Digg's new Reader app and service will allow users to create their own mashups from selected news feeds rather than create mashups on what you read, which is what the Digg service does.
- •Flipboard (flipboard.com) is a popular service that turns your interests into an electronic magazine. Users can create your own virtual magazine based on who you follow on Twitter, from RSS feeds, or from various channels that are managed by Flipboard or one of their partners. Flipboard is available for iOS, Android, Windows Phone, and Blackberry.

Aside from many specialty websites, you can use a search engine to find information on just about any philatelic topic. There are also bloggers dedicated to writing and discussing philatelic information. Blog, which is derived from the term "web log," is the writing of someone with information or an opinion based on the blog's subject matter.

The difference between a blog and a news-based website is that the blog writer, also called a blogger, is not limited to reporting the news. Some bloggers will analyze the news or other issues that affect the numismatic community. Bloggers provide another view into the news, collecting, the stamp collecting community, and the hobby, that adds to the richness of the online information.

Mobile Computing

While there were ways to carry the Internet in your pocket since the late 1990s, the release of the Apple iPhone and the software that runs the phone (iOS) paved the way for creating a new way to view data on the go. Then, with the addition of the Android system and now the new Windows Mobile phones, tablets, and other mobile devices, the possibilities are endless.

The basic use for a smart mobile phone is to use the built-in browser to explore information on the Web. While many websites may not be enhanced for a mobile display, the browsers have the ability to zoom in to the page so it can be read on the smaller screen. Sites that provide an enhanced display for mobile devices may not provide a lot of information in that format, but it is packaged for the collector on the go.

A key area of mobile computing is apps. Apps, short for applications, are programs designed to run on the mobile device that is capable of doing more than what can be done on a website. App markets are a new industry that was pioneered by Apple for its iPhone, iPod Touch, and iPad devices. Google has introduced Google Play for the Android market and Microsoft opened the Windows Store (windows.microsoft.com/en-us/windows-8/apps>) for desktop, tablet, and phones running Windows 8.

Since apps are new, there are not many good apps for collectors. Most of the currently available apps can be found mostly for Apple's devices. Starter lists of apps are as follows:

- •Paris: Art and Stamps (iPhone, iPod Touch, Android)—A mobile-guided tour of 125 famous works of art found throughout the Louvre and Musee d'Orsay that have appeared on stamps.
- •Philately Terms (iPhone, iPod Touch, iPad)—Definitions of stamp collecting terms for your mobile device.
- •Gibbons Stamp Monthly (iPhone, iPod Touch) —Read the British-based *Gibbons Stamp Monthly* on your Apple iDevice. Requires a subscription, which is less expensive than the paper-based magazine.
- •Stamp and Coin Mart (iPhone, iPod Touch, iPad, Android)—Read *Stamp and Coin Mart* magazine on your portable device using this app. It requires a subscription, which is less expensive than the paper-based magazine.

E-books

Amazon.com, probably the most successful electronic commerce (e-commerce) website, pioneered this era of electronic books (e-books) with the invention of the Kindle. Amazon designed the Kindle so that it would use a standard that they controlled so that you can gain access to the books and information sold on Amazon.com. The Kindle family of e-book readers was the first of the current era of tablets and has been successful in moving the publishing industry to make their books available for users of e-readers.

Electronic books are the future of publishing, which can be seen by the phenomenal increase in e-book sales in the last few years. People of all ages are now turning to e-books that allow them to carry libraries with them when they are on the go. Schools and colleges are now turning to e-books to allow students to purchase the most current information they need to support their learning.

As more publishers are providing access to their titles electronically, e-books are key to providing the next generation of collectors and researchers with information in a manner that suits their lives.

E-books are not limited to current editions. There are a number of out of print books online that can be downloaded legally without cost. These are books whose copyrights have expired and have been scanned either through Google's book project (books.google.com) or the Internet Archive Books project (archive.org/details/text).

Another advantage of e-book readers is that if you find something interesting that is in Portable Document Format (PDF), it can be saved on the e-book reader to be used as a reference. If you find an article on a website, you can have it available on your e-reader to read later. If you can create a PDF copy of a webpage, that can also be saved to read later on your e-reader.

Although each of the devices has its own online bookstore where you can buy e-books, Amazon and Barnes & Noble have apps that run on many devices that will read books bought at their stores. The Kindle app can run on your computer as well as your iOS, Android, Blackberry, and Windows phones and tablets. If you buy most of your books from Amazon.com, then a Kindle is the best choice, but the Kindle is very restrictive of the number of devices on which you can read the book.

Family readers can benefit from the Nook by Barnes & Noble where several household members can share an account. The Barnes & Noble Nook app can allow readers to read books bought at bn.com on iPhones, iPads, Android devices, and Windows Phones and tablets.

These options make the best e-reader a matter of personal preference without limiting access to the best electronic reading experience.

Social Media

It has taken a while for the Philatelic community to begin to embrace social media. Some say that the demographic that uses social media tends to be younger than the average collector. While that may be true, there is a growing online community using social media to talk about collecting. Three of the most well-known social media services are Facebook, Twitter, and Pinterest.

Facebook (facebook.com) was not the inventor of social media on the Web, but it has been the most successful because of its ability to adapt to new services. Facebook has made it easy for people of all ages to be social online. Not many collectors have embraced Facebook, or reserve their Facebook activities to maintaining relationships with friends, relatives, and colleagues. Facebook's very public issues with privacy may have collectors thinking about their use of Facebook and restricting what they share.

Twitter (twitter.com) is called a micro-blogging service. A Twitter message can be no longer than 140 characters in length, making brevity a necessity. Twitter is good for short comments and sending links to interesting information to your followers. Similar to making "friends" on Facebook, on Twitter you follow a user's messages, called Tweets. Bloggers use Twitter to announce when content is available. Others use Twitter to point to interesting articles for their followers to read.

Some people can get confused by Twitter's fast pace. The thing to remember about Twitter is that it is a snapshot in time. If you are not reading Twitter during the workday, do not worry. Much of the information will be available in the media or should not be much of a concern. Pick interesting people to follow and you might want to consider looking back on their timeline to see if they had anything interesting to say.

Pinterest (pinterest.com) is the new social media service that calls itself a "Virtual Pinboard." Think of Pinterest as the Twitter for pictures. While you can post pointers to images on Twitter, Pinterest is all about pictures. The Pinterest mobile apps will also allow you to take pictures with your mobile device and upload them to a board you set up for others to see. All three services have mobile apps for both the Apple and Android devices.

Additionally, those interested in creating online photo albums and photo journals can look into photo blogging services like Yahoo's Flickr (flickr .com), Photobucket (photobucket.com), and Google's Picasa (picasa.

google.com). All three have apps for the Apple devices while only Photo-bucket and Picasa have apps for Android. Users of Apple iOS devices can use iCloud to share pictures of their collection.

Buying and Selling Online

Although eBay opened the online world to stamp buying and selling, it is not the only place for a collector to search for stamps. Dealers the world over have embraced online selling and have created e-commerce websites to sell to more people than those in their local area. Their embracing the Web and e-commerce also provides collectors with a wide variety of purchasing options and a way to expand their collections from the comfort of their computers.

A primary option for purchasing current collectibles would be from the manufacturer. For United States coins, that would be the United States Postal Service (usps.com). The U.S. Postal Service will always offer the latest collectibles and offer some stamps from years past as long as they have the inventory to do so. Collectors know that the U.S. Postal Service not only offers stamps but first day covers, special issue covers, and other stamp-related items to make any collector happy.

Auctions

Auctions are the oldest type of marketplace, dating back over 2,500 years, with some auction houses in Europe having been in business since the 18th century. As with most businesses, online and mobile technologies have made it easier to participate in auctions from anywhere in the world.

The excitement behind online auctions goes beyond eBay. Once called traditional, auction houses are now moving auctions online as active plat-forms rather than an entry point for absentee bids to floor auctions. Some hold exclusively online auctions while others have found ways to do live bidding online to extend the auction floor to anywhere in the world.

The auction business has seen the growth of a few different types of businesses from ones that fully embrace technology to those that use it as an extension of their traditional business models. Large auction houses have fully embraced the technology and offer exclusively online auctions along with their live auctions that open with pre-bidding online.

Auctions are not limited to online bidding. Some use technology to extend their mail bid process to the convenience of the online world. Some online mail bid services can give you quicker feedback while others are similar to saving time from mailing or faxing your bids.

Some dealers have found that sponsoring online auctions can profitably help them sell inventory and reach a clientele beyond their hometowns. Using the services from companies like Proxibid (proxibid.com) and Live Auction-eers (liveauctioneers.com) to host their auction and provide transaction sup-port, dealers can take the consignments they obtain locally and offer them to a broader audience to help the seller get the best price for their items.

An auction platform dedicated to the stamp collecting community is the Stamp Auction Network (stampauctionnetwork.com). The Stamp Auction Network has comprehensive listings of auctions, mail bid sales, catalogs, prices realized, and even supports online bidding for some of the companies. There is even a directory of nearly every business that provides stamp auctions and sales. It is a resource for all stamp collectors to bookmark.

For the collector bidding on these auctions, technology gives them access to philatelic items that they would normally not see because of being unable to attend an auction.

Looking into the Future

The first stop on looking into the future is with education. With the number of colleges moving toward online education, there is a lot of software that can support extending education beyond the classroom. The American Philatelic Society (stamps.org) has a number of wonderful resources that collectors should investigate. A collector can find a wealth of information by searching "stamp collecting information" using your favorite search engine.

The next look into the future would be to use the multimedia capabilities that are available to expand education to create virtual clubs. Virtual clubs can be formed around a collecting interest and have international participation from their members. Imagine forming a club for stamp collecting enthusiasts with members from Canada, Europe, and Asia.

Other technologies could help catalog stamps by just taking a picture and providing voice-activated searching. The possibilities are endless!

Your Security Online

When looking at the tools to use to enhance your collecting experience, remember that scammers and other criminals are using the same tools in their activities. Although the technology is helpful, it is not mature enough to trust to keep you safe. Rather than hope that technology will be safe, there are a few guidelines that you should follow to ensure your safety and security:

1. Make sure your software is up-to-date. Whether you have an iPhone or Windows computer, you should learn how to update the software on those devices. Updating your software means more than updating the operating system (Windows, OS X, Android, or iOS), it also means updating the apps so that their bugs cannot be used against you. This includes your browser, which is probably the most used program on your computer.

2. Run an anti-virus and anti-malware program. Malware is "malicious software" that would do harm to your computer. This attack would install malware on your system through your browser. Some service providers offer a free download of an anti-virus program. Take advantage of that offer! If you want a good basic anti-virus program

try the AVG Anti-Virus Free Edition (free.avg.com). It is not as full featured as others, but it provides good protection.

3. Once you install your anti-virus program, make sure you keep it up-to-date! Keeping it up to date means that you download the information about new attacks from the manufacturers of the anti-virus program. Threats are constantly changing and you need to keep up to date. If you are using old information, it is like leaving holes in your defenses for the attackers to get through. Make sure the software keeps updated. Also, pay for the yearly service to keep it updated. Think of it as an insurance policy for your critical data!

4. Desktop and laptop computer systems now come with built-in protections that you should learn how to turn on. If you do not have a relative or friend who can help you, electronic stores provide services to help teach you and set up these features. It is worth spending the time and money for these services to protect your computer from being attacked.

5. Think about what you are doing before you click that link. If you receive a random link in e-mail even from someone you know, contact that person to make sure they sent the link and are not victims of a cyber-attack. If you receive a link in a text message saying that your bank needs for you to verify your account, do not click the link but call your bank and ask if it is a legitimate request—likely it is not.

6. If you do not know what it is, do not investigate and delete or ignore the message. E-mail with attachments, links in tweets, online forum posts can contain links to sites that are ready to infect your system. If there is any doubt, just throw it out!

7. Know how to tell when a site is legitimate by looking at the visual cues. Does the website's address (URL) look right? If you are supposed to be at your bank's website, is there anything else other than the bank's address? Sometimes scammers in another country will make their addresses look like your bank's address (e.g., yourbank.com.cn, providing your bank is not in China). Remember, the number one and lower-case "l" (letter el) look similar and so does an upper case "O" and zero.

8. Just because there is a lock on your browser does not mean the website is secured. It means that the communications between your browser and the server are secured. The same rules for checking the visual cues (above) apply. If there are any errors when trying to begin what you think is a secure session, you should not trust the connection and contact the company you are trying to do business with. Also, look for the clues for sites that are using enhanced security. When you connect to a website that is using the enhanced security, you should see a green lock or other signal that says that your browser confirmed the site you are connected to uses the enhanced security standards and can be trusted.

9. Although Wi-Fi hotspots are convenient, they are also convenient to the scammer. Most Wi-Fi hotspots are not secure and anyone can connect. If you do not have to enter a password to access the Wi-Fi hotspot, it is the network equivalent of standing on a street corner and broadcasting your personal information for anyone to hear. Using a direct connection, such as the cellular data connection on your mobile device is safer than using an unsecured Wi-Fi hotspot.

10. Speaking of Wi-Fi, if you have a wireless network at home you should learn how to properly set it up or get help. Even security professionals who do this for a living often find setting up Wi-Fi networks difficult so do not be afraid of asking for help!

11. Protect your personal information. Understand the information you are being asked to provide and only give what is needed to complete the transaction. For example, there is no reason for anyone to require your social security number for any online transaction. Only fill out the required fields in checkout forms. If there are any questions, find the sites privacy policy and make sure you understand how your personal information will be stored and used.

12. Only use safe payment options like credit cards or a third-party proxy like PayPal (paypal.com). Credit cards are the safest option since the issuers will help if something goes wrong such as a product not being delivered or someone using your card without your permission. Never send cash through the mail or use a money-wiring service since you do not have any recourse if something should go wrong.

Regardless of what you do, keep a record of your online transactions. You should save as much information as possible until the transaction is completed and you are satisfied that everything is in order. Save online receipts by saving the web receipt to a file or keep a printed copy. Save copies of emails and write down all telephone call information during the transaction. Keep this information and verify the transaction on your credit card statement as soon as it arrives. Also, make sure there are not any unauthorized charges. If there are any problems or questions, call the financial institution that issued the credit card immediately.

If you want to learn more about staying safe online, the National Cyber Security Alliance (NCSA) maintains a website (staysafeonline.org) with a lot of good information. NCSA is a consortium of major technology vendors and the U.S. Department of Homeland Security that works hard to keep that site up to date with the latest information. They also sponsor Cyber Security Awareness Month every October to remind everyone that while there is a lot of good in cyberspace you do have to be careful.

Scott Barman is a collector and author of the Coin Collectors Blog (coinsblog .ws). He is also President of the Montgomery County Coin Club (montgomery coinclub.org) and President of the Maryland State Numismatic Society (mdstatenumisassn.org). After more than 30 years in the computer and information security industry, Scott recently started Having-Fun Collectibles to serve collectors in more markets than just numismatics because collecting should be fun. When not out searching for different and interesting collectibles he can be found with his wife and two puggles while they check out his pocket change.

HOW TO USE THIS BOOK

The main section of this book lists U.S. postage stamps with the exception of special issues such as airmail, revenues, etc. Special issues are grouped separately in sections of their own. Please refer to the Table of Contents.

Identification. Illustrations appear together with stamps. In some cases, two or more stamp issues are similar in appearance, but differ only in minor details, such as watermark or gauge of perforation. They are known as face-identical stamps. Listings of face-identical stamps subsequent to the first variety are cross-referenced to the initial listing and its illustration by use of a tilde and the initial catalogue number in parentheses, e.g. Scott number 18 (~5), which indicates that stamp No. 18 possesses the same design as No. 5.

The denomination and a description are given for each stamp. Denominations for non-denominated stamps are given in parentheses, e.g. (15¢) "A" & Eagle.

The type of gum (water activated or self-adhesive) is given only where necessary to distinguish two similar issues.

Prices. Prices are given in columns for unused and used examples, in the median grade of fine to very fine (F-VF). Those of higher quality sell for more; those of lesser quality sell for less. Stamps with faults or defects are worth only a small fraction of catalogue value.

Prices shown are intended to be actual retail selling prices; however, be aware that prices vary with the market and from dealer to dealer. A dash (—) in place of a price indicates that the item is either seldom available or that it does not exist in the form indicated. It should not be assumed, however, that such items are invariably more valuable than those for which prices are shown.

Prices for unused stamps issued before 1935 are for hinged examples. Never-hinged examples sell for more. The never-hinged premium appears in parentheses where applicable, e.g. (NH add 50%). Prices for unused stamps issued after 1935 are for never-hinged (NH) examples. Stated values are a general guide and do not reflect the price of the occasional superb example, such as an early imperforate with four wide margins.

A minimum price of 14¢ has been assigned to the most common stamps, such as those that you might receive on everyday mail. The minimum price reflects the labor incurred by a stamp dealer when filling an order for an individual example, should one be requested. Common stamps can be obtained in packets and bulk mixtures for much less than the listed minimum price.

No prices are given from multiples of used self-adhesive se-tenants, because once the stamps have been removed from their backing paper they cannot be reattached to form a multiple.

A box is provided to the left of each listing for keeping a record of the stamps in your collection.

Plate Blocks. Prices for plate blocks appear in the column headed "Plate Block." Prices for plate blocks of se-tenant issues appear on the line describing the se-tenant multiple under the heading "Plate Block." Plate blocks are assumed to be blocks of four unless otherwise indicated. When the number of stamps is greater than four, it is shown in parentheses following the price of the plate block.

Line Pairs and Plate Number Coil (PNC) Strips. Prices for line pairs are given in the column headed "Line Pair." Prices for plate number coil strips are given in the column headed "PNC Strip (5)." The numeral "5" in parentheses indicates that the price is for a strip of 5 stamps with the plate number located on the center stamp. The standard length for collecting PNC strips is five stamps, although both longer and shorter strips are sometimes collected. In many cases, prices for longer or shorter strips vary only slightly from those for strips of 5; however, some shorter strips (especially early PNCs) are significantly less valuable than strips of five. Check with a dealer active with PNCs for up-to-the-minute prices.

Mint Sheets. Mints sheets are priced in a separate section following the section for stamps.

Se-tenant Stamps. Listings indicate the minimum number of stamps necessary in each instance for a complete se-tenant multiple (block or strip). It is often possible to obtain blocks or strips containing all the designs necessary for a complete multiple but in an order or sequence other than that listed. Only in those cases where the listed sequence is necessary to form a larger design (e.g. No. 1331-32, the Space Twins issue) is the exact order crucial. In all other cases, it is okay to collect se-tenants in whatever order the individual stamps may occur. Some se-tenants can be collected either as blocks or strips; they are indicated in the listings.

HOW TO GRADE STAMPS

A person need not be an expert to judge the quality or grade of a stamp. All he needs is a discerning eye, possibly a small linear measuring device, and the grading instructions listed below.

The major catalogs traditionally list stamps simply as "Unused" or "Used." Auction houses, however, will describe the stamps for sale in a more informative manner. The greater the value of the stamp, the more thoroughly it is described.

There is no officially accepted system of grading stamps. What we have done in this book is essentially to set up a system of grading stamps using the suggestions and practices of stamp dealers from all over the country. Total agreement was made to the following categories and grades of stamps that are most frequently traded.

CATEGORIES

Mint—The perfect stamp with superb centering, no faults, and usually with original gum (if issued with gum).

Unused—Although unused, this stamp may have a hinge mark or may have suffered some change in its gum since it was issued.

Used—Basically this will be the normal stamp that passed through the government postal system and will bear an appropriate cancellation.

Cancelled to Order—These are stamps that have not passed through the postal system but have been carefully cancelled by the government usually for a commemoration. These are generally considered undesirable by collectors.

GRADE—STAMP CENTERING

Average—The perforations cut slightly into the design.

Fine—The perforations do not touch the design at all, but the design will be off center by fifty percent or more of a superb centered stamp.

Very Fine—The design will be off center by less than fifty percent of a superb stamp. The off-centered design will be noticeable.

Extra Fine—The design will be almost perfectly centered. The margin will be off by less than twenty-five percent of a superb stamp.

Superb—This design will be perfectly centered with all four margins exactly the same. On early imperforate issues, superb specimens will have four clear margins that do not touch the design at any point.

GRADE—STAMP GUM

Original Gum—This stamp will have the same gum on it that it had the day it was issued.

Regummed—This stamp will have new gum applied to it as compared to an original gummed stamp. Regummed stamps are worth no more than those with gum missing.

No Gum—This stamp will have had its gum removed or it may have not been issued with gum.

Never Hinged—This stamp has never been hinged so the gum should not have been disturbed in any way.

Lightly Hinged—This stamp has had a hinge applied. A lightly wetted or peelable hinge would do very little damage to the gum when removed.

Heavily Hinged—This stamp has had a hinge applied in such a manner as to secure it to the stamp extremely well. Removal of this hinge proves to be disastrous, in most cases, since either part of the hinge remains on the stamp or part of the stamp comes off on the hinge, causing thin spots on the stamp.

GRADE—STAMP FAULTS

Any fault in a stamp such as thin paper, bad perforations, creases, tears, stains, ink marks, pin holes, etc., depending upon the seriousness of the fault, usually results in grading the stamp to a lower condition.

OTHER STAMP CONSIDERATIONS

CANCELLATIONS

Light Cancel—This stamp has been postally cancelled but the wording and lines are very light and almost unreadable.

Normal Cancel—This stamp has been postally cancelled with just the right amount of pressure. Usually the wording and lines are not distorted and can be made out.

Heavy Cancel—This stamp has been postally cancelled. In the process excessive pressure was used, and the wording and lines are extremely dark and sometimes smeared and in most cases unreadable.

PERFORATIONS

Not to be overlooked in the appearance of a stamp are its perforations. The philatelist might examine these "tear apart" holes with a magnifying glass or microscope to determine the cleanliness of the separations. One must also consider that the different types of paper, upon which the stamp was printed, will sometimes make a difference in the cleanliness of the separations. The term "pulled perf" is used to denote a badly separated stamp in which the perforations are torn or ragged.

COLOR

Other important factors such as color affect the appearance and value of stamps. An expert will have a chart of stamp colors. Chemical changes often occur in inks. Modern printing sometimes uses metallic inks. These "printings" will oxidize upon contact with the natural secretions from human skin.

In some cases, the color of a stamp is deliberately altered by chemicals to produce a rare shade. Overprints can be eliminated. Postmarks may be eradicated. Replacing gum is a simple process. Some stamps have been found to bear forged watermarks. The back of the paper was cut away and then the stamps rebacked with appropriately watermarked paper.

There are stamp experts who earn a living in the business of stamp repairing. They are craftsmen of the first order. A thin spot on a stamp can be repaired by gluing it on a new layer of paper. Missing perforations can be added. Torn stamps can be put back together. Pieces of stamps may be joined.

In some countries it is accepted practice for an expert, upon examination of a stamp, to certify the authenticity by affixing his signature to the back of the stamp. If the stamp is not genuine, it is his right and duty to so designate on the stamp; but these signatures can also be faked.

FACTORS THAT DETERMINE
STAMP VALUES

The collector value (or "market value") of any stamp rests with a variety of factors. Philately becomes a bit less mysterious when one understands the forces at work in the stamp marketplace.

A beginner often assumes that expensive stamps are expensive because of rarity. Certainly there is a great deal of talk about stamp rarities within the hobby, and so it is natural enough to ascribe high prices to the phenomenon of rarity. In fact, rarity is only one of several factors that influence stamp prices, and the influence it carries is not particularly clear-cut.

In this book you will note some stamps (mostly among the early regular issues) with values of $1,000, $2,000, and even higher. Obviously these stamps are rarer than those selling for $10 or $15. But having said that, we have virtually summed up our useful knowledge of rarity and its effect on prices. A comparison of prices between stamps in roughly similar ranges of value does not indicate which is the rarer. A stamp selling for $1,000 is not necessarily rarer than one selling for $500. A $10,000 stamp may actually be more abundant than one which commands $5,000. This hard-to-comprehend fact of philatelic life prevails because of the other factors involved in determining a stamp's price. If rarity were the only factor, one could, of course, easily see which stamps are the rarest by the prices they fetch.

The word "rare" is an elixir to many collectors, not only of stamps but other collectors' items. Sellers are well aware of this, and seldom fail to sprinkle the word liberally in their sales literature. There is no law against calling a stamp rare, as this represents a personal opinion more than anything else and opinions are allowable in advertising. Unfortunately, there is no standard definition for rarity. Does "rare" mean just a handful of specimens in existence, with one reaching the sales portals once in five years? Does it mean 100 in existence, or 1,000, or some other number? Since stamps are—today, at any rate—printed in the multimillions, a thousand surviving specimens might seem a very tiny total to some people. Further complicating this situation is the fact that the specific rarity of most stamps cannot be determined, or even estimated, with any hope of accuracy. The quantities printed are recorded for most of our stamps, going back even into the nineteenth century, but the quantity surviving of any particular stamp is anyone's guess. It is obvious that a stamp that goes through the auction rooms once a year is fairly rare, but this provides no sound basis for guessing the number of specimens in existence. That could only be accomplished if some sort of grand census could be taken, and all specimens tallied. This, of course, is nothing but a pipe dream. Some collectors would not participate in such a census; some might be unaware that it was being conducted. Then, too, there are many scarce or rare stamps in hands other than those of collectors, such as dealers and museums. Additionally, there could be (and probably are) existing specimens of rare stamps yet to be discovered, as fresh discoveries are made periodically in the hobby through attic cleaning and the like.

In terms of influence on price, rarity is outdistanced somewhat by popularity. Some stamps, for one reason or other, are simply more popular than others. They have a sort of innate appeal for hobbyists, either through reputation, exquisite designing, circumstances of issue, oddity, or various other potential reasons. These stamps sell out rapidly from the stocks of dealers, while some stamps that are supposedly scarcer will linger in stock albums for ages and ages waiting to tempt a customer. It is no wonder, then, that the prices of popular stamps rise more quickly than those that are scarce but not in brisk demand. The Columbian series typifies the effect of popularity on stamp values. If stamp prices were fixed by scarcity alone, none of the Columbians would be selling for nearly as much. Much of their value derives from their overwhelming popularity with collectors of U.S. stamps. It would be safe to say, in fact, that all of the Columbians, from the lowest face value to the $5, are more plentiful than other U.S. stamps selling for precisely the same sums. Every dealer has Columbians in stock, and quite a few dealers have the high value of the set, too. They are not "hard to get." But they are very costly.

Popularity, of course, does not remain constant forever. There are shifts in philatelic popularity, usually slight but occasionally extreme. The popularity of commemoratives as a whole versus regular issues as a whole can change from time to time. Then, too, there are swings of popularity for airmails, first-day covers, blocks, coil pairs, mint sheets, and all other philatelic material. A climb or decline in the price of any philatelic item is often an indication of the forces of popularity at work. Then there are activities of investors to consider, whose buying habits seldom reflect those of the pure collector. A great deal of buying by investors in any short period of time (such as occurred during 1979 and 1980, and to less extent in 1981) can make prices seem well out of balance.

Also on the subject of prices, it is important for the beginner to realize that arithmetic is usually futile when dealing with stamp values.

You cannot determine the price of one philatelic item by knowing the value of a similar one. This can best be shown by the relative values of singles and blocks of four. A block of four is, as one would expect, worth more than four times as much as single specimens of that stamp. It is not just four specimens of the stamp, but four of them attached, which lends added scarcity and appeal. The difficulty lies in trying to use mathematics to determine a block's value. Some blocks are worth five times as much as the single stamp; some six times; some ten times as much or even more. Almost all blocks—except very common ones—will vary somewhat in value, in relation to the value of the individual stamp. There is no satisfactory explanation for this, other than the presumption that some blocks are scarcer than others or just in greater demand than others.

In the case of common philatelic items, the value hinges greatly on the method of sale. If you want to buy one specimen of a common cover, you may have to pay $1.50. But if you were willing to buy a hundred common first-day covers of the dealer's choice, you could very likely get them for $75 or 75¢ each. Buying in quantity, and allowing the dealer to make the selections, can save a great deal of money. Of course one may then ask: What is the real value of those covers? Is it $1.50 or 75¢? The only answer is that it depends on how you buy!

If this article seems to raise a great many questions without supplying many answers, it will, hopefully, serve to show that stamp collecting is not bound to rigid formulas. What happens in the stamp market is largely beyond prediction, or precise explanation. This, indeed, is one of the exciting aspects of the hobby.

REPAIRS, FAKES, AND OTHER UNDESIRABLES

Philately, like most hobbies, is not without its pitfalls. The collector who buys from reputable dealers runs very little risk, as today's stamp pros have high principles and are hard to fool. Buying from auction sales and small dealers, who may not have expert knowledge, is another matter. Here the collector must call into play his own expertise and learn to distinguish the bad from the good.

In the early years of philately, stamps provided a playground for fakers and swindlers. They took advantage of the public's gullibility and the general lack of published information about stamps. Copies were printed of rare stamps, as well as of stamps that never existed in the first place. Cancels were bleached from used specimens to make them appear unused. Fake margins were added to imperforates, to allow ordinary copies to be sold as "superb with jumbo margins." Perforated stamps were reperforated to make them better centered. Thin spots in the paper were filled in, tears closed, missing portions of paper replaced. Stamps were doctored and manipulated in more ways than could be imagined, all in the hope of fooling collectors and making anywhere from a few extra cents to thousands of dollars on them. One of the favorite tricks of fakers was to apply bogus overprints or surcharges. By merely using a rubber handstamp and a pad of ink, they could stamp out a hundred or more "rarities" in a few minutes, turning ordinary British or other issues into varieties not found in any catalogue. It was all a great game and proved very profitable, until collectors and the philatelic public at large became wary of such practices. Even though most of these fakes from the hobby's pioneer years have disappeared out of circulation, a few still turn up and must be guarded against.

U.S. stamps have not been faked nearly so extensively as those of many other nations, notably South America and Japan. Still, the collector should learn to watch for fakes and also for repaired specimens.

Total Fake. The counterfeit stamp always varies somewhat from a genuine specimen, though the difference may be very slight. Detection can usually be made if the suspect stamp is examined alongside one known to be genuine. By using a magnifier, the lines of engraving and paper quality can be compared. The ink on a fake is likely to have a fresher appearance and will lie on the surface as a result of being printed at a later date and on less sophisticated equipment; however, this is not always the case. Experts say that when a stamp appears to be a fake, or a reprint, the odds are very good that it is. Some experience is necessary before anyone can get a first-glance reaction to a stamp. The presence or absence of a cancel has no bearing on the likelihood of a stamp being a fake, as cancels can be faked, too.

Faked Cancel. Faked cancels are very rare on U.S. stamps, as nearly all are worth more unused than used. One notable exception is the 90¢, 1857–1861. These are applied either with a fake hand stamp or simply drawn with pen and ink. Skillfully drawn faked cancels can be very deceptive. Faked cancels are much more numerous on covers than loose stamps.

Removed Cancels. So-called cleaned copies of used stamps, sold as unused, were once very plentiful and are still encountered from time to time. The faker, of course, chooses lightly cancelled specimens from which the obliteration can be removed without leaving telltale evidence. In the case of imperforates he may trim down the margins to remove part of the cancel. Rarely will he attempt to clean a stamp whose cancel falls across the face or any important portion of the stamp. Holding the stamp to a strong light may reveal the cancel lines. X-ray examination provides positive proof.

Added Margin(s). When margins have been added to an imperforate stamp, the paper fibers are woven together (after moistening) along the back and at the front where the margin extends beyond the stamp's design. They can usually be detected by looking closely for a seam or joint at the point where the design ends and the margin begins. A magnifying glass will be necessary for this. When held against a light, the reverse side will probably show evidence of the weaving operation. Sometimes the added margins are of a slightly different grade of paper.

Reperforated. A stamp that has been reperforated to improve its centering will usually be slightly smaller than a normal specimen, and this can be revealed by placing it atop an untampered copy.

Filled Thin Spots. If held to a light and examined with a good magnifier, filled-in thin spots will normally appear darker than the remainder of the stamp. Such spots are often mistaken for discoloration by beginners. Thin spots are filled in by making a paste of paper pulp and glue and applying it gradually to the injured area. After drying, the stamp is placed in a vise so that no telltale hills or valleys are left. This is not really considered forgery but honest repair work; it becomes forgery only if done with the intent of selling the stamp as undamaged.

Closed Tears. These are almost always visible against a light with a magnifier, even if small. A routine examination of any rare stamp should include a check of its margins for possible closed or open tears.

Type Identifier

Types of the 1¢ Franklin 1851–1860.

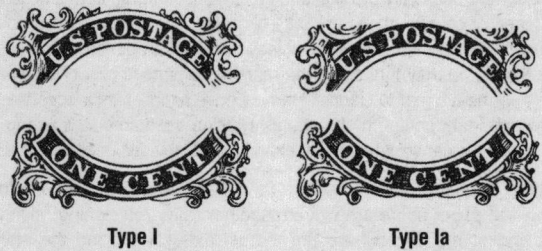

Type I   Type Ia

Type I. The scrollwork on all sides is complete. The curved lines at top and bottom are complete and unbroken. The curls at the bottom scroll-work are complete.

Type Ia. Similar to Type I at bottom, but the line at the top of the inscription is cut away as are the tops of the ornaments.

Type Ib. Similar to Type I at top, but at bottom the curved line below the denomination is partly cut away and the scrollwork is not as complete. (Not illustrated.)

| Type II | Type III |

Type II. The curls and plumes of the bottom ornaments are incomplete. The curved line below the denomination is complete, as are the side ornaments.

Type III. The center portions of the curved lines at both top and bottom are incomplete. Side ornaments are intact.

Type IIIa. Similar to Type III, but only one of the curved lines, either top or bottom, has been cut away. (Not illustrated.)

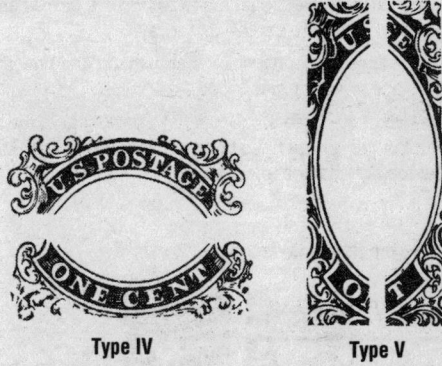

| Type IV | Type V |

Type IV. Similar to Type II, but the curved lines at either top or bottom (or both) are complete and more pronounced, having been reworked.

Type V. Similar to Type III, but the side ornaments are partially cut away.

Types of the 3¢ Washington of 1851–1860 (Scott Nos. 10, 11, 26, 26a, and 41).

Type I. The frame line is complete all around the design.

Type II. No horizontal frame lines along the top and bottom of stamps. Vertical frames at sides, however, are unbroken and continuous.

Type IIa. Similar to Type II except vertical frame lines break between stamps.

Types the 5¢ Jefferson of 1851–1860 (Scott Nos. 12, 27, 28, 28A, 29, 30, 30A and 42).

Type I. The projections at top, bottom and sides are complete.

Type II. The projections at top and bottom are cut away.

Types of the 10¢ Washington of 1851–1860 (Scott Nos. 13, 14, 15, 16, 31, 32, 33, 34, 35 and 43).

Type I. The shells at the lower corners are almost complete. The outer line below the inscription "Ten Cents" is nearly complete. The outer lines at top above "U.S. Postage" and letters "X" at each corner are not complete.

Type II. The outer lines at top above "U.S. Postage" and letters "X" at each corner are complete. The outer line below the inscription "Ten Cents" is broken. The shells at the lower corners are partially cut away.

Type III. The outer lines of the inscriptions at both top and bottom are broken. The outer lines above the letters "X" at top are broken and the shells at the lower corners are partially cut away.

Type IV. The outer lines of the inscriptions at both top and bottom have been recut and appear more pronounced.

Type V. One or two of the three small "pearls" that appear at the sides on the lower part of the design have been cut away. The outer line atop the letter "X" at top right has been cut away.

Secret Marks on the Banknote Issues.

1¢. The secret mark is contained in the ball just to the left of the top of the numeral "1."

2¢. The secret mark is a small diagonal line beneath the scroll above and to left of the letters "U.S."

3¢. The secret mark is additional heavy shading in the ribbon below the letters "RE."

6¢. The secret mark is additional heavy shading of the four vertical lines in the lower left ribbon.

7¢. The secret mark is two semicircles added to the ball ornament at lower right.

10¢. The secret mark is a small semicircle added to the pendant ball at the right end of the denomination tablet.

12¢. The secret mark is the addition of two balls to the numeral "2."

15¢. The secret mark is the strengthening of lines at the "v" at the top left triangle.

Types of the 2¢ Washington of 1894–1898 (Scott Nos. 249, 250, 251, 252, 265, 266 and 267).

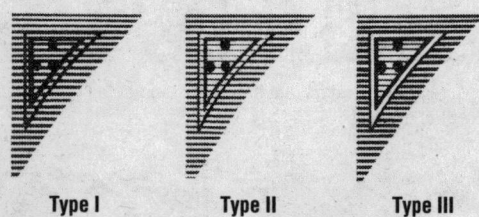

Type I	**Type II**	**Type III**

Type I. Horizontal lines across the triangles at top are of the same thickness throughout.

Type II. Horizontal lines are thin inside the triangles.

Type III. The double frame of the triangles do not contain any lines.

Types of the $1 Perry of 1894–1895 (Scott Nos. 261, 261A, 276 and 276A).

Type I	**Type II**

Type I. Circles around the numeral in the lower corners are broken.

Type II. Circles around the numeral in the lower corners are complete.

Types of the 10¢ Webster of 1898 (Scott Nos. 282C and 283).

| Type I | Type II |

Type I. Circles around the numerals in the lower corners are complete.

Type II. Circles around the numerals in the lower corners are broken.

Types of the 2¢ Washington of 1912–1920.

Type I   Type II

Type I. The tip of the left ribbon contains a single vertical mark. The second curve in the right ribbon contains a single vertical mark. The top line of the toga is faint. Shading lines on the face that terminate at the ear are not joined. Type I occurs on both flat plate and rotary press printings.

Type Ia. Similar to Type I except that the lines atop the toga and toga button are heavy. (Not illustrated).

Type II. Vertical marks in the ribbons are the same as Type I. The line atop the toga and toga button are heavy. A pronounced vertical line joins the shading lines on the face that terminate at the ear. Type II occurs only on rotary press printings.

Type III   **Type IV**

Type III. Similar to Type II except that the ribbons contain two vertical marks instead of one. Type III occurs only on rotary press printings.

Type IV. The top line of the toga is broken. The lines inside the button for the letters "Ɔ I D."

Type V   **Type Va**

Type V. The toga button contains five vertical lines. The top line of the toga is complete. The nose is shaded as illustrated. Type V occurs only on offset printings.

Type Va. Similar to Type V except that the third row of dots from the bottom on the nose contains only four dots rather than six dots. Type Va occurs only on offset printings.

Type VI   **Type VII**

Type VI. Similar to Type V except that the line of shading in the numeral "2" at left is extremely pronounced. Type VI occurs only on offset printings.

Type VII. Contains three vertical rows of dots below the nose. Additional dots of shading have been added to the hair at the top of Washington's head. Type VII occurs only on offset printings.

Types of the 3¢ Washington of 1912–1920.

Type I   **Type II**

Type I. The top of the toga line is weak. The fifth shading line of the toga is partly cut away. The line between the lips is thin. Type I occurs on both flat plate and rotary press printings.

Type II. The top line of the toga is complete and heavy as are the shading lines that join it. Type II occurs on both flat plate and rotary press printings.

Type III   **Type IV**

Type III. Similar to Type II except that the fifth shading line from the left is missing. The letters "P" and "O" in the inscription "Postage" are separated. Type III occurs only on offset printings.

Type IV. Similar to Type III except that the vertical line in the center of the button is a single unbroken vertical line. The letters "P" and "O" in the inscription "Postage" are joined. Type IV occurs only on offset printings.

Types of the 2¢ Washington of 1922 (Scott Nos. 599 and 599A).

Type III   **Type IV**

Type I. Contains thin hair lines atop the head.

Type II. Contains heavy hair lines atop the head.

Watermarks.

 USPS

Double Line Watermark   **Single Line Watermark**

GENERAL ISSUE

Pricing Note: Prices for unused stamps issued before 1890 are for examples without original gum. Examples with original gum command a premium, which can amount to as much as 50 percent or more. Beware regummed examples. Prices are for sound stamps. Those with faults or defects sell for much less.

1
(3)

2
(4)

Scott No.			Unused	Used

1847.

❑ 1	5¢	Red Brown	4200.00	675.00
❑ 2	10¢	Black	—	—

1875. Reproductions of the 1847 Issue, Issued without Gum.

❑ 3	5¢	Red Brown (~1)	800.00	—
❑ 4	10¢	Black (~2)	875.00	—

NOTE: On originals of the 5¢, the white shirt frill falls well below the top of the numeral "5." On reproductions, the top white shirt frill is even with the top of numeral "5." On originals of the 10¢, the left vertical line of Washington's collar falls below the top of the letter "X." On reproductions, it falls above the top of the "X."

5
(5A, 6, 7, 8, 8A, 9, 18, 19, 20, 21, 22, 23, 24, 40)

1851–1856. Imperforate.

❑ 5	1¢	Blue (~5) (type I)	—	—
❑ 5A	1¢	Blue (~5) (type Ib)	RARE	RARE
❑ 6	1¢	Blue (~5) (type Ia)	RARE	RARE

10	**12**	**13**	**17**
(11, 25, 26, 26a, 41)	(27, 28, 28A, 29, 30, 30A, 42)	(14, 15, 16, 31, 32, 33, 34, 35, 43)	(36, 36b, 44)

Scott No.			Unused	Used
❏ 7	1¢	Blue (~5) (type II)	825.00	225.00
❏ 8	1¢	Blue (~5) (type III)	RARE	2500.00
❏ 8A	1¢	Blue (~5) (type IIIa)	RARE	1100.00
❏ 9	1¢	Blue (~5) (type IV)	650.00	175.00
❏ 10	3¢	Orange Brown (type I)	2500.00	175.00
❏ 11	3¢	Dull Red (~10) (type I)	225.00	20.00
❏ 12	5¢	Red Brown (type I)	RARE	725.00
❏ 13	10¢	Green (type I)	RARE	800.00
❏ 14	10¢	Green (~13) (type II)	2500.00	275.00
❏ 15	10¢	Green (~13) (type III)	2500.00	250.00
❏ 16	10¢	Green (~13) (type IV)	RARE	1600.00
❏ 17	12¢	Black	3200.00	375.00

1857–1861. Same Designs as the 1851–1856 Issue, Perforated 15.

❏ 18	1¢	Blue (~5) (type I)	1400.00	675.00
❏ 19	1¢	Blue (~5) (type Ia)	RARE	550.00
❏ 20	1¢	Blue (~5) (type II)	725.00	300.00
❏ 21	1¢	Blue (~5) (type III)	RARE	2200.00
❏ 22	1¢	Blue (~5) (type IIIa)	1400.00	500.00
❏ 23	1¢	Blue (~5) (type IV)	RARE	850.00
❏ 24	1¢	Blue (~5) (type V)	175.00	65.00
❏ 25	3¢	Rose (~10) (type I)	1600.00	100.00
❏ 26	3¢	Dull Red (~10) (type II)	85.00	15.00
❏ 26a	3¢	Dull Red (~10) (type IIa)	300.00	60.00
❏ 27	5¢	Brick Red (~10) (type I)	RARE	1400.00

NOTE: Refer to the Type Identifier for information on types.

37	**38**	**39**
(45)	(46)	(47)

Scott No.			Unused	Used
❑ 28	5¢	Red Brown (~12) (type I)	RARE	950.00
❑ 28A	5¢	Indian Red (~12) (type I)	RARE	2800.00
❑ 29	5¢	Brown (~12) (type I)	RARE	400.00
❑ 30	5¢	Orange Brown (~12) (type II)	1200.00	800.00
❑ 30A	5¢	Brown (~12) (type II)	1100.00	325.00
❑ 31	10¢	Green (~13) (type I)	RARE	1100.00
❑ 32	10¢	Green (~13) (type II)	3000.00	300.00
❑ 33	10¢	Green (~13) (type III)	3000.00	275.00
❑ 34	10¢	Green (~13) (type IV)	RARE	2000.00
❑ 35	10¢	Green (~13) (type IV)	300.00	115.00
❑ 36	12¢	Black (~17) (type I)	925.00	325.00
❑ 36b	12¢	Black (~17) (type II)	525.00	275.00
❑ 37	24¢	Gray Lilac	1000.00	375.00
❑ 38	30¢	Orange	1400.00	450.00
❑ 39	90¢	Blue	2250.00	RARE

1875. Reprints of the 1857–1861 Issue, Perforated 12, Issued without Gum.

❑ 40	1¢	Bright Blue (~5)	710.00	RARE
❑ 41	3¢	Scarlet (~10)	3250.00	RARE
❑ 42	5¢	Orange Brown (~12)	1400.00	RARE
❑ 43	10¢	Blue Green (~13)	3000.00	RARE
❑ 44	12¢	Greenish Black (~17)	2800.00	RARE
❑ 45	24¢	Blackish Violet (~37)	2650.00	RARE
❑ 46	30¢	Yellow Orange (~38)	3200.00	RARE
❑ 47	90¢	Deep Blue (~39)	4650.00	RARE

NOTE: Refer to the Type Identifier for information on types.

63
(63b, 86, 92, 102)

64
(64b, 65, 66, 79, 83, 85, 85C, 88, 94, 104)

67
(75, 76, 95, 105)

68
(62B, 89, 96, 106)

69
(85E, 90, 97, 107)

70
(70b, 70c, 78, 99, 109)

71
(100, 110)

72
(101, 111)

Scott No.			Unused	Used
1861. Perforated 12.				
❏ 62B	10¢	Dark Green (~68)	3800.00	1400.00
1861–1862.				
❏ 63	1¢	Blue	225.00	60.00
❏ 63B	1¢	Dark Blue	500.00	275.00
❏ 64	3¢	Pink	RARE	850.00
❏ 64B	3¢	Rose Pink	525.00	175.00
❏ 65	3¢	Rose	125.00	8.00
❏ 66	3¢	Lake	RARE	RARE
❏ 67	5¢	Buff	1000.00	850.00
❏ 68	10¢	Yellow Green	650.00	75.00
❏ 69	12¢	Black	1100.00	130.00
❏ 70	24¢	Red Lilac	1450.00	275.00
❏ 70b	24¢	Steel Blue	RARE	750.00
❏ 70c	24¢	Violet	RARE	1400.00
❏ 71	30¢	Orange	1400.00	175.00
❏ 72	90¢	Blue	1760.00	425.00

73
(84, 85B, 87, 93, 103)

77
(91, 98, 108)

Scott No.			Unused	Used
1861–1866. New Values or New Colors.				
☐ 73	2¢	Black	500.00	85.00
☐ 75	5¢	Red Brown (~67)	2900.00	450.00
☐ 76	5¢	Brown (~67)	1000.00	125.00
☐ 77	15¢	Black	1200.00	240.00
☐ 78	24¢	Lilac (~70)	900.00	250.00
1867. Same Designs as the 1861–1866 Issue, Grill with Points Up.				
A Grill. Grill Covers Entire Stamp.				
☐ 79	3¢	Rose (~64)	3200.00	1550.00
C Grill. Grill Measures About 13 x 16 mm.				
☐ 83	3¢	Rose (~64)	3000.00	1000.00
1867. Same Designs as the 1861–66 Issue, Grill with Points Down.				
D Grill. Grill Measures About 12 x 14 mm.				
☐ 84	2¢	Black (~73)	RARE	3200.00
☐ 85	3¢	Rose (~64)	RARE	1000.00
Z Grill. Grill Measures About 11 x 14 mm.				
☐ 85B	2¢	Black (~73)	RARE	1400.00
☐ 85C	3¢	Rose (~64)	RARE	2650.00
☐ 85E	12¢	Black (~69)	RARE	1650.00
E Grill. Grill Measures About 11 x 13 mm.				
☐ 86	1¢	Blue (~63)	1775.00	500.00
☐ 87	2¢	Black (~73)	945.00	250.00
☐ 88	3¢	Rose (~64)	600.00	40.00
☐ 89	10¢	Green (~68)	2650.00	300.00
☐ 90	12¢	Black (~69)	2450.00	325.00
☐ 91	15¢	Black (~77)	RARE	625.00

Scott No.			Unused	Used

F Grill. Grill Measures About 9 x 13 mm.

❑ 92	1¢	Blue (~63)	900.00	425.00
❑ 93	2¢	Black (~73)	360.00	75.00
❑ 94	3¢	Red (~64)	250.00	20.00
❑ 95	5¢	Brown (~67)	2035.00	775.00
❑ 96	10¢	Yellow Green (~68)	1800.00	220.00
❑ 97	12¢	Black (~69)	1800.00	225.00
❑ 98	15¢	Black (~77)	2000.00	330.00
❑ 99	24¢	Gray Lilac (~70)	3000.00	1200.00
❑ 100	30¢	Orange (~71)	3500.00	850.00
❑ 101	90¢	Blue (~72)	RARE	2000.00

1875. Re-issue of 1861–1866 Issues, without Grill, Perforated 12, Hard White Paper.

❑ 102	1¢	Blue (~63)	700.00	1225.00
❑ 103	2¢	Black (~73)	2200.00	1100.00
❑ 104	3¢	Brown Red (~64)	2400.00	1650.00
❑ 105	5¢	Light Brown (67)	1760.00	1450.00
❑ 106	10¢	Green (~68)	2640.00	1700.00
❑ 107	12¢	Black (~69)	3080.00	1700.00
❑ 108	15¢	Black (~77)	3080.00	1850.00
❑ 109	24¢	Deep Violet (~70)	3300.00	2500.00
❑ 110	30¢	Brownish Orange (~71)	2900.00	400.00
❑ 111	90¢	Blue (~72)	RARE	3000.00

112
(123, 133)

113
(124)

114
(125)

115
(126)

1869. Pictorial Issue, with Grill.

❑ 112	1¢	Buff	500.00	175.00
❑ 113	2¢	Brown	468.00	100.00
❑ 114	3¢	Ultramarine	350.00	40.00
❑ 115	6¢	Ultramarine	2035.00	275.00

116
(127)

117
(128)

118
(119, 129)

120
(130)

121
(131)

122
(132)

Scott No.			Unused	Used
❏ 116	10¢	Yellow	1375.00	205.00
❏ 117	12¢	Green	1375.00	205.00
❏ 118	15¢	Brown & Blue (type I)	RARE	625.00
❏ 119	15¢	Brown & Blue (~118) (type II)	1760.00	250.00
❏ 120	24¢	Green & Violet	990.00	625.00
❏ 121	30¢	Blue & Carmine	3750.00	575.00
❏ 122	90¢	Carmine & Black	RARE	500.00

NOTE: Type II (No. 119) contains a small diamond-shaped ornament at center just above the central picture. Type I (No. 118) does not contain the diamond-shaped ornament.

1875. Re-issue of the 1869 Pictorial Issue, Hard White Paper, without Grill.

❏ 123	1¢	Buff (~112)	495.00	385.00
❏ 124	2¢	Brown (~113)	800.00	575.00
❏ 125	3¢	Blue (~114)	3080.00	1850.00
❏ 126	6¢	Blue (~115)	1550.00	880.00
❏ 127	10¢	Yellow (~116)	1650.00	1250.00
❏ 128	12¢	Green (~117)	2035.00	1400.00
❏ 129	15¢	Brown & Blue (~118) (type III)	1760.00	1000.00
❏ 130	24¢	Green & Violet (~120)	1850.00	1050.00
❏ 131	30¢	Blue & Carmine (~121)	2475.00	1525.00
❏ 132	90¢	Carmine & Black (~122)	3850.00	1850.00

NOTE: Type III (No. 129) is similar to Type I (No. 118) above except that it does not contain the fringe of brown shading lines around the central picture as does Type I.

134
(145, 156, 182, 206)

135
(146, 157, 178, 183)

136
(147, 158, 184, 207, 214)

137
(148, 159, 186, 208, 208a)

138
(149, 160, 196)

139
(151, 161, 187, 188, 188b, 209, 209b)

140
(151, 162)

141
(152, 163, 189)

142
(153, 164)

143
(154, 165, 190, 217)

144
(155, 166, 191, 218)

Scott No.			Unused	Used
1880. 1869 Pictorial Issue, Soft Porous Paper.				
❏ 133	1¢	Buff (~112)	385.00	305.00
1870–1871. Printed by the National Bank Note Co., with Grill.				
❏ 134	1¢	Ultramarine	1400.00	240.00
❏ 135	2¢	Red Brown	1000.00	100.00
❏ 136	3¢	Green	600.00	35.00
❏ 137	6¢	Carmine	2800.00	550.00
❏ 138	7¢	Vermilion	2000.00	525.00
❏ 139	10¢	Brown	3200.00	725.00
❏ 140	12¢	Light Violet	RARE	3135.00
❏ 141	15¢	Orange	4000.00	1450.00
❏ 142	24¢	Purple	RARE	RARE

Scott No.			Unused	Used
❑ 143	30¢	Black	RARE	3135.00
❑ 144	90¢	Carmine	RARE	2200.00

1870–1871. Same Designs, without Grill.

❑ 145	1¢	Ultramarine (~134)	475.00	33.00
❑ 146	2¢	Red Brown (~135)	330.00	18.00
❑ 147	3¢	Green (~136)	330.00	3.00
❑ 148	6¢	Carmine (~137)	600.00	32.00
❑ 149	7¢	Vermilion (~138)	800.00	125.00
❑ 150	10¢	Brown (~139)	900.00	40.00
❑ 151	12¢	Dull Violet (~140)	1400.00	220.00
❑ 152	15¢	Bright Orange (~141)	1400.00	205.00
❑ 153	24¢	Purple (~142)	1240.00	220.00
❑ 154	30¢	Black (~143)	2600.00	250.00
❑ 155	90¢	Carmine (~144)	2450.00	330.00

1873. Same Designs as the 1870–1871 Issue, Printed by the Continental Bank Note Co., with Secret Marks, Thin Hard Grayish-White Paper.

❑ 156	1¢	Ultramarine (~134)	300.00	6.00
❑ 157	2¢	Brown (~135)	300.00	20.00
❑ 158	3¢	Green (~136)	165.00	8.00
❑ 159	6¢	Dull Pink (~137)	425.00	24.00
❑ 160	7¢	Orange Vermilion (~138)	1000.00	95.00
❑ 161	10¢	Brown (~139)	665.00	28.00
❑ 162	12¢	Black Violet (~140)	1480.00	165.00
❑ 163	15¢	Yellow Orange (141)	1650.00	200.00
❑ 164	24¢	Purple (~142)	RARE	RARE
❑ 165	30¢	Gray Black (~143)	1650.00	125.00
❑ 166	90¢	Rose Carmine (~144)	2500.00	305.00

NOTE: Refer to the Type Identifier for information on secret marks.

179
(185)

1875.

❑ 178	2¢	Vermilion (~135)	300.00	15.00
❑ 179	5¢	Blue, Zachary Taylor	575.00	29.00

Scott No.			Unused	Used

1879. Same Designs as the 1870–1875 Issue, Printed by the American Bank Note Co., Soft Porous Yellowish-White Paper.

			Unused	Used
❏ 182	1¢	Dark Ultramarine (~134)	275.00	5.50
❏ 183	2¢	Vermilion (~135)	135.00	5.00
❏ 184	3¢	Green (~136)	110.00	4.00
❏ 185	5¢	Blue (~179)	425.00	20.00
❏ 186	6¢	Pink (~137)	800.00	25.00
❏ 187	10¢	Brown (~139), without secret mark	1750.00	38.50
❏ 188	10¢	Brown (~139), with secret mark	895.00	28.00
❏ 188b	10¢	Black Brown (~139)	935.00	125.00
❏ 189	15¢	Red Orange (~141)	350.00	25.00
❏ 190	30¢	Full Black (~143)	900.00	75.00
❏ 191	90¢	Carmine (~144)	1650.00	300.00

NOTE: Refer to the Type Identifier for information on secret marks.

205
(216)

1882.

❏ 205	5¢	Yellow Brown, James Garfield	300.00	12.00

1881–1882. Designs of the 1873 Issue, Re-engraved.

❏ 206	1¢	Gray Blue (~134)	110.00	3.00
❏ 207	3¢	Blue Green (~136)	100.00	3.00
❏ 208	6¢	Rose (~137)	300.00	85.00
❏ 208a	6¢	Brown Red (~137)	220.00	110.00
❏ 209	10¢	Brown (~139)	250.00	8.00
❏ 209b	10¢	Black Brown (~139)	495.00	75.00

NOTE: Re-engraved types can be distinguished as follows: The 1¢ is a milky gray blue and lines of shading have been added to the ornament balls in the upper corners. The 3¢ contains a short horizontal line engraved below the "ts" of "cents." The 6¢ contains three vertical lines at the left of the design instead of four. The 10¢ contains four vertical lines between the outer border and portrait oval instead of five.

210
(213)

211
(215)

212

Scott No.			Unused	Used
1883.				
❏ 210	2¢	Red Brown	75.00	4.00
❏ 211	4¢	Blue Green	175.00	18.50
1887.				
❏ 212	1¢	Ultramarine	100.00	3.00
❏ 213	2¢	Green (~210)	55.00	3.00
❏ 214	3¢	Vermilion (~136)	85.00	65.00
1888.				
❏ 215	4¢	Carmine (~211)	225.00	22.00
❏ 216	5¢	Indigo (~205)	225.00	14.00
❏ 217	30¢	Orange Brown (~143)	350.00	100.00
❏ 218	90¢	Purple (~144)	925.00	250.00

PRICING NOTE: From this point forward, prices for unused stamps are for examples with original gum.

219

219D
(220, 220a, 220c)

1890–1893. (NH Add 100%)

❏ 219	1¢	Dull Blue	45.00	3.00
❏ 219D	2¢	Lake	300.00	3.00
❏ 220	2¢	Carmine (~219D)	45.00	3.00
❏ 220a	2¢	Carmine (Cap on left 2)	200.00	14.00
❏ 220c	2¢	Carmine (Cap both 2s)	695.00	25.00

Scott No.			Unused	Used
❑ 221	3¢	Purple	150.00	8.50
❑ 222	4¢	Dark Brown	160.00	7.00
❑ 223	5¢	Chocolate	150.00	7.50
❑ 224	6¢	Brown Red	110.00	22.00
❑ 225	8¢	Lilac	80.00	15.00
❑ 226	10¢	Green	245.00	4.00
❑ 227	15¢	Indigo	275.00	25.00
❑ 228	30¢	Black	425.00	38.50
❑ 229	90¢	Orange	750.00	120.00

1893. Columbian Exposition Issue. (NH Add 100–200%)

❑ 230	1¢	Blue	48.00	1.00
❑ 231	2¢	Violet	48.00	.10–.25
❑ 231c	2¢	"Broken Hat" variety (~231)	85.00	1.50
❑ 232	3¢	Green	100.00	25.00

NOTE: A notch appears at the top of Columbus's hat on the broken hat variety.

233   234   235

236   237   238

239   240   241

242

Scott No.			Unused	Used
❏ 233	4¢	Ultramarine	110.00	8.00
❏ 234	5¢	Chocolate	140.00	10.00
❏ 235	6¢	Purple	140.00	28.00
❏ 236	8¢	Magenta	125.00	14.00
❏ 237	10¢	Black Brown	175.00	12.00
❏ 238	15¢	Dark Green	310.00	110.00
❏ 239	30¢	Orange Brown	375.00	125.00
❏ 240	50¢	Slate Blue	625.00	225.00
❏ 241	$1	Salmon	1475.00	630.00
❏ 242	$2	Brown Red	1475.00	660.00

NOTE: Refer to the Type Identifier for information on types.

	243		244	245

Scott No.			Unused	Used
❑ 243	$3	Yellow Green	3000.00	1100.00
❑ 244	$4	Crimson Lake	3200.00	1400.00
❑ 245	$5	Black	3200.00	1900.00

246
(247, 264, 279)

248
(249, 250, 251, 252, 265,
266, 267, 279B, 279C, 279D)

253
(268)

254
(269, 280)

255
(270, 281)

1894. Similar to the Series of 1890–1893 but with Triangles added in Upper Corners, Unwatermarked. (NH Add 100%)

❑ 246	1¢	Ultramarine	65.00	8.00
❑ 247	1¢	Blue (~246)	85.00	4.00
❑ 248	2¢	Pink (type I)	60.00	8.50
❑ 249	2¢	Carmine Lake (~248) (type I)	210.00	8.00
❑ 250	2¢	Carmine (~248) (type I)	50.00	2.25
❑ 251	2¢	Carmine (~248) (type II)	365.00	12.50
❑ 252	2¢	Carmine (~248) (type III)	200.00	12.50
❑ 253	3¢	Purple	130.00	12.50
❑ 254	4¢	Dark Brown	150.00	8.50
❑ 255	5¢	Chocolate	150.00	8.50

NOTE: Refer to the Type Identifier for information on types.

256	257	258	259
(271, 282, 282a)	(272)	(273, 282C, 283)	(274, 284)

260	261	262	263
(275)	(261A, 276, 276A)	(277)	(278)

Scott No.			Unused	Used
❑ 256	6¢	Dull Brown	185.00	28.50
❑ 257	8¢	Violet Brown	185.00	20.00
❑ 258	10¢	Dark Green	300.00	16.00
❑ 259	15¢	Dark Blue	310.00	65.00
❑ 260	50¢	Orange	600.00	120.00
❑ 261	$1	Black (type I)	1000.00	385.00
❑ 261A	$1	Black (~261) (type II)	2200.00	715.00
❑ 262	$2	Blue	3000.00	1100.00
❑ 263	$5	Dark Green	RARE	2075.00

1895. Same Designs as the 1894 Issue, Double Line Watermark.
(NH Add 100%)

❑ 264	1¢	Blue (~246)	15.00	3.75
❑ 265	2¢	Carmine (~248) (type I)	60.00	4.00
❑ 266	2¢	Carmine (~248) (type II)	40.00	6.00
❑ 267	2¢	Carmine (~248) (type III)	10.00	.10–.25
❑ 268	3¢	Purple (~253)	45.00	3.25
❑ 269	4¢	Dark Brown (~254)	60.00	3.25
❑ 270	5¢	Chocolate (~255)	55.00	3.25
❑ 271	6¢	Dull Brown (~256)	140.00	7.50
❑ 272	8¢	Violet Brown (~257)	85.00	5.00
❑ 273	10¢	Dark Green (~258)	120.00	3.00
❑ 274	15¢	Dark Blue (~259)	200.00	20.00

NOTE: Refer to the Type Identifier for information on types.

Scott No.			Unused	Used
❏ 275	50¢	Dull Orange (~260)	340.00	48.00
❏ 276	$1	Black (~261) (type I)	625.00	90.00
❏ 276A	$1	Black (~261) (type II)	1400.00	200.00
❏ 277	$2	Blue (~262)	1200.00	375.00
❏ 278	$5	Dark Green (~263)	2400.00	575.00

1898. Same Designs as the 1894 Issue but with Changed Colors, Double Line Watermark. (NH Add 100%)

❏ 279	1¢	Deep Green (~246)	15.00	.10–.25
❏ 279B	2¢	Red (~248)	15.00	.10–.25
❏ 279C	2¢	Rose Carmine (~248)	350.00	100.00
❏ 279D	2¢	Orange Red (~248)	25.00	2.00
❏ 280	4¢	Rose Brown (~254)	45.00	4.00
❏ 281	5¢	Dark Blue (~255)	55.00	3.00
❏ 282	6¢	Lake (~256)	70.00	6.25
❏ 282a	6¢	Purplish Lake (~256)	80.00	12.50
❏ 282C	10¢	Brown (~258) (type I)	210.00	7.00
❏ 283	10¢	Orange Brown (~258) (type II)	180.00	7.00
❏ 284	15¢	Olive Green (~259)	160.00	10.00

285   286   287

288   289

1898. Trans-Mississippi Exposition Issue. (NH Add 100%)

❏ 285	1¢	Yellow Green	70.00	6.50
❏ 286	2¢	Copper Red	50.00	4.00
❏ 287	4¢	Orange	210.00	30.00
❏ 288	5¢	Dull Blue	210.00	26.00
❏ 289	8¢	Violet Brown	250.00	45.00

290 291 292

293

Scott No.			Unused	Used
❏ 290	10¢	Gray Violet	220.00	38.00
❏ 291	50¢	Sage Green	825.00	210.00
❏ 292	$1	Black	1850.00	650.00
❏ 293	$2	Orange Brown	2200.00	1050.00

294 295 296

297 298 299

1901. Pan-American Issue. (NH Add 80%)

❏ 294	1¢	Green & Black	75.00	6.00
❏ 295	2¢	Carmine & Black	35.00	3.00
❏ 296	4¢	Chocolate & Black	150.00	25.50
❏ 297	5¢	Ultramarine & Black	150.00	24.00
❏ 298	8¢	Brown Violet Black	175.00	65.50
❏ 299	10¢	Yellow Brown Black	225.00	30.00

300
(314, 316, 318)

301

302

303

304
(315, 317)

305

306

307

308

309

310

311

312
(479)

313
(480)

Scott No.			Unused	Used
1902–1903. Definitives, Perforated 12. (NH Add 100%)				
☐ 300	1¢	Blue Green	18.00	.10–.25
☐ 301	2¢	Carmine	30.00	.10–.25
☐ 302	3¢	Violet	70.00	6.00
☐ 303	4¢	Brown	85.00	3.00
☐ 304	5¢	Blue	85.00	3.00
☐ 305	6¢	Claret	85.00	6.00
☐ 306	8¢	Violet Black	60.00	4.00
☐ 307	10¢	Red Brown	75.00	4.00
☐ 308	13¢	Purple Black	75.00	12.00
☐ 309	15¢	Olive Green	200.00	9.00
☐ 310	50¢	Orange	500.00	28.50
☐ 311	$1	Black	850.00	100.00
☐ 312	$2	Dark Blue	1375.00	175.00
☐ 313	$5	Dark Green	3135.00	630.00

Scott No.				Unused	Used

1906–1908. Designs of the 1902–1903 Issue, Imperforate. (NH Add 80%)

❑ 314	1¢	Blue Green (~300)	45.00	35.00
❑ 315	5¢	Blue (~304)	1400.00	650.00

1908. Coil Stamps, Perforated 12 Horizontally.

❑ 316	1¢	Blue Green (~300)	RARE	RARE
❑ 317	5¢	Blue (~304)	RARE	RARE

1908. Coil Stamp, Perforated 12 Vertically.

❑ 318	1¢	Blue Green (~300)	RARE	3650.00

319
(319a, 320, 320a)

1903. Perforated 12. (NH Add 85%)

❑ 319	2¢	Carmine	10.00	1.00
❑ 319a	2¢	Lake (~319)	—	—

1906. Imperforate. (NH Add 85%)

❑ 320	2¢	Carmine (~319)	45.00	28.00
❑ 320a	2¢	Lake (~319)	70.00	42.50

323   **324**   **325**

1904. Louisiana Purchase Issue. (NH Add 90%)

❑ 323	1¢	Green	48.00	8.00
❑ 324	2¢	Carmine	45.00	7.00
❑ 325	3¢	Violet	110.00	35.00

326 **327**

Scott No.			Unused	Used
❏ 326	5¢	Dark Blue	145.00	32.00
❏ 327	10¢	Red Brown	200.00	35.00

328 **329** **330**

1907. Jamestown Exposition Issue. (NH Add 90%)

❏ 328	1¢	Green	45.00	6.00
❏ 329	2¢	Carmine	45.00	6.00
❏ 330	5¢	Blue	175.00	38.00

331 **332** **333** **334**

(343, 348, 352, 357, 374, 383, 385, 387, 390, 392) (344, 349, 353, 358, 375, 384, 386, 388, 391, 393, 519) (345, 359, 376, 394, 426, 445, 456, 464, 483, 484, 489, 493, 494, 501, 502, 529, 530, 535, 541) (346, 350, 354, 360, 377, 395, 427, 446, 457, 465, 495, 503)

1908–1909. Washington-Franklin Series, Perforated 12, Double Line Watermark. (NH Add 90%)

❏ 331	1¢	Green	18.00	.10–.25
❏ 332	2¢	Carmine	12.00	.10–.25
❏ 333	3¢	Violet	48.00	5.25
❏ 334	4¢	Orange Brown	50.00	3.25

335
(347, 355, 351, 361, 378, 396, 428, 447, 458, 466, 467, 496, 504, 505)

336
(362, 379, 429, 468, 506)

337
(363, 380)

338
(356, 364, 381)

339
(365)

340
(366, 382)

341

342

Scott No.			Line Pair	Unused	Used
❑ 335	5¢	Blue		60.00	3.00
❑ 336	6¢	Red Orange		75.00	6.00
❑ 337	8¢	Olive Green		75.00	6.00
❑ 338	10¢	Yellow		80.00	3.00
❑ 339	13¢	Blue Green		75.00	16.00
❑ 340	15¢	Pale Ultramarine		80.00	10.00
❑ 341	50¢	Violet		325.00	28.50
❑ 342	$1	Violet Black		550.00	125.00

1908–1909. Imperforate, Double Line Watermark. (NH Add 90%)

❑ 343	1¢	Green (~331)		18.00	7.00
❑ 344	2¢	Carmine (~332)		28.00	6.00
❑ 345	3¢	Deep Violet (~333)		60.00	30.00
❑ 346	4¢	Orange Brown (~334)		65.00	45.00
❑ 347	5¢	Blue (~335)		85.00	40.00

1908–1910. Coil Stamps, Perforated 12 Horizontally. (NH Add 90%)

❑ 348	1¢	Green (~331)	235.00	85.00	35.00
❑ 349	2¢	Carmine (~332)	385.00	175.00	85.00
❑ 350	4¢	Orange Brown (~334)	1200.00	275.00	150.00
❑ 351	5¢	Blue (~335)	1200.00	275.00	175.00

Scott No.			Line Pair	Unused	Used

1909. Coil Stamps, Perforated 12 Vertically. (NH Add 90%)

❑ 352	1¢	Green (~331)	675.00	175.00	65.00
❑ 353	2¢	Carmine (~332)	675.00	200.00	25.00
❑ 354	4¢	Orange Brown (~334)	825.00	275.00	100.00
❑ 355	5¢	Blue (~335)	850.00	275.00	100.00
❑ 356	10¢	Yellow (~338)	—	2800.00	1200.00

1909. Washington-Franklin Series, Printed on Bluish Gray Paper.
(NH Add 90%)

				Unused	Used
❑ 357	1¢	Green (~331)		175.00	140.00
❑ 358	2¢	Carmine (~332)		250.00	140.00
❑ 359	3¢	Violet (~333)		3200.00	2000.00
❑ 360	4¢	Orange Brown (~334)		RARE	RARE
❑ 361	5¢	Blue (~335)		RARE	3500.00
❑ 362	6¢	Orange (~336)		1600.00	3500.00
❑ 363	8¢	Olive Green (~337)		RARE	RARE
❑ 364	10¢	Yellow (~338)		RARE	2400.00
❑ 365	13¢	Blue Green (~339)		RARE	2600.00
❑ 366	15¢	Pale Ultramarine (~340)		RARE	1500.00

367
(368, 369)

1909. Lincoln Memorial Issue. (NH Add 85%)

			Unused	Used
❑ 367	2¢	Carmine, perforated 12	18.00	3.00
❑ 368	2¢	Carmine (~367), imperforate	40.00	26.50
❑ 369	2¢	Carmine (~367), perforated 12, on bluish gray paper	400.00	240.00

370
(371)

372
(373)

Scott No.			Line Pair	Unused	Used

1909. Alaska–Yukon Issue. (NH Add 80%)

❏ 370	2¢	Carmine, perforated 12		18.00	3.00
❏ 371	2¢	Carmine (~370), imperforate		50.00	35.50

1909. Hudson–Fulton Issue. (NH Add 80%)

❏ 372	2¢	Carmine, perforated 12		20.00	6.00
❏ 373	2¢	Carmine (~372), imperforate		50.00	35.00

1910–1911. Washington-Franklin Series, Perforated 12, Single Line Watermark. (NH Add 90%)

❏ 374	1¢	Green (~331)		18.00	.10–.45
❏ 375	2¢	Carmine (~332)		18.00	.10–.45
❏ 376	3¢	Deep Violet (~333)		32.00	3.00
❏ 377	4¢	Brown (~334)		48.00	1.00
❏ 378	5¢	Blue (~335)		40.00	1.00
❏ 379	6¢	Red Orange (~336)		55.00	1.00
❏ 380	8¢	Olive Green (~337)		160.00	32.50
❏ 381	10¢	Yellow (~338)		160.00	8.00
❏ 382	15¢	Ultramarine (~340)		325.00	28.00

1910. Washington-Franklin Series, Imperforate, Single Line Watermark. (NH Add 80%)

❏ 383	1¢	Green (~331)		12.00	4.00
❏ 384	2¢	Carmine (~332)		20.00	4.00

1910. Coil Stamps, Perforated 12 Horizontally, Single Line Watermark. (NH Add 90%)

❏ 385	1¢	Green (~331)	500.00	150.00	38.50
❏ 386	2¢	Carmine (~332)	800.00	210.00	55.50

Scott No.			Line Pair	Unused	Used

1910–1911. Coil Stamps, Perforated 12 Vertically, Single Line Watermark. (NH Add 90%)

| ❏ 387 | 1¢ | Green (~331) | 1200.00 | 340.00 | 110.00 |
| ❏ 388 | 2¢ | Carmine (~332) | 4000.00 | 2000.00 | 525.00 |

1910. Coil Stamps, Perforated 8½ Horizontally, Single Line Watermark. (NH Add 90%)

| ❏ 390 | 1¢ | Green (~331) | 42.00 | 22.00 | 7.00 |
| ❏ 391 | 2¢ | Carmine (~332) | 240.00 | 65.00 | 28.00 |

1910–1913. Coil Stamps, Perforated 8½ Vertically, Single Line Watermark. (NH Add 90%)

❏ 392	1¢	Green (~331)	175.00	50.00	35.00
❏ 393	2¢	Carmine (~332)	350.00	65.00	24.00
❏ 394	3¢	Violet (~333)	350.00	100.00	60.00
❏ 395	4¢	Brown (~334)	450.00	100.00	65.00
❏ 396	5¢	Blue (~335)	450.00	100.00	70.00

397
(401)

398
(402)

399
(403)

400
(400A, 404)

1913. Panama–Pacific Issue, Perforated 12. (NH Add 90%)

❏ 397	1¢	Green		35.00	3.00
❏ 398	2¢	Carmine		40.00	1.00
❏ 399	5¢	Blue		120.00	14.00
❏ 400	10¢	Orange Yellow		185.00	28.00
❏ 400A	10¢	Orange		310.00	25.00

Scott No.			**Line Pair**	**Unused**	**Used**

1914–1915. Panama-Pacific Issue, Perforated 10. (NH Add 90%)

❏ 401	1¢	Green (~397)		48.00	8.00
❏ 402	2¢	Carmine (~398)		125.00	4.00
❏ 403	5¢	Blue (~399)		250.00	22.50
❏ 404	10¢	Orange (~400)		1000.00	75.00

405

(408, 410, 412, 424, 441, 443, 448, 452, 462, 481, 486, 490, 498, 525, 531, 536, 538, 542, 543, 544, 545)

406

(409, 411, 413, 425, 442, 444, 449, 450, 453, 454, 455, 459, 461, 463, 482, 487, 488, 491, 492, 499, 500, 526, 527, 528, 528A, 528B, 532, 533, 534, 534A, 534B, 539, 540, 546)

407

(430, 469, 507)

1912–1914. Washington-Franklin Series, Perforated 12, Single Line Watermark. (NH Add 90%)

❏ 405	1¢	Green		14.00	.10–.25
❏ 406	2¢	Carmine		14.00	.10–.25
❏ 407	7¢	Black		110.00	16.50

1912. Washington-Franklin Series, Imperforate, Single Line Watermark. (NH Add 90%)

❏ 408	1¢	Green (~405)		8.00	4.50
❏ 409	2¢	Carmine (~406)		8.00	4.50

1912. Coil Stamps, Perforated 8½ Horizontally, Single Line Watermark. (NH Add 90%)

❏ 410	1¢	Green (~405)	60.00	15.00	8.50
❏ 411	2¢	Carmine (~406)	75.00	15.00	8.50

1912. Coil Stamps, Perforated 8½ Vertically, Single Line Watermark. (NH Add 90%)

❏ 412	1¢	Green (~405)	175.00	40.00	12.00
❏ 413	2¢	Carmine (~406)	285.00	65.00	18.00

414
(431, 470, 508)

415
(432, 471, 509)

416
(433, 472, 497, 510)

417
(435, 435a, 474, 512)

418
(437, 475, 514)

419
(438, 476, 515)

420
(439, 476A, 516)

421
(422, 440, 477, 517)

423
(460, 478, 518, 518b)

Scott No.			Unused	Used

1912–1914. Washington-Franklin Series, Perforated 12, Single Line Watermark. (NH Add 90%)

			Unused	Used
❑ 414	8¢	Olive Green	80.00	2.00
❑ 415	9¢	Salmon Red	80.00	16.50
❑ 416	10¢	Orange Yellow	70.00	1.00
❑ 417	12¢	Claret Brown	70.00	6.50
❑ 418	15¢	Gray	130.00	6.50
❑ 419	20¢	Ultramarine	250.00	22.50
❑ 420	30¢	Orange Red	175.00	32.50
❑ 421	50¢	Violet	525.00	34.50

1912. Franklin Types, Perforated 12, Double Line Watermark. (NH Add 90%)

			Unused	Used
❑ 422	50¢	Violet (~421)	325.00	36.50
❑ 423	$1	Violet Black	575.00	100.00

434
(473, 511)

Scott No.			Line Pair	Unused	Used

1914–1915. Washington-Franklin Series, Perforated 10, Single Line Watermark. (NH Add 90%)

Scott No.			Line Pair	Unused	Used
❑ 424	1¢	Green (~405)		10.00	.10–.25
❑ 425	2¢	Carmine (~406)		10.00	.10–.25
❑ 426	3¢	Deep Violet (~333)		28.00	4.25
❑ 427	4¢	Brown (~334)		60.00	1.00
❑ 428	5¢	Blue (~335)		60.00	1.00
❑ 429	6¢	Orange (~336)		65.00	3.25
❑ 430	7¢	Black (~407)		120.00	8.50
❑ 431	8¢	Olive Green (~414)		65.00	4.25
❑ 432	9¢	Salmon Red (~415)		85.00	15.00
❑ 433	10¢	Orange Yellow (~416)		85.00	3.25
❑ 434	11¢	Dark Green		48.00	14.25
❑ 435	12¢	Claret Brown (~417)		48.00	7.50
❑ 435a	12¢	Copper Red (~417)		48.00	7.50
❑ 437	15¢	Gray (~418)		165.00	10.00
❑ 438	20¢	Ultramarine (~419)		250.00	8.00
❑ 439	30¢	Orange Red (~420)		365.00	18.00
❑ 440	50¢	Violet (~421)		700.00	34.00

1914. Coil Stamps, Perforated 10 Horizontally, Single Line Watermark. (NH Add 90%)

Scott No.			Line Pair	Unused	Used
❑ 441	1¢	Green (~405)	20.00	6.00	3.00
❑ 442	2¢	Carmine (~406)	85.00	28.50	20.00

1914. Coil Stamps, Perforated 10 Vertically, Single Line Watermark. (NH Add 90%)

Scott No.			Line Pair	Unused	Used
❑ 443	1¢	Green (~405)	225.00	48.00	20.00
❑ 444	2¢	Carmine (~406)	325.00	75.00	14.00
❑ 445	3¢	Violet (~333)	800.00	375.00	175.00
❑ 446	4¢	Brown (~334)	800.00	285.00	85.00
❑ 447	5¢	Blue (~335)	300.00	110.00	42.50

Scott No.			Line Pair	Unused	Used

1914–1916. Rotary Press Coil Stamps, Perforated 10 Horizontally, Single Line Watermark. (NH Add 90%)

❑ 448	1¢	Green (~405)		25.00	15.00
❑ 449	2¢	Red (~406) (type I)		2800.00	575.00
❑ 450	2¢	Carmine (~406) (type III)		50.00	14.50

1914–1916. Rotary Press Coils, Perforated 10 Vertically, Single Line Watermark. (NH Add 90%)

❑ 452	1¢	Green (~405)	100.00	30.00	10.00
❑ 453	2¢	Red (~406) (type I)	800.00	165.00	6.00
❑ 454	2¢	Carmine (~406) (type II)	500.00	120.00	14.50
❑ 455	2¢	Carmine (~406) (type III)	100.00	22.00	4.00
❑ 456	3¢	Violet (~333)	1200.00	325.00	175.00
❑ 457	4¢	Brown (~334)	225.00	60.00	40.00
❑ 458	5¢	Blue (~335)	225.00	65.00	40.00

1914. Imperforate, Single Line Watermark. (NH Add 60%)

| ❑ 459 | 2¢ | Carmine (~406) | | 475.00 | 1250.00 |

1915. Franklin Type, Perforated 10, Double Line Watermark. (NH Add 90%)

| ❑ 460 | $1 | Violet Black (~423) | | 1200.00 | 165.00 |

1915. Washington Type, Flat Plate Printing, Perforated 11, Single Line Watermark, Design Measures 18½–19 x 22 mm. (NH Add 90%)

| ❑ 461 | 2¢ | Pale Carmine Red (~406) | | 325.00 | 250.00 |

1916–1917. Washington-Franklin Series, Perforated 10, Unwatermarked. (NH Add 90%)

❑ 462	1¢	Green (~405)		20.00	1.00
❑ 463	2¢	Carmine (~406)		15.00	.10–.25
❑ 464	3¢	Violet (~333)		100.00	20.00
❑ 465	4¢	Orange Brown (~334)		70.00	4.25
❑ 466	5¢	Blue (~335)		110.00	5.00
❑ 467	5¢	Carmine (error) (~335)		800.00	150.00
❑ 468	6¢	Red Orange (~336)		150.00	18.00
❑ 469	7¢	Black (~407)		165.00	28.00
❑ 470	8¢	Olive Green (~414)		110.00	12.00

NOTE: Refer to the Type Identifier for information on types.

Scott No.			Line Pair	Unused	Used
❑ 471	9¢	Salmon Red (~415)		125.00	40.00
❑ 472	10¢	Orange Yellow (~416)		165.00	7.00
❑ 473	11¢	Dark Green (~434)		75.00	40.50
❑ 474	12¢	Claret Brown (~417)		110.00	12.50
❑ 475	15¢	Gray (~418)		350.00	22.00
❑ 476	20¢	Ultramarine (~419)		350.00	20.00
❑ 476A	30¢	Orange Red (~420)		3500.00	—
❑ 477	50¢	Light Violet (~421)		1200.00	100.00
❑ 478	$1	Violet Black (~423)		1050.00	27.50

1916–1917. Designs of 1902–1903, Perforated 10, Unwatermarked.
(NH Add 80%)

❑ 479	$2	Dark Blue (~312)		450.00	62.00
❑ 480	$5	Light Green (~313)		375.00	60.00

**1916–1917. Washington-Franklin Series, Imperforate,
Unwatermarked.** (NH Add 90%)

❑ 481	1¢	Green (~405)		5.00	1.00
❑ 482	2¢	Carmine (~406)		5.00	1.00
❑ 483	3¢	Violet (~333) (type I)		28.00	21.00
❑ 484	3¢	Violet (~333) (type II)		18.00	15.00

**1916–1922. Rotary Press Coil Stamps, Perforated 10 Horizontally,
Unwatermarked.** (NH Add 85%)

❑ 486	1¢	Green (~405)	12.00	4.00	1.00
❑ 487	2¢	Carmine (~406) (type II)	125.00	28.00	18.50
❑ 488	2¢	Carmine (~406) (type III)	35.00	8.00	4.50
❑ 489	3¢	Violet (~333)	50.00	9.00	2.50

**1916–1922. Rotary Press Coil Stamps, Perforated 10 Vertically,
Unwatermarked.** (NH Add 90%)

❑ 490	1¢	Green (~405)	15.00	4.00	1.00
❑ 491	2¢	Carmine (~406) (type II)	1200.00	2500.00	410.00
❑ 492	2¢	Carmine (~406) (type III)	80.00	15.00	1.00
❑ 493	3¢	Violet (~333) (type I)	140.00	34.00	6.00
❑ 494	3¢	Violet (~333) (type II)	80.00	20.00	1.00
❑ 495	4¢	Orange Brown (~334)	100.00	28.00	10.00
❑ 496	5¢	Blue (~335)	65.00	8.00	1.00
❑ 497	10¢	Orange Yellow (~416)	150.00	280.00	16.00

513

Scott No.			Unused	Used

1917–1919. Washington-Franklin Series, Flat Plate Printing, Perforated 11, Unwatermarked. (NH Add 90%)

			Unused	Used
❏ 498	1¢	Green (~405)	3.00	.10–.25
❏ 499	2¢	Rose (~406) (type I)	3.00	.10–.25
❏ 500	2¢	Deep Rose (~406) (type Ia)	350.00	240.00
❏ 501	3¢	Violet (~333) (type I)	25.00	.10–.25
❏ 502	3¢	Violet (~333) (type II)	30.00	2.00
❏ 503	4¢	Brown (~334)	25.00	1.00
❏ 504	5¢	Blue (~335)	18.00	.10–.25
❏ 505	5¢	Rose (error) (~335)	700.00	425.00
❏ 506	6¢	Red Orange (~336)	22.00	1.00
❏ 507	7¢	Black (~407)	35.00	2.25
❏ 508	8¢	Olive Bistre (~414)	24.00	1.00
❏ 509	9¢	Salmon Red (~415)	24.00	5.00
❏ 510	10¢	Orange Yellow (~416)	30.00	.10–.25
❏ 511	11¢	Light Green (~434)	20.00	5.00
❏ 512	12¢	Claret Brown (~417)	22.00	1.00
❏ 513	13¢	Apple Green	20.00	9.00
❏ 514	15¢	Gray (~418)	60.00	2.50
❏ 515	20¢	Ultramarine (~419)	70.00	1.00
❏ 516	30¢	Orange Red (~420)	50.00	2.50
❏ 517	50¢	Red Violet (~421)	85.00	1.00
❏ 518	$1	Violet Brown (~423)	95.00	1.00
❏ 518b	$1	Deep Brown (~423)	2250.00	1150.00

1917. Washington Type, Perforated 11, Double Line Watermark. (NH Add 80%)

❏ 519	2¢	Carmine (~332)	1000.00	800.00

NOTE: Refer to the Type Identifier for information on types.

523
(547)

524

Scott No.			Unused	Used

1918. Washington-Franklin Series, Perforated 11, Unwatermarked. (NH Add 90%)

❑ 523	$2	Orange Red & Black	800.00	475.00
❑ 524	$5	Deep Green & Black	285.00	55.00

1918–1920. Washington-Franklin Series, Offset Printing, Perforated 11, Unwatermarked. (NH Add 90%)

❑ 525	1¢	Gray Green (~405)	10.00	1.00
❑ 526	2¢	Carmine (~406) (type IV)	40.00	5.50
❑ 527	2¢	Carmine (~406) (type V)	40.00	2.50
❑ 528	2¢	Carmine (~406) (type Va)	20.00	1.00
❑ 528A	2¢	Carmine (~406) (type VI)	65.00	2.50
❑ 528B	2¢	Carmine (~406) (type VII)	40.00	.10–.35
❑ 529	3¢	Violet (333) (type III)	15.00	.10–.35
❑ 530	3¢	Purple (~333) (type IV)	8.00	.10–.35

1918–1920. Washington-Franklin Series, Offset Printing, Imperforate, Unwatermarked. (NH Add 90%)

❑ 531	1¢	Gray Green (~405)	28.00	17.50
❑ 532	2¢	Carmine (~406) (type IV)	110.00	75.00
❑ 533	2¢	Carmine (~406) (type V)	350.00	165.00
❑ 534	2¢	Carmine (~406) (type Va)	40.00	27.50
❑ 534A	2¢	Carmine (~406) (type VI)	120.00	75.50
❑ 534B	2¢	Carmine (~406) (type VII)	2100.00	900.00
❑ 535	3¢	Violet (~333)	25.00	14.00

1918–1920. Washington Type, Offset Printing, Perforated 12½, Unwatermarked. (NH Add 90%)

❑ 536	1¢	Gray Green (~405)	50.00	35.00

PLEASE NOTE: Unless otherwise noted, plate blocks are assumed to be blocks of 4. Where the number is more than 4, it appears in parentheses immediately following the price for the plate block. Blocks containing fewer than the appropriate number of stamps are not considered to be plate blocks and sell for much less.

537

Scott No.			Plate Block	Unused	Used
1919. (NH Add 90%)					
❑ 537	3¢	Victory	125.00 (6)	18.00	6.00

1919–1921. Washington-Franklin Series, Rotary Press Printing, Perforated 11 x 10. (NH Add 90%)

❑ 538	1¢	Green (~405)	140.00	22.00	15.00
❑ 539	2¢	Carmine Rose (~406) (type II)	—	2850.00	RARE
❑ 540	2¢	Carmine Rose (~406) (type III)	135.00	30.00	20.00
❑ 541	3¢	Violet (~333)	450.00	70.00	35.00

1920. Washington-Franklin Series, Rotary Press Printing, Perforated 10 x 11, Design Measures 19 x 22½–22½ mm. (NH Add 90%)

❑ 542	1¢	Green (~405)	220.00	25.00	2.00

1921. Washington-Franklin Series, Rotary Press Printing, Perforated 10 x 10, Design Measures 19 x 22½ mm. (NH Add 90%)

❑ 543	1¢	Green (~405)	30.00	4.00	.10–.35

1922. Washington-Franklin Series, Rotary Press Printing, Perforated 11 x 11, Design Measures 19 x 22½ mm. (NH Add 90%)

❑ 544	1¢	Green (~405)	—	RARE	RARE

1921. Washington-Franklin Series, Rotary Press Printing, Perforated 11 x 11, Design Measures 19½–20 x 22 mm. (NH Add 90%)

❑ 545	1¢	Green (~405)	1200.00	350.00	215.00
❑ 546	2¢	Carmine Rose (~406)	800.00	200.00	165.00

1920. Washington-Franklin Series, Flat Press Printing, Perforated 11 x 11. (NH Add 90%)

❑ 547	$2	Carmine & Black (~523)	RARE	375.00	60.00

548	**549**	**550**

Scott No.			Plate Block	Unused	Used

1920. Pilgrim Issue. (NH Add 80%)

			Plate Block	Unused	Used
❏ 548	1¢	Green	75.00 (6)	14.00	6.00
❏ 549	2¢	Carmine Rose	75.00 (6)	14.00	6.00
❏ 550	5¢	Deep Blue	350.00 (6)	55.00	22.00

551	**552**	**553**	**554**
(653)	(575, 578, 581, 597, 604, 532)	(557, 582, 598, 605, 631, 633)	(577, 579, 583, 595, 599, 599A, 606, 634, 634A)

555	**556**	**557**	**558**
(584, 600, 635)	(585, 601, 636)	(586, 602, 637)	(587, 638, 723)

1922–1925. Definitives, Flat Press Printing, Perforated 11.
(NH Add 80%)

❏ 551	½¢	Olive Brown	14.00 (6)	3.00	.10–.35
❏ 552	1¢	Deep Green	42.00 (6)	7.50	.10–.20
❏ 553	1½¢	Yellow Brown	42.00 (6)	7.50	2.50
❏ 554	2¢	Carmine	36.00 (6)	6.50	.10–.20
❏ 555	3¢	Violet	180.00 (6)	30.00	2.50
❏ 556	4¢	Yellow Brown	180.00 (6)	30.00	1.00
❏ 557	5¢	Dark Blue	180.00 (6)	30.00	1.00
❏ 558	6¢	Red Orange	340.00 (6)	55.00	3.00

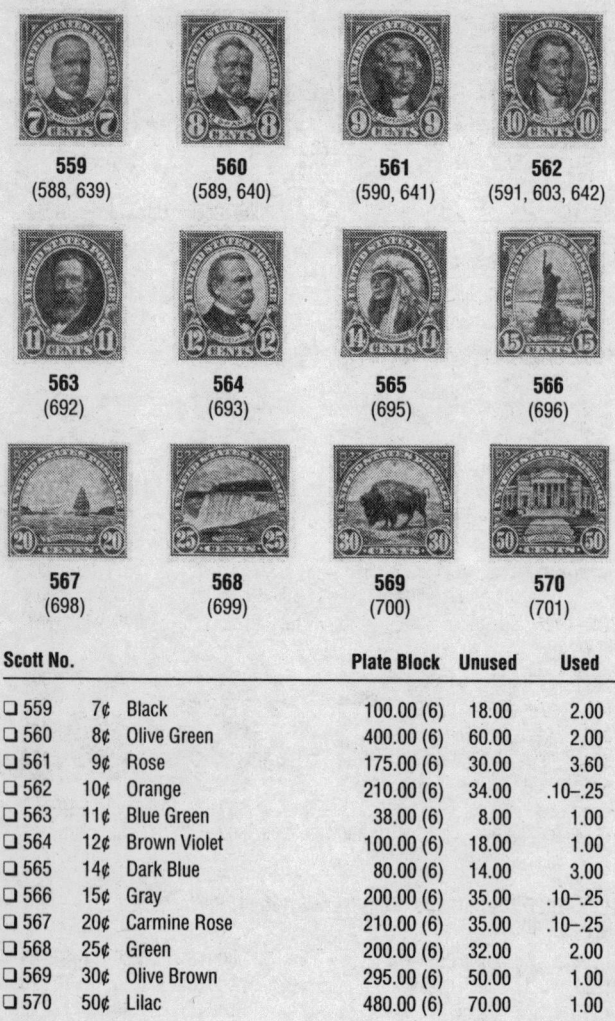

559
(588, 639)

560
(589, 640)

561
(590, 641)

562
(591, 603, 642)

563
(692)

564
(693)

565
(695)

566
(696)

567
(698)

568
(699)

569
(700)

570
(701)

Scott No.			Plate Block	Unused	Used
❑ 559	7¢	Black	100.00 (6)	18.00	2.00
❑ 560	8¢	Olive Green	400.00 (6)	60.00	2.00
❑ 561	9¢	Rose	175.00 (6)	30.00	3.60
❑ 562	10¢	Orange	210.00 (6)	34.00	.10–.25
❑ 563	11¢	Blue Green	38.00 (6)	8.00	1.00
❑ 564	12¢	Brown Violet	100.00 (6)	18.00	1.00
❑ 565	14¢	Dark Blue	80.00 (6)	14.00	3.00
❑ 566	15¢	Gray	200.00 (6)	35.00	.10–.25
❑ 567	20¢	Carmine Rose	210.00 (6)	35.00	.10–.25
❑ 568	25¢	Green	200.00 (6)	32.00	2.00
❑ 569	30¢	Olive Brown	295.00 (6)	50.00	1.00
❑ 570	50¢	Lilac	480.00 (6)	70.00	1.00

571

572

573

Scott No.			Plate Block	Unused	Used
❑ 571	$1	Violet Black	475.00 (6)	75.00	2.00
❑ 572	$2	Deep Blue	850.00 (6)	140.00	11.20
❑ 573	$5	Carmine & Blue	2000.00 (8)	240.00	19.00

Series of 1922–1925, Imperforate. (NH Add 60%)

❑ 575	1¢	Green (~552)	88.00 (6)	14.00	8.50
❑ 576	1½¢	Yellow Brown (~553)	48.00 (6)	6.00	3.00
❑ 577	2¢	Carmine (~554)	40.00 (6)	6.00	5.00

1923–1926. Definitives, Rotary Press Printing, Perforated 11 x 10, Designs Measure 19½ x 22½ mm. (NH Add 60%)

❑ 578	1¢	Green (~552)	850.00	175.00	158.50
❑ 579	2¢	Carmine (~554)	770.00	175.00	140.00

1923–1926. Series of 1922–1925, Rotary Press, Perforated 10. (NH Add 60%)

❑ 581	1¢	Green (~552)	125.00	16.00	1.00
❑ 582	1½¢	Brown (~553)	55.00	8.00	1.00
❑ 583	2¢	Carmine (~554)	55.00	7.00	.10–.25
❑ 584	3¢	Violet (~555)	300.00	35.00	4.45
❑ 585	4¢	Yellow Brown(~556)	275.00	22.00	1.00
❑ 586	5¢	Blue (~557)	250.00	28.00	1.00
❑ 587	6¢	Red Orange (~558)	200.00	28.00	1.00
❑ 588	7¢	Black (~559)	175.00	34.00	10.00
❑ 589	8¢	Olive Green (~560)	250.00	35.00	5.50
❑ 590	9¢	Rose (~561)	100.00	14.00	5.00
❑ 591	10¢	Orange (~562)	550.00	80.00	.45

Scott No.			Line Pair	Unused	Used

1923–1926. Series of 1922–1925, Rotary Press Coil Stamps, Perforated 11. (NH Add 60%)

❑ 595	2¢	Carmine (~554)	2000.00	375.00	350.00

NOTE: No. 595 is a sheet stamp made from coil waste. Its design measures 19½ x 22½ mm.

1923–1929. Series of 1922–1925, Rotary Press Coil Stamps, Perforated 10 Vertically. (NH Add 60%)

❑ 597	1¢	Green (~552)	6.00	3.00	.10–.25
❑ 598	1½¢	Deep Brown (~553)	6.00	3.00	.10–.25
❑ 599	2¢	Carmine (~554) (type I)	6.00	3.00	.10–.25
❑ 599A	2¢	Carmine (~554) (type II)	700.00	160.00	14.50
❑ 600	3¢	Deep Violet (~555)	50.00	12.00	.10–.25
❑ 601	4¢	Yellow Brown (~556)	35.00	8.00	1.00
❑ 602	5¢	Dark Blue (~557)	15.00	6.00	.10–.25
❑ 603	10¢	Orange (~562)	35.00	10.00	.50

NOTE: Refer to the Type Identifier for information on types.

1924–1925. Series of 1922–1925, Coil Stamps, Perforated 10 Horizontally. (NH Add 70%)

❑ 604	1¢	Green (~552)	6.00	3.00	.10–.20
❑ 605	1½¢	Yellow Brown (~553)	6.00	3.00	1.00
❑ 606	2¢	Carmine (~554)	6.00	3.00	1.00

610
(611, 612)

Scott No.			Plate Block	Unused	Used

1923. Harding Memorial Issue. (NH Add 80%)

❑ 610	2¢	Black, perforated 11	21.00 (6)	4.00	.10–.20
❑ 611	2¢	Black (~610), imperforate	116.00 (6)	20.00	9.30
❑ 612	2¢	Black (~610), perforated 10	325.00	26.00	4.50

614 **615** **616**

Scott No.			Plate Block	Unused	Used
1924. Huguenot–Walloon Issue. (NH Add 80%)					
❏ 614	1¢	Green	50.00 (6)	10.00	4.50
❏ 615	2¢	Carmine Rose	50.00 (6)	10.00	4.00
❏ 616	5¢	Dark Blue	300.00 (6)	50.00	32.50

617 **618** **619**

1925. Lexington–Concord Sesquicentennial. (NH Add 60%)					
❏ 617	1¢	Green	65.00 (6)	12.00	6.30
❏ 618	2¢	Carmine Rose	90.00 (6)	16.00	6.50
❏ 619	5¢	Dark Blue	350.00 (6)	55.00	18.25

620 **621**

1925. Norse-American Issue. (NH Add 80%)					
❏ 620	2¢	Carmine & Black	95.00 (8)	12.00	6.50
❏ 621	5¢	Dark Blue & Black	250.00 (8)	30.00	18.00

622
(694)

623
(697)

Scott No.			Plate Block	Unused	Used

1925–1926. 1922–1925 Series New Values, Perforated 11.
(NH Add 80%)

			Plate Block	Unused	Used
❑ 622	13¢	Green	180.00 (6)	30.00	1.00
❑ 623	17¢	Black	230.00 (6)	35.00	.75

627

628

629
(630)

1926. (NH Add 60%)

			Plate Block	Unused	Used
❑ 627	2¢	Sesquicentennial Exposition	48.00 (6)	8.00	1.00
❑ 628	5¢	Ericsson Memorial	100.00 (6)	16.00	5.00
❑ 629	2¢	Battle of White Plains	45.00 (6)	7.00	2.50
❑ 630	2¢	White Plains souvenir sheet (~629)	—	600.00	475.00

1926. Series of 1922–1925, Rotary Press Printing, Imperforate. (NH Add 60%)

			Plate Block	Unused	Used
❑ 631	1½¢	Brown (~553)	75.00	9.00	5.25

1926–1928. Series of 1922–1925, Perforated 11 x 10½.
(NH Add 60%)

			Plate Block	Unused	Used
❑ 632	1¢	Green (~552)	40.00	3.00	.10–.25
❑ 633	1½¢	Yellow Brown (~553)	40.00	7.00	.10–.25
❑ 634	2¢	Carmine (~554) (type I)	20.00	3.00	.10–.25
❑ 634A	2¢	Carmine (~554) (type II)	600.00	400.00	14.75

Scott No.			Plate Block	Unused	Used
❑ 635	3¢	Violet (~555)	20.00	3.00	.10–.25
❑ 636	4¢	Yellow Brown (~556)	80.00	7.00	.10–.25
❑ 637	5¢	Dark Blue (~557)	20.00	7.00	.10–.25
❑ 638	6¢	Red Orange (~558)	25.00	7.00	.10–.25
❑ 639	7¢	Black (~559)	25.00	9.00	.10–.25
❑ 640	8¢	Olive Green (~560)	20.00	7.00	.10–.25
❑ 641	9¢	Orange Red (~561)	22.00	7.00	.10–.25
❑ 642	10¢	Orange (~562)	25.00	7.00	.10–.25

643

644

1927. (NH Add 60%)

❑ 643	2¢	Vermont Sesquicentennial	32.00 (6)	6.00	2.25
❑ 644	2¢	Oriskany - Saratoga	45.00 (6)	8.00	5.00

645

646

647

648

649

650

1928. (NH Add 50–60%)

❑ 645	2¢	Valley Forge	22.00 (6)	4.00	1.00
❑ 646	2¢	Molly Pitcher	40.00	5.00	3.00
❑ 647	2¢	Hawaii	160.00	9.00	6.30
❑ 648	5¢	Hawaii	330.00	30.00	18.75
❑ 649	2¢	Aeronautics Conference	40.00 (6)	7.00	3.00
❑ 650	5¢	Aeronautics Conference	90.00 (6)	16.00	5.00

651

654
(655, 556)

Scott No.			Plate Block	Unused	Used
1929. (NH Add 50%)					
❏ 651	2¢	George Rogers Clark	24.00 (6)	4.50	1.00

1929. Series of 1922–1925, Rotary Press Printing, 11 x 10½.
(NH Add 10–35%)

Scott No.			Plate Block	Unused	Used
❏ 653	½¢	Olive Brown (~551)	8.00	1.25	.10–.25
❏ 654	2¢	Edison - Light Bulb, perforated 11	24.00 (6)	4.00	2.00
❏ 655	2¢	Edison (~654), perforated 11 x 10½	50.00	2.75	.50

Scott No.			Line Pair	Unused	Used
1929. Coil Stamp.					
❏ 656	2¢	Edison – Light Bulb (~654)	80.00	34.00	4.00

657

Scott No.			Plate Block	Unused	Used
1929.					
❏ 657	2¢	Sullivan Expedition	18.00 (6)	3.25	1.50

658

669

Scott No.			Plate Block	Unused	Used

1929. Series of 1922–1925, Perforated 11 x 10½, Overprinted "Kans." (NH Add 50%)

			Plate Block	Unused	Used
❑ 658	1¢	Green	55.00	7.00	5.00
❑ 659	1½¢	Brown	55.00	9.00	6.80
❑ 660	2¢	Carmine	55.00	7.00	1.00
❑ 661	3¢	Violet	235.00	35.00	22.00
❑ 662	4¢	Yellow Brown	235.00	40.00	22.00
❑ 663	5¢	Deep Blue	175.00	22.00	15.00
❑ 664	6¢	Red Orange	450.00	48.00	24.00
❑ 665	7¢	Black	525.00	48.00	32.50
❑ 666	8¢	Olive Green	825.00	125.00	67.50
❑ 667	9¢	Light Rose	325.00	28.00	20.00
❑ 668	10¢	Orange Yellow	325.00	45.00	20.00

1929. Series of 1922–1925, Perforated 11 x 10½, Overprinted "Nebr." (NH Add 50%)

			Plate Block	Unused	Used
❑ 669	1¢	Green	65.00	7.00	6.10
❑ 670	1½¢	Brown	65.00	7.00	5.00
❑ 671	2¢	Carmine	65.00	7.00	1.00
❑ 672	3¢	Violet	210.00	30.00	18.50
❑ 673	4¢	Brown	250.00	35.00	18.00
❑ 674	5¢	Blue	325.00	35.00	24.00
❑ 675	6¢	Orange	475.00	60.00	28.50
❑ 676	7¢	Black	325.00	45.00	30.00
❑ 677	8¢	Olive Green	425.00	70.00	45.00
❑ 678	9¢	Rose	525.00	75.00	45.00
❑ 679	10¢	Orange Yellow	1000.00	150.00	40.00

NOTE: Fakes abound, especially on used stamps.

| **680** | **681** | **682** | **683** |

Scott No.			Plate Block	Unused	Used
1929. (NH Add 35%)					
❑ 680	2¢	Battle of Fallen Timbers	26.00 (6)	4.00	2.00
❑ 681	2¢	Ohio River Canalization	14.00 (6)	2.75	1.00
1930. (NH Add 35%)					
❑ 682	2¢	Massachusetts Bay Colony	40.00 (6)	2.75	1.00
❑ 683	2¢	Charleston, SC	50.00 (6)	6.00	3.50

| **684** | **685** |
| (686) | (687) |

1930. Series of 1922–1925, Rotary Press Printing, Perforated 11 x 10½. (NH Add 35%)

❑ 684	1½¢	Warren G. Harding (full face)	6.00	1.25	.10–.25
❑ 685	4¢	William Howard Taft	20.00	2.75	.10–.25

Scott No.			Line Pair	Unused	Used
1930. Series of 1922–1925, Rotary Press Coil Stamps, Perforated 10 Vertically. (NH Add 40%)					
❑ 686	1½¢	Harding (~684)	12.00	4.25	.10–.25
❑ 687	4¢	Taft (~685)	12.00	6.00	.10–.25

688 **689** **690**

Scott No.			Plate Block	Unused	Used

1930. (NH Add 35%)

❏ 688	2¢	Battle of Braddock's Field	20.00 (6)	3.00	2.00
❏ 689	2¢	Von Steuben	14.00 (6)	2.25	1.00
❏ 690	2¢	Pulaski	8.00 (6)	1.25	.50

1931. Series of 1922–1925, Rotary Press Printing, Perforated 11 x 10½ or 10½ x 11. (NH Add 40%)

❏ 692	11¢	Light Blue (~563)	18.00	8.00	.10–.25
❏ 693	12¢	Brown Violet (~564)	26.00	10.00	.10–.25
❏ 694	13¢	Yellow Green (~622)	20.00	6.00	.80
❏ 695	14¢	Dark Blue (~565)	30.00	10.00	3.00
❏ 696	15¢	Gray (~566)	40.00	18.00	.10–.25
❏ 697	17¢	Black (~623)	35.00	12.00	.50
❏ 698	20¢	Carmine Rose (~567)	42.00	16.00	.10–.25
❏ 699	25¢	Blue Green (~568)	50.00	15.00	.10–.25
❏ 700	30¢	Brown (~569)	80.00	30.00	.10–.25
❏ 701	50¢	Lilac (~570)	185.00	56.00	.10–.25

702 **703**

1931. (NH Add 25%)

❏ 702	2¢	Red Cross	8.00	1.25	.10–.35
❏ 703	2¢	Surrender at Yorktown	8.00	1.25	.50

PLEASE NOTE: Unless otherwise noted, plate blocks are assumed to be blocks of 4. Where the number is more than 4, it appears in parentheses immediately following the price for the plate block. Blocks containing fewer than the appropriate number of stamps are not considered to be plate blocks and sell for much less.

704   705   706   707

708   709   710   711

712   713   714   715

Scott No.			Plate Block	Unused	Used
1932. Washington Bicentennial Set. (NH Add 40%)					
❏ 704	½¢	Olive Brown	6.00	1.05	.10–.35
❏ 705	1¢	Green	8.00	1.05	.10–.35
❏ 706	1½¢	Brown	25.00	1.05	.10–.35
❏ 707	2¢	Carmine	5.00	1.05	.10–.35
❏ 708	3¢	Purple	20.00	1.55	.10–.35
❏ 709	4¢	Light Brown	12.00	1.00	.10–.35
❏ 710	5¢	Blue	20.00	4.25	.10–.35
❏ 711	6¢	Orange	12.00	10.00	.10–.35
❏ 712	7¢	Black	12.00	1.05	.50
❏ 713	8¢	Olive Bistre	75.00	12.00	2.60
❏ 714	9¢	Pale Red	50.00	8.00	.50
❏ 715	10¢	Orange Yellow	100.00	25.00	.10–.25
		Set of 12 (704–715)		70.00	

716	717	718	719	720
				(721, 722)

Scott No.			Plate Block	Unused	Used

1932. (NH Add 30%)

Scott No.			Plate Block	Unused	Used
❑ 716	2¢	Olympics - Lake Placid	8.00 (6)	1.05	.50
❑ 717	2¢	Arbor Day	14.00	1.05	.10–.25
❑ 718	3¢	Olympics - Runner	15.00	5.50	.10–.25
❑ 719	5¢	Olympics - Discus Thrower	25.00	5.50	.50
❑ 720	3¢	George Washington	10.00	1.05	.10–.25

Scott No.			Line Pair	Unused	Used

1932. Coil Stamps. (NH Add 30%)

Scott No.			Line Pair	Unused	Used
❑ 721	3¢	Washington (~720) perf 10 vertically	10.00	5.00	.10–.25
❑ 722	3¢	Washington (~720) perf 10 horizontally	10.00	4.05	.50
❑ 723	6¢	Garfield (~558) perf 10 vertically	50.00	18.00	.10–.35

724	725

Scott No.			Plate Block	Unused	Used

1932. (NH Add 30%)

Scott No.			Plate Block	Unused	Used
❑ 724	3¢	William Penn	14.00 (6)	2.05	.10–.35
❑ 725	3¢	Daniel Webster	16.00 (6)	2.10	.50

726	727	728	729
	(752)	(730, 766)	(731, 767)

Scott No.			Plate Block	Unused	Used
1933. (NH Add 30%)					
❏ 726	3¢	General Oglethorpe	15.00 (6)	2.05	.10–.25
❏ 727	3¢	Washington at Newburgh	7.50	1.05	.10–.25
❏ 728	1¢	Century of Progress - Fort Dearborn	7.50	1.05	.10–.25
❏ 729	3¢	Century of Progress - Skyscrapers	7.50	2.05	.10–.25

730	731

1933. A.P.S. Convention Souvenir Sheets, Imperforate, Ungummed.

Scott No.			Plate Block	Unused	Used
❏ 730	1¢	Sheet of 25 (~728)	—	48.00	—
❏ 730a	1¢	Single stamp	—	2.05	1.00
❏ 731	3¢	Sheet of 25 (~729)	—	40.00	—
❏ 731a	3¢	Single stamp	—	2.00	1.00

732   **733**   **734**

(735, 753, 768)

Scott No.			Plate Block	Unused	Used
1933. (NH Add 20%)					
❑ 732	3¢	National Recovery Act (NRA)	6.00	.80	.10–.25
❑ 733	3¢	Byrd Antarctic Expedition	18.00 (6)	2.05	1.60
❑ 734	5¢	Kosciuszko	18.00 (6)	2.05	1.25

735

1934. National Philatelic Exhibition Souvenir Sheet, Imperforate, Ungummed .

❑ 735	3¢	Sheet of 6 (~733)	—	28.00	—
❑ 735a	3¢	Single stamp	—	6.00	4.00

736

737
(738, 754)

739
(755)

Scott No.			Plate Block	Unused	Used

1934. (NH Add 20%)

❑ 736	3¢	Maryland Tercentenary	8.00 (6)	1.05	.10–.35
❑ 737	3¢	Mother's Day, perf 11 x 10½	4.05	1.05	.10–.25
❑ 738	3¢	Mother's Day (~737), perf 11	8.00 (6)	1.05	.50
❑ 739	3¢	Wisconsin Tercentenary	8.00 (6)	1.05	.10–.25

741
(757)

742
(750, 758, 770)

740
(751, 756, 769)

743
(759)

744
(760)

1934. National Parks Issue, Perforated. (NH Add 25%)

❑ 740	1¢	Yosemite	8.00 (6)	1.05	.10–.25
❑ 741	2¢	Grand Canyon	8.00 (6)	1.05	.10–.25
❑ 742	3¢	Mt. Rainier	8.00 (6)	1.05	.10–.25
❑ 743	4¢	Mesa Verde	14.00 (6)	2.00	.75
❑ 744	5¢	Yellowstone	14.00 (6)	3.00	1.60

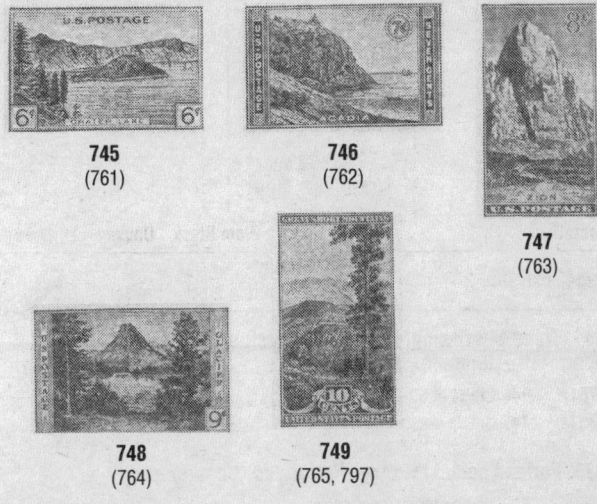

745
(761)

746
(762)

747
(763)

748
(764)

749
(765, 797)

Scott No.			Plate Block	Unused	Used
☐ 745	6¢	Crater Lake	30.00 (6)	4.55	2.25
☐ 746	7¢	Acadia	18.00 (6)	2.30	2.00
☐ 747	8¢	Zion	36.00 (6)	5.50	4.50
☐ 748	9¢	Glacier	36.00 (6)	5.50	2.00
☐ 749	10¢	Smoky Mountains, gray black	46.00 (6)	7.50	3.00
		Set of 10 (740–749)	—	36.00	—

750

1934. A.P.S. Convention Souvenir Sheet, Imperforate, Gummed.
(NH Add 25%)

☐ 750	3¢	Sheet of 6 (~742)	—	65.00	—
☐ 750a	3¢	Single stamp	—	10.00	6.00

751

Scott No.			Plate Block	Unused	Used

1934. Trans-Mississippi Philatelic Exposition Souvenir Sheet, Imperforate, Gummed. (NH Add 25%)

❑ 751	1¢	Sheet of 6 (~740)	—	24.00	—
❑ 751a	1¢	Single stamp	—	4.30	2.10

1935. Farley Special Printing, Perforated, Ungummed.

❑ 752	3¢	Washington at Newburgh (~727)	22.00	1.00	.50
❑ 753	3¢	Byrd Antarctic Expedition (~733)	12.00 (6)	1.65	1.00

1935. Farley Special Printing, Imperforate, Ungummed.

❑ 754	3¢	Mother's Day (~737)	15.00 (6)	2.25	1.75
❑ 755	3¢	Wisconsin Tercentenary (~739)	20.00 (6)	3.00	2.00

1935. Farley Special Printing, National Parks Set, Imperforate, Ungummed.

❑ 756	1¢	Yosemite (~740)	7.00 (6)	1.05	.50
❑ 757	2¢	Grand Canyon (~741)	7.00 (6)	1.05	.50
❑ 758	3¢	Mt. Rainier (~742)	14.00 (6)	2.05	1.00
❑ 759	4¢	Mesa Verde (~743)	32.00 (6)	5.00	2.50
❑ 760	5¢	Yellowstone (~744)	32.00 (6)	5.00	4.00
❑ 761	6¢	Crater Lake (~745)	44.00 (6)	7.00	6.00
❑ 762	7¢	Acadia (~746)	35.00 (6)	5.00	3.00
❑ 763	8¢	Zion (~747)	32.00 (6)	5.00	4.00
❑ 764	9¢	Glacier (~748)	42.00 (6)	6.50	6.00
❑ 765	10¢	Smoky Mountains (~749), gray black	62.00 (6)	10.00	5.75
		Set of 10 (756–765)	—	50.00	—

771

Scott No.			Plate Block	Unused	Used

1935. Farley Special Printing, Imperforate, Ungummed.

❏ 766	1¢	Souvenir sheet of 25 (~730)	—	65.00	—
❏ 767	3¢	Souvenir sheet of 25 (~731)	—	52.00	—
❏ 768	3¢	Souvenir sheet of 6 (~735)	—	32.00	—
❏ 769	1¢	Souvenir sheet of 6 (~751)	—	20.00	—
❏ 770	3¢	Souvenir sheet of 6 (~750)	—	58.00	—
❏ 771	16¢	Airmail Special Delivery	35.00 (6)	5.50	—

NOTE: Farley Special Printing items (752–771) were issued in uncut press sheets. Position pairs and blocks that include guide lines or interpane gutters help distinguish Farley items from their regularly issued counterparts.

NOTE: Prices for stamps from 1935 forward are for never-hinged (NH) examples.

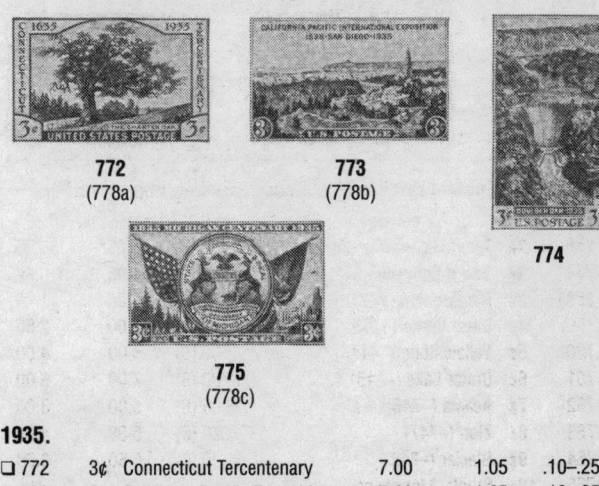

772
(778a)

773
(778b)

774

775
(778c)

1935.

❏ 772	3¢	Connecticut Tercentenary	7.00	1.05	.10–.25
❏ 773	3¢	California Pacific Exposition	7.00	1.05	.10–.25
❏ 774	3¢	Boulder Dam	8.00 (6)	1.05	.10–.25
❏ 775	3¢	Michigan Centenary	8.00	1.05	.10–.25

776
(778d)

777

778

Scott No.			Plate Block	Unused	Used
1936.					
❑ 776	3¢	Texas Centennial	6.00	1.05	.10–.25
❑ 777	3¢	Rhode Island Tercentenary	6.00	1.05	.10–.25
❑ 778	3¢	TIPEX souvenir sheet	—	1.05	—
❑ 778a	3¢	Single Stamp (~772), imperforate	—	1.00	.50
❑ 778b	3¢	Single Stamp (~773), imperforate	—	1.00	.50
❑ 778c	3¢	Single Stamp (~775), imperforate	—	1.00	.50
❑ 778d	3¢	Single Stamp (~776), imperforate	—	1.00	.50

NOTE: Prices for stamps from 1935 forward are for never-hinged (NH) examples.

782 **783** **784**

Scott No.			Plate Block	Unused	Used
❏ 782	3¢	Arkansas Centennial	4.05	1.00	.10–.25
❏ 783	3¢	Oregon Territory Centennial	2.55	1.00	.10–.25
❏ 784	3¢	Susan B. Anthony	2.55	1.00	.10–.25

785 **786**

787 **788**

789 **790**

1936–1937. Army and Navy Issue.

❏ 785	1¢	Washington & Greene	5.00	1.00	.10–.25
❏ 786	2¢	Jackson & Scott	5.00	1.00	.10–.25
❏ 787	3¢	Sherman, Grant & Sheridan	6.00	1.70	.10–.25
❏ 788	4¢	Lee & Stonewall Jackson	12.00	1.70	.50
❏ 789	5¢	West Point	12.00	2.55	.50
❏ 790	1¢	Jones & Barry	5.00	1.00	.10–.25

791

792

793

794

Scott No.			Plate Block	Unused	Used
❏ 791	2¢	Decatur & McDonough	6.00	1.00	.10–.20
❏ 792	3¢	Farragut & Porter	6.00	1.00	.10–.20
❏ 793	4¢	Sampson, Dewey & Schley	12.00	2.05	.50
❏ 794	5¢	Annapolis	12.00	2.55	.50
		Set of 10 (785–779)	—	20.00	—

795

796

797

1937.

❏ 795	3¢	Ordinance of 1787	5.00	1.30	.10–.25
❏ 796	5¢	Virginia Dare	8.00 (6)	1.00	.50
❏ 797	10¢	SPA souvenir sheet (~749), blue green	—	2.05	—

798

799

800

801

802

Scott No.			Plate Block	Unused	Used
❏ 798	3¢	Constitution Sesquicentennial	5.05	2.55	.10–.20
❏ 799	3¢	Hawaii	4.00	1.00	.10–.20
❏ 800	3¢	Alaska	4.00	1.00	.10–.20
❏ 801	3¢	Puerto Rico	4.00	1.00	.10–.20
❏ 802	3¢	Virgin Islands	4.00	1.00	.10–.20

803

804
(839, 848)

805
(840, 849)

806
(841, 850)

807
(842, 851)

1938. Presidential Series.

❏ 803	½¢	Benjamin Franklin	2.00	1.00	.10–.25
❏ 804	1¢	George Washington	2.00	1.00	.10–.25
❏ 805	1½¢	Martha Washington	2.00	1.00	.10–.25
❏ 806	2¢	John Adams	2.00	1.00	.10–.25
❏ 807	3¢	Thomas Jefferson	2.00	1.10	.10–.25

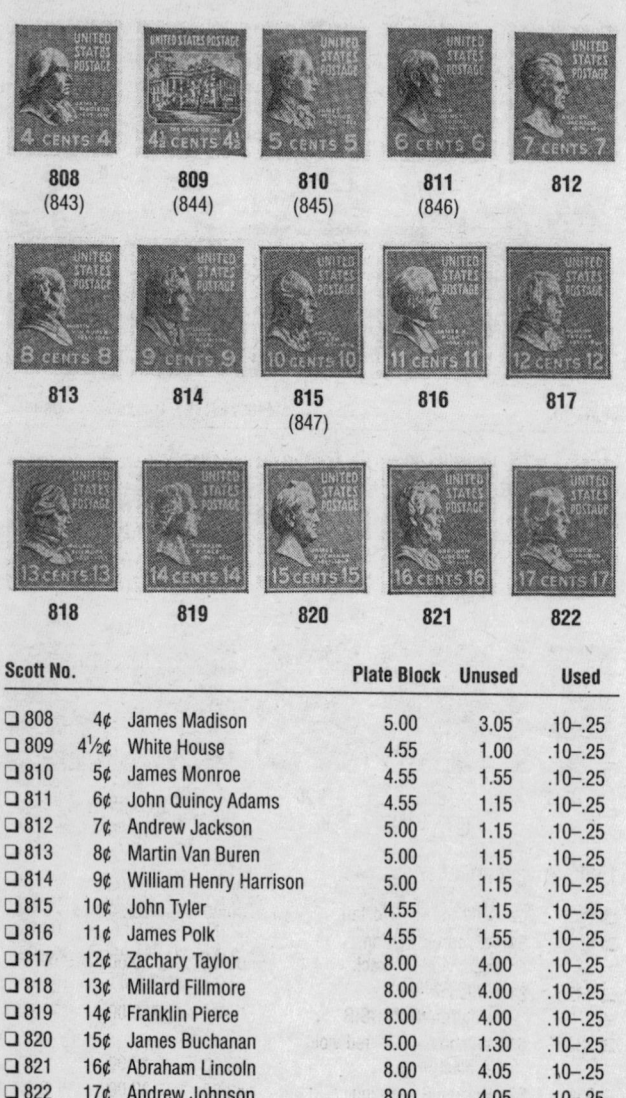

808	809	810	811	812
(843)	(844)	(845)	(846)	

813	814	815	816	817
		(847)		

818	819	820	821	822

Scott No.			Plate Block	Unused	Used
❏ 808	4¢	James Madison	5.00	3.05	.10–.25
❏ 809	4½¢	White House	4.55	1.00	.10–.25
❏ 810	5¢	James Monroe	4.55	1.55	.10–.25
❏ 811	6¢	John Quincy Adams	4.55	1.15	.10–.25
❏ 812	7¢	Andrew Jackson	5.00	1.15	.10–.25
❏ 813	8¢	Martin Van Buren	5.00	1.15	.10–.25
❏ 814	9¢	William Henry Harrison	5.00	1.15	.10–.25
❏ 815	10¢	John Tyler	4.55	1.15	.10–.25
❏ 816	11¢	James Polk	4.55	1.55	.10–.25
❏ 817	12¢	Zachary Taylor	8.00	4.00	.10–.25
❏ 818	13¢	Millard Fillmore	8.00	4.00	.10–.25
❏ 819	14¢	Franklin Pierce	8.00	4.00	.10–.25
❏ 820	15¢	James Buchanan	5.00	1.30	.10–.25
❏ 821	16¢	Abraham Lincoln	8.00	4.05	.10–.25
❏ 822	17¢	Andrew Johnson	8.00	4.05	.10–.25

823 824 825 826 827

828 829 830 831

832
(832b, 832c)

833 834

Scott No.			Plate Block	Unused	Used
❑ 823	18¢	Ulysses S. Grant	12.00	5.25	.10–.25
❑ 824	19¢	Rutherford B. Hayes	8.00	5.25	.10–.25
❑ 825	20¢	James A Garfield	8.00	2.30	.10–.25
❑ 826	21¢	Chester A. Arthur	12.00	5.25	.10–.25
❑ 827	22¢	Grover Cleveland	12.00	4.25	1.05
❑ 828	24¢	Benjamin Harrison	20.00	10.00	.84
❑ 829	25¢	William McKinley	10.00	3.05	.84
❑ 830	30¢	Theodore Roosevelt	20.00	15.00	.84
❑ 831	50¢	William Howard Taft	30.00	20.00	.84
❑ 832	$1	Woodrow Wilson, dark violet & black	60.00	20.00	.10–.25
❑ 832b	$1	Wilson (~832), watermarked "USIR"	—	230.00	71.50
❑ 832c	$1	Wilson, (~832), red violet & black	55.00	15.00	.84
❑ 833	$2	Warren G. Harding	140.00	32.00	8.00
❑ 834	$5	Calvin Coolidge	450.00	160.00	8.00

Scott No.			Plate Block	Unused	Used
1938.					
❑ 835	3¢	Constitution Ratification	6.00	1.75	.10–.25
❑ 836	3¢	Swede-Finn Tercentenary	8.00 (6)	1.05	.10–.25
❑ 837	3¢	Northwest Territory	11.00	1.05	.10–.25
❑ 838	3¢	Iowa Territory Centennial	8.00	1.05	.10–.25

Scott No.			Line Pair	Unused	Used
1939. Presidential Series Coil Stamps, Perforated 10 Vertically.					
❑ 839	1¢	G. Washington (~804)	5.50	.90	.10–.25
❑ 840	1½¢	M. Washington (~805)	5.50	.90	.10–.25
❑ 841	2¢	Adams (~806)	5.50	.90	.10–.25
❑ 842	3¢	Jefferson (~807)	5.50	1.10	.10–.25
❑ 843	4¢	Madison (~808)	30.00	12.00	1.25
❑ 844	4½¢	White House (~809)	5.50	1.50	1.00
❑ 845	5¢	Monroe (~810)	28.00	10.00	1.00
❑ 846	6¢	J. Q. Adams (~811)	8.00	3.05	.10–.30
❑ 847	10¢	Tyler (~815)	50.00	20.00	1.75
1939. Presidential Series Coil Stamps, Perforated 10 Horizontally.					
❑ 848	1¢	G. Washington (~804)	4.30	2.00	.10–.25
❑ 849	1½¢	M. Washington (~805)	4.30	3.55	1.00
❑ 850	2¢	Adams (~806)	7.00	5.00	1.00
❑ 851	3¢	Jefferson (~807)	8.00	5.00	4.00

852   853   854

855   856   857

858

Scott No.			Plate Block	Unused	Used
1939.					
❑ 852	3¢	Golden Gate Exposition	6.25	.90	.10–.25
❑ 853	3¢	New York World's Fair	6.25	.90	.10–.25
❑ 854	3¢	Washington's Inaugural	8.00 (6)	1.30	.10–.25
❑ 855	3¢	Baseball Centennial	10.00	5.00	.10–.25
❑ 856	3¢	Panama Canal	6.25 (6)	.90	.10–.25
❑ 857	3¢	Colonial Printing	6.25	.90	.10–.25
❑ 858	3¢	Washington, Montana & the Dakotas	6.25	.90	.10–.25

NOTE: Prices for stamps from 1935 forward are for never-hinged (NH) examples.

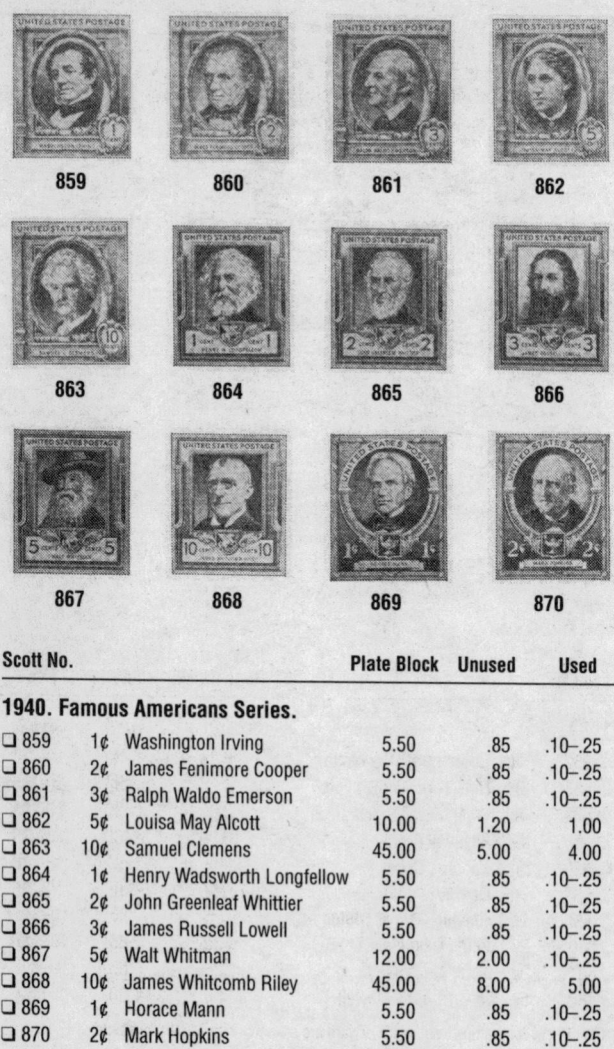

859
860
861
862

863
864
865
866

867
868
869
870

Scott No.			Plate Block	Unused	Used

1940. Famous Americans Series.

☐ 859	1¢	Washington Irving	5.50	.85	.10–.25
☐ 860	2¢	James Fenimore Cooper	5.50	.85	.10–.25
☐ 861	3¢	Ralph Waldo Emerson	5.50	.85	.10–.25
☐ 862	5¢	Louisa May Alcott	10.00	1.20	1.00
☐ 863	10¢	Samuel Clemens	45.00	5.00	4.00
☐ 864	1¢	Henry Wadsworth Longfellow	5.50	.85	.10–.25
☐ 865	2¢	John Greenleaf Whittier	5.50	.85	.10–.25
☐ 866	3¢	James Russell Lowell	5.50	.85	.10–.25
☐ 867	5¢	Walt Whitman	12.00	2.00	.10–.25
☐ 868	10¢	James Whitcomb Riley	45.00	8.00	5.00
☐ 869	1¢	Horace Mann	5.50	.85	.10–.25
☐ 870	2¢	Mark Hopkins	5.50	.85	.10–.25

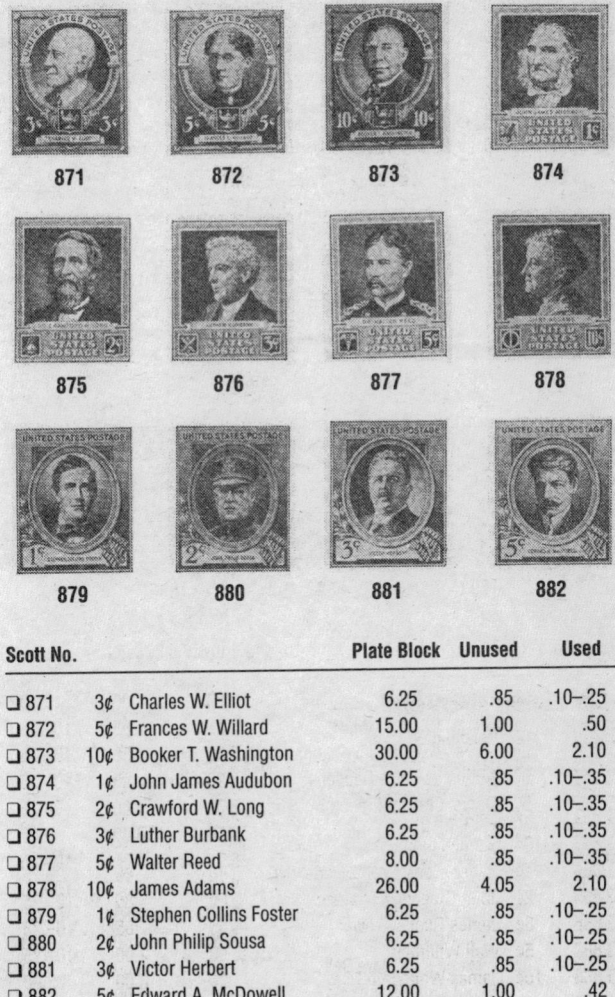

Scott No.			Plate Block	Unused	Used
❏ 871	3¢	Charles W. Elliot	6.25	.85	.10–.25
❏ 872	5¢	Frances W. Willard	15.00	1.00	.50
❏ 873	10¢	Booker T. Washington	30.00	6.00	2.10
❏ 874	1¢	John James Audubon	6.25	.85	.10–.35
❏ 875	2¢	Crawford W. Long	6.25	.85	.10–.35
❏ 876	3¢	Luther Burbank	6.25	.85	.10–.35
❏ 877	5¢	Walter Reed	8.00	.85	.10–.35
❏ 878	10¢	James Adams	26.00	4.05	2.10
❏ 879	1¢	Stephen Collins Foster	6.25	.85	.10–.25
❏ 880	2¢	John Philip Sousa	6.25	.85	.10–.25
❏ 881	3¢	Victor Herbert	6.25	.85	.10–.25
❏ 882	5¢	Edward A. McDowell	12.00	1.00	.42

NOTE: Prices for stamps from 1935 forward are for never-hinged (NH) examples.

Scott No.			Plate Block	Unused	Used
❏ 883	10¢	Ethelbert Nevin	40.00	8.00	2.10
❏ 884	1¢	Gilbert Charles Stuart	5.25	.85	.10–.35
❏ 885	2¢	James A. McNeill Whistler	5.25	.85	.10–.35
❏ 886	3¢	Augustus Saint-Gaudens	5.25	.85	.10–.35
❏ 887	5¢	Daniel Chester French	8.00	4.00	.10–.35
❏ 888	10¢	Frederic Remington	35.00	6.00	2.10
❏ 889	1¢	Eli Whitney	5.25	1.05	.10–.35
❏ 890	2¢	Samuel F. B. Morse	5.25	1.05	.10–.35
❏ 891	3¢	Cyrus McCormick	5.25	1.55	.10–.35
❏ 892	5¢	Elias Howe	15.00	3.00	1.00
❏ 893	10¢	Alexander Graham Bell	80.00	30.00	4.20
		Set of 35 (859–893)	—	100.00	—

NOTE: Prices for stamps from 1935 forward are for never-hinged (NH) examples.

Scott No.			Plate Block	Unused	Used
1940.					
❏ 894	3¢	Pony Express	5.25	1.00	.10–.25
❏ 895	3¢	Pan American Union	5.25	1.00	.10–.25
❏ 896	3¢	Idaho Statehood	5.25	1.00	.10–.25
❏ 897	3¢	Wyoming Statehood	5.25	1.00	.10–.25
❏ 898	3¢	Coronado Expedition	5.25	1.00	.10–.25
❏ 899	1¢	Defense – Statue of Liberty	5.25	1.00	.10–.25
❏ 900	2¢	Defense – Artillery	5.25	1.00	.10–.25
❏ 901	3¢	Defense – Torch of Liberty	5.25	1.00	.10–.25
❏ 902	3¢	13th Amendment	5.25	.95	.10–.25

903

Scott No.			Plate Block	Unused	Used
1941.					
❑ 903	3¢	Vermont Statehood	3.55	1.00	.10–.25

904    **905**    **906**

1942.					
❑ 904	3¢	Kentucky	5.00	.40	.10–.30
❑ 905	3¢	Win the War	5.00	.70	.10–.25
❑ 906	5¢	China	14.00	4.95	2.00

907    **908**

1943.					
❑ 907	2¢	Allied Nations	4.00	.30	.10–.25
❑ 908	1¢	Four Freedoms	4.00	.30	.10–.25

NOTE: Prices for stamps from 1935 forward are for never-hinged (NH) examples.

909

910

911

912

913

914

915

916

Scott No.			Plate Block	Unused	Used
1943–1944. Overrun Countries Issue.					
❑ 909	5¢	Poland	7.00	.40	.10–.30
❑ 910	5¢	Czechoslovakia	5.25	.40	.10–.30
❑ 911	5¢	Norway	5.25	.40	.10–.30
❑ 912	5¢	Luxembourg	5.25	.40	.10–.30
❑ 913	5¢	Netherlands	5.25	.40	.10–.30
❑ 914	5¢	Belgium	5.25	.40	.10–.30
❑ 915	5¢	France	5.25	.40	.10–.30
❑ 916	5¢	Greece	15.00	2.00	1.05

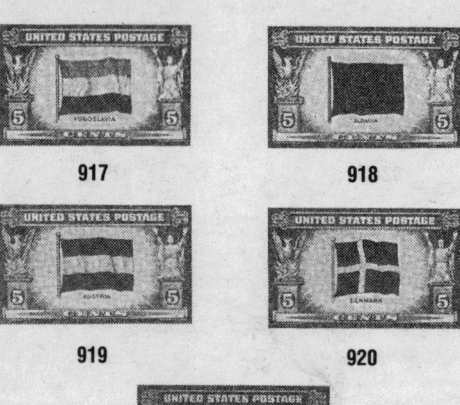

917   918

919   920

921

Scott No.			Plate Block	Unused	Used
❏ 917	5¢	Yugoslavia	8.00	.60	.50
❏ 918	5¢	Albania	8.00	.55	.50
❏ 919	5¢	Austria	6.25	.55	.50
❏ 920	5¢	Denmark	6.25	.55	.50
❏ 921	5¢	Korea	6.25	.55	.50
		Set of 13 (909–921)	—	6.00	4.20

NOTE: Plate blocks of the Overrun Nations Issue are inscribed with the name of country instead of a plate number.

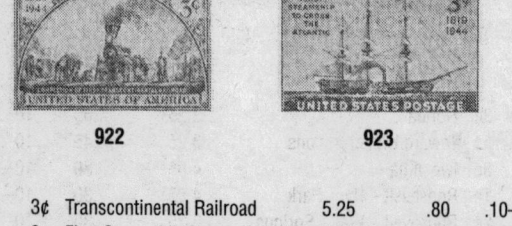

922   923

1944.

❏ 922	3¢	Transcontinental Railroad	5.25	.80	.10–.35
❏ 923	3¢	First Steamship Across Atlantic	5.25	.80	.10–.35

924

925

926

Scott No.			Plate Block	Unused	Used
❏ 924	3¢	Telegraph Centenary	3.25	.45	.10–.30
❏ 925	3¢	Corregidor	3.25	.40	.10–.30
❏ 926	3¢	Motion Pictures	3.25	.40	.10–.30

927

928

929

930

931

1945.

❏ 927	3¢	Florida	3.25	.60	.10–.25
❏ 928	5¢	Toward United Nations	3.25	.45	.10–.25
❏ 929	3¢	Iwo Jima	4.05	.50	.10–.25
❏ 930	1¢	Roosevelt – Hyde Park	4.05	.30	.10–.25
❏ 931	2¢	Roosevelt – Warm Springs	3.25	.30	.10–.25

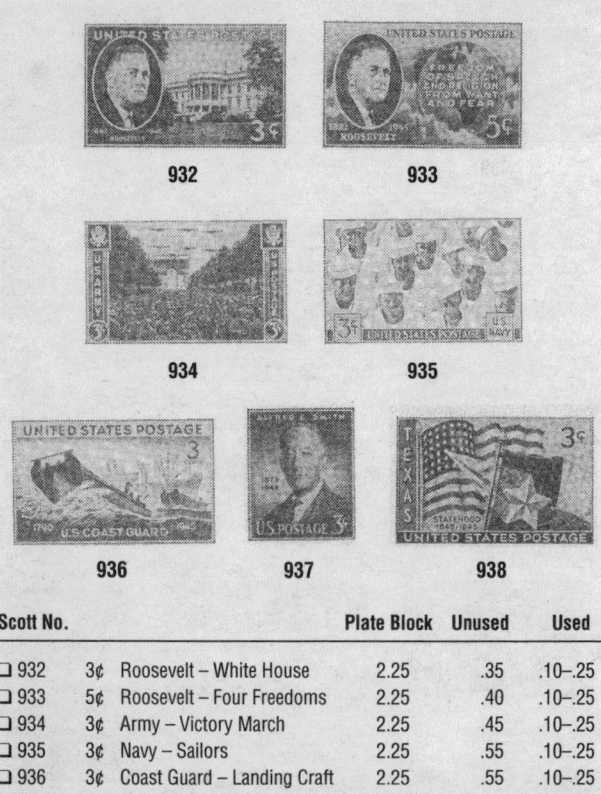

Scott No.			Plate Block	Unused	Used
❏ 932	3¢	Roosevelt – White House	2.25	.35	.10–.25
❏ 933	5¢	Roosevelt – Four Freedoms	2.25	.40	.10–.25
❏ 934	3¢	Army – Victory March	2.25	.45	.10–.25
❏ 935	3¢	Navy – Sailors	2.25	.55	.10–.25
❏ 936	3¢	Coast Guard – Landing Craft	2.25	.55	.10–.25
❏ 937	3¢	Alfred E. Smith	2.25	.55	.10–.25
❏ 938	3¢	Texas Centennial	2.25	.65	.10–.25

NOTE: Prices for stamps from 1935 forward are for never-hinged (NH) examples.

939   **940**   **941**

942   **943**   **944**

Scott No.			Plate Block	Unused	Used
1946.					
☐ 939	3¢	Merchant Marine	2.00	.35	.10–.25
☐ 940	3¢	Discharge Emblem	2.00	.35	.10–.25
☐ 941	3¢	Tennessee Statehood	2.00	1.00	.10–.25
☐ 942	3¢	Iowa Statehood	2.00	.50	.10–.25
☐ 943	3¢	Smithsonian Institution	2.00	.35	.10–.25
☐ 944	3¢	Kearny Expedition	2.00	.45	.10–.25

945   **946**   **947**

1947.					
☐ 945	3¢	Thomas A. Edison	2.00	.65	.10–.25
☐ 946	3¢	Joseph Pulitzer	2.00	.65	.10–.25
☐ 947	3¢	U.S. Stamp Centenary	2.00	.55	.10–.25

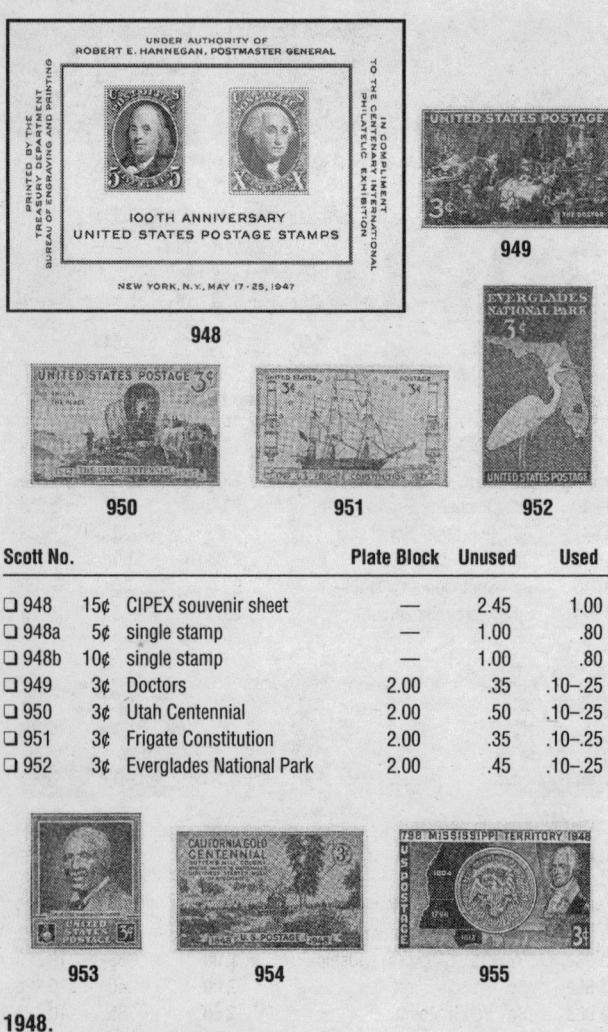

948

949

950

951

952

Scott No.			Plate Block	Unused	Used
❏ 948	15¢	CIPEX souvenir sheet	—	2.45	1.00
❏ 948a	5¢	single stamp	—	1.00	.80
❏ 948b	10¢	single stamp	—	1.00	.80
❏ 949	3¢	Doctors	2.00	.35	.10–.25
❏ 950	3¢	Utah Centennial	2.00	.50	.10–.25
❏ 951	3¢	Frigate Constitution	2.00	.35	.10–.25
❏ 952	3¢	Everglades National Park	2.00	.45	.10–.25

953

954

955

1948.

❏ 953	3¢	George Washington Carver	3.25	.40	.10–.25
❏ 954	3¢	California Gold Rush	3.25	.40	.10–.25
❏ 955	3¢	Mississippi Territory	3.25	.40	.10–.25

956   957   958

959   960   961

962   963   964

965   966   967

Scott No.			Plate Block	Unused	Used
❏ 956	3¢	Immortal Chaplains	4.00	1.00	.10–.25
❏ 957	3¢	Wisconsin Centennial	2.00	.50	.10–.25
❏ 958	5¢	Swedish Pioneers	4.00	.40	.10–.25
❏ 959	3¢	Progress of Women	2.00	.40	.10–.25
❏ 960	3¢	William Allen White	4.00	.40	.10–.25
❏ 961	3¢	U.S. Canada Friendship	2.00	.35	.10–.25
❏ 962	3¢	Francis Scott Key	2.00	.40	.10–.25
❏ 963	3¢	Youth Month	2.00	.35	.10–.25
❏ 964	3¢	Oregon Territory	2.00	.60	.10–.25
❏ 965	3¢	Harlan Fiske Stone	4.00	.85	.10–.25
❏ 966	3¢	Mount Palomar	4.00	.45	.10–.25
❏ 967	3¢	Clara Barton	4.00	.65	.10–.25

968   **969**   **970**

Scott No.			Plate Block	Unused	Used
❑ 968	3¢	Poultry Industry	2.20	.40	.10–.25
❑ 969	3¢	Gold Star Mothers	2.20	.35	.10–.25
❑ 970	3¢	Fort Kearny	2.20	.55	.10–.25

971   **972**   **973**

974   **975**   **976**

1948.

❑ 971	3¢	Volunteer Firemen	4.00	1.00	.10–.25
❑ 972	3¢	Indian Centennial	2.20	.85	.10–.25
❑ 973	3¢	Rough Riders	2.20	.85	.10–.25
❑ 974	3¢	Juliette Low	4.00	.85	.10–.25
❑ 975	3¢	Will Rogers	2.20	.80	.10–.25
❑ 976	3¢	Fort Bliss Centennial	4.00	.80	.10–.25

977

978

979

980

Scott No.			Plate Block	Unused	Used
❑ 977	3¢	Moina Michael	2.20	.35	.10–.25
❑ 978	3¢	Gettysburg Address	4.00	.40	.10–.25
❑ 979	3¢	American Turners	2.20	.35	.10–.25
❑ 980	3¢	Joel Chandler Harris	4.00	.35	.10–.25

981

982

983

984

985

1949.

❑ 981	3¢	Minnesota Centennia	.85	.55	.10–.25
❑ 982	3¢	Washington & Lee University	1.60	.40	.10–.25
❑ 983	3¢	Puerto Rico	1.60	.40	.10–.25
❑ 984	3¢	Annapolis Tercentenary	1.60	.35	.10–.25
❑ 985	3¢	G.A.R.	1.60	.45	.10–.25

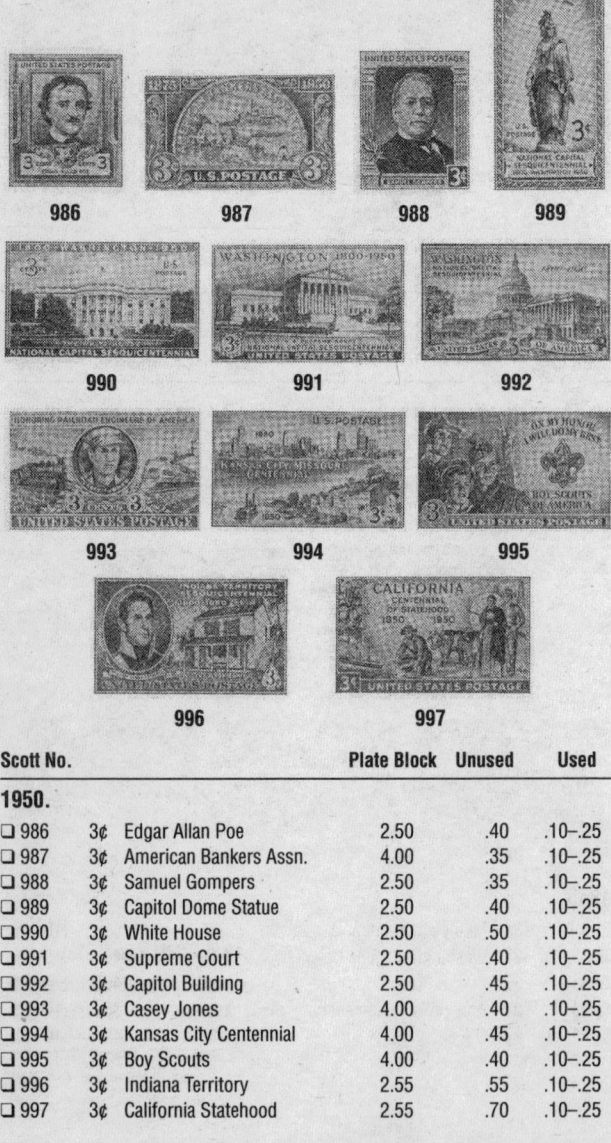

986   987   988   989

990   991   992

993   994   995

996   997

Scott No.			Plate Block	Unused	Used
1950.					
❏ 986	3¢	Edgar Allan Poe	2.50	.40	.10–.25
❏ 987	3¢	American Bankers Assn.	4.00	.35	.10–.25
❏ 988	3¢	Samuel Gompers	2.50	.35	.10–.25
❏ 989	3¢	Capitol Dome Statue	2.50	.40	.10–.25
❏ 990	3¢	White House	2.50	.50	.10–.25
❏ 991	3¢	Supreme Court	2.50	.40	.10–.25
❏ 992	3¢	Capitol Building	2.50	.45	.10–.25
❏ 993	3¢	Casey Jones	4.00	.40	.10–.25
❏ 994	3¢	Kansas City Centennial	4.00	.45	.10–.25
❏ 995	3¢	Boy Scouts	4.00	.40	.10–.25
❏ 996	3¢	Indiana Territory	2.55	.55	.10–.25
❏ 997	3¢	California Statehood	2.55	.70	.10–.25

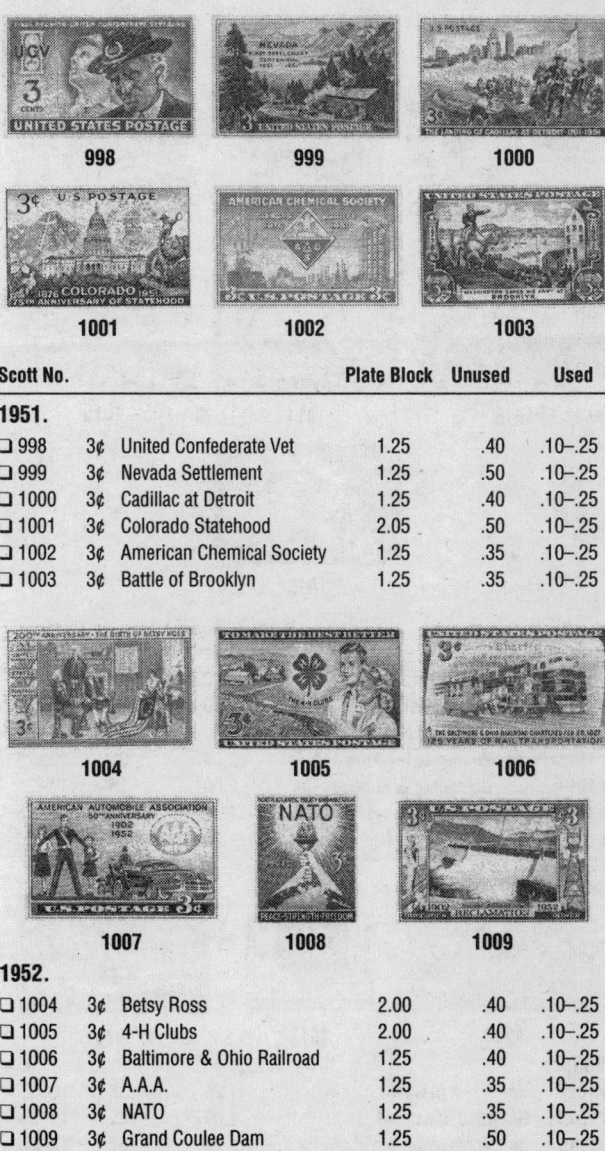

998　　**999**　　**1000**

1001　　**1002**　　**1003**

Scott No.			Plate Block	Unused	Used
1951.					
❏ 998	3¢	United Confederate Vet	1.25	.40	.10–.25
❏ 999	3¢	Nevada Settlement	1.25	.50	.10–.25
❏ 1000	3¢	Cadillac at Detroit	1.25	.40	.10–.25
❏ 1001	3¢	Colorado Statehood	2.05	.50	.10–.25
❏ 1002	3¢	American Chemical Society	1.25	.35	.10–.25
❏ 1003	3¢	Battle of Brooklyn	1.25	.35	.10–.25

1004　　**1005**　　**1006**

1007　　**1008**　　**1009**

1952.					
❏ 1004	3¢	Betsy Ross	2.00	.40	.10–.25
❏ 1005	3¢	4-H Clubs	2.00	.40	.10–.25
❏ 1006	3¢	Baltimore & Ohio Railroad	1.25	.40	.10–.25
❏ 1007	3¢	A.A.A.	1.25	.35	.10–.25
❏ 1008	3¢	NATO	1.25	.35	.10–.25
❏ 1009	3¢	Grand Coulee Dam	1.25	.50	.10–.25

Scott No.			Plate Block	Unused	Used
❏ 1010	3¢	Arrival of Lafayette	2.00	.35	.10–.25
❏ 1011	3¢	Mount Rushmore	1.30	.60	.10–.25
❏ 1012	3¢	Society of Civil Engineers	2.00	.40	.10–.25
❏ 1013	3¢	Women in the Armed Forces	2.00	.35	.10–.25
❏ 1014	3¢	Gutenberg & Printing	2.00	.35	.10–.25
❏ 1015	3¢	Newspaper Boys	1.25	.35	.10–.25
❏ 1016	3¢	International Red Cross	1.25	.35	.10–.25

1953.

❏ 1017	3¢	National Guard	1.25	.35	.10–.25
❏ 1018	3¢	Ohio Statehood	2.00	.35	.10–.25
❏ 1019	3¢	Washington Territory	1.25	.50	.10–.25

Scott No.			Plate Block	Unused	Used
❏ 1020	3¢	Louisiana Purchase	1.65	.40	.10–.25
❏ 1021	5¢	Opening of Japan	2.00	.35	.10–.25
❏ 1022	3¢	American Bar Assn.	1.65	.40	.10–.25
❏ 1023	3¢	Sagamore Hill	1.65	.40	.10–.25
❏ 1024	3¢	Future Farmers	1.65	.40	.10–.25
❏ 1025	3¢	Trucking Industry	1.65	.35	.10–.25
❏ 1026	3¢	George S. Patton	1.65	.35	.10–.25
❏ 1027	3¢	New York City	2.00	.40	.10–.25
❏ 1028	3¢	Gadsden Purchase	1.65	.45	.10–.25

1029

1954.

❏ 1029	3¢	Columbia University	1.30	.40	.10–.25

1030

1031
(1054)

1031A
(1054A)

1032

1033
(1055)

1034
(1056)

1035
(1057)

1036
(1058)

1037
(1059)

1038

1039

1040

1041

Scott No.			Plate Block	Unused	Used
1954–1961. Liberty Series					
❑ 1030	½¢	Benjamin Franklin	1.15	.35	.10–.25
❑ 1031	1¢	George Washington	1.15	.40	.10–.25
❑ 1031A	1¼¢	Palace of Governors	1.15	.35	.10–.25
❑ 1032	1½¢	Mount Vernon	1.15	.40	.10–.25
❑ 1033	2¢	Thomas Jefferson	1.15	.40	.10–.25
❑ 1034	2½¢	Bunker Hill	4.00	.30	.10–.25
❑ 1035	3¢	Statue of Liberty	1.15	.35	.10–.25
❑ 1036	4¢	Abraham Lincoln	1.15	.40	.10–.25
❑ 1037	4½¢	The Hermitage	1.15	.45	.10–.25
❑ 1038	5¢	James Monroe	1.15	.50	.10–.25
❑ 1039	6¢	Theodore Roosevelt	4.00	.50	.10–.25
❑ 1040	7¢	Woodrow Wilson	1.15	.50	.10–.25
❑ 1041	8¢	Statue of Liberty	4.00	.40	.10–.25

1042   **1042A**   **1043**   **1044**

1044A   **1045**   **1046**   **1047**   **1048**
                                                              (1059A)

1049   **1050**   **1051**   **1052**   **1053**

Scott No.			Plate Block	Unused	Used
❏ 1042	8¢	Statue of Liberty (re-engraved)	2.15	.50	.10–.25
❏ 1042A	8¢	John J. Pershing	2.15	.55	.10–.25
❏ 1043	9¢	The Alamo	2.15	.80	.10–.25
❏ 1044	10¢	Independence Hall	5.00	.75	.10–.25
❏ 1044A	11¢	Statue of Liberty	2.15	.60	.10–.25
❏ 1045	12¢	Benjamin Harrison	2.15	.70	.10–.25
❏ 1046	15¢	John Jay	5.00	1.25	.10–.25
❏ 1047	20¢	Monticello	5.00	1.00	.10–.25
❏ 1048	25¢	Paul Revere	6.00	2.25	.10–.25
❏ 1049	30¢	Robert E. Lee	8.00	2.35	.10–.25
❏ 1050	40¢	John Marshall	12.00	4.50	.10–.25
❏ 1051	50¢	S. B. Anthony	12.00	3.30	.10–.25
❏ 1052	$1	Patrick Henry	30.00	9.76	.10–.25
❏ 1053	$5	Alexander Hamilton	400.00	120.00	12.65

Scott No.			Line Pair	Unused	Used

1954–1973. Coil Stamps.

Scott No.			Line Pair	Unused	Used
❏ 1054	1¢	George Washington (~1031)	1.25	.40	.10–.25
❏ 1054A	1¼¢	Palace of Governors (~1031A)	2.00	3.25	.10–.25
❏ 1055	2¢	Thomas Jefferson (~1033)	2.80	.90	.10–.25
❏ 1056	2½¢	Bunker Hill (~1034)	4.00	.45	.10–.25
❏ 1057	3¢	Statue of Liberty (~1035)	1.25	.45	.10–.25
❏ 1058	4¢	Abraham Lincoln (~1036)	1.25	.40	.10–.25
❏ 1059	4½¢	The Hermitage (~1037)	12.00	2.00	1.10
❏ 1059A	25¢	Paul Revere (~1048)	4.00	1.10	.65

1060 **1061** **1062**

1063

1064 **1065** **1066**

Scott No.			Plate Block	Unused	Used

1954.

Scott No.			Plate Block	Unused	Used
❏ 1060	3¢	Nebraska Territory	1.25	.35	.10–.25
❏ 1061	3¢	Kansas Territory	2.00	.60	.10–.25
❏ 1062	3¢	George Eastman	1.25	.40	.10–.25
❏ 1063	3¢	Lewis & Clark	2.00	.85	.10–.25

1955.

❏ 1064	3¢	Pennsylvania Academy	2.00	.50	.10–.25
❏ 1065	3¢	Land Grant Colleges	1.25	.60	.10–.25
❏ 1066	8¢	Rotary International	2.00	.50	.10–.25

1067   **1068**   **1069**

1070   **1071**   **1072**

Scott No.			Plate Block	Unused	Used
❑ 1067	3¢	Armed Forces Reserves	1.15	.35	.10–.25
❑ 1068	3¢	Old Man of the Mountains	1.50	.35	.10–.25
❑ 1069	3¢	Great Lakes Transportation	1.15	.40	.10–.25
❑ 1070	3¢	Atoms for Peace	1.15	.35	.10–.25
❑ 1071	3¢	Fort Ticonderoga	2.00	.35	.10–.25
❑ 1072	3¢	Andrew Mellon	1.15	.40	.10–.25

1073   **1074**

1956.

❑ 1073	3¢	Benjamin Franklin	2.20	.35	.10–.25
❑ 1074	3¢	Booker T. Washington	2.20	.40	.10–.25

1075

1076

1077

1078

1079

1080

Scott No.			Plate Block	Unused	Used
❑ 1075	12¢	FIPEX Souvenir Sheet	—	3.10	—
❑ 1075a	3¢	single stamp	—	2.00	1.50
❑ 1075b	8¢	single stamp	—	2.00	1.50
❑ 1076	3¢	FIPEX	2.25	.40	.10–.25
❑ 1077	3¢	Wild Turkey	2.25	.50	.10–.25
❑ 1078	3¢	Pronghorn Antelope	2.25	.40	.10–.25
❑ 1079	3¢	King Salmon	2.25	.45	.10–.25
❑ 1080	3¢	Pure Food & Drug Act	4.00	.40	.10–.25

1081

1082

1083

1084

1085

Scott No.			Plate Block	Unused	Used
❑ 1081	3¢	Wheatland	2.00	.40	.10–.25
❑ 1082	3¢	Labor Day	1.15	.35	.10–.25
❑ 1083	3¢	Nassau Hall	1.15	.40	.10–.25
❑ 1084	3¢	Devils Tower	1.15	.55	.10–.25
❑ 1085	3¢	Children's Stamp	1.15	.40	.10–.25

1086

1087

1088

1089

1957.

❑ 1086	3¢	Alexander Hamilton	.90	.35	.10–.25
❑ 1087	3¢	Fight Against Polio	.90	.35	.10–.25
❑ 1088	3¢	Coast & Geodetic Survey	.90	.35	.10–.25
❑ 1089	3¢	Architects	.90	.40	.10–.25

1090

1091

1092

1093

1094

1095

1096

1097

1098

1099

Scott No.			Plate Block	Unused	Used
❏ 1090	3¢	American Steel Industry	1.65	.35	.10–.25
❏ 1091	3¢	International Naval Review	1.65	.40	.10–.25
❏ 1092	3¢	Oklahoma Statehood	1.65	.65	.10–.25
❏ 1093	3¢	Teachers of America	1.65	.35	.10–.25
❏ 1094	4¢	48-Star U.S. Flag	1.65	.40	.10–.25
❏ 1095	3¢	Shipbuilding	2.00	.35	.10–.25
❏ 1096	8¢	Ramon Magsaysay	1.65	.40	.10–.25
❏ 1097	3¢	Lafayette Bicentennial	2.00	.35	.10–.25
❏ 1098	3¢	Whooping Cranes	1.65	.35	.10–.25
❏ 1099	3¢	Religious Freedom	1.65	.35	.10–.25

1100 **1104** **1105**

1106 **1107** **1108**

1109 **1110** **1111** **1112**

Scott No.			Plate Block	Unused	Used
1958.					
❑ 1100	3¢	Gardening & Horticulture	2.00	.35	.10–.25
❑ 1104	3¢	Brussels Exhibition	2.00	.35	.10–.25
❑ 1105	3¢	James Monroe	2.00	.50	.10–.25
❑ 1106	3¢	Minnesota Statehood	2.00	.50	.10–.25
❑ 1107	3¢	International Geophysical Year	2.00	.40	.10–.25
❑ 1108	3¢	Gunston Hall	2.00	.35	.10–.25
❑ 1109	3¢	Mackinac Bridge	2.00	.50	.10–.25
❑ 1110	4¢	Simon Bolivar	2.00	.35	.10–.25
❑ 1111	8¢	Simon Bolivar	2.00	.35	.10–.25
❑ 1112	4¢	Atlantic Cable Centennial	2.00	.35	.10–.25

UNITED STATES POSTAGE

1113

UNITED STATES POSTAGE

1114

1115

1116

1117

1118

1119

1120

1121

1122

1123

Scott No.			Plate Block	Unused	Used
❑ 1113	1¢	Youthful Lincoln	1.25	.30	.10–.25
❑ 1114	3¢	Bust of Lincoln	1.25	.35	.10–.25
❑ 1115	4¢	Lincoln-Douglas Debates	2.00	.40	.10–.25
❑ 1116	4¢	Statue of Lincoln	1.25	.40	.10–.25
❑ 1117	4¢	Lajos Kossuth	1.25	.35	.10–.25
❑ 1118	8¢	Lajos Kossuth	2.00	.40	.10–.25
❑ 1119	4¢	Freedom of the Press	1.25	.35	.10–.25
❑ 1120	4¢	Overland Mail	2.00	.35	.10–.25
❑ 1121	4¢	Noah Webster	2.00	.35	.10–.25
❑ 1122	4¢	Forest Conservation	1.25	.40	.10–.25
❑ 1123	4¢	Fort Duquesne	1.25	.35	.10–.25

1124

1125

1126

1127

1128

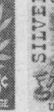
1129

1130

1131

1132

1133

1134

1135

Scott No.			Plate Block	Unused	Used
1959.					
❑ 1124	4¢	Oregon Statehood	1.25	.60	.10–.25
❑ 1125	4¢	Jose de San Martin	.75	.35	.10–.25
❑ 1126	8¢	Jose de San Martin	1.25	.40	.10–.25
❑ 1127	4¢	NATO	.75	.35	.10–.25
❑ 1128	4¢	Arctic Exploration	1.25	.40	.10–.25
❑ 1129	8¢	Peace Through Trade	1.25	.45	.10–.25
❑ 1130	4¢	Silver Centennial	.75	.55	.10–.25
❑ 1131	4¢	St. Lawrence Seaway	1.25	1.55	.10–.25
❑ 1132	4¢	49-Star U.S. Flag	.75	.40	.10–.25
❑ 1133	4¢	Soil Conservation	.75	.45	.10–.25
❑ 1134	4¢	Petroleum Industry	1.25	.40	.10–.25
❑ 1135	4¢	Dental Health	1.25	.40	.10–.25

1136　　　**1137**　　　**1138**

Scott No.			Plate Block	Unused	Used
❏ 1136	4¢	Ernst Reuter	2.00	.40	.10–.25
❏ 1137	8¢	Ernst Reuter	2.00	.35	.10–.25
❏ 1138	4¢	Ephraim McDowell	2.00	.35	.10–.25

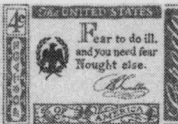
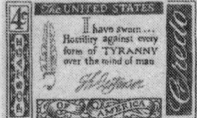

1139　　　**1140**　　　**1141**

1142　　　**1143**　　　**1144**

1145

1960.

❏ 1139	4¢	Credo – Washington	1.25	.55	.10–.25
❏ 1140	4¢	Credo – Franklin	1.25	.40	.10–.25
❏ 1141	4¢	Credo – Jefferson	1.25	.50	.10–.25
❏ 1142	4¢	Credo – Key	2.00	.40	.10–.25
❏ 1143	4¢	Credo – Lincoln	1.25	.35	.10–.25
❏ 1144	4¢	Credo – Henry	1.25	.40	.10–.25
❏ 1145	4¢	Boy Scouts	2.00	.45	.10–.25

1146   **1147**   **1148**   **1149**

1150   **1151**   **1152**

1153   **1154**   **1155**   **1156**

Scott No.			Plate Block	Unused	Used
❏ 1146	4¢	Winter Olympics	1.60	.35	.10–.25
❏ 1147	4¢	Thomas G. Masaryk	.85	.35	.10–.25
❏ 1148	8¢	Thomas G. Masaryk	1.60	.40	.10–.25
❏ 1149	4¢	World Refugee Year	1.60	.35	.10–.25
❏ 1150	4¢	Water Conservation	.85	.40	.10–.25
❏ 1151	4¢	SEATO	.85	.35	.10–.25
❏ 1152	4¢	American Women	.80	.35	.10–.25
❏ 1153	4¢	50-Star U.S. Flag	4.00	.40	.10–.25
❏ 1154	4¢	Pony Express	.85	.35	.10–.25
❏ 1155	4¢	Employ the Handicapped	1.60	.35	.10–.25
❏ 1156	4¢	World Forestry Congress	.85	.50	.10–.25

1157 1158 1159 1160

1161 1162 1163

1164 1165 1166 1167

Scott No.			Plate Block	Unused	Used
❑ 1157	4¢	Mexican Independence	.85	.35	.10–.25
❑ 1158	4¢	U.S.-Japan Treaty	.85	.45	.10–.25
❑ 1159	4¢	Ignacy Jan Paderewski	4.00	.35	.10–.25
❑ 1160	8¢	Ignacy Jan Paderewski	4.00	.40	.10–.25
❑ 1161	4¢	Robert A. Taft	1.25	.35	.10–.25
❑ 1162	4¢	Wheels of Freedom	.85	.40	.10–.25
❑ 1163	4¢	Boys' Clubs	1.25	.35	.10–.25
❑ 1164	4¢	First Automated P.O.	4.00	.40	.10–.25
❑ 1165	4¢	Gustaf Mannerheim	1.25	.35	.10–.25
❑ 1166	8¢	Gustaf Mannerheim	4.00	.40	.10–.25
❑ 1167	4¢	Campfire Girls	4.00	.60	.10–.25

1168   **1169**   **1170**   **1171**

1172   **1173**

Scott No.			Plate Block	Unused	Used
❏ 1168	4¢	Guiseppe Garibaldi	.85	.35	.10–.25
❏ 1169	8¢	Guiseppe Garibaldi	4.00	.35	.10–.25
❏ 1170	4¢	Walter F. George	4.00	.35	.10–.25
❏ 1171	4¢	Andrew Carnegie	1.20	.35	.10–.25
❏ 1172	4¢	John Foster Dulles	1.20	.35	.10–.25
❏ 1173	4¢	Echo I Satellite	4.00	.40	.10–.25

1174   **1175**   **1176**

1961.

❏ 1174	4¢	Mahatma Gandhi	2.00	.35	.10–.25
❏ 1175	8¢	Mahatma Gandhi	2.00	.50	.10–.25
❏ 1176	4¢	Range Conservation	.90	.50	.10–.25
❏ 1177	4¢	Horace Greeley	2.00	.40	.10–.25

1177

1178

1179

1180

1181

1182

1183

1184

1185

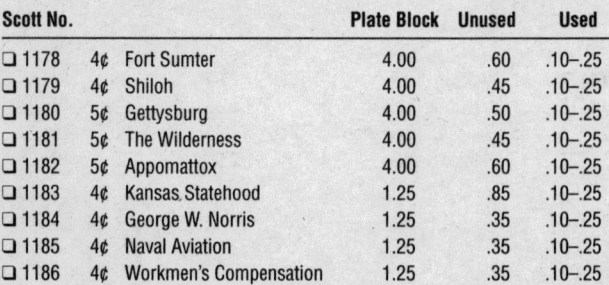
1186

Scott No.			Plate Block	Unused	Used
❏ 1178	4¢	Fort Sumter	4.00	.60	.10–.25
❏ 1179	4¢	Shiloh	4.00	.45	.10–.25
❏ 1180	5¢	Gettysburg	4.00	.50	.10–.25
❏ 1181	5¢	The Wilderness	4.00	.45	.10–.25
❏ 1182	5¢	Appomattox	4.00	.60	.10–.25
❏ 1183	4¢	Kansas Statehood	1.25	.85	.10–.25
❏ 1184	4¢	George W. Norris	1.25	.35	.10–.25
❏ 1185	4¢	Naval Aviation	1.25	.35	.10–.25
❏ 1186	4¢	Workmen's Compensation	1.25	.35	.10–.25

| 1187 | 1188 | 1189 | 1190 |

Scott No.			Plate Block	Unused	Used
❑ 1187	4¢	Frederick Remington	1.25	.40	.10–.25
❑ 1188	4¢	Republic of China	1.25	.80	.10–.25
❑ 1189	4¢	Naismith – Basketball	4.00	.40	.10–.25
❑ 1190	4¢	Nursing	4.00	.35	.10–.25

| 1191 | 1192 |

| 1193 | 1194 | 1195 |

1962.

❑ 1191	4¢	New Mexico Statehood	.90	.55	.10–.25
❑ 1192	4¢	Arizona Statehood	.90	.55	.10–.25
❑ 1193	4¢	Project Mercury	1.15	.40	.10–.25
❑ 1194	4¢	Malaria Eradication	.90	.35	.10–.25
❑ 1195	4¢	Charles Evans Hughes	.90	.40	.10–.25

1196

1197

1198

1199

1200

1201

1202

1203

1204

Scott No.			Plate Block	Unused	Used
❑ 1196	4¢	Seattle World's Fair	.80	.50	.10–.25
❑ 1197	4¢	Louisiana Statehood	2.00	.45	.10–.25
❑ 1198	4¢	The Homestead Act	1.30	.40	.10–.25
❑ 1199	4¢	Girl Scouts	1.25	.40	.10–.25
❑ 1200	4¢	Brien McMahon	1.25	.35	.10–.25
❑ 1201	4¢	Apprenticeship Act	.90	.35	.10–.25
❑ 1202	4¢	Sam Rayburn	1.25	.45	.10–.25
❑ 1203	4¢	Dag Hammarskjold	.80	.35	.10–.25
❑ 1204	4¢	Hammarskjold, yellow inverted	1.25	.35	.10–.25

1205

1206

1207

Scott No.			Plate Block	Unused	Used
❏ 1205	4¢	Christmas Wreath	.85	.35	.10–.25
❏ 1206	4¢	Higher Education	1.25	.35	.10–.25
❏ 1207	4¢	Winslow Homer	1.25	.35	.10–.25

1208

1209
(1225)

1213
(1229)

1962–1963. Definitives.

❏ 1208	5¢	U.S. Flag	.85	.35	.10–.25
❏ 1209	1¢	Andrew Jackson	.85	.35	.10–.25
❏ 1213	5¢	George Washington	.85	.40	.10–.25

Scott No.			Line Pair	Unused	Used

Coil Stamps.

❏ 1225	1¢	Andrew Jackson (~1209)	2.00	.40	.10–.25
❏ 1229	5¢	George Washington (~1213)	4.00	1.50	.10–.25

1230

1231

1232

1233

1234

1235

1236

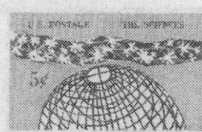
1237

1238

Scott No.			Plate Block	Unused	Used
1963.					
❑ 1230	5¢	Carolina Charter	2.00	.40	.10–.25
❑ 1231	5¢	Food for Peace	.80	.35	.10–.25
❑ 1232	5¢	West Virginia Statehood	1.25	.60	.10–.25
❑ 1233	5¢	Emancipation Proclamation	1.25	.35	.10–.25
❑ 1234	5¢	Alliance for Progress	.80	.35	.10–.25
❑ 1235	5¢	Cordell Hull	4.00	.35	.10–.25
❑ 1236	5¢	Eleanor Roosevelt	1.25	.35	.10–.25
❑ 1237	5¢	The Sciences	1.25	.35	.10–.25
❑ 1238	5¢	City Mail Delivery	1.25	.35	.10–.25

1239

1240

1241

Scott No.			Plate Block	Unused	Used
❑ 1239	5¢	International Red Cross	.85	.35	.10–.25
❑ 1240	5¢	Christmas Tree	1.00	.40	.10–.25
❑ 1241	5¢	John James Audubon	2.00	.35	.10–.25

1242

1243

1244

1245

1246

1247

1964.

❑ 1242	5¢	Sam Houston	1.25	.70	.10–.25
❑ 1243	5¢	Charles M. Russell	4.00	.50	.10–.25
❑ 1244	5¢	New York World's Fair	1.25	.35	.10–.25
❑ 1245	5¢	John Muir	.85	.50	.10–.25
❑ 1246	5¢	John F. Kennedy	4.25	.40	.10–.25
❑ 1247	5¢	New Jersey Statehood	4.25	.35	.10–.25

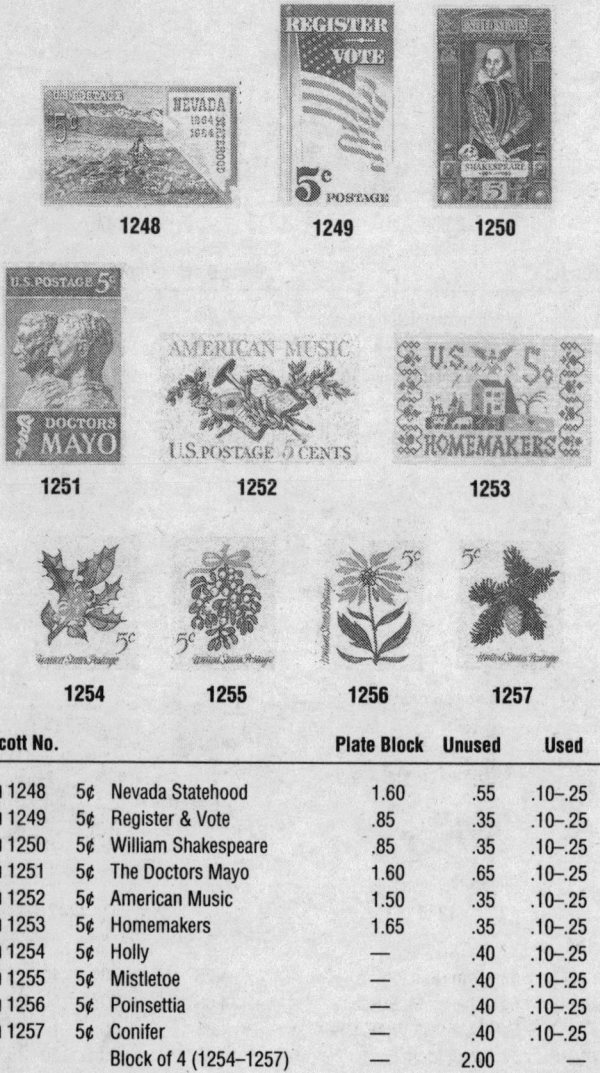

1248 1249 1250

1251 1252 1253

1254 1255 1256 1257

Scott No.			Plate Block	Unused	Used
❏ 1248	5¢	Nevada Statehood	1.60	.55	.10–.25
❏ 1249	5¢	Register & Vote	.85	.35	.10–.25
❏ 1250	5¢	William Shakespeare	.85	.35	.10–.25
❏ 1251	5¢	The Doctors Mayo	1.60	.65	.10–.25
❏ 1252	5¢	American Music	1.50	.35	.10–.25
❏ 1253	5¢	Homemakers	1.65	.35	.10–.25
❏ 1254	5¢	Holly	—	.40	.10–.25
❏ 1255	5¢	Mistletoe	—	.40	.10–.25
❏ 1256	5¢	Poinsettia	—	.40	.10–.25
❏ 1257	5¢	Conifer	—	.40	.10–.25
		Block of 4 (1254–1257)	—	2.00	—

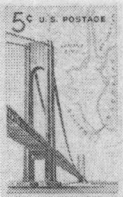

| 1258 | 1259 | 1260 |

Scott No.			Plate Block	Unused	Used
❑ 1258	5¢	Verrazano Bridge	4.00	.35	.10–.25
❑ 1259	5¢	Modern Art	1.25	.35	.10–.25
❑ 1260	5¢	Amateur Radio	1.30	.50	.10–.25

1261

| 1262 | 1263 |

1264

1265

1266

1965.

❑ 1261	5¢	Battle of New Orleans	4.00	.40	.10–.25
❑ 1262	5¢	Fitness – Discus Thrower	1.15	.35	.10–.25
❑ 1263	5¢	Crusade Against Cancer	.85	.35	.10–.25
❑ 1264	5¢	Winston Churchill	1.15	.35	.10–.25
❑ 1265	5¢	Magna Carta	1.15	.35	.10–.25
❑ 1266	5¢	International Cooperation Year	.85	.35	.10–.25

1267

1268

1269

1270

1271

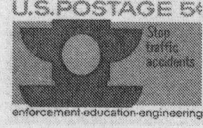
1272

1273

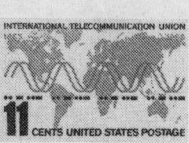
1274

1275

1276

Scott No.			Plate Block	Unused	Used
❏ 1267	5¢	Salvation Army	1.25	.35	.10–.25
❏ 1268	5¢	Dante Alighieri	.85	.35	.10–.25
❏ 1269	5¢	Herbert Hoover	1.25	.50	.10–.25
❏ 1270	5¢	Robert Fulton	1.15	.35	.10–.25
❏ 1271	5¢	Florida Settlement	1.15	.45	.10–.25
❏ 1272	5¢	Traffic Safety	1.15	.45	.10–.25
❏ 1273	5¢	John Singleton Copley	1.25	.35	.10–.25
❏ 1274	11¢	I.T.U.	5.00	.85	.50
❏ 1275	5¢	Adlai E. Stevenson	.85	.35	.10–.25
❏ 1276	5¢	Christmas Angel & Trumpet	.85	.35	.10–.25

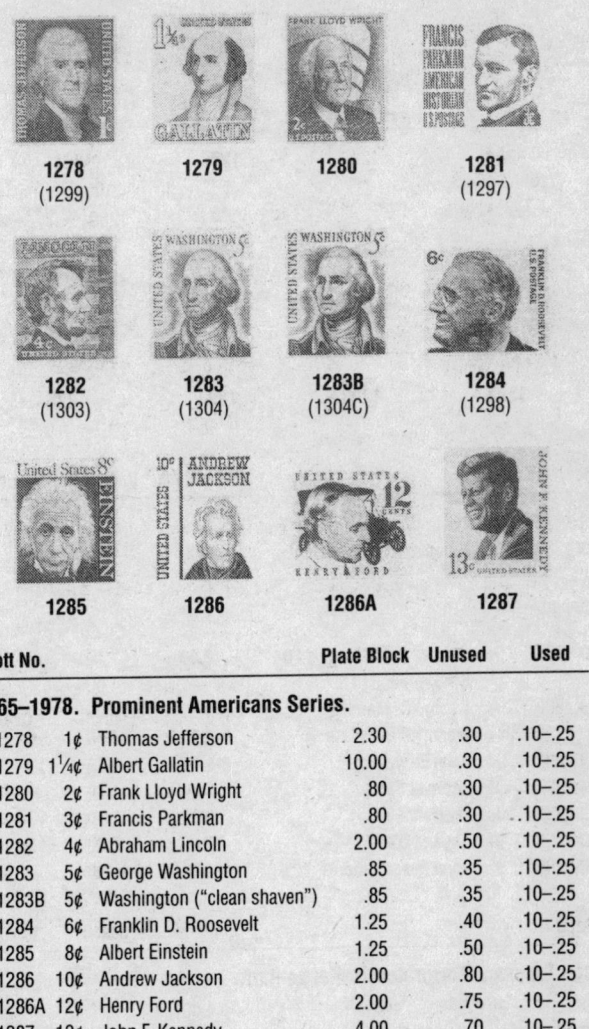

1278
(1299)

1279

1280

1281
(1297)

1282
(1303)

1283
(1304)

1283B
(1304C)

1284
(1298)

1285

1286

1286A

1287

Scott No.			Plate Block	Unused	Used

1965–1978. Prominent Americans Series.

			Plate Block	Unused	Used
☐ 1278	1¢	Thomas Jefferson	2.30	.30	.10–.25
☐ 1279	1¼¢	Albert Gallatin	10.00	.30	.10–.25
☐ 1280	2¢	Frank Lloyd Wright	.80	.30	.10–.25
☐ 1281	3¢	Francis Parkman	.80	.30	.10–.25
☐ 1282	4¢	Abraham Lincoln	2.00	.50	.10–.25
☐ 1283	5¢	George Washington	.85	.35	.10–.25
☐ 1283B	5¢	Washington ("clean shaven")	.85	.35	.10–.25
☐ 1284	6¢	Franklin D. Roosevelt	1.25	.40	.10–.25
☐ 1285	8¢	Albert Einstein	1.25	.50	.10–.25
☐ 1286	10¢	Andrew Jackson	2.00	.80	.10–.25
☐ 1286A	12¢	Henry Ford	2.00	.75	.10–.25
☐ 1287	13¢	John F. Kennedy	4.00	.70	.10–.25

1288
(1288d, 1288B,
1305E)

1289

1290

1291

1292

1293

1294
(1305C)

1295

Scott No.			Plate Block	Unused	Used
❏ 1288	15¢	Oliver Wendell Holmes (type I)	2.00	.55	.10–.25
❏ 1288d	15¢	Holmes (~1288) (type II)	12.00	1.10	.10–.25

Type I: The tip of the necktie touches the coat. Type II: The tip of the necktie is well clear of the coat.

Scott No.			Plate Block	Unused	Used
❏ 1288B	15¢	Holmes (~1288), perf 10	8.00	.70	.10–.25
		Booklet pane of 8	—	4.00	—
❏ 1289	20¢	George C. Marshall	4.00	.90	.10–.25
❏ 1290	25¢	Frederick Douglass	4.00	1.30	.10–.25
❏ 1291	30¢	John Dewey	6.00	1.85	.10–.25
❏ 1292	40¢	Thomas Paine	5.00	1.70	.10–.25
❏ 1293	50¢	Lucy Stone	6.00	2.00	.10–.25
❏ 1294	$1	Eugene O'Neill	15.00	4.60	.10–.25
❏ 1295	$5	John Bassett Moore	60.00	19.00	2.65

Scott No.			Line Pair	Unused	Used
Coil Stamps. Perforated 10 Horizontally.					
❏ 1297	3¢	Francis Parkman (~1281).	2.00	.30	.10–.25
❏ 1298	6¢	Franklin D. Roosevelt (~1284)	2.00	.35	.10–.25

1305

Scott No.			Line Pair	Unused	Used
Coil Stamps. Perforated 10 Vertically.					
❏ 1299	1¢	Thomas Jefferson (~1278)	1.00	.70	.10–.25
❏ 1303	4¢	Abraham Lincoln (~1282)	1.00	.45	.10–.25
❏ 1304	5¢	George Washington (~1283)	.90	.35	.10–.25
❏ 1304C	5¢	Washington ("clean shaven") (~1283B)	2.00	.50	.10–.25
❏ 1305	6¢	Franklin D. Roosevelt	1.00	.40	.10–.25
❏ 1305C	$1	Eugene O'Neill (~1294)	7.00	4.00	2.10
❏ 1305E	15¢	Holmes (~1288)	4.05	.60	.10–.25

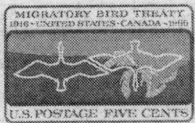

1306

1307

1308

1309

Scott No.			Plate Block	Unused	Used
1966.					
❏ 1306	5¢	Migratory Bird Treaty	1.00	.35	.10–.25
❏ 1307	5¢	Humane Treatment of Animals	1.00	.35	.10–.25
❏ 1308	5¢	Indiana Statehood	1.00	.45	.10–.25
❏ 1309	5¢	Circus Clown	1.15	.50	.10–.25

1310

1311

1312

1313

1314

Scott No.			Plate Block	Unused	Used
❏ 1310	5¢	SIPEX	1.15	.35	.10–.25
❏ 1311	5¢	SIPEX souvenir sheet	1.15	.35	—
❏ 1312	5¢	Bill of Rights	.90	.40	.10–.25
❏ 1313	5¢	Polish Millennium	.90	.35	.10–.25
❏ 1314	5¢	National Park Service	1.15	.55	.10–.25

| 1315 | 1316 | 1317 |

| 1318 | 1319 | 1320 |

| 1321 | 1322 |

Scott No.			Plate Block	Unused	Used
❑ 1315	5¢	Marine Corps Reserve	.90	.45	.10–.25
❑ 1316	5¢	Women's Clubs	.90	.30	.10–.25
❑ 1317	5¢	Johnny Appleseed	4.00	.40	.10–.25
❑ 1318	5¢	Beautification	1.00	.55	.10–.25
❑ 1319	5¢	Great River Road	.90	.55	.10–.25
❑ 1320	5¢	Servicemen & Savings Bonds	1.00	.35	.10–.25
❑ 1321	5¢	Christmas – Madonna	.90	.35	.10–.25
❑ 1322	5¢	Mary Cassatt	1.00	.35	.10–.25

1323

1324

1325

1326

1327

1328

1329

1330

Scott No.			Plate Block	Unused	Used
1967.					
❏ 1323	5¢	Grange Centenary	2.00	.35	.10–.25
❏ 1324	5¢	Canada Centennial	.85	.35	.10–.25
❏ 1325	5¢	Erie Canal	1.15	.40	.10–.25
❏ 1326	5¢	Search for Peace	4.00	.35	.10–.25
❏ 1327	5¢	Henry David Thoreau	1.15	.40	.10–.25
❏ 1328	5¢	Nebraska Statehood	4.00	.60	.10–.25
❏ 1329	5¢	Voice of America	1.20	.40	.10–.25
❏ 1330	5¢	Davy Crockett	1.20	.40	.10–.25

1331–1332

1333

1334

1335

1336

1337

Scott No.			Plate Block	Unused	Used
❏ 1331	5¢	Astronaut EVA	—	.90	.10–.25
❏ 1332	5¢	Gemini Capsule	—	.90	.10–.25
		Se-tenant pair (1331–1332)	—	1.75	—
❏ 1333	5¢	Urban Planning	.90	.35	.10–.25
❏ 1334	5¢	Finland Independence	2.00	.35	.10–.25
❏ 1335	5¢	Thomas Eakins	2.00	.35	.10–.25
❏ 1336	5¢	Christmas – Madonna	.90	.35	.10–.25
❏ 1337	5¢	Mississippi Statehood	4.00	.50	.10–.25

1338
(1338A, 1338D)

1338F
(1338G)

Scott No.			Plate Block	Unused	Used
1968. Definitive.					
☐ 1338	6¢	U.S. Flag, perf 11	1.00	.35	.10–.25

Scott No.			Line Pair	Unused	Used
Coil Stamp.					
☐ 1338A	6¢	U.S. Flag (~1338)	7.00	.50	.10–.25

Scott No.			Plate Block	Unused	Used
1970–1971.					
☐ 1338D	6¢	U.S. Flag (~1338), perf 11x10½	10.00 (20)	.35	.10–.25
☐ 1338F	8¢	U.S. Flag, perf 11 x 10½	5.00	.40	.10–.25

Scott No.			Line Pair	Unused	Used
Coil Stamp.					
☐ 1338G	8¢	U.S. Flag (~1338F)	4.30	.45	.10–.25

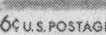

1339

1340

1341

1342

1343

1344

Scott No.			Plate Block	Unused	Used
1968.					
❏ 1339	6¢	Illinois Statehood	4.00	.45	.10–.25
❏ 1340	6¢	Hemisfair '68	.85	.35	.10–.25
❏ 1341	$1	Airlift	12.00	3.60	2.10
❏ 1342	6¢	Support Our Youth	1.15	.35	.10–.25
❏ 1343	6¢	Law & Order	1.15	.50	.10–.25
❏ 1344	6¢	Register & Vote	1.15	.35	.10–.25

Scott No.			Plate Block	Unused	Used
❑ 1345	6¢	Fort Moultrie Flag	—	.45	.85
❑ 1346	6¢	Fort McHenry Flag	—	.45	.85
❑ 1347	6¢	Washington's Cruisers Flag	—	.45	.85
❑ 1348	6¢	Bennington Flag	—	.45	.85
❑ 1349	6¢	Rhode Island Flag	—	.45	.85
❑ 1350	6¢	First Stars & Stripes	—	.45	.85
❑ 1351	6¢	Bunker Hill Flag	—	.45	.85
❑ 1352	6¢	Grand Union Flag	—	.45	.85
❑ 1353	6¢	Philadelphia Light Horse Flag	—	.45	.85
❑ 1354	6¢	First Navy Jack	—	.45	.85
		Strip of 10 (1345–1354)	—	4.20	—

Scott No.			Plate Block	Unused	Used
❑ 1355	6¢	Walt Disney	4.15	1.20	.10–.25
❑ 1356	6¢	Father Marquette	4.15	.50	.10–.25
❑ 1357	6¢	Daniel Boone	4.15	.40	.10–.25
❑ 1358	6¢	Arkansas River Navigation	4.15	.60	.10–.25
❑ 1359	6¢	Leif Erikson	1.30	.35	.10–.25
❑ 1360	6¢	Cherokee Strip Land Rush	4.00	.60	.10–.25
❑ 1361	6¢	John Trumball	4.00	.40	.10–.25
❑ 1362	6¢	Waterfowl Conservation	1.25	.55	.10–.25
❑ 1363	6¢	Christmas – Madonna	6.00 (10)	.35	.10–.25
❑ 1364	6¢	Chief Joseph	2.00	.60	.10–.25

1365–1368

1369   **1370**   **1371**

1372

Scott No.			Plate Block	Unused	Used
1969.					
❑ 1365	6¢	Beautification – Cities	—	.65	.10–.25
❑ 1366	6¢	Beautification – Parks	—	.65	.10–.25
❑ 1367	6¢	Beautification – Highways	—	.65	.10–.25
❑ 1368	6¢	Beautification – Streets	—	.65	.10–.25
		Block of 4 (1365–1368)	—	2.60	—
❑ 1369	6¢	American Legion	.90	.35	.10–.25
❑ 1370	6¢	Grandma Moses	.90	.35	.10–.25
❑ 1371	6¢	Apollo 8	1.25	.55	.10–.25
❑ 1372	6¢	W. C. Handy	4.00	.45	.10–.25

1374

1375

1373

1376–1379

1380

1381

1382

Scott No.			Plate Block	Unused	Used
❏ 1373	6¢	Settlement of California	2.25	.50	.10–.25
❏ 1374	6¢	John Wesley Powell	4.00	.65	.10–.25
❏ 1375	6¢	Alabama Statehood	2.00	.45	.10–.25
❏ 1376	6¢	Pseudotsuga menziesii	—	.75	.10–.25
❏ 1377	6¢	Cypridedium reginae	—	.75	.10–.25
❏ 1378	6¢	Fouquieria splendens	—	.75	.10–.25
❏ 1379	6¢	Franklinia alatamaha	—	.75	.10–.25
		Block of 4 (1376–1379)	—	3.00	.10–.25
❏ 1380	6¢	Daniel Webster	2.25	.40	.10–.25
❏ 1381	6¢	Professional Baseball	4.00	.75	.10–.25
❏ 1382	6¢	Intercollegiate Football	4.00	.50	.10–.25

DWIGHT D.
EISENHOWER

1383

1384

1385

1386

Scott No.			Plate Block	Unused	Used
❏ 1383	6¢	Dwight D. Eisenhower	-.85	.60	.10–.25
❏ 1384	6¢	Christmas – Winter Scene	4.00 (10)	.35	.10–.25
❏ 1385	6¢	Hope for the Crippled	.85	.35	.10–.25
❏ 1386	6¢	William Harnett Painting	.85	.35	.10–.25

1376–1379

1970.

❏ 1387	6¢	American Bald Eagle	—	.35	.10–.25
❏ 1388	6¢	African Elephant Herd	—	.35	.10–.25
❏ 1389	6¢	Haida Ceremonial Canoe	—	.35	.10–.25
❏ 1390	6¢	The Age of Reptiles	—	.35	.10–.25
		Block of 4 (1387–1390)	1.40	—	—

1391

1392

Scott No.			Plate Block	Unused	Used
❑ 1391	6¢	Maine Statehood	2.00	.40	.10–.25
❑ 1392	6¢	Conservation – Bison	2.00	.80	.10–.25

1393
(1401)

1393D

1394
(1395, 1402)

1396

1970–1974. Definitives.

❑ 1393	6¢	Dwight D. Eisenhower	.85	.35	.10–.25
		Booklet pane of 5 + label	—	1.75	.10–.25
		Booklet pane of 8	—	2.00	.10–.25
❑ 1393D	7¢	Benjamin Franklin	2.00	.55	.10–.25
❑ 1394	8¢	Eisenhower, red, black & blue	2.00	.40	.10–.25
❑ 1395	8¢	Eisenhower (~1394), claret	—	.45	.10–.25
		Booklet pane of 4 + 2 labels	—	2.00	.10–.25
		Booklet pane of 6	—	2.00	.10–.25
		Booklet pane of 7 + 1 label	—	4.00	.10–.25
		Booklet pane of 8	—	4.00	.10–.25
❑ 1396	8¢	U.S.P.S. Emblem	5.00	.35	.10–.25

| 1397 | 1398 | 1399 | 1400 |

Scott No.			Plate Block	Unused	Used
❏ 1397	14¢	Fiorello LaGuardia	2.00	.50	.10–.25
❏ 1398	16¢	Ernie Pyle	2.00	.65	.10–.25
❏ 1399	18¢	Elizabeth Blackwell	2.00	.65	.10–.25
❏ 1400	21¢	Amadeo P. Giannini	4.00	.80	.10–.25

Scott No.			Line Pair	Unused	Used

Coil Stamps. Perforated 10 Vertically.

❏ 1401	6¢	Eisenhower (~1393)	.90	.35	.10–.25
❏ 1402	8¢	Eisenhower (~1394) claret	.90	.40	.10–.25

| 1406 | 1407 |

| 1405 | | 1408 | 1409 |

Scott No.			Plate Block	Unused	Used

1970.

❏ 1405	6¢	Edgar Lee Masters	2.00	.40	.10–.25
❏ 1406	6¢	Women's Suffrage	1.25	.50	.10–.25
❏ 1407	6¢	South Carolina	2.00	.40	.10–.25
❏ 1408	6¢	Stone Mountain	—	.45	.10–.25
❏ 1409	6¢	Fort Snelling	2.00	.60	.10–.25

1410–1413

1414

1414a

1415–1418

Scott No.			Plate Block	Unused	Used
❑ 1410	6¢	Save Our Soil	—	.45	.10–.25
❑ 1411	6¢	Save Our Cities	—	.45	.10–.25
❑ 1412	6¢	Save Our Water	—	.45	.10–.25
❑ 1413	6¢	Save Our Air	—	.45	.10–.25
		Block of 4 (1410–1413)	1.75	—	.10–.25
❑ 1414	6¢	Christmas – Manger Scene	4.00 (8)	.35	.10–.25
❑ 1414a	6¢	Christmas, precanceled	4.00 (8)	.40	.10–.25
❑ 1415	6¢	Locomotive	—	.45	.10–.25
❑ 1416	6¢	Toy Horse	—	.45	.10–.25
❑ 1417	6¢	Tricycle	—	.45	.10–.25
❑ 1418	6¢	Doll Carriage	—	.45	.10–.25
		Block of 4 (1415–1418)	2.30	—	—

1415a–1418a

1419

1420

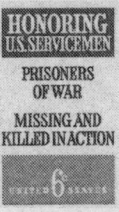

1421   **1422**

Scott No.			Plate Block	Unused	Used
❑ 1415a	6¢	Locomotive, precanceled	—	.85	.10–.25
❑ 1416a	6¢	Toy Horse, precanceled	—	.85	.10–.25
❑ 1417a	6¢	Tricycle, precanceled	—	.85	.10–.25
❑ 1418a	6¢	Doll Carriage, precanceled		.85	.10–.25
		Block of 4 (1415a–1418a)	4.00	—	.10–.25
❑ 1419	6¢	United Nations	1.65	.45	.10–.25
❑ 1420	6¢	Landing of the Pilgrims	1.65	.35	.10–.25
❑ 1421	6¢	Disabled Veterans	—	.40	.10–.25
❑ 1422	6¢	Honoring U.S. Servicemen	—	.40	.10–.25
		Se-tenant pair (1421–1422)	—	.80	—

1425

1423

1424

1426

1427–1430

Scott No.			Plate Block	Unused	Used
1971.					
❏ 1423	6¢	America's Wool	.90	.45	.10–.25
❏ 1424	6¢	Douglas MacArthur	2.00	.50	.10–.25
❏ 1425	6¢	Giving Blood Saves Lives	.90	.35	.10–.25
❏ 1426	8¢	Missouri Statehood	6.00 (12)	.50	.10–.25
❏ 1427	8¢	Trout	—	.55	.10–.25
❏ 1428	8¢	Alligator	—	.55	.10–.25
❏ 1429	8¢	Polar Bear	—	.55	.10–.25
❏ 1430	8¢	California Condor	—	.55	.10–.25
		Block of 4 (1427–1430)	2.00	—	—

1431

1432

1433

1434–1435

1436

1437

1438

1439

Scott No.			Plate Block	Unused	Used
❏ 1431	8¢	Antarctic Treaty	1.25	.35	.10–.25
❏ 1432	8¢	Revolution Bicentennial	1.25	.35	.10–.25
❏ 1433	8¢	John Sloan	1.25	.35	.10–.25
❏ 1434	8¢	Earth & Lander	1.25	.35	.10–.25
❏ 1435	8¢	Lunar Rover	1.25	.35	.10–.25
		Se-tenant pair (1434–1435)	.65	—	.10–.25
❏ 1436	8¢	Emily Dickinson	2.00	.40	.10–.25
❏ 1437	8¢	San Juan, Puerto Rico	1.30	.70	.10–.25
❏ 1438	8¢	Prevent Drug Abuse	3.00 (6)	.35	.10–.25
❏ 1439	8¢	CARE	2.00 (8)	.35	.10–.25

1440–1443

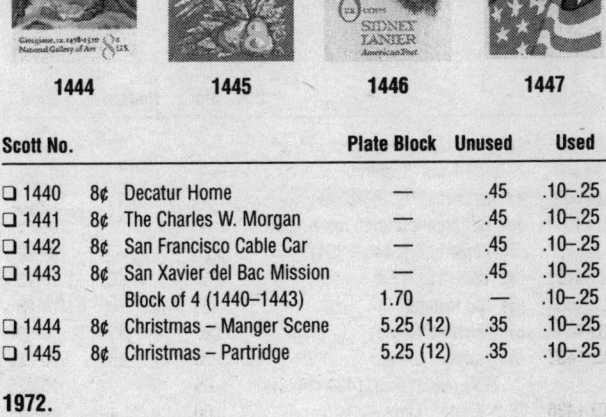

| 1444 | 1445 | 1446 | 1447 |

Scott No.			Plate Block	Unused	Used
❏ 1440	8¢	Decatur Home	—	.45	.10–.25
❏ 1441	8¢	The Charles W. Morgan	—	.45	.10–.25
❏ 1442	8¢	San Francisco Cable Car	—	.45	.10–.25
❏ 1443	8¢	San Xavier del Bac Mission	—	.45	.10–.25
		Block of 4 (1440–1443)	1.70	—	.10–.25
❏ 1444	8¢	Christmas – Manger Scene	5.25 (12)	.35	.10–.25
❏ 1445	8¢	Christmas – Partridge	5.25 (12)	.35	.10–.25
1972.					
❏ 1446	8¢	Sidney Lanier	2.05	.45	.10–.25
❏ 1447	8¢	Peace Corps	2.05 (6)	.35	.10–.25

1448–1451

1452

1453

1454

1455

Scott No.			Plate Block	Unused	Used
❏ 1448	2¢	Hatteras – Shipwreck in Surf	—	.30	.10–.25
❏ 1449	2¢	Hatteras – Lighthouse	—	.30	.10–.25
❏ 1450	2¢	Hatteras – 3 Shorebirds	—	.30	.10–.25
❏ 1451	2¢	Hatteras – Shorebirds & Dunes	—	.30	.10–.25
		Block of 4 (1448–1451)	1.25	—	.10–.25
❏ 1452	6¢	Wolf Trap Farm	4.00	.40	.10–.25
❏ 1453	8¢	Old Faithful	1.25	.70	.10–.25
❏ 1454	15¢	Mount McKinley	4.00	.85	.60
❏ 1455	8¢	Family Planning	1.25	.35	.10–.25

1456–1459

Scott No.			Plate Block	Unused	Used
❑ 1456	8¢	Craftsmen – Glass Blower	—	.30	.10–.25
❑ 1457	8¢	Craftsmen – Silversmith	—	.30	.10–.25
❑ 1458	8¢	Craftsmen – Wigmaker	—	.30	.10–.25
❑ 1459	8¢	Craftsmen – Hatter	—	.30	.10–.25
		Block of 4 (1456–1459)	1.40	—	.10–.25
❑ 1460	6¢	Cycling	2.00 (10)	.35	.10–.25
❑ 1461	8¢	Bobsledding	4.00 (10)	.35	.10–.25
❑ 1462	15¢	Running	4.00 (10)	1.00	.50
❑ 1463	8¢	P.T.A.	1.30	.40	.10–.25
❑ 1463a	8¢	P.T.A., reversed plate number	1.30	—	—

1464–1467

1468

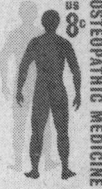

1469

1470

Scott No.			Plate Block	Unused	Used
❑ 1464	8¢	Fur Seal	—	.35	.10–.25
❑ 1465	8¢	Cardinal	—	.35	.10–.25
❑ 1466	8¢	Brown Pelican	—	.35	.10–.25
❑ 1467	8¢	Bighorn Sheep	—	.35	.10–.25
		Block of 4 (1464–1467)	1.25	—	—
❑ 1468	8¢	Mail Order	4.25 (12)	.40	.10–.25
❑ 1469	8¢	Osteopathic Medicine	2.00 (6)	.55	.10–.25
❑ 1470	8¢	Tom Sawyer	2.00	.45	.10–.25

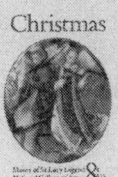

1471

1472

1473

1474

Scott No.			Plate Block	Unused	Used
❑ 1471	8¢	Christmas – Angels	4.00 (12)	.35	.10–.25
❑ 1472	8¢	Christmas – Santa	4.00 (12)	.35	.10–.25
❑ 1473	8¢	Pharmacy	2.25	.50	.10–.25
❑ 1474	8¢	Stamp Collecting	2.25	.35	.10–.25

1475

1476

1477

1478

1479

1973.

❑ 1475	8¢	LOVE	2.00 (6)	.35	.10–.25
❑ 1476	8¢	Colonial Printing Press	1.70	.35	.10–.25
❑ 1477	8¢	Posting a Broadside	1.70	.35	.10–.25
❑ 1478	8¢	Post Rider	1.70	.35	.10–.25
❑ 1479	8¢	Drummer	1.70	.35	.10–.25

1480–1483

| | **1484** | **1485** | |
| | **1486** | **1487** | **1488** |

Scott No.			Plate Block	Unused	Used
❏ 1480	8¢	Tea Party – Dumping Tea	—	.40	.10–.25
❏ 1481	8¢	Tea Party – Ship at Anchor	—	.40	.10–.25
❏ 1482	8¢	Tea Party – Boats & Lantern	—	.40	.10–.25
❏ 1483	8¢	Tea Party – Bystanders on Pier	—	.40	.10–.25
		Block of 4 (1480–1483)	1.55	—	.10–.25
❏ 1484	8¢	George Gershwin	4.25 (12)	.35	.10–.25
❏ 1485	8¢	Robinson Jeffers	4.25 (12)	.35	.10–.25
❏ 1486	6¢	Henry O. Tanner	4.25 (12)	.35	.10–.25
❏ 1487	8¢	Willa Cather	5.00 (12)	.65	.10–.25
❏ 1488	8¢	Copernicus	2.00	.35	.10–.25

1489–1492

1493–1496

1497–1498

Scott No.			Plate Block	Unused	Used
❏ 1489	8¢	Window Clerk	—	.40	.10–.25
❏ 1490	8¢	Collecting Mail	—	.40	.10–.25
❏ 1491	8¢	Conveyor Belt	—	.40	.10–.25
❏ 1492	8¢	Bagging Parcels	—	.40	.10–.25
❏ 1493	8¢	Mail in Trays	—	.40	.10–.25
❏ 1494	8¢	Sorting to Pigeonholes	—	.40	.10–.25
❏ 1495	8¢	Keypunch Operators	—	.40	.10–.25
❏ 1496	8¢	Loading Mail Truck	—	.40	.10–.25
❏ 1497	8¢	Carrier Walking Route	—	.40	.10–.25
❏ 1498	8¢	Rural Delivery Carrier	—	.40	.10–.25
		Strip of 10 (1489–1498)	—	3.60	—

1499

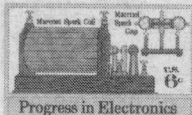

1500

1501

1502

1503

1504

1505

1506

Scott No.			Plate Block	Unused	Used
❑ 1499	8¢	Harry S. Truman	2.15	.55	.10–.25
❑ 1500	6¢	Spark Coil & Spark Gap	2.15	.35	.10–.25
❑ 1501	8¢	Transistors	2.15	.35	.10–.25
❑ 1502	15¢	Microphone & Speaker	2.15	1.00	.85
❑ 1503	8¢	Lyndon B. Johnson	6.00 (12)	.50	.10–.25
❑ 1504	8¢	Angus Cattle	2.20	.50	.10–.25
❑ 1505	10¢	Chautauqua	2.20	.35	.10–.25
❑ 1506	10¢	Winter Wheat	2.20	.60	.10–.25

1507   **1508**

Scott No.			Plate Block	Unused	Used
❏ 1507	8¢	Madonna & Child	4.00 (12)	.35	.10–.25
❏ 1508	8¢	Christmas Tree	4.00 (12)	.35	.10–.25

1509   **1510**   **1511**
(1519)   (1520)

1973–1974. Definitives.

❏ 1509	10¢	Crossed Flags	7.20 (20)	.40	.10–.25
❏ 1510	10¢	Jefferson Memorial	2.25	.55	.10–.25
❏ 1511	10¢	ZIP Code	3.45 (8)	.45	.10–.25

1518

Scott No.			Line Pair	Unused	Used
Coil Stamps.					
❑ 1518	6.3¢	Liberty Bell	.90	.85	.40
❑ 1519	10¢	Crossed Flags (~1509)	—	.50	.10–.25
❑ 1520	10¢	Jefferson Memorial (~1510)	1.00	.55	.10–.25

1525	**1526**	**1527**

1528	**1529**

Scott No.			Plate Block	Unused	Used
1974.					
❑ 1525	10¢	V.F.W.	2.25	.45	.10–.25
❑ 1526	10¢	Robert Frost	2.25	.50	.10–.25
❑ 1527	10¢	Expo '74	6.80 (12)	.60	.10–.25
❑ 1528	10¢	Horse Racing	5.00 (12)	.45	.10–.25
❑ 1529	10¢	Skylab	2.25	.40	.10–.25

1530–1437

Scott No.			Plate Block	Unused	Used
❏ 1530	10¢	UPU – Raphael	—	.80	.45
❏ 1531	10¢	UPU – Hokusai	—	.80	.45
❏ 1532	10¢	UPU – Peto	—	.80	.45
❏ 1533	10¢	UPU – Liotard	—	.80	.45
❏ 1534	10¢	UPU – Terborch	—	.80	.45
❏ 1535	10¢	UPU – Chardin	—	.80	.45
❏ 1536	10¢	UPU – Gainsborough	—	.80	.45
❏ 1537	10¢	UPU – Goya	—	.80	.45
		Block of 8 (1530–1537)	3.25	—	—

1538–1441　　　　　**1542**

1543–1446

Scott No.			Plate Block	Unused	Used
❏ 1538	10¢	Minerals – Petrified Wood	—	.50	.10–.25
❏ 1539	10¢	Minerals – Tourmaline	—	.50	.10–.25
❏ 1540	10¢	Minerals – Amethyst	—	.50	.10–.25
❏ 1541	10¢	Minerals – Rhodochrosite	—	.50	.10–.25
		Block of 4 (1538–1541)	2.00	—	.10–.25
❏ 1542	10¢	Fort Harrod Bicentennial	2.25	.45	.10–.25
❏ 1543	10¢	Carpenters' Hall	—	.45	.10–.25
❏ 1544	10¢	We Ask But For Peace	—	.45	.10–.25
❏ 1545	10¢	Deriving Their Just Powers	—	.45	.10–.25
❏ 1546	10¢	Independence Hall	—	.45	.10–.25
		Block of 4 (1543–1546)	1.70	—	—

1547

1548

1549

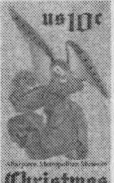
1550

1551

1552

Scott No.			Plate Block	Unused	Used
❑ 1547	10¢	Energy Conservation	3.05	.55	.10–.25
❑ 1548	10¢	Legend of Sleepy Hollow	3.05	.40	.10–.25
❑ 1549	10¢	Retarded Children	3.05	.45	.10–.25
❑ 1550	10¢	Christmas – Angel	3.60 (10)	.35	.10–.25
❑ 1551	10¢	Christmas – Currier & Ives	4.00 (12)	.35	.10–.25
❑ 1552	10¢	Christmas – Weather Vane	8.80 (20)	.45	.10–.25

1553

1554

1555

1556

1557

1558

1559

1560

1561

Scott No.			Plate Block	Unused	Used
1975.					
❏ 1553	10¢	Benjamin West	4.65 (10)	.50	.10–.25
❏ 1554	10¢	Paul Laurence Dunbar	5.60 (10)	.60	.10–.25
❏ 1555	10¢	D. W. Griffith	2.25	.60	.10–.25
❏ 1556	10¢	Pioneer 10	2.25	.45	.10–.25
❏ 1557	10¢	Mariner 10	2.25	.45	.10–.25
❏ 1558	10¢	Collective Bargaining	3.40 (8)	.45	.10–.25
❏ 1559	8¢	Sybil Ludington	11.00 (10)	1.10	.10–.25
❏ 1560	10¢	Salem Poor	4.25 (10)	.45	.10–.25
❏ 1561	10¢	Haym Salomon	7.60 (10)	.80	.10–.25

1562

US Bicentennial IOcents

1563

US Bicentennial IOc

1564

1565–1568

1569–1570

Scott No.			Plate Block	Unused	Used
❑ 1562	18¢	Peter Francisco	6.00 (10)	1.00	.50
❑ 1563	10¢	Lexington & Concord	5.55 (12)	.50	.10–.25
❑ 1564	10¢	Battle of Bunker Hill	5.05 (12)	.45	.10–.25
❑ 1565	10¢	Continental Army	4.60 (12)	.40	.10–.25
❑ 1566	10¢	Continental Navy	4.60 (12)	.40	.10–.25
❑ 1567	10¢	Continental Marines	4.60 (12)	.40	.10–.25
❑ 1568	10¢	American Militia	4.60 (12)	.40	.10–.25
		Block of 4 (1565–1568)	1.60 (12)	—	.10–.25
❑ 1569	10¢	Apollo-Soyuz & Earth	4.35 (12)	.40	.10–.25
❑ 1570	10¢	Apollo-Soyuz & Logo	—	.40	.10–.25
		Pair (1569–1570)	—	.80	—

1571

1572–1575

1576

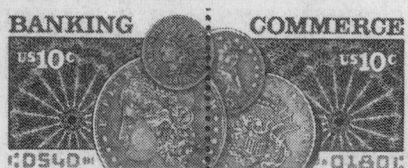

1577–1578

Scott No.			Plate Block	Unused	Used
❏ 1571	10¢	Int'l Women's Year	2.20 (6)	.40	.10–.25
❏ 1572	10¢	Stagecoach	—	.45	.10–.25
❏ 1573	10¢	Steam Engine	—	.45	.10–.25
❏ 1574	10¢	Biplane	—	.45	.10–.25
❏ 1575	10¢	Satellite	—	.45	.10–.25
		Block of 4 (1572–1575)	1.70	—	.10–.25
❏ 1576	10¢	World Peace Thru Law	2.00	.45	.10–.25
❏ 1577	10¢	Banking	—	.50	.10–.25
❏ 1578	10¢	Commerce	—	.50	.10–.25
		Pair (1577–1578)	—	1.00	—

1579

1580
(1580B)

Scott No.			Plate Block	Unused	Used
❏ 1579	10¢	Madonna & Child	5.50 (12)	.50	.10–.25
❏ 1580	10¢	Prang Card, perf 11	5.50 (12)	.50	.10–.25
❏ 1580B	10¢	Prang Card (~1580), perf 10.5 x 11.3	11.55 (12)	1.00	.40

1581
(1811)

1582

1584

1585

1590
(1590A, 1591, 1616)

1975–1981. Americana Series.

❏ 1581	1¢	Inkwell	.75	.30	.10–.25
❏ 1582	2¢	Speaker's Lectern	.75	.30	.10–.25
❏ 1584	3¢	Ballot Box	.75	.40	.10–.25
❏ 1585	4¢	Books & Glasses	.80	.30	.10–.25
❏ 1590	9¢	Capitol Dome, white paper, perf 11 x 10½	—	3.05	2.50
		Pair (1590 & 1623)	—	6.00	—
❏ 1590A	9¢	Capitol Dome, white paper, perf 10	—	16.00	10.00
		Pair (1590A & 1623A)	—	35.00	—
❏ 1591	9¢	Capitol Dome (~1590), gray paper	1.25	.40	.10–.25

1592
(1617)

1593

1594
(1816)

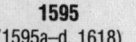

1595
(1595a–d, 1618)

1596

1597
(1598, 1618C)

1599
(1619)

Scott No.			Plate Block	Unused	Used
❏ 1592	10¢	Justice	2.15	.40	.10–.25
❏ 1593	11¢	Printing Press	2.15	.45	.10–.25
❏ 1594	12¢	Torch of Liberty	2.15	.50	.10–.25
❏ 1595	13¢	Liberty Bell, from booklet pane	—	.50	.10–.25
❏ 1595a	13¢	Booklet pane of 6	—	2.50	—
❏ 1595b	13¢	Booklet pane of 7 + label	—	2.50	—
❏ 1595c	13¢	Booklet pane of 8	—	2.50	—
❏ 1595d	13¢	Booklet pane of 5 + label	—	2.50	—
❏ 1596	13¢	Eagle & Shield	5.55 (12)	.50	.10–.25
❏ 1597	15¢	Stars & Stripes	11.20 (20)	.60	.10–.25
❏ 1598	15¢	Stars & Stripes (~1597)	—	.90	.10–.25
		Booklet pane of 8	—	8.00	—
❏ 1599	16¢	Statue of Liberty	4.30	1.25	.85

1603 **1604** **1605** **1606**

1608 **1610** **1611** **1612**

Scott No.			Plate Block	Unused	Used
❏ 1603	24¢	Old North Church	5.15	.90	.10–.25
❏ 1604	28¢	Fort Nisqually	5.15	1.50	.10–.25
❏ 1605	29¢	Sandy Hook Lighthouse	5.15	1.10	.10–.25
❏ 1606	30¢	School House	5.15	1.40	.10–.25
❏ 1608	50¢	Iron Betty Lamp	5.15	1.90	.10–.25
❏ 1610	$1	Rush Lamp	15.00	1.70	.10–.25
❏ 1611	$2	Kerosene Lamp	25.00	6.60	1.35
❏ 1612	$5	Railroad Lantern	50.00	16.40	2.10

1613 **1614** **1615** **1615C**

Scott No.			Line Pair	Unused	Used
Americana Series Coil Stamps.					
❏ 1613	3.1¢	Guitar	1.25	.80	.60
❏ 1614	7.7¢	Saxhorns	2.00	.80	.60
❏ 1615	7.9¢	Drum	1.30	.80	.60
❏ 1615C	8.4¢	Piano	4.00	.80	.60

Scott No.			Line Pair	Unused	Used
❑ 1616	9¢	Capitol Dome (~1590)	1.25	.45	.10–.25
❑ 1617	10¢	Justice (~1592)	1.25	.45	.10–.25
❑ 1618	13¢	Liberty Bell (~1595)	1.45	.50	.10–.25

United States 13c

1622
(1622C, 1625)

USA 13¢

1623
(1623B)

Scott No.			Plate Block	Unused	Used
1975–1977. Definitives.					
❑ 1622	13¢	Flag & Ind. Hall, perf 11 x 10½	10.40 (20)	.55	.10–.25
❑ 1622C	13¢	Flag & Ind. Hall (~1622), perf 11½	64.00 (20)	3.20	.36
❑ 1623	13¢	Flag & Capitol, perf 11 x 10½	—	.55	.36
		Booklet pane of 8 (7 x 1623, 1 x 1590)	—	4.35	—
❑ 1623B	13¢	Flag & Capitol (~1623), perf 10	—	1.10	.36
		Booklet pane of 8 (7 x 1623B, 1 x 1590A)	—	9.00	—

Scott No.			Line Pair	Unused	Used
Coil Stamps.					
❑ 1625	13¢	Flag & Independence Hall (~1622)	7.00	.60	.10–.25

1629–1531

1632

Scott No.			Plate Block	Unused	Used
1976.					
❏ 1629	13¢	Youthful Drummer	—	.55	.10–.25
❏ 1630	13¢	Mature Drummer	—	.55	.10–.25
❏ 1631	13¢	Fief Player	—	.55	.10–.25
		Strip of 3, 1629–1631	—	1.60	.10–.25
❏ 1632	13¢	INTERPHIL '76	2.00	.50	.10–.25

1633–1682

Scott No.			Plate Block	Unused	Used
❏ 1633–1682	13¢	Fifty State Flags	—	32.00 (50)	—
		Any Single Stamp		.65	.40

❏ 1633 Delaware	❏ 1637 Connecticut
❏ 1634 Pennsylvania	❏ 1638 Massachusetts
❏ 1635 New Jersey	❏ 1639 Maryland
❏ 1636 Georgia	❏ 1640 South Carolina

- ❏ 1641 New Hampshire
- ❏ 1642 Virginia
- ❏ 1643 New York
- ❏ 1644 North Carolina
- ❏ 1645 Rhode Island
- ❏ 1646 Vermont
- ❏ 1647 Kentucky
- ❏ 1648 Tennessee
- ❏ 1649 Ohio
- ❏ 1650 Louisiana
- ❏ 1651 Indiana
- ❏ 1652 Mississippi
- ❏ 1653 Illinois
- ❏ 1654 Alabama
- ❏ 1655 Maine
- ❏ 1656 Missouri
- ❏ 1657 Arkansas
- ❏ 1658 Michigan
- ❏ 1659 Florida
- ❏ 1660 Texas
- ❏ 1661 Iowa
- ❏ 1662 Wisconsin
- ❏ 1663 California
- ❏ 1664 Minnesota
- ❏ 1665 Oregon
- ❏ 1666 Kansas
- ❏ 1667 West Virginia
- ❏ 1668 Nevada
- ❏ 1669 Nebraska
- ❏ 1670 Colorado
- ❏ 1671 North Dakota
- ❏ 1672 South Dakota
- ❏ 1673 Montana
- ❏ 1674 Washington
- ❏ 1675 Idaho
- ❏ 1676 Wyoming
- ❏ 1677 Utah
- ❏ 1678 Oklahoma
- ❏ 1679 New Mexico
- ❏ 1680 Arizona
- ❏ 1681 Alaska
- ❏ 1682 Hawaii

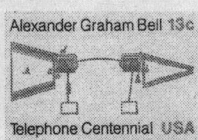

1683

Alexander Graham Bell 13¢
Telephone Centennial USA

Commercial Aviation
USA 13¢ 1926-1976

1684

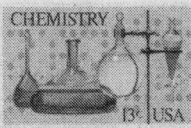

CHEMISTRY
13¢ USA

1685

Scott No.			Plate Block	Unused	Used
❏ 1683	13¢	Telephone Centennial	2.30	.55	.10–.25
❏ 1684	13¢	Commercial Aviation	7.00 (10)	.75	.10–.25
❏ 1685	13¢	Chemistry	6.70 (12)	.60	.10–.25

The Surrender of Lord Cornwallis at Yorktown
From a Painting by John Trumbull

1686

The Declaration of Independence, 4 July 1776 at Philadelphia
From a Painting by John Trumbull

1687

Washington Crossing the Delaware
From a Painting by Emanuel Leutze / Eastman Johnson

1688

Scott No.			Plate Block	Unused	Used
❏ 1686	13¢	Surrender at Yorktown, souvenir sheet	—	8.00	—
❏ 1686a–e		Any single stamp	—	1.65	.40
❏ 1687	18¢	Declaration of Independence, souvenir sheet	—	8.00	—
❏ 1687a–e		Any single stamp	—	1.65	.40
❏ 1688	24¢	Crossing the Delaware, souvenir sheet	—	8.00	—
❏ 1688a–e		Any single stamp	—	1.65	.40

Washington Reviewing His Ragged Army at Valley Forge
From a Painting by William T. Trego

1689

1690

Scott No.			Plate Block	Unused	Used
❑ 1689	31¢	Valley Forge, souvenir sheet	—	8.00	—
❑ 1689a–e		Any single stamp	—	1.65	.40
❑ 1690	13¢	Benjamin Franklin	2.15	.55	.68

JULY 4,1776 ; JULY 4,1776 ; JULY 4,1776 ; JULY 4,1776

1691–1694

1695–1698

Scott No.			Plate Block	Unused	Used
❑ 1691	13¢	Delegates Seated & Standing	—	2.25	.10–.25
❑ 1692	13¢	Delegates Seated	—	2.25	.10–.25
❑ 1693	13¢	Delegates at Desk	—	2.25	.10–.25
❑ 1694	13¢	Seated at Large Chair	—	2.25	.10–.25
		Strip of 4 (1691–1694)	3.20	—	.10–.25
❑ 1695	13¢	Olympics – Diving	—	2.00	.10–.25
❑ 1696	13¢	Olympics – Skiing	—	2.00	.10–.25
❑ 1697	13¢	Olympics – Running	—	2.00	.10–.25
❑ 1698	13¢	Olympics – Skating	—	2.00	.10–.25
		Block of 4 (1695–1698)	2.25	—	—

1701

1699

1700

1702

Scott No.			Plate Block	Unused	Used
❑ 1699	13¢	Clara Maass	6.50 (12)	.55	.10–.25
❑ 1700	13¢	Adolph S. Ochs	4.00	.55	.10–.25
❑ 1701	13¢	Christmas – Manger Scene	5.80 (12)	.50	.10–.25
❑ 1702	13¢	Winter Pastimes (overall tagging)	5.00 (10)	.50	.10–.25
❑ 1703	13¢	Winter Pastimes (~1702) (block tagging)	5.00 (10)	.50	.10–.25

US Bicentennial 13c

1704

13

1705

Scott No.			Plate Block	Unused	Used
1977.					
❑ 1704	13¢	Washington at Princeton	5.20 (10)	.55	.10–.25
❑ 1705	13¢	Sound Recording	5.00	.60	.10–.25

Hopi: Heard Museum Phoenix
Pueblo Art USA 13c · **Pueblo Art** USA 13c
Acoma: School of American Research

Zia: Museum of New Mexico
Pueblo Art USA 13c · **Pueblo Art** USA 13c
San Ildefonso: Denver Art Museum

1706–1709

1710

1711

Scott No.			Plate Block	Unused	Used
❑ 1706	13¢	Zia Pot	—	.60	.10–.25
❑ 1707	13¢	San Ildefonso Pot	—	.60	.10–.25
❑ 1708	13¢	Hopi Pot	—	.60	.10–.25
❑ 1709	13¢	Acoma Pot	—	.60	.10–.25
		Block of 4 (1706–1709)	2.30	—	—
❑ 1710	13¢	Spirit of St. Louis	8.20 (12)	.70	.10–.25
❑ 1711	13¢	Colorado Statehood	5.00	.65	.10–.25

1712–1715

1716

1717–1720

1721

1722

Scott No.			Plate Block	Unused	Used
❑ 1712	13¢	Swallowtail	—	.55	.10–.25
❑ 1713	13¢	Checkerspot	—	.55	.10–.25
❑ 1714	13¢	Dogface	—	.55	.10–.25
❑ 1715	13¢	Orange-Tip	—	.55	.10–.25
		Block of 4 (1712–1715)	2.25 (12)	—	—
❑ 1716	13¢	Lafayette	2.00	.55	.10–.25
❑ 1717	13¢	Seamstress	—	.55	.10–.25
❑ 1718	13¢	Blacksmith	—	.55	.10–.25
❑ 1719	13¢	Wheelwright	—	.55	.10–.25
❑ 1720	13¢	Leatherworker	—	.55	.10–.25
		Block of 4 (1717–1720)	2.25	—	—
❑ 1721	13¢	Peace Bridge	2.00	.55	.10–.25
❑ 1722	13¢	Battle of Oriskany	4.40 (10)	.45	.10–.25

1723–24

1725

1726

1727

US Bicentennial 13 cents

1728

1729

Christmas USA 13¢

1730

Scott No.			Plate Block	Unused	Used
❑ 1723	13¢	Energy Conservation	—	.65	.10–.25
❑ 1724	13¢	Energy Development	—	.65	.10–.25
		Se-tenant pair (1723–1724)	—	1.20	—
❑ 1725	13¢	Alta, California	2.30	.50	.10–.25
❑ 1726	13¢	Articles of Confederation	2.30	.50	.10–.25
❑ 1727	13¢	Talking Pictures	2.30	.55	.10–.25
❑ 1728	13¢	Surrender at Saratoga	5.20 (10)	.55	.10–.25
❑ 1729	13¢	Christmas – Valley Forge	9.60 (20)	.50	.10–.25
❑ 1730	13¢	Christmas – Mailbox	4.80 (10)	.50	.10–.25

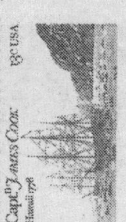

| 1731 | | 1732–1733 | |

Scott No.			Plate Block	Unused	Used
1978.					
❑ 1731	13¢	Carl Sandburg	5.15	.55	.10–.25
❑ 1732	13¢	Captain James Cook	—	.65	.10–.25
❑ 1733	13¢	Ships at Anchor	—	.65	.10–.25
		Se-tenant pair (1732–1733)	—	1.20	—

1734	1735
	(1736, 1743)

Scott No.			Plate Block	Unused	Used
1978–1980.					
❑ 1734	13¢	Indian Head Cent	2.30	.45	.10–.25
❑ 1735	(15¢)	"A" (photogravure)	2.30	.65	.10–.25
Booklet Stamps.					
❑ 1736	(15¢)	"A" (~1735) (engraved)	—	.65	.10–.25
		Booklet pane of 8	—	4.60	—

1737　　　　　　　　　**1738–1742**

Scott No.			Plate Block	Unused	Used
❏ 1737	15¢	Roses	—	.55	.10–.25
		Booklet pane of 8	—	4.30	—
❏ 1738	15¢	Windmill – Virginia	—	.65	.10–.25
❏ 1739	15¢	Windmill – Rhode Island	—	.65	.10–.25
❏ 1740	15¢	Windmill – Massachusetts	—	.65	.10–.25
❏ 1741	15¢	Windmill – Illinois	—	.65	.10–.25
❏ 1742	15¢	Windmill – Texas	—	.65	.10–.25
		Booklet pane of 10 (2 each 1738–1742)	—	6.20	—

Scott No.			Line Pair	Unused	Used
Coil Stamp.					
❏ 1743	(15¢)	"A" (~1735) (engraved)	1.00	.50	.10–.25

1744

Scott No.			Plate Block	Unused	Used
1978.					
❏ 1744	13¢	Harriet Tubman	7.00 (12)	.60	.10–.25

1745–1748

1749–1752

Scott No.			Plate Block	Unused	Used
❏ 1745	13¢	Quilt with Flowers	—	.85	.10–.25
❏ 1746	13¢	Red & White Quilt	—	.85	.10–.25
❏ 1747	13¢	Orange Striped Quilt	—	.85	.10–.25
❏ 1748	13¢	Black Plaid Quilt	—	.85	.10–.25
		Block of 4 (1745–1748)	3.30	—	—
❏ 1749	13¢	Ballet	—	.50	.10–.25
❏ 1750	13¢	Theater	—	.50	.10–.25
❏ 1751	13¢	Folk Dance	—	.50	.10–.25
❏ 1752	13¢	Modern Dance	—	.50	.10–.25
		Block of 4 (1749–1752)	2.05	—	—

1753 **1754** **1755** **1756**

1757

Scott No.			Plate Block	Unused	Used
❏ 1753	13¢	French Alliance	2.00	.45	.10–.25
❏ 1754	13¢	Cancer Detection	4.25	.50	.10–.25
❏ 1755	13¢	Jimmie Rodgers	8.20 (12)	.70	.10–.25
❏ 1756	15¢	George M. Cohan	8.90 (12)	.75	.10–.25
❏ 1757	13¢	CAPEX, block of 8	3.60	—	—
❏ 1757a–h		Any single	—	.90	.75

1758   **1759**

1760–1763

Scott No.			Plate Block	Unused	Used
❑ 1758	15¢	Photography	10.00 (12)	.55	.10–.25
❑ 1759	15¢	Viking Mission to Mars	4.00	.55	.10–.25
❑ 1760	15¢	Great Gray Owl	—	.90	.10–.25
❑ 1761	15¢	Saw-whet Owl	—	.90	.10–.25
❑ 1762	15¢	Barred Owl	—	.90	.10–.25
❑ 1763	15¢	Great Horned Owl	—	.90	.10–.25
		Block of 4 (1760–1763)	3.45	—	—

1764–1767

1768

1769

Scott No.			Plate Block	Unused	Used
❏ 1764	15¢	Giant Sequoia	—	.85	.10–.25
❏ 1765	15¢	White Pine	—	.85	.10–.25
❏ 1766	15¢	White Oak	—	.85	.10–.25
❏ 1767	15¢	Gray Birch	—	.85	.10–.25
		Block of 4 (1764–1767)	3.20	—	—
❏ 1768	15¢	Christmas – Madonna	6.25 (12)	.55	.10–.25
❏ 1769	15¢	Christmas – Rocking Horse	6.25 (12)	.55	.10–.25

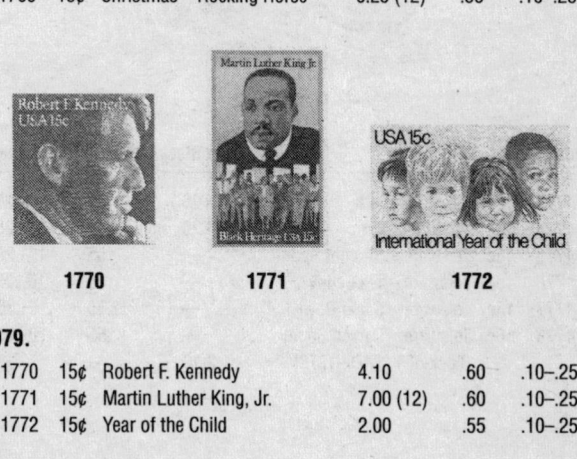

1770

1771

1772

1979.

❏ 1770	15¢	Robert F. Kennedy	4.10	.60	.10–.25
❏ 1771	15¢	Martin Luther King, Jr.	7.00 (12)	.60	.10–.25
❏ 1772	15¢	Year of the Child	2.00	.55	.10–.25

1773   **1774**

1775–1778

Scott No.			Plate Block	Unused	Used
❏ 1773	15¢	John Steinbeck	4.20	.60	.10–.25
❏ 1774	15¢	Albert Einstein	4.20	.70	.10–.25
❏ 1775	15¢	Toleware – Straight Spout	—	.55	.10–.25
❏ 1776	15¢	Toleware – Tea Caddy	—	.55	.10–.25
❏ 1777	15¢	Toleware – Sugar Bowl	—	.55	.10–.25
❏ 1778	15¢	Toleware – Curved Spout	—	.55	.10–.25
		Block of 4 (1775–1778)	2.10	—	—

1779–82

1783–1786

1787

1788

Scott No.			Plate Block	Unused	Used
❏ 1779	15¢	Virginia Rotunda	—	.65	.10–.25
❏ 1780	15¢	Baltimore Cathedral	—	.65	.10–.25
❏ 1781	15¢	Boston State House	—	.65	.10–.25
❏ 1782	15¢	Philadelphia Exchange	—	.65	.10–.25
		Block of 4 (1779–1782)	2.50	—	—
❏ 1783	15¢	Persistent Trillium	—	.60	.10–.25
❏ 1784	15¢	Hawaiian Wild Broadbean	—	.60	.10–.25
❏ 1785	15¢	Contra Costa Wallflower	—	.60	.10–.25
❏ 1786	15¢	Evening Primrose	—	.60	.10–.25
		Block of 4 (1783–1786)	2.25	—	—
❏ 1787	15¢	Seeing for Me	10.80 (20)	.55	.10–.25
❏ 1788	15¢	Special Olympics	5.80 (10)	.60	.10–.25

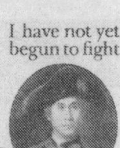

1789
(1789A, 1789B)

1791–1794

1790

1795–1798

Scott No.			Plate Block	Unused	Used
❑ 1789	15¢	John Paul Jones, perf 11 x 12	5.80 (10)	.60	.10–.25
❑ 1789A	15¢	Jones (~1789), perf 11	10.00 (10)	1.00	.10–.25
❑ 1789B	15¢	Jones (~1789), perf 12	14000.00	2000.00	685.00
❑ 1790	10¢	Olympics – Decathlon	4.10 (12)	.35	.10–.25
❑ 1791	15¢	Olympics – Runners	—	.65	.10–.25
❑ 1792	15¢	Olympics – Swimmers	—	.65	.10–.25
❑ 1793	15¢	Olympics – Rowers	—	.65	.10–.25
❑ 1794	15¢	Olympics – Equestrian	—	.65	.10–.25
		Block of 4 (1791–1794)	7.45 (12)	—	—
❑ 1795	15¢	Olympics – Skater	—	.60	.10–.25
❑ 1796	15¢	Olympics – Skier	—	.60	.10–.25
❑ 1797	15¢	Olympics – Ski Jumper	—	.60	.10–.25
❑ 1798	15¢	Olympics – Hockey	—	.60	.10–.25
		Block of 4 (1795–1795)	6.75 (12)	—	—

1799

1800

1801

1802

Scott No.			Plate Block	Unused	Used
❑ 1799	15¢	Christmas – Madonna	6.50 (12)	.55	.10–.25
❑ 1800	15¢	Gingerbread Santa	5.80 (12)	.50	.10–.25
❑ 1801	15¢	Will Rogers	7.45 (12)	.65	.10–.25
❑ 1802	15¢	Vietnam Veterans	7.40 (10)	.75	.10–.25

1803

1804

1980.

❑ 1803	15¢	W. C. Fields	7.00 (12)	.60	.10–.25
❑ 1804	15¢	Benjamin Banneker	9.15 (12)	.80	.10–.25

1805–1810

Scott No.			Plate Block	Unused	Used
❑ 1805	15¢	Letters Preserve Memories	—	.70	.10–.25
❑ 1806	15¢	P. S. Write Soon (violet & pink)	—	.70	.10–.25
❑ 1807	15¢	Letters Lift Spirits	—	.70	.10–.25
❑ 1808	15¢	P.S. (green & yellow green)	—	.70	.10–.25
❑ 1809	15¢	Letters Shape Opinions	—	.70	.10–.25
❑ 1810	15¢	P.S. (scarlet & blue)	—	.70	.10–.25
		Strip of 6 (1805–1810)	—	4.10	•—

1813

Scott No.			Line Pair	Unused	Used
1980. Americana Series Coil Stamps.					
❑ 1811	1¢	Inkwell (~1581)	.65	.30	.10–.25
❑ 1813	3.5¢	Violins	1.00	.35	.39
❑ 1816	12¢	Torch of Liberty (~1594)	2.10	.55	.46

1818
(1819, 1820)

Scott No.		Plate Block	Unused	Used
1981.				
❏ 1818 (18¢)	"B" (photogravure)	2.00	.65	.10–.25
❏ 1819 (18¢)	"B" (~1818) (engraved)	4.00	.90	.10–.25
	Booklet pane of 8	—	5.00	—

Scott No.		Line Pair	Unused	Used
Coil Stamp.				
❏ 1820 (18¢)	"B" (~1818) (engraved)	1.55	.75	.10–.25

1821	1822	1823	1824

Scott No.			Plate Block	Unused	Used
1980.					
❏ 1821	15¢	Francis Perkins	2.25	.55	.10–.25
❏ 1822	15¢	Dolley Madison	2.25	.65	.10–.25
❏ 1823	15¢	Emily Bissell	4.10	.60	.10–.25
❏ 1824	15¢	Helen Keller – Anne Sullivan	4.10	.70	.10–.25

1825

1826

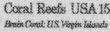

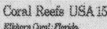

1827–1830

1831

1832

1833

Scott No.			Plate Block	Unused	Used
❑ 1825	15¢	Veterans Administration	4.15	.50	.10–.25
❑ 1826	15¢	General Bernardo de Galvez	4.15	.70	.10–.25
❑ 1827	15¢	Brain Coral	—	.70	.10–.25
❑ 1828	15¢	Elkhorn Coral	—	.70	.10–.25
❑ 1829	15¢	Chalice Coral	—	.70	.10–.25
❑ 1830	15¢	Finger Coral	—	.70	.10–.25
		Block of 4 (1827–1830)	2.75	—	—
❑ 1831	15¢	Organized Labor	11.30 (12)	.95	.10–.25
❑ 1832	15¢	Edith Wharton	2.00	.60	.10–.25
❑ 1833	15¢	Learning Never Ends	3.25 (6)	.55	.10–.25

1834–1837

1838–1841

Scott No.			Plate Block	Unused	Used
❏ 1834	15¢	Mask – Heiltsuk, Bella Bella	—	.75	.10–.25
❏ 1835	15¢	Mask – Chilkat Tlingit	—	.75	.10–.25
❏ 1836	15¢	Mask – Tlingit	—	.75	.10–.25
❏ 1837	15¢	Mask – Bella Coola	—	.75	.10–.25
		Block of 4 (1834–1837)	2.90	—	—
❏ 1838	15¢	Architecture – Smithsonian	—	.75	.10–.25
❏ 1839	15¢	Architecture – Trinity Church	—	.75	.10–.25
❏ 1840	15¢	Architecture – Penn Academy	—	.75	.10–.25
❏ 1841	15¢	Architecture – Lyndhurst	—	.75	.10–.25
		Block of 4 (1838–1841)	2.80	—	—

Christmas USA 15c

1842

USA 15c
Season's Greetings

1843

Scott No.			Plate Block	Unused	Used
❏ 1842	15¢	Christmas – Madonna & Child	6.50 (12)	.55	.10–.25
❏ 1843	15¢	Christmas – Wreath & Drum	10.40 (20)	.55	.10–.25

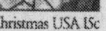

1844   **1845**   **1846**   **1847**   **1848**

1849   **1850**   **1851**   **1852**   **1853**

1980–1985. Great Americans Series.

❏ 1844	1¢	Dorothea Dix	5.20 (20)	.30	.10–.25
❏ 1845	2¢	Igor Stravinsky	.90	.30	.10–.25
❏ 1846	3¢	Henry Clay	.90	.35	.10–.25
❏ 1847	4¢	Carl Schurz	.90	.30	.10–.25
❏ 1848	5¢	Pearl Buck	.90	.75	.10–.25
❏ 1849	6¢	Walter Lippmann	5.20 (20)	.30	.10–.25
❏ 1850	7¢	Abraham Baldwin	9.20 (20)	.50	.10–.25
❏ 1851	8¢	Henry Knox	2.15	.45	.10–.25
❏ 1852	9¢	Sylvanus Thayer	7.60 (20)	.40	.50
❏ 1853	10¢	Richard Russell	19.60 (20)	1.00	.50

| 1854 | 1855 | 1856 | 1857 |

| 1858 | 1859 | 1860 | 1861 |

| 1862 | 1863 | 1864 | 1865 |

Scott No.			Plate Block	Unused	Used
❑ 1854	11¢	Alden Partridge	4.30	.75	.10–.25
❑ 1855	13¢	Crazy Horse	2.00	.70	.10–.25
❑ 1856	14¢	Sinclair Lewis	17.60 (20)	.90	.10–.25
❑ 1857	17¢	Rachel Carson	4.30	.70	.10–.25
❑ 1858	18¢	George Mason	4.30	.75	.10–.25
❑ 1859	19¢	Sequoyah	4.30	1.00	.65
❑ 1860	20¢	Ralph Bunche	4.30	1.00	.10–.25
❑ 1861	20¢	Thomas H. Gallaudet	4.30	1.10	.10–.25
❑ 1862	20¢	Harry S. Truman	16.40 (20)	.85	.10–.25
❑ 1863	22¢	John J. Audubon	18.80 (20)	.95	.10–.25
❑ 1864	30¢	Frank C. Laubach	21.60 (20)	1.10	.10–.25
❑ 1865	35¢	Charles R. Drew M.D.	6.50	1.90	.65

| | | 1866 | 1867 | 1868 | 1869 |

Scott No.			Plate Block	Unused	Used
❑ 1866	37¢	Robert Millikan	8.00	1.50	.10–.25
❑ 1867	39¢	Grenville Clark	29.60 (20)	1.50	.10–.25
❑ 1868	40¢	Lillian M. Gilbreth	29.60 (20)	1.50	.10–.25
❑ 1869	50¢	Chester W. Nimitz	12.00	1.70	.10–.25

NOTE: See Nos. 2168–2197 and 2933–2943 for other Great Americans Series stamps.

| | 1874 | 1875 |

1876–1879

1981.

❑ 1874	15¢	Everett M. Dirksen	2.25	.55	.10–.25
❑ 1875	15¢	Whitney Moore Young	2.25	.65	.10–.25
❑ 1876	18¢	Rose	—	.75	.10–.35
❑ 1877	18¢	Camellia	—	.75	.10–.35
❑ 1878	18¢	Dahlia	—	.75	.10–.35
❑ 1879	18¢	Lily	—	.75	.10–.35
		Block of 4 (1876–1879)	2.90	—	—

1880–1889

Scott No.			Plate Block	Unused	Used
Booklet Pane.					
❑ 1880	18¢	Bighorn Sheep	—	1.15	.10–.25
❑ 1881	18¢	Mountain Lion	—	1.15	.10–.25
❑ 1882	18¢	Harbor Seal	—	1.15	.10–.25
❑ 1883	18¢	Bison	—	1.15	.10–.25
❑ 1884	18¢	Brown Bear	—	1.15	.10–.25
❑ 1885	18¢	Polar Bear	—	1.15	.10–.25
❑ 1886	18¢	Elk	—	1.15	.10–.25
❑ 1887	18¢	Moose	—	1.15	.10–.25
❑ 1888	18¢	White-tailed Deer	—	1.15	.10–.25
❑ 1889	18¢	Pronghorn Antelope	—	1.15	.10–.25
		Booklet pane of 10 (1880–1889)	—	11.20	—

1890   **1891**

981. Definitive.

Scott No.			Plate Block	Unused	Used
❑ 1890	18¢	Flag – Amber Waves of Grain	15.60 (20)	.80	.10–.25

Scott No.			PNC Strip (5)	Unused	Used
Coil Stamp.					
❑ 1891	18¢	Flag – Sea to Shining Sea	2.00	.85	.10–.25

1892   **1893**   **1894**
                                   (1895, 1896)

Scott No.			Plate Block	Unused	Used
1981. Definitives.					
❑ 1892	6¢	Numeral in Circle of Stars	—	4.00	2.50
❑ 1893	18¢	Flag – Purple Mountain Majesties	—	.80	.50
		Booklet pane of 8 (two 1892; six 1893)	—	5.45	—
❑ 1894	20¢	Flag over Supreme Court	23.60 (20)	1.20	.10–.25

Scott No.			PNC Strip (5)	Unused	Used
1981. Coil Stamp.					
❑ 1895	20¢	Flag over Supreme Court (~1894)	12.00	.65	.10–.25

Scott No.			Plate Block	Unused	Used
1981. Booklet Stamp.					
❑ 1896	20¢	Flag over Supreme Court (~1894)	—	.90	.10–.25
		Booklet pane of 6	—	5.30	—
		Booklet pane of 10	—	8.80	—

Omnibus 1880s USA 1c	Locomotive 1870s USA 2c	Handcar 1880s USA 3c	Stagecoach 1890s USA 4c	Motorcycle 1913 USA 5c
1897	**1897A**	**1898**	**1898A**	**1899**

Sleigh 1880s USA 5.2c Nonprofit Org.	Bicycle 1870s USA 5.9c Nonprofit Org.	Baby Buggy 1880s USA 7.4c	Mail Wagon 1880s USA 9.3c	Hansom Cab 1890s USA 10.9c
1900	**1901**	**1902**	**1903**	**1904**

RR Caboose 1890's USA 11c Bulk Rate	Electric Auto 1917 USA 17c	Surrey 1890s USA 18c	Fire Pumper 1860s USA 20c
1905	**1906**	**1907**	**1908**

Scott No.			PNC Strip (5)	Unused	Used

1981–1984. Transportation Series Coil Stamps.

Scott No.			PNC Strip (5)	Unused	Used
❏ 1897	1¢	Omnibus	.90	.30	.10–.25
❏ 1897A	2¢	Locomotive	.90	.30	.10–.25
❏ 1898	3¢	Handcar	.90	.30	.10–.25
❏ 1898A	4¢	Stagecoach	2.05	.35	.10–.25
❏ 1899	5¢	Motorcycle	2.05	.30	.10–.25
❏ 1900	5.2¢	Sleigh	5.00	.35	.10–.25
❏ 1901	5.9¢	Bicycle	6.00	.85	.45
❏ 1902	7.4¢	Baby Buggy	8.00	.85	.45
❏ 1903	9.3¢	Mail Wagon	8.00	1.25	.50
❏ 1904	10.9¢	Hansom Cab	12.00	1.25	.50
❏ 1905	11¢	Caboose	5.00	.75	.10–.25
❏ 1906	17¢	Electric Auto	5.00	.70	.10–.25
❏ 1907	18¢	Surrey	4.25	.80	.10–.25
❏ 1908	20¢	Fire Pumper	4.25	.65	.10–.25

NOTE: Some values of the above exist Bureau precanceled. Prices are the same as unprecanceled examples. See Nos. 2123–2136, 2225–2231, 2252–2266, and 2451–2468 for other Transportation Series coil stamps.

| | 1909 | | 1910 | | 1911 |

1912–1919

Scott No.			Plate Block	Unused	Used
1981.					
❑ 1909	$9.35	Express Mail	—	40.00	—
		Booklet pane of 3	—	125.35	—
❑ 1910	18¢	American Red Cross	4.00	.65	.10–.25
❑ 1911	18¢	Savings & Loan	2.00	.60	.10–.25
❑ 1912	18¢	Exploring the Moon	—	.75	.10–.35
❑ 1913	18¢	Shuttle Jettisoning Boosters	—	.75	.10–.35
❑ 1914	18¢	Shuttle Deploying Satellite	—	.75	.10–.35
❑ 1915	18¢	Understanding the Sun	—	.75	.10–.35
❑ 1916	18¢	Probing the Planets	—	.75	.10–.35
❑ 1917	18¢	Shuttle – Vertical Ascent	—	.75	.10–.35
❑ 1918	18¢	Shuttle – Landing Gear Down	—	.75	.10–.35
❑ 1919	18¢	Comprehending the Universe	—	.75	.10–.35
		Block of 8 (1912–1919)	6.00 (8)	—	—

1920

1921–1924

1925

1926

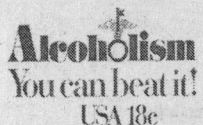

1927

Scott No.			Plate Block	Unused	Used
☐ 1920	18¢	Professional Management	4.00	.60	.10–.25
☐ 1921	18¢	Save Wetland Habitats	—	1.30	.10–.25
☐ 1922	18¢	Save Grassland Habitats	—	1.30	.10–.25
☐ 1923	18¢	Save Mountain Habitats	—	1.30	.10–.25
☐ 1924	18¢	Save Woodland Habitats	—	1.30	.10–.25
		Block of 4 (1921–1924)	5.20	—	—
☐ 1925	18¢	Disabled Persons	2.60	.65	.10–.25
☐ 1926	18¢	Edna St. Vincent Millay	2.60	.70	.10–.25
☐ 1927	18¢	Alcoholism	12.80 (20)	.65	.10–.25

1928–1931

1934

1932   **1933**

Scott No.			Plate Block	Unused	Used
❏ 1928	18¢	NYU Library – New York	—	.90	.10–.25
❏ 1929	18¢	Biltmore – Asheville, NC	—	.90	.10–.25
❏ 1930	18¢	Palace of Arts – San Francisco	—	.90	.10–.25
❏ 1931	18¢	Bank – Owatonna, MN	—	.90	.10–.25
		Block of 4 (1928–1931)	3.45	—	—
❏ 1932	18¢	Babe Zaharias	4.25	.95	.10–.25
❏ 1933	18¢	Bobby Jones	6.00	1.30	.10–.25
❏ 1934	18¢	Frederick Remington	4.00	.95	.10–.25

1935

1936

1937–1938

1939

1940

John Hanson
President Continental Congress
USA 20c

1941

Scott No.			Plate Block	Unused	Used
❏ 1935	18¢	James Hoban	4.25	1.50	.75
❏ 1936	20¢	James Hoban	4.25	.70	.10–.25
❏ 1937	18¢	Yorktown Map	—	1.75	.60
❏ 1938	18¢	Virginia Capes Map	—	1.75	.60
		Se-tenant pair (1937–1938)	—	4.00	—
❏ 1939	(20¢)	Christmas – Madonna & Child	4.25	.70	.10–.25
❏ 1940	(20¢)	Christmas – Teddy Bear	4.25	.70	.10–.25
❏ 1941	20¢	John Hanson	4.25	.70	.10–.25

1942–1945

1946
(1947, 1948)

Scott No.			Plate Block	Unused	Used
❏ 1942	20¢	Cactus – Barrel Cactus	—	.90	.10–.25
❏ 1943	20¢	Cactus – Agave	—	.90	.10–.25
❏ 1944	20¢	Cactus – Beavertail Cactus	—	.90	.10–.25
❏ 1945	20¢	Cactus – Saguaro	—	.90	.10–.25
		Block of 4 (1942–1945)	3.55	—	—
❏ 1946	(20¢)	"C" & Eagle	2.00	.80	.10–.25

Scott No.			Line Pair	Unused	Used
Coil Stamp.					
❏ 1947	(20¢)	"C" & Eagle (~1946)	1.75	.85	.10–.25

Scott No.			Plate Block	Unused	Used
Booklet Stamps.					
❏ 1948	(20¢)	"C" & Eagle (~1946)	—	.80	.10–.25
		Booklet pane of 10	—	7.80	—

1949

Scott No.			Plate Block	Unused	Used
❏ 1949	20¢	Bighorn Sheep	—	1.00	.10–.25
		Booklet pane of 10	—	10.00	—

1951
(1951A)

1950

1952

1982.

❏ 1950	20¢	Franklin D. Roosevelt	4.25	.70	.10–.25
❏ 1951	20¢	Love – Flowers	2.00	.80	.10–.25
❏ 1952	20¢	George Washington	4.25	1.00	.10–.25

1953–2002

Scott No.		Plate Block	Unused	Used
❏ 1953– 20¢ 2002	State Birds & Flowers, perf 10½ x 11¼	—	44.00	—
❏ 1953– 2002 20¢	Any single stamp	—	.90	.40
❏ 1953A– 2002A 20¢	State Birds & Flowers, perf 11¼ x 11	—	50.00	—
❏ 1953A– 2002A 20¢	Any single stamp	—	1.00	.40

❏ 1953 Alabama
❏ 1954 Alaska
❏ 1955 Arizona
❏ 1956 Arkansas
❏ 1957 California
❏ 1958 Colorado
❏ 1959 Connecticut
❏ 1960 Delaware
❏ 1961 Florida

❏ 1962 Georgia
❏ 1963 Hawaii
❏ 1964 Idaho
❏ 1965 Illinois
❏ 1966 Indiana
❏ 1967 Iowa
❏ 1968 Kansas
❏ 1969 Kentucky
❏ 1970 Louisiana

- 1971 Maine
- 1972 Maryland
- 1973 Massachusetts
- 1974 Michigan
- 1975 Minnesota
- 1976 Mississippi
- 1977 Missouri
- 1978 Montana
- 1979 Nebraska
- 1980 Nevada
- 1981 New Hampshire
- 1982 New Jersey
- 1983 New Mexico
- 1984 New York
- 1985 North Carolina
- 1986 North Dakota

- 1987 Ohio
- 1988 Oklahoma
- 1989 Oregon
- 1890 Pennsylvania
- 1991 Rhode Island
- 1992 South Carolina
- 1993 South Dakota
- 1994 Tennessee
- 1995 Texas
- 1996 Utah
- 1997 Vermont
- 1998 Virginia
- 1999 Washington
- 2000 West Virginia
- 2001 Wisconsin
- 2002 Wyoming

2003

2004

Scott No.			Plate Block	Unused	Used
2003	20¢	Netherlands	12.00 (20)	.65	.10–.25
2004	20¢	Library of Congress	4.00	.90	.10–.25

2005

Scott No.			PNC Strip (5)	Unused	Used
Coil Stamp.					
2005	20¢	Consumer Education	8.00	1.50	.10–.25

2006–2009

2010

2011

2012

2013

2014

Scott No.			Plate Block	Unused	Used
1982.					
❏ 2006	20¢	Solar Energy	—	.85	.10–.25
❏ 2007	20¢	Synthetic Fuels	—	.85	.10–.25
❏ 2008	20¢	Breeder Reactor	—	.85	.10–.25
❏ 2009	20¢	Fossil Fuels	—	.85	.10–.25
		Block of 4 (2006–2009)	3.30	—	—
❏ 2010	20¢	Horatio Alger	4.00	.65	.10–.25
❏ 2011	20¢	Aging Together	2.75	.65	.10–.25
❏ 2012	20¢	The Barrymores	2.75	.65	.10–.25
❏ 2013	20¢	Dr. Mary Walker	2.75	.65	.10–.25
❏ 2014	20¢	International Peace Garden	2.75	1.50	.10–.25

2015

2016

2017

2018

2019–2022

Scott No.			Plate Block	Unused	Used
❑ 2015	20¢	America's Libraries	4.25	.65	.10–.25
❑ 2016	20¢	Jackie Robinson	8.00	2.30	.10–.25
❑ 2017	20¢	Touro Synagogue	20.00 (20)	1.00	.10–.25
❑ 2018	20¢	Wolf Trap Farm Park	4.25	.65	.10–.25
❑ 2019	20¢	Architecture – Frank Lloyd Wright	—	1.00	.10–.25
❑ 2020	20¢	Architecture – Mies van der Rohe	—	1.00	.10–.25
❑ 2021	20¢	Architecture – Walter Gropius	—	1.00	.10–.25
❑ 2022	20¢	Architecture – Eero Saarinen	—	1.00	.10–.25
		Block of 4 (2019–2022)	4.00	—	—

2023

2024

2025

2026

2027–2030

Science & Industry USA 20c

2031

Scott No.			Plate Block	Unused	Used
❏ 2023	20¢	Francis of Assisi	4.25	.70	.10–.25
❏ 2024	20¢	Ponce de Leon	22.40 (20)	1.15	.10–.25
❏ 2025	13¢	Christmas – Kitten & Puppy	2.00	.55	.10–.25
❏ 2026	20¢	Christmas – Madonna & Child	13.60 (20)	.70	.10–.25
❏ 2027	20¢	Christmas – Sledding	—	1.00	.10–.25
❏ 2028	20¢	Christmas – Snowman	—	1.00	.10–.25
❏ 2029	20¢	Christmas – Ice Skating	—	1.00	.10–.25
❏ 2030	20¢	Christmas – Trimming Tree	—	1.00	.10–.25
		Block of 4 (2027–2030)	3.95	—	—
❏ 2031	20¢	Science & Industry	4.25	.65	.10–.25

2032–2035

Scott No.			Plate Block	Unused	Used
❑ 2032	20¢	Ballooning – Intrepid	—	1.00	.10–.25
❑ 2033	20¢	Ballooning – Hot Air Balloon	—	1.00	.10–.25
❑ 2034	20¢	Ballooning – Hot Air Balloon	—	1.00	.10–.25
❑ 2035	20¢	Ballooning – Explorer II	—	1.00	.10–.25
		Block of 4 (2032–2035)	4.00	—	—

2036

2037

2038

2039

2040

1983.

❑ 2036	20¢	USA – Sweden	5.25	1.00	.10–.25
❑ 2037	20¢	Civilian Conservation Corps	5.25	1.00	.10–.25
❑ 2038	20¢	Joseph Priestley	5.25	1.00	.10–.25
❑ 2039	20¢	Volunteer – Lend a Hand	20.00 (20)	1.00	.10–.25
❑ 2040	20¢	German Immigration	2.50	1.00	.10–.25

2041

2042

2043

2044

2045

2046

2047

Scott No.			Plate Block	Unused	Used
❏ 2041	20¢	Brooklyn Bridge	6.00	1.00	.10–.25
❏ 2042	20¢	Tennessee Valley Authority	20.00 (20)	1.00	.10–.25
❏ 2043	20¢	Physical Fitness	20.00 (20)	1.00	.10–.25
❏ 2044	20¢	Scott Joplin	6.00	1.00	.10–.25
❏ 2045	20¢	Medal of Honor	6.00	1.00	.10–.25
❏ 2046	20¢	Babe Ruth	12.00	2.25	.10–.25
❏ 2047	20¢	Nathaniel Hawthorne	6.00	1.00	.10–.25

2048–2051

2052

2053

2054

Scott No.			Plate Block	Unused	Used
☐ 2048	13¢	Olympics – Discus	—	1.25	.10–.25
☐ 2049	13¢	Olympics – High Jump	—	1.25	.10–.25
☐ 2050	13¢	Olympics – Archery	—	1.25	.10–.25
☐ 2051	13¢	Olympics – Boxing	—	1.25	.10–.25
		Block of 4 (2048–2051)	5.00	—	—
☐ 2052	20¢	Treaty of Paris	4.25	1.00	.10–.25
☐ 2053	20¢	Civil Service	20.00 (20)	1.00	.10–.25
☐ 2054	20¢	Metropolitan Opera	4.25	1.00	.10–.25

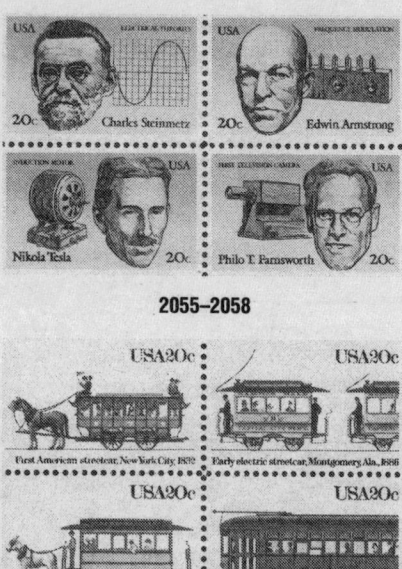

2055–2058

2059–2062

Scott No.			Plate Block	Unused	Used
❏ 2055	20¢	Charles Steinmetz	—	1.50	.10–.25
❏ 2056	20¢	Edwin Armstrong	—	1.50	.10–.25
❏ 2057	20¢	Nikola Tesla	—	1.50	.10–.25
❏ 2058	20¢	Philo T. Farnsworth	—	1.50	.10–.25
		Block of 4 (2055–2058)	6.00	—	—
❏ 2059	20¢	Streetcars – First American	—	1.50	.10–.25
❏ 2060	20¢	Streetcars – Electric Trolley	—	1.50	.10–.25
❏ 2061	20¢	Streetcars – Bobtail Horsecar	—	1.50	.10–.25
❏ 2062	20¢	Streetcars – St. Charles Coach	—	1.50	.10–.25
		Block of 4 (2059–2062)	6.00	—	—

NOTE. Prices for stamps from 1935 to date are for never-hinged (NH) examples.

| **2063** | **2064** | **2065** |

Scott No.			Plate Block	Unused	Used
❑ 2063	20¢	Christmas – Madonna	4.00	1.00	.10–.25
❑ 2064	20¢	Christmas – Santa Claus	20.00 (20)	1.00	.10–.25
❑ 2065	20¢	Martin Luther	4.00	1.00	.10–.25

2066

2067–70

1984.

❑ 2066	20¢	Alaska Statehood	5.00	1.10	.10–.25
❑ 2067	20¢	Olympics – Ice Dancing	—	1.10	.10–.25
❑ 2068	20¢	Olympics – Downhill Skiing	—	1.10	.10–.25
❑ 2069	20¢	Olympics – Cross Country Skiing	—	1.10	.10–.25
❑ 2070	20¢	Olympics – Hockey	—	1.10	.10–.25
		Block of 4 (2067–2070)	5.00	—	—

2071

2072

2073

2074

2075

2076–2079

2080

Scott No.			Plate Block	Unused	Used
❏ 2071	20¢	FDIC	4.25	1.00	.10–.25
❏ 2072	20¢	Love	20.00 (20)	1.00	.10–.25
❏ 2073	20¢	Carter G. Woodson	4.25	1.00	.10–.25
❏ 2074	20¢	Soil & Water Conservation	4.25	1.00	.10–.25
❏ 2075	20¢	Credit Union	4.25	1.00	.10–.25
❏ 2076	20¢	Orchids – Wild Pink	—	1.25	.10–.25
❏ 2077	20¢	Orchids – Yellow Lady Slipper	—	1.25	.10–.25
❏ 2078	20¢	Orchids – Spreading Pogonia	—	1.25	.10–.25
❏ 2079	20¢	Orchids – Pacific Calypso	—	1.25	.10–.25
		Block of 4 (2076–2079)	5.00	—	—
❏ 2080	20¢	Hawaii Statehood	4.25	1.00	.10–.25

2081

2082–2085

2086

2087

2088

Scott No.			Plate Block	Unused	Used
❏ 2081	20¢	National Archives	4.25	1.30	.10–.25
❏ 2082	20¢	Olympics – Men's Diving	—	1.30	.10–.25
❏ 2083	20¢	Olympics – Long Jump	—	1.30	.10–.25
❏ 2084	20¢	Olympics – Wrestling	—	1.30	.10–.25
❏ 2085	20¢	Olympics – Kayaking	—	1.30	.10–.25
		Block of 4 (2081–2084)	6.50	—	—
❏ 2086	20¢	Louisiana World's Exposition	4.25	1.00	.10–.25
❏ 2087	20¢	Health Research	4.25	.75	.10–.25
❏ 2088	20¢	Douglas Fairbanks	28.00 (20)	1.40	.10–.25

2091

2089   **2090**

2092   **2093**   **2094**

2095   **2096**   **2097**

Scott No.			Plate Block	Unused	Used
❑ 2089	20¢	Jim Thorpe	4.25	1.80	.10–.25
❑ 2090	20¢	John McCormack	4.25	1.50	.10–.25
❑ 2091	20¢	St. Lawrence Seaway	4.25	1.80	.10–.25
❑ 2092	20¢	Preserving Wetlands	4.25	1.00	.10–.25
❑ 2093	20¢	Roanoke Voyages	4.25	1.00	.10–.25
❑ 2094	20¢	Herman Melville	4.25	1.00	.10–.25
❑ 2095	20¢	Horace Moses	20.00 (20)	1.00	.10–.25
❑ 2096	20¢	Smokey the Bear	4.25	1.00	.10–.25
❑ 2097	20¢	Roberto Clemente	12.00	3.10	.10–.25

2098–2101   **2102**

2103   **2104**   **2105**

Scott No.			Plate Block	Unused	Used
❑ 2098	20¢	Beagle & Boston Terrier	—	1.25	.10–.25
❑ 2099	20¢	Retriever & Cocker Spaniel	—	1.25	.10–.25
❑ 2100	20¢	Malamute & Collie	—	1.25	.10–.25
❑ 2101	20¢	Coonhound & Foxhound	—	1.25	.10–.25
		Block of 4 (2098–2101)	5.00	—	—
❑ 2102	20¢	Crime Prevention	4.25	1.00	.10–.25
❑ 2103	20¢	Hispanic Americans	4.25	1.00	.10–.25
❑ 2104	20¢	Family Unity	20.00 (20)	1.00	.10–.25
❑ 2105	20¢	Eleanor Roosevelt	4.25	1.00	.10–.25

| 2106 | 2107 | 2108 |

2109

Scott No.			Plate Block	Unused	Used
❏ 2106	20¢	Nation of Readers	4.25	1.00	.10–.25
❏ 2107	20¢	Christmas – Madonna & Child	4.25	1.00	.10–.25
❏ 2108	20¢	Christmas – Santa Claus	4.25	1.00	.10–.25
❏ 2109	20¢	Vietnam Veterans Memorial	4.25	1.30	.10–.25

2110	2111
	(2112, 2113)

1985.

❏ 2110	22¢	Jerome Kern	4.25	1.00	.10–.25
❏ 2111	(22¢)	"D" & Eagle	32.00 (20)	1.30	.10–.25

Scott No.		PNC Strip (5)	Unused	Used

1985. Coil Stamp.

❏ 2112 (22¢)	"D" & Eagle (~2111)	14.00	1.10	.40

2114
(2115)

Scott No.		Plate Block	Unused	Used

1985.

❏ 2113 (22¢)	"D" & Eagle (~2111)	—	1.50	.10–.25
	Booklet pane of 10	—	15.00	—
❏ 2114	22¢	Flag over Capitol	4.00	1.50	.10–.25

Scott No.		PNC Strip (5)	Unused	Used

1985. Coil Stamps.

❏ 2115	22¢ Flag over Capitol (~2114)	4.00	.90	.10–.25
❏ 2115b	With small letter "T" at bottom	4.00	.90	.10–.25

2116

Scott No.		Plate Block	Unused	Used

1985.

❏ 2116	22¢	Flag over Capitol	—	1.10	.10–.25
	Booklet pane of 5	—	5.50	—

2117–2121

2122

Scott No.			Plate Block	Unused	Used
❑ 2117	22¢	Seashells – Frilled Dogwinkle	—	1.00	.10–.25
❑ 2118	22¢	Seashells – Reticulated Dogwinkle	—	1.00	.10–.25
❑ 2119	22¢	Seashells – New England Neptune	—	1.00	.10–.25
❑ 2120	22¢	Seashells – Calico Scallop	—	1.00	.10–.25
❑ 2121	22¢	Seashells – Lightning Whelk	—	1.00	.10–.25
		Booklet pane of 10 (2 each 2117–2121)	—	10.00	—
❑ 2122	$10.75	Express Mail (type I)	—	40.00	10.00
		Booklet pane of 3	—	120.00	—
❑ 2122b	$10.75	Express Mail (~2122) (type II)	—	50.00	16.80
		Booklet pane of 3	—	150.00	—

NOTE: Type I (Plate No. 11111) appears washed-out. Type II (Plate No. 22222) appears brighter and more intensely colored.

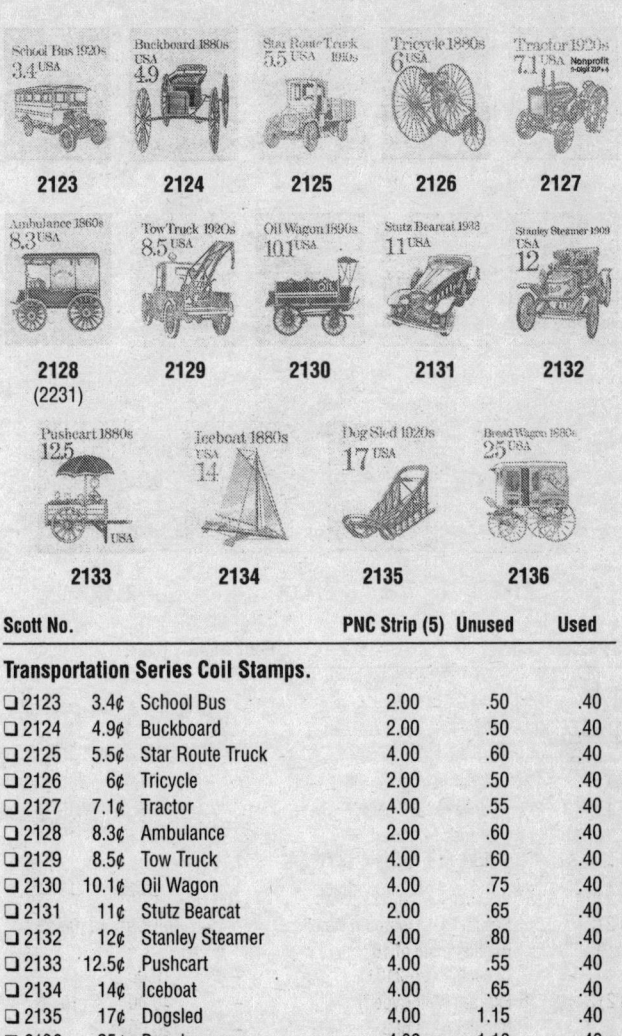

Scott No.			PNC Strip (5)	Unused	Used

Transportation Series Coil Stamps.

Scott No.			PNC Strip (5)	Unused	Used
❏ 2123	3.4¢	School Bus	2.00	.50	.40
❏ 2124	4.9¢	Buckboard	2.00	.50	.40
❏ 2125	5.5¢	Star Route Truck	4.00	.60	.40
❏ 2126	6¢	Tricycle	2.00	.50	.40
❏ 2127	7.1¢	Tractor	4.00	.55	.40
❏ 2128	8.3¢	Ambulance	2.00	.60	.40
❏ 2129	8.5¢	Tow Truck	4.00	.60	.40
❏ 2130	10.1¢	Oil Wagon	4.00	.75	.40
❏ 2131	11¢	Stutz Bearcat	2.00	.65	.40
❏ 2132	12¢	Stanley Steamer	4.00	.80	.40
❏ 2133	12.5¢	Pushcart	4.00	.55	.40
❏ 2134	14¢	Iceboat	4.00	.65	.40
❏ 2135	17¢	Dogsled	4.00	1.15	.40
❏ 2136	25¢	Breadwagon	4.00	1.10	.40

NOTE: Some values of the above exist Bureau precanceled. Prices are the same as unprecanceled examples.

See Nos. 1897–1908, 2225–2231, 2252–2266, and 2451–2468 for other Transportation Series coil stamps.

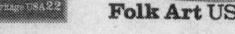

2137

2138–2141

2142

2143

2144

Scott No.			Plate Block	Unused	Used
1985.					
❑ 2137	22¢	Mary McLeod Bethune	4.25	1.40	.10–.30
❑ 2138	22¢	Broadbill Decoy	—	1.95	.10–.30
❑ 2139	22¢	Mallard Decoy	—	1.95	.10–.30
❑ 2140	22¢	Canvasback Decoy	—	1.95	.10–.30
❑ 2141	22¢	Redhead Decoy	—	1.95	.10–.30
		Block of 4 (2138–2141)	7.70	—	—
❑ 2142	22¢	Winter Special Olympics	4.25	1.25	.10–.25
❑ 2143	22¢	Love	4.25	1.25	.10–.25
❑ 2144	22¢	Rural Electrification	25.00 (20)	1.25	.10–.25

| 2145 | 2146 | 2147 |

Scott No.			Plate Block	Unused	Used
❏ 2145	22¢	AMERIPEX	5.00	1.25	.10–.25
❏ 2146	22¢	Abigail Adams	5.00	1.25	.10–.25
❏ 2147	22¢	F. A. Bartholdi	5.00	1.25	.10–.25

| 2149 | 2149a | 2150 | 2150a |

Scott No.			PNC Strip (5)	Unused	Used
Coil Stamps.					
❏ 2149	18¢	George Washington	6.00	.85	.10–.25
❏ 2149a	18¢	Washington & "Presorted First-Class"	4.25	.95	.10–.25
❏ 2150	21.1¢	Envelopes	5.00	1.30	.10–.25
❏ 2150a	21.1¢	Envelopes & "ZIP + 4"	6.00	1.30	.10–.25

2152   **2153**

2154

2155–2158   **2159**

Scott No.			Plate Block	Unused	Used
1985.					
❑ 2152	22¢	Korean War Veterans	4.25	1.10	.10–.25
❑ 2153	22¢	Social Security	4.25	.75	.10–.25
❑ 2154	22¢	World War I Veterans	4.25	1.00	.10–.25
❑ 2155	22¢	Quarter Horse	—	2.30	.40
❑ 2156	22¢	Morgan Horse	—	2.30	.40
❑ 2157	22¢	Saddlebred Horse	—	2.30	.40
❑ 2158	22¢	Appaloosa	—	2.30	.40
		Block of 4 (2155–2158)	9.20	—	—
❑ 2159	22¢	Public Education	8.00	2.50	.10–.25

2160–2163

2164

2165

2166

2167

Scott No.			Plate Block	Unused	Used
❏ 2160	22¢	Youth Year – YMCA	—	1.40	.40
❏ 2161	22¢	Youth Year – Boy Scouts	—	1.40	.40
❏ 2162	22¢	Youth Year – Big Brothers	—	1.40	.40
❏ 2163	22¢	Youth Year – Campfire Girls	—	1.40	.40
		Block of 4 (2160–2163)	5.60	—	—
❏ 2164	22¢	Help End Hunger	4.25	1.00	.10–.25
❏ 2165	22¢	Christmas – Madonna & Child	4.25	1.00	.10–.25
❏ 2166	22¢	Christmas – Poinsettia	4.25	1.00	.10–.25
1986.					
❏ 2167	22¢	Arkansas Statehood	4.25	1.40	.10–.25

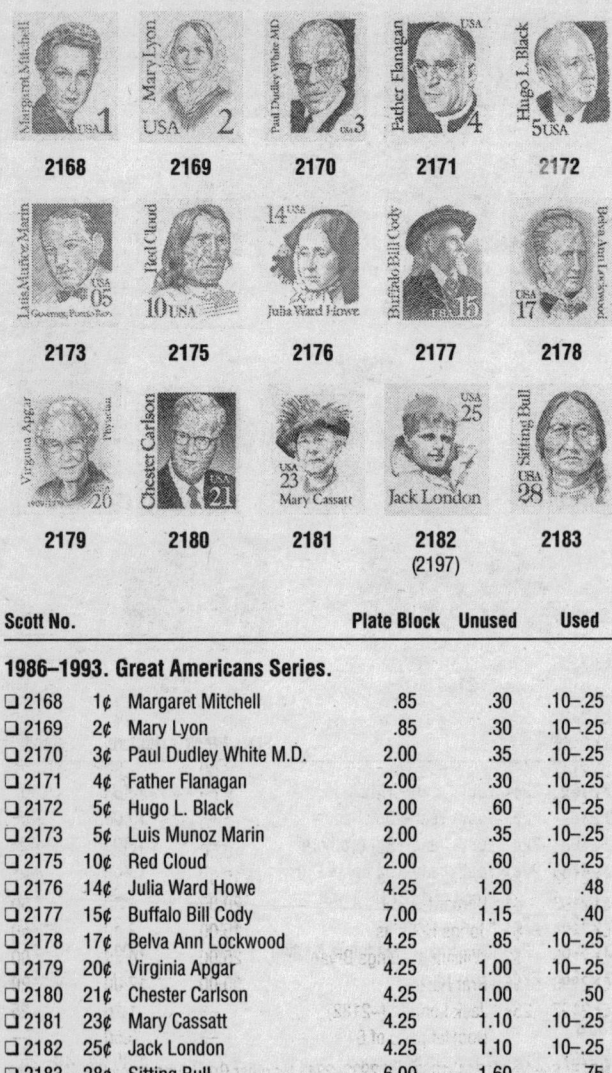

2168	2169	2170	2171	2172
2173	2175	2176	2177	2178
2179	2180	2181	2182 (2197)	2183

Scott No.			Plate Block	Unused	Used
1986–1993. Great Americans Series.					
❏ 2168	1¢	Margaret Mitchell	.85	.30	.10–.25
❏ 2169	2¢	Mary Lyon	.85	.30	.10–.25
❏ 2170	3¢	Paul Dudley White M.D.	2.00	.35	.10–.25
❏ 2171	4¢	Father Flanagan	2.00	.30	.10–.25
❏ 2172	5¢	Hugo L. Black	2.00	.60	.10–.25
❏ 2173	5¢	Luis Munoz Marin	2.00	.35	.10–.25
❏ 2175	10¢	Red Cloud	2.00	.60	.10–.25
❏ 2176	14¢	Julia Ward Howe	4.25	1.20	.48
❏ 2177	15¢	Buffalo Bill Cody	7.00	1.15	.40
❏ 2178	17¢	Belva Ann Lockwood	4.25	.85	.10–.25
❏ 2179	20¢	Virginia Apgar	4.25	1.00	.10–.25
❏ 2180	21¢	Chester Carlson	4.25	1.00	.50
❏ 2181	23¢	Mary Cassatt	4.25	1.10	.10–.25
❏ 2182	25¢	Jack London	4.25	1.10	.10–.25
❏ 2183	28¢	Sitting Bull	6.00	1.60	.75

Scott No.			Plate Block	Unused	Used
☐ 2184	29¢	Earl Warren	4.25	1.35	1.00
☐ 2185	29¢	Thomas Jefferson	4.25	1.50	.10–.25
☐ 2186	35¢	Dennis Chavez	5.00	1.30	1.00
☐ 2187	40¢	Claire Chenault	7.00	1.60	.10–.25
☐ 2188	45¢	Dr. Harvey Cushing	7.00	1.80	.10–.25
☐ 2189	52¢	Hubert Humphrey	8.00	2.00	.10–.25
☐ 2190	56¢	John Harvard	8.00	2.30	1.75
☐ 2191	65¢	H. H. "Hap" Arnold	8.50	2.40	1.75
☐ 2192	75¢	Wendell Wilkie	10.00	3.00	.47
☐ 2193	$1	Bernard Revel	20.00	4.30	.50
☐ 2194	$1	Johns Hopkins	15.00	3.40	.50
☐ 2195	$2	William Jennings Bryan	25.00	6.70	4.00
☐ 2196	$5	Bret Harte	50.00	17.00	4.20
☐ 2197	25¢	Jack London (~2182)	—	1.10	.10–.25
		Booklet pane of 6	—	6.50	—

NOTE: See Nos. 1844–1869 and 2933–2943 for other Great Americans Series stamps.

2198–2201

| 2202 | 2203 | 2204 |

Scott No.			Plate Block	Unused	Used
1986.					
❏ 2198	22¢	AMERIPEX – Vintage Hand Cancel	—	1.00	.50
❏ 2199	22¢	AMERIPEX – Boy Stamp Collector	—	1.00	.50
❏ 2200	22¢	AMERIPEX – Magnifying Glass	—	1.00	.50
❏ 2201	22¢	AMERIPEX – Modern Hand Cancel	—	1.00	.50
		Booklet pane of 4 (2198–2201)	—	4.00	—
❏ 2202	22¢	Love – Puppy	4.25	1.20	.10–.25
❏ 2203	22¢	Sojourner Truth	4.25	1.35	.10–.25
❏ 2204	22¢	Republic of Texas	4.25	1.35	.10–.25

2210

2211

2205–2209

Scott No.			Plate Block	Unused	Used
❑ 2205	22¢	Fish – Muskellunge	—	2.10	.10–.30
❑ 2206	22¢	Fish – Atlantic Cod	—	2.10	.10–.30
❑ 2207	22¢	Fish – Largemouth Bass	—	2.10	.10–.30
❑ 2208	22¢	Fish – Bluefin Tuna	—	2.10	.10–.30
❑ 2209	22¢	Fish – Catfish	—	2.10	.10–.30
		Booklet pane of 5 (2205–2209)	—	10.50	—
❑ 2210	22¢	Public Hospitals	4.25	.85	.10–.25
❑ 2211	22¢	Duke Ellington	4.25	1.05	.10–.25

2216

2218

2217

2219

Scott No.			Plate Block	Unused	Used
❏ 2216	22¢	AMERIPEX – Presidents I	—	10.00	—
❏ 2216a-i		Any single stamp	—	1.10	.40
❏ 2217	22¢	AMERIPEX – Presidents II	—	10.00	—
❏ 2217a-i		Any single stamp	—	1.10	.40
❏ 2218	22¢	AMERIPEX – Presidents III	—	10.00	—
❏ 2218a-i		Any single stamp	—	1.10	.40
❏ 2219	22¢	AMERIPEX – Presidents IV	—	10.00	—
❏ 2219a-i		Any single stamp	—	1.10	.40

	2220–2223			2224	

Scott No.			Plate Block	Unused	Used
❏ 2220	22¢	Elisha Kane Kent	—	1.60	.40
❏ 2221	22¢	Adolphus W. Greely	—	1.60	.40
❏ 2222	22¢	Vilhjalmur Stefansson	—	1.60	.40
❏ 2223	22¢	Peary & Henson	—	1.60	.40
		Block of 4 (2220–2223)	6.40	—	—
❏ 2224	22¢	Statue of Liberty	9.50	1.55	.10–.25

2225	2226	2228

Scott No.			PNC Strip (5)	Unused	Used

1986–1987. Transportation Series Coil Stamps.

Scott No.			PNC Strip (5)	Unused	Used
❏ 2225	1¢	Omnibus, no ¢ symbol	1.00	.30	.10–.25
❏ 2226	2¢	Locomotive, no ¢ symbol	1.00	.30	.10–.25
❏ 2228	4¢	Stagecoach (~1898A)	2.00	.35	.10–.25
❏ 2231	8.3¢	Ambulance (~2128)	10.00	.35	.10–.25

NOTE: See Nos. 1897–1897A for designs similar to Nos. 2225–2226 except with ¢ symbol,

2235–2238

2239

2240–2243

Scott No.			Plate Block	Unused	Used
1986.					
❏ 2235	22¢	Navajo Carpet – Four Crosses	—	1.40	.10–.25
❏ 2236	22¢	Navajo Carpet – Vertical Diamonds	—	1.40	.10–.25
❏ 2237	22¢	Navajo Carpet – Lowe Art Museum	—	1.40	.10–.25
❏ 2238	22¢	Navajo Carpet – Eight Diamonds	—	1.40	.10–.25
		Block of 4 (2235–2238)	5.60	—	—
❏ 2239	22¢	T. S. Eliot	4.25	1.15	.10–.25
❏ 2240	22¢	Highlander Figure	—	1.25	.10–.25
❏ 2241	22¢	Ship Figurehead	—	1.25	.10–.25
❏ 2242	22¢	Nautical Figure	—	1.25	.10–.25
❏ 2243	22¢	Cigar Store Figure	—	1.25	.10–.25
		Block of 4 (2240–2243)	5.00	—	—

2244

2245

Scott No.			Plate Block	Unused	Used
❑ 2244	22¢	Christmas – Madonna & Child	4.25	1.00	.10–.25
❑ 2245	22¢	Christmas – Village Scene	4.25	1.00	.10–.25

2247

2248

2246

2249

2250

2251

1987.

❑ 2246	22¢	Michigan Statehood	4.25	1.00	.10–.25
❑ 2247	22¢	Pan American Games	4.25	1.00	.10–.25
❑ 2248	22¢	Love	4.25	1.00	.10–.25
❑ 2249	22¢	Jean Baptiste Pointe du Sable	4.25	1.00	.10–.25
❑ 2250	22¢	Enrico Caruso	2.50	1.00	.10–.25
❑ 2251	22¢	Girl Scouts	4.25	1.00	.10–.25

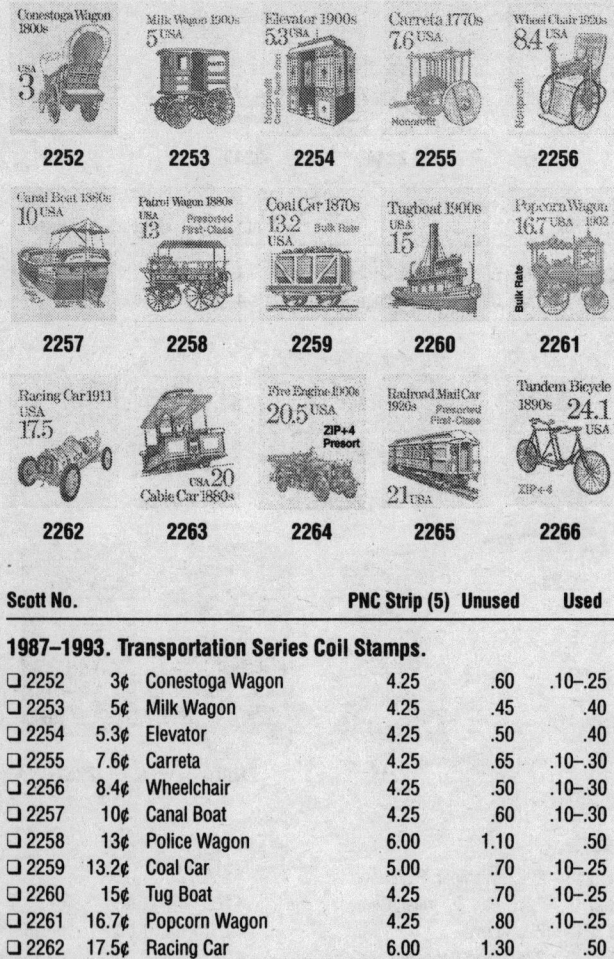

Scott No.			PNC Strip (5)	Unused	Used

1987–1993. Transportation Series Coil Stamps.

			PNC Strip (5)	Unused	Used
❑ 2252	3¢	Conestoga Wagon	4.25	.60	.10–.25
❑ 2253	5¢	Milk Wagon	4.25	.45	.40
❑ 2254	5.3¢	Elevator	4.25	.50	.40
❑ 2255	7.6¢	Carreta	4.25	.65	.10–.30
❑ 2256	8.4¢	Wheelchair	4.25	.50	.10–.30
❑ 2257	10¢	Canal Boat	4.25	.60	.10–.30
❑ 2258	13¢	Police Wagon	6.00	1.10	.50
❑ 2259	13.2¢	Coal Car	5.00	.70	.10–.25
❑ 2260	15¢	Tug Boat	4.25	.70	.10–.25
❑ 2261	16.7¢	Popcorn Wagon	4.25	.80	.10–.25
❑ 2262	17.5¢	Racing Car	6.00	1.30	.50
❑ 2263	20¢	Cable Car	5.00	1.00	.50
❑ 2264	20.5¢	Fire Engine	12.00	1.60	.40
❑ 2265	21¢	Railroad Mail Car	8.00	1.10	.40
❑ 2266	24.1¢	Tandem Bicycle	8.00	1.30	.78

See Nos. 1897–1908, 2123–2136, 2225–2231, and 2451–2468 for other Transportation Series coil stamps.

2267–2274

Scott No.			Plate Block	Unused	Used
1987.					
❑ 2267	22¢	Congratulations!	—	2.20	.40
❑ 2268	22¢	Get Well!	—	2.20	.40
❑ 2269	22¢	Thank You!	—	2.20	.40
❑ 2270	22¢	Love You, Dad!	—	2.20	.40
❑ 2271	22¢	Best Wishes!	—	2.20	.40
❑ 2272	22¢	Happy Birthday!	—	2.20	.40
❑ 2273	22¢	Love You, Mother!	—	2.20	.40
❑ 2274	22¢	Keep in Touch!	—	2.20	.40
		Booklet pane of 10 (2267–2271)	—	18.00	—

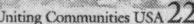

2275	**2276**	**2277** (2279, 2282)

2278 (2285A)

Scott No.			Plate Block	Unused	Used
❑ 2275	22¢	United Way	4.25	1.25	.10–.25
❑ 2276	22¢	Flag & Fireworks	4.25	1.25	.10–.25
		Booklet pane of 20	—	20.00	—
❑ 2277	(25¢)	"E" & Earth	4.25	1.25	.10–.25
❑ 2278	25¢	Flag & Clouds, perf 10	4.25	1.25	.10–.25

2280	**2281**	**2283**	**2284**	**2285**

Scott No.			PNC Strip (5)	Unused	Used
Coil Stamps.					
❑ 2279	(25¢)	"E" & Earth (~2277)	4.25	.90	.10–.25
❑ 2280	25¢	Flag over Yosemite	5.00	1.00	.10–.25
❑ 2281	25¢	Honey Bee	6.00	1.00	.10–.25
Booklet Stamps.					
❑ 2282	(25¢)	"E" & Earth (~2277)	—	1.30	.40
		Booklet pane of 10	—	13.00	—
❑ 2283	25¢	Pheasant	—	1.50	.10–.25
		Booklet pane of 10	—	15.00	—
❑ 2284	25¢	Grosbeak	—	1.00	.10–.25
❑ 2285	25¢	Owl	—	1.00	.10–.25
		Booklet pane of 10, (5 each 2284 & 2285)	—	9.60	—
❑ 2285A	25¢	Flag & Clouds (2278), perf 10x11	—	1.00	.10–.25
		Booklet pane of 6	—	5.90	—

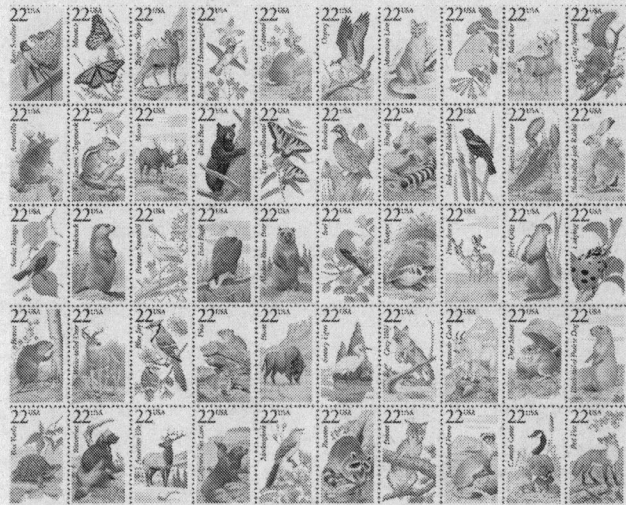

2286–2335

Scott No.	Plate Block	Unused	Used
1987.			
❏ 2286–2335 22¢ Wildlife, pane of 50	—	32.00	—
❏ 2286–2335 Any single stamp	—	.65	.10–.25

❏ 2286 Barn Swallow

❏ 2287 Monarch Butterfly

❏ 2288 Bighorn Sheep

❏ 2289 Broad-tailed Hummingbird

❏ 2290 Cottontail

❏ 2291 Osprey

❏ 2292 Mountain Lion

❏ 2293 Luna Moth

❏ 2294 Mule Deer

❏ 2295 Gray Squirrel

❏ 2296 Armadillo

❏ 2297 Eastern Chipmunk

❏ 2298 Moose

❏ 2299 Black Bear

❏ 2300 Tiger Swallowtail

❏ 2301 Bobwhite

❏ 2302 Ringtail

❏ 2303 Red-wing Blackbird

❏ 2304 Lobster

❏ 2305 Black-tailed Jack Rabbit

❏ 2306 Scarlet Tanager

❏ 2307 Woodchuck

❏ 2308 Roseate Spoonbill

❏ 2309 Bald Eagle

❏ 2310 Alaskan Brown Bear

❏ 2311 Iiwi

- ❑ 2312 Badger
- ❑ 2313 Pronghorn
- ❑ 2314 River Otter
- ❑ 2315 Ladybug
- ❑ 2316 Beaver
- ❑ 2317 White-tail Deer
- ❑ 2318 Blue Jay
- ❑ 2319 Pika
- ❑ 2320 Buffalo
- ❑ 2321 Snowy Egret
- ❑ 2322 Gray Wolf
- ❑ 2323 Mountain Goat

- ❑ 2324 Deer Mouse
- ❑ 2325 Black-tailed Prairie Dog
- ❑ 2326 Box Turtle
- ❑ 2327 Wolverine
- ❑ 2328 Elk
- ❑ 2329 California Sea Lion
- ❑ 2330 Mockingbird
- ❑ 2331 Raccoon
- ❑ 2332 Bobcat
- ❑ 2333 Black-footed Ferret
- ❑ 2334 Canada Goose
- ❑ 2335 Red Fox

2336

2337

2338

2339

2340

2341

2342

Scott No.			Plate Block	Unused	Used
❑ 2336	22¢	Delaware	5.75	1.50	.10–.30
❑ 2337	22¢	Pennsylvania	5.75	1.50	.10–.30
❑ 2338	22¢	New Jersey	5.75	1.50	.10–.30
❑ 2339	22¢	Georgia	5.75	1.50	.10–.30
❑ 2340	22¢	Connecticut	5.75	1.50	.10–.30
❑ 2341	22¢	Massachusetts	5.75	1.50	.10–.30
❑ 2342	22¢	Maryland	5.75	1.50	.10–.30

May 23, 1788
South Carolina
2343

June 21, 1788
New Hampshire
2344

June 25, 1788
Virginia
2345

July 26, 1788
New York
2346

November 21, 1789
North Carolina
2347

May 29, 1790
Rhode Island
2348

Friendship with Morocco 1787–1987
USA 22
2349

William Faulkner
2350

Scott No.			Plate Block	Unused	Used
❏ 2343	22¢	South Carolina	5.75	1.50	.10–.30
❏ 2344	22¢	New Hampshire	5.75	1.50	.10–.30
❏ 2345	22¢	Virginia	5.75	1.50	.10–.30
❏ 2346	22¢	New York	5.75	1.50	.10–.30
❏ 2347	22¢	North Carolina	5.75	1.50	.10–.30
❏ 2348	22¢	Rhode Island	5.75	1.50	.10–.30
❏ 2349	22¢	Friendship with Morocco	5.75	1.50	.10–.30
❏ 2350	22¢	William Faulkner	5.75	1.50	.10–.30

2351–2354

2355–2359

Scott No.			Plate Block	Unused	Used
☐ 2351	22¢	Lace	—	1.25	.10–.35
☐ 2352	22¢	Lace	—	1.25	.10–.35
☐ 2353	22¢	Lace	—	1.25	.10–.35
☐ 2354	22¢	Lace	—	1.25	.10–.35
		Block of 4 (2351–2354)	5.00	—	—
☐ 2355	22¢	Constitution – "Bicentennial"	—	1.60	.10–.25
☐ 2356	22¢	Constitution – "We the People"	—	1.60	.10–.25
☐ 2357	22¢	Constitution – "Establish Justice"	—	1.60	.10–.25
☐ 2358	22¢	Constitution – "And Secure"	—	1.60	.10–.25
☐ 2359	22¢	Constitution – "Do Ordain"	—	1.60	.10–.25
		Booklet pane of 5 (1255–2359)	—	7.80	—

2360

2361

2362–2366

2367

2368

Scott No.			Plate Block	Unused	Used
❏ 2360	22¢	U. S. Constitution	5.00	1.40	.10–.25
❏ 2361	22¢	CPAs	14.00	2.50	.10–.25
❏ 2362	22¢	Stourbridge Lion	—	1.30	.10–.25
❏ 2363	22¢	Best Friend of Charleston	—	1.30	.10–.25
❏ 2364	22¢	John Bull	—	1.30	.10–.25
❏ 2365	22¢	Brother Jonathan	—	1.30	.10–.25
❏ 2366	22¢	Gowan & Marx	—	1.30	.10–.25
		Booklet pane of 5 (2362–2367)	—	6.50	—
❏ 2367	22¢	Christmas – Madonna & Child	4.25	1.25	.10–.25
❏ 2368	22¢	Christmas – Ornament	4.25	1.25	.10–.25

2369   2370   2371

2372–2375

Scott No.			Plate Block	Unused	Used
1988.					
❏ 2369	22¢	Olympics – Downhill Skier	4.25	1.70	.10–.25
❏ 2370	22¢	Australia Bicentennial	4.25	1.75	.10–.25
❏ 2371	22¢	James Weldon Johnson	4.25	1.15	.10–.25
❏ 2372	22¢	Cats – Siamese & Exotic Short Hair	—	1.50	.50
❏ 2373	22¢	Cats – Abyssinian & Himalayan	—	1.50	.50
❏ 2374	22¢	Cats – Maine Coon & Burmese	—	1.50	.50
❏ 2375	22¢	Cats – American Shorthair & Persian	—	1.50	.50
		Block of 4 (2372–2375)	6.00	—	—

Scott No.			Plate Block	Unused	Used
❏ 2376	22¢	Knute Rockne	4.25	1.15	.50
❏ 2377	25¢	Francis Ouimet	5.00	1.25	.50
❏ 2378	25¢	Love – Rose	4.00	.85	.10–.25
❏ 2379	45¢	Love – Rose	6.00	1.55	.10–.25
❏ 2380	25¢	Olympics – Gymnast on Rings	5.00	1.10	.10–.25
❏ 2381	25¢	Autos – Locomobile	—	2.40	.10–.25
❏ 2382	25¢	Autos – Pierce Arrow	—	2.40	.10–.25
❏ 2383	25¢	Autos – Cord	—	2.40	.10–.25
❏ 2384	25¢	Autos – Packard	—	2.40	.10–.25
❏ 2385	25¢	Autos – Duesenberg	—	2.40	.10–.25
		Booklet pane of 5 (2381–2385)	—	12.00	—

2386–2389

2394

2390–2393

Scott No.			Plate Block	Unused	Used
❑ 2386	25¢	Nathaniel Palmer	—	1.40	.40
❑ 2387	25¢	Lt. Charles Wilkes	—	1.40	.40
❑ 2388	25¢	Richard E. Byrd	—	1.40	.40
❑ 2389	25¢	Lincoln Ellsworth	—	1.40	.40
		Block of 4 (2386–2389)	5.60	—	—
❑ 2390	25¢	Carousel – Deer	—	1.50	.10–.25
❑ 2391	25¢	Carousel – Horse	—	1.50	.10–.25
❑ 2392	25¢	Carousel – Camel	—	1.50	.10–.25
❑ 2393	25¢	Carousel – Goat	—	1.50	.10–.25
		Block of 4 (2390–2393)	6.00	—	—
❑ 2394	$8.75	Express Mail	100.00	30.00	10.50

2395   **2396**

2397   **2398**

2399   **2400**

Scott No.			Plate Block	Unused	Used
❑ 2395	25¢	Happy Birthday	—	1.30	.40
❑ 2396	25¢	Best Wishes	—	1.30	.40
		Booklet pane of 6 (3 each 2395 & 2396)	—	8.00	—
❑ 2397	25¢	Thinking of You	—	1.25	.40
❑ 2398	25¢	Love You	—	1.25	.40
		Booklet pane of 6 (3 each 2397 & 2398)	—	6.00	—
❑ 2399	25¢	Christmas – Madonna & Child	4.25	1.25	.10–.25
❑ 2400	25¢	Christmas – Winter Scene	4.25	1.25	.10–.25

2401

2402

2405–2409

2403

2404

Scott No.			Plate Block	Unused	Used
1989.					
❏ 2401	25¢	Montana	4.25	1.70	.10–.25
❏ 2402	25¢	A. Philip Randolph	4.25	1.70	.10–.25
❏ 2403	25¢	North Dakota Statehood	4.25	1.70	.10–.25
❏ 2404	25¢	Washington Statehood	4.25	1.85	.10–.25
❏ 2405	25¢	Steamboats – Experiment	—	1.50	.10–.25
❏ 2406	25¢	Steamboats – Phoenix	—	1.50	.10–.25
❏ 2407	25¢	Steamboats – New Orleans	—	1.50	.10–.25
❏ 2408	25¢	Steamboats – Washington	—	1.50	.10–.25
❏ 2409	25¢	Steamboats – Walk in the Water	—	1.50	.10–.25
		Booklet pane of 5 (2404–2409)	—	7.50	—

2410

2411

2412

2413

2414

2415

2416

Scott No.			Plate Block	Unused	Used
❑ 2410	25¢	World Stamp Expo '89	4.25	1.25	.10–.25
❑ 2411	25¢	Arturo Toscanini	4.25	1.25	.10–.25
❑ 2412	25¢	Bicentennial – House of Representatives	5.00	1.25	.10–.25
❑ 2413	25¢	Bicentennial – U. S. Senate	5.00	1.25	.10–.25
❑ 2414	25¢	Bicentennial – Executive Branch	5.00	1.25	.10–.25
❑ 2415	25¢	Bicentennial – Supreme Court	4.25	1.25	.10–.25
❑ 2416	25¢	South Dakota Statehood	4.25	1.25	.10–.25

2417

2418

2419

2420

2422–2425

2421

Scott No.			Plate Block	Unused	Used
❑ 2417	25¢	Lou Gehrig	5.00	1.30	.10–.25
❑ 2418	25¢	Ernest Hemingway	5.00	1.30	.10–.25
❑ 2419	$2.40	Moon Landing	32.00	14.00	10.00
❑ 2420	25¢	Letter Carriers	4.25	.85	.10–.25
❑ 2421	25¢	Bill of Rights	4.50	1.10	.10–.25
❑ 2422	25¢	Dinosaurs – Tyrannosaurus	—	1.50	.10–.25
❑ 2423	25¢	Dinosaurs – Pteranodon	—	1.50	.10–.25
❑ 2424	25¢	Dinosaurs – Stegosaurus	—	1.50	.10–.25
❑ 2425	25¢	Dinosaurs – Brontosaurus	—	1.50	.10–.25
		Block of 4 (2421–2425)	6.00	5.00	—

2426

2427

2428
(2429)

2431

2433

Scott No.			Plate Block	Unused	Used
❏ 2426	25¢	Southwest Carving	4.25	1.25	.10–.25
❏ 2427	25¢	Christmas – Madonna	4.25	1.25	.10–.25
❏ 2428	25¢	Christmas – Sleigh	4.25	1.25	.10–.25
❏ 2429	25¢	Christmas – Sleigh (~2428)	—	1.25	.10–.25
		Booklet pane of 10	—	5.00	—
❏ 2431	25¢	Eagle & Shield	—	1.35	.50
		Booklet pane of 18	—	24.00	—
❏ 2433	$3.60	Lincoln Essays, souvenir sheet	—	28.00	—
❏ 2433a-d		Any single stamp	—	5.25	2.30

2434–2437

20th Universal Postal Congress

A review of historical methods of delivering the mail in the United States is the theme of these four stamps issued in commemoration of the convening of the 20th Universal Postal Congress in Washington, D.C. from November 13 through December 14, 1989. The United States, as host nation to the Congress for the first time in ninety-two years, welcomed more than 1,000 delegates from most of the member nations of the Universal Postal Union to the major international event.

©USPS 1989

2438

Scott No.			Plate Block	Unused	Used
❑ 2434	25¢	Stagecoach	—	1.40	.10–.25
❑ 2435	25¢	Paddlewheel Steamer	—	1.40	.10–.25
❑ 2436	25¢	Biplane	—	1.40	.10–.25
❑ 2437	25¢	Automobile	—	1.40	.10–.25
		Block of 4 (2434–2437)	5.60	—	—
❑ 2438	$1	Souvenir sheet (~2434–2437)	—	8.00	—
❑ 2438a-d		Any single stamp	—	2.00	4.50

2439

2440
(2441)

2442

2443

2445–2448

2444

Scott No.			Plate Block	Unused	Used
1990.					
❏ 2439	25¢	Idaho Statehood	4.25	1.80	.10–.25
❏ 2440	25¢	Love	4.25	1.30	.10–.25
❏ 2441	25¢	Love (~2440)	—	1.30	.10–.25
		Booklet pane of 10	—	13.00	—
❏ 2442	25¢	Ida B. Wells	4.25	1.70	.10–.25
❏ 2443	25¢	Beach Umbrella	—	.55	.10–.25
		Booklet pane of 10	—	5.00	—
❏ 2444	25¢	Wyoming Statehood	4.25	2.00	.10–.30
❏ 2445	25¢	Films – Wizard of Oz	—	2.75	.10–.30
❏ 2446	25¢	Films – Gone with the Wind	—	2.75	.10–.30
❏ 2447	25¢	Films – Beau Geste	—	2.75	.10–.30
❏ 2448	25¢	Films – Stagecoach	—	2.75	.10–.30
		Block of 4 (2445–2448)	11.00	—	—

2449

Scott No.			Plate Block	Unused	Used
❑ 2449	25¢	Marianne Moore	4.25	2.00	.10–.25

2451	2452	2452D	2453	2457
	(2452B)		(2454)	(2458)

Scott No.			PNC Strip (5)	Unused	Used
1990. Transportation Series Coil Stamps.					
❑ 2451	4¢	Steam Carriage	2.15	.30	.10–.25
❑ 2452	5¢	Circus Wagon (05) (engraved)	2.15	.35	.10–.25
❑ 2452B	5¢	Circus Wagon (~2452) (05) (photogravure)	2.15	.45	.10–.25
❑ 2452D	5¢	Circus Wagon (~2452) (5¢)	2.15	.40	.10–.25
❑ 2453	5¢	Canoe, brown (engraved)	2.15	.45	.10–.25
❑ 2454	5¢	Canoe, red (~2453) (photogravure)	4.25	.55	.10–.25
❑ 2457	10¢	Tractor Trailer (engraved)	4.25	.50	.10–.25
❑ 2458	10¢	Tractor Trailer (~2457) (photogravure)	4.25	1.00	.75

| **2463** | **2464** | **2466** | **2468** |

Scott No.			PNC Strip (5)	Unused	Used
☐ 2463	20¢	Cog Railway	6.00	.80	.10–.25
☐ 2464	23¢	Lunch Wagon	5.00	1.00	.10–.25
☐ 2466	32¢	Ferryboat	8.00	1.20	.10–.25
☐ 2468	$1	Seaplane	20.00	4.00	1.00

NOTE: Some values of the above exist Bureau precanceled. Prices are the same as unprecanceled examples.

See Nos. 1897–1908, 2123–2136, and 2225–2231 for other Transportation Series coil stamps.

2470–2474

Scott No.			Plate Block	Unused	Used
1990.					
☐ 2470	25¢	Lighthouses – Admiralty Head	—	3.00	.10–.25
☐ 2471	25¢	Lighthouses – Cape Hatteras	—	3.00	.10–.25
☐ 2472	25¢	Lighthouses – West Quoddy Head	—	3.00	.10–.25
☐ 2473	25¢	Lighthouses – American Shoals	—	3.00	.10–.25
☐ 2474	25¢	Lighthouses – Sandy Hook	—	3.00	.10–.25
		Booklet pane of 5 (2470–2474)	—	15.00	—

2475

2476

2477
(3031, 3031A,
3044)

2478

2479

2480

2481

2482

Scott No.			Plate Block	Unused	Used
❏ 2475	25¢	Stylized Flag	—	1.25	.10–.25
		Booklet pane of 12	—	14.50	
❏ 2476	1¢	Kestrel ("01" numeral)	1.00	.35	.10–.25
❏ 2477	1¢	Kestrel ("1¢" numeral)	1.00	.35	.10–.25
❏ 2478	3¢	Bluebird ("03" numeral)	2.25	.35	.10–.25
❏ 2479	19¢	Fawn	2.25	.70	.10–.25
❏ 2480	30¢	Cardinal	4.00	1.05	.40
❏ 2481	45¢	Sunfish	6.00	1.50	.80
❏ 2482	$2	Bobcat	20.00	5.00	.80

2483
(3048, 3053)

1991–1995. Booklet Stamps.

❏ 2483	20¢	Blue Jay	—	.95	.40
		Booklet pane of 10	—	9.20	—

2484

2486

2487
(2493, 2495)

2488
(2494, 2495A)

2489

2490

2491

2492

Scott No.			Plate Block	Unused	Used
☐ 2484	29¢	Wood Duck, black numerals	—	1.10	.10–.25
		Booklet pane of 10	—	11.00	—
☐ 2485	29¢	Wood Duck, red numerals	—	1.15	.10–.25
		Booklet pane of 10	—	11.00	—
☐ 2486	29¢	African Violets	—	1.10	.10–.25
		Booklet pane of 10	—	11.00	—
☐ 2487	32¢	Peach	—	1.30	.10–.25
☐ 2488	32¢	Pear	—	1.35	.10–.25
		Booklet pane of 10 (5 each of 2487–2488)	—	13.20	—
☐ 2489	29¢	Red Squirrel	—	1.10	.10–.25
		Booklet pane of 18	—	20.00	—
☐ 2490	29¢	Red Rose	—	1.10	.10–.25
		Booklet pane of 18	—	20.00	—
☐ 2491	29¢	Pine Cone	—	1.10	.10–.25
		Booklet pane of 18	—	20.00	—
☐ 2492	32¢	Pink Rose	—	1.25	.10–.25
		Booklet pane of 20	—	24.50	—
		Booklet pane of 18	—	22.00	—
		Booklet pane of 16	—	19.50	—
		Booklet pane of 14	—	17.10	—
☐ 2493	32¢	Peach (~2487)	—	1.25	.10–.25
☐ 2494	32¢	Pear (~2488)	—	1.25	.10–.25
		Booklet pane of 20 (10 each 2493–2494)	—	24.40	—

Scott No.			PNC Strip (5)	Unused	Used

1995. Coil Stamps.

Scott No.			PNC Strip (5)	Unused	Used
❑ 2495	32¢	Peach (~2487)	—	3.25	1.00
❑ 2495A	32¢	Pear (~2488)	—	3.25	1.00
		Se-tenant pair (2495–2495A)	—	7.00	—

2496–2500

Scott No.			Plate Block	Unused	Used

1990.

Scott No.			Plate Block	Unused	Used
❑ 2496	25¢	Olympians – Jesse Owens	—	5.00	1.75
❑ 2497	25¢	Olympians – Ray Ewry	—	1.40	.75
❑ 2498	25¢	Olympians – Hazel Wightman	—	1.40	.75
❑ 2499	25¢	Olympians – Eddie Eagan	—	1.40	.75
❑ 2500	25¢	Olympians – Helene Madison	—	1.40	.75
		Strip of 5 (2496–2500)	17.60 (10)	10.75	—

2501–2505

 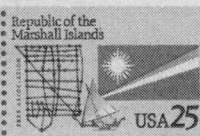

2506–2507

Scott No.			Plate Block	Unused	Used
❑ 2501	25¢	Headdress – Assiniboine	—	2.60	.10–.25
❑ 2502	25¢	Headdress – Cheyenne	—	2.60	.10–.25
❑ 2503	25¢	Headdress – Comanche	—	2.60	.10–.25
❑ 2504	25¢	Headdress – Flathead	—	2.60	.10–.25
❑ 2505	25¢	Headdress – Shoshone	—	2.60	.10–.25
		Booklet pane of 10 (5 each 2501–2505)	—	26.00	—
❑ 2506	25¢	Micronesia	—	1.50	.10–.25
❑ 2507	25¢	Marshall Islands	—	1.50	.10–.25
		Se-tenant pair (2506–2507)	—	3.00	—

2508–2511

2512　　　　　　　**2513**

Scott No.			Plate Block	Unused	Used
❏ 2508	25¢	Killer Whale	—	2.00	.10–.25
❏ 2509	25¢	Northern Sea Lion	—	2.00	.10–.25
❏ 2510	25¢	Sea Otter	—	2.00	.10–.25
❏ 2511	25¢	Dolphin	—	2.00	.10–.25
		Block of 4 (2508–2511)	8.00	—	—
❏ 2512	25¢	Grand Canyon	4.00	1.75	.10–.25
❏ 2513	25¢	Dwight D. Eisenhower	5.00	1.75	.10–.25

2514   **2515**   **2517**
       (2516)   (2518–2520)

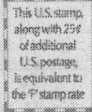 

                 2522

2521

Scott No.			Plate Block	Unused	Used
❏ 2514	25¢	Christmas – Madonna	4.25	1.20	.10–.25
❏ 2515	25¢	Christmas Tree	4.25	.95	.10–.25
❏ 2516	25¢	Christmas Tree	—	1.40	.10–.25
		Booklet pane of 10	—	14.00	—
❏ 2517	(29¢)	"F" & Flower	4.25	1.60	.10–.25

Scott No.			PNC Strip (5)	Unused	Used
Coil Stamp.					
❏ 2518	(29¢)	"F" & Flower (~2517)	5.00	1.10	.10–.25

Scott No.			Plate Block	Unused	Used
1991.					
❏ 2519	(29¢)	"F" & Flower (~2517)	—	1.25	.10–.25
		Booklet pane of 10	—	12.40	—
❏ 2520	(29¢)	"F" & Flower (~2517)	—	5.00	1.50
		Booklet pane of 10	—	50.00	—

NOTE: No. 2519 has a pale green leaf; No. 2520, a bright green leaf.

❏ 2521	(4¢)	Make Up Rate	2.00	.30	.10–.25
❏ 2522	(29¢)	"F" & Stylized Flag	—	1.50	.40
		Booklet pane of 10	—	14.80	—

2523	2524	2528	2529
(2523A)	(2524A, 2525–2527)		(2529C)

Scott No.	PNC Strip (5)	Unused	Used

1991. Coil Stamps.

			PNC Strip (5)	Unused	Used
❑ 2523	29¢	Flag over Mt. Rushmore (engraved)	7.00	1.90	.10–.25
❑ 2523A	29¢	Flag over Mt. Rushmore (photogravure)	6.00	1.50	.50

Scott No.	Plate Block	Unused	Used

1991. Sheet Stamps.

			Plate Block	Unused	Used
❑ 2524	29¢	Tulip, perforated 11	4.00	1.10	.10–.25
❑ 2524A	29¢	Tulip, perforated 13 x 12½	5.00	2.10	.10–.25

Scott No.	PNC Strip (5)	Unused	Used

1991. Coil Stamps.

			PNC Strip (5)	Unused	Used
❑ 2525	29¢	Tulip (~2524), rouletted	6.50	1.10	.10–.25
❑ 2526	29¢	Tulip (~2524), perforated 10	7.00	1.30	.75

Scott No.	Plate Block	Unused	Used

1991. Booklet Stamps.

			Plate Block	Unused	Used
❑ 2527	29¢	Tulip (~2524)	—	1.15	.10–.25
		Booklet pane of 10	—	11.20	—
❑ 2528	29¢	Flag & Olympic Rings	—	1.15	.10–.25
		Booklet pane of 10	—	11.20	—

Scott No.	PNC Strip (5)	Unused	Used

1991. Coil Stamps.

			PNC Strip (5)	Unused	Used
❑ 2529	19¢	Fishing Boat	5.00	.80	.10–.25
❑ 2529C	19¢	Fishing Boat (~2529)	10.00	1.30	.10–.25

NOTE: No. 2529C contains only one loop of rope on the dock pole.

2530   2531   2531A   2532

2533   2534   2535   2537
              (2535A, 2536)

Scott No.			Plate Block	Unused	Used
1991. Booklet Stamp.					
❑ 2530	19¢	Ballooning	—	.80	.10–.25
		Booklet pane of 10	—	8.00	—
1991.					
❑ 2531	29¢	Flags on Parade	4.25	1.15	.10–.25
❑ 2531A	29¢	Torch of Liberty	—	1.30	.10–.25
❑ 2532	50¢	Switzerland	7.00	2.00	.40
❑ 2533	29¢	Vermont Statehood	7.00	1.85	.10–.25
❑ 2534	29¢	Savings Bonds	4.25	1.30	.10–.25
❑ 2535	29¢	Love, perforated 12½ x 13	4.25	1.30	.10–.25
❑ 2535A	29¢	Love, perforated 11 (all sides)	5.00	1.30	.10–.25
❑ 2536	29¢	Love, perforated 11 (2 or 3 sides)	—	1.40	.10–.25
		Booklet pane of 10	—	14.00	—
❑ 2537	52¢	Love Birds	7.00	1.90	.40

2538

2539

2540

2541

2542

2543

2544

2544A

Scott No.			Plate Block	Unused	Used
❏ 2538	29¢	William Saroyan	4.00	1.10	.10–.25
❏ 2539	$1	Olympic Rings	12.00	3.60	2.00
❏ 2540	$2.90	Eagle & Olympic Rings	35.00	14.60	4.50
❏ 2541	$9.95	Express Mail	100.00	36.00	12.60
❏ 2542	$14	Express Mail	140.00	48.00	10.00
❏ 2543	$2.90	Futuristic Spacecraft	35.00	12.00	2.00
❏ 2544	$3	Space Shuttle "Enterprise"	32.00	10.00	2.00
❏ 2544A	$10.75	Shuttle Blasting Off	100.00	28.00	6.00

2545–2549

2550

2551
(2552)

Scott No.			Plate Block	Unused	Used
❑ 2545	29¢	Fishing Flies – Royal Wulff	—	3.00	.10–.25
❑ 2546	29¢	Fishing Flies – Jock Scott	—	3.00	.10–.25
❑ 2547	29¢	Fishing Flies – Apte Tarpon Fly	—	3.00	.10–.25
❑ 2548	29¢	Fishing Flies – Lefty's Deceiver	—	3.00	.10–.25
❑ 2549	29¢	Fishing Flies – Muddler Minnow	—	3.00	.10–.25
		Booklet pane of 5 (2545–2549)	—	15.00	—
❑ 2550	29¢	Cole Porter	4.25	1.15	.10–.25
❑ 2551	29¢	Desert Storm	4.25	1.15	.10–.25
❑ 2552	29¢	Desert Storm, booklet stamp	—	1.30	.10–.25
		Booklet pane of 5	—	6.50	—

2553–2557

2558

Scott No.			Plate Block	Unused	Used
❑ 2553	29¢	Olympics – High Jump	—	1.75	.60
❑ 2554	29¢	Olympics – Discus	—	1.75	.60
❑ 2555	29¢	Olympics – Sprint	—	1.75	.60
❑ 2556	29¢	Olympics – Javelin	—	1.75	.60
❑ 2557	29¢	Olympics – Hurdles	—	1.75	.60
		Strip of 5 (2553–2557)	13.00 (10)	9.00	—
❑ 2558	29¢	Numismatics	7.50	1.40	.10–.25

2559

2560

2561

Scott No.			Plate Block	Unused	Used
❑ 2559	29¢	World War II, 1941, pane of 10	—	14.00	—
❑ 2559a–j	29¢	Any single stamp	—	1.30	.10–.25
❑ 2560	29¢	Basketball	5.25	1.50	.10–.25
❑ 2561	29¢	District of Columbia	5.25	1.10	.10–.25

2562–2566

2567

Scott No.			Plate Block	Unused	Used
1991.					
☐ 2562	29¢	Comedians – Laurel & Hardy	—	2.00	.40
☐ 2563	29¢	Comedians – Bergen & McCarthy	—	2.00	.40
☐ 2564	29¢	Comedians – Jack Benny	—	2.00	.40
☐ 2565	29¢	Comedians – Fanny Brice	—	2.00	.40
☐ 2566	29¢	Comedians – Abbott & Costello	—	2.00	.40
		Booklet pane of 10 (2 each 1561–2566)	—	20.00	—
☐ 2567	29¢	Jan E. Matzeliger	4.25	1.35	.10–.30

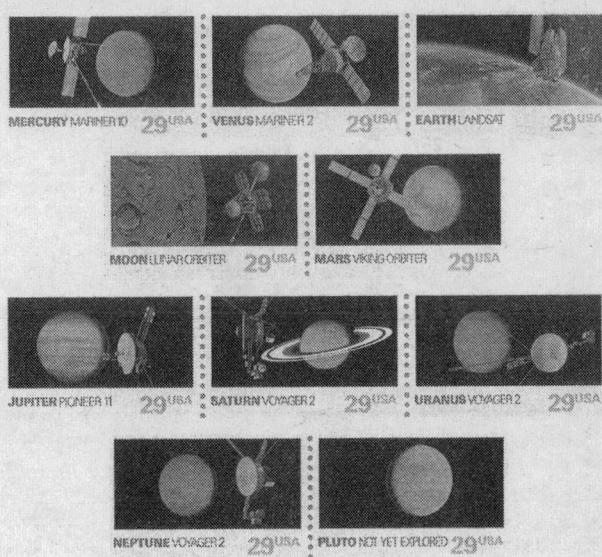

2568–2577

Scott No.			Plate Block	Unused	Used
❑ 2568	29¢	Mercury	—	2.00	.40
❑ 2569	29¢	Venus	—	2.00	.40
❑ 2570	29¢	Earth	—	2.00	.40
❑ 2571	29¢	Moon	—	2.00	.40
❑ 2572	29¢	Mars	—	2.00	.40
❑ 2573	29¢	Jupiter	—	2.00	.40
❑ 2574	29¢	Saturn	—	2.00	.40
❑ 2575	29¢	Uranus	—	2.00	.40
❑ 2576	29¢	Neptune	—	2.00	.40
❑ 2577	29¢	Pluto	—	2.00	.40
		Booklet pane of 10 (2568–2577)	—	20.00	—

2578

2579
(2580–2581)

2582

2583

2584

2585

Scott No.		Plate Block	Unused	Used
❏ 2578 (29¢)	Christmas – Madonna & Child	4.25	1.00	.10–.25
	Booklet pane of 10	—	11.00	—
❏ 2579 (29¢)	Santa in Chimney, perforated all sides	4.25	1.10	.10–.25
❏ 2580 (29¢)	Santa in Chimney (~2579)	—	2.30	.40
❏ 2581 (29¢)	Santa in Chimney (~2579)	—	2.30	.10–.25
	Booklet pane of 4 (2 each of 2580–2581)	—	10.00	—

NOTE: Examples of 2580 contain part of an extra brick on the left side of the top row of bricks; examples of 2581 do not. Nos. 2580–2581 are booklet stamps and contain perforations on only 2 or 3 sides.

❏ 2582 (29¢)	Santa with List	—	1.75	.10–.25
	Booklet pane of 4	—	7.00	—
❏ 2583 (29¢)	Santa and Package	—	1.75	.10–.25
	Booklet pane of 4	—	7.00	—
❏ 2584 (29¢)	Santa and Fireplace	—	1.75	.10–.25
	Booklet pane of 4	—	7.00	—
❏ 2585 (29¢)	Santa and Sleigh	—	1.75	.10–.25
	Booklet pane of 4	—	7.00	—

2587

2590

2592

Scott No.			Plate Block	Unused	Used
1994–1995.					
❑ 2587	32¢	James Polk	4.25	1.30	.10–.25
❑ 2590	$1	Surrender of General Burgoyne	12.00	5.00	.75
❑ 2592	$5	Washington & Jackson	40.00	18.50	2.50

2593
(2593B, 2594)

2595
(2596–2597)

1992–1993. Booklet Stamps.

❑ 2593	29¢	Flag, black numeral, perforated 10	—	1.20	.10–.25
		Booklet pane of 10	—	12.00	—
❑ 2593B	29¢	Flag (~2593), black numeral, perforated 11 x 10	—	3.60	.10–.25
		Booklet pane of 10	—	36.00	—
❑ 2594	29¢	Flag (~2593, red numeral	—	1.60	.10–.25
		Booklet pane of 10	—	16.00	—
❑ 2595	29¢	Eagle & Shield, brown numeral	—	1.30	.10–.25
		Booklet pane of 17	—	22.50	—
❑ 2596	29¢	Eagle & Shield (~2595), green numeral	—	1.30	.10–.25
		Booklet pane of 17	—	22.50	—
❑ 2597	29¢	Eagle & Shield (~2595), red numeral	—	1.25	.10–.25
		Booklet pane of 17	—	21.00	—

2598   **2599**

Scott No.			Plate Block	Unused	Used
❑ 2598	29¢	Eagle with Wings Upraised	—	1.30	.10–.25
		Booklet pane of 18	—	22.50	—
❑ 2599	29¢	Statue of Liberty	—	1.15	.10–.25
		Booklet pane of 18	—	20.50	—

2602   **2603**   **2605**   **2606**   **2609**
        (2604)   **(2607–2608)**

Scott No.			PNC Strip (5)	Unused	Used

1991–1993. Coil Stamps.

❑ 2602	(10¢)	Bulk Rate USA, "USA" in red	4.25	.55	.10–.25
❑ 2503	(10¢)	USA Bulk Rate, "USA" in blue, bright gold	4.25	.45	.10–.25
❑ 2504	(10¢)	USA Bulk Rate (~2504), "USA" in blue & dull gold	4.25	.45	.10–.25

NOTE: See Nos. 3270–3271 for Eagle & Shield stamps inscribed "USA Presort Std."

❑ 2605	23¢	Flag Presorted First–Class	6.25	1.00	.10–.35
❑ 2606	23¢	Flag & Chrome, bright blue	6.25	1.00	.10–.35
❑ 2607	23¢	Flag & Chrome (~2606), dark blue	6.25	1.00	.10–.35
❑ 2608	23¢	Flag & Chrome (~2606), violet blue	6.25	1.10	.10–.35
❑ 2609	29¢	Flag & White House	6.25	1.40	.10–.35

2611–2615

2616   2617   2618

Scott No.			Plate Block	Unused	Used
1992.					
❏ 2611	29¢	Olympics – Hockey	—	1.10	.10–.25
❏ 2612	29¢	Olympics – Figure Skating	—	1.10	.10–.25
❏ 2613	29¢	Olympics – Speed Skating	—	1.10	.10–.25
❏ 2614	29¢	Olympics – Downhill Skiing	—	1.10	.10–.25
❏ 2615	29¢	Olympics – Bobsledding	—	1.10	.10–.25
		Strip of 5 (2611–2615)	11.50 (10)	5.50	—
❏ 2616	29¢	World Columbian Stamp Expo	4.25	1.40	.10–.25
❏ 2617	29¢	W. E. B. DuBois	4.25	1.40	.10–.25
❏ 2618	29¢	Love	4.25	1.40	.10–.25

2619

2620–2623

Scott No.			Plate Block	Unused	Used
❑ 2619	29¢	Olympic Baseball	5.25	1.40	.10–.25
❑ 2620	29¢	Seeking Isabella's Support	—	1.40	.10–.25
❑ 2621	29¢	Crossing the Atlantic	—	1.40	.10–.25
❑ 2622	29¢	Approaching Land	—	1.40	.10–.25
❑ 2623	29¢	Coming Ashore	—	1.40	.10–.25
		Block of 4 (2620–2623)	5.60	—	—

2624   2625

2626   2627

Scott No.		Plate Block	Unused	Used
1992. Columbian Souvenir Sheets.				
❑ 2624 $1.05	Sheet of 3			
	(1¢, 4¢ & $1 denominations)	—	8.20	—
❑ 2625 $4.05	Sheet of 3			
	(2¢, 3¢ & $4 denominations)	—	8.20	—
❑ 2626 85¢	Sheet of 3			
	(5¢, 30¢ & 50¢ denominations)	—	8.20	—
❑ 2627 $3.14	Sheet of 3			
	(6¢, 8¢ & $3 denominations)	—	8.20	—

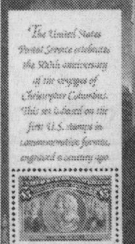

| | 2628 | | 2629 | |

Scott No.		Plate Block	Unused	Used
❑ 2628 $2.25	Sheet of 3			
	(10¢, 15¢ & $2 denominations)	—	8.20	—
❑ 2629 $5	Sheet of 1 ($5 denomination)	—	8.20	—
	Set of 6 sheets	—	50.00	—

2630

2631–2634

2635

2636

Scott No.			Plate Block	Unused	Used
❑ 2630	29¢	N. Y. Stock Exchange	4.25	1.10	.10–.25
❑ 2631	29¢	Cosmonaut	—	1.20	.10–.25
❑ 2632	29¢	Astronaut	—	1.20	.10–.25
❑ 2633	29¢	Apollo Spacecraft	—	1.20	.10–.25
❑ 2634	29¢	Soyuz Spacecraft	—	1.20	.10–.25
		Block of 4 (2631–2634)	5.00	—	—
❑ 2635	29¢	Alaska Highway	4.25	1.10	.10–.25
❑ 2636	29¢	Kentucky Statehood	4.25	1.10	.10–.25

2637–2641

2642–2646

Scott No.			Plate Block	Unused	Used
❏ 2637	29¢	Olympics – Soccer	—	1.10	.75
❏ 2638	29¢	Olympics – Gymnastics	—	1.10	.75
❏ 2639	29¢	Olympics – Volleyball	—	1.10	.75
❏ 2640	29¢	Olympics – Boxing	—	1.10	.75
❏ 2641	29¢	Olympics – Diving	—	1.10	.75
		Strip of 5 (2637–2641)	11.00 (10)	5.50	—
❏ 2642	29¢	Ruby-throated Hummingbird	—	1.10	.10–.25
❏ 2643	29¢	Broad-billed Hummingbird	—	1.10	.10–.25
❏ 2644	29¢	Costa's Hummingbird	—	1.10	.10–.25
❏ 2645	29¢	Rufous Hummingbird	—	1.10	.10–.25
❏ 2646	29¢	Calliope Hummingbird	—	1.10	.10–.25
		Booklet pane of 5 (2642–2646)	—	5.50	—

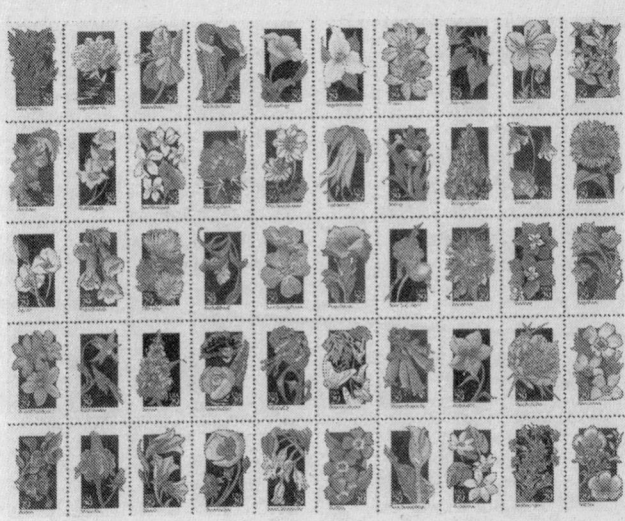

2647–2696

Scott No.		Plate Block	Unused	Used
❏ 2647–2696	29¢ Wildflowers, pane of 50	—	70.00	—
❏ 2647–2696	Any single stamp	—	1.40	.40

❏ 2647 Indian Paintbrush
❏ 2648 Fragrant Water Lily
❏ 2649 Meadow Beauty
❏ 2650 Jack-in-the-Pulpit
❏ 2651 California Poppy
❏ 2652 Large Flower Trillium
❏ 2653 Tickseed
❏ 2654 Shooting Star
❏ 2655 Stream Violet
❏ 2656 Bluets
❏ 2657 Herb Robert
❏ 2658 Marsh Marigold
❏ 2659 Sweet White Violet
❏ 2660 Claret Cup Cactus
❏ 2661 White Mountain Avens

❏ 2662 Sessile Bellwort
❏ 2663 Blue Flag
❏ 2664 Harlequin Lupine
❏ 2665 Twin Flower
❏ 2666 Common Sunflower
❏ 2667 Sego Lily
❏ 2668 Virginia Bluebells
❏ 2669 Ohi'a Lehua
❏ 2670 Rosebud Orchid
❏ 2671 Showy Evening Primrose
❏ 2672 Fringed Gentian
❏ 2673 Yellow Lady's Slipper
❏ 2674 Passion Flower
❏ 2675 Bunch Berry
❏ 2676 Pasque Flower

❑ 2677 Round-Lobed Hepatica
❑ 2678 Wild Columbine
❑ 2679 Firewood
❑ 2680 Indian Pond Lily
❑ 2681 Turk's Cap Lily
❑ 2682 Dutchman's Breeches
❑ 2683 Trumpet Honeysuckle
❑ 2684 Jacob's Ladder
❑ 2685 Plains Prickly Pear
❑ 2686 Mots Campion

❑ 2687 Bearberry
❑ 2688 Mexican Hat
❑ 2689 Harebell
❑ 2690 Desert Five Spot
❑ 2691 Smooth Solomon's Seal
❑ 2692 Red Maids
❑ 2693 Yellow Skunk Cabbage
❑ 2694 Rue Anemone
❑ 2695 Standing Cypress
❑ 2696 Wild Flax

2697

Scott No.			Plate Block	Unused	Used
❑ 2697	29¢	World War II, 1942, pane of 10	—	14.00	—
❑ 2697a–j	29¢	Any single stamp	—	1.30	.10–.25

2698   **2699**

2700–2703   **2704**

Scott No.			Plate Block	Unused	Used
❏ 2698	29¢	Dorothy Parker	4.25	1.50	.10–.25
❏ 2699	29¢	Theodore von Kármán	4.25	1.10	.10–.25
❏ 2700	29¢	Minerals – Azurite	—	1.80	.10–.25
❏ 2701	29¢	Minerals – Copper	—	1.80	.10–.25
❏ 2702	29¢	Minerals – Variscite	—	1.80	.10–.25
❏ 2703	29¢	Minerals – Wulfenite	—	1.80	.10–.25
		Block of 4 (2700–2703)	7.40	—	—
❏ 2704	29¢	Juan Rodríguez Cabrillo	4.25	1.25	.10–.25

Giraffe

Giant Panda

Flamingo

King Penguins

White Bengal Tiger

2705–2709

CHRISTMAS

Bellini c.1460 National Gallery

2710

Scott No.			Plate Block	Unused	Used
❏ 2705	29¢	Giraffe	—	1.10	.10–.25
❏ 2706	29¢	Giant Panda	—	1.10	.10–.25
❏ 2707	29¢	Flamingo	—	1.10	.10–.25
❏ 2708	29¢	King Penguins	—	1.10	.10–.25
❏ 2709	29¢	White Bengal Tiger	—	1.10	.10–.25
		Booklet pane of 5 (2705–2709)	—	5.50	—
❏ 2710	29¢	Christmas – Madonna & Child	—	1.10	.10–.25
		Booklet pane of 10	—	11.00	—

2711–2714
(2715–2718)

2719

2720

Scott No.			Plate Block	Unused	Used
❑ 2711	29¢	Christmas – Horse, perf 11½ x 11	—	1.30	.10–.25
❑ 2712	29¢	Christmas – Locomotive, perf 11½ x 11	—	1.30	.10–.25
❑ 2713	29¢	Christmas – Fire Pumper, perf 11½ x 11	—	1.30	.10–.25
❑ 2714	29¢	Christmas – Boat, perf 11½ x 11	—	1.30	.10–.25
		Block of 4 (2711–2714)	—	5.50	—

1992. Booklet Stamps.

❑ 2715	29¢	Christmas – Horse (~2711), perf 11	—	1.80	.10–.25
❑ 2716	29¢	Christmas – Locomotive (~2712), perf 11	—	1.80	.10–.25
❑ 2717	29¢	Christmas – Fire Pumper (~2713), perf 11	—	1.80	.10–.25
❑ 2718	29¢	Christmas – Boat (~2714), perf 11	—	1.80	.10–.25
		Booklet pane of 4 (2715–2718)	—	7.50	—
❑ 2719	29¢	Christmas – Locomotive (~2712), self-adhesive	—	1.30	.50
		Booklet pane of 18	—	23.00	.40
❑ 2720	29¢	Year of the Rooster	4.00	1.40	.10–.25

2721

2722

2723
(2723A)

Scott No.			Plate Block	Unused	Used
1993.					
☐ 2721	29¢	Elvis (no "Presley")	5.25	1.10	.10–.25
☐ 2722	29¢	Oklahoma! (no black frameline)	5.25	1.10	.10–.25

NOTE: See also No. 2769.

☐ 2723	29¢	Hank Williams, perf 10	5.25	2.25	.10–.25
☐ 2723A	29¢	Hank Williams, perf 11.2 x 11.4	150.00	25.00	12.00

NOTE: The inscription on Nos. 2723 and 2723A measures 27½ mm. See also Nos. 2771 and 2775.

2724–2730
(2731–2737)

Scott No.			Plate Block	Unused	Used
❏ 2724	29¢	Elvis (with "Presley")	—	2.20	1.00
❏ 2725	29¢	Bill Haley	—	2.20	1.00
❏ 2726	29¢	Clyde McPhatter	—	2.20	1.00
❏ 2727	29¢	Ritchie Valens	—	2.20	1.00
❏ 2728	29¢	Otis Redding	—	2.20	1.00
❏ 2729	29¢	Buddy Holly	—	2.20	1.00
❏ 2730	29¢	Dinah Washington	—	2.20	1.00
		Strip of 7 (2724–2730)	22.00 (10)	15.00	—

NOTE: Nos. 2724–2730 lack a black frameline around stamps. See also No. 2731–2737.

Scott No.			Plate Block	Unused	Used
❑ 2731	29¢	Elvis (~2724) (with "Presley")	—	1.45	.40
❑ 2732	29¢	Bill Haley (~2725)	—	1.45	.40
❑ 2733	29¢	Clyde McPhatter (~2726)	—	1.45	.40
❑ 2734	29¢	Ritchie Valens (~2727)	—	1.45	.40
❑ 2735	29¢	Otis Redding (~2728)	—	1.45	.40
❑ 2736	29¢	Buddy Holly (~2729)	—	1.45	.40
❑ 2737	29¢	Dinah Washington (~2730)	—	1.45	.40
		Booklet pane of 8 (1 x 2731; 2 each 2737)	—	11.50	—
		Booklet pane of 4 (2731 & 2735–2737)	—	6.00	—

NOTE: Nos. 2731–2737 have a black frameline around stamps.

2741–2745

❑ 2741	29¢	Planet & Rings	—	1.25	.10–.25
❑ 2742	29¢	Flying Saucers	—	1.25	.10–.25
❑ 2743	29¢	Jet Backpacks	—	1.25	.10–.25
❑ 2744	29¢	Winged Spacecraft	—	1.25	.10–.25
❑ 2745	29¢	Stubby-winged Spacecraft	—	1.25	.10–.25
		Booklet pane of 5 (2741–2745)	—	6.25	—

2746

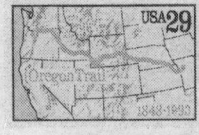

2747

2748

2749

2754

2750–2753

Scott No.			Plate Block	Unused	Used
❑ 2746	29¢	Percy Lavon Julian	5.25	1.40	.10–.25
❑ 2747	29¢	Oregon Trail	5.25	1.40	.10–.25
❑ 2748	29¢	World University Games	5.25	1.10	.10–.25
❑ 2749	29¢	Grace Kelly	5.25	1.30	.10–.25
❑ 2750	29¢	Clown	—	2.00	.10–.25
❑ 2751	29¢	Ringmaster	—	2.00	.10–.25
❑ 2752	29¢	Trapeze Artist	—	2.00	.10–.25
❑ 2753	29¢	Elephant	—	2.00	.10–.25
		Block of 4 (2750–2753)	12.00 (6)	8.00	—
❑ 2754	29¢	Cherokee Strip	5.25	1.45	.10–.25

2755

2756–2759

2760–2764

Scott No.			Plate Block	Unused	Used
❏ 2755	29¢	Dean Acheson	4.00	1.50	.10–.25
❏ 2756	29¢	Steeplechase	—	1.50	.75
❏ 2757	29¢	Thoroughbred Racing	—	1.50	.75
❏ 2758	29¢	Harness Racing	—	1.50	.75
❏ 2759	29¢	Polo	—	1.50	.75
		Block of 4 (2554–2557)	6.00	—	—
❏ 2760	29¢	Hyacinth	—	1.50	.10–.25
❏ 2761	29¢	Daffodil	—	1.50	.10–.25
❏ 2762	29¢	Tulip	—	1.50	.10–.25
❏ 2763	29¢	Iris	—	1.50	.10–.25
❏ 2764	29¢	Lilac	—	1.50	.10–.25
		Booklet pane of 5 (2760–2764)	—	7.50	—

2765

2766

Scott No.			Plate Block	Unused	Used
❑ 2765	29¢	World War II, 1943, pane of 10	—	14.00	—
❑ 2765a–j	29¢	Any single stamp	—	1.40	.38
❑ 2766	29¢	Joe Louis	4.50	1.25	.10–.25

2767–2770

Scott No.			Plate Block	Unused	Used
❑ 2767	29¢	Show Boat	—	1.10	.10–.25
❑ 2768	29¢	Porgy & Bess	—	1.10	.10–.25
❑ 2769	29¢	Oklahoma! (~2722) (black frameline)	—	1.10	.10–.25
❑ 2770	29¢	My Fair Lady	—	1.10	.10–.25
		Booklet pane of 4 (2767–2770)	—	5.00	—

2771–2774
(2775–2778)

2779–2782

Scott No.			Plate Block	Unused	Used
❏ 2771	29¢	Hank Williams (~2723) (no frameline)	—	2.00	1.00
❏ 2772	29¢	Patsy Cline (no frameline)	—	2.00	1.00
❏ 2773	29¢	Carter Family (no frameline)	—	2.00	1.00
❏ 2774	29¢	Bob Wills (no frameline)	—	2.00	1.00
		Block or strip of 4 (2771–2774)	8.00	6.00	—

NOTE: The inscription on No. 2771 measures 27mm. See also Nos. 2723, 2723A and 2778.

❏ 2775	29¢	Hank Williams (~2723) (black frameline)	—	1.10	.10–.25
❏ 2776	29¢	Patsy Cline (~2772) (black frameline)	—	1.10	.10–.25
❏ 2777	29¢	Carter Family (~2773) (black frameline)	—	1.10	.10–.25
❏ 2778	29¢	Bob Wills (~2774) (black frameline)	—	1.10	.10–.25
		Booklet pane of 4 (2775–2778)	—	4.50	—

NOTE: The inscription on No. 2775 measures 22mm. See also Nos. 2723, 2723A and 2771.

❏ 2779	29¢	Benjamin Franklin	—	1.40	.10–.25
❏ 2780	29¢	Drummer	—	1.40	.10–.25
❏ 2781	29¢	Charles Lindbergh	—	1.40	.10–.25
❏ 2782	29¢	Rare Stamps	—	1.40	.10–.25
		Block of 4 (2779–2782)	6.00	—	—

2783–84

2785–2788

Scott No.			Plate Block	Unused	Used
❑ 2783	29¢	Deafness – Mother & Child	—	1.10	.10–.25
❑ 2784	29¢	American Sign Language	—	1.10	.10–.25
		Se-tenant pair (2783–2784)	4.00	1.10	—
❑ 2785	29¢	Rebecca of Sunnybrook Farm	—	2.00	1.00
❑ 2786	29¢	Little House on the Prairie	—	2.00	1.00
❑ 2787	29¢	Huckleberry Finn	—	2.00	1.00
❑ 2788	29¢	Little Women	—	2.00	1.00
		Block of 4 (2785–2788)	8.00	—	—

2789

2791–2794
(2795–2803)

Scott No.			Plate Block	Unused	Used
❏ 2789	29¢	Christmas – Madonna & Child	5.00	1.20	.10–.25
❏ 2790	29¢	Madonna & Child (~2789)	—	1.20	.10–.25
		Booklet pane of 4	—	4.80	—

NOTE: The design of No.2789 is slightly cropped in No. 2790, the booklet version.

❏ 2791	29¢	Christmas – Jack in the Box	—	1.40	.10–.25
❏ 2792	29¢	Christmas – Reindeer	—	1.40	.10–.25
❏ 2793	29¢	Christmas – Snowman	—	1.40	.10–.25
❏ 2794	29¢	Christmas – Toy Soldier	—	1.40	.10–.25
		Block or strip of 4 (2791–2794)	6.00	—	—
❏ 2795	29¢	Toy Soldier (~2794)	—	1.40	.10–.25
❏ 2796	29¢	Snowman (~2793)	—	1.40	.10–.25
❏ 2797	29¢	Reindeer (~2792)	—	1.40	.10–.25
❏ 2798	29¢	Jack in the Box (~2791)	—	1.40	.10–.25
		Booklet pane of 10 (2 or 3 of each design)	—	14.00	—
❏ 2799	29¢	Snowman (~2793) self-adhesive	—	1.80	.10–.25
❏ 2800	29¢	Toy Soldier (~2794) self-adhesive	—	1.80	.10–.25
❏ 2801	29¢	Jack in the Box (~2791) self-adhesive	—	1.80	.10–.25
❏ 2802	29¢	Reindeer (~2792) self-adhesive	—	1.80	.10–.25
		Booklet pane of 12 (3 each 2799–2802)	—	22.00	—

NOTE: Nos. 2799–2802 measure 19½ x 26½ mm.

Scott No.			Plate Block	Unused	Used
❑ 2803	29¢	Snowman (~2793)			
		self-adhesive	—	1.30	.75
		Booklet pane of 18	—	23.00	—

NOTE: No. 2803 measures 17 x 20 mm.

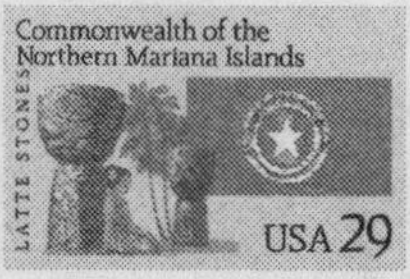

2804

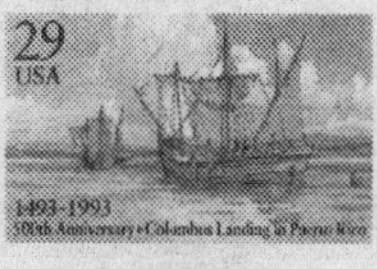

2805

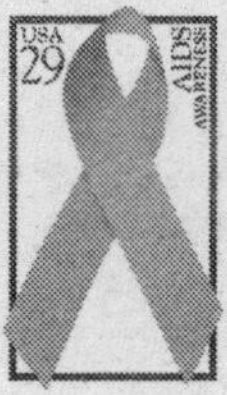

2806

❑ 2804	29¢	Mariana Islands	4.25	1.50	.10–.25
❑ 2805	29¢	Columbus Landing	4.25	1.10	.10–.25
❑ 2806	29¢	AIDS Awareness	4.25	1.10	.10–.25
❑ 2806b	29¢	Booklet pane of 5 (~2806)	—	5.50	

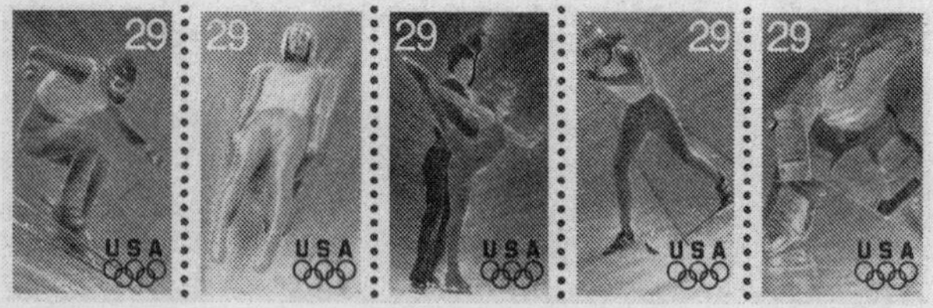

2807–2811

1994.

❑ 2807	29¢	Slalom	—	1.25	.75
❑ 2808	29¢	Luge	—	1.25	.75
❑ 2809	29¢	Ice Dancing	—	1.25	.75
❑ 2810	29¢	Skiing	—	1.25	.75
❑ 2811	29¢	Hockey	—	1.25	.75
		Strip of 5 (2807–2811)	11.00 (10)	6.25	—

2812

2813

2814
(2814C)

2815

2816

2817

2818

Scott No.			Plate Block	Unused	Used
☐ 2812	29¢	Edward R. Murrow	4.25	2.15	.10–.25
☐ 2813	29¢	Love – Sunshine Heart	6.00	1.30	.10–.25
		Booklet pane of 18	—	22.50	—
☐ 2814	29¢	Love – Dove (photogravure)	—	1.10	.10–.25
		Booklet pane of 10	—	11.00	—
☐ 2814C	29¢	Love (~2814) (lithographed			
		& engraved)	4.25	1.20	.10–.25
☐ 2815	52¢	Love – Doves	5.00	1.80	.10–.25
☐ 2816	29¢	Dr. Allison Davis	4.25	1.40	.10–.25
☐ 2817	29¢	Year of the Dog	5.00	2.00	.10–.25
☐ 2818	29¢	Buffalo Soldiers	4.25	1.25	.10–.25

2819–2828

Scott No.			Plate Block	Unused	Used
❏ 2819	29¢	Rudolph Valentino	—	2.00	1.00
❏ 2820	29¢	Clara Bow	—	2.00	1.00
❏ 2821	29¢	Charlie Chaplin	—	2.00	1.00
❏ 2822	29¢	Lon Chaney	—	2.00	1.00
❏ 2823	29¢	John Gilbert	—	2.00	1.00
❏ 2824	29¢	Zasu Pitts	—	2.00	1.00
❏ 2825	29¢	Harold Lloyd	—	2.00	1.00
❏ 2826	29¢	Keystone Cops	—	2.00	1.00
❏ 2827	29¢	Theda Bara	—	2.00	1.00
❏ 2828	29¢	Buster Keaton	—	2.00	1.00
		Block of 10 (2819–2828)	20.00 (10)	—	—

2829–2833

2837

Scott No.			Plate Block	Unused	Used
❏ 2829	29¢	Lily	—	1.40	.10–.25
❏ 2830	29¢	Zinnia	—	1.40	.10–.25
❏ 2831	29¢	Gladiola	—	1.40	.10–.25
❏ 2832	29¢	Marigold	—	1.40	.10–.25
❏ 2833	29¢	Rose	—	1.40	.10–.25
		Booklet pane of 5 (2830–2833)	—	7.00	—
❏ 2834	29¢	World Cup Soccer	4.00	1.40	.10–.25
❏ 2835	40¢	World Cup Soccer	5.00	1.40	.10–.25
❏ 2836	50¢	World Cup Soccer	6.00	1.70	.10–.25
❏ 2837	$1.19	Souvenir Sheet of 3 (2834–2836)	—	6.50	—

2838

Scott No.			Plate Block	Unused	Used
❑ 2838	29¢	World War II, 1944, pane of 10	—	30.00	—
❑ 2838a–j		Any single stamp	—	3.00	.42

2839

2840

Scott No.			Plate Block	Unused	Used
❑ 2839	29¢	Norman Rockwell	5.00	1.10	.10–.25
❑ 2840	50¢	Rockwell souvenir sheet	—	7.50	—
❑ 2840a–d	50¢	Any single stamp	—	1.60	.42

First Moon Landing, 1969

2841

25th Anniversary   First Moon Landing, 1969

2842

George Meany

Labor Leader USA 29

2848

2843–2847

Scott No.			Plate Block	Unused	Used
❏ 2841	29¢	Moon Landing	—	1.45	.50
❏ 2842	$9.95	Moon Landing	80.00	42.00	16.80
❏ 2843	29¢	Hudson's General	—	1.30	.10–.25
❏ 2844	29¢	McQueen's Jupiter	—	1.30	.10–.25
❏ 2845	29¢	Eddy's No. 242	—	1.30	.10–.25
❏ 2846	29¢	Ely's No. 10	—	1.30	.10–.25
❏ 2847	29¢	Buchanan's No. 999	—	1.30	.10–.25
		Booklet pane of 5 (2843–2847)	—	6.50	—
❏ 2848	29¢	George Meany	35.00	1.10	.10–.25

2849–2853

Scott No.			Plate Block	Unused	Used
1995.					
❑ 2849	29¢	Al Jolson	—	1.80	.75
❑ 2850	29¢	Bing Crosby	—	1.80	.75
❑ 2851	29¢	Ethel Waters	—	1.80	.75
❑ 2852	29¢	Nat "King" Cole	—	1.80	.75
❑ 2853	29¢	Ethel Merman	—	1.80	.75
		Strip of 5 (2849–2853)	18.00 (10)	9.00	—

2854–2861

Scott No.			Plate Block	Unused	Used
❏ 2854	29¢	Bessie Smith	—	2.00	1.00
❏ 2855	29¢	Muddy Waters	—	2.00	1.00
❏ 2856	29¢	Billie Holiday	—	2.00	1.00
❏ 2857	29¢	Robert Johnson	—	2.00	1.00
❏ 2858	29¢	Jimmy Rushing	—	2.00	1.00
❏ 2859	29¢	"Ma" Rainey	—	2.00	1.00
❏ 2860	29¢	Mildred Bailey	—	2.00	1.00
❏ 2861	29¢	Howlin' Wolf	—	2.00	1.00
		Block of 9 (2854–3861 + any 1 extra stamp)	20.00 (10)	—	—

2862

2863–2866

2867–2868

Scott No.			Plate Block	Unused	Used
❏ 2862	29¢	James Thurber	4.00	1.25	.50
❏ 2863	29¢	Motorboat & Diver	—	1.20	.50
❏ 2864	29¢	Three–masted Ship	—	1.20	.50
❏ 2865	29¢	Diver & Sunken Wheel	—	1.20	.50
❏ 2866	29¢	Fish & Coral	—	1.20	.50
		Block of 4 (2863–2866)	5.00	—	—
❏ 2867	29¢	Black-necked Crane	—	1.10	.10–.30
❏ 2868	29¢	Whooping Crane	—	1.10	.10–.30
		Se-tenant pair (2867–2868)	5.00	2.50	—

2869

2869g

2870g

Scott No.		Plate Block	Unused	Used
❑ 2869	29¢ Legends of the West	—	27.00	—
❑ 2869a–j	29¢ Any single stamp	—	1.35	.42
❑ 2870	29¢ Recalled Legends	—	375.00	—
❑ 2870a–j	29¢ Any single stamp	—	16.00	14.70

NOTE: The Bill Pickett stamps in Nos. 2869 and 2870 differ. The Pickett stamp in No. 2870 shows a handkerchief in the vest pocket. Other stamps in the two panes are similar except that the framelines on No. 2869 are thicker than on No. 2870.

2871
(2871A)   **2872**   **2873**   **2874**

2875

Scott No.			Plate Block	Unused	Used
☐ 2871	29¢	Madonna & Child, perf 11½	5.00	1.10	.10–.25
☐ 2871A	29¢	Madonna & Child (~2871), perf 9½ x 11	—	1.10	.10–.25
		Booklet pane of 10	—	9.00	—
☐ 2872	29¢	Teddy Bear in Stocking	5.00	1.10	.10–.25
☐ 2872a	29¢	Booklet pane of 20	—	22.00	—
☐ 2873	29¢	Santa Claus	—	1.40	.10–.25
		Booklet pane of 12	—	16.00	—
☐ 2874	29¢	Cardinal	—	1.20	.50
		Booklet pane of 18	—	22.00	—
☐ 2875	$2	B.E.P. souvenir sheet	—	28.00	—
		Single stamp	—	7.00	1.00

2876

2877
(2878)

2879
(2880)

2881
(2882–2887,
2889–2892)

Scott No.			Plate Block	Unused	Used
❑ 2876	29¢	Year of the Boar	5.00	1.40	.75
❑ 2877	(4¢)	G Rate Make-up Stamp	2.00	.30	.10–.25
❑ 2878	(4¢)	G Rate Make-up Stamp (~2877)	2.00	.30	.10–.25

NOTE: No. 2877 is printed with bright blue; No. 2878 is printed with dark blue.

❑ 2879	(20¢)	Yellow with Black G	5.00	1.10	.10–.25
❑ 2880	(20¢)	Yellow with Red G (~2879)	10.00	1.10	.10–.25
❑ 2881	(32¢)	White with Black G, perf 11.2 x 11.1	12.00	4.50	.10–.25
		Booklet pane of 10	—	45.00	—
❑ 2882	(32¢)	White with Red G (~2881)	5.00	1.25	.10–.25

Booklet Stamps.

❑ 2883	(32¢)	White with Black G (~2881), perf 10 x 9.9	—	1.40	.10–.25
		Booklet pane of 10	—	14.00	—
❑ 2884	(32¢)	White with Blue G (~2881)	—	1.40	.10–.25
		Booklet pane of 10	—	14.00	—
❑ 2885	(32¢)	White with Red G (~2881)	—	1.80	.10–.25
		Booklet pane of 10	—	18.00	—
❑ 2886	(32¢)	White with Black G (~2881), self-adhesive	—	1.30	.10–.25
		Booklet pane of 18	—	24.00	—
		PNC strip of 5 (see note)	6.50	—	—

NOTE: No.2886 also exists as a coil stamp. Booklet examples and coil examples alike possess straight die cutting and, therefore, are indistinguishable once removed from their backing paper.

Scott No.		Plate Block	Unused	Used
❑ 2887 (32¢)	White with Black G (~2881),			
	self-adhesive	—	1.80	.50
	Booklet pane of 18	—	32.50	—

NOTE: No. 2887 contains noticeable blue shading in the white stripes below the field of stars; No. 2886 does not.

2888

2893

Scott No.		PNC Strip (5)	Unused	Used
Coil Stamps.				
❑ 2888 (25¢)	Blue with Black G	10.00	1.60	.50
❑ 2889 (32¢)	White with Black G (~2881)	12.00	4.00	1.00
❑ 2890 (32¢)	White with Blue G (~2881)	8.00	1.30	.10–.25
❑ 2891 (32¢)	White with Red G (~2881)	8.00	1.80	.10–.25
❑ 2892 (32¢)	White with Red G (~2881),			
	rouletted	10.00	1.70	.10–.25
❑ 2893 (5¢)	Green with Black G	4.00	.85	.10–.25

2897
(2913–2915, 2920, 3113)

Scott No.		Plate Block	Unused	Used
1995.				
❑ 2897 32¢	Flag over Porch, perforated	5.00	1.40	.10–.25

2902	**2903**	**2905**	**2908**	**2911**
(2902B)	(2904, 2904A)	(2906)	(2909–2910)	(2912, 2912A, 3132)

Scott No.		PNC Strip (5)	Unused	Used

Coil Stamps.

❏ 2902 (5¢)	Butte, Non-Profit, perforated	2.00	.65	.10–.25
❏ 2902B (5¢)	Butte, Non-Profit, die cut	4.00	.50	.10–.25
❏ 2903 (10¢)	Mountain, purple cast, perforated	4.00	.40	.10–.25
❏ 2904 (10¢)	Mountain, bluish cast (~2903), perforated	4.00	.45	.10–.25
❏ 2904A (10¢)	Mountain, purple cast (~2903), die cut	4.00	.50	.10–.25
❏ 2905 (10¢)	Automobile, Bulk rate, perforated	4.00	.45	.10–.25
❏ 2906 (10¢)	Automobile (~2905), die cut	3.00	.70	.10–.25
❏ 2908 (15¢)	Tail Fin, orange-yellow cast, perforated	5.00	.55	.52
❏ 2909 (15¢)	Tail Fin (~2908), buff cast, perforated	4.00	.55	.52
❏ 2910 (15¢)	Tail Fin (~2908), self-adhesive	4.00	.60	.52
❏ 2911 (25¢)	Juke Box, perforated	6.00	1.00	.68
❏ 2912 (25¢)	Juke Box (~2911), perforated	6.00	1.00	.68
❏ 2912A (25¢)	Juke Box (~2911), die cut	6.00	1.10	.68
❏ 2913 32¢	Flag over Porch (~2897), perforated	7.00	1.30	.75
❏ 2914 32¢	Flag over Porch (~2897), perforated	8.00	2.00	.75

NOTE: The tan color on No. 2913 appears tan; it appears yellow brown on No. 2914.

❏ 2915 32¢	Flag over porch, die cut (~2897)	14.00	2.00	.75

2919

Scott No.			Plate Block	Unused	Used

Booklet Stamps.

❑ 2916	32¢	Flag over Porch (~2897), water-activated gum	—	1.90	.10–.25
		Booklet pane of 10	—	19.00	—
❑ 2919	32¢	Flag over Field, self-adhesive	—	1.45	.75
		Booklet pane of 18	—	26.00	—
❑ 2920	32¢	Flag over Porch (~2897), self-adhesive	—	1.45	.10–.25
		Booklet pane of 20	—	28.50	—

2933    **2934**    **2935**    **2936**    **2938**

1995–1996. Great Americans Series.

❑ 2933	32¢	Milton Hershey	4.00	1.30	1.00
❑ 2934	32¢	Cal Farley	4.00	1.45	1.00
❑ 2935	32¢	Henry R. Luce	4.00	1.30	1.00
❑ 2936	32¢	Lila & DeWitt Wallace	4.00	1.40	1.00
❑ 2938	46¢	Ruth Benedict	4.50	1.80	1.00

| 2940 | 2941 | 2942 | 2943 |

Scott No.			Plate Block	Unused	Used
❏ 2940	55¢	Alice Hamilton M.D.	7.00	1.80	.10–.35
❏ 2941	55¢	Justin S. Morrill	6.00	2.30	.10–.35
❏ 2942	77¢	Mary Breckinridge	7.00	2.80	.10–.35
❏ 2943	78¢	Alice Paul	8.00	2.80	.10–.35

| 2948 | 2949 | 2950 |

1995.

❏ 2948	(32¢)	Love – Cherub, perforated	4.00	1.10	.10–.25
❏ 2949	(32¢)	Love – Cherub, self-adhesive	—	1.30	.10–.25
		Booklet pane of 20	—	26.00	—
❏ 2950	32¢	Florida Statehood	5.00	2.00	.10–.25

2951–2954

2955

2956

2957
(2959)

2958
(2960)

Scott No.			Plate Block	Unused	Used
❑ 2951	32¢	Globe in a Tub	—	1.15	.10–.25
❑ 2952	32¢	Sun & Electrical Cord	—	1.15	.10–.25
❑ 2953	32¢	Planting a Tree	—	1.15	.10–.25
❑ 2954	32¢	Clean-up at the Beach	—	1.15	.10–.25
		Block of 4 (2952–2954)	4.50	—	—
❑ 2955	32¢	Richard M. Nixon	4.25	1.45	.10–.25
❑ 2956	32¢	Bessie Coleman	4.25	1.80	.10–.25
❑ 2957	32¢	Love – Cherub, perforated	4.25	1.10	.10–.25
❑ 2958	55¢	Love – Cherubs, perforated	4.25	1.90	.42
❑ 2959	32¢	Love – Cherub, self-adhesive	—	1.30	.10–.25
		Booklet pane of 10	—	13.00	—
❑ 2960	55¢	Love – Cherubs, self-adhesive	—	1.30	.42
		Booklet pane of 20	—	36.00	—

2961–2965

2966

2967

2968

Scott No.			Plate Block	Unused	Used
❏ 2961	32¢	Volleyball	—	1.20	.85
❏ 2962	32¢	Softball	—	1.20	.85
❏ 2963	32¢	Bowling	—	1.20	.85
❏ 2964	32¢	Tennis	—	1.20	.85
❏ 2965	32¢	Golf	—	1.20	.85
		Strip of 5 (2961–2965)	12.00 (10)	6.00	—
❏ 2966	32¢	POW – MIA	4.00	1.10	.10–.25
❏ 2967	32¢	Marilyn Monroe	6.00	2.50	.10–.25
❏ 2968	32¢	Texas Statehood	4.00	1.40	.10–.25

2969–2973

2974

Scott No.			Plate Block	Unused	Used
❑ 2969	32¢	Split Rock Lighthouse	—	2.10	.10–.25
❑ 2970	32¢	St. Joseph Lighthouse	—	2.10	.10–.25
❑ 2971	32¢	Spectacle Reef Lighthouse	—	2.10	.10–.25
❑ 2972	32¢	Marblehead Lighthouse	—	2.10	.10–.25
❑ 2973	32¢	Thirty Mile Point Lighthouse	—	2.10	.10–.25
		Booklet pane of 5 (2969–1973)	—	10.50	—
❑ 2974	32¢	United Nations	5.00	1.10	.10–.25

2975

Scott No.			Plate Block	Unused	Used
❏ 2975	32¢	Civil War, pane of 20	—	40.00	—
❏ 2975a–t		Any single stamp	—	1.90	.42

2976–2979

2980

Scott No.			Plate Block	Unused	Used
❏ 2976	32¢	Carousel Horse – Gold	—	1.25	.10–.25
❏ 2977	32¢	Carousel Horse – Black & Gold	—	1.25	.10–.25
❏ 2978	32¢	Carousel Horse – Silver	—	1.25	.10–.25
❏ 2979	32¢	Carousel Horse – Brown	—	1.25	.10–.25
		Block of 4 (2976–2979)	5.00	4.00	—
❏ 2980	32¢	Women's Suffrage	4.00	1.10	.10–.25

2981

2982

Scott No.			Plate Block	Unused	Used
☐ 2981	32¢	World War II, 1945, pane of 10	—	22.50	—
☐ 2981a–j	32¢	Any single stamp	—	2.25	.65
☐ 2982	32¢	Louis Armstrong (white "32¢")	5.00	1.70	.10–.25

2983–2992

Scott No.			Plate Block	Unused	Used
❏ 2983	32¢	Coleman Hawkins	—	4.00	3.00
❏ 2984	32¢	Louis Armstrong (black "32¢")	—	4.00	3.00
❏ 2985	32¢	James P. Johnson	—	4.00	3.00
❏ 2986	32¢	Jelly Roll Morton	—	4.00	3.00
❏ 2987	32¢	Charlie Parker	—	4.00	3.00
❏ 2988	32¢	Eubie Blake	—	4.00	3.00
❏ 2989	32¢	Charles Mingus	—	4.00	3.00
❏ 2990	32¢	Thelonious Monk	—	4.00	3.00
❏ 2991	32¢	John Coltrane	—	4.00	3.00
❏ 2992	32¢	Errol Garner	—	4.00	3.00
		Block of 10 (2983–2992)	40.00 (10)	15.00	—

2993–2997

2998

2999

Scott No.			Plate Block	Unused	Used
❏ 2993	32¢	Aster	—	1.10	.10–.25
❏ 2994	32¢	Chrysanthemum	—	1.10	.10–.25
❏ 2995	32¢	Dahlia	—	1.10	.10–.25
❏ 2996	32¢	Hydrangea	—	1.10	.10–.25
❏ 2997	32¢	Rudbeckia	—	1.10	.10–.25
		Booklet pane of 5 (2993–2997)	—	4.50	—
❏ 2998	60¢	Eddie Rickenbacker	8.00	2.00	.10–.30
❏ 2999	32¢	Republic of Palau	4.00	1.10	.10–.30

3000

3001   **3002**

Scott No.			Plate Block	Unused	Used
❏ 3000	32¢	Comic Strip Classics	—	28.00	—
❏ 3000a–t	32¢	Any single stamp	—	1.10	.10–.25
❏ 3001	32¢	U.S. Naval Academy	4.25	1.80	.10–.25
❏ 3002	32¢	Tennessee Williams	6.00	1.70	.10–.25

3003
(3003A)

3004–3007
(3008–3011, 3014–3017)

3012
(3018)

3013

Scott No.			Plate Block	Unused	Used
❏ 3003	32¢	Madonna & Child, perf 11.2	4.00	1.25	.10–.25
❏ 3003A	32¢	Madonna & Child, perf 9.8 x 11.9	—	1.25	.10–.25
		Booklet pane of 10	—	12.50	—
❏ 3004	32¢	Santa & Chimney, perforated	—	1.50	.10–.25
❏ 3005	32¢	Jack-in-the-Box, perforated	—	1.50	.10–.25
❏ 3006	32¢	Boy & Christmas Tree, perforated	—	1.50	.10–.25
❏ 3007	32¢	Santa in Workshop, perforated	—	1.50	.10–.25
		Block or strip of 4	6.00	—	—
		Booklet pane of 10 (2 or 3 each 3004–3007)	—	15.00	—
❏ 3008	32¢	Santa in Workshop (~3007), self-adhesive	—	2.50	.10–.25
❏ 3009	32¢	Jack-in-the-Box (~3005), self-adhesive	—	2.50	.10–.25
❏ 3010	32¢	Santa & Chimney (~3004), self-adhesive	—	2.50	.10–.25
❏ 3011	32¢	Boy & Christmas Tree (~3006), self-adhesive	—	2.50	.10–.25
		Booklet pane of 20 (5 each 3008–3011)	—	50.00	—
❏ 3012	32¢	Christmas – Midnight Angel	—	1.10	.10–.25
		Booklet pane of 20	—	22.00	—
❏ 3013	32¢	Christmas – Children Sledding	—	1.25	.10–.25
		Booklet pane of 18	—	22.50	—

Scott No.			PNC Strip (5)	Unused	Used

Coil Stamps.

Scott No.			PNC Strip (5)	Unused	Used
❏ 3014	32¢	Santa in Workshop (~3007), self-adhesive	—	6.20	1.25
❏ 3015	32¢	Jack-in-the-Box (~3005), self-adhesive	—	6.20	1.25
❏ 3016	32¢	Santa & Chimney (~3004), self-adhesive	—	6.20	1.25
❏ 3017	32¢	Boy & Christmas Tree (~3006), self-adhesive	—	6.20	1.25
		Strip of 4 (3014–3017)	12.00	25.00	—
❏ 3018	32¢	Christmas – Midnight Angel, self-adhesive	12.00	1.70	1.25

3019–3023

Scott No.			Plate Block	Unused	Used

1995.

Scott No.			Plate Block	Unused	Used
❏ 3019	32¢	1893 Duryea	—	1.50	1.00
❏ 3020	32¢	1894 Haynes	—	1.50	1.00
❏ 3021	32¢	1898 Columbia	—	1.50	1.00
❏ 3022	32¢	1899 Winton	—	1.50	1.00
❏ 3023	32¢	1901 White	—	1.50	1.00
		Strip of 5 (3019–3023)	15.00 (10)	7.50	—

3024

3025–3029

3030

Scott No.			Plate Block	Unused	Used
1996.					
☐ 3024	32¢	Utah Statehood	4.00	1.90	.10–.25
☐ 3025	32¢	Crocus	—	1.30	.10–.25
☐ 3026	32¢	Winter Aconite	—	1.30	.10–.25
☐ 3027	32¢	Pansy	—	1.30	.10–.25
☐ 3028	32¢	Snowdrop	—	1.30	.10–.25
☐ 3029	32¢	Anemone	—	1.30	.10–.25
		Booklet pane of 5 (3024–3029)	—	6.50	—
☐ 3030	32¢	Love – Cherub, self adhesive	—	1.40	.10–.25
		Booklet pane of 15	—	21.00	—
		Booklet pane of 20	—	28.00	—

3032
(3045)

3033

3036

Scott No.			Plate Block	Unused	Used
❑ 3031	1¢	Kestrel, die cut 10½ ("1¢")	1.00	.30	.10–.25
❑ 3031A	1¢	Kestrel, die cut 11½ ("1¢")	1.00	.30	.10–.25
❑ 3032	2¢	Woodpecker	1.00	.50	.10–.25
❑ 3033	3¢	Blue Bird ("3¢")	1.00	.50	.10–.25
❑ 3036	$1	Red Fox	10.00	10.00	1.00

NOTE: See Nos. 2476 and 2478 for 1¢ and 3¢ stamps denominated "01" and "03."

Scott No.			PNC Strip (5)	Unused	Used
Coil Stamps.					
❑ 3044	1¢	Kestrel ("1¢")	1.50	.30	.10–.25
❑ 3045	2¢	Woodpecker	2.00	.40	.10–.25

3048

3049
(3054)

Scott No.			Plate Block	Unused	Used
1996. Booklet Stamps.					
❑ 3048	20¢	Blue Jay (~2483), self-adhesive	—	.80	.10–.25
		Booklet pane of 10	—	8.00	—
❑ 3049	32¢	Yellow Rose (~2490), self-adhesive	—	1.30	.10–.25
		Booklet pane of 20	—	25.50	—

3050
(3051, 3055)

3052
(3052E)

Scott No.			Plate Block	Unused	Used
❑ 3050	20¢	Pheasant, die cut 11½	—	1.10	.10–.25
		Booklet pane of 10	—	8.80	—
❑ 3051	20¢	Pheasant (~3050), die cut 10½ x 11	—	1.70	1.00
		Booklet pane of 5 (& one 3051a)	—	10.00	—
❑ 3051a	20¢	Pheasant, die cut 10½	—	12.50	.10–.25
❑ 3052	32¢	Coral Pink Rose, die cut 11½ x 11½	—	1.70	.10–.25
		Booklet pane of 20	—	34.00	—
❑ 3052E	32¢	Coral Pink Rose (~3052), die cut 10½ x 10½	—	1.60	.10–.25
		Booklet pane of 20	—	32.00	—

Scott No.			PNC Strip (5)	Unused	Used

Coil Stamps.

			PNC Strip (5)	Unused	Used
❑ 3053	20¢	Blue Jay (~2483), die cut 11½	6.00	1.30	.42
❑ 3054	32¢	Yellow Rose (~2490), die cut 9½	8.00	1.30	.10–.35
❑ 3055	20¢	Pheasant (~3051), die cut 9½	5.00	1.10	.10–.35

3058

3061–3064

3059

3060

3065

3066

3067

Scott No.			Plate Block	Unused	Used
1996.					
❑ 3058	32¢	Ernest E. Just	4.00	1.50	.10–.25
❑ 3059	32¢	Smithsonian Institution	4.00	1.10	.10–.25
❑ 3060	32¢	Year of the Rat	5.00	1.50	.10–.25
❑ 3061	32¢	Edweard Muybridge	—	1.50	1.00
❑ 3062	32¢	Ottmar Mergenthaler	—	1.50	1.00
❑ 3063	32¢	Frederick E. Ives	—	1.50	1.00
❑ 3064	32¢	William Dickson	—	1.50	1.00
		Block of 4 (3061–3064)	6.00	—	—
❑ 3065	32¢	Fulbright Scholarships	4.00	2.00	.10–.25
❑ 3066	50¢	Jacqueline Cochran	6.00	1.70	.42
❑ 3067	32¢	Marathon	4.00	1.10	.10–.25

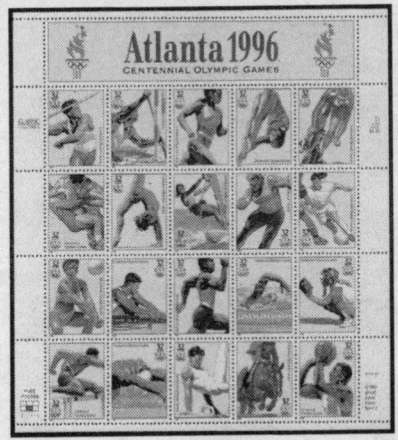

3069

3070
(3071)

3068

3072–3076

Scott No.			Plate Block	Unused	Used
❑ 3068	32¢	Olympics 1996, pane of 20	—	25.00	—
		Any single stamp	—	1.25	.42
❑ 3069	32¢	Georgia O'Keeffe	5.00	1.60	.10–.25
❑ 3070	32¢	Tennessee, perforated	4.00	1.30	.10–.25
❑ 3071	32¢	Tennessee (~3070), self-adhesive	—	1.45	.10–.25
		Booklet pane of 20	—	28.50	—
❑ 3072	32¢	Fancy Dance	—	1.80	1.00
❑ 3073	32¢	Butterfly Dance	—	1.80	1.00
❑ 3074	32¢	Traditional Dance	—	1.80	1.00
❑ 3075	32¢	Raven Dance	—	1.80	1.00
❑ 3076	32¢	Hoop Dance	—	1.80	1.00
		Strip of 5 (3072–3076)	18.00 (10)	9.00	—

3077–3080

3081

3082

Scott No.			Plate Block	Unused	Used
❑ 3077	32¢	Eohippus	—	1.40	.10–.25
❑ 3078	32¢	Woolly Mammoth	—	1.40	.10–.25
❑ 3079	32¢	Mastodon	—	1.40	.10–.25
❑ 3080	32¢	Saber-tooth Cat	—	1.40	.10–.25
		Block of 4 (3077–3080)	5.60	—	—
❑ 3081	32¢	Breast Cancer Awareness	6.00	1.30	.10–.25
❑ 3082	32¢	James Dean	6.00	1.70	.10–.25

3087

3088
(3089)

3089

3083–3086

Scott No.			Plate Block	Unused	Used
❑ 3083	32¢	Mighty Casey	—	1.65	1.00
❑ 3084	32¢	Paul Bunyan	—	1.65	1.00
❑ 3085	32¢	John Henry	—	1.65	1.00
❑ 3086	32¢	Pecos Bill	—	1.65	1.00
		Block of 4 (3083–3086)	6.50	—	—
❑ 3087	32¢	Discus Thrower	4.25	1.50	.10–.30
❑ 3088	32¢	Iowa Statehood, water activated	4.25	1.80	.10–.30
❑ 3089	32¢	Iowa (~3088), self-adhesive	—	1.80	.10–.30
		Booklet pane of 20	—	36.00	—
❑ 3090	32¢	RFD – Rural Free Delivery	4.25	2.00	.10–.30

3091–3095

Scott No.			Plate Block	Unused	Used
❑ 3091	32¢	Riverboat – Robert E. Lee	—	1.20	.10–.25
❑ 3092	32¢	Riverboat – Sylvan Dell	—	1.20	.10–.25
❑ 3093	32¢	Riverboat – Far West	—	1.20	.10–.25
❑ 3094	32¢	Riverboat – Rebecca Everingham	—	1.20	.10–.25
❑ 3095	32¢	Riverboat – Bailey Gatzert	—	1.20	.10–.25
		Strip of 5 (3091–3096)	12.00 (10)	6.00	—

3096–3099

3100–3103

Scott No.			Plate Block	Unused	Used
❑ 3096	32¢	Count Basie	—	1.70	1.00
❑ 3097	32¢	Tommy & Jimmy Dorsey	—	1.70	1.00
❑ 3098	32¢	Glenn Miller	—	1.70	1.00
❑ 3099	32¢	Benny Goodman	—	1.70	1.00
		Block or strip of 4 (3096–3099)	7.00	—	—
❑ 3100	32¢	Harold Arlen	—	1.25	1.00
❑ 3101	32¢	Johnny Mercer	—	1.25	1.00
❑ 3102	32¢	Dorothy Fields	—	1.25	1.00
❑ 3103	32¢	Hoagy Carmichael	—	1.25	1.00
		Block or strip of 4 (3100–3103)	5.00	—	—

F SCOTT FITZGERALD
23
USA

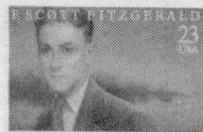

3104

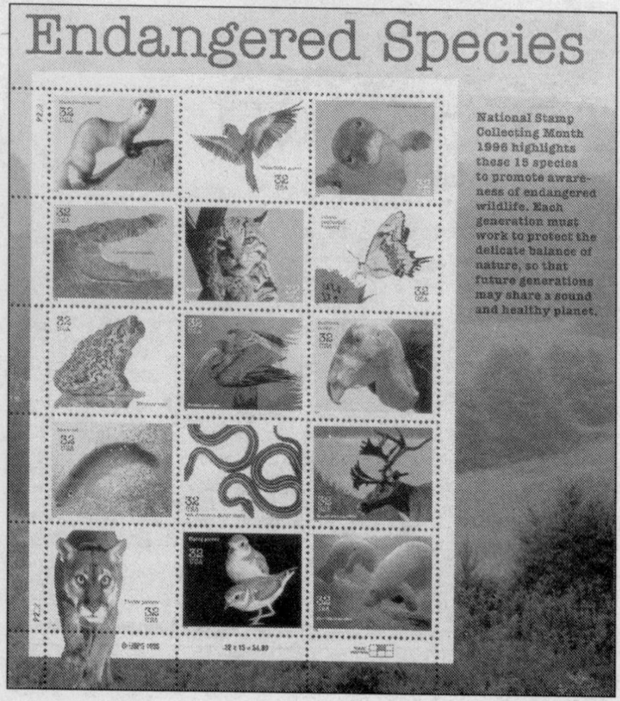
Endangered Species
National Stamp
Collecting Month
1996 highlights
these 15 species
to promote aware-
ness of endangered
wildlife. Each
generation must
work to protect the
delicate balance of
nature, so that
future generations
may share a sound
and healthy planet.

3105

Scott No.			Plate Block	Unused	Used
❑ 3104	23¢	F. Scott Fitzgerald	4.00	1.20	.10–.25
❑ 3105	32¢	Endangered Species, pane of 15	—	24.00	—
❑ 3105a–o		Any single stamp	—	1.10	.42

3106 **3107**
(3112)

3108–3111
(3113–3116)

Scott No.			Plate Block	Unused	Used
❏ 3106	32¢	Computer Technology	4.00	1.10	.10–.25
❏ 3107	32¢	Christmas – Madonna & Child	4.00	1.10	.10–.25
❏ 3108	32¢	Family & Fireplace	—	1.10	.10–.25
❏ 3109	32¢	Decorating Christmas Tree	—	1.60	.10–.25
❏ 3110	32¢	Dreaming of Santa	—	1.60	.10–.25
❏ 3111	32¢	Christmas Shopping	—	1.60	.10–.25
		Block or strip of 4 (3108–3111)	6.50	—	—
❏ 3112	32¢	Madonna & Child (~3107), self-adhesive	—	1.20	.10–.25
		Booklet pane of 20	—	22.00	—
❏ 3113	32¢	Family & Fireplace (~3108), self-adhesive	—	1.20	.10–.25
❏ 3114	32¢	Decorating Tree (~3109) , self-adhesive	—	1.20	.10–.25
❏ 3115	32¢	Dreaming of Santa (~3110) , self-adhesive	—	1.20	.10–.25
❏ 3116	32¢	Christmas Shopping (~3111) , self-adhesive	—	1.20	.10–.25
		Booklet pane of 20 (5 each of 3113–3116)	—	24.00	—

3117

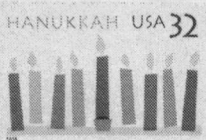

3118

3119

Scott No.			Plate Block	Unused	Used
❏ 3117	32¢	Christmas – Skaters	—	1.30	.10–.25
		Booklet pane of 18	—	23.00	.10–.25
❏ 3118	32¢	Hanukkah	4.00	1.10	.10–.25
❏ 3119	$1	Cycling, souvenir sheet of 2	—	4.00	—
		Any single stamp	—	1.10	.10–.25

3120

3121

3122

3123

3124

3125

Scott No.			Plate Block	Unused	Used
1997.					
❑ 3120	32¢	Year of the Ox	4.25	1.35	.10–.25
❑ 3121	32¢	Benjamin O. Davis, Sr.	4.25	1.50	.10–.25
❑ 3122	32¢	Statue of Liberty	—	1.35	.10–.25
		Booklet pane of 20	—	27.00	—
❑ 3123	32¢	Swans	—	1.30	.10–.25
		Booklet pane of 20	—	26.00	—
❑ 3124	55¢	Swans	—	2.10	.42
		Booklet pane of 20	—	42.00	—
❑ 3125	32¢	Helping Children Learn	4.25	1.10	.10–.25

3126
(3128)

3127
(3129)

3130

3131

Scott No.			Plate Block	Unused	Used
❏ 3126	32¢	Citron	—	1.10	.10–.25
❏ 3127	32¢	Flowering Pineapple	—	1.10	.10–.25
		Booklet pane of 20 (10 each 3126–3127)	—	22.00	—
❏ 3128	32¢	Citron (~3126)	—	2.00	1.00
❏ 3129	32¢	Flowering Pineapple (~3127)	—	2.00	1.00
		Booklet pane of 5 (2 of 3128; 3 of 3129)	—	10.00	—

NOTE: Nos. 3126–3127 measure 19½ x 26½ mm; Nos. 3128–3129 measure 18½ x 24 mm.

❏ 3130	32¢	Pacific 97 – Ship	—	1.10	.10–.25
❏ 3131	32¢	Pacific 97 – Stagecoach	—	1.10	.10–.25
		Se-tenant pair (3130–3131)	—	3.00	—

Scott No.			PNC Strip (5)	Unused	Used

Coil Stamps. Linerless Self-Adhesive.

❏ 3132	(25¢)	Jukebox (~2911)	16.00	2.30	.75
❏ 3133	32¢	Flag over Porch (~2897)	7.00	1.80	1.00

NOTE: Nos. 3121 and 3122 are not mounted on backing paper (liner) as are other self-adhesive coil stamps.

3134   3135

3136

Scott No.			Plate Block	Unused	Used
1997.					
❏ 3134	32¢	Thornton Wilder	4.25	1.10	.44
❏ 3135	32¢	Raoul Wallenberg	4.25	1.10	.10–.25
❏ 3136	32¢	Dinosaurs, pane of 15	—	20.00	—
❏ 3136a–o		Any single stamp	—	1.10	.70

3137
(3138)

Scott No.			Plate Block	Unused	Used
☐ 3137	32¢	Bugs Bunny		1.10	.10–.25
		Pane of 10	—	12.00	—

NOTE: Die cutting on No. 3137 does not cut into backing.

☐ 3138	32¢	Bugs Bunny (~3137)	—	2.00	.10–.25
		Pane of 10	—	20.00	—

NOTE: Die cutting on No. 3138 cuts through the backing. Used examples of Nos. 3137 and 3138 are identical in appearance. Once removed from backing paper they cannot be distinguished from one another.

☐ 3138	32¢	Booklet pane of 10,			
		right stamp w/o die cut	—	175.00	—

3139

3140

Scott No.			Plate Block	Unused	Used
❏ 3139	50¢	Franklin, pane of 12	—	20.00	—
❏		Single stamp	—	2.00	.42
❏ 3140	60¢	Washington, pane of 12	—	20.00	—
		Single stamp	—	2.30	.42

3141

3142

Scott No.			Plate Block	Unused	Used
❏ 3141	32¢	Marshall Plan	4.00	1.10	.10–.25
❏ 3142	32¢	Classic Aircraft, pane of 20	—	24.00	—
❏ 3142a–t		Any single stamp	—	1.10	.10–.25

3143–3146

3147	3148

3149	3150

Scott No.			Plate Block	Unused	Used
❏ 3143	32¢	Bear Bryant	—	1.40	1.00
❏ 3144	32¢	Pop Warner	—	1.40	1.00
❏ 3145	32¢	Vince Lombardi	—	1.40	1.00
❏ 3146	32¢	George Halas	—	1.40	1.00
		Block of 4 (3143–3146)	6.00	—	—
❏ 3147	32¢	Vince Lombardi	4.25	1.40	1.00
❏ 3148	32¢	Bear Bryant	4.25	1.25	1.00
❏ 3149	32¢	Pop Warner	4.25	1.25	1.00
❏ 3150	32¢	George Halas	4.25	1.25	1.00

NOTE: Nos. 3147–3150 were issued in individual (not se-tenant) panes and stamps contain a red stripe above the coach's name. Nos. 3143–3146 were issued in se-tenant panes and do not contain a red stripe above the coach's name.

3151

Scott No.			Plate Block	Unused	Used
❏ 3151	32¢	American Dolls, pane of 15	—	25.00	—
❏ 3151a–o		Any single stamp	—	1.10	.10–.25

3152   3153

3154–3157

Scott No.			Plate Block	Unused	Used
❏ 3152	32¢	Humphrey Bogart	4.25	1.50	.10–.25
❏ 3153	32¢	Stars & Stripes Forever	4.25	1.25	.10–.25
❏ 3154	32¢	Lily Pons	—	1.50	1.00
❏ 3155	32¢	Richard Tucker	—	1.50	1.00
❏ 3156	32¢	Lawrence Tibbett	—	1.50	1.00
❏ 3157	32¢	Rosa Ponselle	—	1.50	1.00
		Block or strip of 4 (3154–3157)	5.00	—	—

3158–3165

3166

3167

Scott No.			Plate Block	Unused	Used
❑ 3158	32¢	Leopold Stokowski	—	1.70	1.00
❑ 3159	32¢	Arthur Fiedler	—	1.70	1.00
❑ 3160	32¢	George Szell	—	1.70	1.00
❑ 3161	32¢	Eugene Ormandy	—	1.70	1.00
❑ 3162	32¢	Samuel Barber	—	1.70	1.00
❑ 3163	32¢	Ferde Grofé	—	1.70	1.00
❑ 3164	32¢	Charles Ives	—	1.70	1.00
❑ 3165	32¢	Louis Moreau Gottschalk	—	1.70	1.00
		Block of 8 (3158–3163)	14.00 (8)	—	—
❑ 3166	32¢	Padre Félix Varela	5.00	1.10	1.00
❑ 3167	32¢	U.S. Air Force	5.00	1.10	.10–.25

3168–3172

3173   **3174**   **3175**

3176   **3177**

Scott No.			Plate Block	Unused	Used
❏ 3168	32¢	Phantom of the Opera	—	1.50	1.00
❏ 3169	32¢	Dracula	—	1.50	1.00
❏ 3170	32¢	Frankenstein	—	1.50	1.00
❏ 3171	32¢	The Mummy	—	1.50	1.00
❏ 3172	32¢	Wolf Man	—	1.50	1.00
		Strip of 5 (3168–3172)	—	7.50	—
❏ 3173	32¢	Supersonic Flight	5.50	1.10	.10–.25
❏ 3174	32¢	Women in the Military	5.50	1.10	.10–.25
❏ 3175	32¢	Kwanzaa	5.50	1.00	.10–.25
❏ 3176	32¢	Christmas – Madonna & Child	—	1.10	.10–.25
		Booklet pane of 20	—	22.00	—
❏ 3177	32¢	Christmas – Holly	—	1.10	.10–.25
		Booklet pane of 20	—	22.00	—

3178

3179

3180

3181

Scott No.			Plate Block	Unused	Used
❏ 3178	$3	Mars Rover, souvenir sheet	—	10.00	—
1998.					
❏ 3179	32¢	Year of the Tiger	4.00	1.40	.10–.25
❏ 3180	32¢	Alpine Skiing	5.00	1.40	.10–.25
❏ 3181	32¢	Madam C.J. Walker	4.00	1.40	.10–.25

3182

3183

3184

3185

Scott No.		Plate Block	Unused	Used
Celebrate the Century.				
❑ 3182	32¢ 1900s, pane of 15	—	15.00	—
❑ 3182a–o	Any single stamp	—	1.00	.10–.25
❑ 3183	32¢ 1910s, pane of 15	—	15.00	—
❑ 3183a–o	Any single stamp	—	1.00	.10–.25
❑ 3184	32¢ 1920s, pane of 15	—	15.00	—
❑ 3184a–o	Any single stamp	—	1.00	.10–.25
❑ 3185	32¢ 1930s, pane of 15	—	15.00	—
❑ 3185a–o	Any single stamp	—	1.00	.10–.25

3186

3187

3188

3189

Scott No.		Plate Block	Unused	Used
❑ 3186	33¢ 1940s, pane of 15	—	15.00	—
❑ 3186a–o	Any single stamp	—	1.00	.10–.25
❑ 3187	33¢ 1950s, pane of 15	—	15.00	—
❑ 3187a–o	Any single stamp	—	1.00	.10–.25
❑ 3188	33¢ 1960s, pane of 15	—	15.00	—
❑ 3188a–o	Any single stamp	—	1.00	.10–.25
❑ 3189	33¢ 1970s, pane of 15	—	15.00	—
❑ 3189a–o	Any single stamp	—	1.00	.10–.25

3190   **3191**

Scott No.		Plate Block	Unused	Used
❑ 3190	33¢ 1980s, pane of 15	—	15.00	—
❑ 3190a–o	Any single stamp	—	1.00	.10–.25
❑ 3191	33¢ 1990s, pane of 15	—	15.00	—
❑ 3191a–o	Any single stamp	—	1.00	.10–.25

3192

3193–3197

 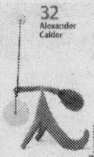   

3198–3202

Scott No.			Plate Block	Unused	Used
1998.					
❏ 3192	32¢	Remember the Maine	5.00	1.10	.10–.25
❏ 3193	32¢	Southern Magnolia	—	1.40	.10–.25
❏ 3194	32¢	Blue Paloverde	—	1.40	.10–.25
❏ 3195	32¢	Yellow Poplar	—	1.40	.10–.25
❏ 3196	32¢	Prairie Crab Apple	—	1.40	.10–.25
❏ 3197	32¢	Pacific Dogwood	—	1.40	.10–.25
		Strip of 5 (3193-3197)	14.00 (10)	8.50	—
❏ 3198	32¢	Black Cascade, 13 Verticals, 1959	—	1.25	—
❏ 3199	32¢	Untitled, 1965	—	1.25	1.00
❏ 3200	32¢	Rearing Stallion, 1928	—	1.25	1.00
❏ 3201	32¢	Portrait of a Young Man, c. 1945	—	1.25	1.00
❏ 3202	32¢	Un Effet du Japonais, 1945	—	1.25	1.00
		Strip of 5 (3198-3202)	—	7.00	—

3203

3204
(3205)

Scott No.			Plate Block	Unused	Used
❏ 3203	32¢	Cinco de Mayo	5.00	1.10	.10–.25
❏ 3204	32¢	Sylvester & Tweety	—	1.30	.10–.25
		Pane of 10	—	12.50	—
❏ 3205	32¢	Sylvester & Tweety	—	1.30	.10–.25
		Pane of 10 no die cutting	—	24.00	—

NOTE: The stamp in the right panel of No. 3204 contains a die cut; the stamp in the right panel of No. 3205 does not.

3206

Scott No.			Plate Block	Unused	Used
❏ 3206	32¢	Wisconsin Statehood	4.00	1.40	.42

3207
(3207A)

3208
(3208A)

Scott No.			PNC Strip (5)	Unused	Used
Coil Stamps.					
❏ 3207	(5¢)	Wetlands—Nonprofit Org.	4.15	.35	.10–.25
❏ 3207A	(5¢)	Wetlands (~3207), self-adhesive	4.15	.35	.10–.25
❏ 3208	(25¢)	Diner—Presorted First-Class	7.00	1.10	.42
❏ 3208A	(25¢)	Diner (3208), self-adhesive	7.00	1.10	.42

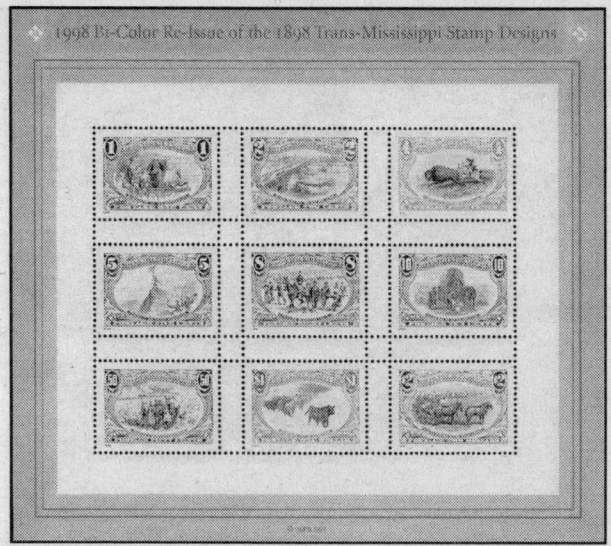

3209

Scott No.			Plate Block	Unused	Used
1998.					
❏ 3209		1989 Trans-Mississippi reissue Sheet of 9	—	20.00	—
❏ 3209a	1¢	Marquette on the Mississippi	—	1.10	.10–.25
❏ 3209b	2¢	Farming in the West	—	1.10	.10–.25
❏ 3209c	4¢	Indian Hunting Buffalo	—	1.10	.10–.25
❏ 3209d	5¢	Fremont on Rocky Mountains	—	1.10	.10–.25
❏ 3209e	8¢	Troops Guarding Train	—	1.10	.10–.25
❏ 3209f	10¢	Hardships of Emigration	—	1.10	.10–.25
❏ 3209g	50¢	Western Mining Prospector	—	1.10	.10–.25
❏ 3209h	$1	Western Cattle in Storm	—	1.10	.10–.25
❏ 3209l	$2	Mississippi Bridge	—	1.10	.10–.25

NOTE: The reissued stamps are bicolor and contain the date "1998" in the lower right corner. Stamps of the original issue of 1898 are monocolor and contain no date at lower right. Once separated from their respective sheets, Nos. 3209h and 3210 are indistinguishable.

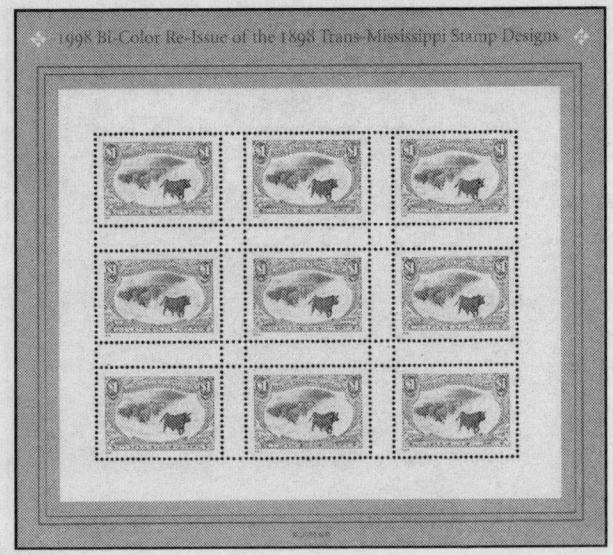

3210

Scott No.			Plate Block	Unused	Used
❑ 3210	$1	Cattle in Storm, sheet of 9	—	30.00	—

3211

3212–3215

Scott No.			Plate Block	Unused	Used
❑ 3211	32¢	Berlin Airlift	4.00	1.10	.10–.25
❑ 3212	32¢	Leadbelly	—	1.90	1.00
❑ 3213	32¢	Woody Guthrie	—	1.90	1.00
❑ 3214	32¢	Sonny Terry	—	1.90	1.00
❑ 3215	32¢	Josh White	—	1.90	1.00
		Block or strip of 4 (3212-3215)	7.60	7.60	—

3216–3219

3220

3221

Scott No.			Plate Block	Unused	Used
❏ 3216	32¢	Mahalia Jackson	—	1.90	1.00
❏ 3217	32¢	Roberta Martin	—	1.90	1.00
❏ 3218	32¢	Clara Ward	—	1.90	1.00
❏ 3219	32¢	Sister Rosetta	—	1.90	1.00
		Block or strip of 4 (3216–3219)	7.60	7.60	—
❏ 3220	32¢	Spanish Settlement	4.00	1.10	.10–.25
❏ 3221	32¢	Stephen Vincent Benét	—	1.10	.10–.25

3222–3225

3226

3227

3228
(3229)

Scott No.			Plate Block	Unused	Used
❏ 3222	32¢	Antillean Euphonia	—	1.75	.50
❏ 3223	32¢	Green-throated Carib	—	1.75	.50
❏ 3224	32¢	Crested Honeycreeper	—	1.75	.50
❏ 3225	32¢	Cardinal Honeyeater	—	1.75	.50
		Block of 4 (3222–3225)	5.00	4.00	—
❏ 3226	32¢	Alfred Hitchcock	4.00	1.80	.10–.20
❏ 3227	32¢	Organ & Tissue Donation	4.00	1.10	.10–.20

Scott No.			PNC Strip (5)	Unused	Used
Coil Stamps.					
❏ 3228	(10¢)	Bicycle Handlebar, self-adhesive	6.00	.45	.10–.25
❏ 3229	(10¢)	Bicycle (~3228), water-activated gum	6.00	.45	.10–.25

3230–3234

3235

Scott No.			Plate Block	Unused	Used
1998.					
❑ 3230	32¢	Bright Eyes - Dog	—	1.90	.42
❑ 3231	32¢	Bright Eyes - Fish	—	1.90	.42
❑ 3232	32¢	Bright Eyes - Cat	—	1.90	.42
❑ 3233	32¢	Bright Eyes - Parakeet	—	1.90	.42
❑ 3234	32¢	Bright Eyes - Hamster	—	1.90	.42
		Strip of 5 (3230–3234)	19.00 (10)	9.50	—
❑ 3235	32¢	Klondike Gold Rush	5.00	1.25	.10–.25

3236

Scott No.			Plate Block	Unused	Used
❏ 3236	32¢	American Art, pane of 20	—	38.00	—
❏ 3236a–t		Any single stamp	—	1.10	.10–.25

3237

3238–3242

3243

3244

Scott No.			Plate Block	Unused	Used
❏ 3237	32¢	Ballet	5.00	1.45	.10–.25
❏ 3238	32¢	Futuristic Truck	—	1.20	1.00
❏ 3239	32¢	Pod-craft in Flight	—	1.20	1.00
❏ 3240	32¢	Observer in Space Suit	—	1.20	1.00
❏ 3241	32¢	Planet Rover	—	1.20	1.00
❏ 3242	32¢	Spaceport Dome	—	1.20	1.00
		Strip of 5 (3238-3242)	—	6.00	—
❏ 3243	32¢	Giving & Sharing	5.00	1.10	.10–.25
❏ 3244	32¢	Christmas - Madonna & Child	—	1.00	.10–.25
		Booklet pane of 20	—	20.00	—

3245–3248
(3249–3252)

3257
(3258)

Scott No.			Plate Block	Unused	Used
❏ 3245	32¢	Evergreen Wreath	—	2.50	1.00
❏ 3246	32¢	Victorian Wreath	—	2.50	1.00
❏ 3247	32¢	Chili Pepper Wreath	—	2.50	1.00
❏ 3248	32¢	Tropical Wreath	—	2.50	1.00
		Booklet pane of 20 (3245-3248)	—	50.00	—
❏ 3249	32¢	Evergreen Wreath (~3245)	—	2.50	1.00
❏ 3250	32¢	Victorian Wreath (~3246)	—	2.50	1.00
❏ 3251	32¢	Chili Pepper Wreath (~3247)	—	2.50	1.00
❏ 3252	32¢	Tropical Wreath (~3248)	—	2.50	1.00
		Block or strip of 4 (3249–3252)	10.00	10.00	—

NOTE: Nos. 3249–3252 measure 23 x 30 mm.

❏ 3257	(1¢)	Weather Vane, white "U.S.A."	1.00	.30	.10–.25
❏ 3258	(1¢)	Weather Vane, blue "U.S.A."	1.00	.30	.10–.25

3259
(3263, 3353)

3260
(3264–3269)

3261

3262

Scott No.			Plate Block	Unused	Used
❏ 3259	22¢	Uncle Sam	5.00	.75	.10–.35
❏ 3260	(33¢)	Uncle Sam's Hat	5.00	1.10	.42
❏ 3261	$3.20	Space Shuttle	30.00	10.75	5.00
❏ 3262	$11.75	Space Shuttle Piggyback	110.00	38.00	15.00

Scott No.			PNC Strip (5)	Unused	Used
Coil Stamps.					
❏ 3263	22¢	Uncle Sam (~3259)	6.00	.95	.10–.35
❏ 3264	(33¢)	Uncle Sam's Hat (~3260), water-activated gum	8.00	1.00	.75
❏ 3265	(33¢)	Hat (~3260), self-adhesive, square corners	8.00	1.50	.10–.25
❏ 3266	(33¢)	Hat (~3260), self-adhesive, rounded corners	9.00	3.00	2.00

Scott No.			Plate Block	Unused	Used
Booklet Stamps.					
❏ 3267	(33¢)	Hat (~3260), die cut 9.9	—	1.35	.10–.25
		Booklet pane of 10	—	14.00	—
❏ 3268	(33¢)	Hat (~3260), die cut 11 or 11½	—	1.50	.10–.25
		Booklet pane of 10	—	15.00	—
		Booklet pane of 20	—	30.00	—

Scott No.			Plate Block	Unused	Used
❑ 3269	(33¢)	Hat (~3260), die cut 8	—	1.40	1.00
		Booklet pane of 10	—	14.00	—
		Booklet pane of 18	—	25.00	—

3270
(3271)

Scott No.			PNC Strip (5)	Unused	Used
Coil Stamps.					
❑ 3270	(10¢)	Eagle & Shield, water-activated gum, perforated	4.00	.60	.10–.25
❑ 3271	(10¢)	Eagle & Shield, self-adhesive, die cut	5.00	.50	.10–.25

NOTE: See Nos. 2602–2604 for Eagle & Shield stamps inscribed "USA Bulk Rate" or "Bulk Rate USA."

3272

3273

Scott No.			Plate Block	Unused	Used
1999.					
❑ 3272	33¢	Year of the Rabbit	4.00	1.40	.10–.25
❑ 3273	33¢	Malcolm X	5.00	1.65	.10–.25

3274   **3275**   **3276**   **3277**
(3278, 3279–
3282)

Scott No.			Plate Block	Unused	Used
❑ 3274	33¢	Love - Lacy Valentine	—	1.25	.10–.25
		Booklet pane of 20	—	20.00	.10–.25
❑ 3275	55¢	Love - Lacy Valentine	—	1.80	.10–.25
❑ 3276	33¢	Hospice Care	5.00	1.15	.10–.25
❑ 3277	33¢	Flag & City, water-activated gum, perforated	8.00	3.00	1.00
❑ 3278	33¢	Flag & City (~3277), self-adhesive, black date	—	1.15	.50
		Booklet pane of 10	—	12.00	—
		Booklet pane of 20	—	22.00	—
❑ 3279	33¢	Flag & City (~3277), self-adhesive, red date	—	1.50	.10–.25
		Booklet pane of 10	—	15.00	—

Scott No.			PNC Strip (5)	Unused	Used

Coil Stamps.

❑ 3280	33¢	Flag & City (~3277), water-activated gum, perforated	8.00	1.30	.10–.35
❑ 3281	33¢	Flag & City (~3277), self-adhesive, square corners	8.00	1.50	.10–.35
❑ 3282	33¢	Flag & City (~3277), self-adhesive, rounded corners	9.00	1.50	.10–.35

3283

3286

3287

3288–3292

Scott No.			Plate Block	Unused	Used
1999.					
❏ 3283	33¢	Flag & Chalkboard, self-adhesive	—	1.45	.42
		Booklet pane of 18	—	26.00	—
❏ 3286	33¢	Irish Immigration	5.00	1.20	.10–.25
❏ 3287	33¢	Alfred Lunt & Lynn Fontanne	5.00	1.25	.10–.25
❏ 3288	33¢	Arctic Hare	—	1.25	1.00
❏ 3289	33¢	Arctic Fox	—	1.25	1.00
❏ 3290	33¢	Snowy Owl	—	1.25	1.00
❏ 3291	33¢	Polar Bear	—	1.25	1.00
❏ 3292	33¢	Gray Wolf	—	1.25	1.00
		Strip of 5 (3288-3293)	12.50 (10)	6.25	—

3293

Scott No.			Plate Block	Unused	Used
❑ 3293	33¢	Sonoran Desert, pane of 10	—	20.00	—
❑ 3293a–j		Any single stamp	—	2.00	.78

3294–3297
(3298–3301, 3302–3305)

Scott No.			Plate Block	Unused	Used
❏ 3294	33¢	Blueberries	—	1.50	.10–.25
❏ 3295	33¢	Raspberries	—	1.50	.10–.25
❏ 3296	33¢	Strawberries	—	1.50	.10–.25
❏ 3297	33¢	Blackberries	—	1.50	.10–.25
		Booklet pane of 20 (3294-3297)	—	30.00	—

NOTE: Nos. 3294–3297 exist dated either 1999 or 2000. Prices are the same for both. Nos. 3294–3297 are die cut 11½ x 11½. Nos. 3298–3301 are die cut 9½ x 10.

❏ 3298	33¢	Blueberries (~3294)	—	1.50	.10–.25
❏ 3299	33¢	Raspberries (~3295)	—	1.50	.10–.25
❏ 3300	33¢	Strawberries (~3296)	—	1.50	.10–.25
❏ 3301	33¢	Blackberries (~3297)	—	1.50	.10–.25
		Booklet pane (3298-3301)	—	6.00	—

Scott No.			PNC Strip (5)	Unused	Used

Coil Stamps.

❏ 3302	33¢	Blueberries (~3294)	—	1.50	.10–.35
❏ 3303	33¢	Raspberries (~3295)	—	1.50	.10–.35
❏ 3304	33¢	Strawberries (~3296)	—	1.50	.10–.35
❏ 3305	33¢	Blackberries (~3297)	—	1.50	.10–.35
		Strip of 4 (3302-3305)	—	6.00	—

NOTE: See also Nos. 3404–3407. Nos. 3302–3305 contain straight edges at top and bottom; Nos. 3404–3407 contain straight edges at sides.

3306
(3307)

Scott No.			Plate Block	Unused	Used
1999.					
❏ 3306	33¢	Daffy Duck	—	1.30	.10–.25
		Pane of 10	—	13.00	
❏ 3307	33¢	Daffy Duck	—	1.30	.10–.25
		Pane of 10, right stamp w/o die cut	—	18.00	—

3308

3309

3310–3313

Scott No.			Plate Block	Unused	Used
❑ 3308	33¢	Ayn Rand	5.00	1.10	.10–.25
❑ 3309	33¢	Cinco de Mayo	5.00	1.10	.10–.25
❑ 3310	33¢	Bird of Paradise	—	1.45	.10–.25
❑ 3311	33¢	Royal Poinciana	—	1.45	.10–.25
❑ 3312	33¢	Gloriosa	—	1.45	.10–.25
❑ 3313	33¢	Chinese Hibiscus	—	1.45	.10–.25
		Booklet pane of 20			
		(3310-3315)	—	28.50	—

3316

3314   **3315**

3317–3320

Scott No.			Plate Block	Unused	Used
❏ 3314	33¢	John & William Bartram	5.00	1.10	.10–.25
❏ 3315	33¢	Prostate Cancer Awareness	5.00	1.10	.10–.25
❏ 3316	33¢	California Gold Rush	5.00	1.10	.10–.25
❏ 3317	33¢	Fish - Yellow & Red Fish	—	1.35	.42
❏ 3318	33¢	Fish - Fish & Thermometer	—	1.35	.42
❏ 3319	33¢	Fish - Blue Fish	—	1.35	.42
❏ 3320	33¢	Fish - Hermit Crab	—	1.35	.42
		Strip of 4 (3317-3320)	—	5.50	—

3321–3324

3325–3328

Scott No.			Plate Block	Unused	Used
❏ 3321	33¢	Extreme Sports – Skateboarding	—	1.50	.42
❏ 3322	33¢	Extreme Sports – BMX Biking	—	1.50	.42
❏ 3323	33¢	Extreme Sports – Snowboarding	—	1.50	.42
❏ 3324	33¢	Extreme Sports – Inline Skating	—	1.50	.42
		Block of 4 (3321–3324)	6.00	4.00	.42
❏ 3325	33¢	Free-blown Glass	—	1.90	.42
❏ 3326	33¢	Mold-blown Glass	—	1.90	.42
❏ 3327	33¢	Pressed Glass	—	1.90	.42
❏ 3328	33¢	Art Glass	—	1.90	.42
		Block or strip of 4 (3225–3228)	7.50	7.50	—

3329   **3330**

3331

3332

3333–3337

Scott No.			Plate Block	Unused	Used
❑ 3329	33¢	James Cagney	4.00	1.65	.10–.25
❑ 3330	33¢	General Billy Mitchell	6.00	1.75	.50
❑ 3331	33¢	Honoring Those Who Served	5.00	1.55	.10–.25
❑ 3332	45¢	Universal Postal Union	6.00	1.75	.75
❑ 3333	33¢	Trains – the "Daylight"	—	1.30	.42
❑ 3334	33¢	Trains – the "Congressional"	—	1.30	.42
❑ 3335	33¢	Trains – the "20th Century Limited"	—	1.30	.42
❑ 3336	33¢	Trains – the "Hiawatha"	—	1.30	.42
❑ 3337	33¢	Trains – the "Super Chief"	—	1.30	.42
		Strip of 5 (3333–3337)	13.00 (10)	6.50	—

3338

3339–3344

Scott No.			Plate Block	Unused	Used
❑ 3338	33¢	Frederick Law Olmsted	4.00	1.10	.10–.25
❑ 3339	33¢	Max Steiner	—	1.50	1.00
❑ 3340	33¢	Dmitri Tiomkin	—	1.50	1.00
❑ 3341	33¢	Bernard Herrmann	—	1.50	1.00
❑ 3342	33¢	Franz Waxman	—	1.00	1.00
❑ 3343	33¢	Alfred Newman	—	1.50	1.00
❑ 3344	33¢	Erich Wolfgang Korngold	—	1.75	1.00
		Block of 6 (3339–3344)	8.00 (6)	7.50	—

3345–3350

Scott No.			Plate Block	Unused	Used
❑ 3345	33¢	Ira & George Gershwin	—	1.35	1.00
❑ 3346	33¢	Lerner & Loewe	—	1.35	1.00
❑ 3347	33¢	Lorenz Hart	—	1.35	1.00
❑ 3348	33¢	Rodgers & Hammerstein	—	1.35	1.00
❑ 3349	33¢	Meredith Willson	—	1.35	1.00
❑ 3350	33¢	Frank Loesser	—	1.35	1.00
		Block of 6 (3345–3350)	8.00 (6)	8.00	—

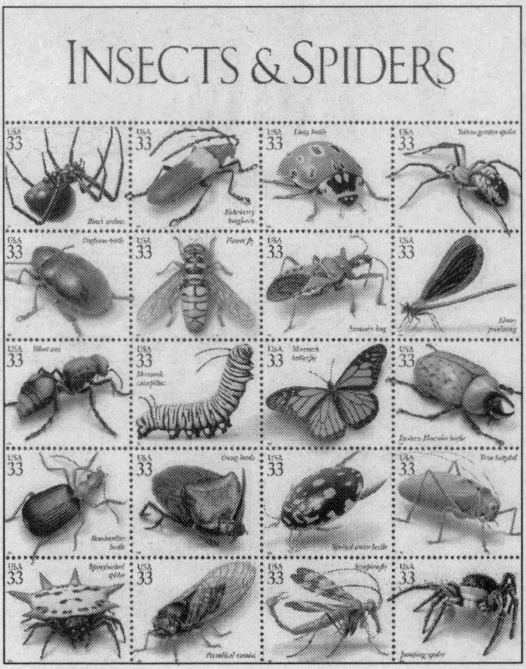

INSECTS & SPIDERS

3351

Scott No.			Plate Block	Unused	Used
❏ 3351	33¢	Insects & Spiders, pane of 20	—	18.00	—
❏ 3351a–t		Any single stamp	—	1.10	.10–.25

3352

Scott No.			Plate Block	Unused	Used
❑ 3352	33¢	Hanukkah	4.00	1.10	.10–.25

Scott No.			PNC Strip (5)	Unused	Used

Coil Stamp.

❑ 3353	22¢	Uncle Sam (~3259), water-activated gum, perforated	6.00	1.10	.42

3354   **3355**

Scott No.			Plate Block	Unused	Used
1999.					
❑ 3354	33¢	NATO 50th Anniversary	5.00	1.10	.10–.25
❑ 3355	33¢	Christmas – Madonna & Child	—	1.10	.10–.25
		Booklet pane of 20	—	21.00	—

3356–3359
(3360–3363, 3364–3367)

Scott No.			Plate Block	Unused	Used
❑ 3356	33¢	Leaping Stag, maroon & gold	—	1.75	.42
❑ 3357	33¢	Leaping Stag, blue & gold	—	1.75	.42
❑ 3358	33¢	Leaping Stag, violet & gold	—	1.75	.42
❑ 3359	33¢	Leaping Stag, green & gold	—	1.75	.42
		Block or strip of 4			
		(3356–3359)	7.00	7.00	—
❑ 3360	33¢	Stag, maroon & gold (~3356)	—	1.75	.10–.35
❑ 3361	33¢	Stag, blue & gold (~3357)	—	1.75	.10–.35
❑ 3362	33¢	Stag, violet & gold (~3358)	—	1.75	.10–.35
❑ 3363	33¢	Stag, green & gold (3359)	—	1.75	.10–.35
		Booklet pane of 20			
		(3360–3363)	—	35.00	—

NOTE: The frameline on Nos. 3356–3369 is narrower than the frameline on Nos. 3360–3363.

❑ 3364	33¢	Stag, maroon & gold (~3356)	—	1.75	.42
❑ 3365	33¢	Stag, blue & gold (~3357)	—	1.75	.42
❑ 3366	33¢	Stag, violet & gold (~3358)	—	1.75	.42
❑ 3367	33¢	green & gold (3359)	—	1.75	.42
		Booklet pane of 20			
		(3364–3367)	—	35.00	—

NOTE: Nos. 3364–3367 measure 21 x 18 mm.

3368

3369

3370

3371

Scott No.			Plate Block	Unused	Used
❏ 3368	33¢	Kwanzaa	5.35	1.10	.10–.25
❏ 3369	33¢	Infant New Year	5.35	1.10	.10–.25
❏ 3370	33¢	Year of the Dragon	5.35	1.10	.10–.25
❏ 3371	33¢	Patricia Roberts Harris	5.35	1.10	.10–.25

3372

3373–3377

Scott No.			Plate Block	Unused	Used
❑ 3372	33¢	Los Angeles Class Submarine	5.00	1.25	.10–.25
❑ 3373	22¢	S Class Submarine	—	1.50	.10–.25
❑ 3374	33¢	Los Angeles Class Submarine	—	1.75	.10–.25
❑ 3375	55¢	Ohio Class Submarine	—	3.00	1.35
❑ 3376	60¢	USS Holland	—	3.25	1.65
❑ 3377	$3.20	Gato Class Submarine	—	17.50	5.50
		Booklet pane of 5 (3373–3377)	—	20.00	—
		Intact booklet with 2 panes (3373–3377)		18.00	—

NOTE: No. 3372 contains microprinted letters "USPS" at the base of its conning tower; No. 3374 does not. Each of the two booklet panes in the booklet contain a different marginal text.

3378

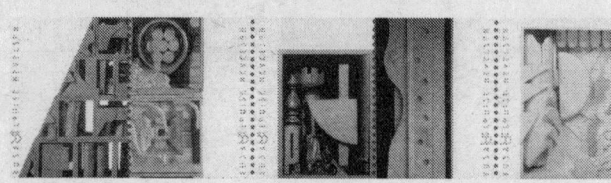

3379–3383

Scott No.			Plate Block	Unused	Used
❑ 3378	33¢	Rain Forest, pane of 10	—	11.00	—
❑ 3378a–j		Any single stamp	—	1.25	.75
❑ 3379	33¢	Nevelson – Silent Music I	1.40	1.25	.75
❑ 3380	33¢	Nevelson – Royal Tide I	—	1.25	.75
❑ 3381	33¢	Nevelson – Black Chord	—	1.25	.75
❑ 3382	33¢	Nevelson – Nightsphere Light	—	1.25	.75
❑ 3383	33¢	Nevelson – Wedding Chapel I	—	1.25	.75
		Strip of 5 (3379–3381)	18.00 (10)	4.10	—

3384–3388

3389

3390

Scott No.			Plate Block	Unused	Used
❏ 3384	33¢	Eagle Nebula	—	1.25	.42
❏ 3385	33¢	Ring Nebula	—	1.25	.42
❏ 3386	33¢	Lagoon Nebula	—	1.25	.42
❏ 3387	33¢	Egg Nebula	—	1.25	.42
❏ 3388	33¢	Galaxy NGC 1316	—	1.25	.42
		Strip of 5 (3384–3388)	6.25 (5)	6.25	—
❏ 3389	33¢	American Samoa	5.00	1.25	.42
❏ 3390	33¢	Library of Congress	5.00	1.25	.10–.25

3391
(3392)

Scott No.			Plate Block	Unused	Used
❑ 3391	33¢	Roadrunner & Wile E. Coyote	—	1.10	.10–.25
		Pane of 10	—	11.00	—
❑ 3392	33¢	Roadrunner & Wile E. Coyote	—	1.10	.42
		Pane of 10, right stamp			
		w/o die cut	—	20.00	—

3393–3396

3397

3398

Scott No.			Plate Block	Unused	Used
❏ 3393	33¢	Major General John Hines	—	1.25	.42
❏ 3394	33¢	General Omar Bradley	—	1.25	.42
❏ 3395	33¢	Sergeant Alvin York	—	1.25	.42
❏ 3396	33¢	Second Lt. Audie Murphy	—	1.25	.42
		Block or strip of 4 (3393–3396)	5.00	4.00	—
❏ 3397	33¢	Summer Sports – Runners	1.30	1.25	.10–.25
❏ 3398	33¢	Adoption	1.30	1.25	.10–.25

3399–3402

Scott No.			Plate Block	Unused	Used
❏ 3399	33¢	Basketball	1.40	1.35	.42
❏ 3400	33¢	Football	—	1.35	.42
❏ 3401	33¢	Soccer	—	1.35	.42
❏ 3402	33¢	Baseball	—	1.35	.42
		Block or strip of 4			
		(3399–3402)	5.50	5.50	—

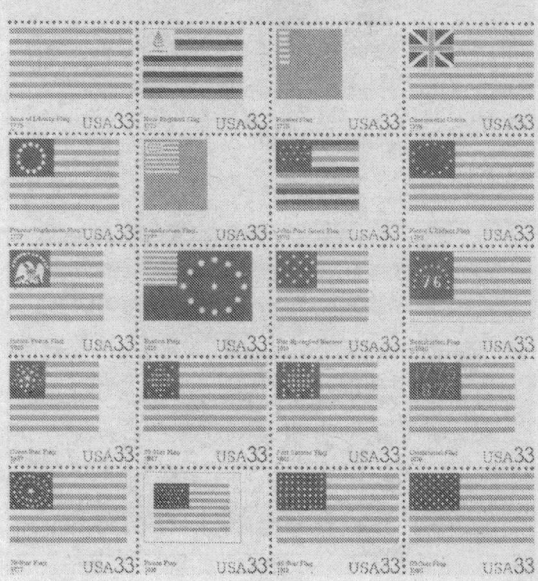

3403

Scott No.			Plate Block	Unused	Used
❑ 3403	33¢	American Flags, pane of 20	—	20.00	—
❑ 3403a–t	33¢	Any single stamp	—	1.10	.10–.25

Scott No.			PNC Strip (5)		

Coil Stamps.

❑ 3404	33¢	Blueberries (~3294)	1.50	1.10	.42
❑ 3405	33¢	Strawberries (~3296)	—	1.10	.42
❑ 3406	33¢	Blackberries (~3297)	—	1.10	.42
❑ 3407	33¢	Raspberries (~3295)	—	1.10	.42
		Strip of 4 (3404–3407)	—	4.50	—

NOTE: Nos. 3404–3407 contain straight edges at sides; Nos. 3302–3305 contain straight edges at top and bottom.

3408

Scott No.			Plate Block	Unused	Used
2000.					
❑ 3408	33¢	Baseball, pane of 20	—	20.00	—
❑ 3408a–t	33¢	Any single stamp	—	1.10	.10–.25

3409

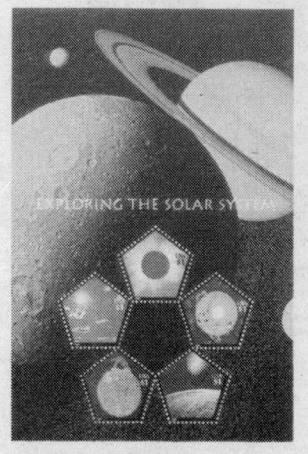

| | | 3410 | | 3411 | |
Scott No.			Plate Block	Unused	Used
❑ 3409	60¢	Probing the Vastness of Space, souvenir sheet of 6	—	25.00	—
		Any single stamp	—	4.00	1.00
❑ 3410	$1.00	Exploring the Solar System, souvenir sheet of 5	—	30.00	—
		Any single stamp	—	6.00	2.00
❑ 3411	$3.20	Escaping the Gravity of Earth, souvenir sheet of 2	—	40.00	—
		Any single stamp	—	2.00	1.00

3412

3413

Scott No.	Plate Block	Unused	Used
❏ 3412 $11.75 Space Achievement & Exploration, souvenir sheet of 1	—	40.00	—
❏ 3413 $11.75 Landing on the Moon, souvenir sheet of 1	—	40.00	—

3414–3417

Scott No.			Plate Block	Unused	Used
❏ 3414	33¢	Space Figures	—	1.25	.42
❏ 3415	33¢	Heart	—	1.25	.42
❏ 3416	33¢	Mommy Are We There Yet	—	1.25	.42
❏ 3417	33¢	Space Dog	—	1.25	.42
		Strip of 4 (3414–3417)	10.00 (8)	5.00	—

3420	**3426**	**3431**	**3432**

Distinguished Americans Series.

❏ 3420	10¢	General Joseph W. Stillwell	2.00	.55	.10–.25
❏ 3426	33¢	Claude Pepper	4.00	1.25	.44
❏ 3431	76¢	Hattie W. Caraway	7.00	3.50	.44
❏ 3432	83¢	Edna Ferber	8.00	2.50	1.05

3438

3439–3443

Scott No.			Plate Block	Unused	Used
2000.					
❑ 3438	33¢	California Statehood	4.00	1.75	.44
❑ 3439	33¢	Fanfin Anglefish	—	1.75	1.00
❑ 3440	33¢	Sea Cucumber	—	1.75	1.00
❑ 3441	33¢	Fangtooth	—	1.75	1.00
❑ 3442	33¢	Amphipod	—	1.75	1.00
❑ 3443	33¢	Medusa	—	1.75	1.00
		Strip of 5 (3438–3443)	17.50 (10)	8.75	—

3444

3445

3446

Scott No.			Plate Block	Unused	Used
❑ 3444	33¢	Thomas Wolfe	4.25	1.25	.10–.25
❑ 3445	33¢	White House	4.25	1.25	.10–.25
❑ 3446	33¢	Edward G. Robinson	4.25	3.00	2.00

3447

Scott No.		PNC Strip (5)	Unused	Used
Coil Stamp.				
❑ 3447 (10¢)	New York Public Library Lion	4.00	.80	.10–.25

3448
(3449–3450)

3451

Scott No.		Plate Block	Unused	Used
2000.				
❏ 3448 (34¢)	Flag over Farm, water-activated gum	4.00	1.10	.58
❏ 3449 (34¢)	Flag over Farm (~3448), self-adhesive, die cut 11½	5.00	1.10	.10–.25
❏ 3450 (34¢)	Flag over Farm (~3448), self-adhesive, die cut 8	—	1.10	.44
	Booklet pane of 8	—	1.10	—
❏ 3451 (34¢)	Statue of Liberty, self-adhesive	—	1.10	.10–.25
	Booklet pane of 20	—	22.00	—

3452
(3453)

Scott No.		PNC Strip (5)	Unused	Used
Coil Stamps.				
❏ 3452 (34¢)	Statue of Liberty, water-activated gum	10.00	1.10	.10–.25
❏ 3453 (34¢)	Statue of Liberty, self-adhesive	10.00	1.10	.10–.25

3454–3457
(3458–3461)

3466
(3476–3477)

Scott No.			Plate Block	Unused	Used
2000.					
❑ 3454 (34¢)	Flower – Purple		—	1.10	.10–.25
❑ 3455 (34¢)	Flower – Tan		—	1.10	.10–.25
❑ 3456 (34¢)	Flower – Green		—	1.10	.10–.25
❑ 3457 (34¢)	Flower – Red		—	1.10	.10–.25
	Booklet pane of 20 (3454–3457)		—	20.00	—
❑ 3458 (34¢)	Flower – Purple (~3454)		—	1.75	.42
❑ 3459 (34¢)	Flower – Tan (~3455)		—	1.75	.42
❑ 3460 (34¢)	Flower – Green (~3456)		—	1.75	.42
❑ 3461 (34¢)	Flower – Red (~3457)		—	1.25	.42
	Booklet pane of 6 (3458–3461)		—	6.50	—

Scott No.			PNC Strip (5)	Unused	Used
Coil Stamps.					
❑ 3462 (34¢)	Flower – Green (~3456)		—	1.75	.10–.25
❑ 3463 (34¢)	Flower – Red (~3457)		—	1.75	.10–.25
❑ 3464 (34¢)	Flower – Tan (~3455)		—	1.75	.10–.25
❑ 3465 (34¢)	Flower – Purple (~3454)		—	1.75	.10–.25
	Strip of 4 (3462–3465)		10.00	1.75	.10–.25
❑ 3466	34¢	Statue of Liberty, self-adhesive, rounded corners	5.00	1.25	.42

See also No. 3477.

3467
(3468, 3475, 3484, 3484A)

3468A
(3475A)

3469
(3470, 3495)

3471

3472

3473

Scott No.			Plate Block	Unused	Used
2001.					
❑ 3467	21¢	Buffalo, water-activated gum	5.00	1.10	.42
❑ 3468	21¢	Buffalo, self-adhesive	4.25	1.10	.42
❑ 3468A	23¢	George Washington, self-adhesive	4.25	1.10	.42
❑ 3469	34¢	Flag over Farm, water-activated gum	4.25	1.10	.42
❑ 3470	34¢	Flag over Farm (~3470), self-adhesive, die cut 11½	4.25	1.10	.42
❑ 3471	55¢	Art Deco Eagle	7.00	1.50	.75
❑ 3471A	57¢	Art Deco Eagle (~3471)	7.00	1.50	.75
❑ 3472	$3.50	Capitol Dome	35.00	12.00	4.20
❑ 3473	$12.25	Washington Monument	125.00	32.00	10.00

3487–3490

Scott No.			PNC Strip (5)	Unused	Used
Coil Stamps.					
❑ 3475	21¢	Buffalo (~3467), self-adhesive	6.00	1.00	.10–.25
❑ 3475A	23¢	George Washington (~3468A), self-adhesive	4.00	1.00	.10–.25
❑ 3476	34¢	Statue of Liberty (~3466), water-activated gum	8.00	1.50	.10–.25
❑ 3477	34¢	Liberty (~3466), self-adhesive, square corners	7.00	1.65	.10–.25
❑ 3478	34¢	Flower – Green	—	1.50	.10–.25
❑ 3479	34¢	Flower – Red	—	1.50	.10–.25
❑ 3480	34¢	Flower – Tan	—	1.50	.10–.25
❑ 3481	34¢	Flower – Purple	—	1.50	.10–.25
		Strip of 4 (3478–3481)	6.00	6.00	—

3482
(3483)

Scott No.			Plate Block	Unused	Used
2001.					
❑ 3482	20¢	George Washington, self-adhesive, die cut 11½	—	1.10	.42
		Booklet pane of 10	—	6.00	—
❑ 3483	20¢	Washington (~3482), self-adhesive, die cut 10½ x 11½	—	5.00	1.45
		Booklet pane of 10	—	20.00	—

3485	**3491** (3493)	**3492** (3494)

Scott No.			Plate Block	Unused	Used
❏ 3484	21¢	Buffalo (~3467), self-adhesive, die cut 11½	—	1.10	.75
		Booklet pane of 10	—	6.00	—
❏ 3484A	21¢	Buffalo (~3467), self-adhesive, die cut 10½ x 11½	—	5.00	1.85
		Booklet pane of 10	—	20.00	—
❏ 3485	34¢	Statue of Liberty, self-adhesive, die cut 11	—	1.10	.10–.25
		Booklet pane of 10	—	8.00	—
		Booklet pane of 20	—	16.00	—
❏ 3487	34¢	Flower – Purple (~3481)	—	1.10	.10–.25
❏ 3488	34¢	Flower – Tan (~3480)	—	1.10	.10–.25
❏ 3489	34¢	Flower – Green (~3478)	—	1.10	.10–.25
❏ 3490	34¢	Flower – Red (~3479)	—	1.10	.10–.25
		Booklet pane of 20 (3487–3480)	—	20.00	—
❏ 3491	34¢	Apple, self-adhesive, die cut 11½	—	1.25	.10–.25
❏ 3492	34¢	Orange, self-adhesive, die cut 11½	—	1.25	.10–.25
		Booklet pane of 20 (3491–3492)	—	25.00	—
❏ 3493	34¢	Apple (~3491), self-adhesive, die cut 10½ x 11½	—	1.25	.50
❏ 3494	34¢	Orange (~3492)), self-adhesive, die cut 10½ x 11½	—	1.25	.50
		Booklet pane of 20 (3493–3494)	—	4.00	—
❏ 3495	34¢	Flag over Farm (~3469), self-adhesive, die cut 8	—	1.35	.50
		Booklet pane of 18	—	24.50	—

3496

3497
(3498)

3499

3500

3501

Scott No.			Plate Block	Unused	Used
❏ 3496 (34¢)		Love – Rose	—	1.10	.10–.25
		Booklet pane of 20	—	20.00	—
❏ 3497	34¢	Love – Rose	—	1.10	.10–.25
		Booklet pane of 20	—	20.00	—
❏ 3498	34¢	Love – Rose	—	1.10	.10–.25
		Booklet pane of 20	—	20.00	—

NOTE: No. 3497 measures 19½ x 26½ mm; No. 3498 measures 18 x 21 mm.

❏ 3499	55¢	Love – Rose	6.00	2.00	.42

NOTE: No. 3551 for 57¢ stamp of similar design.

❏ 3500	34¢	Year of the Snake	5.00	1.25	.10–.25
❏ 3501	34¢	Roy Wilkins	4.00	1.75	.10–.25

3502

3503   **3504**

Scott No.			Plate Block	Unused	Used
❏ 3502	34¢	Illustrators, pane of 20	—	18.00	—
❏ 3502a–t		Any single stamp	—	1.10	.10–.25
❏ 3503	34¢	Diabetes Awareness	5.00	1.10	.10–.25
❏ 3504	34¢	Nobel Prize 1901–2001	5.00	1.10	.10–.25

3505

Scott No.			Plate Block	Unused	Used
❏ 3505	34¢	Pan-American Inverts, souvenir sheet	—	10.00	—
❏ 3505a	1¢	Ship Inverted	—	1.10	.84
❏ 3505b	2¢	Train Inverted	—	1.10	.84
❏ 3505c	4¢	Automobile Inverted	—	1.10	.84
❏ 3505d	80¢	Exposition Seal	—	4.00	2.10

NOTE: Nos. 3505a–3505c can be distinguished from the original errors by the date 2001 at lower left.

3506

3507

3508

3509

Scott No.			Plate Block	Unused	Used
❏ 3506	34¢	Great Plains Prairie, pane of 10	—	12.00	—
❏ 3506a–j		Any single stamp	—	1.10	.10–.25
❏ 3507	34¢	Snoopy	5.00	1.50	.10–.25
❏ 3508	34¢	Honoring Veterans	4.25	1.00	.10–.25
❏ 3509	34¢	Frida Kahlo	4.25	1.10	.10–.25

3510–3519

Scott No.			Plate Block	Unused	Used
❏ 3510	34¢	Ebbets Field	—	1.10	.42
❏ 3511	34¢	Tiger Stadium	—	1.10	.42
❏ 3512	34¢	Crosley Field	—	1.10	.42
❏ 3513	34¢	Yankee Stadium	—	1.10	.42
❏ 3514	34¢	Polo Grounds	—	1.10	.42
❏ 3515	34¢	Forbes Field	—	1.10	.42
❏ 3516	34¢	Fenway Park	—	1.10	.42
❏ 3517	34¢	Comisky Park	—	1.10	.42
❏ 3518	34¢	Shibe Park	—	1.10	.42
❏ 3519	34¢	Wrigley Field	—	1.10	.42
		Block of 10 (3510–3519)	11.00 (10)	11.00	—

3520

3521

3522

Scott No.		PNC Strip (5)	Unused	Used
Coil Stamp.				
❑ 3520 (10¢)	Atlas Statue, self-adhesive	4.25	.45	.10–.25

Scott No.		Plate Block	Unused	Used
2001.				
❑ 3521 34¢	Leonard Bernstein	4.25	1.40	.42

Scott No.		PNC Strip (5)	Unused	Used
Coil Stamp.				
❑ 3522 (15¢)	Woody Wagon, self-adhesive	4.25	.80	.42

3523

Scott No.		Plate Block	Unused	Used
2001.				
❑ 3523 34¢	Lucille Ball	5.00	1.80	.10–.25

 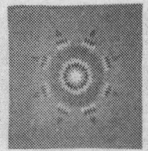  

AMISH QUILT 34 USA   AMISH QUILT 34 USA   AMISH QUILT 34 USA   AMISH QUILT 34 USA

3524–3527

Venus Flytrap   Yellow Trumpet   Cobra Lily   English Sundew   Venus Flytrap

3528–3531

Scott No.			Plate Block	Unused	Used
❏ 3524	34¢	Amish quilt – Diamond in Square	—	1.25	.38
❏ 3525	34¢	Amish quilt – Starburst	—	1.25	.38
❏ 3526	34¢	Amish quilt – Diamond Pattern	—	1.25	.38
❏ 3427	34¢	Amish quilt – Double Ninepatch Pattern	—	1.25	.38
		Block or strip of 4 (3424–3427)	5.00	4.00	—
❏ 3528	34¢	Venus Flytrap	—	1.50	.38
❏ 3529	34¢	Yellow Trumpet	—	1.50	.38
❏ 3530	34¢	Cobra Lily	—	1.50	.38
❏ 3531	34¢	English Sundew	—	1.50	.38
		Block or strip of 4 (3528–3531)	6.00	6.00	—

3532   **3533**

3534
(3535)

Scott No.			Plate Block	Unused	Used
❏ 3532	34¢	Eid Mubarak	4.25	1.10	.10–.30
❏ 3533	34¢	Enrico Fermi	4.25	1.10	.10–.30
❏ 3534	34¢	Porky Pig	—	1.10	.10–.25
		Pane of 10	—	10.00	—
❏ 3535	34¢	Porky Pig	—	1.50	.42
		Pane of 10, right stamp w/o die cut	—	40.00	—

3536

3537–3540
(3541–3544)

Scott No.			Plate Block	Unused	Used
❑ 3536	34¢	Christmas – Madonna & Child	—	1.10	.38
		Booklet pane of 20	—	16.00	.38
❑ 3537	34¢	Santa & Rocking Horse, black inscription	—	1.25	.38
❑ 3538	34¢	Santa & Tree on Shoulder, black inscription	—	1.25	.38
❑ 3539	34¢	Santa Holding Tree, black inscription	—	1.25	.38
❑ 3540	34¢	Santa Garland on Cap, black inscription	—	1.25	.38
		Block of 4 (3537–3540)	5.00	5.00	—
		Booklet pane of 4 (3537–3540)	—	5.00	—

NOTE: Year date at lower right is smaller on booklet stamps than on those from pane of 20.

❑ 3541	34¢	Santa & Rocking Horse, red & green inscription	—	1.25	.42
❑ 3542	34¢	Santa & Tree on Shoulder, red & green inscription	—	1.25	.42
❑ 3543	34¢	Santa Holding Tree, red & green inscription	—	1.25	.42
❑ 3544	34¢	Santa Garland on Cap, red & green inscription	—	1.25	.42
		Booklet pane of 4 (3541–3544)	—	5.00	—

3545

3546

3547

3548

3549
(3550–3550A)

Scott No.			Plate Block	Unused	Used
❏ 3545	34¢	James Monroe	5.00	1.25	.10–.25
❏ 3546	34¢	We Give Thanks	5.00	1.25	.10–.25
❏ 3547	34¢	Hanukkah (~ 3118)	5.00	1.25	.10–.25
❏ 3548	34¢	Kwanzaa (~3175)	5.00	1.25	.10–.25
❏ 3549	34¢	United We Stand	—	1.25	.10–.25
		Booklet Pane of 20	—	25.00	—

Scott No.			PNC Strip (5)	Unused	Used

Coils Stamps.

Scott No.			PNC Strip (5)	Unused	Used
❏ 3550	34¢	United We Stand (~3549), self-adhesive, square corners	8.50	1.75	.10–.25
❏ 3550A	34¢	United We Stand (~3549), self-adhesive, rounded corners	10.00	1.75	1.00

Scott No.			Plate Block	Unused	Used

2001.

Scott No.			Plate Block	Unused	Used
❏ 3551	57¢	Love – Rose (~3499)	6.00	2.00	.84

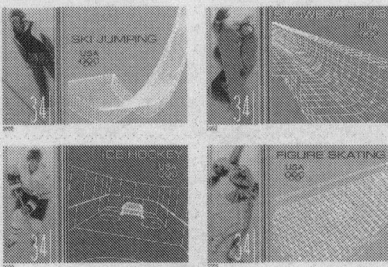

3552–3555

3556

3557

3558

3559

3560

Scott No.			Plate Block	Unused	Used
❑ 3552	34¢	Olympics – Ski Jumping	—	1.25	.42
❑ 3553	34¢	Olympics – Snowboarding	—	1.25	.42
❑ 3554	34¢	Olympics – Ice Hockey	—	1.25	.42
❑ 3555	34¢	Olympics – Figure Skating	—	1.25	.42
		Block or strip of 4 (3551–3555)	5.00	5.00	—
❑ 3556	34¢	Mentoring a Child	4.75	1.25	.10–.25
❑ 3557	34¢	Langston Hughes	4.75	1.25	.10–.25
❑ 3558	34¢	Happy Birthday	4.75	1.25	.10–.25
❑ 3559	34¢	Year of the Horse	4.75	1.50	.10–.25
❑ 3560	34¢	West Point	4.75	1.50	.10–.25

3561–3610

Scott No.				Plate Block	Unused	Used
❏ 3561–						
3610	34¢	Greetings from America		—	40.00	—
		Any single stamp		—	1.10	.10–.25

3611

3612

3613
(3614)

Scott No.			Plate Block	Unused	Used
❑ 3611	34¢	Pine Forest, pane of 10	—	22.00	—
❑ 3611a–j		Any single stamp	—	1.10	.10–.25

Scott No.			PNC Strip (5)	Unused	Used
Coil Stamp.					
❑ 3612	(5¢)	American Toleware	4.00	.55	.10–.25
2002.					
❑ 3613	3¢	Red, white & blue Star	5.00	.55	.42
❑ 3614	3¢	Red, white & blue Star (~3613)	4.00	.55	.42

NOTE: On No. 3613 the date appears at lower left; on No. 3614 it appears at lower right.

3620
(3621–3625)

3626–3629

Scott No.		Plate Block	Unused	Used
❏ 3620 (37¢)	Flag, water activated	8.00	1.35	1.00
❏ 3621 (37¢)	Flag (~3620), self-adhesive	4.00	1.35	1.00

Scott No.		PNC Strip (5)	Unused	Used
❏ 3622 (37¢)	Flag (~3620), self-adhesive	8.00	1.35	.10–.25

Scott No.		Plate Block	Unused	Used
❏ 3623 (37¢)	Flag (~3620), die cut 11.25	—	1.35	.10–.25
	Booklet pane of 20	—	27.00	—
❏ 3624 (37¢)	Flag (~3620), die cut 10½ x 10¾	—	1.35	.42
	Booklet pane of 4	—	5.50	—
	Booklet pane of 20	—	27.00	—
❏ 3625 (37¢)	Flag (~3620), die cut 8	—	1.35	.42
	Booklet pane of 18	—	25.00	—
❏ 3626 (37¢)	Mail Wagon	—	1.35	.42
❏ 3627 (37¢)	Locomotive	—	1.35	.42
❏ 3628 (37¢)	Automobile	—	1.35	.42
❏ 3629 (37¢)	Fire Engine	—	1.35	.42
	Booklet pane of 20 (3626-3629)	—	27.00	—

3630
(3631–3636)

Scott No.			Plate Block	Unused	Used
❑ 3630	37¢	Flag	5.00	1.75	.42

Scott No.			PNC Strip (5)	Unused	Used
❑ 3631	37¢	Flag (~3630), water activated	7.00	1.50	.42
❑ 3632	37¢	Flag (~3630), self-adhesive, die cut 10	8.00	1.50	.42
❑ 3633	37¢	Flag (~3630), self-adhesive, die cut 8	7.00	2.50	.42

Scott No.			Plate Block	Unused	Used
❑ 3635	37¢	Flag (~3630), die cut 11.25	—	1.50	.42
		Booklet pane of 20	—	30.00	—
❑ 3636	37¢	Flag (~3630), die cut 10½ x 10¾	—	1.50	.42
		Booklet pane of 20	—	30.00	—

3638–3641

Scott No.			PNC Strip (5)	Unused	Used
Coil Stamp.					
❑ 3638	37¢	Locomotive	—	1.35	.42
❑ 3639	37¢	Mail Wagon	—	1.35	.42
❑ 3640	37¢	Fire Engine	—	1.35	.42
❑ 3641	37¢	Automobile	—	1.35	.42
		Strip of 4 (3638–3642)	16.00	5.50	—

Scott No.			Plate Block	Unused	Used
❑ 3642	37¢	Mail Wagon (~3639)	—	1.50	.10–.25
❑ 3643	37¢	Locomotive (~3638)	—	1.50	.10–.25
❑ 3644	37¢	Automobile (~3641)	—	1.50	.10–.25
❑ 3644	37¢	Fire Engine (~3640)	—	1.50	.10–.25
		Booklet pane of 4 (3642-3644)	—	6.00	—
		Booklet pane of 20 (3642-3644)	—	30.00	—

3646

3647

3648

❑ 3646	60¢	Eagle	6.00	2.00	.10–.30
❑ 3647	$3.85	Jefferson Memorial	35.00	12.00	10.00
❑ 3648	$13.65	Capitol Dome	100.00	35.00	10.00

3649

3650

3651

Scott No.			Plate Block	Unused	Used
❑ 3649	37¢	Photography, pane of 20	—	20.00	—
❑ 3649a–t		Any single stamp	—	1.10	.10–.25
❑ 3650	37¢	John James Audubon	6.00	1.10	.10–.25
❑ 3651	37¢	Harry Houdini	6.00	1.10	.10–.25

3652

3653　　**3654**　　**3655**　　**3656**

Scott No.			Plate Block	Unused	Used
❏ 3652	37¢	Andy Warhol	4.25	1.30	.10–.25
❏ 3653-56	37¢	Teddy Bears	4.25	1.75	.42

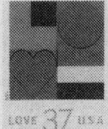   

3657　　　　**3658**　　　　**3659**

Scott No.			Plate Block	Unused	Used
❏ 3657	37¢	Love	—	1.35	.10–.25
		Pane of 20	—	24.00	—
❏ 3658	60¢	Love	6.00	2.00	.60
❏ 3659	37¢	Ogden Nash	5.00	1.35	.10–.25

3660

| **3661** | **3662** | **3663** | **3664** |

Scott No.			Plate Block	Unused	Used
❑ 3660	37¢	Duke Kahanamoku	12.00	1.25	.10–.25
❑ 3661-64	37¢	American Bats	4.00	1.50	.42
		Strip of 4	—	6.00	—

| **3665** | **3666** | **3667** | **3668** |

Scott No.			Plate Block	Unused	Used
❑ 3665	37¢	Nellie Bly	—	1.50	.42
❑ 3666	37¢	Ida M. Tarbell	—	1.50	.42
❑ 3667	37¢	Ethel L. Payne	—	1.50	.42
❑ 3668	37¢	Marguerite Higgins	—	1.50	.42
		Block of 4	6.00	—	—

3669

3670-71

Scott No.			Plate Block	Unused	Used
❑ 3669	37¢	Irving Berlin	5.00	1.50	.10–.25
❑ 3670	37¢	Neuter and Spay	6.00	1.75	.42
❑ 3671	37¢	Neuter and Spay	6.00	1.75	.42

3672

3673

3674

3675

Scott No.			Plate Block	Unused	Used
❑ 3672	37¢	Hanukkah SA	4.25	1.35	.10–.25
❑ 3673	37¢	Kwanzaa SA	4.25	1.35	.10–.25
❑ 3674	37¢	Islamic Festival	4.25	1.35	.10–.25
❑ 3675	37¢	Madonna	4.25	1.35	.10–.25
		Pane of 20	—	27.00	—

3676 **3677** **3678** **3679**

3680 **3681** **3682** **3683**

Scott No.			Plate Block	Unused	Used
❏ 3676-79	37¢	Snowman	4.00	1.10	.42
❏ 3680-83	37¢	Snowman	—	1.10	.60
		Strip of 5	—	6.00	—

3684 **3685** **3686** **3687**

3688 **3689** **3690** **3691**

Scott No.			Plate Block	Unused	Used
❏ 3684-87	37¢	Snowman	5.00	1.10	.42
❏ 3688-91	37¢	Snowman	5.00	1.10	.60

3692

3693

3694

3695

Scott No.			Plate Block	Unused	Used
❑ 3692	37¢	Cary Grant	6.00	1.25	.42
❑ 3693	5¢	Sea Coast	6.00	1.10	.10–.25
		Strip of 5	—	6.00	—
❑ 3694	37¢	Hawaiian Missionary	—	1.10	—
		Pane of 4	—	6.00	—
❑ 3695	37¢	Happy Birthday	6.00	1.10	.10–.25

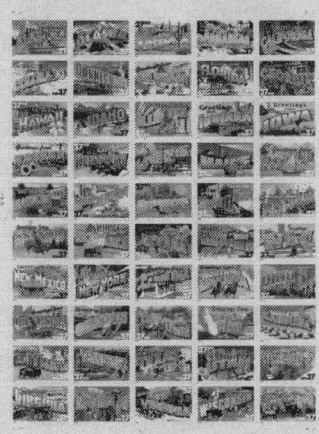

3696-3745

3746

3747

3748

3749

Scott No.			Plate Block	Unused	Used
❏ 3696-3745	37¢	Greetings From America	—	35.00	—
		Any single stamp	—	1.25	.42
❏ 3746	37¢	Thurgood Marshall SA	4.25	1.30	.10–.20
❏ 3747	37¢	Year of the Ram SA	4.25	1.30	.10–.20
❏ 3748	37¢	Zora Neale Hurston SA	4.25	1.30	.10–.20
❏ 3749	2¢	Navajo jewelry	4.25	1.30	.10–.20

3751

3757

3759

3766

3769

3770

Scott No.			Plate Block	Unused	Used
❏ 3751	10¢	U.S. Clock	1.50	.40	.10–.25
❏ 3757	1¢	Tiffany Lamp		.40	.10–.25
❏ 3759	3¢	Silver Coffeepot		.40	.10–.25
❏ 3766	$1	Wisdom	10.00	2.50	.53
❏ 3769	10¢	New York Public Library	—	.45	.36
❏ 3770	10¢	Atlas	—	.45	.10–.25

3771

3772

Scott No.			Plate Block	Unused	Used
❏ 3771	80¢	Special Olympics	—	3.50	1.00
❏ 3772	37¢	American Filmmaking		1.00	.10–.25
		Pane of 10	—	12.00	—

3773

3774

3775

3776–80

Scott No.			Plate Block	Unused	Used
❑ 3773	37¢	Ohio Statehood	4.50	1.25	.10–.25
❑ 3774	37¢	Pelican Island	4.50	1.25	.10–.25
❑ 3775	50¢	Seacoast	—	.45	.10–.25
		Strip of 5	—	2.10	—
❑ 3776–80	37¢	Old Glory	—	1.25	1.00
		Strip of 5	—	6.25	—

3781

3782

Scott No.			Plate Block	Unused	Used
❑ 3781	37¢	Cesar Chavez SA	4.50	1.20	.10–.25
❑ 3782	37¢	Louisiana Purchase SA	4.50	1.20	.10–.25

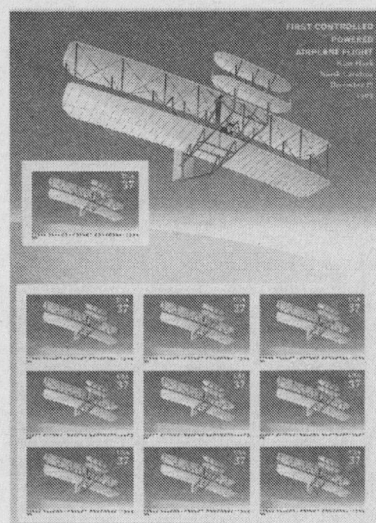

3783

3784

3784A

3785

Scott No.			Plate Block	Unused	Used
❑ 3783	37¢	First Flight	8.00	1.20	.10–.25
		Pane of 10	—	12.00	—
❑ 3784	37¢	Purple Heart	4.00	1.25	.42
❑ 3785	37¢	Sea Coast	4.00	1.35	.10–.25

3786

3787–91

Scott No.			Plate Block	Unused	Used
❏ 3786	37¢	Audrey Hepburn	—	1.75	.10–.25
		Pane of 20	—	35.00	—
❏ 3787–91	37¢	Cape Henry Lighthouse	—	1.50	.60
		Strip of 5	—	7.50	—

3792-96

3797–3801

Scott No.			Plate Block	Unused	Used
Coil.					
❏ 3792–96	25¢	Presorted First Class	—	1.10	.75
❏ 3797–3801	25¢	Presorted (Strip of 10)	—	12.00	—

3802

3803

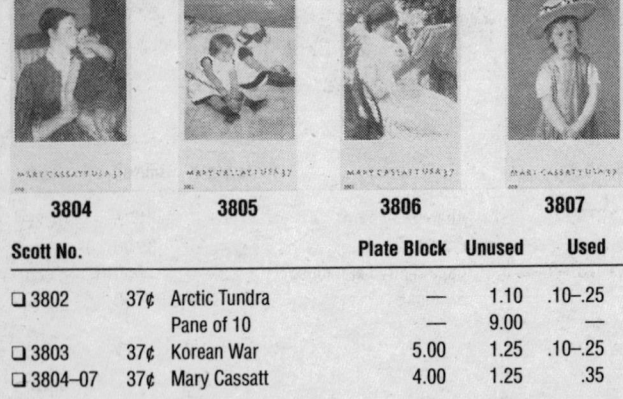

3804	**3805**	**3806**	**3807**

Scott No.			Plate Block	Unused	Used
❏ 3802	37¢	Arctic Tundra	—	1.10	.10–.25
		Pane of 10	—	9.00	—
❏ 3803	37¢	Korean War	5.00	1.25	.10–.25
❏ 3804–07	37¢	Mary Cassatt	4.00	1.25	.35

3808–11

3812

3813

3814–18

Scott No.			Plate Block	Unused	Used
❏ 3808–11	37¢	Early Football Heroes	9.00	1.25	.42
		Pane of 4	—	5.00	—
❏ 3812	37¢	Roy Acuff	8.00	1.25	.42
❏ 3813	37¢	District of Columbia	9.00	1.25	.42
❏ 3814–18	37¢	Reptile (Strip of 5)	9.00	1.25	.42

3819

3820

3821

3822

3823

3824

3821–24

3825

3826

3827

3828

Scott No.			Plate Block	Unused	Used
❏ 3819	37¢	Washington	7.00	1.10	.42
❏ 3820	37¢	J. Gossaett Christmas	7.00	1.10	.42
❏ 3821–24	37¢	Christmas (Strip of 4)	—	5.00	.42
❏ 3821	37¢	Christmas	—	1.25	.75
❏ 3822	37¢	Christmas	—	1.25	.75
❏ 3823	37¢	Christmas	—	1.25	.75
❏ 3824	37¢	Christmas	—	1.25	.75
❏ 3825	37¢	Christmas SA	—	1.25	1.00
❏ 3826	37¢	Christmas SA	—	1.25	1.00
❏ 3827	37¢	Christmas SA	—	1.25	1.00
❏ 3828	37¢	Christmas SA	—	1.25	1.00

3829

3830

3831

3832

3833

3834

Scott No.			Plate Block	Unused	Used
❏ 3829	37¢	Egret	8.00	1.25	.42
❏ 3830	37¢	American Flag	8.00	1.25	.10–.25
❏ 3831	37¢	Pacific Coral Reefs	—	1.10	.10–.25
		Sheet of 10	—	12.00	—
❏ 3832	37¢	Year of the Monkey	4.25	1.25	.10–.25
❏ 3833	37¢	Candy Hearts Love	—	1.25	.10–.25
❏ 3834	37¢	Paul Robeson	4.25	1.25	.10–.25

3835

3835 (Sheet)

3836

3838

3839

Scott No.			Plate Block	Unused	Used
❑ 3835	37¢	Dr. Seuss	4.50	1.25	.10–.25
		Sheet of 20	—	25.00	—
❑ 3836	37¢	Garden Blossoms	4.50	1.25	.10–.25
❑ 3838	37¢	U. S. Air Force Academy	4.50	1.25	.10–.25
❑ 3839	37¢	Henry Mancini	4.50	1.25	.10–.25

3840–3843

3855

3856

Scott No.			Plate Block	Unused	Used
❏ 3840	37¢	Martha Graham	—	1.25	.50
❏ 3841	37¢	Alvin Ailey	—	1.25	.50
❏ 3842	37¢	Agnes de Mille	—	1.25	.50
❏ 3843	37¢	George Balanchine	—	1.25	.50
❏ 3855	37¢	Lewis	—	1.25	.50
❏ 3856	37¢	Clark	—	1.25	.50

3857–3861

3857–3861 (Pane)

Scott No.			Plate Block	Unused	Used
❑ 3857	37¢	Isamu Noguchi-Akari	—	1.25	1.00
❑ 3858	37¢	Isamu Noguchi-Margaret La Farge Osborn	—	1.25	1.00
❑ 3859	37¢	Isamu Noguchi-Black Sun	—	1.25	1.00
❑ 3860	37¢	Isamu Noguchi-Mother & Child	—	1.25	1.00
❑ 3861	37¢	Isamu Noguchi-Figure	—	1.25	1.00
		Sheet of 20	—	25.00	—

3862

3863

3864

3865

Scott No.			Plate Block	Unused	Used
☐ 3862	37¢	World War II Memorial	—	1.25	.10–.25
☐ 3863	37¢	Summer Olympic Games	—	1.25	.10–.25
☐ 3864	5¢	Sea Coast	—	.35	.10–.25
☐ 3865	37¢	Art of Disney–Goofy, Mickey, Donald	—	1.25	.40

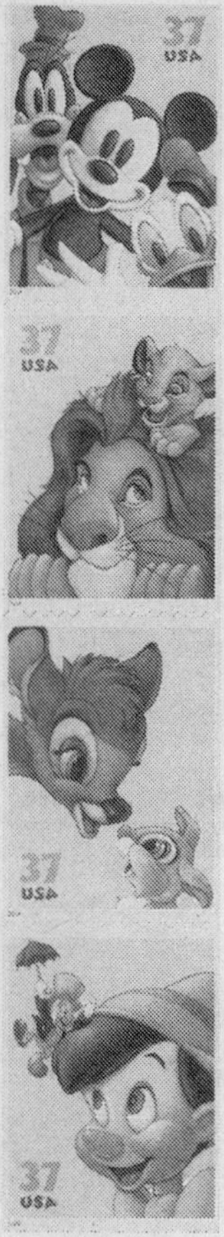

3865–68 (Sheet)

3865-3868

3869

3870

Scott No.			Plate Block	Unused	Used
❑ 3866	37¢	Art of Disney-Bambi, Thumper	—	1.25	.40
❑ 3867	37¢	Art of Disney-Mufasa, Simba	—	1.25	.40
❑ 3868	37¢	Art of Disney-Jiminy, Pinocchio	—	1.25	.40
		Sheet of 20	—	25.00	—
❑ 3869	37¢	USS Constellation	—	1.25	.10–.25
❑ 3870	37¢	Buckminster Fuller	—	1.25	.10–.25

3871

3872

3873 a–j

3874

3875

Scott No.			Plate Block	Unused	Used
❑ 3871	37¢	James Baldwin	—	1.10	.10–.25
❑ 3872	37¢	Martin Johnson Heade	—	1.10	.10–.25
❑ 3873	37¢	American Indian Art	—	1.10	.10–.25
❑ 3874	37¢	Sea Coast	—	.35	.10–.25
❑ 3875	37¢	Sea Coast	—	.35	.10–.25

3876   3876 (Sheet)

3877   3878

Scott No.			Plate Block	Unused	Used
❑ 3876	37¢	John Wayne	—	1.75	.10–.30
		Sheet of 20	—	35.00	—
❑ 3877	37¢	Sickle Cell	—	1.10	.10–.30
❑ 3878	37¢	Cloudscapes	—	1.10	.10–.30
		Sheet of 15	—	18.00	—

3879

3880

3881

3882

Scott No.			Plate Block	Unused	Used
❏ 3879	37¢	Madonna & Child	—	1.25	.10–.30
❏ 3880	37¢	Hanukkah	—	1.25	.10–.30
❏ 3881	37¢	Kwanzaa	—	1.25	.10–.30
❏ 3882	37¢	Moss Hart	—	1.25	.10–.30

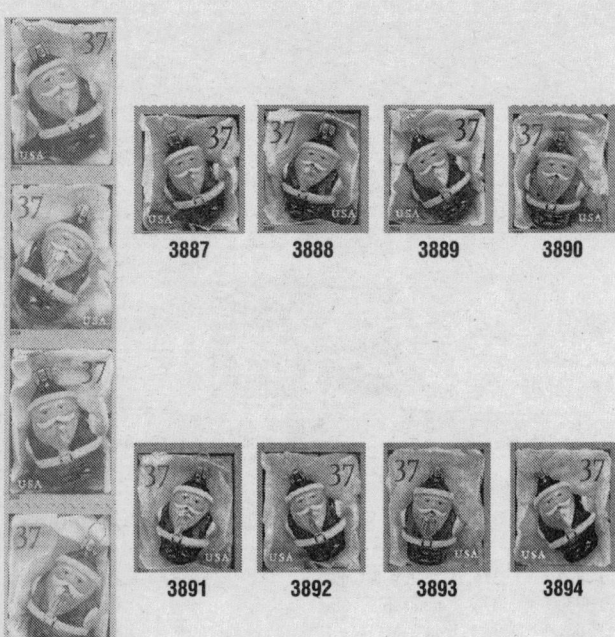

3887 3888 3889 3890

3891 3892 3893 3894

3883–3886

Scott No.			Plate Block	Unused	Used
❏ 3883–94	37¢	Holiday Ornaments	—	1.25	.10–.35

3895

3896

3897

3898

Scott No.			Plate Block	Unused	Used
❏ 3895	37¢	Lunar New Year	—	1.10	.10–.25
		Pane of 12	—	14.00	—
❏ 3896	37¢	Marian Anderson	—	1.25	.10–.25
❏ 3897	37¢	Ronald Reagan	—	1.25	.10–.25
❏ 3898	37¢	Love Bouquet	—	1.25	.10–.25

3899

3900

3901

3902

3903

3904

3905

Scott No.			Plate Block	Unused	Used
❑ 3899	37¢	Northeast Deciduous Forest	—	1.00	.10–.25
		Sheet of 10 stamps	—	10.00	.10–.30
❑ 3900–03	37¢	Spring Flowers	—	1.50	.10–.30
❑ 3904	37¢	Robert Penn Warren	—	1.25	.10–.30
❑ 3905	37¢	Yip Harburg	—	1.25	.10–.30

3906–3909

3910

3911

Scott No.			Plate Block	Unused	Used
❏ 3906–09	37¢	American Scientists	—	1.25	.10–.25
		Strip of 4 stamps	—	5.00	—
❏ 3910	37¢	American Architecture	—	1.25	.10–.25
		Sheet of 12 stamps	—	15.00	—
❏ 3911	37¢	Henry Fonda	—	1.40	.10–.25
		Sheet of 20 stamps	—	28.00	—

3912–3915

3916–3925

Scott No.			Plate Block	Unused	Used
❑ 3912–15	37¢	Disney	—	1.25	.42
❑ 3916–25	37¢	Aviation	—	1.25	1.00

3926

3927

3928

3929

3930

3931

3932

3933

3934

3935

Scott No.			Plate Block	Unused	Used
❑ 3926–29	37¢	Rio Blankets	—	1.40	.50
❑ 3930	37¢	Presidential Libraries	—	1.25	.10–.30
❑ 3931–35	37¢	Sporty Cars	—	1.50	.42

3936

3937

3938

3939 **3940** **3941** **3942**

Scott No.			Plate Block	Unused	Used
❏ 3936	37¢	Arthur Ashe	—	1.25	.10–.30
❏ 3937	37¢	Civil Rights	—	1.10	.10–.30
		Sheet of 10	—	10.00	—
❏ 3938	37¢	Child Health	—	1.10	.10–.30
❏ 3939–42	37¢	Dance	—	1.40	1.00

3943

3944

Scott No.			Plate Block	Unused	Used
❑ 3943	37¢	Greta Garbo	—	1.10	.10–.30
❑ 3944	37¢	Muppets	—	1.10	.10–.30
		Pane of 11	—	10.00	—

3953

3954

3955

3956

3957

3958

3959

3960

3949-3952

3945-48

Scott No.			Plate Block	Unused	Used
❑ 3945–48	37¢	Constellations	—	1.25	.80
❑ 3949–60	37¢	Holiday Cookies	—	1.25	.42

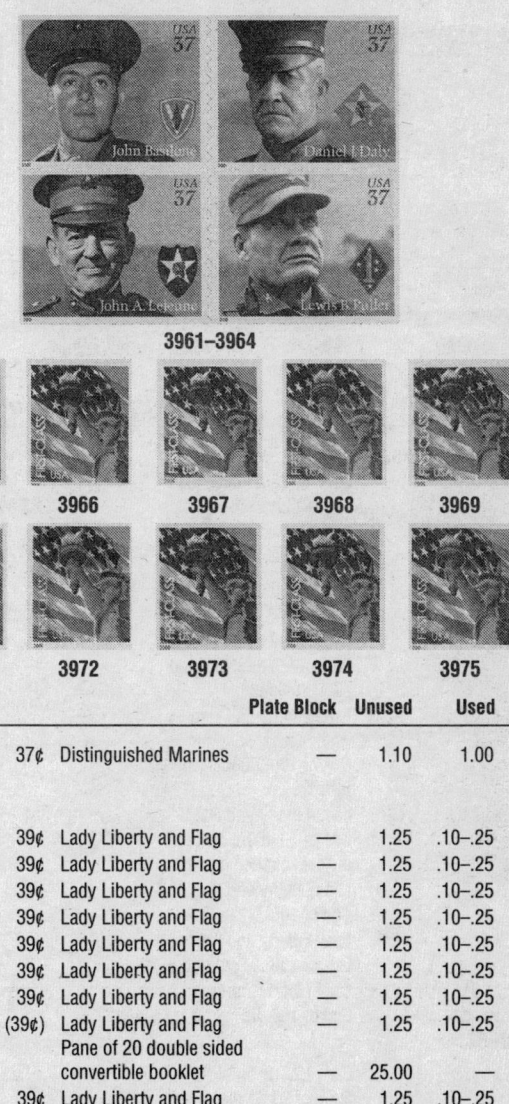

3961–3964

| 3965 | 3966 | 3967 | 3968 | 3969 |

| 3970 | 3972 | 3973 | 3974 | 3975 |

Scott No.			Plate Block	Unused	Used
❏ 3961–64	37¢	Distinguished Marines	—	1.10	1.00
2007.					
❏ 3965	39¢	Lady Liberty and Flag	—	1.25	.10–.25
❏ 3966	39¢	Lady Liberty and Flag	—	1.25	.10–.25
❏ 3967	39¢	Lady Liberty and Flag	—	1.25	.10–.25
❏ 3968	39¢	Lady Liberty and Flag	—	1.25	.10–.25
❏ 3969	39¢	Lady Liberty and Flag	—	1.25	.10–.25
❏ 3970	39¢	Lady Liberty and Flag	—	1.25	.10–.25
❏ 3972	39¢	Lady Liberty and Flag	—	1.25	.10–.25
❏ 3973	(39¢)	Lady Liberty and Flag	—	1.25	.10–.25
		Pane of 20 double sided			
		convertible booklet	—	25.00	—
❏ 3974	39¢	Lady Liberty and Flag	—	1.25	.10–.25
❏ 3975	39¢	Lady Liberty and Flag	—	1.25	.10–.25

| 3976 | | | 3978 | 3979 |

| 3980 | 3981 | 3982 | 3983 | 3985 |

Scott No.			Plate Block	Unused	Used
❏ 3976	(39¢)	Love True Blue	—	1.10	.10–.30
		Pane of 20 double sided convertible booklet	—	22.00	—
Coil Stamp.					
❏ 3978	39¢	Lady Liberty and Flag	—	1.75	.10–.30
		Pane of 20 double sided convertible booklet	—	35.00	—
		Pane of 20 double cut	—	35.00	—
		Pane of 10 double sided convertible booklet	—	18.00	—
❏ 3979	39¢	Lady Liberty and Flag water activated Coil of 100/3,000/10,000/ Strip 25	—	1.25	.10–.30
❏ 3980	39¢	Lady Liberty and Flag Coil of 10,000/strip of 25, die cut rounded corners	—	1.25	.10–.30
❏ 3981	39¢	Lady Liberty and Flag Coil of 100	—	1.25	.10–.30
❏ 3982	39¢	Lady Liberty and Flag Coil of 100 die cut gauge 10	—	1.25	.10–.30
❏ 3983	39¢	Lady Liberty and Flag Coil of 100 die cut gauge 8.5	—	1.25	.10–.30
2007.					
❏ 3985	39¢	Lady Liberty and Flag Pane of 20 double sided convertible booklet	—	1.25	.10–.30
			—	25.00	—

3987–3994

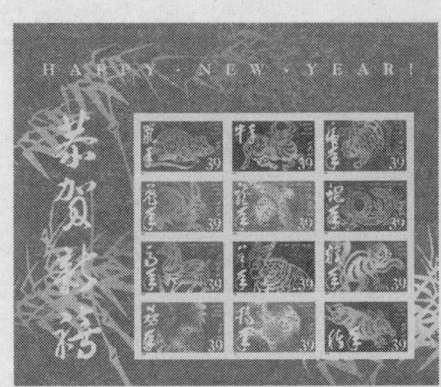

3995

3996

3997

Scott No.			Plate Block	Unused	Used
❑ 3987–94	39¢	Favorite Children's Book Animals			
		Pane of 16	—	18.00	—
		Any single stamp	—	1.10	.42
❑ 3995	39¢	2006 Olympic Games			
		Pane of 20	—	22.00	—
		Any single stamp	—	1.10	.42
❑ 3996	39¢	Black Heritage-Hattie McDaniel			
		Pane of 20	—	22.00	—
		Any single stamp	—	1.10	.42
❑ 3997	39¢	Lunar New Year			
		Pane of 12	—	14.00	—
		Any single stamp	—	1.10	.42

3998

3999

4003

Scott No.			Plate Block	Unused	Used
❏ 3998	39¢	Our Wedding Purple Dove	—	1.10	.10–.25
		Pane of 20 convertible booklet	—	22.00	—
❏ 3999	63¢	Our Wedding Green Dove	—	2.00	1.00
		Pane of 40 convertible booklet			
		20/39¢ & 20/63¢	—	45.00	—
❏ 4000	24¢	Common Buckeye	—	.80	.10–.25
		Pane of 100, water activated,			
		perforated	—	75.00	—
❏ 4001	24¢	Common Buckeye	—	.80	.10–.25
		Pane of 20 self-adhesive	—	15.00	—
❏ 4001a		Pane of 10 self-adhesive	—	7.50	—
		Booklet of 10 self-adhesive	—	7.50	—
Coil.					
❏ 4002	24¢	Common Buckeye Coil	—	.80	.10–.25
		Coil of 100 self-adhesive	—	52.00	—
❏ 4003	39¢	Crops of America–Pepper	—	1.25	.10–.25
		Coil of 100	—	125.00	—

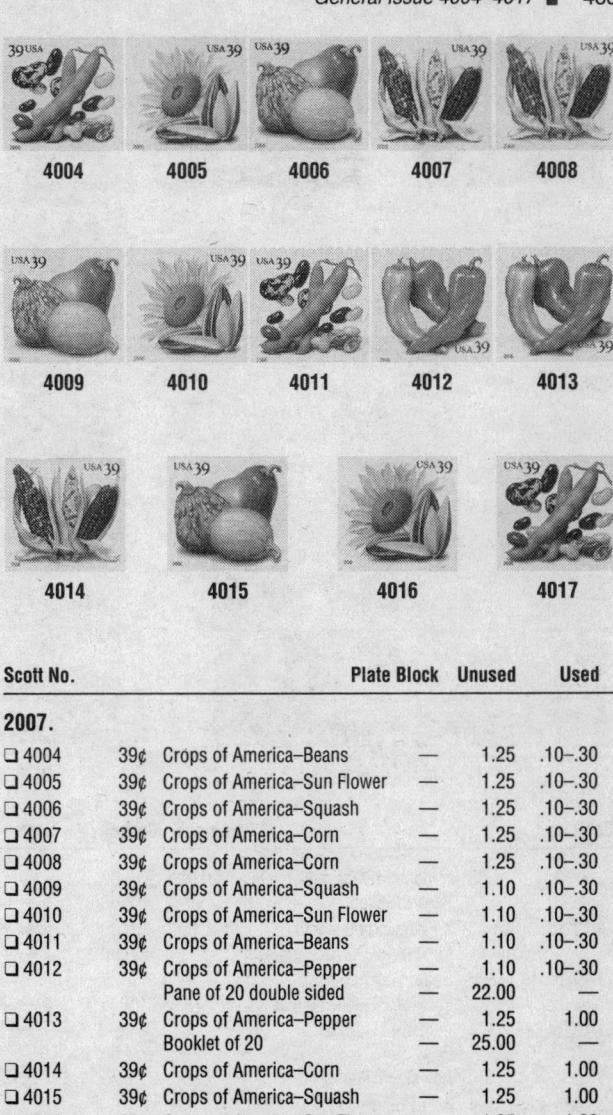

Scott No.			Plate Block	Unused	Used
2007.					
❏ 4004	39¢	Crops of America–Beans	—	1.25	.10–.30
❏ 4005	39¢	Crops of America–Sun Flower	—	1.25	.10–.30
❏ 4006	39¢	Crops of America–Squash	—	1.25	.10–.30
❏ 4007	39¢	Crops of America–Corn	—	1.25	.10–.30
❏ 4008	39¢	Crops of America–Corn	—	1.25	.10–.30
❏ 4009	39¢	Crops of America–Squash	—	1.10	.10–.30
❏ 4010	39¢	Crops of America–Sun Flower	—	1.10	.10–.30
❏ 4011	39¢	Crops of America–Beans	—	1.10	.10–.30
❏ 4012	39¢	Crops of America–Pepper	—	1.10	.10–.30
		Pane of 20 double sided	—	22.00	—
❏ 4013	39¢	Crops of America–Pepper	—	1.25	1.00
		Booklet of 20	—	25.00	—
❏ 4014	39¢	Crops of America–Corn	—	1.25	1.00
❏ 4015	39¢	Crops of America–Squash	—	1.25	1.00
❏ 4016	39¢	Crops of America–Sun Flower	—	1.25	1.00
❏ 4017	39¢	Crops of America–Beans	—	1.25	1.00

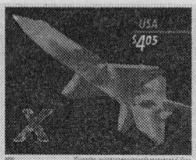
4018

4019

4020

4021–4024

4025–4028

Scott No.			Plate Block	Unused	Used
❏ 4018	4.05	X Plane Priority Mail	40.00	10.00	7.35
		Pane of 20	—	2.00	—
❏ 4019	14.40	X Plane Express Mail	120.00	30.00	16.80
		Pane of 20	—	600.00	—
❏ 4020	39¢	Sugar Ray Robinson	—	1.25	.10–.25
		Pane of 20	—	25.00	—
❏ 4021–24	39¢	Benjamin Franklin			
		Pane of 4	—	7.00	—
		Any single stamp	—	1.75	1.00
❏ 4025–28	39¢	Art of Disney			
		Pane of 20	—	25.00	—
		Any single stamp	—	1.25	.42

4029

4030

4031

4032

4033–4072

Scott No.			Plate Block	Unused	Used
❏ 4029	39¢	Love True Blue	—	1.25	.10–.25
		Pane of 20 double sided convertible booklet	—	25.00	—
❏ 4030	39¢	Katherine Anne Porter–Literary Arts Services	—	1.25	.10–.25
		Pane of 20	—	25.00	—
❏ 4031	39¢	Amber Alert	—	1.25	.10–.25
		Pane of 20	—	25.00	—
❏ 4032	39¢	Purple Heart	—	1.25	.10–.25
		Pane of 20	—	25.00	—
❏ 4033–72	39¢	Wonders of America			
		Pane of 40	—	48.00	—
		Any single stamp	—	1.10	.10–.25

4073

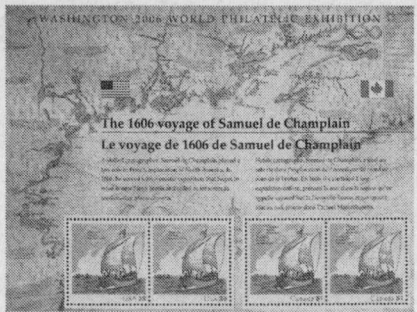

4074

4075

4076a–f

Scott No.			Plate Block	Unused	Used
❑ 4073	39¢	1606 Voyage of Samuel Champlain	—	1.25	.10–.25
		Pane of 20 self-adhesive		25.00	—
❑ 4074	39¢	1606 Voyage of Samuel Champlain			
		Souvenir sheet of 4 water activated	—	5.00	—
❑ 4074a		Any single stamp	—	1.10	.32
❑ 4075a	$1	Washington 2006 World Philatelic Exhibition	—	2.25	.78
❑ 4075b	$2	Washington 2006 World Philatelic Exhibition	—	4.50	2.50
❑ 4075c	$5	Washington 2006 World Philatelic Exhibition	—	9.00	5.00
		Souvenir sheet of 3 ($1$2$5) water activated	—	20.00	—
❑ 4076a–f	39¢	Distinguished American Diplomats			
		Pane of 6	—	8.00	—
		Any single stamp	—	1.25	.10–.30

4077

4078

4080–4084

4079

Scott No.			Plate Block	Unused	Used
❑ 4077	39¢	Judy Garland–Legends of Hollywood	—	1.25	.50
		Pane of 20	—	25.00	—
❑ 4078	39¢	Ronald Reagan	—	1.25	.10–.25
		Pane of 20	—	25.00	—
❑ 4079	39¢	Happy Birthday–Holiday Celebrations	—	1.25	.32
		Pane of 20	—	25.00	—
❑ 4081–84	39¢	Baseball Sluggers			
		Pane of 4	—	5.00	—
		Any single stamp	—	1.25	.42

4084a–t

4085–4088

Scott No.			Plate Block	Unused	Used
❏ 4084a–t	39¢	DC Comics Super Heroes			
		Pane of 20	—	24.00	—
		Any single stamp	—	1.20	.10–.30
❏ 4085–88	39¢	American Motorcycles			
		Souvenir sheet of 4	—	6.00	—
		Any single stamp	—	1.25	.42

4089   **4090**   **4091**   **4092**   **4093**

4094   **4095**   **4096**   **4097**   **4098**

4099

4100

Scott No.			Plate Block	Unused	Used
❑ 4089–98	39¢	Quilts of Gee's Bend			
		Pane of 20 double sided	—	25.00	—
		Any single stamp	—	1.30	.50
❑ 4099	39¢	Southern Florida Wetlands	—	1.30	.42
		Pane of 10	—	14.00	—
❑ 4100	39¢	Christmas Madonna	—	1.10	.42
		Pane of 20 double sided	—	22.00	—

4105 **4106** **4107** **4108**

4109 **4110** **4111** **4112**

4101-4104

4113 **4114** **4115** **4116**

Scott No.			Plate Block	Unused	Used
☐ 4101–16	39¢	Snowflakes	—	2.00	.75

4117

4118

4119

Scott No.			Plate Block	Unused	Used
❑ 4117	39¢	Eid	—	1.25	1.00
		Pane of 20	—	25.00	—
❑ 4118	39¢	Hanukkah	—	1.25	.10–.30
		Pane of 20	—	25.00	—
❑ 4119	39¢	Kwanzaa	—	1.25	.10–.30
		Pane of 20	—	25.00	—

4120

4121

4122

Scott No.			Plate Block	Unused	Used
2008.					
❑ 4120	39¢	Ella Fitzgerald, Black Heritage Series	—	1.25	.10–.25
❑ 4121	39¢	Oklahoma Statehood	—	1.25	.10–.25
❑ 4122	39¢	Love Hershey Kiss	—	1.25	.10–.25

4123a

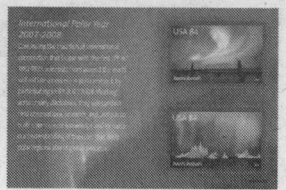

4123a

4124

4125

4126

4127

4128

4129

4130

Scott No.			Plate Block	Unused	Used
❏ 4123a	84¢	International Polar Year, Aurora Borealis & Aurora Australis,	—	2.25	1.35
		Souvenir sheet 2 stamps	—	4.00	—
❏ 4124	39¢	Henry Wadsworth Longfellow	—	1.75	.10–.25
❏ 4125	41¢	Forever–Liberty Bell large	—	1.25	.75
❏ 4126	41¢	Forever–Liberty Bell small	—	1.25	.10–.25
❏ 4127	41¢	Forever–Liberty Bell medium	—	1.25	.10–.25
❏ 4128	41¢	Forever–Liberty Bell large, booklet	—	1.25	.50
❏ 4129	41¢	American Flag, perforated	—	1.25	1.00
❏ 4130	41¢	American Flag, die cut 11.25x10.75	—	1.25	.42

4131 **4132** **4133** **4134** **4135**

4136

4137 **4138** **4139**

Scott No.			Plate Block	Unused	Used
Coil Stamp.					
❑ 4131	41¢	American Flag, coil	—	1.25	.42
❑ 4132	41¢	American Flag, coil die cut 9.5	—	1.25	.42
❑ 4133	41¢	American Flag, coil die cut 11	—	1.25	.42
❑ 4134	41¢	American Flag, coil die cut 8.4	—	1.25	.42
❑ 4135	41¢	American Flag, coil die cut 11	—	1.25	.42
❑ 4136	41¢	Settlement of Jamestown	—	2.00	.10–.30
❑ 4137	26¢	Florida Panther, water-activated stamp	—	.80	.10–.30
❑ 4138	17¢	Big Horn Sheep	—	.70	.10–.30
❑ 4139	26¢	Florida Panther	—	.80	.10–.30

4140

4141

4142

Scott No.			PNC Strip	Unused	Used

Coil Stamps

			PNC Strip	Unused	Used
❏ 4140	17¢	Big Horn Sheep, coil of 100	—	.60	.10–.35
❏ 4141	26¢	Florida Panther, coil of 100	—	.80	.10–.35
❏ 4142	26¢	Florida Panther	—	.60	.10–.35

4143

Scott No.			Plate Block	Unused	Used
❏ 4143	41¢	Star Wars–Darth Vader	—	1.25	.10–.25
		Pane of 15	—	20.00	—

4144   **4145**

Scott No.			Plate Block	Unused	Used
❏ 4144	$4.60	Air Force One, Priority Mail	—	14.00	12.00
❏ 4145	$16.25	Marine One, Express Mail	—	45.00	32.00

4146–50

4151   **4152**

Scott No.			Plate Block	Unused	Used
❏ 4146	41¢	Pacific Lighthouses, Diamond Head	—	1.35	.42
❏ 4147	41¢	Pacific Lighthouses, Five Finger	—	1.35	.42
❏ 4148	41¢	Pacific Lighthouses, Grays Harbor	—	1.35	.42
❏ 4149	41¢	Pacific Lighthouses, Umpqua River	—	1.35	.42
❏ 4150	41¢	Pacific Lighthouses, St. George Reef	—	1.35	.42
		5 stamp set	—	6.75	—
❏ 4151	41¢	Love Series–Purple Heart, water activated stamp	—	1.25	.42
❏ 4152	58¢	Love Series–Silver Heart, for 2 ounce rate	—	2.00	.42

4153

4154

4155

4156

Scott No.			Plate Block	Unused	Used
❏ 4153	41¢	Pollination, Bumble Bees	—	1.25	.42
❏ 4154	41¢	Pollination, Calliope Hummingbird	—	1.25	.42
❏ 4155	41¢	Pollination, Lesser Long-nosed Bat	—	1.25	.42
❏ 4156	41¢	Pollination, Southern Dogfaced Butterfly	—	1.25	.42
		set of 4 stamps	—	5.00	—

4157

4158

Scott No.			PNC Strip	Unused	Used

Coil Stamps

Scott No.			PNC Strip	Unused	Used
❏ 4157	10¢	Patriotic Banner, non denominated definitive stamp coil of 3000, rounded corners	—	.45	.10–.25
❏ 4158	10¢	Patriotic Banner, non denominated definitive stamp coil of 3000, regular corners	—	.45	.10–.25

4159

Scott No.			Plate Block	Unused	Used
❏ 4159	41¢	Marvel Comics, 20 stamps, Spider Man, The Hulk, Sub Mariner, The Thing, Captain America, Silver Surfer, Spider Woman, Iron Man, Elektra, Wolverine, Amazing Spider Man cover, Incredible Hulk cover, Sub Mariner cover, Fantastic Four cover, Captain America cover, Silver Surfer cover, Spider Woman cover, Iron Man cover, Elektra cover, X-Men cover	—	1.10	.32
		Pane of 20	—	25.00	—

4160–4163

4164

LOUIS COMFORT TIFFANY

4165

Scott No.			Plate Block	Unused	Used
❑ 4160	41¢	Vintage Mahogany Speedboats, Hitchinson	—	1.25	.75
❑ 4161	41¢	Vintage Mahogany Speedboats, Chris Craft	—	1.25	.75
❑ 4162	41¢	Vintage Mahogany Speedboats, Hacker Craft	—	1.25	.75
❑ 4163	41¢	Vintage Mahogany Speedboats, Gar Wood	—	1.25	.75
		set of 4 stamps	—	5.50	—
❑ 4164	41¢	Purple Heart	—	1.25	.10–.35
❑ 4165	41¢	Louis Comfort Tiffany, single	—	1.25	.10–.35

4166

4167

4168

4169

4170

4171

4172

4173

4174

4175

Scott No.			PNC Strip	Unused	Used
Coil Stamps					
❑ 4166	41¢	Flower Blossom–Iris, coil of 10	—	1.25 12.50	.10–.35
❑ 4167	41¢	Flower Blossom–Dahlia, coil of 10	—	1.25 12.50	.10–.35
❑ 4168	41¢	Flower Blossom–Vulcan Magnolia, coil of 10	—	1.25 12.50	.10–.35
❑ 4169	41¢	Flower Blossom–Red Gerber Daisy, coil of 10	—	1.25 12.50	.10–.35
❑ 4170	41¢	Flower Blossom–Purple Coneflower, coil of 10	—	1.25 12.50	.10–.35
❑ 4171	41¢	Flower Blossom–Tulip, coil of 10	—	1.25 12.50	.10–.35
❑ 4172	41¢	Flower Blossom–Water Lily coil of 10	—	1.25 12.50	.10–.35
❑ 4173	41¢	Flower Blossom–Poppy, coil of 10	—	1.25 12.50	.10–.35
❑ 4174	41¢	Flower Blossom–Spider Chrysanthemum coil of 10	—	1.25 12.50	.10–.35
❑ 4175	41¢	Flower Blossom–Orange Gerber Daisy coil of 10	—	1.25 12.50	.10–.35

Scott No.			Plate Block	Unused	Used
❑ 4176	41¢	Flower Blossom– Spider Chrysanthemum	—	1.25	.10–.35
❑ 4177	41¢	Flower Blossom– Orange Gerber Daisy	—	1.25	.10–.35
❑ 4178	41¢	Flower Blossom–Iris	—	1.25	.10–.35
❑ 4179	41¢	Flower Blossom–Dahlia	—	1.25	.10–.35
❑ 4180	41¢	Flower Blossom– Vulcan Magnolia	—	1.25	.10–.35
❑ 4181	41¢	Flower Blossom– Red Gerber Daisy	—	1.25	.10–.35
❑ 4182	41¢	Flower Blossom–Water Lily	—	1.25	.10–.35
❑ 4183	41¢	Flower Blossom–Poppy	—	1.25	.10–.35
❑ 4184	41¢	Flower Blossom– Purple Coneflower	—	1.25	.10–.35
❑ 4185	41¢	Flower Blossom–Tulip	—	1.25	.10–.35

4186

4187

4188

4189

Scott No.			PNC Strip	Unused	Used
Coil Stamps					
❑ 4186	41¢	American Flag, 9.5 die cut, coil of 100	—	1.25	.10–.35
❑ 4187	41¢	American Flag, 11 die cut, coil of 100	—	1.25	.10–.35
❑ 4188	41¢	American Flag, coil of 100	—	1.25	.10–.35
❑ 4189	41¢	American Flag, coil of 3,000/10,000	—	1.25	.10–.35

4190

4191

Booklet			Plate Block	Unused	Used
❑ 4190	41¢	American Flag, gray pole, booklet of 10	—	1.25	.10–.35
❑ 4191	41¢	American Flag, black pole, booklet of 20	—	1.25	.10–.35

4192

4194

4194

4195

4196

4192–4195

Scott No.			Plate Block	Unused	Used
❑ 4192	41¢	The Art of Disney Magic– Mickey Mouse	—	1.25	.42
❑ 4193	41¢	The Art of Disney Magic– Tinker Bell & Peter Pan	—	1.25	.42
❑ 4194	41¢	The Art of Disney Magic– Dumbo & Timothy Mouse	—	1.25	.42
❑ 4195	41¢	The Art of Disney Magic– Aladdin & Genie	—	1.25	.42
		set of 4 stamps	—	5.00	—
❑ 4196	41¢	Celebrate	—	1.25	.10–.25

4197

Scott No.			Plate Block	Unused	Used
❏ 4197	41¢	Legends of Hollywood–			
		James Stewart	—	1.40	.42
		Sheet of 20	—	28.00	—

4198

Scott No.			Plate Block	Unused	Used
❑ 4198	41¢	Nature of America Series– Alpine Tundra, elk, golden eagle, yellow bellied marmot, America pika, bighorn sheep, Magdalena alpine butterfly, white-tailed ptarmigan, Rocky Mountain parnassian butterfly, Melissa artic butterfly, brown capped rosy finch	—	1.10	.42
		Pane of 10	—	12.00	—

4199

Scott No.			Plate Block	Unused	Used
❑ 4199	41¢	Gerald R. Ford	—	1.25	.42

4200

4201

4202

4203

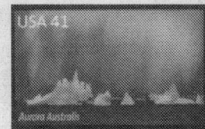

4204

4205

4206

Scott No.			Plate Block	Unused	Used
❏ 4200	41¢	Jury Duty–Serve with Pride	—	1.25	.10–.35
❏ 4201	41¢	Mendez v. Westminster School District	—	1.25	.10–.35
❏ 4202	41¢	Holiday Celebrations–Eid	—	1.25	.10–.35
❏ 4203	41¢	Polar Lights–Aurora Borealis	—	1.25	.10–.35
❏ 4204	41¢	Polar Lights–Aurora Australis	—	1.25	.10–.35
		2 stamp set	—	2.50	—
❏ 4205	41¢	Star Wars–Yoda	—	1.25	.10–.35
❏ 4206	41¢	Madonna & Child by Luini	—	1.25	.10–.35

4211

4212

4213

4214

4207–4210

Scott No.			Plate Block	Unused	Used
❏ 4207	41¢	Christmas Knits–deer	—	1.25	.42
❏ 4208	41¢	Christmas Knits–Christmas tree	—	1.25	.42
❏ 4209	41¢	Christmas Knits–snowman	—	1.25	.42
❏ 4210	41¢	Christmas Knits–bear	—	1.25	.42
		Strip of 4 stamps	—	5.60	—
		vending booklet of 20	—	35.00	—

Booklet			Plate Block	Unused	Used
❏ 4211	41¢	Christmas Knits–deer	—	1.25	.42
		vending booklet of 20	—	28.00	—
❏ 4212	41¢	Christmas Knits–Christmas tree	—	1.25	.42
		vending booklet of 20	—	28.00	—
❏ 4213	41¢	Christmas Knits–snowman	—	1.25	.42
		vending booklet of 20	—	28.00	—
❏ 4214	41¢	Christmas Knits–bear	—	1.25	.42
		vending booklet of 20	—	28.00	—

4215

4216

4217

4218

4219

4220

4221

4222

4223

Booklet			Plate Block	Unused	Used
❏ 4215	41¢	Christmas Knits–deer	—	1.25	.42
		atm convert. booklet of 20	—	25.00	—
❏ 4216	41¢	Christmas Knits–Christmas tree	—	1.25	.42
		atm convert. booklet of 20	—	25.00	—
❏ 4217	41¢	Christmas Knits–snowman	—	1.25	.42
		atm convert. booklet of 20	—	25.00	—
❏ 4218	41¢	Christmas Knits–bear	—	1.25	.42
		atm convert. booklet of 20	—	25.00	—

Scott No.			Plate Block	Unused	Used
❏ 4219	41¢	Holiday Celebrations–Hanukkah	—	1.25	.42
❏ 4220	41¢	Holiday Celebrations–Kwanzaa	—	1.25	.42
2009.					
❏ 4221	41¢	New Year	—	1.25	.10–.35
❏ 4222	41¢	Charles Chestnutt	—	1.25	.10–.35
❏ 4223	41¢	Marjorie Rawlings	—	1.25	.10–.35

4224–27

4228–31

4231   4232–35

4236–39

Scott No.			Plate Block	Unused	Used
❏ 4224	41¢	Gerti Cori	—	1.25	.42
❏ 4225	41¢	Linus Pauling	—	1.25	.42
❏ 4226	41¢	Edwin Hubble	—	1.25	.42
❏ 4227	41¢	John Bardeen	—	1.25	.42
❏ 4228	42¢	Flag Dusk	—	1.25	.42
❏ 4229	42¢	Flag Night	—	1.25	.42
❏ 4230	42¢	Flag Dawn	—	1.25	.42
❏ 4231	42¢	Flag Midday	—	1.25	.42
Coil Stamp.					
❏ 4232-35	42¢	Flag Coil 9.5 each	—	1.25	.42
❏ 4236-39	42¢	Flag Coil 11 each	—	1.25	.42

4240–43

4244–47

 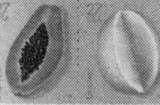 

4253–57   **4248–52**

Scott No.			Plate Block	Unused	Used
❑ 4240-43	42¢	Flag Coil 8.5 each	—	1.25	.42
❑ 4244-47	42¢	Flag Coil R11 each	—	1.25	.42
❑ 4248	42¢	Martha Gelhom	—	1.25	.42
❑ 4249	42¢	John Hersey	—	1.25	.42
❑ 4250	42¢	George Polk	—	1.25	.42
❑ 4251	42¢	Ruben Salazar	—	1.25	.42
❑ 4252	42¢	Eric Sevareid	—	1.25	.42
❑ 4253	27¢	Pomegranate	—	1.10	.32
❑ 4254	27¢	Star Fruit	—	1.10	.32
❑ 4255	27¢	Kiwi	—	1.10	.32
❑ 4256	27¢	Papaya	—	1.10	.32
❑ 4257	27¢	Guava	—	1.10	.32

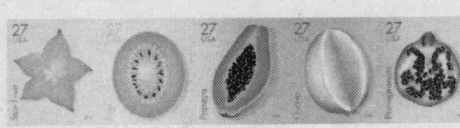

4258–62

4263   4264   4265   4266   4267

4268   4269   4270

Scott No.			Plate Block	Unused	Used
Coil Stamp.					
❏ 4258	27¢	Papaya Coil	—	1.10	.32
❏ 4259	27¢	Guava Coil	—	1.10	.32
❏ 4260	27¢	Pomegranate Coil	—	1.10	.32
❏ 4261	27¢	Star Fruit Coil	—	1.10	.32
❏ 4262	27¢	Kiwi Coil	—	1.10	.32
❏ 4263	42¢	Purple Heart wa	—	1.25	.10–.25
❏ 4264	42¢	Purple Heart sa	—	1.25	.10–.25
❏ 4265	42¢	Sinatra	—	1.25	.10–.25
❏ 4266	42¢	Minnesota Statehood	—	1.25	.10–.25
❏ 4267	62¢	Dragonfly	—	1.75	.42
❏ 4268	$4.80	Mt. Rushmore	—	14.00	12.00
❏ 4269	$16.50	Hoover Dam	—	38.00	34.00
❏ 4270	42¢	Love Heart	—	1.25	.10–.25

4271

4272

4273

4274

4275

4276

4277

4278

4279

4280

4281

4282

4283

Booklet			Plate Block	Unused	Used
❏ 4271	42¢	Hearts Booklet	—	1.00	.10–.25
		Pair	—	2.00	—

Scott No.			Plate Block	Unused	Used
❏ 4272	59¢	Hearts	—	1.50	.42
❏ 4273	42¢	American Flag	—	1.25	.42
❏ 4274	42¢	Alabama	—	1.25	.42
❏ 4275	42¢	Alaska	—	1.25	.42
❏ 4276	42¢	American Samoa	—	1.25	.42
❏ 4277	42¢	Arizona	—	1.25	.42
❏ 4278	42¢	Arkansas	—	1.25	.42
❏ 4279	42¢	California	—	1.25	.42
❏ 4280	42¢	Colorado	—	1.25	.42
❏ 4281	42¢	Connecticut	—	1.25	.42
❏ 4282	42¢	Delaware	—	1.25	.42
❏ 4283	42¢	Washington DC	—	1.25	.42

Scott No.			Plate Block	Unused	Used
❑ 4284	42¢	Florida	—	1.25	.42
❑ 4285	42¢	Georgia	—	1.25	.42
❑ 4286	42¢	Guam	—	1.25	.42
❑ 4287	42¢	Hawaii	—	1.25	.42
❑ 4288	42¢	Idaho	—	1.25	.42
❑ 4289	42¢	Illinois	—	1.25	.42
❑ 4290	42¢	Indiana	—	1.25	.42
❑ 4291	42¢	Iowa	—	1.25	.42
❑ 4292	42¢	Kansas	—	1.25	.42
❑ 4323	42¢	Texas	—	1.25	.42
❑ 4324	42¢	Utah	—	1.25	.42
❑ 4325	42¢	Vermont	—	1.25	.42

4326

4327

4328

4329

4330

4331

4332

4333

Scott No.			Plate Block	Unused	Used
❑ 4326	42¢	Virgin Islands	—	1.25	.42
❑ 4327	42¢	Virginia	—	1.25	.42
❑ 4328	42¢	Washington	—	1.25	.42
❑ 4329	42¢	West Virginia	—	1.25	.42
❑ 4330	42¢	Wisconsin	—	1.25	.42
❑ 4331	42¢	Wyoming	—	1.25	.42
❑ 4332	42¢	Fruited Plains	—	1.25	.42
❑ 4333	42¢	Charles & Ray Eames	—	1.25	.42
		Sheet of 16	—	16.50	—

4334

4335

4336–40

4336–40

4338

4341

Scott No.			Plate Block	Unused	Used
❏ 4334	42¢	Olympics	—	1.25	.42
❏ 4335	42¢	Celebrate	—	1.25	.42
❏ 4336	42¢	Black Cinema	—	1.25	.42
❏ 4337	42¢	Black Cinema—Gods	—	1.25	.42
❏ 4338	42¢	Black Cinema—Tam Tam	—	1.25	.42
❏ 4339	42¢	Black Cinema—Caldonia	—	1.25	.42
❏ 4340	42¢	Black Cinema—Hallelujah	—	1.25	.42
❏ 4341	42¢	Ballgame	1.00	1.25	.42

4343

4342–45

4342–45   **4346**   **4347**   **4348**

4349

Scott No.			Plate Block	Unused	Used
❏ 4342	42¢	Disney Pongo	—	1.25	.42
❏ 4343	42¢	Steamboat Willie	—	1.25	.42
❏ 4344	42¢	Princesses	—	1.25	.42
❏ 4345	42¢	Mowgli and Baloo	—	1.25	.42
❏ 4346	42¢	Albert Bierstadt	—	1.25	.42
❏ 4347	42¢	Sunflower	—	1.25	.42
❏ 4348	5¢	Sun Coast	—	1.25	.42
❏ 4349	42¢	Latin Jazz	—	1.25	.42

4351

4350

4350

4352

4353–57

Scott No.			Plate Block	Unused	Used
❏ 4350	42¢	Bette Davis	—	1.10	.42
		Sheet of 20	—	20.00	—
❏ 4351	42¢	EID	—	1.10	.42
❏ 4352	42¢	Great Lakes Dunes	—	1.20	.42
		Sheet of 10	—	12.00	—
❏ 4353	42¢	Tail Fins and Chrome	—	1.25	.42
❏ 4354	42¢	Tail Fins and Chrome	—	1.25	.42
❏ 4355	42¢	Tail Fins and Chrome	—	1.25	.42
❏ 4356	42¢	Tail Fins and Chrome	—	1.25	.42
❏ 4357	42¢	Tail Fins and Chrome	—	1.25	.42

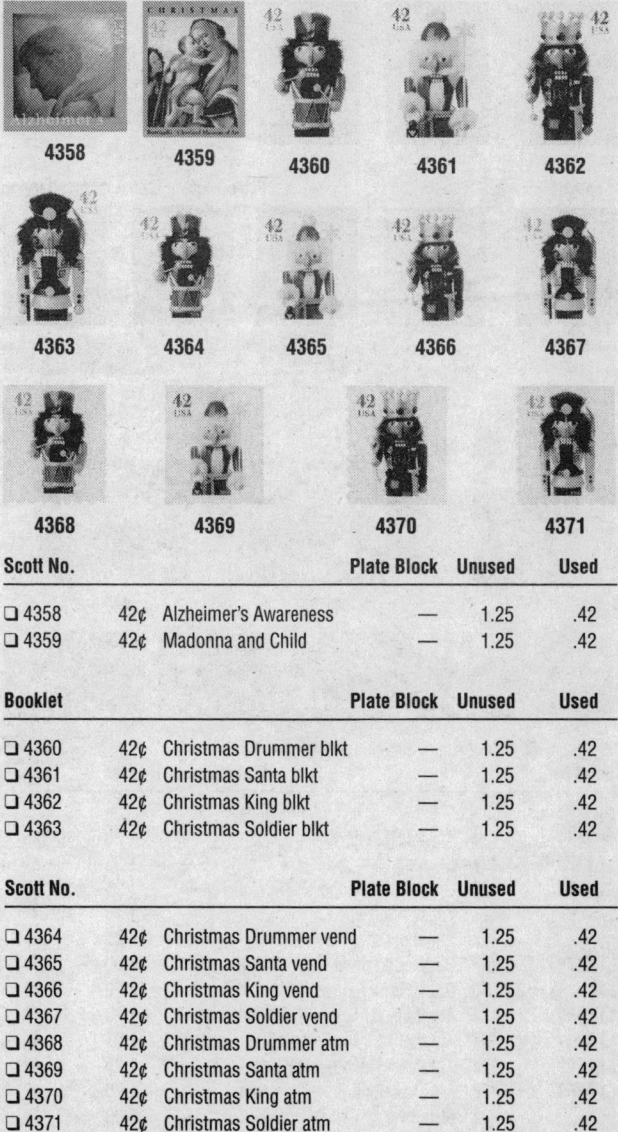

4358

4359

4360

4361

4362

4363

4364

4365

4366

4367

4368

4369

4370

4371

Scott No.			Plate Block	Unused	Used
❏ 4358	42¢	Alzheimer's Awareness	—	1.25	.42
❏ 4359	42¢	Madonna and Child	—	1.25	.42

Booklet			Plate Block	Unused	Used
❏ 4360	42¢	Christmas Drummer blkt	—	1.25	.42
❏ 4361	42¢	Christmas Santa blkt	—	1.25	.42
❏ 4362	42¢	Christmas King blkt	—	1.25	.42
❏ 4363	42¢	Christmas Soldier blkt	—	1.25	.42

Scott No.			Plate Block	Unused	Used
❏ 4364	42¢	Christmas Drummer vend	—	1.25	.42
❏ 4365	42¢	Christmas Santa vend	—	1.25	.42
❏ 4366	42¢	Christmas King vend	—	1.25	.42
❏ 4367	42¢	Christmas Soldier vend	—	1.25	.42
❏ 4368	42¢	Christmas Drummer atm	—	1.25	.42
❏ 4369	42¢	Christmas Santa atm	—	1.25	.42
❏ 4370	42¢	Christmas King atm	—	1.25	.42
❏ 4371	42¢	Christmas Soldier atm	—	1.25	.42

| 4372 | 4373 |

Scott No.			Plate Block	Unused	Used
❏ 4372	42¢	Hanukkah	—	1.25	.65
❏ 4373	42¢	Kwanzaa	—	1.25	.65

| 4374 | 4375 | 4376 |

| 4377 | 4378 | 4379 |

4380–83

Scott No.			Plate Block	Unused	Used
2010.					
❏ 4374	42¢	Alaska Statehood	—	1.25	.10–.25
❏ 4375	42¢	Chinese New Year—Ox	—	1.25	.10–.25
❏ 4376	42¢	Oregon Statehood	—	1.25	.10–.25
❏ 4377	42¢	Edgar Allan Poe	—	1.25	.10–.25
		Sheet of 20	—	25.00	—
❏ 4378	$4.95	Redwood Forest Priority Mail	—	13.00	10.00
❏ 4379	$17.50	Old Faithful Express Mail	—	38.00	30.00
❏ 4380	42¢	Abraham Lincoln— Rail Splitter	—	1.25	.42
❏ 4381	42¢	Abraham Lincoln—Lawyer	—	1.25	.42
❏ 4382	42¢	Abraham Lincoln—Politician	—	1.25	.42
❏ 4383	42¢	Abraham Lincoln—President	—	1.25	.42
		Strip of 4	—	5.00	—

4384

Scott No.			Plate Block	Unused	Used
❑ 4384	42¢	Civil Rights Pioneers pane	—	1.25	.10–.35
		Sheet of 6	—	8.00	—

4385

Scott No.			PNC Strip	Unused	Used

Coil Stamp.

❑ 4385	10¢	Patriotic Banner	—	.55	.10–.35

| **4386** | **4387** | **4388** | **4389** | **4390** |

Scott No.			Plate Block	Unused	Used
❑ 4386	61¢	Richard Wright	—	1.25	.42
❑ 4387	28¢	Polar Bear	—	1.00	.42
❑ 4388	64¢	Dolphin	—	1.60	.42
❑ 4389	28¢	Polar Bear	—	1.00	.42
❑ 4390	44¢	Purple Heart	—	1.25	.42

| 4391 | 4392 | 4393 | 4394 | 4395 | 4396 |

Scott No.			PNC Strip	Unused	Used

Coil Stamp.

❏ 4391	44¢	Flag coil	1.25	.32
❏ 4392	44¢	Flag coil—11 perf	1.25	.32
❏ 4393	44¢	Flag coil—9 1/2 perf	1.25	.32
❏ 4394	44¢	Flag coil—8 1/2 perf	1.25	.32
❏ 4395	44¢	Flag coil—11 perf	1.25	.32
❏ 4396	44¢	Flag coil—11 1/4 perf—10 3/4	1.25	.32

4397

4399–4403

4398

4404–05

Scott No.			Plate Block	Unused	Used
❏ 4397	44¢	Wedding Rings	—	1.25	.42
❏ 4398	61¢	Wedding Cake	—	1.50	.42
❏ 4399	44¢	Homer Simpson	—	1.25	.42
❏ 4400	44¢	Marge Simpson	—	1.25	.42
❏ 4401	44¢	Bart Simpson	—	1.25	.42
❏ 4402	44¢	Lisa Simpson	—	1.25	.42
❏ 4403	44¢	Maggie Simpson	—	1.25	.42
		Strip of 5	—	6.25	—
❏ 4404	44¢	Love—King of Hearts	—	1.25	.10–.25
❏ 4405	44¢	Love—Queen of Hearts	—	1.25	.10–.25
		Pair	—	2.50	—

4433

4434

No.			Plate Block	Unused	Used
33	44¢	Hanukkah		1.25	.42
34	44¢	Kwanzaa		1.25	.42

4435

4436

4437

4438

4439

Scott No.			Plate Block	Unused	Used
2011.					
☐4435	44¢	Lunar New Year—The Year of the Tiger	—	1.75	.10–.25
☐4436	44¢	Vancouver 2010 Winter Games Snowboarder	—	1.25	.10–.25

Booklet			Plate Block	Unused	Used
☐4437	44¢	Liberty Bell	—	1.00	.42
		booklet of 18		18.00	—

Scott No.			Plate Block	Unused	Used
☐4438	$4.90	Mackinac Bridge	—	12.00	10.00
☐4439	$18.30	Bixby Creek	—	38.00	30.00

4406

4407

4408

4409–13

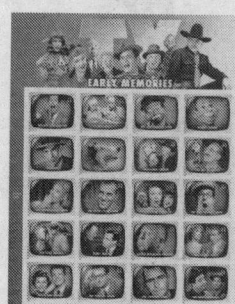

4414

Scott No.			Plate Block	Unused	Used
☐ 4406	44¢	Bob Hope	—	1.50	.10–.35
		Sheet of 20	—	30.00	—
☐ 4407	44¢	Celebrate!	—	1.10	.10–.35
☐ 4408	44¢	Anna Julia Cooper	—	1.10	.10–.35
☐ 4409	44¢	Matagorda Island—Texas	—	2.00	.10–.35
☐ 4410	44¢	Sabine Pass, Louisiana	—	2.00	.10–.35
☐ 4411	44¢	Biloxi, Mississippi	—	2.00	.10–.35
☐ 4412	44¢	Sand Island, Alabama	—	2.00	.10–.35
☐ 4413	44¢	Fort Jefferson, Florida	—	2.00	.10–.35
		Strip of 4	—	8.50	—
☐ 4414	44¢	Early TV Memories	—	1.25	.32
		Sheet of 20	—	25.00	—

4415

4416

4417–20

4421

4422

Scott No.			Plate Block	Unused	Used
❑ 4415	44¢	Hawaii Statehood	—	1.25	.42
❑ 4416	44¢	EID	—	1.25	.42
❑ 4417	44¢	Thanksgiving Day Parade— Crowd	—	1.10	.42
❑ 4418	44¢	Thanksgiving Day Parade— Drum Major	—	1.10	.42
❑ 4419	44¢	Thanksgiving Day Parade— Musicians	—	1.10	.42
❑ 4420	44¢	Thanksgiving Day Parade— Turkey Ball	—	1.10	.42
		Strip of 4	—	4.50	—
❑ 4421	44¢	Gary Cooper	—	1.10	.42
		Sheet of 20	—	22.00	—
❑ 4422	44¢	Supreme Court Justices	—	1.25	.42
		Sheet of 4	—	5.00	—

KELP FOREST

4423

4424

4425

4426

4427

4429

4430

4431

Scott No.			Plate Block	Unused	
❑ 4423	44¢	Kelp Forest	—	1.45	
		Sheet of 10	—	14.50	
❑ 4424	44¢	Christmas—Madonna	—	1.25	
❑ 4425	44¢	Winter Holidays—Reindeer	—	1.25	.4
❑ 4426	44¢	Winter Holidays—Snowman	—	1.25	.42
❑ 4427	44¢	Winter Holidays—Gingerbread	—	1.25	.42
❑ 4428	44¢	Winter Holidays—Toy Soldier	—	1.25	.42
		Strip of 4	—	5.00	—
❑ 4429	44¢	Winter Holidays—Reindeer	—	1.25	.42
❑ 4430	44¢	Winter Holidays—Snowman	—	1.25	.42
❑ 4431	44¢	Winter Holidays—Gingerbread Man	—	1.25	.42
❑ 4432	44¢	Winter Holidays—Toy Soldier	—	1.25	.42
		Strip of 4	—	5.00	—

4440–43

4440   4441   4442   4443

4444

BILL MAULDIN

4445

4446

4446–49

Scott No.			Plate Block	Unused	Used
❏4440	44¢	Distinguished Sailors—William S. Sims	—	1.50	.42
❏4441	44¢	Distinguished Sailors—Arleigh A. Burke	—	1.50	.42
❏4442	44¢	Distinguished Sailors—John McCloy	—	1.50	.42
❏4443	44¢	Distinguished Sailors—Doris Miller	—	1.50	.42
		Strip of 4 (4440-43)	—	6.00	—
❏4444	44¢	Abstract Expressionists	—	1.40	.42
		Sheet of 10 (a–j)	—	12.00	—
❏4445	44¢	Bill Mauldin Cartoonist	—	1.25	.10–.25
❏4446	44¢	Cowboys of the Silver Screen—Roy Rogers	—	1.25	.42

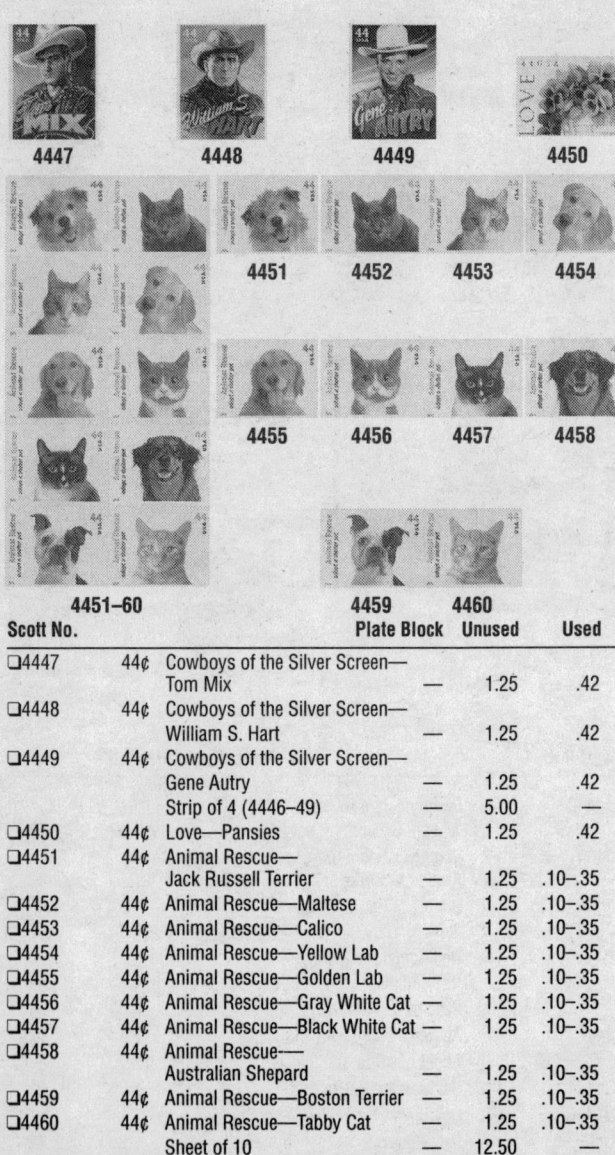

4447　　**4448**　　**4449**　　**4450**

4451　　**4452**　　**4453**　　**4454**

4455　　**4456**　　**4457**　　**4458**

4451–60　　**4459**　　**4460**

Scott No.			Plate Block	Unused	Used
❏4447	44¢	Cowboys of the Silver Screen—Tom Mix	—	1.25	.42
❏4448	44¢	Cowboys of the Silver Screen—William S. Hart	—	1.25	.42
❏4449	44¢	Cowboys of the Silver Screen—Gene Autry	—	1.25	.42
		Strip of 4 (4446–49)	—	5.00	—
❏4450	44¢	Love—Pansies	—	1.25	.42
❏4451	44¢	Animal Rescue—Jack Russell Terrier	—	1.25	.10–.35
❏4452	44¢	Animal Rescue—Maltese	—	1.25	.10–.35
❏4453	44¢	Animal Rescue—Calico	—	1.25	.10–.35
❏4454	44¢	Animal Rescue—Yellow Lab	—	1.25	.10–.35
❏4455	44¢	Animal Rescue—Golden Lab	—	1.25	.10–.35
❏4456	44¢	Animal Rescue—Gray White Cat	—	1.25	.10–.35
❏4457	44¢	Animal Rescue—Black White Cat	—	1.25	.10–.35
❏4458	44¢	Animal Rescue—Australian Shepard	—	1.25	.10–.35
❏4459	44¢	Animal Rescue—Boston Terrier	—	1.25	.10–.35
❏4460	44¢	Animal Rescue—Tabby Cat	—	1.25	.10–.35
		Sheet of 10	—	12.50	—

4461

4461

4462

4463

4464

4465–66

4465

4466

Scott No.			Plate Block	Unused	Used
☐4461	44¢	Katharine Hepburn	—	1.25	.10–.30
		Sheet of 20	—	25.00	—
☐4462	44¢	Monarch Butterfly	—	1.35	.42
☐4463	44¢	Kate Smith	—	1.25	.10–.35
☐4464	44¢	Black Heritage Series-Oscar Micheaux		1.25	.10–.35
☐4465	44¢	Negro League Baseball	—	1.25	.10–.35
		Strip of 2 (4465–66)	—	2.50	—
☐4466	44¢	Negro League Baseball—Rube Foster		1.25	.10–.35

4467

4468   **4468**   **4469**   **4470**   **4471**

4472

4473

Scott No.			Plate Block	Unused	Used
☐4467	44¢	Beetle Bailey	—	1.25	.42
		Strip of 5 (4467–71)	—	6.50	—
☐4468	44¢	Calvin Hobbes	—	1.25	.42
☐4469	44¢	Archie	—	1.25	.42
☐4470	44¢	Garfield	—	1.25	.42
☐4471	44¢	Dennis the Menace	—	1.25	.42
☐4472	44¢	Scouting	—	1.25	.42
☐4473	44¢	Winslow Homer	—	1.25	.42

4474

4475

4476

4477

4478–81

Scott No.			Plate Block	Unused	Used
☐4474	44¢	Nature of America—Hawaiian			
		Rain Forest	—	1.50	.32
		Sheet of 10 (a-j)	—	15.00	—
☐4475	44¢	Mother Teresa	—	1.25	.42
☐4476	44¢	Julia de Burgos	—	1.25	.42
☐4477	44¢	Angel with Lute	—	1.25	.42
☐4478	44¢	Evergreens—Ponderosa Pine	—	1.00	.10–.35
☐4479	44¢	Evergreens—Eastern Red Cedar	—	1.00	.10–.35
☐4480	44¢	Evergreens—Blue Spruce	—	1.00	.10–.35
☐4481	44¢	Evergreens—Balsam Fir	—	1.00	.10–.35
		Block of 4	4.00	—	—

Scott No.			Plate Block	Unused	Used
☐4482-85	44¢	Evergreens—	—	1.25	.10–.35
		Block of 4	5.00	—	—

4492

4492

4493

4494

4495

4496

Scott No.			Plate Block	Unused	Used
2012.					
❏4492	44¢	Year of the Rabbit	—	1.10	.10–.30
		Sheet of 12	—	13.00	—
❏4493	44¢	Kansas Statehood	—	1.10	.10–.30
		Pane of 20	—	22.00	—
❏4494	44¢	Ronald Reagan	—	1.10	.10–.30
		Pane of 20	—	22.00	—

Coil			Plate Block	Unused	Used
❏4495	5¢	Art Deco Bird	—	.35	.10–.30
❏4496	44¢	Patriotic Quill & Inkwell	—	1.00	.10–.30

4497–4501

4502

4503

4504

4505–09

Scott No.			Plate Block	Unused	Used
❏4497	44¢	Latin Music Legends—Tito Puente	—	1.00	.10–.30
❏4498	44¢	Latin Music Legends—Carmen Miranda	—	1.00	.10–.30
❏4499	44¢	Latin Music Legends—Selena	—	1.00	.10–.30
❏4500	44¢	Latin Music Legends—Carlos Gardel	—	1.00	.10–.30
❏4501	44¢	Latin Music Legends—Celia Cruz	—	1.00	.10–.30
		Strip of 5	—	5.00	—
❏4502	44¢	Neon Celebrate	—	1.00	.10–.30
		Pane of 20	—	20.00	—
❏4503	44¢	Jazz	—	1.00	.10–.30
		Pane of 20	—	20.00	—
❏4504	20¢	George Washington	—	.55	.10–.30
		Pane of 20	—	10.00	—
❏4505	29¢	Herbs—Oregano	—	.65	.10–.30
❏4506	29¢	Herbs—Flax	—	.65	.10–.30
❏4507	29¢	Herbs—Foxglove	—	.65	.10–.30
❏4508	29¢	Herbs—Lavender	—	.65	.10–.30
❏4509	29¢	Herbs—Sage	—	.65	.10–.30
		Strip of 5	—	3.00	—

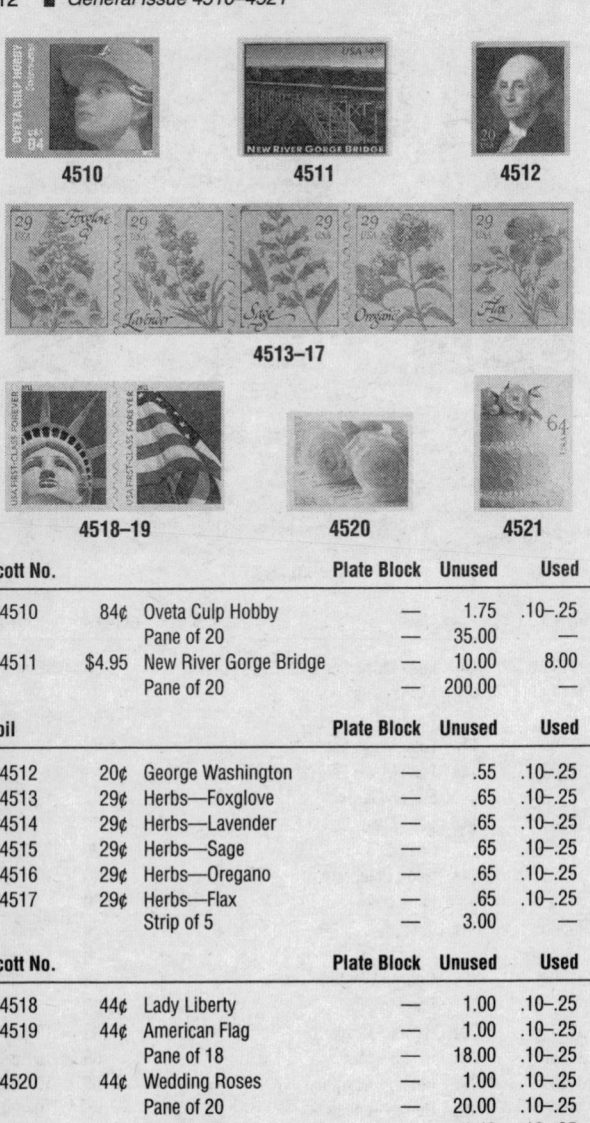

4510

4511

4512

4513–17

4518–19

4520

4521

Scott No.			Plate Block	Unused	Used
❏4510	84¢	Oveta Culp Hobby	—	1.75	.10–.25
		Pane of 20	—	35.00	—
❏4511	$4.95	New River Gorge Bridge	—	10.00	8.00
		Pane of 20	—	200.00	—

Coil			Plate Block	Unused	Used
❏4512	20¢	George Washington	—	.55	.10–.25
❏4513	29¢	Herbs—Foxglove	—	.65	.10–.25
❏4514	29¢	Herbs—Lavender	—	.65	.10–.25
❏4515	29¢	Herbs—Sage	—	.65	.10–.25
❏4516	29¢	Herbs—Oregano	—	.65	.10–.25
❏4517	29¢	Herbs—Flax	—	.65	.10–.25
		Strip of 5	—	3.00	—

Scott No.			Plate Block	Unused	Used
❏4518	44¢	Lady Liberty	—	1.00	.10–.25
❏4519	44¢	American Flag	—	1.00	.10–.25
		Pane of 18	—	18.00	.10–.25
❏4520	44¢	Wedding Roses	—	1.00	.10–.25
		Pane of 20	—	20.00	.10–.25
❏4521	64¢	Wedding Cake	—	1.40	.10–.25
		Pane of 20	—	28.00	.10–.25

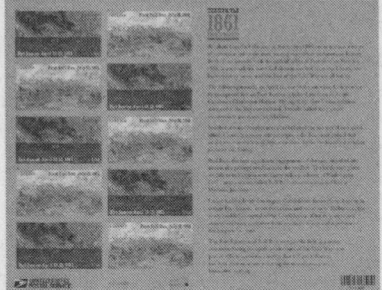

4522

4522

4523

4523

4524a   **4524b**   **4524c**   **4524d**   **4524e**

Scott No.			Plate Block	Unused	Used
❑4522	44¢	The Civil War—Fort Sumter	—	1.00	.10–.35
		Sheet of 12	—	12.00	—
❑4523	44¢	The Civil War—Bull Run	—	1.00	.10–.35
		Sheet of 12	—	12.00	.10–.35
❑4524a	44¢	Go Green—Buy Local Produce	—	1.00	.10–.35
❑4524b	44¢	Go Green—Fix Water Leaks	—	1.00	.10–.35
❑4524c	44¢	Go Green—Share Rides	—	1.00	.10–.35
❑4524d	44¢	Go Green—Turn Off Lights	—	1.00	.10–.35
❑4524e	44¢	Go Green—Choose to Walk	—	1.00	.10–.35

4524f

4524g

4524h

4524i

4524j

4524k

4524l

4524m

4524n

4524o

4524p

4525

Scott No.			Plate Block	Unused	Used
☐4524f	44¢	Go Green—Go Green	—	1.00	.10–.25
☐4524g	44¢	Go Green—Compost	—	1.00	.10–.25
☐4524h	44¢	Go Green—Let Nature Do the Work	—	1.00	.10–.25
☐4524i	44¢	Go Green—Recycle More	—	1.00	.10–.25
☐4524j	44¢	Go Green—Ride a Bike	—	1.00	.10–.25
☐4524k	44¢	Go Green—Plant Trees	—	1.00	.10–.25
☐4524l	44¢	Go Green—Insulate the Home	—	1.00	.10–.25
☐4524m	44¢	Go Green—Use Public Transportation	—	1.00	.10–.25
☐4524n	44¢	Go Green—Use Efficient Light Bulbs	—	1.00	.10–.25
☐4524o	44¢	Go Green—Adjust the Thermostat	—	1.00	.10–.25
☐4524p	44¢	Go Green—Maintain Tire Pressure	—	1.00	.10–.25
		Pane of 16	—	16.00	—
☐4525	44¢	Helen Hayes	—	1.00	.10–.25
		Pane of 20	—	20.00	—

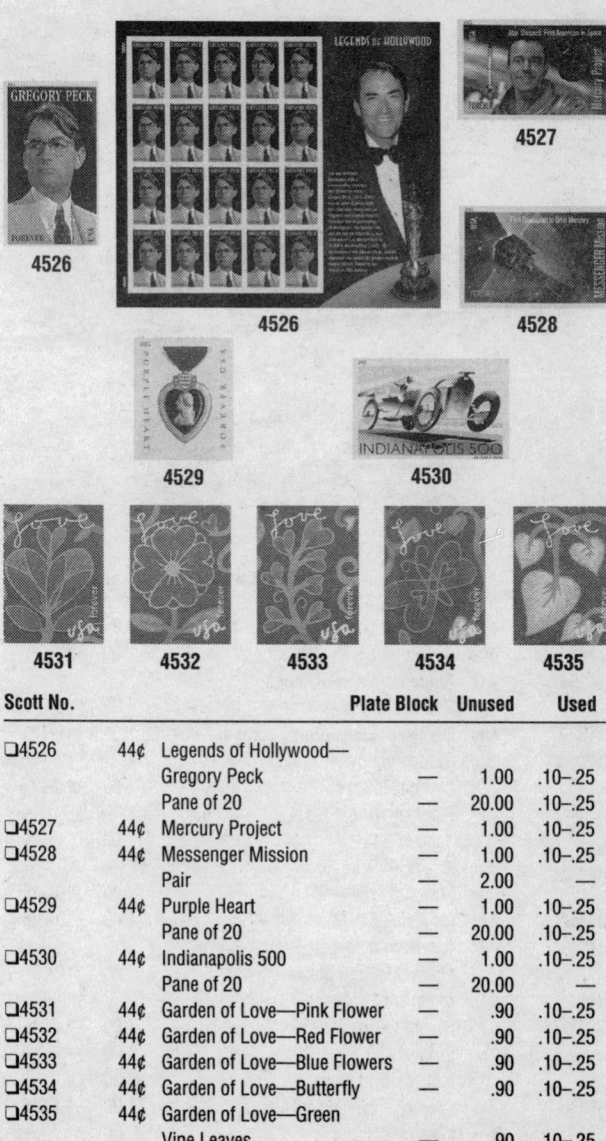

4526

4527

4528

4529

4530

4531

4532

4533

4534

4535

Scott No.			Plate Block	Unused	Used
❑4526	44¢	Legends of Hollywood—			
		Gregory Peck	—	1.00	.10–.25
		Pane of 20	—	20.00	.10–.25
❑4527	44¢	Mercury Project	—	1.00	.10–.25
❑4528	44¢	Messenger Mission	—	1.00	.10–.25
		Pair	—	2.00	—
❑4529	44¢	Purple Heart	—	1.00	.10–.25
		Pane of 20	—	20.00	.10–.25
❑4530	44¢	Indianapolis 500	—	1.00	.10–.25
		Pane of 20	—	20.00	—
❑4531	44¢	Garden of Love—Pink Flower	—	.90	.10–.25
❑4532	44¢	Garden of Love—Red Flower	—	.90	.10–.25
❑4533	44¢	Garden of Love—Blue Flowers	—	.90	.10–.25
❑4534	44¢	Garden of Love—Butterfly	—	.90	.10–.25
❑4535	44¢	Garden of Love—Green			
		Vine Leaves	—	.90	.10–.25

4536

4537

4538

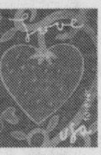
4539

4540

4541

4542

4543

4544

4545

Scott No.			Plate Block	Unused	Used
❑4536	44¢	Garden of Love—Blue Flower	—	.90	.10–.25
❑4537	44¢	Garden of Love—Doves	—	.90	.10–.25
❑4538	44¢	Garden of Love—Orange Red Flowers	—	.90	.10–.25
❑4539	44¢	Garden of Love—Strawberries	—	.90	.10–.25
❑4540	44¢	Garden of Love—Yellow Orange Flowers	—	.90	.10–.25
		Block of 10	8.50	—	—
		Pane of 20	—	17.00	—
❑4541	44¢	American Scientists— Melvin Calvin	—	1.00	.10–.25
❑4542	44¢	American Scientists—Asa Gray	—	1.00	.10–.25
❑4543	44¢	American Scientists— Maria Goeppart Mayer	—	1.00	.10–.25
❑4544	44¢	American Scientists— Severo Ochoa	—	1.00	.10–.25
		Strip of 4	—	4.00	—
		Pane of 20	—	20.00	—
❑4545	44¢	Literary Arts—Mark Twain	—	1.00	.10–.25
		Pane of 20	—	20.00	—

4546a

4546b

4546c

4546d

4546

4546e

4546f

4546g

4546h

Scott No.			Plate Block	Unused	Used
☐4546a	44¢	Pioneers of American Industrial Design—Peter Muller-Munk	—	1.00	.10–.25
☐4546b	44¢	Pioneers of American Industrial Design—Frederick Hurten Rhead	—	1.00	.10–.25
☐4546c	44¢	Pioneers of American Industrial Design—Raymond Loewy	—	1.00	.10–.25
☐4546d	44¢	Pioneers of American Industrial Design—Donald Deskey	—	1.00	.10–.25
☐4546e	44¢	Pioneers of American Industrial Design—Walter Dorwin Teague	—	1.00	.10–.25
☐4546f	44¢	Pioneers of American Industrial Design—Henry Dreyfuss	—	1.00	.10–.25
☐4546g	44¢	Pioneers of American Industrial Design—Norman Bel Geddes	—	1.00	.10–.25
☐4546h	44¢	Pioneers of American Industrial Design—Dave Chapman	—	1.00	.10–.25

4546i

4546j

4546k

4546l

4547

4548–51

4548

4549

4550

4551

Scott No.			Plate Block	Unused	Used
☐4546i	44¢	Pioneers of American Industrial Design—Greta von Nessen	—	1.00	.10–.25
☐4546j	44¢	Pioneers of American Industrial Design—Eliot Noyes	—	1.00	.10–.25
☐4546k	44¢	Pioneers of American Industrial Design—Russel Wright	—	1.00	.10–.25
☐4546l	44¢	Pioneers of American Industrial Design—Gilbert Rohde	—	1.00	.10–.25
		Sheet of 12	—	12.00	—
☐4547	44¢	Owney the Postal Dog	—	1.50	.10–.25
		Pane of 20	—	30.00	—
☐4548	44¢	US Merchant Marine—Clipper Ship	—	1.00	.10–.25
☐4549	44¢	US Merchant Marine—Auxiliary Steamship	—	1.00	.10–.25
☐4550	44¢	US Merchant Marine—Liberty Ship	—	1.00	.10–.25
☐4551	44¢	US Merchant Marine—Container Ship	—	1.00	.10–.25
		Sheet of 20	—	20.00	—

4552

4553 **4554** **4555** **4556** **4557**

4553–57

4558

Scott No.			Plate Block	Unused	Used
☐4552	44¢	Eid	—	1.00	.10–.25
		Pane of 20	—	20.00	—
☐4553	44¢	Pixar Films: Send a Hello—Cars	—	1.25	.10–.25
☐4554	44¢	Pixar Films: Send a Hello—Ratatouille	—	1.25	.10–.25
☐4555	44¢	Pixar Films: Send a Hello—Toy Story	—	1.25	.10–.25
☐4556	44¢	Pixar Films: Send a Hello—Up	—	1.25	.10–.25
☐4557	44¢	Pixar Films: Send a Hello—Wall-E	—	1.25	.10–.25
		Strip of 4	—	5.00	—
		Pane of 20	—	25.00	—
☐4558	44¢	American Treasures—Edward Hopper	—	1.00	.10–.25
		Pane of 20	—	20.00	—

4559   4560   4561   4562   4563   4564

4565   4566   4567   4568   4569

Scott No.			Plate Block	Unused	Used
❑4559	44¢	Lady Liberty	—	1.00	.10–.25
❑4560	44¢	American Flag	—	1.00	.10–.25
❑4561	44¢	Lady Liberty	—	1.00	.10–.25
❑4562	44¢	American Flag	—	1.00	.10–.25
❑4563	44¢	Lady Liberty	—	1.00	.10–.25
❑4564	44¢	American Flag	—	1.00	.10–.25
		Pane of 20	—	20.00	—
❑4565	44¢	Black Heritage—Barbara Jordan	—	1.00	.10–.25
		Pane of 20	—	20.00	.10–.25
❑4566	44¢	Romare Bearden—Conjunction	—	1.00	.10–.25
❑4567	44¢	Romare Bearden—Odysseus	—	1.00	.10–.25
❑4568	44¢	Romare Bearden—Prevalence of Ritual	—	1.00	.10–.25
❑4569	44¢	Romare Bearden—Falling Star	—	1.00	.10–.25
		Strip of 4	—	4.00	—
		Sheet of 16	—	16.00	—

Scott No.			Plate Block	Unused	Used
❑ 4570	44¢	Madonna of the Candelabra	—	1.00	.10–.25
❑ 4571	44¢	Holiday Baubles	—	1.00	.10–.25
❑ 4572	44¢	Holiday Baubles	—	1.00	.10–.25
❑ 4573	44¢	Holiday Baubles	—	1.00	.10–.25
❑ 4574	44¢	Holiday Baubles	—	1.00	.10–.25
		Block of 4	4.00	—	—
❑ 4575	44¢	Holiday Baubles	—	1.00	.10–.25
❑ 4576	44¢	Holiday Baubles	—	1.00	.10–.25
❑ 4577	44¢	Holiday Baubles	—	1.00	.10–.25
❑ 4578	44¢	Holiday Baubles	—	1.00	.10–.25
		Block of 4	4.00	—	—
❑ 4579	44¢	Holiday Baubles	—	1.00	.10–.25
❑ 4580	44¢	Holiday Baubles	—	1.00	.10–.25
❑ 4581	44¢	Holiday Baubles	—	1.00	.10–.25
❑ 4582	44¢	Holiday Baubles	—	1.00	.10–.25
		Block of 4	4.00	—	—
❑ 4583	44¢	Hanukkah	—	1.00	.10–.25
❑ 4584	44¢	Kwanzaa	—	1.00	.10–.25

4585   4586   4587

4588   4589   4590

Scott No.			Plate Block	Unused	Used
Coil.					
❑ 4585	44¢	Spectrum Eagle—Green	—	1.00	.10–.25
❑ 4586	44¢	Spectrum Eagle—Blue	—	1.00	.10–.25
❑ 4587	44¢	Spectrum Eagle—Purple	—	1.00	.10–.25
❑ 4588	44¢	Spectrum Eagle—Red	—	1.00	.10–.25
❑ 4589	44¢	Spectrum Eagle—Yellow	—	1.00	.10–.25
❑ 4590	44¢	Spectrum Eagle—Green	—	1.00	.10–.25
		Horizontal strip of 6	—	6.00	—

Scott No.			Plate Block	Unused	Used
2012.					
❑ 4591	44¢	New Mexico Statehood	—	1.00	.10–.25
❑ 4592	32¢	Aloha Shirts—Surfers/Palm Trees	—	1.00	.10–.25
❑ 4593	32¢	Aloha Shirts—Surfers	—	1.00	.10–.25
❑ 4594	32¢	Aloha Shirts—Bird of Paradise	—	1.00	.10–.25
❑ 4595	32¢	Aloha Shirts—Kilauea Volcano	—	1.00	.10–.25
❑ 4596	32¢	Aloha Shirts—Fish/Star Fish	—	1.00	.10–.25
		Horizontal strip of 5	—	5.00	.10–.25
❑ 4597	32¢	Aloha Shirts—Fish/Star Fish	—	1.00	.10–.25
❑ 4598	32¢	Aloha Shirts—Surfers/Palm Trees	—	1.00	.10–.25
❑ 4599	32¢	Aloha Shirts—Surfers	—	1.00	.10–.25
❑ 4600	32¢	Aloha Shirts—Bird of Paradise	—	1.00	.10–.25
❑ 4601	32¢	Aloha Shirts—Kilauea Volcano	—	1.00	.10–.25
		Horizontal strip of 5	—	5.00	.10–.25
		Pane of 20	—	20.00	—
❑ 4602	65¢	Wedding Cake	—	1.50	.10–.25
❑ 4603	65¢	Baltimore Checkerspot Butterfly	—	1.70	.10–.25
❑ 4604	65¢	Dogs at Work—Seeing Eye	—	1.35	.10–.25
❑ 4605	65¢	Dogs at Work—Therapy	—	1.35	.10–.25
❑ 4606	65¢	Dogs at Work—Military	—	1.35	.10–.25
❑ 4607	65¢	Dogs at Work—Rescue	—	1.35	.10–.25
		Block of 4	5.50	—	—
		Pane of 20	—	27.00	—

	4608	4609	4610	4611	4612

Scott No.			Plate Block	Unused	Used
❏ 4608	85¢	Birds of Prey—Northern Goshawk	—	2.00	.10–.25
❏ 4609	85¢	Birds of Prey—Peregrine Falcon	—	2.00	.10–.25
❏ 4610	85¢	Birds of Prey—Golden Eagle	—	2.00	.10–.25
❏ 4611	85¢	Birds of Prey—Osprey	—	2.00	.10–.25
❏ 4612	85¢	Birds of Prey—Northern Harrier	—	2.00	.10–.25
		Strip of 5	—	10.00	—
		Pane of 20	—	40.00	—

	4613	4614	4615	4616	4617

	4618	4619	4620	4621	4622

Scott No.			Plate Block	Unused	Used

Coil.

❏ 4613	45¢	Weather Vanes—Rooster w/Perch	—	1.10	.10–.25
❏ 4614	45¢	Weather Vanes—Cow	—	1.10	.10–.25
❏ 4615	45¢	Weather Vanes—Eagle	—	1.10	.10–.25
❏ 4616	45¢	Weather Vanes—Rooster wo/Perch	—	1.10	.10–.25
❏ 4617	45¢	Weather Vanes—Centaur	—	1.10	.10–.25
		Horizontal strip of 5	—	5.50	—
❏ 4618	45¢	Bonsai—Sierra Juniper	—	1.10	.10–.25
❏ 4619	45¢	Bonsai—Black Pine	—	1.10	.10–.25
❏ 4620	45¢	Bonsai—Banyan	—	1.10	.10–.25
❏ 4621	45¢	Bonsai—Trident Maple	—	1.10	.10–.25
❏ 4622	45¢	Bonsai—Azalea	—	1.10	.10–.25
		Horizontal strip of 5	—	5.50	—
		Double sided pane of 20	—	22.00	—

4623

4624

4625

4626

4627

4628

Scott No.			Plate Block	Unused	Used
❏ 4623	45¢	Year of the Dragon	—	1.00	.10–.25
❏ 4624	45¢	Black Heritage Series—			
		John H. Johnson	—	1.00	.10–.25
		Sheet of 12	—	12.00	—
❏ 4625	45¢	Heart Health	—	1.00	.10–.25
		Pane of 20	—	20.00	—
❏ 4626	45¢	Love Ribbons	—	1.00	.10–.25
		Pane of 20	—	20.00	—
❏ 4627	45¢	Arizona Statehood 1912–2012	—	1.00	.10–.25
		Pane of 20	—	20.00	—
❏ 4628	45¢	Danny Thomas	—	1.00	.10–.25
		Pane of 20	—	20.00	—

4629	4630	4631	4632
Equality FOREVER	Justice FOREVER	Freedom FOREVER	Liberty FOREVER

4633	4634	4635	4636
Equality FOREVER	Justice FOREVER	Freedom FOREVER	Liberty FOREVER

4637	4638	4639	4640
Equality FOREVER	Justice FOREVER	Freedom FOREVER	Liberty FOREVER

4641	4642	4643	4644
Freedom FOREVER	Liberty FOREVER	Equality FOREVER	Justice FOREVER

Scott No.			Plate Block	Unused	Used
Coil.					
❏ 4629	45¢	Four Flags—Equality (AVR)	—	1.00	.10–.25
❏ 4630	45¢	Four Flags—Justice (AVR)	—	1.00	.10–.25
❏ 4631	45¢	Four Flags—Freedom (AVR)	—	1.00	.10–.25
❏ 4632	45¢	Four Flags—Liberty (AVR)	—	1.00	.10–.25
		Horizontal strip of 4	—	4.00	—
❏ 4633	45¢	Four Flags—Equality (APU)	—	1.00	.10–.25
❏ 4634	45¢	Four Flags—Justice (APU)	—	1.00	.10–.25
❏ 4635	45¢	Four Flags—Freedom (APU)	—	1.00	.10–.25
❏ 4636	45¢	Four Flags—Liberty (APU)	—	1.00	.10–.25
		Horizontal strip of 4	—	4.00	—
❏ 4637	45¢	Four Flags—Equality (SSP)	—	1.00	.10–.25
❏ 4638	45¢	Four Flags—Justice (SSP)	—	1.00	.10–.25
❏ 4639	45¢	Four Flags—Freedom (SSP)	—	1.00	.10–.25
❏ 4640	45¢	Four Flags—Liberty (SSP)	—	1.00	.10–.25
		Horizontal strip of 4	—	4.00	—
❏ 4641	45¢	Four Flags—Freedom, colored dots	—	1.00	.10–.25
❏ 4642	45¢	Four Flags—Liberty, colored dots	—	1.00	.10–.25
❏ 4643	45¢	Four Flags—Equality, colored dots	—	1.00	.10–.25
❏ 4644	45¢	Four Flags—Justice, colored dots	—	1.00	.10–.25
		Block of 4	—	4.00	—

4645

4646

4647

4648

4649

4650

4651–52

Scott No.			Plate Block	Unused	Used
❏ 4645	45¢	Four Flags—Freedom	—	1.00	.10–.25
❏ 4646	45¢	Four Flags—Liberty	—	1.00	.10–.25
❏ 4647	45¢	Four Flags—Equality	—	1.00	.10–.25
❏ 4648	45¢	Four Flags—Justice	—	1.00	.10–.25
		Block of 4	—	4.00	—
		Double sided pane of 20	—	20.00	—
❏ 4649	$5.15	Priority Mail—Sunshine Parkway Bridge	—	12.00	6.00
❏ 4650	$18.95	Express Mail—Carmel Mission	—	30.00	10.00
❏ 4651	45¢	Cherry Blossom Centennial—Washington Monument	—	1.00	.10–.25
❏ 4652	45¢	Cherry Blossom Centennial—Jefferson Monument	—	1.00	.10–.25
		Horizontal pair	—	2.00	—
		Pane of 20	—	20.00	—

4653

4654–63

Scott No.			Plate Block	Unused	Used
❏ 4653	45¢	American Treasure Series— William H. Johnson	—	1.60	.10–.25
❏ 4654	45¢	Twentieth Century Poets— Joseph Brodsky	—	1.00	.10–.25
❏ 4655	45¢	Twentieth Century Poets— Gwendolyn Brooks	—	1.00	.10–.25
❏ 4656	45¢	Twentieth Century Poets— William Carlos Williams	—	1.00	.10–.25
❏ 4657	45¢	Twentieth Century Poets— Robert Hayden	—	1.00	.10–.25
❏ 4658	45¢	Twentieth Century Poets— Sylvia Plath	—	1.00	.10–.25
❏ 4659	45¢	Twentieth Century Poets— Elizabeth Bishop	—	1.00	.10–.25
❏ 4660	45¢	Twentieth Century Poets— Wallace Stevens	—	1.00	.10–.25
❏ 4661	45¢	Twentieth Century Poets— Denise Levertov	—	1.00	.10–.25
❏ 4662	45¢	Twentieth Century Poets— e. e. cummings	—	1.00	.10–.25
❏ 4663	45¢	Twentieth Century Poets— Theodore Roethke	—	1.00	.10–.25
		Block of 10	10.00	—	—
		Sheet of 20	—	20.00	—

4664

4665

4666

4667

4668–71

Scott No.			Plate Block	Unused	Used
❑ 4664	45¢	Civil War 1862—New Orleans	—	1.00	.10–.25
❑ 4665	45¢	Civil War 1862—Antietam	—	1.00	.10–.25
		Horizontal pair	—	2.00	—
		Vertical pair	—	2.00	—
❑ 4666	45¢	Distinguished American Series— José Ferrer, Actor	—	1.00	.10–.25
❑ 4667	45¢	Louisiana Statehood 1812	—	1.00	.10–.25
❑ 4668	45¢	Great Film Directors—John Ford	—	1.10	.10–.25
❑ 4669	45¢	Great Film Directors—Frank Capra	—	1.10	.10–.25
❑ 4670	45¢	Great Film Directors—Billy Wilder	—	1.10	.10–.25
❑ 4671	45¢	Great Film Directors—John Houston	—	1.10	.10–.25
		Block of 4	4.50	—	—
		Pane of 20	—	20.00	—

4672

4673–76

4677–81

Scott No.			Plate Block	Unused	Used
❏ 4672	1¢	Bobcat	—	1.00	.10–.25

Scott No.			Plate Block	Unused	Used
Coil.					
❏ 4673	45¢	Four Flags—Freedom	—	1.00	.10–.25
❏ 4674	45¢	Four Flags—Liberty	—	1.00	.10–.25
❏ 4675	45¢	Four Flags—Equality	—	1.00	.10–.25
❏ 4676	45¢	Four Flags—Justice	—	1.00	.10–.25
		Block of 4	4.00	—	—

Scott No.			Plate Block	Unused	Used
❏ 4677	45¢	Pixar Mail A Smile—A Bugs Life	—	1.00	.10–.25
❏ 4678	45¢	Pixar Mail A Smile—The Incredibles	—	1.00	.10–.25
❏ 4679	45¢	Pixar Mail A Smile—Finding Nemo	—	1.00	.10–.25
❏ 4680	45¢	Pixar Mail A Smile—Toy Story 2	—	1.00	.10–.25
❏ 4681	45¢	Pixar Mail A Smile—Monsters, Inc.	—	1.00	.10–.25
		Horizontal strip of 5	—	5.00	—
		Pane of 20	—	20.00	—

4682   **4683**   **4684**   **4685**   **4686**

4687–90

4691

4692   **4693**

Scott No.			Plate Block	Unused	Used
❏ 4682	32¢	Aloha Shirts—Surfers/Palm Trees	—	1.00	.10–.25
❏ 4683	32¢	Aloha Shirts—Bird of Paradise	—	1.00	.10–.25
❏ 4684	32¢	Aloha Shirts—Fish/Star Fish	—	1.00	.10–.25
❏ 4685	32¢	Aloha Shirts—Surfers	—	1.00	.10–.25
❏ 4686	32¢	Aloha Shirts—Kilauea Volcano	—	1.00	.10–.25
		Vertical strip of 5	—	5.00	.10–.25
		Pane of 10	—	10.00	
❏ 4687	45¢	Bicycling—Child	—	1.00	.10–.25
❏ 4688	45¢	Bicycling—Commuter	—	1.00	.10–.25
❏ 4689	45¢	Bicycling—Road Racer	—	1.00	.10–.25
❏ 4690	45¢	Bicycling—BMX Rider	—	1.00	.10–.25
		Horizontal strip of 4	—	4.00	—
		Pane of 20	—	20.00	—
❏ 4691	45¢	Celebrate Scouting	—	1.00	.10–.25
❏ 4692	45¢	Edith Piaf	—	1.00	.10–.25
❏ 4693	45¢	Miles Davis	—	1.00	.10–.25
		Horizontal pair	—	2.00	—
		Sheet of 20	—	20.00	—

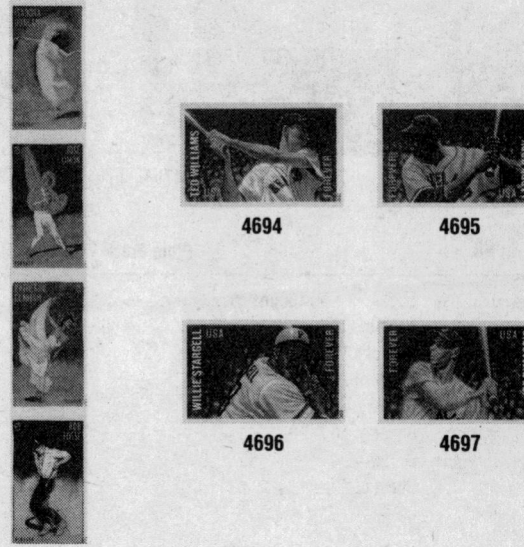

4694

4695

4696

4697

4698–4701

Scott No.			Plate Block	Unused	Used
❏ 4694	45¢	Major League Baseball All-Stars—Ted Williams	—	1.00	.10–.25
❏ 4695	45¢	Major League Baseball All-Stars—Larry Doby	—	1.00	.10–.25
❏ 4696	45¢	Major League Baseball All-Stars—Willie Stargell	—	1.00	.10–.25
❏ 4697	45¢	Major League Baseball All-Stars—Joe DiMaggio	—	1.00	.10–.25
		Block of 4	—	4.00	—
		Sheet of 20	—	20.00	—
❏ 4698	45¢	Innovative Choreographers—Isadora Duncan	—	1.00	.10–.25
❏ 4699	45¢	Innovative Choreographers—Jose Limon	—	1.00	.10–.25
❏ 4700	45¢	Innovative Choreographers—Katherine Dunham	—	1.00	.10–.25
❏ 4701	45¢	Innovative Choreographers—Bob Fosse	—	1.00	.10–.25
		Vertical strip of 4	—	4.00	—
		Pane of 20	—	20.00	—

4702

4703

4704

4705

Scott No.			Plate Block	Unused	Used
☐ 4702	45¢	Edgar Rice Burroughs	—	1.00	.10–.25
		Pane of 20	—	20.00	—
☐ 4703	45¢	War of 1812	—	1.00	.10–.25
		Sheet of 20	—	20.00	—
☐ 4704	45¢	Purple Heart	—	1.00	.10–.25
		Sheet of 20	—	20.00	—
☐ 4705	45¢	O. Henry	—	1.00	.10–.25
		Sheet of 20	—	20.00	—

4706

4707

4708

4709

Scott No.			Plate Block	Unused	Used
Coil.					
☐ 4706	45¢	Four Flags—Freedom	—	1.00	.10–.25
☐ 4707	45¢	Four Flags—Liberty	—	1.00	.10–.25
☐ 4708	45¢	Four Flags—Equality	—	1.00	.10–.25
☐ 4709	45¢	Four Flags—Justice	—	1.00	.10–.25
		Block of 4	4.00	—	—

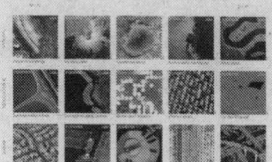

4710

4711

4712

4713

4716

4714

4715

Scott No.			Plate Block	Unused	Used
❏ 4710	45¢	Earthscapes single stamp	—	1.00	.10–.25
		Sheet of 15	—	14.00	—
		Imperforate sheet of 15	—	35.00	—
❏ 4711	45¢	Christmas Holy Family	—	1.00	.10–.25
		Double–sided pane of 20	—	20.00	—
❏ 4712	45¢	Reindeer Moon	—	1.00	.10–.25
❏ 4713	45¢	Santa Sleigh	—	1.00	.10–.25
		Block of 4	4.00	—	—
❏ 4714	45¢	Reindeer Roof	—	1.00	.10–.25
❏ 4715	45¢	Village	—	1.00	.10–.25
❏ 4716	45¢	Lady Bird Johnson	—	1.00	.10–.25
		Sheet of 6	—	6.00	—

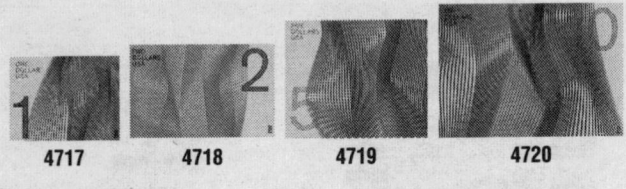

4717   4718   4719   4720

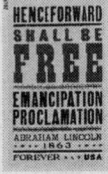

4721

4722–25

4726

Scott No.			Plate Block	Unused	Used
❑ 4717	$1	Waves of Color	—	1.00	.10–.25
❑ 4718	$2	Waves of Color	—	2.00	.10–.25
❑ 4719	$5	Waves of Color	—	5.00	.10–.25
❑ 4720	$10	Waves of Color	—	10.00	.10–.25

2013.

Scott No.			Plate Block	Unused	Used
❑ 4721	45¢	Emancipation	—	1.00	.10–.25
		Pane of 20	—	20.00	—
❑ 4722	46¢	Kaleidoscope Flowers—yellow	—	1.00	.10–.25
❑ 4723	46¢	Kaleidoscope Flowers—yellow green	—	1.00	.10–.25
❑ 4724	46¢	Kaleidoscope Flowers—red violet	—	1.00	.10–.25
❑ 4725	46¢	Kaleidoscope Flowers—red	—	1.00	.10–.25
❑ 4726	45¢	Year of the Snake	—	1.00	.10–.25
		Pane of 12	—	12.00	—

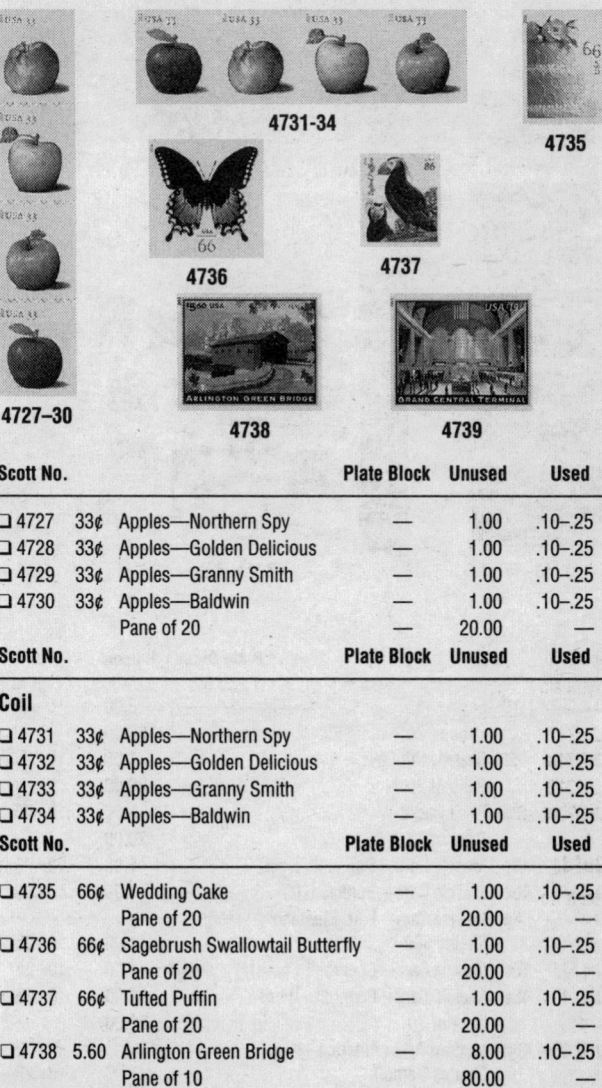

4731-34

4735

4736

4737

4727-30

4738

4739

Scott No.			Plate Block	Unused	Used
❏ 4727	33¢	Apples—Northern Spy	—	1.00	.10–.25
❏ 4728	33¢	Apples—Golden Delicious	—	1.00	.10–.25
❏ 4729	33¢	Apples—Granny Smith	—	1.00	.10–.25
❏ 4730	33¢	Apples—Baldwin	—	1.00	.10–.25
		Pane of 20	—	20.00	—

Scott No.			Plate Block	Unused	Used

Coil

❏ 4731	33¢	Apples—Northern Spy	—	1.00	.10–.25
❏ 4732	33¢	Apples—Golden Delicious	—	1.00	.10–.25
❏ 4733	33¢	Apples—Granny Smith	—	1.00	.10–.25
❏ 4734	33¢	Apples—Baldwin	—	1.00	.10–.25

Scott No.			Plate Block	Unused	Used
❏ 4735	66¢	Wedding Cake	—	1.00	.10–.25
		Pane of 20		20.00	—
❏ 4736	66¢	Sagebrush Swallowtail Butterfly	—	1.00	.10–.25
		Pane of 20		20.00	—
❏ 4737	66¢	Tufted Puffin	—	1.00	.10–.25
		Pane of 20		20.00	—
❏ 4738	5.60	Arlington Green Bridge	—	8.00	.10–.25
		Pane of 10		80.00	—
❏ 4739	19.95	Grand Central Terminal	—	22.00	.10–.25
		Pane of 10		220.00	—

4740

4741

4742

4743–47

MODERN ART IN AMERICA

4748a–48l

Scott No.			Plate Block	Unused	Used
❑ 4740	1.10	Earth	—	3.00	.10–.25
		Pane of 20		60.00	—
❑ 4741	46¢	Sealed with Love	—	1.00	.10–.25
		Pane of 20		20.00	—
❑ 4742	46¢	Rosa Parks	—	1.00	.10–.25
		Pane of 20		20.00	—
❑ 4743	46¢	Muscle Cars—Dodge Charger	—	1.00	.10–.25
❑ 4744	46¢	Muscle Cars—Pontiac GTO	—	1.00	.10–.25
❑ 4745	46¢	Muscle Cars—Ford Mustang			
		Shelby 500	—	1.00	.10–.25
❑ 4746	46¢	Muscle Cars—Chevrolet Chevel	—	1.00	.10–.25
❑ 4747	46¢	Muscle Cars—Plymouth Hemi	—	1.00	.10–.25
		Pane of 20		20.00	—
❑ 4748a	46¢	Modern Art in America—			
		Charles Demoth	—	1.00	.10–.25
❑ 4748b	46¢	Modern Art in America—John Marin	—	1.00	.10–.25
❑ 4748c	46¢	Modern Art in America—Stuart Davis	—	1.00	.10–.25

Scott No.			Plate Block	Unused	Used
❑ 4748d	46¢	Modern Art in America—Marsden Hartley	—	1.00	.10–.25
❑ 4748e	46¢	Modern Art in America—Georgia O'Keeffe	—	1.00	.10–.25
❑ 4748f	46¢	Modern Art in America—Man Ray	—	1.00	.10–.25
❑ 4748g	46¢	Modern Art in America—Aaron Douglas	—	1.00	.10–.25
❑ 4748h	46¢	Modern Art in America—Charles Sheeter	—	1.00	.10–.25
❑ 4748i	46¢	Modern Art in America—Joseph Stella	—	1.00	.10–.25
❑ 4748j	46¢	Modern Art in America—Gerald Murphy	—	1.00	.10–.25
❑ 4748k	46¢	Modern Art in America—Marcel Duchamp	—	1.00	.10–.25
❑ 4748l	46¢	Modern Art in America—Arthur Dove	—	1.00	.10–.25
		Pane of 12		12.00	—

4749

4750–53

Scott No.			Plate Block	Unused	Used

Coil

Scott No.			Plate Block	Unused	Used
❑ 4749	46¢	Patriotic Star	—	1.00	.10–.25

Scott No.			Plate Block	Unused	Used
❑ 4750	46¢	La Florida—hibiscus	—	1.00	.10–.25
❑ 4751	46¢	La Florida—yellow cannas	—	1.00	.10–.25
❑ 4752	46¢	La Florida—morning glories	—	1.00	.10–.25
❑ 4753	46¢	La Florida—passion flowers	—	1.00	.10–.25
		Pane of 16		16.00	—

4754   4755   4756   4757   4758   4759   4760

4761   4762   4763

4764   4765

4766–69

Scott No.			Plate Block	Unused	Used
❑ 4754	46¢	Vintage Seed Packets—phlox	—	1.00	.10–.25
❑ 4755	46¢	Vintage Seed Packets—calendula	—	1.00	.10–.25
❑ 4756	46¢	Vintage Seed Packets—digitalis	—	1.00	.10–.25
❑ 4757	46¢	Vintage Seed Packets—linum	—	1.00	.10–.25
❑ 4758	46¢	Vintage Seed Packets—alyssum	—	1.00	.10–.25
❑ 4759	46¢	Vintage Seed Packets—zinnias	—	1.00	.10–.25
❑ 4760	46¢	Vintage Seed Packets—pinks	—	1.00	.10–.25
❑ 4761	46¢	Vintage Seed Packets—cosmos	—	1.00	.10–.25
❑ 4762	46¢	Vintage Seed Packets—aster	—	1.00	.10–.25
❑ 4763	46¢	Vintage Seed Packets—primrose	—	1.00	.10–.25
		Pane of 20		20.00	—
❑ 4764	46¢	Wedding Series— Where Dreams Blossom	—	1.00	.10–.25
❑ 4765	66¢	Yes I Do	—	1.00	.10–.25
❑ 4766	46¢	A Flag For All Seasons—autumn	—	1.00	.10–.25
❑ 4767	46¢	A Flag For All Seasons—winter	—	1.00	.10–.25
❑ 4768	46¢	A Flag For All Seasons—spring	—	1.00	.10–.25
❑ 4769	46¢	A Flag For All Seasons—summer	—	1.00	.10–.25

4770–73　　　　**4774–77**

4778　**4779**　**4780**　**4781**　**4782**　**4783**　**4784**　**4785**

4786　　　　**4787**

Scott No.			Plate Block	Unused	Used
☐ 4770	46¢	A Flag For All Seasons—autumn	—	1.00	.10–.25
☐ 4771	46¢	A Flag For All Seasons—winter	—	1.00	.10–.25
☐ 4772	46¢	A Flag For All Seasons—spring	—	1.00	.10–.25
☐ 4773	46¢	A Flag For All Seasons—summer	—	1.00	.10–.25
☐ 4774	46¢	A Flag For All Seasons—winter	—	1.00	.10–.25
☐ 4775	46¢	A Flag For All Seasons—spring	—	1.00	.10–.25
☐ 4776	46¢	A Flag For All Seasons—summer	—	1.00	.10–.25
☐ 4777	46¢	A Flag For All Seasons—autumn	—	1.00	.10–.25
☐ 4778	46¢	A Flag For All Seasons—spring	—	1.00	.10–.25
☐ 4779	46¢	A Flag For All Seasons—summer	—	1.00	.10–.25
☐ 4780	46¢	A Flag For All Seasons—autumn	—	1.00	.10–.25
☐ 4781	46¢	A Flag For All Seasons—winter	—	1.00	.10–.25
☐ 4782	46¢	A Flag For All Seasons—spring	—	1.00	.10–.25
☐ 4783	46¢	A Flag For All Seasons—summer	—	1.00	.10–.25
☐ 4784	46¢	A Flag For All Seasons—autumn	—	1.00	.10–.25
☐ 4785	46¢	A Flag For All Seasons—winter	—	1.00	.10–.25
		Pane of 20		20.00	—
☐ 4786	46¢	The Civil War—Vicksburg	—	1.00	.10–.25
☐ 4787	46¢	The Civil War—Gettysburg	—	1.00	.10–.25
☐ 4788	46¢	Double sided pane of 12		12.00	—

4789   **4790**   **4791–95**

4796   **4797**   **4798**   **4799**

Scott No.			Plate Block	Unused	Used
❑ 4789	46¢	Johnny Cash	—	1.00	.10–.25
		Pane of 16		16.00	—
❑ 4790	46¢	West Virginia Statehood	—	1.00	.10–.25
		Pane of 20		20.00	—
❑ 4791	46¢	New England Coastal Lighthouse— Portland Head	—	1.00	.10–.25
❑ 4792	46¢	New England Coastal Lighthouse— Portsmouth Harbor	—	1.00	.10–.25
❑ 4793	46¢	New England Coastal Lighthouse— Boston Harbor	—	1.00	.10–.25
❑ 4794	46¢	New England Coastal Lighthouse— Point Judith	—	1.00	.10–.25
❑ 4795	46¢	New England Coastal Lighthouse— New London Harbor	—	1.00	.10–.25
		Pane of 20		20.00	—
❑ 4796	46¢	A Flag For All Seasons—Spring	—	1.00	.10–.25
❑ 4797	46¢	A Flag For All Seasons—Summer	—	1.00	.10–.25
❑ 4798	46¢	A Flag For All Seasons—Fall	—	1.00	.10–.25
❑ 4799	46¢	A Flag For All Seasons—Winter	—	1.00	.10–.25
		Pane of 20		20.00	—

4800a–4800k

4801

4802

Scott No.			Plate Block	Unused	Used
❏ 4800a	46¢	Made in America—airplane mechanic	—	1.00	.10–.25
❏ 4800b	46¢	Made in America—derrick man	—	1.00	.10–.25
❏ 4800c	46¢	Made in America—millinery apprentice	—	1.00	.10–.25
❏ 4800d	46¢	Made in America—man on hoisting ball	—	1.00	.10–.25
❏ 4800e	46¢	Made in America—linotype operator	—	1.00	.10–.25
❏ 4800f	46¢	Made in America—welder	—	1.00	.10–.25
❏ 4800g	46¢	Made in America—coal miner	—	1.00	.10–.25
❏ 4800h	46¢	Made in America—riveter	—	1.00	.10–.25
❏ 4800i	46¢	Made in America—railroad track walker	—	1.00	.10–.25
❏ 4800j	46¢	Made in America—textile worker	—	1.00	.10–.25
❏ 4800k	46¢	Made in America—man guiding beam	—	1.00	.10–.25
		5 panes of 12		60.00	—
❏ 4801	46¢	Eid	—	1.00	.10–.25
		Pane of 20		20.00	—
❏ 4802	1¢	Bobcat	—	1.00	.10–.25
		Pane of 20		20.00	—

4803 4804 4805 4806

4807 4808 4813 4814

4815 4816 4817 4818 4819 4820 4821

Scott No.			Plate Block	Unused	Used
❑ 4803	46¢	Althea Gibson	—	1.00	.10–.25
		Pane of 14		14.00	—
❑ 4804	46¢	March On Washington	—	1.00	.10–.25
		Pane of 20		20.00	—
❑ 4805	46¢	War of 1812 Battle of Lake Erie	—	1.00	.10–.25
		Pane of 20		20.00	—
❑ 4806	46¢	Jenny Invert	—	1.00	.10–.25
❑ 4807	46¢	Ray Charles	—	1.00	.10–.25
❑ 4808	46¢	Snowflakes	—	1.00	.10–.25
❑ 4813	46¢	Holy Family	—	1.00	.10–.25
❑ 4814	46¢	Christmas Wreath	—	1.00	.10–.25
❑ 4815	46¢	Madonna & Child	—	1.00	.10–.25
❑ 4816	46¢	Poinsettia	—	1.00	.10–.25
❑ 4817	46¢	Gingerbread House—red	—	1.00	.10–.25
❑ 4818	46¢	Gingerbread House—blue	—	1.00	.10–.25
❑ 4819	46¢	Gingerbread House—green	—	1.00	.10–.25
❑ 4820	46¢	Gingerbread House—yellow	—	1.00	.10–.25
❑ 4821	46¢	Poinsettia	—	1.00	.10–.25

NW138

NW139

NW1310a

NW1310b

NW1310c

NW1310d

NW1310e

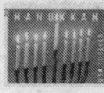
NW1311

NW1312

Scott No.			Plate Block	Unused	Used
❏	46¢	Medal of Honor Navy	—	1.00	.10–.25
❏	46¢	Medal of Honor Army	—	1.00	.10–.25
❏	46¢	Early Years	—	1.00	.10–.25
❏	46¢	Creatures	—	1.00	.10–.25
❏	46¢	Hogwart—Classes	—	1.00	.10–.25
❏	46¢	Hogwart—Spells	—	1.00	.10–.25
❏	46¢	Hogwart—Horcruxes	—	1.00	.10–.25
❏	46¢	Hanukkah	—	1.00	.10–.25
❏	46¢	Kwanzaa	—	1.00	.10–.25

SEMIPOSTAL STAMPS

NOTE: The listings include the initial postage value and surtax. The postage value changes to match first class postage as rates increase. In most cases, the surtax decreases by a corresponding amount. When the surtax falls below a certain amount, the Postal Service raises the price of a stamp, such as was the case for the Breast Cancer stamp, which rose from 40¢ to 45¢.

B1

Scott No.			Plate Block	Unused	Used
1998.					
❏ B1	(32¢+8¢)	Breast Cancer	21.00	1.25	.48

B2

Scott No.			Plate Block	Unused	Used
2002.					
❏ B2	(34¢+11¢)	Heroes of 2001	5.25	1.65	.48

AIRMAIL STAMPS

C1
(C2–C3)

Scott No.			Plate Block	Unused	Used
1918. (NH Add 60%)					
❏ C1	6¢	Orange	1575.00 (6)	70.00	58.80
❏ C2	16¢	Green (~C1)	2310.00 (6)	180.00	65.10
❏ C3	24¢	Carmine & Blue (~C1)	2625.00 (12)	215.00	65.10

C4	**C5**	**C6**

Scott No.			Plate Block	Unused	Used
1923. (NH Add 60%)					
❏ C4	8¢	Dark Green	575.00 (6)	38.00	15.75
❏ C5	16¢	Dark Blue	3675.00 (6)	115.00	47.25
❏ C6	24¢	Carmine	4200.00 (6)	158.00	47.25

C7
(C8–C9)

Scott No.			Plate Block	Unused	Used
1926–1927. (NH Add 60%)					
❏ C7	10¢	Biplanes & Map	105.00 (6)	6.75	2.10
❏ C8	15¢	Biplanes & Map (~C7)	105.00 (6)	6.75	4.25
❏ C9	20¢	Biplanes & Map (~C7)	210.00 (6)	14.50	5.25

C10

Scott No.			Plate Block	Unused	Used
1927. (NH Add 60%)					
❑ C10	10¢	Lindbergh	315.00 (6)	13.50	5.35
		Booklet Pane of 3	—	80.00	—

C11

1928. (NH Add 50%)					
❑ C11	5¢	Beacon	340.00 (8)	8.75	1.00

C12
(C16)

1930. Flat Plate Press. (NH Add 60%)					
❑ C12	5¢	Winged Globe, perf 11	265.00 (6)	16.50	1.50

C13

C14

C15

Scott No.			Plate Block	Unused	Used
1930. (NH Add 50%)					
☐ C13	65¢	Graf Zeppelin	4200.00 (6)	345.00	250.00
☐ C14	$1.30	Graf Zeppelin	RARE (6)	660.00	480.00
☐ C15	$2.60	Graf Zeppelin	RARE (6)	850.00	750.00

C17

1931–1932. Rotary Press. (NH Add 60%)

			Plate Block	Unused	Used
☐ C16	5¢	Winged Globe (~C12), perf 10½ x 11	168.00	10.50	1.00
☐ C17	8¢	Winged Globe, perf 10½ x 11	63.00	6.75	.75

C18

1933. (NH Add 50%)

			Plate Block	Unused	Used
☐ C18	50¢	Zeppelin	1627.00 (6)	148.00	100.00

C19

Scott No.			Plate Block	Unused	Used
1934. (NH Add 30%)					
❑ C19	6¢	Winged Globe	65.00	6.75	.10–.35

NOTE: Prices for stamps from 1935 forward are for never-hinged (NH) examples.

C20    **C21**    **C22**

			Plate Block	Unused	Used
1935–1937.					
❑ C20	25¢	Pan-Am Clipper	45.00 (6)	6.00	3.20
❑ C21	20¢	Pan-Am Clipper	158.00 (6)	16.00	3.50
❑ C22	50¢	Clipper	184.00 (6)	17.00	6.50

C23    **C24**

			Plate Block	Unused	Used
1938.					
❑ C23	6¢	Eagle & Shield	28.00	2.10	.10–.35
1939.					
❑ C24	30¢	Transatlantic Airmail	285.00 (6)	15.00	3.00

C25
(C26–C31)

Scott No.			Plate Block	Unused	Used
1941–1944. Transport Plane Series.					
❑ C25	6¢	Carmine	5.75	.75	.10–.30
❑ C26	8¢	Olive Green (~C25)	5.75	.75	.10–.30
❑ C27	10¢	Violet (~C25)	12.50	3.15	.10–.30
❑ C28	15¢	Brown Carmine (~C25)	14.75	6.50	.10–.30
❑ C29	20¢	Bright Green (~C25)	12.50	5.75	.10–.30
❑ C30	30¢	Blue (~C25)	14.75	5.75	.10–.30
❑ C31	50¢	Orange (~C25)	84.00	18.00	4.20

C32   **C33**   **C34**
               (C37)

C35   **C36**

1946–1947.					
❑ C32	5¢	DC-4 Skymaster, large	2.50	.75	.10–.30
❑ C33	5¢	DC-4 Skymaster, small	2.50	.75	.10–.30
❑ C34	10¢	Pan American Union Building	2.50	.75	.10–.30
❑ C35	15¢	New York Skyline	2.50	1.00	.10–.30
❑ C36	25¢	Golden Gate	4.70	2.00	.10–.30

Scott No.			Line Pair	Unused	Used
1948. Coil Stamp.					
☐ C37	5¢	DC-4 Skymaster (~C33)	11.50	3.75	2.36

C38

Scott No.			Plate Block	Unused	Used
1948.					
☐ C38	5¢	New York City	6.00	1.10	.10–.30

C39
(C41)

C40

Scott No.			Plate Block	Unused	Used
1949.					
☐ C39	6¢	DC-4 Skymaster	1.75	1.10	.10–.30
☐ C40	6¢	Alexandria	1.75	1.10	.10–.30

Scott No.			Line Pair	Unused	Used
1949. Coil Stamp.					
☐ C41	6¢	DC-4 Skymaster (~C39)	15.00	4.50	.10–.30

C42

C43

C44

C45

Scott No.			Plate Block	Unused	Used
1949.					
❑ C42	10¢	UPU Centennial	3.00	.75	.52
❑ C43	15¢	UPU Centennial	3.00	1.00	.63
❑ C44	25¢	UPU Centennial	6.30	1.35	.89
❑ C45	6¢	Wright Brothers	3.00	1.00	.52

C46

C47

C48
(C50)

Scott No.			Plate Block	Unused	Used
1952.					
❑ C46	80¢	Diamond Head	32.50	9.75	2.25
1953.					
❑ C47	6¢	Wright Brothers	3.00	.75	.10–.25
1954.					
❑ C48	4¢	Eagle in Flight	3.00	.75	.10–.25

C49

C51
(C52, C60–C61)

1957.

❏ C49	6¢	50th Anniversary – Air Force	2.50	.75	.10–.35

1958.

❏ C50	5¢	Eagle in Flight (~C48)	2.50	.75	.10–.35
❏ C51	7¢	Jetliner Silhouette, blue	2.50	.75	.10–.35

Scott No.			Line Pair	Unused	Used

1958. Coil Stamp.

❏ C52	7¢	Jetliner Silhouette (~C51), blue	19.50	4.50	.10–.35

C53

C54

C55

Scott No.			Plate Block	Unused	Used

1959.

❏ C53	7¢	Alaska Statehood	2.00	1.00	.10–.35
❏ C54	7¢	Balloon Jupiter	2.25	1.00	.10–.35
❏ C55	7¢	Hawaii Statehood	2.00	1.00	.10–.35

C56

Scott No.			Plate Block	Unused	Used
❏ C56	10¢	Pan American Games	2.25	1.25	.80

C57

C58

C59

1959–1961.

❏ C57	10¢	Liberty Bell	8.50	2.25	1.05
❏ C58	15¢	Statue of Liberty	2.25	1.25	.10–.35
❏ C59	25¢	Abraham Lincoln	4.50	1.25	.10–.35

1960.

❏ C60	7¢	Jetliner Silhouette (~C51), carmine	1.25	.65	.10–.35

Scott No.			Line Pair	Unused	Used

Coil Stamp.

❏ C61	7¢	Jetliner Silhouette (~C51), carmine	42.00	9.00	.85

C62   **C63**   **C64**
                              (C65)

Scott No.			Plate Block	Unused	Used
1961.					
❑ C62	13¢	Liberty Bell	2.50	1.35	.10–.25
❑ C63	15¢	Statue of Liberty	2.50	1.35	.10–.25

NOTE: No. C58 contains a border extension around the Statue of Liberty; No. C63 does not.

1962.					
❑ C64	8¢	Jetliner over Capitol	2.25	.75	.10–.25

Scott No.			Line Pair	Unused	Used
Coil Stamp.					
❑ C65	8¢	Jetliner over Capitol (~C64)	7.25	1.10	.10–.25

C66   **C67**   **C68**

Scott No.			Plate Block	Unused	Used
1963.					
❑ C66	15¢	Montgomery Blair	6.75	2.35	1.05
❑ C67	6¢	Eagle Perched on Rock	3.00	.75	.10–.35
❑ C68	8¢	Amelia Earhart	3.00	.65	.10–.35

C69

Scott No.			Plate Block	Unused	Used
1964.					
❑ C69	8¢	Robert Goddard	2.25	1.35	.10–.25

C70   **C71**   **C72**
                                   (C73)

Scott No.			Plate Block	Unused	Used
1967.					
❑ C70	8¢	Alaska Purchase	2.85	1.10	.10–.25
❑ C71	20¢	Columbia Jays	4.20	1.75	.10–.25
❑ C72	10¢	Runway of Stars	3.00	1.10	.10–.25

Scott No.			Line Pair	Unused	Used
1968. Coil Stamp.					
❑ C73	10¢	Runway of Stars (~C72)	2.75	1.15	.10–.25

C74   **C75**

Scott No.			Plate Block	Unused	Used
1968.					
❏ C74	10¢	50th Anniversary of Airmail	4.75	1.45	.10–.25
❏ C75	20¢	USA & Jet	4.75	1.45	.10–.25

C76

1969.					
❏ C76	10¢	First Man on the Moon	2.25	1.10	.10–.35

C77   **C78**   **C79**   **C80**
             (C82)   (C83)

1971–1973.					
❏ C77	9¢	Delta Wing	2.75	.50	.10–.35
❏ C78	11¢	Jetliner	2.75	.60	.10–.35
❏ C79	13¢	Winged Letter	2.75	.60	.10–.35
❏ C80	17¢	Statue of Liberty	2.75	.85	.10–.35

C81

Scott No.			Plate Block	Unused	Used
❑ C81	21¢	USA & Jet	3.25	.85	.10–.25

Scott No.			Line Pair	Unused	Used
Coil Stamps.					
❑ C82	11¢	Jetliner (~C78)	1.45	.65	.10–.25
❑ C83	13¢	Winged Letter (~C79)	2.20	.70	.10–.25

C84

C85

C86

Scott No.			Plate Block	Unused	Used
1972.					
❑ C84	11¢	City of Refuge	3.00	.75	.10–.35
❑ C85	11¢	Olympics—Skiers	4.35	.75	.10–.35
1973.					
❑ C86	11¢	Progress in Electronics	2.85	.75	.10–.35

C87

C88

C89

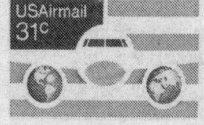

C90

Scott No.			Plate Block	Unused	Used
1974.					
☐ C87	18¢	Statue of Liberty	3.25	.85	.10–.35
☐ C88	26¢	Mount Rushmore	4.75	1.40	.10–.35
1976.					
☐ C89	25¢	Jetliner & Globes	4.85	1.00	.10–.35
☐ C90	31¢	Jetliner—Stars & Stripes	4.85	1.10	.10–.35

C91–92

1979.					
☐ C91	31¢	Wright Bros., large portraits	—	1.35	1.00
☐ C92	31¢	Wright Bros., small portraits	—	1.35	1.00
		Pair (C91–C92)	6.60	2.65	—

C93–94   **C95–96**   **C97**

Scott No.			Plate Block	Unused	Used
❑ C93	21¢	Octave Chanute, large portrait	—	2.00	1.50
❑ C94	21¢	Octave Chanute, small portrait	—	2.00	1.50
		Pair (C93–C93)	6.50	4.25	1.10

1980.

❑ C95	25¢	Wiley Post, large portrait	—	3.40	2.90
❑ C96	25¢	Wiley Post, small portrait	—	4.25	2.90
		Pair (C95–C96)	5.35	3.85	—
❑ C97	31¢	Olympics—High Jumper	12.60	1.85	1.00

C98   **C99**   **C100**
(C98A)

1981.

❑ C98	40¢	Philip Mazzei, perf 11	16.75	1.50	.10–.35
❑ C98A	40¢	Philip Mazzei, perf 10½ x 11½	12.75	6.50	2.15
❑ C99	28¢	Blanche Stuart Scott	12.75	1.20	.10–.35
❑ C100	35¢	Glenn Curtiss	14.75	1.35	.10–.35

C101–104

C105–108

Scott No.			Plate Block	Unused	Used
1983.					
❑ C101	28¢	Olympics—Gymnastics	—	2.50	1.00
❑ C102	28¢	Olympics—Hurdles	—	2.50	1.00
❑ C103	28¢	Olympics—Basketball	—	2.50	1.00
❑ C104	28¢	Olympics—Soccer	—	2.50	1.00
		Block of 4 (C101–C104)	10.00	—	—
❑ C105	40¢	Olympics—Shot Put	—	2.50	1.00
❑ C106	40¢	Olympics—Gymnast on Rings	—	2.50	1.00
❑ C107	40¢	Olympics—Swimming	—	2.50	1.00
❑ C108	40¢	Olympics—Weight Lifting	—	2.50	1.00
		Block of 4 (C105–C108)	10.00	—	—

C109–112

Scott No.			Plate Block	Unused	Used
❏ C109	35¢	Olympics—Fencing	—	2.45	1.50
❏ C110	35¢	Olympics—Cycling	—	2.45	1.50
❏ C111	35¢	Olympics—Volleyball	—	2.45	1.50
❏ C112	35¢	Olympics—Pole Vault	—	2.45	1.50
		Block of 4 (C109–C112)	7.35	—	—

C113

C114

C115

C116

1985.

❏ C113	33¢	Alfred V. Verville	5.35	1.20	.70
❏ C114	39¢	Lawrence & Elmer Sperry	5.35	1.35	.70
❏ C115	44¢	Transatlantic Airmail Clipper	7.35	2.40	.70
❏ C116	44¢	Junipero Serra	10.50	2.25	.80

C117

C118

C119

Scott No.			Plate Block	Unused	Used
1988.					
❏ C117	44¢	New Sweden	10.75	3.00	1.00
❏ C118	45¢	Samuel Langley	8.50	1.60	1.00
❏ C119	36¢	Igor Sikorsky	8.50	1.25	1.00

C120

C121

1989.					
❏ C120	45¢	French Revolution	6.45	2.75	1.60
❏ C121	45¢	Carved Figure	7.35	2.00	1.40

C122–125

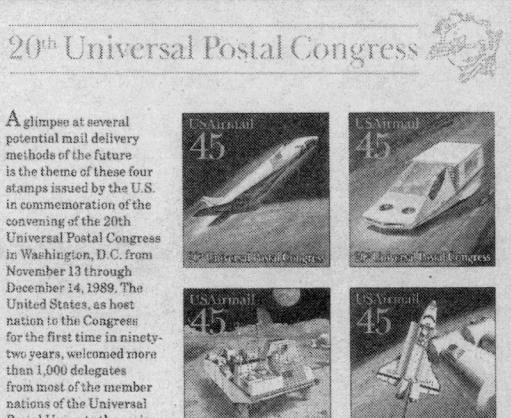

C126

Scott No.			Plate Block	Unused	Used
❏ C122	45¢	Shuttle in Flight	—	1.85	1.00
❏ C123	45¢	Hovercraft	—	1.85	1.00
❏ C124	45¢	Moon Rover	—	1.85	1.00
❏ C125	45¢	Shuttle Docking	—	1.85	1.00
		Block of 4 (C122–C125)	8.00	—	—
❏ C126	$1.80	Souvenir sheet (~C122–C125)	—	8.75	5.30
❏ C126a-d		Any single stamp, imperforate	—	2.10	1.25

C127

Scott No.			Plate Block	Unused	Used
1990.					
❏ C127	45¢	Tropical Beach	8.75	2.75	1.08

C128

C129
(C132)

C130

C131

1991.					
❏ C128	50¢	Harriet Quimby	8.65	1.85	.75
❏ C129	40¢	William Piper	6.50	1.65	.75
❏ C130	50¢	Antarctic Treaty	8.65	2.15	1.00
❏ C131	50¢	Crossing from Asia	8.65	2.85	1.00
❏ C132	40¢	William Piper (~C129)	34.00	6.75	3.00

NOTE: On No. C132, the top of Piper's hair touches the top of the stamp; on No. C129, it does not.

C133

C134

C135

C136

C137

C138

Scott No.			Plate Block	Unused	Used
1993.					
☐ C133	48¢	Niagara Falls	6.40	1.90	.80
☐ C134	40¢	Rio Grande	5.35	1.50	.80
☐ C135	60¢	Grand Canyon	7.35	2.00	.10–.35
☐ C136	70¢	Nine Mile Prairie	8.50	2.65	1.00
☐ C137	80¢	Mount McKinley	9.50	3.10	.80
☐ C138	60¢	Acadia National Park	6.50	2.75	.80

AIRMAIL SPECIAL DELIVERY STAMPS

CE1
(CE2)

Scott No.			Plate Block	Unused	Used
❑ CE1	16¢	Great Seal, blue	19.75 (6)	1.85	2.05
❑ CE2	16¢	Seal (~CE1), red & blue	11.00 (6)	1.85	.90

SPECIAL DELIVERY STAMPS

E1

E2
(E3)

E4
(E5)

E6
(E08–E11)

Scott No.			Plate Block	Unused	Used
1885. (NH Add 100%)					
❑ E1	10¢	Blue, inscribed "At Any Special Delivery Office"	—	340.00	48.00
1888. (NH Add 100%)					
❑ E2	10¢	Blue, inscribed "At Any Post Office"	—	210.00	22.25
1893. (NH Add 100%)					
❑ E3	10¢	Orange (~E2)	—	155.00	19.25
1894. (NH Add 100%)					
❑ E4	10¢	Blue, line below "Ten Cents"	—	485.00	37.00
1895. Double Line Watermark. (NH Add 100%)					
❑ E5	10¢	Blue (~E4)	—	175.00	9.00
1902. Double Line Watermark. (NH Add 100%)					
❑ E6	10¢	Bicycle Messenger	—	140.00	8.95

E7	**E12**	**E14**
(E08–E11)	(E13, E15–E18)	(E19)

Scott No.			Plate Block	Unused	Used

1908. (NH Add 80%)

❏ E7	10¢	Mercury's Helmet	—	70.00	42.00

1911. Perforated 12, Single Line Watermark. (NH Add 80%)

❏ E8	10¢	Bicycle Messenger (~E6)	—	108.00	13.25

1914. Perforated 10, Single Line Watermark. (NH Add 80%)

❏ E9	10¢	Bicycle Messenger (~E6)	—	185.00	13.25

1916. Perforated 10, Unwatermarked. (NH Add 80%)

❏ E10	10¢	Pale Ultramarine (~E6)	—	265.00	31.50

1917. Perforated 11, Unwatermarked. (NH Add 80%)

❏ E11	10¢	Ultramarine (~E6)	155.00 (6)	32.50	6.85

1922–1925. Perforated 11. (NH Add 80%)

❏ E12	10¢	Motorcycle Messenger	300.00 (6)	42.00	1.32
❏ E13	10¢	Deep Orange (~E12)	240.00 (6)	34.50	6.85
❏ E14	20¢	Special Delivery Truck	40.00 (6)	8.25	6.85

1927–1951. Perforated 11 x 10$^1\!/\!_2$. (NH Add 50%)

❏ E15	10¢	Gray Violet (~E12)	6.40	1.65	.70
❏ E16	15¢	Orange (~E12)	6.40	1.65	.70
❏ E17	13¢	Blue (~E12)	5.25	1.65	.70
❏ E18	17¢	Yellow (~E12)	21.00	6.45	4.25
❏ E19	20¢	Black (~E14)	9.00	2.10	.70

NOTE: Prices for stamps from 1935 forward are for never-hinged (NH) examples.

E20
(E21)

E22
(E23)

Scott No.			Plate Block	Unused	Used
1954-1971.					
❏ E20	20¢	Letter & Hand, blue	4.50	1.00	.55
❏ E21	30¢	Letter & Hand (~E20), maroon	4.50	1.95	.55
❏ E22	45¢	Stylized Arrows	7.45	2.75	.55
❏ E23	60¢	Stylized Arrows (~E22)	7.45	2.75	.55

REGISTERED MAIL STAMP

F1

Scott No.			Plate Block	Unused	Used
1911.					
❏ F1	10¢	Eagle	31.50 (6)	17.50	10.50

CERTIFIED MAIL STAMP

FA1

Scott No.			Plate Block	Unused	Used
1955.					
❏ FA1	10¢	Letter Carrier	8.50	1.95	1.35

POSTAGE DUE STAMPS

NOTE: Prices for unused stamps issued before 1890 are for examples without original gum. Examples with original gum command a premium, which can amount to as much as fifty percent or more. Beware regummed examples. Prices are for sound stamps. Those with faults or defects sell for much less.

J1
(J2–J28)

Scott No.			Unused	Used
1879.				
❏ J1	1¢	Brown	52.50	10.50
❏ J2	2¢	Brown (~J1)	236.00	10.50
❏ J3	3¢	Brown (~J1)	52.50	10.50
❏ J4	5¢	Brown (~J1)	400.00	26.25
❏ J5	10¢	Brown (~J1)	520.00	21.00
❏ J6	30¢	Brown (~J1)	290.00	33.60
❏ J7	50¢	Brown (~J1)	440.00	36.75
1884–1889.				
❏ J15	1¢	Red Brown (~J1)	70.00	10.50
❏ J16	2¢	Red Brown (~J1)	70.00	10.50
❏ J17	3¢	Red Brown (~J1)	525.00	105.00
❏ J18	5¢	Red Brown (~J1)	340.00	21.00
❏ J19	10¢	Red Brown (~J1)	325.00	21.00
❏ J20	30¢	Red Brown (~J1)	150.00	42.00
❏ J21	50¢	Red Brown (~J1)	850.00	105.00
1891–1893.				
❏ J22	1¢	Bright Claret (~J1)	35.00	10.50
❏ J23	2¢	Bright Claret (~J1)	35.00	10.50
❏ J24	3¢	Bright Claret (~J1)	60.00	10.50
❏ J25	5¢	Bright Claret (~J1)	95.00	12.75
❏ J26	10¢	Bright Claret (~J1)	132.00	21.00
❏ J27	30¢	Bright Claret (~J1)	315.00	105.00
❏ J28	50¢	Bright Claret (~J1)	315.00	131.25

J29
(J30–J68)

Scott No.			Unused	Used
1894. (NH Add 60%)				
❑ J29	1¢	Vermilion	1785.00	472.00
❑ J30	2¢	Vermilion (~J29)	720.00	236.00
❑ J31	1¢	Claret (~J29)	110.00	10.50
❑ J32	2¢	Claret (~J29)	110.00	8.50
❑ J33	3¢	Claret (~J29)	210.00	48.00
❑ J34	5¢	Claret (~J29)	290.00	48.00
❑ J35	10¢	Claret (~J29)	280.00	32.00
❑ J36	30¢	Claret (~J29)	368.00	148.00
❑ J37	50¢	Claret (~J29)	1390.00	384.00
1895. Perforated 12, Double Line Watermark. (NH Add 60%)				
❑ J38	1¢	Claret (~J29)	20.00	5.50
❑ J39	2¢	Claret (~J29)	20.00	5.50
❑ J40	3¢	Claret (~J29)	68.00	5.50
❑ J41	5¢	Claret (~J29)	55.00	5.50
❑ J42	10¢	Claret (~J29)	85.00	6.40
❑ J43	30¢	Claret (~J29)	472.00	58.00
❑ J44	50¢	Claret (~J29)	368.00	42.00
1910–1912. Perforated 12, Single Line Watermark. (NH Add 60%)				
❑ J45	1¢	Claret (~J29)	45.00	5.85
❑ J46	2¢	Claret (~J29)	45.00	5.85
❑ J47	3¢	Claret (~J29)	475.00	26.25
❑ J48	5¢	Claret (~J29)	100.00	15.75
❑ J49	10¢	Claret (~J29)	150.00	19.50
❑ J50	50¢	Claret (~J29)	840.00	120.00

Scott No.			Unused	Used

1914–1916. Perforated 10, Single Line Watermark. (NH Add 50%)

			Unused	Used
❏ J52	1¢	Carmine (~J29)	65.00	16.00
❏ J53	2¢	Carmine (~J29)	65.00	6.80
❏ J54	3¢	Carmine (~J29)	785.00	53.00
❏ J55	5¢	Carmine (~J29)	45.00	6.85
❏ J56	10¢	Carmine (~J29)	75.00	6.85
❏ J57	30¢	Carmine (~J29)	225.00	21.00
❏ J58	50¢	Carmine (~J29)	7000.00	865.00

1916. Perforated 10, Unwatermarked. (NH Add 80%)

			Unused	Used
❏ J59	1¢	Rose (~J29)	2000.00	275.00
❏ J60	2¢	Rose (~J29)	150.00	35.00

Scott No.			Plate Block	Unused	Used

1917–1926. Perforated 11, Unwatermarked. (NH Add 60%)

			Plate Block	Unused	Used
❏ J61	1¢	Carmine Rose (~J29)	43.00 (6)	2.75	.58
❏ J62	2¢	Carmine Rose (~J29)	43.00 (6)	2.75	.58
❏ J63	3¢	Carmine Rose (~J29)	132.00 (6)	21.50	.52
❏ J64	5¢	Carmine Rose (~J29)	132.00 (6)	21.50	.52
❏ J65	10¢	Carmine Rose (~J29)	132.00 (6)	21.50	.48
❏ J66	30¢	Carmine Rose (~J29)	420.00 (6)	95.00	.96
❏ J67	50¢	Carmine Rose (~J29)	710.00 (6)	105.00	.58
❏ J68	½¢	Dull Red (~J29)	26.00 (6)	6.75	.58

J69
(J70–J76, J79–J66)

1930–1931. Perforated 11. (NH Add 60%)

❏ J69	½¢	Carmine	58.00 (6)	7.75	2.65
❏ J70	1¢	Carmine (~J69)	58.00 (6)	7.75	1.35
❏ J71	2¢	Carmine (~J69)	52.00 (6)	7.75	1.35
❏ J72	3¢	Carmine (~J69)	252.00 (6)	26.00	4.20
❏ J73	5¢	Carmine (~J69)	252.00 (6)	25.00	2.60

J77
(J78, J87)

Scott No.			Plate Block	Unused	Used
❏ J74	10¢	Carmine (~J69)	525.00 (6)	52.00	3.20
❏ J75	30¢	Carmine (~J69)	1300.00 (6)	158.00	2.10
❏ J76	50¢	Carmine (~J69)	1300.00 (6)	158.00	3.20
❏ J77	$1	Carmine	236.00 (6)	35.00	3.20
❏ J78	$5	Carmine (~J77)	336.00 (6)	48.00	3.20

1931–1956. Perforated 10½ x 11 or 11 x 10½. (NH Add 45%)

❏ J79	½¢	Carmine (~J69)	27.00	2.60	.10–.35
❏ J80	1¢	Carmine (~J69)	6.75	3.00	.10–.35
❏ J81	2¢	Carmine (~J69)	6.75	3.00	.10–.35
❏ J82	3¢	Carmine (~J69)	6.75	3.00	.10–.35
❏ J83	5¢	Carmine (~J69)	6.75	1.65	.10–.35
❏ J84	10¢	Carmine (~J69)	15.00	1.60	.10–.35
❏ J85	30¢	Carmine (~J69)	79.00	10.50	.10–.35
❏ J86	50¢	Carmine (~J69)	84.00	15.00	.10–.35
❏ J87	$1	Red (~J77)	252.00	52.00	.10–.35

NOTE: Prices for stamps from this point forward are for never-hinged (NH) examples.

J89
(J88, J90–J104)

Scott No.			Plate Block	Unused	Used
1959.					
❏ J88	½¢	Red & Black (~J89)	210.00	1.95	.10–.35
❏ J89	1¢	Red & Black	2.45	.75	.10–.35

Scott No.			Plate Block	Unused	Used
❑ J90	2¢	Red & Black (~J89)	1.35	.35	.10–.20
❑ J91	3¢	Red & Black (~J89)	1.35	.50	.10–.35
❑ J92	4¢	Red & Black (~J89)	1.35	.40	.10–.20
❑ J93	5¢	Red & Black (~J89)	1.35	.40	.10–.20
❑ J94	6¢	Red & Black (~J89)	2.35	.40	.10–.20
❑ J95	7¢	Red & Black (~J89)	2.35	.40	.10–.20
❑ J96	8¢	Red & Black (~J89)	2.35	.45	.10–.20
❑ J97	10¢	Red & Black (~J89)	2.35	.35	.10–.20
❑ J98	30¢	Red & Black (~J89)	5.25	1.00	.10–.35
❑ J99	50¢	Red & Black (~J89)	7.35	1.75	.10–.35
❑ J100	$1	Red & Black (~J89)	12.75	3.65	.60
❑ J101	$5	Red & Black (~J89)	63.00	12.75	8.00

1978.

❑ J102	11¢	Red & Black (~J89)	5.50	.50	.10–.35
❑ J103	13¢	Red & Black (~J89)	5.50	.40	.10–.20

1985.

❑ J104	17¢	Red & Black (~J89)	42.00	.85	.10–.25

U.S. OFFICES IN CHINA

K1 Surcharge Style 1   **K1 Surcharge Style 2**

Scott No.			Plate Block	Unused	Used

1919. New values surcharged (Style 1) on Washington-Franklin Series Stamps. (NH Add 75%)

			Plate Block	Unused	Used
☐ K1	2¢	On 1¢ green	130.00 (6)	80.00	45.00
☐ K2	4¢	On 2¢ rose	130.00 (6)	80.00	45.00
☐ K3	6¢	On 3¢ violet	170.00 (6)	85.00	45.00
☐ K4	8¢	On 4¢ brown	170.00 (6)	85.00	45.00
☐ K5	10¢	On 5¢ blue	170.00 (6)	85.00	45.00
☐ K6	12¢	On 6¢ orange	210.00 (6)	100.00	75.00
☐ K7	14¢	On 7¢ black	350.00 (6)	130.00	115.00
☐ K8	16¢	On 8¢ olive bistre	235.00 (6)	75.00	80.00
☐ K8a	16¢	On 8¢ olive green	235.00 (6)	85.00	80.00
☐ K9	18¢	On 9¢ orange red	235.00 (6)	105.00	80.00
☐ K10	20¢	On 10¢ yellow orange	235.00 (6)	105.00	80.00
☐ K11	24¢	On 12¢ brown carmine	195.00 (6)	105.00	80.00
☐ K11a	24¢	On 12¢ claret brown	340.00 (6)	130.00	115.00
☐ K12	30¢	On 15¢ gray	340.00 (6)	130.00	115.00
☐ K13	40¢	On 20¢ ultramarine	525.00 (6)	175.00	140.00
☐ K14	60¢	On 30¢ orange red	525.00 (6)	165.00	140.00
☐ K15	$1	On 50¢ violet	890.00 (6)	445.00	80.00
☐ K16	$2	On $1 violet brown	790.00 (6)	445.00	340.00

1922. New Values Surcharged (Style 2) on Washington-Franklin Series Stamps. (NH Add 75%)

			Plate Block	Unused	Used
☐ K17	2¢	On 1¢ green	250.00 (6)	130.00	100.00
☐ K18	4¢	On 2¢ carmine	250.00 (6)	130.00	100.00

OFFICIAL STAMPS

NOTE: Prices for unused stamps issued before 1890 are for examples without original gum. Examples with original gum command a premium, which can amount to as much as 50 percent or more. Beware regummed examples. Prices are for sound stamps. Those with faults or defects sell for much less.

Official stamps of the nineteenth century (O1–O120) for the various departments utilize the same portraits with each group inscribed for its department. The Post Office Department stamps (O47–O56) are the exception and utilize a different design.

| 01 | 02 | 03 | 04 | 05 |

| 06 | 07 | 08 | 09 |

Scott No.			Unused	Used

1873. Agriculture Department, Continental Bank Note Co. Printing, Hard Thin Paper.

			Unused	Used
❏ O1	1¢	Yellow	150.00	135.00
❏ O2	2¢	Yellow	150.00	80.00
❏ O3	3¢	Yellow	150.00	45.00
❏ O4	6¢	Yellow	150.00	45.00
❏ O5	10¢	Yellow	150.00	95.00
❏ O6	12¢	Yellow	225.00	180.00
❏ O7	15¢	Yellow	225.00	180.00
❏ O8	24¢	Yellow	225.00	135.00
❏ O9	30¢	Yellow	225.00	210.00

| | O10 | O15 | O24 | O25 |

Scott No.			Unused	Used

1873. Same Portraits as O1–O5, but inscribed Executive Department, Continental Bank Note Co. Printing, Hard Thin Paper.

			Unused	Used
☐ O10	1¢	Carmine	575.00	250.00
☐ O11	2¢	Carmine	450.00	240.00
☐ O12	3¢	Carmine	450.00	240.00
☐ O13	6¢	Carmine	685.00	395.00
☐ O14	10¢	Carmine	775.00	450.00

1873. Same Portraits as Nos. O1–O7, but inscribed Interior Department, Continental Bank Note Co. Printing, Hard Thin Paper.

			Unused	Used
☐ O15	1¢	Vermilion (~O1)	80.00	16.00
☐ O16	2¢	Vermilion (~O2)	80.00	19.00
☐ O17	3¢	Vermilion (~O3)	90.00	16.00
☐ O18	6¢	Vermilion (~O4)	90.00	16.00
☐ O19	10¢	Vermilion	75.00	19.00
☐ O20	12¢	Vermilion	85.00	16.00
☐ O21	15¢	Vermilion	75.00	21.00
☐ O22	24¢	Vermilion	70.00	19.00
☐ O23	30¢	Vermilion	85.00	21.00
☐ O24	90¢	Vermilion	90.00	40.00

1873. Same Portraits as Nos. O1–O9, but inscribed Department of Justice, Continental Bank Note Co. Printing, Hard Thin Paper.

			Unused	Used
☐ O25	1¢	Purple	160.00	100.00
☐ O26	2¢	Purple	175.00	60.00
☐ O27	3¢	Purple	175.00	55.00
☐ O28	6¢	Purple	175.00	50.00
☐ O29	10¢	Purple	175.00	65.00
☐ O30	12¢	Purple	175.00	70.00
☐ O31	15¢	Purple	200.00	160.00
☐ O32	24¢	Purple	650.00	240.00
☐ O33	30¢	Purple	525.00	210.00
☐ O34	90¢	Purple	775.00	370.00

035   047

Scott No.			Unused	Used

1873. Same Portraits as Nos. O1–O9, but inscribed Navy Department, Continental Bank Note Co. Printing, Hard Thin Paper.

			Unused	Used
❑ 035	1¢	Ultramarine	125.00	115.00
❑ 036	2¢	Ultramarine	125.00	60.00
❑ 037	3¢	Ultramarine	125.00	40.00
❑ 038	6¢	Ultramarine	125.00	40.00
❑ 039	7¢	Ultramarine	290.00	185.00
❑ 040	10¢	Ultramarine	135.00	70.00
❑ 041	12¢	Ultramarine	160.00	85.00
❑ 042	15¢	Ultramarine	175.00	90.00
❑ 043	24¢	Ultramarine	175.00	75.00
❑ 044	30¢	Ultramarine	175.00	80.00
❑ 045	90¢	Ultramarine	475.00	185.00

1873. Post Office Department, Continental Bank Note Co. Printing, Hard Thin Paper.

			Unused	Used
❑ 047	1¢	Black	60.00	16.00
❑ 048	2¢	Black (~047)	60.00	7.00
❑ 049	3¢	Black (~047)	25.00	13.00
❑ 050	6¢	Black (~047)	50.00	19.00
❑ 051	10¢	Black (~047)	80.00	42.00
❑ 052	12¢	Black (~047)	60.00	16.00
❑ 053	15¢	Black (~047)	60.00	37.00
❑ 054	24¢	Black (~047)	85.00	37.00
❑ 055	30¢	Black (~047)	85.00	37.00
❑ 056	90¢	Black (~047)	85.00	37.00

O57	**O68** (069–071)	**O72**

Scott No.			Unused	Used

1873. Same Portraits as Nos. O1–O9, but inscribed State Department, Continental Bank Note Co. Printing, Hard Thin Paper.

			Unused	Used
❑ O57	1¢	Green	140.00	63.00
❑ O58	2¢	Green	210.00	90.00
❑ O59	3¢	Green	140.00	34.00
❑ O60	6¢	Green	140.00	34.00
❑ O61	7¢	Green	185.00	63.00
❑ O62	10¢	Green	160.00	63.00
❑ O63	12¢	Green	235.00	100.00
❑ O64	15¢	Green	220.00	80.00
❑ O65	24¢	Green	400.00	195.00
❑ O66	30¢	Green	400.00	175.00
❑ O67	90¢	Green	680.00	220.00
❑ O68	$2	Green	790.00	—
❑ O69	$5	Green & Black (~O68)	4850.00	2500.00
❑ O70	$10	Green & Black (~O68)	2800.00	1750.00
❑ O71	$20	Green & Black (~O68)	3000.00	1600.00

1873. Same Portraits as Nos. O1–O9, but inscribed Treasury Department, Continental Bank Note Co. Printing, Hard Thin Paper.

			Unused	Used
❑ O72	1¢	Brown	55.00	13.00
❑ O73	2¢	Brown	75.00	11.00
❑ O74	3¢	Brown	75.00	11.00
❑ O75	6¢	Brown	75.00	6.50
❑ O76	7¢	Brown	160.00	27.00
❑ O77	10¢	Brown	185.00	17.00
❑ O78	12¢	Brown	190.00	17.00
❑ O79	15¢	Brown	185.00	11.00
❑ O80	24¢	Brown	500.00	80.00

Scott No.			Unused	Used
❑ O81	30¢	Brown	175.00	16.00
❑ O82	90¢	Brown	175.00	19.00

O83

1873. Same Portraits as Nos. O1–O9, but inscribed War Department, Continental Bank Note Co. Printing, Hard Thin Paper.

❑ O83	1¢	Rose	175.00	19.00
❑ O84	2¢	Rose	175.00	17.00
❑ O85	3¢	Rose	190.00	11.00
❑ O86	6¢	Rose	340.00	13.00
❑ O87	7¢	Rose	125.00	80.00
❑ O88	10¢	Rose	80.00	19.00
❑ O89	12¢	Rose	185.00	11.00
❑ O90	15¢	Rose	70.00	19.00
❑ O91	24¢	Rose	70.00	19.00
❑ O92	30¢	Rose	80.00	11.00
❑ O93	90¢	Rose	130.00	40.00

1879. Agriculture Department, American Bank Note Co. Printing, Soft Porous Paper.

❑ O94	1¢	Yellow (~O1)	3000.00	—
❑ O95	3¢	Yellow (~O3)	2000.00	105.00

1879. Same Portraits as Nos. O1–O8, but inscribed Interior Department, American Bank Note Co. Printing, Soft Porous Paper.

❑ O96	1¢	Vermilion	210.00	105.00
❑ O97	2¢	Vermilion	12.00	6.50
❑ O98	3¢	Vermilion	12.00	6.50
❑ O99	6¢	Vermilion	12.00	11.00
❑ O100	10¢	Vermilion	100.00	80.00
❑ O101	12¢	Vermilion	185.00	105.00
❑ O102	15¢	Vermilion	275.00	210.00
❑ O103	24¢	Vermilion	2450.00	—

Scott No.			Unused	Used

1879. Same Portraits as Nos. O3 & O4, but inscribed Department of Justice, American Bank Note Co. Printing, Soft Porous Paper.

❏ O106	3¢	Purple	110.00	80.00
❏ O107	6¢	Purple	340.00	185.00

1879. Post Office Department, American Bank Note Co. Printing, Soft Porous Paper.

❏ O108	3¢	Black (~O47)	20.00	12.00

1879. Same Portraits as Nos. O3–O9, but inscribed Treasury Department, American Bank Note Co. Printing, Soft Porous Paper.

❏ O109	3¢	Brown	70.00	9.00
❏ O110	6¢	Brown	125.00	40.00
❏ O111	10¢	Brown	185.00	80.00
❏ O112	30¢	Brown	1025.00	325.00
❏ O113	90¢	Brown	1400.00	370.00

1879. Same Portraits as Nos. O1–O9, but inscribed War Department, American Bank Note Co. Printing, Soft Porous Paper.

❏ O114	1¢	Rose	10.00	6.50
❏ O115	2¢	Rose	10.00	6.50
❏ O116	3¢	Rose	10.00	6.50
❏ O117	6¢	Rose	16.00	6.50
❏ O118	10¢	Rose	80.00	35.00
❏ O119	12¢	Rose	65.00	16.00
❏ O120	30¢	Rose	130.00	80.00

0121
(O122–O126)

0127
(O128–O152)

Scott No.			Unused	Used
1910–1911. Postal Savings Stamps. Double Line Watermark.				
☐ O121	2¢	Black	20.00	5.25
☐ O122	50¢	Dark Green (~121)	185.00	55.00
☐ O123	$1	Ultramarine (~121)	168.00	21.00
Postal Savings Stamps. Single Line Watermark.				
☐ O124	1¢	Dark Violet (~121)	12.00	5.25
☐ O125	2¢	Black (~121)	80.00	8.50
☐ O126	10¢	Carmine (~121)	35.00	5.25

Scott No.			Plate Block	Unused	Used
1983–1985. Engraved.					
☐ O127	1¢	Great Seal	1.60	.40	.10–.20
☐ O128	4¢	Great Seal (~O127)	1.60	.40	.10–.20
☐ O129	13¢	Great Seal (~O127)	4.20	.60	.10–.35
☐ O130	17¢	Great Seal (~O127)	4.20	.85	.10–.35
☐ O132	$1	Great Seal (~O127)	13.00	4.40	2.10
☐ O133	$5	Great Seal (~O127)	55.00	15.00	7.35

Scott No.			PNC Strip (5)	Unused	Used
Coil Stamps.					
☐ O135	20¢	Great Seal (~O127)	19.00	1.75	.40
☐ O136	22¢	Great Seal (~O127)	17.00	1.75	.40

Scott No.			Plate Block	Unused	Used
1985.					
☐ O138 (14¢)		"D" & Great Seal (~O127)	48.00	5.00	4.00

Scott No.			PNC Strip (5)	Unused	Used
Coil Stamps.					
❑ O138A 15¢	Great Seal (~O127)		—	1.10	.10–.35
❑ O138B 20¢	Great Seal (~O127)		—	1.85	.80
❑ O139 (22¢)	"D" & Great Seal (~O127)		55.00	5.50	4.20
❑ O140 (25¢)	"E" & Great Seal (~O127)		—	2.00	1.50
❑ O141 25¢	Great Seal (~O127)		—	1.60	.80

Scott No.			Plate Block	Unused	Used
1989. Lithographed.					
❑ O143 1¢	Great Seal (~O127)		—	.40	.10–.25

Scott No.			PNC Strip (5)	Unused	Used
Coil Stamps.					
❑ O144 29¢	Great Seal (~O127)		—	4.50	1.60
❑ O145 29¢	Great Seal (~O127)		—	1.60	.78

Scott No.			Plate Block	Unused	Used
1991. Lithographed.					
❑ O146 4¢	Great Seal (~O127)		—	.60	.10–.35
❑ O146A 10¢	Great Seal (~O127)		—	.80	.10–.35
❑ O147 19¢	Great Seal (~O127)		—	1.35	.10–.35
❑ O148 23¢	Great Seal (~O127)		—	1.35	.10–.35
❑ O151 $1	Great Seal (~O127)		—	10.00	8.00

0153
(O154–O157)

Scott No.	PNC Strip (5)	Unused	Used
Coil Stamps.			
❑ O152 (32¢) "G" & Great Seal (~O127)	—	1.75	1.60
❑ O153 32¢ Great Seal	—	3.50	1.00

NOTE: No. O153 contains a line of micro-type below the Great Seal.

Scott No.	Plate Block	Unused	Used
1995-2001.			
❑ O154 1¢ Great Seal (~O153)	—	.65	.10–.35
❑ O155 20¢ Great Seal (~O153)	—	1.10	.10–.35
❑ O156 23¢ Great Seal (~O153)	—	1.60	.80

NOTE: Nos. O154–O156 contain a line of micro-type below the Great Seal.

Scott No.	PNC Strip (5)	Unused	Used
1999-2002. Coil Stamps.			
❑ O157 33¢ Great Seal (~O153)	—	3.20	1.00
❑ O158 34¢ Great Seal (~O127)	—	2.50	1.00

NOTE: No. O157 contains a line of micro-type below the Great Seal.

PARCEL POST STAMPS

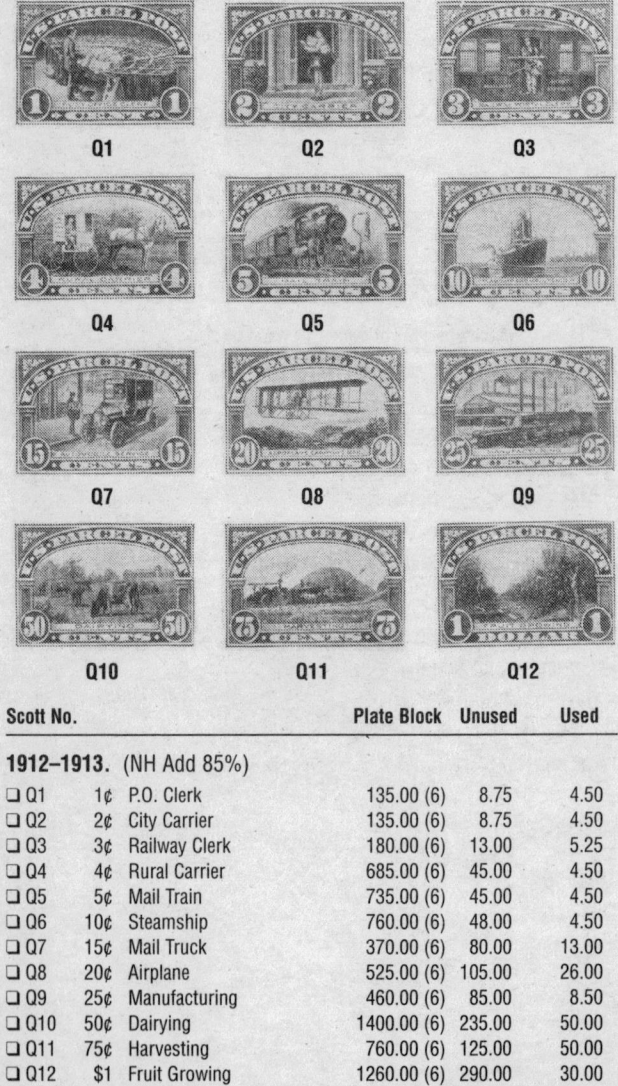

Scott No.			Plate Block	Unused	Used
1912–1913. (NH Add 85%)					
❑ Q1	1¢	P.O. Clerk	135.00 (6)	8.75	4.50
❑ Q2	2¢	City Carrier	135.00 (6)	8.75	4.50
❑ Q3	3¢	Railway Clerk	180.00 (6)	13.00	5.25
❑ Q4	4¢	Rural Carrier	685.00 (6)	45.00	4.50
❑ Q5	5¢	Mail Train	735.00 (6)	45.00	4.50
❑ Q6	10¢	Steamship	760.00 (6)	48.00	4.50
❑ Q7	15¢	Mail Truck	370.00 (6)	80.00	13.00
❑ Q8	20¢	Airplane	525.00 (6)	105.00	26.00
❑ Q9	25¢	Manufacturing	460.00 (6)	85.00	8.50
❑ Q10	50¢	Dairying	1400.00 (6)	235.00	50.00
❑ Q11	75¢	Harvesting	760.00 (6)	125.00	50.00
❑ Q12	$1	Fruit Growing	1260.00 (6)	290.00	30.00

PARCEL POST POSTAGE DUE STAMPS

JQ1
(JQ2–JQ5)

Scott No.			Plate Block	Unused	Used
1912.	(NH Add 80%)				
❑ JQ1	1¢	Dark Green	420.00 (6)	12.00	6.75
❑ JQ2	2¢	Dark Green (~JQ1)	500.00 (6)	85.00	14.00
❑ JQ3	5¢	Dark Green (~JQ1)	500.00 (6)	20.00	6.75
❑ JQ4	10¢	Dark Green (~JQ1)	1155.00 (6)	160.00	55.00
❑ JQ5	25¢	Dark Green (~JQ1)	790.00 (6)	110.00	6.75

SPECIAL HANDLING STAMPS

QE1
(QE2–QE5)

Scott No.			Plate Block	Unused	Used
1925–1929.	(NH Add 66%)				
❑ QE1	10¢	Yellow Green	50.00 (6)	3.75	1.75
❑ QE2	15¢	Yellow Green (~QE1)	50.00 (6)	3.75	1.75
❑ QE3	20¢	Yellow Green (~QE1)	65.00 (6)	5.50	1.75
❑ QE4	25¢	Yellow Green (~QE1)	230.00 (6)	32.00	6.00
❑ QE4A	25¢	Deep Green (~QE1)	290.00 (6)	22.00	13.00

FEDERAL DUCK STAMPS

Courtesy of Bob and Rita Dumaine at the Sam Houston Duck Company
P. O. Box 820087, Houston, TX 77282
(Specialized duck catalog $5.00, refundable with purchase; or available
as a free download at Shduck.com)

JUST WHAT ARE DUCK STAMPS?

The federal duck stamp was created through a wetlands conservation
program. President Herbert Hoover signed the Migratory Bird Conservation Act in 1929 to authorize the acquisition and preservation of wetlands as waterfowl habitat.

The law, however, did not provide a permanent source of funds to
buy and preserve wetlands. On March 16, 1934, Congress passed, and
President Franklin Roosevelt signed, the Migratory Bird Hunting Stamp
Act. Popularly known as the Duck Stamp Act, the bill's whole purpose
was to generate revenue designated for one specific use: acquiring wetlands for what is now known as the National Refuge System.

It has been proven that sales of duck stamps increase when the
public has been informed of how the revenue generated through stamp
sales is used.

Jay N. "Ding" Darling, a conservationist and Pulitzer Prize–winning polit-
ical cartoonist, was appointed the head of the Duck Stamp Program. Darling's pencil sketch of mallards alighting was used on the first duck stamp.
The same design was reproduced on Scott 2092, a commemorative marking the 50th anniversary of the Migratory Bird Hunting Stamp Act.

In reality, a "duck stamp" is a permit to hunt, basically a receipt for payment of fees collected. Funds generated are used for the preservation
and conservation of wetlands.

The term "duck stamp" is a shortened term for the message "Migratory Bird Hunting and Conservation Stamp," which appears on the federal duck stamp.

In fact, use of the word "duck" is inaccurate, since many migratory
waterfowl, including geese, swans, brants, and more, are intended to
benefit from the sale of duck stamps.

WHO ISSUES DUCK STAMPS?

Federal duck stamps are now issued by the U.S. Fish and Wildlife Service, Department of the Interior United States Government, and have been issued by all states. Currently, thirty-three states issue duck stamps.

Many foreign countries, including Canada and its provinces, Sweden, Australia, Russia, Iceland, the United Kingdom, Costa Rica, Hungary, Venezuela, Italy, Argentina, Belgium, Mexico, Ireland, Spain, Denmark, Israel, Croatia, and New Zealand have issued duck stamps.

The issuing authorities within the various governments that release duck stamps are usually conservation and wildlife departments. These programs must be created by some form of legislation for the resulting stamps to be accepted as a valid governmental issue.

Labels featuring ducks are also issued by various special interest groups, such as Ducks Unlimited, the National Fish and Wildlife Foundation, the National Duck Stamp Collectors Society, and the National Wildlife Federation. Their issues are referred to as "society stamps." These items technically are not duck stamps, because the fee structure and disposition of funds are not legislated. However, society stamps are very collectible and often appreciate in value. Funds raised by these organizations are also used for waterfowl and conservation efforts.

Valid organizations and societies of this type perform a major service to conservation by their donations and efforts, and they merit public support.

WHEN ARE DUCK STAMPS ISSUED?

Duck stamps are issued once a year. In most states, hunters are required to purchase both a federal and state stamp before hunting waterfowl.

Waterfowl hunting seasons vary, but most begin in September or October, so naturally, stamps are needed prior to opening day of the hunting season.

Currently, the federal stamp and more than half of the state stamps are issued in July. Some are issued on the first day of the new year, and a few at the last minute in September or early October.

THE COST OF DUCK STAMPS

The annual federal duck stamp had a face value of $1 in 1934, jumped to $2 in 1949, and to $3 in 1959. In 1972 the price increased to $5, then up to $7.50 in 1979, $10 in 1987, $12.50 in 1989, and to $15 beginning in 1991.

For every $15 stamp sold, the federal government retains $14.70 for wetlands acquisition and conservation, so very little gets lost in the system for overhead.

Most state conservation stamps have a face value of $5. Alaska, Colorado and Michigan are the lowest price at $5.00 and Louisiana's non-resident is the highest at $25.00.

Funds generated from state stamps are designated for wetlands restoration and preservation, much like the federal funds, but with a more localized purpose.

Most state agencies sell their stamps at face value. However, some also charge a premium to collectors buying single stamps, to help cover overhead costs. Some states also produce special limited editions for collectors.

FORMAT OF STAMPS

The federal stamp is presently issued in panes of twenty stamps. Originally, the stamps were issued in panes of twenty-eight, but because of a change in the printing method (and to make stamps easier to count) the 30-stamp format was adopted in 1959. Then switched to twenty in 2000.

Beginning in 1998, the department of the Interior also issued a single-sheet, self-adhesive Federal stamp to be used in ATM machines and to ease handling in sporting good stores.

Most states and foreign governments follow the federal format. Many states issue a ten-stamp pane for ease of handling and mailing to field offices.

TYPES OF STAMPS

Currently, thirty-three states issue stamps, of which nine issue one for collectors and another for hunter use. Arkansas, Louisiana and Mississippi have a non-resident issue.

Collector stamps are usually in panes of ten or thirty without tabs. Hunter-type stamps are usually issued in panes of five or ten, many with tabs attached. Hunters use the tabs to list their name, address, age, and other data. Some states use only serial numbers to designate their hunter-type stamp.

State stamps are therefore referred to as either collector stamps or hunter-type stamps. Most dealers will distinguish between these types on their price lists. Separate albums exist for both types and are available from most dealers.

Plate blocks, better described as control number blocks, are designations given to a block of stamps, usually four, with a plate or control number present on the selvage. Such a block is usually located in one or all four corners of a pane. Federal stamps prior to 1959 plus the 1964 issue are collected in blocks of six and must have selvage on two sides.

Governors' Editions have been issued by several state agencies as a means of raising additional income. These stamps are printed in small quantities, most fewer than 1,000. They have a face value of approximately $50, and are imprinted with the name of the state governor.

Governors also hand-sign a limited number of stamps. These are usually available at a premium, generally twice the price of normal singles. Hand-signed or autographed stamps are issued in very small quantities and are scarce to rare.

Governors' Editions are valid for hunting by all issuing states thus far. Obviously none would be used for that purpose, however, as it would destroy the mint condition and lower the value of the stamp.

Artist-Signed Stamps are mint examples of duck stamps autographed by the artist responsible for the artwork on the stamp. Such stamps are rapidly gaining popularity with collectors, and most can be purchased for a small premium over mint examples.

Early federal stamps are particularly valuable and difficult to acquire. Signed stamps by artists now deceased also command a substantial premium.

Printed Text Stamps are another popular collectible. Generally, these preceded the later pictorial issues. The term is applied to stamps required for duck hunting that contain only writing but no waterfowl illustration.

Certain American Indian reservations and tribes also issue waterfowl hunting stamps. The stamps of these sovereign Indian nations allow holders to hunt on that reservation when a federal stamp also is purchased. Reservation stamps are becoming increasingly popular with collectors as more people discover their existence.

ERRORS

With the printing of such a large number of stamps year after year by many different states and printing agencies, errors do occur, but are seldom found. A few federal stamps are known to exist with major errors, but only a few, namely on the 1934, 1946, 1955, 1957, 1959, 1962, 1982, 1985, 1986, 1990, 1991, 1993, and 2003 issues. In addition, the Federal duck stamp minisheets exist missing the artist's signature, which qualifies as a major error.

Stamps without perforations, with missing or incorrect color, missing or inverted writing on the reverse are all major errors. Smaller flaws, such as color shifts, misplaced perforations, hickeys (or donuts), and other such anomalies are termed freaks, rather than errors. These, too, are collectible and have value, but they do not command the same attention as major errors. Major errors are extremely rare and exist in small numbers. All errors and freaks on duck stamps are very desirable and add a great deal of interest and value to a collection.

HOW TO COLLECT DUCK STAMPS

The first basic rule is to remember that stamp collecting is very personal. You can make your own rules.

Most collectors prefer to collect mint condition duck stamps. Others prefer collecting stamps on licenses, autographed stamps, plate blocks, stamps signed by hunters, art prints, souvenir cards, first day covers, or a combination. The bottom line, however, is to collect what interests you.

Quality is a very important factor in a stamp collection. This applies not only to duck stamps, but all types. Preserving the mint condition of a stamp is crucial for determining value. A perfectly centered stamp will usually sell for a substantial premium over a stamp with normal centering. Very fine is the norm in stamp collecting, and is the condition priced by Scott.

Care should be taken not to damage a stamp, including the gum. The mint state of a stamp includes the freshness and original gum, so stamp mounts should be utilized when placing a stamp in your album. When a stamp has never been hinged, the abbreviation "NH" is used by dealers.

COLLECTORS ORGANIZATION

The National Duck Stamp Collectors Society exists for the benefit of those who collect duck stamps. Dues are $20 a year and are tax exempt. The NDSCS issues a quarterly newsletter. Send your $20 directly to the NDSCS, Membership Chairman, P.O. Box 43, Harleysville, PA 19438.

Bob Dumaine is a recognized expert in duck stamps, founder of the National Duck Stamp Collectors Society, publisher of *The Duck Report,* a past judge in the Federal Duck Stamp Contest and several Federal junior duck stamp contests, and serves on the expertizing committee of Professional Stamp Experts and co-authored an award-winning 208 page book, *The Duck Stamp Story.* In 2008 Mr. Dumaine was inducted in to the Philatelic Writer's Hall of Fame. In 2012, he was added to the American Stamp Dealers Association. Hall of Fame. Rita Dumaine has also served as a judge in the Federal Duck Stamp and Junior Duck Stamp contests. She has served as the editor of "Duck Tracks," the newsletter of the National Duck Stamp Collectors Society. Dumaine is the owner of Sam Houston Duck Co., a firm that specializes in duck stamps and related material.

Request your copy of their award-winning Duck Stamp Catalog—eighty color illustrated pages jam-packed with information on federal and state duck stamps, artist-signed stamps, prints, conservation issues and much more. Catalog $5.00, refundable with first order. Free download at shduck.com

Sam Houston Duck Company, P.O. Box 820087, Houston, TX 77282; 1-800-231-5926; Fax 1-281-496-1445. Visit our Web site at www. shduck.com.

FEDERAL DUCK STAMP DUCKLINGS

The Federal Junior Duck Stamp Program, a nonprofit organization to promote interest among young people, unveiled the design of its first federal junior duck stamp in 1993. The program also includes a conservation education curriculum that helps students of all ages. It focuses on wildlife conservation and management, wildlife art, and philately.

The resulting stamp, unlike the federal issue, is not valid as a revenue, but emulates the federal program in terms of art selection and the creation of stamps, prints, and other items for sale. All proceeds from the junior duck stamp go to the United States Fish and Wildlife Foundation to further its efforts, along with scholarship awards.

DUCK STAMP AGENCIES

Courtesy of Sam Houston Duck Co.
(approximate issue month follows state name)

Alabama, (8) Duck Stamp, Dept. of Conservation & Natural Resources, 64 N. Union, Montgomery, AL 36130, (334) 242-3829.

Alaska, (7) Alaska Dept. of Fish & Game, Licensing Section, P.O. Box 25525, Juneau, AK 99802-5525, (907) 465-6089.

Arizona, (7) Game & Fish Dept., 5000 W. Carefree Hwy., Phoenix, AZ 85086, (623) 236-7213.

Arkansas, (7) Game & Fish Commission, Collector Stamps, 2 Natural Resources Dr., Little Rock, AR 72205, (501) 223-6300.

California, (7) Dept. of Fish & Game, License Section, 1740 N. Market Blvd., Sacramento, CA 95834, (916) 928-5805.

Colorado, (7) Colorado Wildlife Heritage Foundation, P.O. Box 211512, Denver, CO 80022, (303) 291-7212

Connecticut, (8) Wildlife Division, Dept. of Environmental Protection, 79 Elm St., Hartford, CT 06106, (860) 424-3011.

Delaware, (7) Divison of Fish & Wildlife, 89 Kings Hwy., Dover, DE 19901, (302) 739-9911.

Florida, (-) Game & Fish Comm, Finance, Sect., 620 S. Meridian St., Tallahassee, FL 32399-1600, (850) 488-5878. (Last stamp issued 2003.)

Georgia, (-) Dept. of Natural Resources, 2189 North Lake Pkwy. Bldg. 10 Ste. 108, Tucker, GA 30084, (770) 414-3333. (Last stamp issued 1999.)

Hawaii, (9) Division of Forestry & Wildlife, 1151 Punch Bowl St., Room 325, Honolulu, HI 96813, (808) 587-0166.

Idaho, (-) Collector Stamps, Idaho Dept. of Fish & Game, Box 25, Boise, ID 83707, (208) 334-3717. (Last stamp issued 1998.)

Illinois, (-) Illinois Dept. of Natural Resources, License Section, P.O. Box 19459, Springfield, IL 62794-9459, (217) 782-2191. (Last stamp issued 2010.)

Indiana, (6) Indiana Division of Fish & Wildlife, License Section (Stamp). 402 W. Washington Rm. W273, Indianapolis, IN 46204-2267, (317) 232-4080.

Iowa, (6) Dept. of Natural Resources, License Section, Wallace State Office Building, Des Moines, IA 50319, (515) 281-5918.

Kansas, (-) Fish & Game, Pratt Headquarters, 512 SE 25th Ave., Pratt, KS 67124, (316) 672-0735. (Last stamp issued 2004)

Kentucky, (12) Dept. of Fish & Wildlife Resources, 1 Sportsman Lane, Frankfort, KY 40601, (502) 564-3400. Online orders only, http://fw.ky.gov.

Louisiana, (6) Dept. of Wildlife & Fisheries, P.O. Box 98000, ATTN: Licensing Section, Baton Rouge, LA 70898-9000, (225) 765-2887.

Maine, (8) Dept. of Inland Fisheries & Wildlife, 284 State St., State House Station 41, Augusta, ME 04333, (207) 287-8000.

Maryland, (8) Dept. of Natural Resources, Licensing & Registration Services, Box 1869, Annapolis, MD 21404, (410) 260-3220.

Massachusetts, (-) Division of Fisheries & Game, License Section, 251 Causeway St., Suite 400, Boston, MA 02114-2104, (617) 626-1577. (Last stamp issued 2011.)

Michigan, (5) Duck Hunters Assn., P.O. Box 20, Midland, MI 48640, (989) 631-5079.

Minnesota, (3) Dept. of Natural Resources, License Bureau, 500 Lafayette Rd., St. Paul, MN 55155-4026, (651) 297-1230.

Mississippi, (7) Dept. of Wildlife, Fish & Parks, Waterfowl Stamp Coordinator, Box 451, Jackson, MS 39205-0451, (601) 432-2263.

Missouri, (-) Dept. of Conservation, Fiscal Section, Box 180, Jefferson, MO 65105, (573) 751-4115. (Last stamp issued in 1996.)

Montana, (-) Dept. of Fish, Wildlife & Parks, P.O. Box 200701, Helena, MT 59620-0701, (406) 444-2612 (Last stamp issued 2003.)

Nebraska, (-) Game & Parks Commission, License Section, P.O. Box 30370, Lincoln, NE 68503, (402) 471-0641. (Last stamp issued 2009.)

Nevada, (6) Div. of Wildlife, ATTN: License Office, Stamp Sales, 4600 Kietzke Ln., Suite D-135, Reno, NV 89502, (775) 688-1513.

New Hampshire, (-) Fish & Game Dept., License Section, 2 Hazen Dr., Concord, NH 03301, (603) 271-6832. (Last stamp issued 2007.)

New Jersey, (-) Division of Fish & Wildlife, Waterfowl Stamp, P.O. Box 400, Trenton, NJ 08625-0400, (609) 292-2965. (Last stamp issued 2008.)

New Mexico, (-) Dept. of Game & Fish, State Capitol, Villagra Bldg., Santa Fe, NM 87503, (505) 827-7920. (Last stamp issued in 1994.)

New York, (-) Dept. of Conservation, Division Headquarters, 625 Broadway, Albany, NY 12233-4750, (518) 457-4480. (Last stamp issued in 2002.)

North Carolina, (7) Wildlife Resources Commission, Direct Sales Unit, 1710 Mail Service Ctr., Raleigh, NC 27699, (919) 707-0288.

North Dakota, (7) Game & Fish Dept., Collector Stamps 100 N. Bismark Expressway, Bismark, ND 58501, (701) 328-6334.

Ohio, (8) Division of Wildlife, License Section, 2045 Morse Rd., Bldg "G", Columbus, OH 43229-6693, (614) 265-7036.

Oklahoma, (8) Dept. of Wildlife Conservation, P.O. Box 53465, Oklahoma City, OK 73152, (405) 522-3649.

Oregon, (9) Dept. of Fish & Wildlife, ATTN: Licensing Services, 3406 Cherry Ave. NE, Salem, Oregon 97303, (503) 947-6101.

Pennsylvania, (3) Game Commission, License Section, 2001 Elmerton Ave., Harrisburg, PA 17110-9797, (888) 888-3459.

Rhode Island, (8) Rhode Island Fish & Wildlife, Division of Fish & Wildlife, 277 Great Neck Rd., West Kingston, RI, 02892, (401) 789-0281.

South Carolina, (7) Dept. of Natural Resources, License Section, P.O. Box 11710, Columbia, SC 29211, (803) 734-4585.

South Dakota, (-) Game, Fish & Parks, License Division, 412 W. Missouri, Pierre, SD 57501, (605) 773-5527. (Last stamp issued 2007.)

Tennessee, (7) Wildlife Resources Agency, ATTN.: Wildlife Stamps, Box 40747, Nashville, TN 37204, (615) 781-6585.

Texas, (8) Parks & Wildlife Dept., License Office, 4200 Smith School Rd., Austin, TX 78744, (512) 389-8250.

Utah, (-) Division of Wildlife Resources, 1596 W. North Temple, Salt Lake City, UT 84116-3195, (801) 538-4841. (Last stamp issued in 1997.)

Vermont, (9) Dept. of Fish & Wildlife, Stamp Order, 103 S. Main St., 10 South, Waterbury, VT 05671-0501, (802) 878-1564.

Virginia, (10) c/o VA. Ducks Unlimited, P.O. Box 1054, Warrenton, VA 20188, (202) 720-1764.

Washington, (7) Washington Waterfowl Assoc., 12556-120th Ave, NE, #352, Kirkland, WA 98034, (425) 883-1150.

West Virginia, (-) Dept. of Natural Resources, Waterfowl Stamp Program, Box 67, Elkins, WV 26241, (304) 637-0245. (Last stamp issued in 1996.)

Wisconsin, (8) Dept. of Natural Resources, Box 7924, Madison, WI 53707, (608) 264-6137.

Wyoming, (1) Game & Fish Dept., ATTN: Alternative Enterprises, 5440 Bishop Blvd., Cheyenne, WY 82006, (307) 777-4570.

FEDERAL & INTERNATIONAL AGENCIES

U.S. Dept. of Wildlife, (7) Duck Stamp Office, 4401 North Fairfax Drive, 4th Floor, Arlington, VA 22203, (703) 358-2000.

Argentina, (-) National Art Publishing Corp., 11000 Metro Pkwy. Ste #32, Ft. Myers, FL 33912-1293, (941) 939-7518. (Last stamp issued 1996.)

Australia, (-) Jan Sec Fine Stamps, 4/358 Pacific Hwy., Linfield NSW 2070, Australia - P.O. Box 214. (Last stamp issued 1996.)

Canada, (8) Wildlife Habitat Canada, 9 Hinton Ave. North Ste. #200, Ottawa, Ontario, Canada K1Y 4P1.

Quebec, Rosseau Timbres 585, Rue Sainte Catherine Ouest Rez-de-Chausse'e Montréal, QC HB3 3Y5 Canada (514)284-8686

Croatia, (-) Duck Stamp Fulfillment Center, P.O. Box 17, Sullivan, IL 61951, (217)797-6770. (Last stamp issued 1997.)

Denmark, (-) Duck Stamp Fulfillment Center, 1015 West Jackson, Sullivan, IL 61951, (217)728-8321. (Last stamp issued 1997.)

Ireland, (-) Duck Stamp Fulfillment Center, 1015 West Jackson, Sullivan, IL 61951, (217)728-8321. (Last stamp issued 1998.)

Israel, (-) Mystic Stamp Co, NY. (Last stamp issued 1998.)

Italy, (-) Duck Stamp Fulfillment Center, 1015 West Jackson, Sullivan, IL 61951, (217)728-8321. (Last stamp issued 1998.)

Mexico, (-) Duck Stamp Fulfillment Center, 1015 West Jackson, Sullivan, IL 61951, (217)728-8321. (Last stamp issued 1997.)

New Zealand, (9) Duck Stamp Fulfillment Center, 1015 West Jackson, Sullivan, IL 61951, (217)728-8321. (Last stamp issued 1997.)

Russia, Mystic Stamp Co., NY (Last stamp issued 2006)

Spain, (-) National Art Publishing Corp., 11000 Metro Pkwy. Ste. #32, Ft. Myers, FL 33912-1293, (941)939-7518. (Last stamp issued 1996.)

Sweden, (-) Duck Stamp Fulfillment Center, 1015 West Jackson, Sullivan, IL 61951, (217)728-8321. (Last stamp issued 1997.)

United Kingdom, Wildlife Habitat Trust, c/o BASC, Marford Mill, Rossett, Wrexham, LL12 0 HC United Kingdom 44-573-014, Fax 44-573-013.

Venezuela, (-) National Art Publishing Corp., 11000 Metro Pkwy. Ste. #32, Ft. Myers, FL 33912-129, (941)939-7518. (Last stamp issued 1996.)

FEDERAL MIGRATORY BIRD HUNTING STAMPS

NOTE: The year of issue appears in parentheses. Stamps are inscribed with an expiration date, which is one year later than the issue date; for example, the 1934 stamp reads, "Void After June 30, 1935." Stamps are canceled (used) by the application of the hunter's signature.

PRICING NOTE: Prices are for very fine (VF) never-hinged (NH) examples.

RW1

Scott No.			Plate Block	NH Mint	Used
❑ RW1	$1	Mallards (1934), blue	17500.00 (6)	850.00	150.00
❑ RW2	$1	Canvasbacks (1935), rose lake	19500.00 (6)	950.00	225.00
❑ RW3	$1	Canada Geese (1936), brown black	3750.00 (6)	400.00	90.00
❑ RW4	$1	Scaups (1937), light green	3500.00 (6)	425.00	70.00
❑ RW5	$1	Pintails (1938), light violet	4500.00 (6)	475.00	70.00
❑ RW6	$1	Green-Winged Teal (1939), chocolate	3000.00 (6)	250.00	60.00
❑ RW7	$1	Black Ducks (1940), sepia	2500.00 (6)	250.00	60.00
❑ RW8	$1	Ruddy Ducks (1941), brown carmine	2650.00 (6)	260.00	60.00
❑ RW9	$1	Widgeon (1942), violet brown	2650.00 (6)	260.00	60.00
❑ RW10	$1	Wood Ducks (1943), deep rose	775.00 (6)	150.00	60.00
❑ RW11	$1	White Fronted Geese (1944), red orange	825.00 (6)	150.00	45.00
❑ RW12	$1	Shovelers (1945), black	525.00 (6)	110.00	35.00

Scott No.			Plate Block	NH Mint	Used
❑ RW13	$1	Redheads (1946), red brown	365.00 (6)	55.00	16.00
❑ RW14	$1	Snow Geese (1947), black	365.00 (6)	60.00	16.00
❑ RW15	$1	Buffleheads (1948), bright blue	365.00 (6)	60.00	16.00
❑ RW16	$2	Goldeneyes (1949), bright green	425.00 (6)	85.00	16.00
❑ RW17	$2	Trumpeter Swans (1950), violet	600.00 (6)	100.00	16.00
❑ RW18	$2	Gadwalls (1951), gray black	600.00 (6)	100.00	16.00
❑ RW19	$2	Harlequins (1952), ultramarine	600.00 (6)	100.00	16.00
❑ RW20	$2	Blue-winged Teal (1953), dark rose brown	625.00 (6)	100.00	16.00
❑ RW21	$2	Ring-necked Ducks (1954), black	625.00 (6)	100.00	14.00
❑ RW22	$2	Blue Geese (1955), dark blue	625.00 (6)	100.00	14.00
❑ RW23	$2	Mergansers (1956), black	625.00 (6)	100.00	14.00
❑ RW24	$2	American Eider (1957), emerald	625.00 (6)	100.00	14.00
❑ RW25	$2	Canada Geese (1958), black	625.00 (6)	100.00	14.00
❑ RW26	$3	Labrador (1959) multicolored	600.00	130.00	16.00
❑ RW27	$3	Redheads (1960), multicolored	500.00	100.00	15.00
❑ RW28	$3	Mallards (1961), multicolored	550.00	115.00	15.00
❑ RW29	$3	Pintails (1962), multicolored	625.00	125.00	15.00
❑ RW30	$3	American Brant (1963), multicolored	625.00	125.00	15.00
❑ RW31	$3	Nene Geese (1964), multicolored	2000.00 (6)	125.00	15.00

RW32

Scott No.			Plate Block	NH Mint	Used
❑ RW32	$3	Canvasbacks (1965), multicolored	500.00	115.00	15.00
❑ RW33	$3	Whistling Swans (1966), multicolored	525.00	115.00	15.00
❑ RW34	$3	Oldsquaws (1967), multicolored	625.00	125.00	15.00
❑ RW35	$3	Mergansers (1968), multicolored	350.00	75.00	14.00
❑ RW36	$3	White-winged Scoters (1969), multicolored	350.00	75.00	12.00
❑ RW37	$3	Ross' Geese (1970), multicolored	350.00	85.00	12.00
❑ RW38	$3	Cinnamon Teal (1971), multicolored	210.00	50.00	10.00
❑ RW39	$5	Emperor Geese (1972), multicolored	120.00	30.00	8.00
❑ RW40	$5	Steller's Eiders (1973), multicolored	100.00	22.00	8.00
❑ RW41	$5	Wood Ducks (1974), multicolored	85.00	20.00	8.00
❑ RW42	$5	Decoy/Canvasbacks (1975), multicolored	80.00	18.00	8.00
❑ RW43	$5	Canada Geese (1976), emerald & black	75.00	18.00	8.00
❑ RW44	$5	Ross' Geese (1977), multicolored	75.00	18.00	8.00
❑ RW45	$5	Mergansers (1978), multicolored	65.00	16.00	8.00
❑ RW46	$7.50	Green-winged Teal (1979), multicolored	65.00	16.00	8.00

Scott No.			Plate Block	NH Mint	Used
❏ RW47	$7.50	Mallards (1980), multicolored	75.00	18.00	8.00
❏ RW48	$7.50	Ruddy Ducks (1981), multicolored	75.00	18.00	8.00
❏ RW49	$7.50	Canvasbacks (1982), multicolored	75.00	18.00	8.00
❏ RW50	$7.50	Pintails (1983), multicolored	75.00	18.00	8.00
❏ RW51	$7.50	Widgeons (1984), multicolored	75.00	18.00	8.00
❏ RW52	$7.50	Cinnamon Teal (1985), multicolored	75.00	18.00	8.00
❏ RW53	$7.50	Fulvous Whistling Duck (1986), multicolored	75.00	18.00	8.00
❏ RW54	$10	Redheads (1987), multicolored	80.00	20.00	8.00
❏ RW55	$10	Snow Goose (1988), multicolored	80.00	20.00	8.00
❏ RW56	$12.50	Lesser Scaup (1989), multicolored	95.00	30.00	12.00
❏ RW57	$12.50	Black-bellied Whistling Duck (1990), multicolored	95.00	30.00	12.00
❏ RW58	$15	King Eider (1991), multicolored	125.00	40.00	12.50
❏ RW59	$15	Spectacled Eiders (1992), multicolored	125.00	40.00	12.50
❏ RW60	$15	Canvasbacks (1993), multicolored	125.00	40.00	12.50
❏ RW61	$15	Red-breasted Mergansers (1994), multicolored	125.00	40.00	12.50
❏ RW62	$15	Mallards (1995), multicolored	125.00	40.00	12.50
❏ RW63	$15	Sun Scoter (1996), multicolored	125.00	40.00	12.50

RW64

Scott No.			Plate Block	NH Mint	Used
❏ RW64	$15	Canada Goose (1997), multicolored	135.00	32.00	12.00
❏ RW65	$15	Barrow Golden Eyes (1998), multicolored	200.00	50.00	22.50
❏ RW65A		PSA Type (1998)	—	35.00	16.00
❏ RW66	$15	Greater Scaup (1999), multicolored	160.00	50.00	16.00
❏ RW66A		PSA Type (1999)	—	28.00	16.00
❏ RW67	$15	Mottled duck (2000), multicolored	145.00	40.00	20.00
❏ RW67A		PSA Type (2000)	—	30.00	14.00
❏ RW68	$15	Pintail (2001), multicolored	145.00	32.00	20.00
❏ RW68A		PSA Type (2001)	—	28.00	14.00
❏ RW69	$15	Black Scoter (2002), multicolored	145.00	32.00	18.00
❏ RW69A		PSA Type (2002)	—	28.00	15.00
❏ RW70	$15	Snow Goose (2003), multicolored	135.00	32.00	20.00
❏ RW70A		PSA Type (2003)	—	28.00	12.00
❏ RW71	$15	Red Heads (2004), multicolored	130.00	32.00	20.00
❏ RW71		PSA Type (2004)	—	30.00	14.00
❏ RW71A		PSA Type (2004)	—	28.00	14.00
❏ RW72		Hooded Mergansers (2005)	125.00	26.00	14.00
❏ RW72C		Type II w/frame line (2005)	125.00	24.00	14.00
❏ RW72A		PSA Type (2005)	—	26.00	14.00

RW72B

Scott No.		Plate Block	NH Mint	Used
❏ RW72B	Pane of one (2005) s/s (a (1,000 issued)	—	2000.00	
❏ RW72B	variation approximately 150 signed in blue ink	3250.00		2200.00
	variation approximately 100 signed in gold ink	2950.00		2350.00

RW73B

Scott No.		Plate Block	NH Mint	Used
❏ RW73	Ross's Goose (2006)	130.00	26.00	15.00
❏ RW73A	PSA Type (2006)	—	22.00	15.00
❏ RW73B	Pane of one (2006) s/s (a/s) (10,000 issued)	—	200.00	—
❏ RW73B	Pane of one, 2 signatures	—	265.00	—
❏ RW73C	Error—Missing signature*		3500.00	—
❏ RW74	Ringed neck ducks (2007)	130.00	26.00	15.00
❏ RW74A	PSA Type (2007)	—	24.00	15.00

*Only 10 known to exist

RW74B

Scott No.		Plate Block	NH Mint	Used
❑ RW74B	Pane of one (2007) s/s (a/s) (10,000 issued)	—	225.00	200.00
❑ RW74C	Missing signature*	—	3000.00	—

*Approximately 120 known to exist

RW75B

Scott No.		Plate Block	NH Mint	Used
❑ RW75	Northern Pintails (2008)	130.00	26.00	15.00
❑ RW75A	PSA Type (2008)	—	24.00	15.00
❑ RW75B	Pane of one (2008) s/s (a/s) (10,000 issued)	—	85.00	—
❑ RW75C	Missing signature*	—	650.00	—
❑ RW75	Souvenir Sheet of 2 (2008)	—	85.00	—
❑ RW76	Long tailed duck (2009)	130.00	26.00	15.00
❑ RW76A	PSA type (2009)	—	24.00	15.00
❑ RW76B	Pane of one (2009) s/s (a/s) (10,000 issued)	—	110.00	15.00
❑ RW76C	Missing signature	—	550.00	—

* Quantity unknown estimate 50–75

RW77B

Scott No.		Plate Block	NH Mint	Used
❏ RW77	Wigeon (2010)	125.00	24.00	15.00
❏ RW77A	PSA type (2010)	—	24.00	15.00
❏ RW77B	Pane of one (2010) s/s (a/s)	—	70.00	—
❏ RW77C	Missing signature	—	195.00	—

RW78B

Scott No.		Plate Block	NH Mint	Used
❏ RW78	White-Fronted Geese (2011)	125.00	24.00	15.00
❏ RW78A	PSA type (2011)	—	24.00	15.00
❏ RW78B	Pane of one (2011) s/s (a/s)	—	70.00	—
❏ RW78C	Missing signature	—	275.00	—

RW79B

Scott No.		Plate Block	NH Mint	Used
❏ RW79	Wood Duck (2012)	110.00	24.00	15.00
❏ RW79A	PSA type (2012)	—	24.00	15.00
❏ RW79B	Pane of one (2012) s/s (a/s)	—	75.00	—
❏ RW79C	Missing signature	—	1750.00	—

FEDERAL JUNIOR STAMPS

Scott No.		Single	Plate of 4
❑ JDS1	Redhead 1993	95.00	450.00
❑ JDS2	Hooded Merganser 1994	225.00	1000.00
❑ JDS3	Pintail 1995	475.00	1850.00
❑ JDS4	Canvasback 1996	575.00	2150.00
❑ JDS5	Canada Goose 1997	550.00	2450.00
❑ JDS6	Black Duck 1998	550.00	2450.00
❑ JDS7	Wood Duck 1999	550.00	2450.00
❑ JDS8	Pintail 2000	375.00	1450.00
❑ JDS9	Trumpeter Swan 2001	100.00	350.00
❑ JDS10	Mallard 2002	60.00	200.00
❑ JDS11	Green-winged Teal 2003	40.00	180.00
❑ JDS12	Fulvous Whistling 2004	30.00	180.00
❑ JDS13	Ringed-neck Duck 2005	28.00	125.00
❑ JDS14	Redhead 2006	18.00	70.00
❑ JDS15	Wigeon 2007	14.00	60.00
❑ JDS16	Hawaiian Nene Goose 2008	14.00	60.00
❑ JDS17	Wood Duck 2009	14.00	60.00
❑ JDS18	Hooded Merganser 2010	14.00	60.00
❑ JDS19	Ring-necked Duck 2011	14.00	60.00
❑ JDS20	Northern Pintail 2012	14.00	60.00

MINT SHEETS

❏ 643	2¢	Vermont	340.00
❏ 644	2¢	Burgoyne	340.00
❏ 645	2¢	Valley Forge	236.00
❏ 646	2¢	Molly Pitcher	236.00
❏ 647	2¢	Hawaii	890.00
❏ 648	5¢	Hawaii	2310.00
❏ 649	2¢	Aeronautics	170.00
❏ 650	5¢	Aeronautics	450.00
❏ 651	2¢	George R. Clark	158.00
❏ 653	½¢	Hale	53.00
❏ 654	2¢	Edison-Flat	221.00
❏ 655	2¢	Edison-Rotary	1470.00
❏ 657	2¢	Sullivan	263.00
❏ 680	2¢	Fallen Timbers	263.00
❏ 681	2¢	Ohio Canal	147.00
❏ 682	2¢	Mass. Bay	132.00
❏ 683	2¢	Carolina-Charleston	195.00
❏ 684	1½¢	Harding	79.00
❏ 685	4¢	Taft	147.00
❏ 688	2¢	Braddock	221.00
❏ 689	2¢	Von Steuben	105.00
❏ 690	2¢	Pulaski	63.00
❏ 702	2¢	Red Cross	41.00
❏ 703	2¢	Yorktown	41.00
❏ 704	½¢	Wash. Bicent'l	41.00
❏ 705	1¢	Wash. Bicent'l	41.00
❏ 706	1½¢	Wash. Bicent'l	79.00
❏ 707	2¢	Wash. Bicent'l	36.00
❏ 708	3¢	Wash. Bicent'l	105.00
❏ 709	4¢	Wash. Bicent'l	58.00
❏ 710	5¢	Wash. Bicent'l	289.00
❏ 711	6¢	Wash. Bicent'l	525.00
❏ 712	7¢	Wash. Bicent'l	105.00
❏ 713	8¢	Wash. Bicent'l	525.00
❏ 714	9¢	Wash. Bicent'l	525.00
❏ 715	10¢	Wash. Bicent'l	1730.00
❏ 716	2¢	Lake Placid	105.00
❏ 717	2¢	Arbor Day	52.00
❏ 718	2¢	Olympics	236.00
❏ 719	5¢	Olympics	368.00
❏ 720	3¢	Washington	63.00
❏ 724	3¢	Penn	84.00
❏ 725	3¢	Webster	105.00
❏ 726	3¢	Oglethorpe	84.00
❏ 727	3¢	Newburgh	51.00
❏ 728	1¢	Chicago	51.00
❏ 729	3¢	Chicago	51.00
❏ 732	3¢	N.R.A.	51.00
❏ 733	3¢	Byrd	58.00
❏ 734	5¢	Kosciuszko	158.00
❏ 736	3¢	Maryland	42.00
❏ 737	3¢	Mother's Day Rotary	21.00
❏ 738	3¢	Mother's Day Flat	27.00
❏ 739	3¢	Wisconsin	23.00
❏ 740	1¢	Nat'l. Parks	23.00
❏ 741	2¢	Nat'l. Parks	23.00
❏ 742	3¢	Nat'l. Parks	23.00
❏ 743	4¢	Nat'l. Parks	42.00
❏ 744	5¢	Nat'l. Parks	79.00
❏ 745	6¢	Nat'l. Parks	105.00
❏ 746	7¢	Nat'l. Parks	84.00
❏ 747	8¢	Nat'l. Parks	221.00
❏ 748	9¢	Nat'l. Parks	221.00
❏ 749	10¢	Nat'l. Parks	263.00
❏ 752	3¢	Newburg	420.00
❏ 753	3¢	Byrd	630.00
❏ 754	3¢	Mother's Day	231.00
❏ 755	3¢	Wisconsin	184.00
❏ 756	1¢	Park	116.00
❏ 757	2¢	Park	116.00
❏ 758	3¢	Park	158.00
❏ 759	4¢	Park	315.00
❏ 760	5¢	Park	525.00
❏ 761	6¢	Park	630.00
❏ 762	7¢	Park	265.00
❏ 763	8¢	Park	630.00
❏ 764	9¢	Park	840.00
❏ 765	10¢	Park	1050.00
❏ 766a	1¢	Chicago	525.00
❏ 767a	3¢	Chicago	525.00
❏ 768a	3¢	Byrd	630.00
❏ 769	1¢	Park	289.00

❑ 770	3¢	Park	735.00		❑ 862	5¢	Alcott	48.00
❑ 771	16¢	Air Spec. Deal	840.00		❑ 863	10¢	Clemens	210.00
❑ 772	3¢	Connecticut	21.00		❑ 864	1¢	Longfellow	37.00
❑ 773	3¢	San Diego	20.00		❑ 865	2¢	Whittier	32.00
❑ 774	3¢	Boulder Dam	20.00		❑ 866	3¢	Lowell	32.00
❑ 775	3¢	Michigan	21.00		❑ 867	5¢	Whitman	63.00
❑ 776	3¢	Texas	21.00		❑ 868	10¢	Riley	252.00
❑ 777	3¢	Rhode Island	37.00		❑ 869	1¢	Mann	23.00
❑ 782	3¢	Arkansas	21.00		❑ 870	2¢	Hopkins	23.00
❑ 783	3¢	Oregon	20.00		❑ 871	3¢	Elliot	23.00
❑ 784	3¢	Susan B. Anthony	27.00		❑ 872	5¢	Willard	63.00
❑ 785	1¢	Army	27.00		❑ 873	10¢	B.T. Washington	210.00
❑ 786	2¢	Army	16.00		❑ 874	1¢	Audubon	27.00
❑ 787	3¢	Army	27.00		❑ 875	2¢	Long	21.00
❑ 788	4¢	Army	53.00		❑ 876	3¢	Burbank	27.00
❑ 789	5¢	Army	53.00		❑ 877	5¢	Reed	53.00
❑ 790	1¢	Navy	13.00		❑ 878	10¢	Addams	158.00
❑ 791	2¢	Navy	16.00		❑ 879	1¢	Fosters	27.00
❑ 792	3¢	Navy	20.00		❑ 880	2¢	Sousa	23.00
❑ 793	4¢	Navy	48.00		❑ 881	3¢	Herbert	23.00
❑ 794	5¢	Navy	53.00		❑ 882	5¢	MacDowell	69.00
❑ 795	3¢	N.W. Territory	37.00		❑ 883	10¢	Nevin	368.00
❑ 796	5¢	Virginia Dare	37.00		❑ 884	1¢	Sturat	28.00
❑ 798	3¢	Constitution	37.00		❑ 885	2¢	Whistler	28.00
❑ 799	3¢	Hawaii	21.00		❑ 886	3¢	St. Gaudens	28.00
❑ 800	3¢	Alaska	28.00		❑ 887	5¢	French	53.00
❑ 801	3¢	Puerto Rico	28.00		❑ 888	10¢	Remington	210.00
❑ 802	3¢	Virgin Islands	28.00		❑ 889	1¢	Whitney	27.00
❑ 835	3¢	Ratification	32.00		❑ 890	2¢	Morse	27.00
❑ 836	3¢	Swede-Finn	19.00		❑ 891	3¢	McCormick	32.00
❑ 837	3¢	N.W. Territory	42.00		❑ 892	5¢	Howe	105.00
❑ 838	3¢	Iowa	27.00		❑ 893	10¢	Bell	1575.00
❑ 852	3¢	Golden Gate	21.00		❑ 894	3¢	Pony Express	37.00
❑ 853	3¢	N.Y. Fair	21.00		❑ 895	3¢	Pan America	37.00
❑ 854	3¢	Inauguration	53.00		❑ 896	3¢	Idaho	28.00
❑ 855	3¢	Baseball	158.00		❑ 897	3¢	Wyoming	28.00
❑ 856	3¢	Canal Zone	28.00		❑ 898	3¢	Coronado	23.00
❑ 857	3¢	Printing	28.00		❑ 899	1¢	Defense	29.00
❑ 858	3¢	Four States	28.00		❑ 900	2¢	Defense	29.00
❑ 859	1¢	Irving	28.00		❑ 901	3¢	Defense	29.00
❑ 860	2¢	Cooper	28.00		❑ 902	3¢	Emancipation	29.00
❑ 861	3¢	Emerson	16.00		❑ 903	3¢	Vermont	29.00

☐ 904	3¢	Kentucky	27.00	☐ 945	3¢	Edison	23.00
☐ 905	3¢	Win the War	27.00	☐ 946	3¢	Pulitzer	21.00
☐ 906	5¢	China	78.00	☐ 947	3¢	CIPEX	21.00
☐ 907	2¢	Allied Nations	22.00	☐ 949	3¢	Doctors	21.00
☐ 908	1¢	Four Freedoms	22.00	☐ 950	3¢	Utah	9.00
☐ 909	5¢	Poland	15.00	☐ 951	3¢	Constitution	11.00
☐ 910	5¢	Czechoslovakia	16.00	☐ 952	3¢	Everglades	15.00
☐ 911	5¢	Norway	15.00	☐ 953	3¢	Carver	17.00
☐ 912	5¢	Luxembourg	23.00	☐ 954	3¢	Gold Rush	16.00
☐ 913	5¢	Netherlands	23.00	☐ 955	3¢	Mississippi	16.00
☐ 914	5¢	Belgium	23.00	☐ 956	3¢	Chaplains	16.00
☐ 915	5¢	France	13.00	☐ 957	3¢	Wisconsin	16.00
☐ 916	5¢	Greece	42.00	☐ 958	5¢	Swedish Pioneer	16.00
☐ 917	5¢	Yugoslavia	31.00	☐ 959	3¢	Women	16.00
☐ 918	5¢	Albania	31.00	☐ 960	3¢	White	15.00
☐ 919	5¢	Austria	23.00	☐ 961	3¢	U.S. Canada	13.00
☐ 920	5¢	Denmark	27.00	☐ 962	3¢	Key	16.00
☐ 921	5¢	Korea	23.00	☐ 963	3¢	Youth	13.00
☐ 909–21		Set of 13	262.00	☐ 964	3¢	Oregon	13.00
☐ 922	3¢	Railroad	23.00	☐ 965	3¢	Stone	17.00
☐ 923	3¢	Steamship	27.00	☐ 966	3¢	Palomar	17.00
☐ 924	3¢	Telegraph	21.00	☐ 967	3¢	Barton	17.00
☐ 925	3¢	Corregidor	21.00	☐ 968	3¢	Poultry	17.00
☐ 926	3¢	Motion Pictures	21.00	☐ 969	3¢	Gold Star	9.00
☐ 927	3¢	Florida	21.00	☐ 970	3¢	Fort Kearny	11.00
☐ 928	5¢	United Nations	21.00	☐ 971	3¢	Firemen	16.00
☐ 929	3¢	Iwo Jima	23.00	☐ 972	3¢	Indian Centennial	16.00
☐ 930	1¢	Roosevelt	13.00	☐ 973	3¢	Rough Riders	16.00
☐ 931	2¢	Roosevelt	13.00	☐ 974	3¢	Juliette Low	16.00
☐ 932	3¢	Roosevelt	13.00	☐ 975	3¢	Will Rogers	17.00
☐ 933	5¢	Roosevelt	16.00	☐ 976	3¢	Fort Bliss	17.00
☐ 934	3¢	Army	21.00	☐ 977	3¢	Moina Michael	17.00
☐ 935	3¢	Navy	21.00	☐ 978	3¢	Gettysburg	16.00
☐ 936	3¢	Coast Guard	21.00	☐ 979	3¢	Turners	16.00
☐ 937	3¢	Alfred E. Smith	23.00	☐ 980	3¢	Harris	19.00
☐ 938	3¢	Texas	17.00	☐ 981	3¢	Minnesota	15.00
☐ 939	3¢	Merchant Marine	16.00	☐ 982	3¢	Washington & Lee	15.00
☐ 940	3¢	Discharge Emblem	23.00	☐ 983	3¢	Puerto Rico	13.00
☐ 941	3¢	Tennessee	21.00	☐ 984	3¢	Annapolis	16.00
☐ 942	3¢	Iowa	17.00	☐ 985	3¢	G.A.R.	16.00
☐ 943	3¢	Smithsonian	17.00	☐ 986	3¢	Poe	23.00
☐ 944	3¢	Kearny	11.00	☐ 987	3¢	Bankers	23.00

❏ 988	3¢	Gompers	20.00	❏ 1030	½¢	Franklin	15.00
❏ 989	3¢	Capitol Statue	20.00	❏ 1031	1¢	Washington	15.00
❏ 990	3¢	White House	20.00	❏ 1031A	1¼¢	Palace of Governors	15.00
❏ 991	3¢	Supreme Court	20.00	❏ 1032	1½¢	Mount Vernon	28.00
❏ 992	3¢	Capitol Building	13.00	❏ 1033	2¢	Jefferson	16.00
❏ 993	3¢	Casey Jones	16.00	❏ 1034	2½¢	Bunker Hill	23.00
❏ 994	3¢	Kansas City	20.00	❏ 1035	3¢	Liberty	16.00
❏ 995	3¢	Boy Scouts	20.00	❏ 1036	4¢	Lincoln	34.00
❏ 996	3¢	Indiana	20.00	❏ 1037	4½¢	Hermitage	34.00
❏ 997	3¢	California	13.00	❏ 1038	5¢	Monroe	34.00
❏ 998	3¢	Confederate	16.00	❏ 1039	6¢	Roosevelt	37.00
❏ 999	3¢	Nevada	16.00	❏ 1040	7¢	Wilson	34.00
❏ 1000	3¢	Cadillac at Detroit	16.00	❏ 1041	8¢	Liberty	37.00
❏ 1001	3¢	Colorado	16.00	❏ 1042	8¢	Liberty (re-engraved)	34.00
❏ 1002	3¢	Chemical	16.00	❏ 1042A	8¢	Pershing	37.00
❏ 1003	3¢	Battle of Brooklyn	15.00	❏ 1043	9¢	Alamo	53.00
❏ 1004	3¢	Betsy Ross	15.00	❏ 1044	10¢	Independence Hall	53.00
❏ 1005	3¢	4-H Clubs	20.00	❏ 1044A	11¢	Liberty	53.00
❏ 1006	3¢	B&O Railroad	16.00	❏ 1045	12¢	Harrison	63.00
❏ 1007	3¢	A.A.A.	16.00	❏ 1046	15¢	Jay	105.00
❏ 1008	3¢	NATO	16.00	❏ 1047	20¢	Monticello	84.00
❏ 1009	3¢	Grand Coulee Dam	15.00	❏ 1048	25¢	Revere	184.00
❏ 1010	3¢	Lafayette	20.00	❏ 1049	30¢	Lee	247.00
❏ 1011	3¢	Rushmore	15.00	❏ 1050	40¢	Marshall	342.00
❏ 1012	3¢	Engineers	15.00	❏ 1051	50¢	Stone	247.00
❏ 1013	3¢	Armed Forces Women	11.00	❏ 1052	$1	Henry	630.00
❏ 1014	3¢	Gutenberg	9.00	❏ 1053	$5	Hamilton	814.00
❏ 1015	3¢	Newspaper Boys	13.00	❏ 1060	3¢	Nebraska	15.00
❏ 1016	3¢	Red Cross	13.00	❏ 1061	3¢	Kansas	15.00
❏ 1017	3¢	National Guard	13.00	❏ 1062	3¢	George Eastman	17.00
❏ 1018	3¢	Ohio	28.00	❏ 1063	3¢	Lewis & Clark	17.00
❏ 1019	3¢	Washington	11.00	❏ 1064	3¢	Penn Academy	17.00
❏ 1020	3¢	Louisiana	17.00	❏ 1065	3¢	Colleges	17.00
❏ 1021	5¢	Opening of Japan	17.00	❏ 1066	8¢	Rotary	17.00
❏ 1022	3¢	Bar Association	16.00	❏ 1067	3¢	Reserves	15.00
❏ 1023	3¢	Sagamore Hill	16.00	❏ 1068	3¢	Vermont	17.00
❏ 1024	3¢	Future Farmers	16.00	❏ 1069	3¢	Great Lakes	17.00
❏ 1025	3¢	Trucking	16.00	❏ 1070	3¢	Atoms for Peace	17.00
❏ 1026	3¢	Patton	16.00	❏ 1071	3¢	Ft. Ticonderoga	17.00
❏ 1027	3¢	New York City	16.00	❏ 1072	3¢	Andrew Mellon	28.00
❏ 1028	3¢	Gadsden Purchase	16.00	❏ 1073	3¢	Benj. Franklin	16.00
❏ 1029	3¢	Columbia U.	16.00	❏ 1074	3¢	B. T. Washington	16.00

❏ 1076	3¢	FIPEX	15.00	❏ 1121	4¢	Webster	17.00
❏ 1077	3¢	Wild Turkey	15.00	❏ 1122	4¢	Forest Conserv.	11.00
❏ 1078	3¢	Antelope	9.00	❏ 1123	4¢	Ft. Duquesne	15.00
❏ 1079	3¢	King Salmon	13.00	❏ 1124	4¢	Oregon	11.00
❏ 1080	3¢	Pure Food & Drug	11.00	❏ 1125	4¢	San Martin	13.00
❏ 1081	3¢	Wheatland	13.00	❏ 1126	8¢	San Martin	17.00
❏ 1082	3¢	Labor Day	16.00	❏ 1127	4¢	NATO	17.00
❏ 1083	3¢	Nassau Hall	16.00	❏ 1128	4¢	Arctic Exploration	17.00
❏ 1084	3¢	Devils Tower	12.00	❏ 1129	8¢	World Peace	17.00
❏ 1085	3¢	Children	12.00	❏ 1130	4¢	Silver Centennial	17.00
❏ 1086	3¢	Hamilton	12.00	❏ 1131	4¢	Seaway	15.00
❏ 1087	3¢	Polio	12.00	❏ 1132	4¢	49-Star Flag	12.00
❏ 1088	3¢	Geodetic	12.00	❏ 1133	4¢	Soil Conserv.	12.00
❏ 1089	3¢	Architects	12.00	❏ 1134	4¢	Petroleum	15.00
❏ 1090	3¢	Steel Industry	12.00	❏ 1135	4¢	Dental Health	17.00
❏ 1091	3¢	Naval Review	12.00	❏ 1136	4¢	Reuter	17.00
❏ 1092	3¢	Oklahoma	12.00	❏ 1137	8¢	Reuter	17.00
❏ 1093	3¢	Teachers	12.00	❏ 1138	4¢	McDowell	20.00
❏ 1094	4¢	48-Star Flag	12.00	❏ 1139	4¢	Credo – Washington	17.00
❏ 1095	3¢	Shipbuilding	17.50	❏ 1140	4¢	Credo – Franklin	17.00
❏ 1096	8¢	Magsaysay	13.00	❏ 1141	4¢	Credo – Jefferson	17.00
❏ 1097	3¢	Lafayette	17.50	❏ 1142	4¢	Credo – Key	17.00
❏ 1098	3¢	Whooping Cranes	13.00	❏ 1143	4¢	Credo – Lincoln	17.00
❏ 1099	3¢	Religious Freedom	11.00	❏ 1144	4¢	Credo – Henry	17.00
❏ 1100	3¢	Horticulture	11.00	❏ 1145	4¢	Boy Scouts	17.00
❏ 1104	3¢	Brussels Exhib.	11.00	❏ 1146	4¢	Winter Olympics	9.00
❏ 1105	3¢	James Monroe	13.00	❏ 1147	4¢	Masaryk	13.00
❏ 1106	3¢	Minnesota	11.00	❏ 1148	8¢	Masaryk	17.00
❏ 1107	3¢	Geophysical Year	11.00	❏ 1149	4¢	Refugee Year	15.00
❏ 1108	3¢	Gunston Hall	11.00	❏ 1150	4¢	Water Conserv.	15.00
❏ 1109	3¢	Mackinac Bridge	11.00	❏ 1151	4¢	SEATO	15.00
❏ 1110	4¢	Bolivar	13.00	❏ 1152	4¢	Women	11.00
❏ 1111	8¢	Bolivar	17.00	❏ 1153	4¢	50-Star Flag	11.00
❏ 1112	4¢	Atlantic Cable	12.00	❏ 1154	4¢	Pony Express	15.00
❏ 1113	1¢	Lincoln	12.00	❏ 1155	4¢	Handicapped	11.00
❏ 1114	3¢	Lincoln	15.00	❏ 1156	4¢	Forestry	11.00
❏ 1115	4¢	Lincoln-Douglas	16.00	❏ 1157	4¢	Mexican Ind.	11.00
❏ 1116	4¢	Lincoln	15.00	❏ 1158	4¢	U.S.-Japan	11.00
❏ 1117	4¢	Kossuth	13.00	❏ 1159	4¢	Paderewski	13.00
❏ 1118	8¢	Kossuth	20.00	❏ 1160	8¢	Paderewski	23.00
❏ 1119	4¢	Free Press	11.00	❏ 1161	4¢	Robert Taft	23.00
❏ 1120	4¢	Overland Mail	15.00	❏ 1162	4¢	Wheels of Freedom	13.00

❏ 1163	4¢	Boys' Clubs	17.00
❏ 1164	4¢	Automated P.O.	20.00
❏ 1165	4¢	Mannerheim	16.00
❏ 1166	8¢	Mannerheim	23.00
❏ 1167	4¢	Campfire Girls	18.00
❏ 1168	4¢	Garibaldi	18.00
❏ 1169	8¢	Garibaldi	18.00
❏ 1170	4¢	George	18.00
❏ 1171	4¢	Carnegie	23.00
❏ 1172	4¢	Dulles	23.00
❏ 1173	4¢	Echo I	23.00
❏ 1174	4¢	Gandhi	13.00
❏ 1175	8¢	Gandhi	23.00
❏ 1176	4¢	Range Conserv.	13.00
❏ 1177	4¢	Greeley	23.00
❏ 1178	4¢	Ft. Sumter	26.00
❏ 1179	4¢	Shiloh	20.00
❏ 1180	5¢	Gettysburg	23.00
❏ 1181	5¢	Wilderness	20.00
❏ 1182	5¢	Appomattox	37.00
❏ 1183	4¢	Kansas	15.00
❏ 1184	4¢	Norris	17.00
❏ 1185	4¢	Naval Aviation	15.00
❏ 1186	4¢	Workmen's Comp.	15.00
❏ 1187	4¢	Remington	15.00
❏ 1188	4¢	China	15.00
❏ 1189	4¢	Basketball	17.00
❏ 1190	4¢	Nursing	17.00
❏ 1191	4¢	New Mexico	13.00
❏ 1192	4¢	Arizona	13.00
❏ 1193	4¢	Project Mercury	13.00
❏ 1194	4¢	Malaria	13.00
❏ 1195	4¢	Hughes	13.00
❏ 1196	4¢	Seattle Fair	13.00
❏ 1197	4¢	Louisiana	17.00
❏ 1198	4¢	Homestead	11.00
❏ 1199	4¢	Girl Scouts	9.00
❏ 1200	4¢	McMahon	15.00
❏ 1201	4¢	Apprenticeship	9.00
❏ 1202	4¢	Rayburn	13.00
❏ 1203	4¢	Hammarskjold	9.00
❏ 1204	4¢	Hammarskjold invert	15.00
❏ 1205	4¢	Christmas Wreath	17.00
❏ 1206	4¢	Education	13.00
❏ 1207	4¢	Winslow Homer	17.00
❏ 1208	5¢	U.S. Flag	17.00
❏ 1209	1¢	Jackson	13.00
❏ 1213	5¢	Washington	23.00
❏ 1230	5¢	Carolina	23.00
❏ 1231	5¢	Food for Peace	17.00
❏ 1232	5¢	West Virginia	17.00
❏ 1233	5¢	Emancipation	17.00
❏ 1234	5¢	Alliance for Progress	17.00
❏ 1235	5¢	Hull	17.00
❏ 1236	5¢	E. Roosevelt	15.00
❏ 1237	5¢	Sciences	13.00
❏ 1238	5¢	City Mail	13.00
❏ 1239	5¢	Red Cross	13.00
❏ 1240	5¢	Christmas Tree	23.00
❏ 1241	5¢	Audubon	15.00
❏ 1242	5¢	Sam Houston	13.00
❏ 1243	5¢	Russell	17.00
❏ 1244	5¢	World's Fair	13.00
❏ 1245	5¢	John Muir	13.00
❏ 1246	5¢	J.F.K.	32.00
❏ 1247	5¢	New Jersey	17.00
❏ 1248	5¢	Nevada	13.00
❏ 1249	5¢	Register & Vote	13.00
❏ 1250	5¢	Shakespeare	13.00
❏ 1251	5¢	Doctors Mayo	15.00
❏ 1252	5¢	Music	12.00
❏ 1253	5¢	Homemakers	12.00
❏ 1254–57	5¢	Christmas	38.00
❏ 1258	5¢	Verrazano Bridge	17.00
❏ 1259	5¢	Modern Art	11.00
❏ 1260	5¢	Amateur Radio	17.00
❏ 1261	5¢	New Orleans	23.00
❏ 1262	5¢	Physical Fitness	13.00
❏ 1263	5¢	Fight Cancer	13.00
❏ 1264	5¢	Churchill	17.00
❏ 1265	5¢	Magna Carta	17.00
❏ 1266	5¢	Cooperation Year	13.00
❏ 1267	5¢	Salvation Army	13.00
❏ 1268	5¢	Dante Alighieri	13.00

❑ 1269	5¢	Herbert Hoover	15.00	❑ 1321	5¢	Christmas	13.00
❑ 1270	5¢	Robert Fulton	15.00	❑ 1322	5¢	Cassatt	13.00
❑ 1271	5¢	Florida	15.00	❑ 1323	5¢	Grange	13.00
❑ 1272	5¢	Traffic Safety	11.00	❑ 1324	5¢	Canada	9.00
❑ 1273	5¢	John S. Copley	15.00	❑ 1325	5¢	Erie Canal	17.00
❑ 1274	11¢	I.T.U.	32.00	❑ 1326	5¢	Peace	23.00
❑ 1275	5¢	Stevenson	13.00	❑ 1327	5¢	Thoreau	23.00
❑ 1276	5¢	Christmas	16.00	❑ 1328	5¢	Nebraska	23.00
❑ 1278	1¢	Jefferson	10.00	❑ 1329	5¢	Voice of America	11.00
❑ 1279	1¼¢	Gallatin	23.00	❑ 1330	5¢	Davy Crockett	16.00
❑ 1280	2¢	Wright	13.00	❑ 1331–32	5¢	Space Twins	37.00
❑ 1281	3¢	Parkman	13.00	❑ 1333	5¢	Urban Planning	13.00
❑ 1282	4¢	Lincoln	34.00	❑ 1334	5¢	Finland	13.00
❑ 1283	5¢	Washington	23.00	❑ 1335	5¢	Eakins	16.00
❑ 1283B	5¢	Washington	16.00	❑ 1336	5¢	Christmas	11.00
❑ 1284	6¢	Roosevelt	34.00	❑ 1337	5¢	Mississippi	23.00
❑ 1285	8¢	Einstein	37.00	❑ 1338	6¢	Flag	23.00
❑ 1286	10¢	Jackson	44.00	❑ 1338D	6¢	Flag	19.00
❑ 1286A	12¢	Ford	37.00	❑ 1338F	8¢	Flag	28.00
❑ 1287	13¢	Kennedy	52.00	❑ 1339	6¢	Illinois	19.00
❑ 1288	15¢	Holmes (type I)	42.00	❑ 1340	6¢	Hemisfair '68	11.00
❑ 1288A	15¢	Holmes (type II)	121.00	❑ 1341	$1	Airlift	155.00
❑ 1289	20¢	Marshall	121.00	❑ 1342	6¢	Youth	9.00
❑ 1290	25¢	Douglass	121.00	❑ 1343	6¢	Law & Order	13.00
❑ 1291	30¢	Dewey	147.00	❑ 1344	6¢	Register & Vote	13.00
❑ 1292	40¢	Paine	163.00	❑ 1345–54	6¢	Flags	23.00
❑ 1293	50¢	Stone	163.00	❑ 1355	6¢	Disney	52.00
❑ 1294	$1	O'Neill	315.00	❑ 1356	6¢	Marquette	20.00
❑ 1306	5¢	Migratory Bird	13.00	❑ 1357	6¢	Daniel Boone	20.00
❑ 1307	5¢	Humane Treatment	13.00	❑ 1358	6¢	Arkansas River	20.00
❑ 1308	5¢	Indiana	16.00	❑ 1359	6¢	Leif Erikson	20.00
❑ 1309	5¢	Clown	15.00	❑ 1360	6¢	Cherokee Strip	20.00
❑ 1310	5¢	SIPEX	15.00	❑ 1361	6¢	Trumball	20.00
❑ 1312	5¢	Bill of Rights	15.00	❑ 1362	6¢	Waterfowl	16.00
❑ 1313	5¢	Poland	15.00	❑ 1363	6¢	Christmas	13.00
❑ 1314	5¢	Park Service	15.00	❑ 1364	6¢	Chief Joseph	19.00
❑ 1315	5¢	Marine Reserve	15.00	❑ 1365–68	6¢	Beautification	28.00
❑ 1316	5¢	Women's Clubs	15.00	❑ 1369	6¢	American Legion	15.00
❑ 1317	5¢	J. Appleseed	15.00	❑ 1370	6¢	Grandma Moses	15.00
❑ 1318	5¢	Beautification	15.00	❑ 1371	6¢	Apollo 8	16.00
❑ 1319	5¢	Great River Road	16.00	❑ 1372	6¢	W. C. Handy	17.00
❑ 1320	5¢	Servicemen	13.00	❑ 1373	6¢	California	15.00

❏ 1374	6¢	Powell	22.00	❏ 1433	8¢	John Sloan	14.20
❏ 1375	6¢	Alabama	22.00	❏ 1434–35	8¢	Space Achiev.	14.75
❏ 1376–79	6¢	Botanical	37.00	❏ 1436	8¢	Dickinson	16.85
❏ 1380	6¢	Webster	16.00	❏ 1437	8¢	Puerto Rico	15.75
❏ 1381	6¢	Baseball	47.00	❏ 1438	8¢	Drug Abuse	15.75
❏ 1382	6¢	Football	31.50	❏ 1439	8¢	CARE	15.75
❏ 1383	6¢	Eisenhower	10.50	❏ 1440	8¢	Landmarks	15.75
❏ 1384	6¢	Christmas	14.75	❏ 1444	8¢	Christmas	15.75
❏ 1385	6¢	Hope	14.75	❏ 1445	8¢	Partridge	15.75
❏ 1386	6¢	Harnett	14.75	❏ 1446	8¢	Lanier	22.50
❏ 1387–90	6¢	Conservation	10.50	❏ 1447	8¢	Peace Corps	14.75
❏ 1391	6¢	Maine	14.75	❏ 1448–51	2¢	Cape Hatteras	14.75
❏ 1392	6¢	Bison	14.75	❏ 1452	6¢	Wolf Trap	14.75
❏ 1393	6¢	Eisenhower	22.50	❏ 1453	8¢	Old Faithful	14.20
❏ 1393D	7¢	Franklin	26.25	❏ 1454	15¢	Mt. McKinley	23.10
❏ 1394	8¢	Eisenhower	25.25	❏ 1455	8¢	Family Planning	15.75
❏ 1395	8¢	Eisenhower	25.25	❏ 1456–59	8¢	Craftsmen	15.75
❏ 1396	8¢	U.S.P.S. Logo	26.25	❏ 1460	6¢	Cycling	10.50
❏ 1397	14¢	LaGuardia	36.75	❏ 1461	8¢	Bobsledding	14.75
❏ 1398	16¢	Pyle	52.50	❏ 1462	15¢	Running	23.10
❏ 1399	18¢	Blackwell	78.75	❏ 1463	8¢	P.T.A.	16.85
❏ 1400	21¢	Giannini	78.75	❏ 1464	8¢	Wildlife	14.75
❏ 1405	6¢	Masters	18.50	❏ 1468	8¢	Mail Order	15.75
❏ 1406	6¢	Suffrage	18.50	❏ 1469	8¢	Osteopath	23.10
❏ 1407	6¢	South Carolina	18.50	❏ 1470	8¢	Tom Sawyer	16.85
❏ 1408	6¢	Stone Mountain	15.75	❏ 1471	8¢	Christmas	16.85
❏ 1409	6¢	Fort Snelling	14.20	❏ 1472	8¢	Santa	14.75
❏ 1410–13	6¢	Conservation	18.50	❏ 1473	8¢	Pharmacy	23.10
❏ 1414	6¢	Christmas	15.75	❏ 1474	8¢	Stamp Collecting	16.85
❏ 1414a	6¢	Precanceled	15.75	❏ 1475	8¢	LOVE	14.25
❏ 1415–18	6¢	Toys	26.25	❏ 1476	8¢	Printing Press	14.25
❏ 1415a–18a	6¢	Toys precancel	36.75	❏ 1477	8¢	Broadside	14.25
❏ 1419	6¢	U.N.	15.75	❏ 1478	8¢	Post Rider	14.20
❏ 1420	6¢	Pilgrims	15.75	❏ 1479	8¢	Drummer	15.75
❏ 1421–22	6¢	Veterans	15.75	❏ 1480–83	8¢	Tea Party	16.85
❏ 1423	6¢	Wool	15.75	❏ 1484	8¢	Gershwin	14.25
❏ 1424	6¢	MacArthur	16.85	❏ 1485	8¢	Jeffers	14.20
❏ 1425	6¢	Give Blood	15.75	❏ 1486	6¢	Tanner	14.25
❏ 1426	8¢	Missouri	15.75	❏ 1487	8¢	Cather	14.20
❏ 1427–30	8¢	Wildlife	15.75	❏ 1488	8¢	Copernicus	14.25
❏ 1431	8¢	Antarctic	14.20	❏ 1489–98	8¢	Postal People	16.85
❏ 1432	8¢	Bicentennial	15.75	❏ 1499	8¢	Truman	16.85

❑ 1500	6¢	Electronics	16.80
❑ 1501	8¢	Electroncs	16.80
❑ 1502	15¢	Electronics	22.50
❑ 1503	8¢	L.B. J.	12.75
❑ 1504	8¢	Angus Cattle	15.75
❑ 1505	10¢	Chautauqua	15.75
❑ 1506	10¢	Winter Wheat	22.50
❑ 1507	8¢	Christmas	15.75
❑ 1508	8¢	Christmas Tree	15.75
❑ 1509	10¢	Crossed Flags	40.00
❑ 1510	10¢	Jeff. Memorial	40.00
❑ 1511	10¢	ZIP Code	40.00
❑ 1525	10¢	V.F.W.	15.75
❑ 1526	10¢	Robert Frost	27.80
❑ 1527	10¢	Expo '74	15.75
❑ 1528	10¢	Horse Racing	22.50
❑ 1529	10¢	Skylab	15.75
❑ 1530–37	10¢	UPU	15.75
❑ 1538–41	10¢	Minerals	15.75
❑ 1542	10¢	Ft. Harrod	27.80
❑ 1543–46	10¢	Independence	27.80
❑ 1547	10¢	Energy	15.75
❑ 1548	10¢	Sleepy Hollow	15.75
❑ 1549	10¢	Retarded Children	15.75
❑ 1550	10¢	Christmas	15.75
❑ 1551	10¢	Currier & Ives	15.75
❑ 1552	10¢	Weather Vane	16.80
❑ 1553	10¢	West	27.30
❑ 1554	10¢	Dunbar	27.30
❑ 1555	10¢	Griffith	27.30
❑ 1556	10¢	Pioneer 10	20.00
❑ 1557	10¢	Mariner 10	16.80
❑ 1558	10¢	Bargaining	15.75
❑ 1559	8¢	Ludington	15.75
❑ 1560	10¢	Poor	15.75
❑ 1561	10¢	Salomon	16.80
❑ 1562	18¢	Francisco	27.80
❑ 1563	10¢	Lexington-Concord	14.75
❑ 1564	10¢	Bunker Hill	16.80
❑ 1565–68	10¢	Armed Forces	16.80
❑ 1569–70	10¢	Apollo-Soyuz	15.75
❑ 1571	10¢	Women's Year	15.75
❑ 1572–75	10¢	Transportation	16.80
❑ 1576	10¢	Peace Thru Law	20.00
❑ 1577–78	10¢	Banking/Commerce	20.00
❑ 1579	10¢	Christmas	15.75
❑ 1580	10¢	Prang	20.00
❑ 1580B	10¢	Prang	36.75
❑ 1581	1¢	Inkwell	14.75
❑ 1582	2¢	Lectern	14.75
❑ 1584	3¢	Ballot Box	14.75
❑ 1585	4¢	Books	14.75
❑ 1591	9¢	Capitol Dome	36.75
❑ 1592	10¢	Justice	36.75
❑ 1593	11¢	Printing Press	36.75
❑ 1594	12¢	Torch	36.75
❑ 1596	13¢	Eagle	36.75
❑ 1597	15¢	U.S. Flag	57.75
❑ 1599	16¢	Liberty	57.75
❑ 1603	24¢	North Church	68.25
❑ 1604	28¢	Ft. Nisqually	84.00
❑ 1605	29¢	Lighthouse	131.25
❑ 1606	30¢	School House	131.25
❑ 1608	50¢	Lamp	141.75
❑ 1610	$1	Lamp	346.50
❑ 1611	$2	Lamp	551.25
❑ 1612	$5	Lantern	1312.50
❑ 1622	13¢	Flag & Hall	52.50
❑ 1622C	13¢	Flag & Hall	183.75
❑ 1629–31	13¢	Fife & Drum	36.75
❑ 1632	13¢	Interphil	36.75
❑ 1633–82	13¢	State Flags	36.75
❑ 1683	13¢	Telephone	26.25
❑ 1684	13¢	Aviation	26.25
❑ 1685	13¢	Chemistry	31.50
❑ 1691–94	13¢	Signers	36.75
❑ 1695–98	13¢	Olympics	33.60
❑ 1699	13¢	Maass	23.10
❑ 1700	13¢	Ochs	16.80
❑ 1701	13¢	Christmas	26.25
❑ 1702	13¢	Winter Pastime	26.25
❑ 1703	13¢	Winter Pastime	26.25
❑ 1704	13¢	Princeton	26.25
❑ 1705	13¢	Recording	26.25

❏ 1706–09	13¢	Pottery	15.75		❏ 1789	15¢	Jones, 11x12	27.80
❏ 1710	13¢	Spirit of St. Louis	27.80		❏ 1789A	15¢	Jones, 11	36.75
❏ 1711	13¢	Colorado	27.80		❏ 1789B	15¢	Jones, 12	—
❏ 1712–15	13¢	Butterflies	27.80		❏ 1790	10¢	Olympics	21.00
❏ 1716	13¢	Lafayette	27.80		❏ 1791–94	15¢	Olympics	33.60
❏ 1717–20	13¢	Craftsmen	27.80		❏ 1795–98	15¢	Olympics	33.60
❏ 1721	13¢	Peace Bridge	27.80		❏ 1799	15¢	Madonna	47.25
❏ 1722	13¢	Oriskany	23.10		❏ 1800	15¢	Santa	47.25
❏ 1723–24	13¢	Energy	23.10		❏ 1801	15¢	Rogers	26.25
❏ 1725	13¢	Alta	27.80		❏ 1802	15¢	Vietnam Vets	33.60
❏ 1726	13¢	Confederation	27.80		❏ 1803	15¢	W. C. Fields	21.00
❏ 1727	13¢	Talking Pictures	27.80		❏ 1804	15¢	Banneker	40.00
❏ 1728	13¢	Saratoga	21.00		❏ 1805–10	15¢	Letters	40.00
❏ 1729	13¢	Valley Forge	47.25		❏ 1818	(18¢)	"B" Stamp	52.50
❏ 1730	13¢	Mailbox	47.25		❏ 1821	15¢	Perkins	42.00
❏ 1731	13¢	Sandburg	22.80		❏ 1822	15¢	Madison	99.75
❏ 1732–33	13¢	Cook	31.50		❏ 1823	15¢	Bissell	33.60
❏ 1734	13¢	Indian	68.25		❏ 1824	15¢	Keller	31.50
❏ 1735	(15¢)	"A" Stamp	47.25		❏ 1825	15¢	V.A.	33.60
❏ 1744	13¢	Tubman	42.00		❏ 1826	15¢	Galvez	31.50
❏ 1745–48	13¢	Quilts	21.00		❏ 1827–30	15¢	Coral	27.80
❏ 1753	13¢	French Alliance	15.75		❏ 1831	15¢	Labor	27.80
❏ 1754	13¢	Pap Test	27.80		❏ 1832	15¢	Wharton	27.80
❏ 1755	13¢	Rodgers	40.00		❏ 1833	15¢	Learning	37.80
❏ 1756	15¢	Cohan	36.75		❏ 1834–37	15¢	Masks	37.80
❏ 1757	13¢	CAPEX	23.10		❏ 1838–41	15¢	Architecture	37.80
❏ 1758	15¢	Photography	23.10		❏ 1842	15¢	Madonna	23.10
❏ 1759	15¢	Viking	27.80		❏ 1843	15¢	Drum & Wreath	23.10
❏ 1760–63	15¢	Owls	27.80		❏ 1844	1¢	Dix	15.75
❏ 1764–67	15¢	Trees	21.00		❏ 1845	2¢	Stravinsky	12.60
❏ 1768	15¢	Madonna	47.25		❏ 1846	3¢	Clay	19.00
❏ 1769	15¢	Rocking Horse	47.25		❏ 1847	4¢	Schurz	19.00
❏ 1770	15¢	R. F. Kennedy	36.75		❏ 1848	5¢	Buck	19.00
❏ 1771	15¢	M.L. King.	36.75		❏ 1849	6¢	Lippmann	21.00
❏ 1772	15¢	Year of Child	36.75		❏ 1850	7¢	Baldwin	36.75
❏ 1773	15¢	Steinbeck	27.80		❏ 1851	8¢	Knox	36.75
❏ 1774	15¢	Einstein	36.75		❏ 1852	9¢	Thayer	36.75
❏ 1775–78	15¢	Toleware	36.75		❏ 1853	10¢	Russell	42.00
❏ 1779–82	15¢	Architecture	36.75		❏ 1854	11¢	Partridge	68.25
❏ 1783–86	15¢	Flowers	36.75		❏ 1855	13¢	Horse	68.25
❏ 1787	15¢	Seeing for Me	36.75		❏ 1856	14¢	Lewis	68.25
❏ 1788	15¢	Spec. Olympics	27.80		❏ 1857	17¢	Carson	68.25

❏ 1858	18¢	Mason	52.50
❏ 1859	19¢	Sequoyah	73.50
❏ 1860	20¢	Bunche	73.50
❏ 1861	20¢	Gallaudet	78.75
❏ 1862	20¢	Truman	68.25
❏ 1863	22¢	Audubon	84.00
❏ 1864	30¢	Laubach	105.00
❏ 1865	35¢	Drew	132.80
❏ 1866	37¢	Millikan	105.00
❏ 1867	39¢	Clark	132.80
❏ 1868	40¢	Gilbreth	132.80
❏ 1869	50¢	Nimitz	132.80
❏ 1874	15¢	Dirksen	26.25
❏ 1875	15¢	Young	26.25
❏ 1876–79	18¢	Flowers	40.40
❏ 1890	18¢	Flag-Grain	68.25
❏ 1894	20¢	Flag-Court	105.00
❏ 1910	18¢	Red Cross	40.40
❏ 1911	18¢	Savings & Loan	26.25
❏ 1912–19	18¢	Space	40.40
❏ 1920	18¢	Management	40.40
❏ 1921–24	18¢	Habitats	40.40
❏ 1925	18¢	Disabled	40.40
❏ 1926	18¢	Millay	40.40
❏ 1927	18¢	Alcoholism	63.00
❏ 1928–31	18¢	Architecture	47.25
❏ 1932	18¢	Zaharias	47.25
❏ 1933	18¢	Jones	78.75
❏ 1934	18¢	Remington	31.50
❏ 1935	18¢	Hoban	40.40
❏ 1936	20¢	Hoban	40.40
❏ 1937–38	18¢	Yorktown Map	40.40
❏ 1939	(20¢)	Madonna	52.50
❏ 1940	(20¢)	Teddy Bear	31.50
❏ 1941	20¢	Hanson	40.40
❏ 1942–45	20¢	Cactus	31.50
❏ 1946	(20¢)	"C" Stamp	57.75
❏ 1950	20¢	F.D.R.	31.50
❏ 1951	20¢	Love	42.00
❏ 1952	20¢	Washington	40.42
❏ 1953–02	20¢	State Birds	63.00
❏ 1953A–02A	20¢	State Birds	63.00
❏ 2003	20¢	Netherlands	40.42
❏ 2004	20¢	Library of Congress	33.60
❏ 2006–09	20¢	Energy	42.00
❏ 2010	20¢	Alger	42.00
❏ 2011	20¢	Aging	40.42
❏ 2012	20¢	Barrymores	40.42
❏ 2013	20¢	Walker	40.42
❏ 2014	20¢	Peace Garden	40.42
❏ 2015	20¢	Libraries	31.50
❏ 2016	20¢	Robinson	105.00
❏ 2017	20¢	Touro	63.00
❏ 2018	20¢	Wolf Trap	33.60
❏ 2019	20¢	Architecture	40.42
❏ 2023	20¢	Francis of Assisi	31.50
❏ 2024	20¢	de Léon	44.10
❏ 2025	13¢	Kitten & Puppy	33.60
❏ 2026	20¢	Madonna	40.42
❏ 2027	20¢	Christmas	40.80
❏ 2031	20¢	Science/Industry	33.60
❏ 2032–35	20¢	Ballooning	40.42
❏ 2036	20¢	Sweden	40.42
❏ 2037	20¢	C.C.C.	40.42
❏ 2038	20¢	Priestley	40.42
❏ 2039	20¢	Volunteer	40.42
❏ 2040	20¢	German Immigr.	40.42
❏ 2041	20¢	Brooklyn Bridge	40.42
❏ 2042	20¢	T.V.A.	40.42
❏ 2043	20¢	Fitness	33.60
❏ 2044	20¢	Joplin	33.60
❏ 2045	20¢	Medal of Honor	40.42
❏ 2046	20¢	Babe Ruth	132.80
❏ 2047	20¢	Hawthorne	42.00
❏ 2048	13¢	Olympics	40.42
❏ 2052	20¢	Treaty of Paris	26.25
❏ 2053	20¢	Civil Service	52.50
❏ 2054	20¢	The Met	40.00
❏ 2055–58	20¢	Inventors	47.25
❏ 2059–62	20¢	Streetcars	47.25
❏ 2063	20¢	Madonna	31.50
❏ 2064	20¢	Santa Claus	40.42
❏ 2065	20¢	Martin Luther	40.42
❏ 2066	20¢	Alaska	40.42

❏ 2067–70	20¢	Olympics	42.00	❏ 2152	22¢	Korea Veterans	57.75
❏ 2071	20¢	FDIC	36.75	❏ 2153	22¢	Social Security	42.00
❏ 2072	20¢	Love	36.75	❏ 2154	22¢	WW I Veterans	47.25
❏ 2073	20¢	Woodson	36.75	❏ 2155–58	22¢	Horses	132.80
❏ 2074	20¢	Conservation	36.75	❏ 2159	22¢	Education	78.75
❏ 2075	20¢	Credit Union	36.75	❏ 2160–63	22¢	Youth Year	68.25
❏ 2076–79	20¢	Orchids	36.75	❏ 2164	22¢	Hunger	57.75
❏ 2080	20¢	Hawaii	36.75	❏ 2165	22¢	Madonna	57.75
❏ 2081	20¢	Archives	35.70	❏ 2166	22¢	Poinsettia	57.75
❏ 2082–85	20¢	Olympics	57.75	❏ 2167	22¢	Arkansas	68.25
❏ 2086	20¢	Louisiana Expo	42.00	❏ 2168	1¢	Mitchell	16.80
❏ 2087	20¢	Health Research	42.00	❏ 2169	2¢	Lyon	16.80
❏ 2088	20¢	Fairbanks	42.00	❏ 2170	3¢	White	16.80
❏ 2089	20¢	Thorpe	42.00	❏ 2171	4¢	Flanagan	16.80
❏ 2090	20¢	McCormack	33.60	❏ 2172	5¢	Black	36.75
❏ 2091	20¢	Seaway	42.00	❏ 2173	5¢	Marin	26.25
❏ 2092	20¢	Wetlands	57.75	❏ 2175	10¢	Red Cloud	44.10
❏ 2093	20¢	Roanoke	36.75	❏ 2176	14¢	Howe	47.25
❏ 2094	20¢	Melville	57.75	❏ 2177	15¢	Cody	105.00
❏ 2095	20¢	Moses	57.75	❏ 2178	17¢	Lockwood	57.75
❏ 2096	20¢	Smokey	42.00	❏ 2179	20¢	Apgar	78.75
❏ 2097	20¢	Clemente	147.00	❏ 2180	21¢	Carlson	78.75
❏ 2098–01	20¢	Dogs	33.60	❏ 2181	23¢	Cassatt	78.75
❏ 2102	20¢	Anti-Crime	33.60	❏ 2182	25¢	London	78.75
❏ 2103	20¢	Hispanic	26.25	❏ 2183	28¢	Sitting Bull	131.25
❏ 2104	20¢	Family Unity	47.25	❏ 2184	29¢	Warren	132.80
❏ 2105	20¢	E. Roosevelt	36.75	❏ 2185	29¢	Jefferson	132.80
❏ 2106	20¢	Readers	36.75	❏ 2186	35¢	Chavez	132.80
❏ 2107	20¢	Madonna	33.60	❏ 2187	40¢	Chenault	132.80
❏ 2108	20¢	Santa Claus	33.60	❏ 2188	45¢	Cushing	157.50
❏ 2109	20¢	Vietnam Memorial	42.00	❏ 2189	52¢	Humphrey	183.75
❏ 2110	22¢	Kern	36.75	❏ 2190	56¢	Harvard	183.75
❏ 2111	(22¢)	"D" Stamp	147.00	❏ 2191	65¢	Arnold	183.75
❏ 2114	22¢	Flag	63.00	❏ 2192	75¢	Wilkie	231.00
❏ 2137	22¢	Bethune	57.75	❏ 2193	$1	Revel	367.50
❏ 2138–41	22¢	Decoys	132.80	❏ 2194	$1	Hopkins	89.25
❏ 2142	22¢	Special Olympics	33.60	❏ 2195	$2	Bryan	561.75
❏ 2143	22¢	Love	36.75	❏ 2196	$5	Harte	288.75
❏ 2144	22¢	Electrification	63.00	❏ 2202	22¢	Love	57.75
❏ 2145	22¢	AMERIPEX	37.80	❏ 2203	22¢	Truth	57.75
❏ 2146	22¢	Adams	37.80	❏ 2204	22¢	Texas	42.00
❏ 2147	22¢	Bartholdi	29.40	❏ 2210	22¢	Hospitals	42.00

❑ 2211	22¢	Ellington	44.10		❑ 2376	22¢	Rockne	47.25
❑ 2220–23	22¢	Explorers	63.00		❑ 2377	25¢	Ouimet	52.50
❑ 2224	22¢	Liberty	57.75		❑ 2378	25¢	Love	78.75
❑ 2235–38	22¢	Navajo Carpets	57.75		❑ 2379	45¢	Love	78.75
❑ 2239	22¢	Eliot	57.75		❑ 2380	25¢	Gymnast	52.50
❑ 2240–43	22¢	Carvings	57.75		❑ 2386–89	25¢	Explorers	63.00
❑ 2244	22¢	Madonna	69.80		❑ 2390–93	25¢	Carousel	78.75
❑ 2245	22¢	Village Scene	69.80		❑ 2394	$8.75	Express Mail	567.00
❑ 2246	22¢	Michigan	40.00		❑ 2399	25¢	Madonna	44.10
❑ 2247	22¢	Pan Am Games	40.00		❑ 2400	25¢	Winter Scene	44.10
❑ 2248	22¢	Love	63.00		❑ 2401	25¢	Montana	52.50
❑ 2249	22¢	du Sable	47.25		❑ 2402	25¢	Randolph	52.50
❑ 2250	22¢	Caruso	47.25		❑ 2403	25¢	North Dakota	47.25
❑ 2251	22¢	Girl Scouts	31.50		❑ 2404	25¢	Washington	44.10
❑ 2275	22¢	United Way	31.50		❑ 2410	25¢	Stamp Expo '89	44.10
❑ 2277	(25¢)	"E" Stamp	89.25		❑ 2411	25¢	Toscanini	37.80
❑ 2278	25¢	Flag	78.75		❑ 2412	25¢	House of Reps.	47.25
❑ 2286–35	22¢	Wildlife	101.30		❑ 2413	25¢	Senate	57.75
❑ 2336	22¢	Delaware	57.75		❑ 2414	25¢	Executive Br.	57.75
❑ 2337	22¢	Pennsylvania	57.75		❑ 2415	25¢	Supreme Court	57.75
❑ 2338	22¢	New Jersey	57.75		❑ 2416	25¢	South Dakota	57.75
❑ 2339	22¢	Georgia	47.25		❑ 2417	25¢	Gehrig	63.00
❑ 2340	22¢	Connecticut	52.50		❑ 2418	25¢	Hemingway	52.50
❑ 2341	22¢	Massachusetts	52.50		❑ 2419	$2.40	Moon Landing	194.25
❑ 2342	22¢	Maryland	69.80		❑ 2420	25¢	Letter Carriers	26.25
❑ 2343	22¢	South Carolina	69.80		❑ 2421	25¢	Bill of Rights	52.50
❑ 2344	22¢	New Hampshire	69.80		❑ 2422–25	25¢	Dinosaurs	69.80
❑ 2345	22¢	Virginia	69.80		❑ 2426	25¢	Southwest	36.75
❑ 2346	22¢	New York	69.80		❑ 2427	25¢	Madonna	52.50
❑ 2347	22¢	North Carolina	69.80		❑ 2428	25¢	Sleigh	52.50
❑ 2348	22¢	Rhode Island	69.80		❑ 2434	25¢	UPU	52.50
❑ 2349	22¢	Morocco	36.75		❑ 2439	25¢	Idaho	44.10
❑ 2350	22¢	Faulkner	52.50		❑ 2440	25¢	Love	44.10
❑ 2351–54	22¢	Lace	44.10		❑ 2442	25¢	Wells	47.25
❑ 2360	22¢	Constitution	52.50		❑ 2444	25¢	Wyoming	44.10
❑ 2361	22¢	CPAs	183.75		❑ 2445–49	25¢	Films	105.00
❑ 2367	22¢	Madonna	69.80		❑ 2449	25¢	Moore	31.50
❑ 2368	22¢	Ornament	89.25		❑ 2476	1¢	Kestrel	15.75
❑ 2369	22¢	Skier	44.10		❑ 2477	1¢	Kestrel	15.75
❑ 2370	22¢	Australia	33.60		❑ 2478	3¢	Bluebird	15.75
❑ 2371	22¢	Johnson	36.75		❑ 2479	19¢	Fawn	52.50
❑ 2372–75	22¢	Cats	47.25		❑ 2480	30¢	Cardinal	78.75

☐ 2481	45¢	Sunfish	132.80	☐ 2616	29¢	Stamp Expo	36.75
☐ 2482	$2	Bobcat	132.80	☐ 2617	29¢	DuBois	63.00
☐ 2496	25¢	Olympians	44.10	☐ 2618	29¢	Love	63.00
☐ 2506–07	25¢	Micronesia	49.35	☐ 2619	29¢	Baseball	63.00
☐ 2508–11	25¢	Sea Mammals	44.10	☐ 2620–23	29¢	Columbus	49.35
☐ 2512	25¢	Grand Canyon	52.50	☐ 2630	29¢	Stock Exchange	49.35
☐ 2513	25¢	Eisenhower	52.50	☐ 2631–24	29¢	Space	52.50
☐ 2514	25¢	Madonna	36.75	☐ 2635	29¢	Alaska Hiway	36.75
☐ 2515	25¢	Christmas Tree	49.35	☐ 2636	29¢	Kentucky	52.50
☐ 2517	(29¢)	"F" Stamp	84.00	☐ 2637–41	29¢	Olympics	52.50
☐ 2521	(4¢)	Make Up Rate	19.00	☐ 2647–96	29¢	Wildflowers	52.50
☐ 2524	29¢	Tulip	84.00	☐ 2697	29¢	WW II, 1942	26.25
☐ 2524A	29¢	Tulip	152.25	☐ 2698	29¢	Parker	63.00
☐ 2531	29¢	Flags	152.25	☐ 2699	29¢	von Kármán	63.00
☐ 2531A	29¢	Torch	84.00	☐ 2700	29¢	Minerals	63.00
☐ 2532	50¢	Switzerland	68.25	☐ 2704	29¢	Cabrillo	49.35
☐ 2533	29¢	Vermont	63.00	☐ 2711–14	29¢	Christmas	52.50
☐ 2534	29¢	Savings Bonds	52.50	☐ 2720	29¢	Rooster	21.00
☐ 2535	29¢	Love	52.50	☐ 2721	29¢	Elvis	49.35
☐ 2535A	29¢	Love	52.50	☐ 2722	29¢	Oklahoma!	36.75
☐ 2537	52¢	Love Birds	89.25	☐ 2723	29¢	Williams	42.00
☐ 2538	29¢	Saroyan	63.00	☐ 2723A	29¢	Williams	84.00
☐ 2539	$1	Olympic Rings	63.00	☐ 2724–30	29¢	Singers	52.50
☐ 2540	$2.90	Eagle	225.00	☐ 2746	29¢	Julian	42.00
☐ 2541	$9.95	Express Mail	525.00	☐ 2747	29¢	Oregon Trail	63.00
☐ 2542	$14	Express Mail	787.50	☐ 2748	29¢	Univ. Games	63.00
☐ 2543	$2.90	Spacecraft	367.50	☐ 2749	29¢	Grace Kelly	42.00
☐ 2544	$3	Space Shuttle	189.00	☐ 2750–53	29¢	Circus	52.50
☐ 254A	$10.75	Space Shuttle	525.00	☐ 2754	29¢	Cherokee Strip	21.00
☐ 2550	29¢	Porter	63.00	☐ 2755	29¢	Acheson	44.10
☐ 2551	29¢	Desert Storm	57.75	☐ 2756–59	29¢	Horse Racing	44.10
☐ 2553–57	29¢	Olympics	63.00	☐ 2765	29¢	WWar II, 1943	42.00
☐ 2558	29¢	Numismatics	63.00	☐ 2766	29¢	Louis	52.50
☐ 2559	29¢	WWar II, 1941	26.25	☐ 2771–74	29¢	Singers	36.75
☐ 2560	29¢	Basketball	52.50	☐ 2779–82	29¢	Postal Museum	36.75
☐ 2561	29¢	D.C.	52.50	☐ 2783–84	29¢	Deafness	23.10
☐ 2567	29¢	Matzeliger	52.50	☐ 2785–88	29¢	Literature	52.50
☐ 2579	(29¢)	Santa	36.25	☐ 2789	29¢	Madonna	42.00
☐ 2587	32¢	Polk	89.25	☐ 2791–94	29¢	Christmas	63.00
☐ 2590	$1	Burgoyne	52.50	☐ 2804	29¢	Mariana Is.	26.25
☐ 2592	$5	Washington/Jackson	315.00	☐ 2805	29¢	Columbus	52.50
☐ 2611–15	29¢	Olympics	49.35	☐ 2806	29¢	AIDS	52.50

❑ 2807–11	29¢	Olympics	26.25	❑ 2950	32¢	Florida	26.25
❑ 2812	29¢	Murrow	36.75	❑ 2951–54	32¢	Environment	23.10
❑ 2814C	29¢	Love	63.00	❑ 2955	32¢	Nixon	52.50
❑ 2815	52¢	Love	78.75	❑ 2956	32¢	Coleman	52.50
❑ 2816	29¢	Davis	36.75	❑ 2957	32¢	Love	52.50
❑ 2817	29¢	Year of Dog	36.75	❑ 2958	55¢	Love	78.75
❑ 2818	29¢	Buffalo Soldiers	22.50	❑ 2961–65	32¢	Sports	34.10
❑ 2819–28	29¢	Film Stars	36.75	❑ 2966	32¢	POW - MIA	34.10
❑ 2834	29¢	Soccer	26.25	❑ 2967	32¢	Marilyn	34.10
❑ 2835	40¢	Soccer	26.25	❑ 2968	32¢	Texas	26.25
❑ 2836	50¢	Soccer	36.75	❑ 2974	32¢	U.N.	22.50
❑ 2838	29¢	WW II, 1944	34.10	❑ 2975	32¢	Civil War	19.00
❑ 2839	29¢	Rockwell	52.50	❑ 2976–79	32¢	Carousel	26.25
❑ 2842	29¢	Moon	735.00	❑ 2980	32¢	Suffrage	36.75
❑ 2848	29¢	Meany	52.50	❑ 2981	32¢	WW II, 1945	36.75
❑ 2849–53	29¢	Singers	26.25	❑ 2982	32¢	Armstrong	36.75
❑ 2854–61	29¢	Singers	52.50	❑ 2983–92	32¢	Singers	36.75
❑ 2862	29¢	Thurber	52.50	❑ 2998	60¢	Rickenbacker	89.25
❑ 2863–66	29¢	Sea Wonders	52.50	❑ 2999	32¢	Palau	42.00
❑ 2867–68	29¢	Cranes	26.25	❑ 3000	32¢	Comics	34.10
❑ 2869	29¢	Legends	26.25	❑ 3001	32¢	Annapolis	34.10
❑ 2870	29¢	Legends	183.75	❑ 3002	32¢	Williams	34.10
❑ 2871	29¢	Madonna	47.25	❑ 3003	32¢	Christmas	42.00
❑ 2872	29¢	Stocking	47.25	❑ 3004–07	32¢	Christmas	47.25
❑ 2876	29¢	Year of Boar	22.05	❑ 3019–23	32¢	Autos	26.25
❑ 2877	(4¢)	Make-up Rate	22.05	❑ 3024	32¢	Utah	47.25
❑ 2878	(4¢)	Make-up Rate	22.05	❑ 3031	1¢	Kestrel	15.75
❑ 2879	(20¢)	"G" Stamp	78.75	❑ 3031A	1¢	Kestrel	15.75
❑ 2880	(20¢)	"G" Stamp	78.75	❑ 3032	2¢	Woodpecker	15.75
❑ 2881	(32¢)	"G" Stamp	265.50	❑ 3033	3¢	Blue Bird	15.75
❑ 2882	(32¢)	"G" Stamp	152.25	❑ 3036	$1	Red Fox	52.50
❑ 2897	32¢	Flag	152.25	❑ 3058	32¢	Just	26.25
❑ 2933	32¢	Hershey	84.00	❑ 3059	32¢	Smithsonian	26.25
❑ 2934	32¢	Farley	105.00	❑ 3060	32¢	Year of Rat	36.75
❑ 2935	32¢	Luce	26.25	❑ 3061–64	32¢	Scientists	26.25
❑ 2936	32¢	Wallace	26.25	❑ 3065	32¢	Scholarships	52.50
❑ 2938	46¢	Benedict	131.25	❑ 3066	50¢	Cochran	78.75
❑ 2940	55¢	Hamilton	141.75	❑ 3067	32¢	Marathon	22.05
❑ 2941	55¢	Morrill	47.25	❑ 3068	32¢	Olympics	22.05
❑ 2942	77¢	Breckinridge	47.25	❑ 3069	32¢	O'Keeffe	22.05
❑ 2943	78¢	Paul	220.50	❑ 3070	32¢	Tennessee	42.00
❑ 2948	(32¢)	Love	47.25	❑ 3072–76	32¢	Dance	23.10

❑ 3077–80	32¢	Prehistoric	26.25	❑ 3179	32¢	Year of Tiger	18.90
❑ 3081	32¢	Breast Cancer	36.75	❑ 3180	32¢	Skiing	26.25
❑ 3082	32¢	Dean	36.75	❑ 3181	32¢	Walker	26.25
❑ 3083–86	32¢	Folk Heroes	36.75	❑ 3182	32¢	1900s	16.80
❑ 3087	32¢	Olympics	23.10	❑ 3183	32¢	1910s	16.80
❑ 3088	32¢	Iowa	42.00	❑ 3184	32¢	1920s	14.70
❑ 3090	32¢	RFD	23.10	❑ 3185	32¢	1930s	14.70
❑ 3091–95	32¢	Riverboats	23.10	❑ 3186	33¢	1940s	17.85
❑ 3096–99	32¢	Musicians	26.25	❑ 3187	33¢	1950s	17.85
❑ 3100–03	32¢	Composers	26.25	❑ 3188	33¢	1960s	17.85
❑ 3104	23¢	Fitzgerald	42.00	❑ 3189	33¢	1970s	12.60
❑ 3105	32¢	Endangered	23.10	❑ 3190	33¢	1980s	18.90
❑ 3106	32¢	Computers	36.75	❑ 3191	33¢	1990s	18.90
❑ 3107	32¢	Madonna	42.00	❑ 3192	32¢	The Maine	23.10
❑ 3108–11	32¢	Christmas	52.50	❑ 3193–87	32¢	Flowers	16.80
❑ 3118	32¢	Hanukkah	16.80	❑ 3198–02	32¢	Calder	23.10
❑ 3120	32¢	Year of Ox	26.25	❑ 3203	32¢	Cinco de Mayo	19.00
❑ 3121	32¢	Davis	26.25	❑ 3209	1¢–$2	Trans-Mississippi	14.70
❑ 3125	32¢	Learning	26.25	❑ 3210	$1	Cattle in Storm	42.00
❑ 3130–31	32¢	Pacific 97	26.25	❑ 3211	32¢	Airlift	16.80
❑ 3134	32¢	Wilder	23.10	❑ 3212–19	32¢	Singers	25.20
❑ 3135	32¢	Wallenberg	23.10	❑ 3220	32¢	Spanish Settlement	25.20
❑ 3136	32¢	Dinosaurs	16.80	❑ 3221	32¢	Benét	25.20
❑ 3139	50¢	Pacific 97	16.80	❑ 3226	32¢	Hitchcock	23.10
❑ 3140	60¢	Pacific 97	23.10	❑ 3227	32¢	Organ Donors	23.10
❑ 3141	32¢	Marshall Plan	23.10	❑ 3230–34	32¢	Bright Eyes	26.25
❑ 3142	32¢	Aircraft	23.10	❑ 3235	32¢	Klondike	21.00
❑ 3147	32¢	Lombardi	25.20	❑ 3236	32¢	Art	16.80
❑ 3148	32¢	Bryant	25.20	❑ 3237	32¢	Ballet	23.10
❑ 3149	32¢	Warner	23.10	❑ 3238–42	32¢	Future Space	23.10
❑ 3150	32¢	Halas	23.10	❑ 3243	32¢	Giving	23.10
❑ 3151	32¢	Dolls	15.75	❑ 3249–52	32¢	Wreaths	23.10
❑ 3152	32¢	Bogart	23.10	❑ 3257	(1¢)	Weather Vane	8.50
❑ 3153	32¢	Stars & Strips	42.00	❑ 3258	(1¢)	Weather Vane	8.50
❑ 3154–57	32¢	Opera	26.25	❑ 3259	22¢	Uncle Sam	10.50
❑ 3158–65	32¢	Composers	26.25	❑ 3260	(33¢)	Hat	42.00
❑ 3166	32¢	Varela	26.25	❑ 3261	$3.20	Space Shuttle	241.50
❑ 3167	32¢	Air Force	16.80	❑ 3262	$11.75	Space Shuttle	787.50
❑ 3168–72	32¢	Monsters	23.10	❑ 3272	33¢	Year of Rabbit	25.20
❑ 3173	32¢	Flight	23.10	❑ 3273	33¢	Malcolm X	25.20
❑ 3174	32¢	Military Women	23.10	❑ 3276	33¢	Hospice	15.75
❑ 3175	32¢	Kwanzaa	44.10	❑ 3277	33¢	Flag	105.00

❏ 3286	33¢	Irish	23.10
❏ 3287	33¢	Lunt & Fontanne	23.10
❏ 3288–92	33¢	Arctic Animals	23.10
❏ 3293	33¢	Desert	12.60
❏ 3308	33¢	Rand	18.90
❏ 3309	33¢	Cinco de Mayo	18.90
❏ 3314	33¢	Bartram	18.90
❏ 3315	33¢	Prostate Cancer	18.90
❏ 3316	33¢	Gold Rush	18.90
❏ 3317–20	33¢	Fish	18.90
❏ 3321–24	33¢	Extreme Sports	18.90
❏ 3325	33¢	Glass	18.90
❏ 3329	33¢	Cagney	18.90
❏ 3330	33¢	Mitchell	33.60
❏ 3331	33¢	Who Served	33.60
❏ 3332	45¢	U.P.U.	33.60
❏ 3333–37	33¢	Trains	23.10
❏ 3338	33¢	Olmsted	23.10
❏ 3339–44	33¢	Composers	23.10
❏ 3345–50	33¢	Composers	23.10
❏ 3351	33¢	Insects	23.10
❏ 3352	33¢	Hanukkah	23.10
❏ 3354	33¢	NATO	23.10
❏ 3356–59	33¢	Stag	23.10
❏ 3369	33¢	New Year	23.10
❏ 3370	33¢	Year of Dragon	23.10
❏ 3371	33¢	Harris	16.80
❏ 3372	33¢	Submarine	16.80
❏ 3378	33¢	Rain Forest	16.80
❏ 3379–83	33¢	Nevelson	23.10
❏ 3385–88	33¢	Hubble	23.10
❏ 3389	33¢	Samoa	23.10
❏ 3390	33¢	Library of Cong.	23.10
❏ 3393	33¢	War Heroes	23.10
❏ 3397	33¢	Runners	23.10
❏ 3398	33¢	Adoption	16.80
❏ 3399–02	33¢	Sports	16.80
❏ 3403	33¢	Flags	16.80
❏ 3408	33¢	Baseball	16.80
❏ 3414–17	33¢	Drawings	16.80
❏ 3420	10¢	Stillwell	16.80
❏ 3426	33¢	Pepper	16.80
❏ 3431	76¢	Caraway	36.75
❏ 3632	37¢	Ferber	26.25
❏ 3438	33¢	California	18.90
❏ 3439–43	33¢	Fish	17.85
❏ 3444	33¢	Wolfe	17.85
❏ 3445	33¢	White House	17.85
❏ 3446	33¢	Robinson	17.85
❏ 3448	(34¢)	Flag	23.10
❏ 3449	(34¢)	Flag	23.10
❏ 3467	21¢	Buffalo	52.50
❏ 3468	21¢	Buffalo	16.80
❏ 3468A	23¢	Washington	18.90
❏ 3469	34¢	Flag	18.90
❏ 3470	34¢	Flag	23.10
❏ 3471	55¢	Eagle	33.60
❏ 3471A	57¢	Eagle	33.60
❏ 3472	$3.50	Capitol Dome	23.10
❏ 3473	$12.25	Wash. Monument	588.00
❏ 3499	55¢	Love	26.25
❏ 3500	34¢	Year of Snake	23.10
❏ 3501	34¢	Wilkins	23.10
❏ 3502	34¢	Illustrators	23.10
❏ 3503	34¢	Diabetes	15.75
❏ 3504	34¢	Nobel Prize	16.80
❏ 3505		Inverts	15.75
❏ 3506	34¢	Prairie	15.75
❏ 3507	34¢	Snoopy	23.10
❏ 3508	34¢	Veterans	18.90
❏ 3509	34¢	Kahlo	18.90
❏ 3510–19	34¢	Stadiums	18.90
❏ 3521	34¢	Bernstein	18.90
❏ 3523	34¢	Ball	18.90
❏ 3524–27	34¢	Quilts	16.80
❏ 3528–31	34¢	Carniverous	16.80
❏ 3532	34¢	Eid	16.80
❏ 3533	34¢	Fermi	12.60
❏ 3537–40	34¢	Christmas	18.90
❏ 3545	34¢	Monroe	18.90
❏ 3546	34¢	Thanks	23.10
❏ 3547	34¢	Hanukkah	18.90
❏ 3548	34¢	Kwanzaa	18.90
❏ 3551	57¢	Love	23.10

❑ 3552–55	34¢	Olympics	18.90
❑ 3556	34¢	Mentoring	18.90
❑ 3557	34¢	Hughes	18.90
❑ 3558	34¢	Birthday	18.90
❑ 3559	34¢	Year of Horse	18.90
❑ 3560	34¢	West Point	18.90
❑ 3561–10	34¢	Greetings	36.75
❑ 3611	34¢	Pine Forest	15.75
❑ 3613	3¢	Star	15.75
❑ 3614	3¢	Star	15.75
❑ 3646	60¢	Eagle	26.25
❑ 3647	$3.85	Jefferson Memorial	187.20
❑ 3648	$13.65	Capitol Dome	525.00
❑ 3649	37¢	Photography	18.90
❑ 3650	37¢	Audubon	18.90
❑ 3651	37¢	Houdini	18.90
❑ 3652	37¢	Andy Warhol	18.90
❑ 3653–56	37¢	Teddy Bears	18.90
❑ 3657	37¢	Love Pane of 20	32.55
❑ 3659	37¢	Ogden Nash SA	26.25
❑ 3660	37¢	Duke Kahanamoku	26.25
❑ 3661–64	37¢	American Bats	26.25
❑ 3665–68	37¢	Nellie Bly	26.25
❑ 3669	37¢	Irving Berlin	26.25
❑ 3670–71	37¢	Neuter and Spay	26.25

❑ 3672	37¢	Hanukkah SA	23.10
❑ 3673	37¢	Kwanzaa SA	23.10
❑ 3674	37¢	Islamic Festival	23.10
❑ 3675	37¢	Madonna (pane of 20)	23.10
❑ 3676–79	37¢	Snowman	23.10
❑ 3692	37¢	Cary Grant	23.10
❑ 3695	37¢	Happy Birthday	23.10
❑ 3746	37¢	Thurgood Marshall SA	23.10
❑ 3747	37¢	Year of the Ram SA	23.10
❑ 3748	37¢	Zora Neale Hurston SA	23.10
❑ 3751	10¢	U.S. Clock	5.25
❑ 3757	1¢	Tiffany Lamp	42.00
❑ 3771	80¢	Special Olympics	31.50
❑ 3773	37¢	Ohio Statehood	23.10
❑ 3774	37¢	Pelican Island	18.90
❑ 3781	37¢	Cesar Chavez SA	21.00
❑ 3782	37¢	Louisiana Purchase SA	15.75
❑ 3784	37¢	Purple Heart	21.00
❑ 3785	37¢	Sea Coast	21.00
❑ 3786	37¢	Audrey Hepburn	21.00
❑ 3787–91	37¢	Cape Henry Lighthouse	21.00
❑ 3803	37¢	Korean War	21.00
❑ 3812	37¢	Roy Acuff	21.00

SEMIPOSTAL STAMPS

❑ B1	(32¢+8¢)	Breast Cancer	31.50
❑ B2	(34¢+11¢)	Heroes of 2001	26.25

AIRMAIL

❑ C25	6¢	Transport	19.95
❑ C26	8¢	Transport	19.95
❑ C27	10¢	Transport	78.75
❑ C28	15¢	Transport	183.75
❑ C29	20¢	Transport	157.50
❑ C30	30¢	Transport	157.50
❑ C31	50¢	Transport	787.50
❑ C32	5¢	DC-4, large	15.75
❑ C33	5¢	DC-4, small	19.95
❑ C34	10¢	Building	19.95
❑ C35	15¢	N.Y. Skyline	31.50
❑ C36	25¢	Golden Gate	63.00

❑ C38	5¢	New York	33.60
❑ C39	6¢	DC-4	26.25
❑ C40	6¢	Alexandria	18.90
❑ C42	10¢	UPU	21.00
❑ C43	15¢	UPUI	29.40
❑ C44	25¢	UPUI	44.10
❑ C45	6¢	Wright Bros.	15.75
❑ C46	80¢	Diamond Head	351.75
❑ C47	6¢	Flight	18.90
❑ C48	4¢	Eagle	18.90
❑ C49	6¢	Air Force	14.70
❑ C50	5¢	Eagle	18.90

❑ C51	7¢	Jetliner, blue	23.10
❑ C53	7¢	Alaska	20.00
❑ C54	7¢	Balloon Jupiter	20.00
❑ C55	7¢	Hawaii	14.70
❑ C56	10¢	Pan Am Games	15.75
❑ C57	10¢	Liberty Bell	84.00
❑ C58	15¢	Statue of Liberty	36.75
❑ C59	25¢	Abraham Lincoln	36.75
❑ C60	7¢	Jetliner, carmine	26.25
❑ C62	13¢	Liberty Bell	26.25
❑ C63	15¢	Statue of Liberty	26.25
❑ C64	8¢	Jetliner-Capitol	26.25
❑ C66	15¢	Blair	36.75
❑ C67	6¢	Eagle	26.25
❑ C68	8¢	Amelia Earhart	26.25
❑ C69	8¢	Robert Goddard	26.25
❑ C70	8¢	Alaska Purchase	16.80
❑ C71	20¢	Columbia Jays	47.25
❑ C72	10¢	Runway of Stars	31.50
❑ C74	10¢	Biplane	20.00
❑ C75	20¢	USA & Jet	26.25
❑ C76	10¢	Moon Landing	20.00
❑ C77	9¢	Delta Wing	42.00
❑ C78	11¢	Jetliner	42.00
❑ C79	13¢	Winged Letter	42.00
❑ C80	17¢	Statue of Liberty	26.25
❑ C81	21¢	USA & Jet	36.75
❑ C84	11¢	City of Refugee	26.25
❑ C85	11¢	Skiers	23.10
❑ C86	11¢	Electronics	23.10
❑ C87	18¢	Statue of Liberty	26.25
❑ C88	26¢	Mt. Rushmore	47.25
❑ C89	25¢	Jetliner & Globes	47.25
❑ C90	31¢	Jetliner	57.75

❑ C91–92	31¢	Wright Bros.	132.80
❑ C93–94	21¢	Chanute	132.80
❑ C95–96	25¢	Post	183.75
❑ C97	31¢	High Jumper	68.25
❑ C98	40¢	Mazzei, perf 11	68.25
❑ C98A	40¢	Mazzei, perf 10½ x11½	57.75
❑ C99	28¢	Scott	68.25
❑ C100	35¢	Curtiss	57.75
❑ C101–4	28¢	Olympics	84.00
❑ C105–8	40¢	Olympics	84.00
❑ C109–12	35¢	Olympics	84.00
❑ C113	33¢	Verville	68.25
❑ C114	39¢	Sperry	68.25
❑ C115	44¢	Clipper	68.25
❑ C116	44¢	Serra	89.25
❑ C117	44¢	New Sweden	89.25
❑ C118	45¢	Langley	68.25
❑ C119	36¢	Sikorsky	57.75
❑ C120	45¢	French Revolution	57.75
❑ C121	45¢	Carved Figure	99.75
❑ C122–5	45¢	Space Travel	99.75
❑ C127	45¢	Tropical Beach	99.75
❑ C128	50¢	Quimby	99.75
❑ C129	40¢	Piper	99.75
❑ C130	50¢	Antarctic	99.75
❑ C131	50¢	Asia Crossing	99.75
❑ C132	40¢	Piper	115.50
❑ C133	48¢	Niagara Falls	26.25
❑ C134	40¢	Rio Grande	23.10
❑ C135	60¢	Grand Canyon	47.25
❑ C136	70¢	Nine Mile Prairie	47.25
❑ C137	80¢	Mount McKinley	47.25
❑ C138	60¢	Acadia National Park	26.25

SPECIAL DELIVERY

❑ E20	20¢	Letter, blue	47.25
❑ E21	30¢	Letter, maroon	47.25

❑ E22	45¢	Arrows	78.75
❑ E23	60¢	Arrows	84.00

CERTIFIED MAIL

❑ FA1	10¢	Letter Carrier	36.75

POSTAGE DUE

❏ J88	½¢	Red & Black	430.50		❏ J97	10¢	Red & Black	44.10
❏ J89	1¢	Red & Black	14.70		❏ J98	30¢	Red & Black	126.00
❏ J90	2¢	Red & Black	14.70		❏ J99	50¢	Red & Black	131.25
❏ J91	3¢	Red & Black	15.75		❏ J100	$1	Red & Black	346.50
❏ J92	4¢	Red & Black	21.00		❏ J101	$5	Red & Black	1050.00
❏ J93	5¢	Red & Black	15.75		❏ J102	11¢	Red & Black	47.25
❏ J94	6¢	Red & Black	36.75		❏ J103	13¢	Red & Black	47.25
❏ J95	7¢	Red & Black	36.75		❏ J104	17¢	Red & Black	105.00
❏ J96	8¢	Red & Black	36.75					

OFFICIAL STAMPS

❏ O127	1¢	Great Seal	20.00		❏ O146	4¢	Great Seal	19.00
❏ O128	4¢	Great Seal	20.00		❏ O146A	10¢	Great Seal	26.25
❏ O129	13¢	Great Seal	47.25		❏ O147	19¢	Great Seal	68.25
❏ O130	17¢	Great Seal	68.25		❏ O148	23¢	Great Seal	78.75
❏ O132	$1	Great Seal	346.50		❏ O151	$1	Great Seal	472.50
❏ O133	$5	Great Seal	918.75		❏ O154	1¢	Great Seal	18.90
❏ O138	(14¢)	"D"	446.25		❏ O155	20¢	Great Seal	78.75
❏ O143	1¢	Great Seal	15.75		❏ O156	23¢	Great Seal	84.00

AMERICAN FIRST DAY COVERS
THE AMERICAN FIRST DAY COVER SOCIETY

The **American First Day Cover Society** is the largest not-for-profit organization of FDC collectors in the world and has members as far away as Australia. It publishes its award-winning journal *First Days* eight times a year, as well as handbooks and other works.

It recently archived every issue of its journal from its start in 1955 through 2011—395 issues and almost 35,000 pages—in a searchable PDF archive. It's a valuable resource for researchers, authors, exhibitors, philatelic judges, and just anyone who enjoys first day covers. The archive is available either on a DVD ($79) or flash drive ($89). It may be purchased on the AFDCS website, www.afdcs.org.

The AFDCS also produces an annual Court of Honor series, showcasing the best cachet artists in the hobby and occasional FDCs for other issues. These, too, are available for purchase on the website.

The Society holds an annual show and convention, Americover, a World Series of Philately show at which first day covers are featured. Americover is held in a different location every year. Americover 2013 is August 16–18 in Independence, Ohio (near Cleveland), and Americover 2014 is in Somerset, NJ, August 15–17.

Other services include a mentor program, cachetmakers directory, "donation auctions" with many unique FDCs, and audio-visual presentations. The AFDCS also represents the interests of first day cover collectors and dealers to other stamp collecting organizations and postal agencies.

A variety of membership plans are available from $24 a year for adults. Junior and Family memberships are also available.

Contact information:

AFDCS Central Office
PO Box 16277
Tucson, AZ 85732
(520) 321-0880
AFDCS@afdcs.org
www.afdcs.org

#3: Baltimore Philatelic Society: Attn: Librarian, 1224 N. Calvert Street, Baltimore, MD 21202, www.balpex.org

#5: Motor City Stamp Club: Bob Quintero, 22608 Poplar Court, Hazel Park, MI 48030, www.motorcitystampandcover.com

#6: Chicagoland FDC Society: Eliot A. Landau, 515 Ogden Ave., Suite 101, Downers Grove IL 60515

#7: West Suburban Stamp Club: AFDCS Chapter Representative, PO Box 700049, Plymouth, MI 48170, www.thewssc.com/

#9: Harford County Stamp Club: 8 Crestmont Drive, Aberdeen, MD 21001

#17: Robert C. Graebner Chapter: Otto Thamasett, 6025 Sherborn Lane, Springfield, VA 22152, Facebook group

#25: Coryell's Ferry Stamp Club: Mrs. Frank Davis, PO Box 52, Penns Park, PA 18943-0052

#26: Ft. Findlay Stamp Club: Scott E. Little, 10339 Columbus Grove Road, Bluffton, OH 45817

#34: Columbus Philatelic Club: Paul Gault, PO Box 20711, Columbus, OH 43220

#36: Autograph Chapter: George Haggas, PO Box 1463, Merchantville, NJ 08109

#41: FDC Unit Clifton Stamp Society: Andrew Boyajian, PO Box 229, Hasbrouck Height, NJ 07604, mysite.verizon.net/vzevmv97/index.html

#43: George Washington Masonic Stamp Club: John R. Allen, 2831 Swanhurst Drive, Midlothian, VA 23113, gwmsc.tripod.com/

#44: Hamilton Township Philatelic Society: John Ranto, 10 Cranbrook Road, Hamilton, NJ 08690-2506, www.hamiltonphilatelic.org/

#45: Joplin Stamp Club: Frederic L. Roesel, 3322 Willow Lane, Joplin, MO 64801

#48: Claude C. Ries Chapter: Rick Whyte, 2870 N. Towne Ave, Apt. 155, Pomona, CA 91767, www.rieschapterafdcs.com

#50: The 7/1/71 Affair: David Wallman, 6740 Shadow Ridge Road, Lincoln, NE 68512

#53: Central NY FDC Society: Rick Kase, 6 Starwood Drive, Rochester, NY 14625-2631

#54: JAPOS Study Group: Cletus Delvaux, 800 E. River Dr., Unit B, De Pere, WI 54115

#56: Fred Sawyer North Texas Chapter of the AFDCS: Paul Benson, 201 Willow Creek Circle, Allen, TX 75002-3509, www.afdcschap56.org

#58: American Ceremony Program Society: Mark Gereb, 555 North Avenue #9J, Fort Lee, NJ 07024, stampceremony.org/

#65: Cachet Makers Association: Fred Fowler, PO Box 392, Niles, MI 49120-0392, cachetmakers.org/

#67: Maximum Card Study Unit: Gary Denis, PO Box 766, Patuxent River, MD 20670

#69: Rochester Philatelic Association: Joe Doles, 105 Lawson Road, Rochester, NY 14616-1444, www.rpastamps.org/

#70: Tucson Stamp Club: Alex Lutgendorf, PO Box 50603, Tucson, AZ 85703, tucsonstampclub.blogspot.com/

#71: North Carolina Chapter of AFDCS: Eric Wile, 2202 Jane Street, Greensboro, NC 27407

#72: Gay & Lesbian History on Stamps Club: PO Box 190842, Dallas, TX 75219-0842, www.glhsc.org/

#75: American Indian Philatelic Society: Dean Lilly, 5460 Margie Lane, Oak Forest, IL 60542-3727

#77: Molly Pitcher Stamp Club: 94 Cumberland Avenue, Verona, NJ 07044-2119

#78: National Duck Stamp Collectors Society: NDSCS Secretary, PO Box 43, Harleysville, PA 19438-0043, www.ndscs.org/

#79: Art Cover Exchange (ACE): Joseph Doles, 105 Lawson Road, Rochester, NY 14616, www.artcoverexchange.org

#80: Waterbury Stamp Club: AFDCS Representative, PO Box 581, Waterbury, CT 06720

#83: Dayton Stamp Club: Mr. L. William Streisel, 2741 Symphony Way, Dayton, OH 45449, www.daytonstampclub.com

#84: The Virtual Stamp Club: Lloyd A. de Vries, PO Box 1249, Twp. of Washington, NJ 07676-1249, www.virtualstampclub.com

#85: Connecticut Cover Club: Joseph Connolly, 571 Treat Lane, Orange, CT, 06477, jccachet@optonline.net, Facebook group

#87: American Society for Philatelic Pages and Panels: Gerald Blankenship, 539 North Gum Gully, Crosby, TX 77532, www.asppp.org/

#88: Stamp Collectors' Club of Toledo: Cliff Campbell, 544 Garfield Drive, Perrysburg, OH 43551-1617, www.toledostampclub.org

#90: Australian Cover Society: Noel Almeida, PO Box 768, Dandenong 3175, Australia, www.acs-inc.com.au/home.html

#91: Ebony Society of Philatelic Events & Reflections: Don Neal, PO Box 5245, Somerset, NJ 08875-5245, www.esperstamps.org

#92: Rattlesnake Island Local Post Society: Larry Lafoe, 228 Knoll Circle, Apt D, Crawfordsville, IN 47933-6510

A GLOSSARY OF
FIRST DAY COVER TERMS

Compiled by FIRST DAYS Staff

Add-on—A cachet design added to a cover which was originally uncacheted. An add-on cachet should be identified by maker and date so that it is clear that it is not contemporary with the cover. Unfortunately, many add-ons are not so identified.

Aerogramme—Postal stationery characterized by a single sheet which may be folded into an envelope, sealed, and then sent at a rate less than the airmail letter rate. Postage is usually but not always imprinted. Also known as aerogram.

AFDCS—American First Day Cover Society.

All-over cachet—A cachet design that covers most of or the entire face (front) of the envelope, as compared to one that occupies just the left side.

All-purpose cachet—A cachet with a general design that can be used for any stamp subject. It has no specific theme. Also, General Purpose.

Alternate cancel—Any First Day cancellation from the official First Day city, other than the official First Day of Issue postmarks supplied by the USPS. (These are sometimes referred to as semi-officials, or by the specific name of the cancel, such as plug, slogan, show, or ship cancels, etc.)

AMF—Air Mail Field. Found in many postmarks of postal facilities located in airports.

Autographed—An autographed envelope bears one or more signatures of individuals who are usually associated with the stamp. The autograph relationships may be the stamp subject, the designer, the local postmaster, dignitaries present at the dedication ceremony, etc. Authenticity and possible mechanical application of an autograph are significant considerations.

Auxiliary markings—Postal markings which are occasionally found on First Day Covers such as "Registered," "Insured," "Return to Sender," "Postage Due ——¢," etc.

B/4—Block of four stamps. Also B4.

Back stamp—The arrival mark of the destination city which usually appears on the reverse of the cover. Most registered covers are back-stamped on arrival.

Booklet pane—A sheetlet of stamps removed from a stamp booklet which may have one or more such panes. On FDC it is desirable to include the tab which is used to bind the pane into the booklet. This may not be possible with some modern issues.

Bullseye—also, bull's-eye. 1) The dial or circular portion of a postmark used by itself as a cancel. 2) Any circular postmark struck directly on the center of a stamp. (See Socked-on-the-nose.)

Cachet—Any textual or graphic design which has been applied to a cover usually, but not always, on the left side of the envelope. A cachet may be produced by any means—printed, rubber stamped, hand drawn, etc. A First Day cachet should be related specifically to the stamp on the cover.

Cachetmaker—One who designs and/or produces cacheted envelopes. Cachets may be identified by the artist's name, brand name, or manufacturing firm.

Cancel—The portion of a postmark which defaces or "kills" the stamp. Often loosely used interchangeably with "postmark."

CDS—Circular date stamp, ie. the dial or circular portion of the postmark.

Ceremony program—The printed program usually distributed by the Post Office or sponsoring organization at the First Day dedication of a new stamp. These are usually collected with the new stamp affixed and cancelled on the First Day.

Classic—The period prior to 1930 during which few First Day Covers were serviced and cachets were not common.

Coil—Stamps produced in rolls for use in vending machines. They are characterized by two opposite edges being straight or imperforate. A horizontal coil stamp is imperforate top and bottom and a vertical coil is straight-edged at the left and right sides.

Combo—One or more thematically related stamps affixed to a FDC. Also, combination cover.

Commemorative—A stamp, usually of large format, which is issued to salute or honor a person, event, state, organization, place, etc. Typically issued on an anniversary in a multiple of 10, 50, 100 years, etc. and produced in limited quantities. Contrasted with "definitive."

Commercial FDCs—FDCs sponsored by an individual, company, or organization used for promoting a service, product or as a gesture of goodwill.

Contract station—A sub-unit of a larger post office which is contracted to a private individual. Most contract stations are located in private business establishments.

Corner card—The imprint at the upper left corner of a cover which may be the return address or other identification of the sender.

Counterfeit—A stamp, postmark, or cachet created in direct imitation of a genuine item and intended to deceive. It is a Federal offense to counterfeit any postal marking or postal issue.

Cover—An envelope that has seen postal service or has a cancelled stamp on it, usually one with philatelic interest. May exemplify some segment of postal history or simply be a souvenir of an event or a place.

Crash cover—Any cover or FDC salvaged from the crash of a plane or vehicle in which it was carried. Usually bears postal markings explaining its damaged condition.

CXL—Abbreviation for "cancel." Also, cxl.

Definitive—Stamp issued for an indefinite period in an indefinite quantity to meet an ordinary postal rate. Designs do not usually honor a specific time dated event or person; most frequently in small format. Contrasted with "commemorative." Also known as "regular issue."

Designated First Day—The date officially announced by the Post Office for the sale of a new postal issue. Many issues prior to 1922 had no designated First Day. Covers cancelled prior to the designated dates are predates.

Dial—Circular portion of a postmark, usually containing the city, date and time. See bullseye.

Dual cancel—Two related or unrelated cancellations on a cover, each cancelling a stamp. One or both cancels may be for a First Day.

Duplex cancel—A metal handstamp containing both cancel and postmark in a single unit. Often found on FDCs before the mid-1930s.

EDC—Earliest documented cover. The earliest known postmark on a postal issue which had no designated First Day. Used interchangeably with EKU.

EFO—Errors, Freaks, and Oddities, i.e., stamps, cachets, cancellations, etc. that contain unintended mistakes or design faults.

EKU—Earliest known use. A designation for the earliest identified postmark on a stamp for which a first day of issue was not designated.

Electric eye (EE)—An electronic device which guides the perforating equipment during stamp manufacture. This is accomplished by heavy ink dashes in the selvage, which are used for detection and alignment. FDCs of EE stamps must have the selvage with dashes attached to the stamps.

Embossing—The process of impressing a design in relief into the paper of an envelope.

Engraved—A method of printing in which the lines of the design are cut into metal, which are recessed to retain the ink. The paper is forced under pressure into these lines to pick up the ink. Hence engraved cachets appear to have the design raised above the paper surface.

Error—A consistent abnormal variety created by a mistake in the production of a stamp or postmark. For example, the name of a city may be misspelled in the First Day cancel. Used in contrast to "freak."

Esoterica—Any item, other than a cover or envelope, that has been First Day cancelled that doesn't fit any of the regular collecting categories.

Event cover—A cacheted cover, not a FDC, prepared as a souvenir of a specific event or an anniversary of an event.

Event program—A list of events or speakers in any program related to the stamp release, such as a stamp show, any function at which a stamp is released, or any event honoring the same event as the stamp.

Fancy cancel—A cancellation which is or includes a design. The term is normally used for 19th-century cancels which were created by local postal officials according to personal whim. Also, see Pictorial.

Favor cancel—Any postal marking supplied as a favor or accommodation for a stamp collector.

FD—First Day.

FDC—First Day Cover. (FDCs—plural)

FDOI—First Day Of Issue. The slogan found in most First Day cancellations since Sc. 795, released in 1937.

FFC—First flight cover, ie. a cover flown on the inaugural flight of a new air route.

Filler—A stiff piece of paper, cardboard, or plastic found inside a First Day Cover. It provides necessary stiffness for a clearer cancellation. It also protects the cover from bending when it travels through the mail stream. Fillers, also termed stuffers, occasionally are imprinted with an advertising message or information pertaining to the stamp or cachet on the cover.

First cachet—The initial cachet commercially produced by a cachetmaker.

First Day—The day on which a stamp for the first time is officially sold by the Post Office.

First Day cover—Cover with a new stamp(s) or postal indicia, cancelled on the First Day.

Flag cancel—A cancellation used during the early 20th century incorporating a flag design. The stripes of the flag are the killer bars. Also, any more recent cancel with a similar design.

Flocked—A cachet production method in which powdered cloth is adhered to the envelope in the desired design.

Forgery—A fraudulently produced or altered philatelic item intended to deceive the collector.

Frank—A stamp, mark, or signature that shows payment of postage on a piece of mail. (A signature, with no stamp or paid marking, is called a Free Frank. Free as available to Congress and the President.)

Freak—An abnormal variety created by an unusual circumstance and not repeated with regularity. For example, a FDC may bear only a portion of a postmark because the cover was misfed into the cancelling machine. Used in contrast to "error."

General purpose (GP)—A cachet with a general design that is non-specific and may be used with any stamp subject. Also, All-purpose.

Hand cancel (HC)—A canceller which is applied to stamps individually and by hand. May be manufactured of plastic, rubber, or steel and is similar to a rubber stamp.

Hand-drawn (H/D)—A cachet applied to a cover by hand with pen, pencil, brush, chalk, or other art media. Each cachet is made individually and is an original.

Handmade (H/M)—A cachet applied to a cover by hand by adding seals, pasteups, collage, or similar materials. Each cachet is made individually and is an original.

Hand-painted (H/P) or Hand-colored (H/C)—A printed, hand-drawn or handmade cachet to which hand painting or hand coloring has been added.

HC, H/C, H/D, H/M, H/P—See preceding definitions.

HPO—Highway Post Office. The Post Office sorted mail on special motor vehicles in transit between cities. This system was in use from the late 1930s through the mid-1970s. FDCs were occasionally cancelled with HPO markings.

IA—Ink addressed. Refers to the method of addressing a cover.

Inaugural cover—A cover cancelled on the day that a president is sworn into office. Since 1957 the words INAUGURATION DAY have been incorporated into the cancel. The site was usually Washington, D.C., although other locations, like the President's city of birth, are now being designated. (In 1957 and 1985 the inauguration date fell on a Sunday. In both cases, covers of January 20, the private swearing-in ceremony, and January 21, the date of the public ceremony, both exist, and both are considered collectible.)

Indicia—An imprint on postal stationery indicating prepayment of postage. The plural is also "indicia."

Joint issue—Two or more stamps issued by different countries to commemorate the same event, topic, place, or person. Officially sanctioned joint issues are intentionally issued with the cooperation of the postal services of the countries involved.

Killer bars—The horizontal lines of a postmark which cancel the stamp. Since 1937 the FIRST DAY OF ISSUE slogan has appeared between the bars of most First Day cancels.

LA—Label addressed. Refers to the addressing method on a cover.

Last Day—The final day of a postal rate, post office operation, or similar occurrence. A cover cancelled on this day is referred to as a last day cover.

Lithography, or litho—A common method of printing stamps and cachets in which the design is transferred from a smooth plate by selective inks which wet only the design portion of the printing plate.

LL—Lower left. Refers to the plate number or marginal marking position on a sheet of stamps.

LR—Lower right. Refers to the marginal marking position.

LSASE—A legal-sized, stamped, self-addressed envelope. See SASE.

Luminescent—The condition of a stamp or postal stationery which has been treated with chemicals which are sensitive to and glow under ultraviolet (UV) light. This permits automatic cancelling equipment to detect the position of the postage on the cover and to orient it for rapid mechanical cancelling.

Machine cancel (MC)—A cancellation applied by an automatic cancelling device or machine.

Maximum card—A picture (post)card with a reproduction of the stamp or related subject from which the stamp was derived. Maximum card specialists prefer that the card and the stamp be as directly related as possible, but not be reproduced. The attempt is to achieve maximum agreement or concordance between the stamp subject and postcard. The stamp and cancel are usually placed on the illustrated side. This may be cancelled on the First Day of the stamp. See "Souvenir card."

Mellone catalog—A series of cachet catalogs for various time periods. They feature cachet illustrations with assigned code numbers for identification.

Mylar—Dupont's trademark for a durable plastic (polyester) film often recommended for storing stamps or covers because of its excellent chemical stability and the protection offered.

Nondenominated—Stamp or postal stationery without denomination or value in the design. These were created by the Post Office in anticipation of postal rate change when the exact rates could not be determined in advance.

Obliterator—Another term for the cancel portion of a postmark which defaces or obliterates the stamp.

OE—An abbreviation which indicates that a cover has been opened at the end or side.

Official—1) Of or related to the Federal government. USPS postmarks are official markings. 2) Stamps or stationery issued for use by government departments in the course of official business.

Official cachet—1) A cachet produced and applied by or for postal administrations. Official cachets are rare on U.S. FDCs but are common for many other countries. 2) Loosely used to refer to cachets authorized or sponsored by an organization closely associated with the issuance of a stamp, more properly called a sponsored cachet. The word "official" is abused by some cachetmakers.

Official FDC—Any First Day Cover with an official government postmark. This term is often misused for covers with sponsored cachets.

Offset—A printing method in which the design is transferred by ink from the image to another surface and then applied to the paper.

OT—An abbreviation indicating that a cover has been opened at the top.

PA—Pencil addressed. Refers to the method of cover addressing.

Patriotic or patriotic cachet—Design with patriotic or nationalistic theme, most often used to bolster public spirit during periods of war or national stress.

PB—Plate block. A group of stamps with the plate number in the selvage. May contain four or more stamps depending on the configuration of the printed numbers.

Peelable label—A self-stick label that can be easily removed from a cover without leaving adhesive or blemish. Used for addressing covers—later removed to create unaddressed covers.

Philatelic center—A post office window or station where most currently available stamps may be purchased by collectors. Created for the convenience of stamp collectors. Also postique.

Photocachet—A cachet consisting in part or entirely of a photograph.

Pictorial—A cancellation incorporating a pictorial design. Pictorial First Day cancels were used by the United States from 1958 to 1962 and are becoming more widespread on FDC issues of the 1980s and '90s. Many postiques each have a unique pictorial cancel. Many non-FD pictorial cancels are available nationwide, and are used for a limited time at special public or philatelic events.

Planty Catalogue—Catalog of U.S. cachets, for various year periods in individual volumes, assembled by Prof. Earl Planty. Planty identification designations are referred to as Planty Numbers.

Plug cancel—Colloquial name for a round, double circle marking, officially known as a validator stamp. The plug is chiefly used on postal receipts and registered envelopes. Also called a registry cancel or round-dater.

PNC—1) Plate Number Coil, ie. a coil stamp with a plate number thereon. 2) Philatelic-numismatic cover, ie. a cover with a cancelled stamp and a visible coin on the front, both thematically related. May be a FDC for the stamp.

POD—Post Office Department, the predecessor of the USPS. Also USPOD.

Polysleeve—Any of a variety of generally clear plastic sleeves, usually closed on two or three sides, to contain covers so they may be handled without soiling or damage.

Postage due—Stamps issued to indicate a penalty for insufficient postage. Postage due stamps are not used to pay postage, yet some issues are known on FDCs. These FDCs were cancelled inadvertently or by favor.

Postal card—A government produced postcard with an indicia indicating prepayment of postage.

Postal stationery—Postal cards, aerogrammes, and envelopes on which postage has been imprinted. Created as a convenience for the public so postage need not be applied.

Post-cancelled (post-dated, back-dated)—A cover which has been cancelled on a date later than that indicated on the postmark.

Postcard—A privately produced card usually bearing an illustration on one side and spaces for message, address, and postage on the other.

Postique—A special station or location at a post office where collectors may obtain currently available stamps. Each office usually has its own pictorial cancellation.

Postmark—A postal marking which indicates the time and point of origin of the mail to which it is applied. Often loosely used interchangeably with "Cancel."

PR—Pair of stamps.

Precancel—Stamps or stationery issued by the Post Office with words or lines printed thereon which prevent further use of the stamp. Precancelled stamps need not be cancelled again during mail handling. The standard First Day postmarks, however, are applied to FDCs of precancels.

Predate—A cover with a stamp cancelled earlier than the officially designated First Day of sale. Predates usually are created when stamps are sold prior to the official release date, contrary to postal regulations. Predates can exist only for issues with a designated First Day date.

Presentation album—Album containing a pane of a new stamp which is distributed to each dignitary at a First Day dedication ceremony. The album may have the recipient's name engraved on it. The first album is always for the President of the United States.

Presidentials—The 1938 series of definitive stamps featuring the Presidents of the United States.

Prexy—An information alternative term to designate the Presidential series of definitives.

Printed cachets—A cachet design type that is produced by printing, using any one of many methods.

Program—See Ceremony program.

Rag content—Pertains to the use of cotton fiber rather than wood pulp in the manufacture of envelopes. High rag content or 100 percent rag envelopes resist the ravages of time much better than do wood fiber covers, which contain processing chemicals that eventually discolor the paper and make the envelope more brittle.

Registry cancel—See Plug cancel.

Regular issue—Stamp issued for an indefinite period and quantity for ordinary postal use. See definitive.

RPO—Railway post office. A system once used by the POD to process mail in railroad cars enroute between cities. A distinctive cancel was used and FDCs exist with RPO postmarks.

RSA—Rubber-stamp addressed. A cover addressing method.

RSC—Rubber-stamp cachet.

Rubber stamps (R/S) cachet—A cachet applied to a cover using a rubber stamp. This method or device was very popular in the 1930s.

SASE—Self-addressed stamped envelope or SAE—self-addressed envelope. See also "LSASE."

Scott—Philatelic Publishing Company which produces Scott catalogs. A Scott (Sc.) number refers to a Scott catalog number to identify a stamp—a widely accepted practice.

Second-Day cover—A cover postmarked on the day following the First Day Of Issue. These were popular in the 1940s when the stamps were available at the Philatelic Agency in Washington, DC, on the second day.

Self-adhesive—A pre-gummed postage stamp on a peelable backing which requires no moisture for affixing to an envelope.

Selvage—The edges of a stamp pane beyond the perforations—including the portions that contain marginal markings as plate numbers, copyright notice, and other symbols/text. The plain selvage is usually removed from stamps when preparing FDCs, except for plate numbers and other collectible markings. Also spelled "selvedge."

Service—The act of affixing a stamp to and having it cancelled on a cover.

Servicer—One who performs the act of servicing. Frequently a person who does so on a commercial and large volume basis.

SGL—Single stamp. Also "sgl."

Ship cancel—A cancellation applied aboard a vessel—most frequently U.S. Navy although there are others. Ship cancels are fairly common but such strikes on FDCs are considered unusual because they represent a special effort in order to be obtained.

Show cancel—Special Post Office cancellation designed for and applied at a philatelic show or exhibition station.

Silk cachet—A cachet type with a pictorial design printed on a piece of fabric with a silky finish.

Slogan cancel—A cancellation with a message incorporated, such as—"Mail Early Before Christmas" or "Fight Tuberculosis."

Socked-on-the-nose (SOTN)—Designation for a stamp where the circle of the postmark falls exactly on the center. Another designation for "bullseye."

Souvenir card—A commemorative card, usually with reproductions of previously issued stamps and an inscription, issued by postal authorities in conjunction with a special philatelic event. The card or stamp units cannot be used for postal purposes but are often enhanced by collectors with an actual stamp and cancel.

Souvenir program—See Ceremony program.

Sponsor (cachet)—Individual or organization that has commissioned an established cachetmaker to prepare a special design in addition to the regular cachet for a particular issue. The term is sometimes used interchangeably with "cachetmaker."

Sponsored cachet—A cachet authorized or sponsored by an organization closely associated with the issuance of a stamp. See also "Official cachet," No. 2.

Station cancel—A cancellation applied at a temporary postal station established for a convention, exhibition, or other special event.

Stuffer—See Filler.

Tagged—Stamp or postal stationery which has had the postage area treated with a material sensitive to ultraviolet (UV) light, so that the cover can be mechanically oriented for canceling. Also luminescent.

Thermography—A printing method for producing raised designs by use of a special powder and heat. Often called, "poor man's embossing."

Tied—The cancellation overlaps the stamp, falling on both the postage and the cover thus affirming that the stamp was affixed prior to the postmarking. Also may be applied to non-postal labels or adhesives to show contemporaneous usage.

Toning—A deleterious condition of a cover resembling darkening or discoloration caused by excess gum at the edge of the stamp or a stain from the gum of the envelope flap. May also result from chemicals used in the production of inexpensive envelopes.

Trade name—A name or identification assigned to a cachet line by the producer. Example: Washington Press produces Artcraft Cachets.

UA—Unaddressed. A cover which does not have an address.

UL—Upper left. Refers to the position of stamp marginal markings.

Unaddressed (UA)—A cover which has no address.

Uncacheted—A cover which has no cachet design.

Unofficial cancel—A private, non-postal marking, usually resembling an official postmark, applied to a stamp or cover.

Unofficial FDC (UO)—A FDC cancelled with other than the official FIRST DAY OF ISSUE slogan cancel or official First Day pictorial cancelled supplied by the USPS for the First Day. For FDCs before the initial use of the FDOI slogan, this term refers to any city other than that which was officially designated. (There is much controversy among specialists and purists about this definition. Some dislike the use of the word "unofficial" as all postmarks are official cancellations of the USPS. Some would like to make a further distinction between stamps purchased in the official FD city, versus stamps sold in error on or before the FD in cities other than the FD city. Both of these are points well taken, but basically UOs are any FDC serviced in the city of issue or another location with any cancel other than the official FD cancel supplied by the USPS. A UO FDC must have the correct First Day date.)

UO—Unofficial First Day cover.

UR—Upper right. Refers to the position of the marginal markings on stamp selvage.

USPS—United States Postal Service, established in 1971.

Validator—See Plug.

FIRST DAY COVERS

NOTE: "D.C." indicates Washington, D.C., as the official city and date of issue. Other cities with significantly different values are also listed. When no city is indicated, the number of cities in which the stamps were issued is indicated.

Scott No.			Single	Block of 4
Uncacheted.				
❑ 551	½¢	Hale (D.C. & New Haven, CT, 4/4/25)	22.05	30.50
❑ 552	1¢	Franklin (D.C., 1/17/23)	27.30	48.80
❑ 552	1¢	Franklin (Philadelphia, PA)	59.30	65.60
❑ 553	1½¢	Harding (D.C., 3/19/25)	37.80	44.10
❑ 554	2¢	Washington (D.C., 1/15/23)	49.85	55.10
❑ 555	3¢	Lincoln (D.C., 2/12/23)	48.30	71.40
❑ 555	3¢	Lincoln (Hodgenville, KY)	220.50	380.60
❑ 556	4¢	Martha Washington (D.C., 1/15/23)	81.90	131.70
❑ 557	5¢	Roosevelt (D.C., 10/27/22)	131.70	197.40
❑ 557	5¢	Roosevelt (New York, NY)	288.75	446.25
❑ 557	5¢	Roosevelt (Oyster Bay, NY)	2257.50	—
❑ 558	6¢	Garfield (D.C., 11/20/22)	241.50	328.10
❑ 559	7¢	McKinley (D.C., 5/1/23)	214.20	278.25
❑ 559	7¢	McKinley (Niles, OH)	220.50	—
❑ 560	8¢	Grant (D.C., 5/1/23)	214.20	247.80
❑ 561	9¢	Jefferson (D.C., 1/15/23)	214.20	285.60
❑ 562	10¢	Monroe (D.C., 1/15/23)	191.60	285.60
❑ 563	11¢	Hayes (D.C., 10/4/22)	1097.25	RARE
❑ 563	11¢	Hayes (Fremont, OH)	3350.00	—
❑ 564	12¢	Cleveland (D.C., Boston, MA, Caldwell, NJ, 3/20/23)	273.00	412.10
❑ 565	14¢	Indian (D.C., 5/1/23)	411.60	556.50
❑ 565	14¢	Indian (Muskogee, OK)	2625.00	RARE
❑ 566	15¢	Statue of Liberty (D.C., 11/11/22)	546.00	934.50
❑ 567	20¢	Golden Gate (5/1/23)	656.25	1375.50
❑ 567	20¢	Golden Gate (San Francisco)	3920.00	—
❑ 568	25¢	Niagara Falls (D.C., 11/11/22)	714.00	1375.50
❑ 569	30¢	Bison (D.C., 3/20/23)	934.50	1648.50
❑ 570	50¢	Arlington (D.C., 11/11/22)	1732.50	—
❑ 571	$1	Lincoln Memorial (D.C., Springfield, IL 2/12/23)	RARE	RARE
❑ 572	$2	U.S. Capitol (D.C., 3/20/23)	RARE	—

Scott No.			Single	Block of 4
❏ 573	$5	America (D.C., 3/20/23)	RARE	—
❏ 576	1½¢	Harding (D.C., 4/4/25)	54.60	92.90
❏ 581	1¢	Franklin (D.C., 10/17/23)	798.00	—
❏ 582	1½¢	Harding (D.C., 3/19/25)	65.60	59.30
❏ 583a	2¢	Washington (booklet pane, D.C., 8/27/26)	1548.75	—
❏ 584	3¢	Lincoln (D.C., 8/1/25)	71.40	113.90
❏ 585	4¢	Martha Washington (D.C., 4/4/25)	71.40	113.90
❏ 586	5¢	Roosevelt (D.C., 4/4/25)	71.40	113.90
❏ 587	6¢	Garfield (D.C., 4/4/25)	71.40	113.90
❏ 588	7¢	McKinley (D.C., 5/29/26)	71.40	113.90
❏ 589	8¢	Grant (D.C., 5/29/26)	92.90	121.25
❏ 590	9¢	Jefferson (D.C., 5/29/26)	92.90	121.25
❏ 591	10¢	Monroe (D.C., 6/8/25)	113.40	164.30
❏ 597	1¢	Franklin (coil, D.C., 7/18/23)	819.00	—
❏ 598	1½¢	Harding (coil, D.C., 3/19/25)	546.00	—
❏ 599	2¢	Washington (coil, D.C., 1/15/23)	2992.50	—
❏ 600	3¢	Lincoln (coil, D.C., 5/10/24)	136.50	—
❏ 602	5¢	Roosevelt (coil, D.C., 3/5/24)	120.75	—
❏ 603	10¢	Monroe (coil, D.C., 2/1/24)	131.25	—
❏ 604	1¢	Franklin (coil, D.C., 7/19/24)	107.10	—
❏ 605	1½¢	Harding (coil, D.C., 5/9/25)	86.60	—
❏ 606	2¢	Washington (coil, D.C., 12/31/23)	164.30	—
❏ 610	2¢	Harding (D.C., Marion, OH 9/1/25)	43.55	65.60
❏ 611	2¢	Harding (imperf., D.C., 11/15/23)	153.80	180.60
❏ 612	2¢	Harding (perf. 10, D.C., 9/12/23)	153.80	180.60
❏ 614	1¢	Huguenot-Walloon (5/1/24)	55.10	82.40
❏ 615	2¢	Huguenot-Walloon (5/1/24)	55.10	82.40
❏ 616	5¢	Huguenot-Walloon (5/1/24)	82.00	142.30
❏ 614–616		Huguenot-Walloon, set on one cover (5/1/24), from any of the following cities: Albany, NY, Allentown, PA, Charleston, SC, Jacksonville, FL, Lancaster, PA, Mayport, FL, New Rochelle, NY, New York, NY, Philadelphia, PA, Reading, PA, and Washington, D.C.	163.80	—
❏ 617	1¢	Lexington-Concord (4/4/25)	44.10	71.90
❏ 618	2¢	Lexington-Concord (4/4/25)	44.10	71.90
❏ 619	5¢	Lexington-Concord (4/4/25)	76.10	107.60

Scott No.			Single	Block of 4
❑ 617–619		Lexington-Concord, set on one cover (4/4/25), from any of the following cities: Boston, MA, Cambridge, MA, Concord, MA, Lexington, MA, or Washington, D.C. Concord, MA sells for 25% more.	164.30	—
❑ 620	2¢	Norse-American (5/18/25)	22.58	55.10
❑ 621	5¢	Norse-American (5/18/25)	43.55	65.60
❑ 620–621		Norse-American, set on one cover (5/18/25) from any of the following cities: Angola, IN, Benson, MN, Decoran, IA, Minneapolis, MN, Northfield, MN, St. Paul, MN, or Washington, D.C.	65.60	110.65
❑ 622	13¢	Harrison	27.80	61.40
❑ 622	13¢	Harrison (Indianapolis, IN, 1/11/26)	27.80	61.40
❑ 622	13¢	Harrison (North Bend, OH, 1/11/26)	153.80	336.50
❑ 623	17¢	Wilson (New York, NY, Princeton, NJ, Staunton, VA, Washington, D.C., 12/28/25)	22.55	43.55
❑ 627	2¢	Sesquicentennial (Boston, MA, Philadelphia,PA, D.C., 5/10/26)	16.25	27.80
❑ 628	5¢	Erikson (Chicago, IL, Minneapolis, MN, New York, NY, D.C. 5/29/26)	23.60	27.80
❑ 629	2¢	White Plains (White Plains, NY, New York, NY, Philadelphia, PA Expo 10/18/26)	13.35	16.25
❑ 630	2¢	White Plains (complete sheet, 10/18/26)	1659.00	—
❑ 631	1½¢	Harding (D.C., 8/27/26)	59.30	79.80
❑ 632	1¢	Franklin (D.C., 6/10/27)	59.30	79.80
❑ 632a	1¢	Franklin booklet of 6 (D.C. 11/2/27)	3850.00	
❑ 633	1½¢	Harding (D.C., 5/17/27)	54.60	77.15
❑ 634	2¢	Washington (D.C., 12/10/26)	50.40	70.85
❑ 635	3¢	Lincoln (D.C., 2/3/27)	49.62	65.60
❑ 635a	3¢	Bright Violet (D.C., 2/7/34)	49.62	65.60
❑ 636	4¢	Martha Washington (D.C., 5/17/27)	49.62	65.60
❑ 637	5¢	Roosevelt (D.C., 3/24/27)	38.30	49.35
❑ 638	6¢	Garfield (D.C., 7/27/27)	49.10	65.60

Scott No.			Single	Block of 4
❏ 639	7¢	McKinley (D.C., 3/24/27)	49.60	54.60
❏ 640	8¢	Grant (D.C., 6/10/27)	54.60	82.15
❏ 641	9¢	Jefferson (D.C., 5/17/27)	66.15	55.35
❏ 642	10¢	Monroe (D.C., 2/3/27)	54.60	115.50
❏ 643	2¢	Vermont (Burlington, VT, D.C., 8/3/27)	15.25	19.45
❏ 644	2¢	Burgoyne (Albany, NY, Rome, NY, Syracuse, NY, Utica, NY, and D.C., 8/3/27)	15.25	19.45
❏ 645	2¢	Valley Forge (Cleveland Phil Sta., OH, Lancaster, PA, Norriston, PA, Philadelphia, PA, Valley Forge, PA, West Chester, PA, and D.C., 5/26/28)	5.50	8.90
❏ 646	2¢	Molly Pitcher (Freehold, NJ, Red Bank, NJ, D.C., 10/20/18)	6.80	16.25
❏ 647	2¢	Hawaii (Honolulu, HI, D.C., 8/13/28)	24.40	27.80
❏ 648	5¢	Hawaii (Honolulu, HI, D.C., 8/13/28)	24.40	—
❏ 647–648		Hawaii set on one cover (8/13/28)	44.10	72.20
❏ 649	2¢	Aero Conf. (D.C., 12/12/28)	8.65	13.40
❏ 650	5¢	Aero Conf. (D.C., 12/12/28)	11.05	15.25
❏ 649–650		Areo Conf. set on one cover (12/12/18)	13.15	22.60
❏ 651	2¢	Clark (Vincennes, IN, 2/25/29)	5.50	11.30
❏ 653	½¢	Hale (D.C., 5/25/29)	—	22.60
❏ 654	2¢	Electric Light (Menlopark, NJ, 6/5/29)	11.30	15.25
❏ 655	2¢	Electric Light (D.C., 6/11/29)	76.90	101.75
❏ 656	2¢	Electric Light (coil, 6/11/29)	138.60	—
❏ 657	2¢	Sullivan (16 different New York cities and D.C., 6/17/29)	4.75	8.90
❏ 658	1¢	Kansas (D.C., 5/1/29)	27.80	32.80
❏ 659	1½¢	Kansas (D.C., 5/1/29)	43.60	48.55
❏ 660	2¢	Kansas (D.C., 5/1/29)	43.60	48.55
❏ 661	3¢	Kansas (D.C., 5/1/29)	43.60	48.55
❏ 662	4¢	Kansas (D.C., 5/1/29)	71.40	93.95
❏ 663	5¢	Kansas (D.C., 5/1/29)	71.40	93.95
❏ 664	6¢	Kansas (D.C., 5/1/29)	234.75	113.40
❏ 665	7¢	Kansas (D.C., 5/1/29)	143.30	164.30
❏ 666	8¢	Kansas (D.C., 5/1/29)	143.30	164.30
❏ 667	9¢	Kansas (D.C., 5/1/29)	111.80	153.80
❏ 668	10¢	Kansas (D.C., 5/1/29)	111.80	153.80
❏ 658–668		Kansas set on one cover (D.C., 5/1/29)	1128.75	—

Scott No.			Single	Block of 4
❏ 669	1¢	Nebraska (D.C., 5/1/29)	55.10	65.60
❏ 670	1½¢	Nebraska (D.C., 5/1/29)	55.10	65.60
❏ 671	2¢	Nebraska (D.C., 5/1/29)	55.10	65.60
❏ 672	3¢	Nebraska (D.C., 5/1/29)	49.05	70.85
❏ 673	4¢	Nebraska (D.C., 5/1/29)	59.55	70.85
❏ 674	5¢	Nebraska (D.C., 5/1/29)	65.60	70.85
❏ 675	6¢	Nebraska (D.C., 5/1/29)	86.60	126.50
❏ 676	7¢	Nebraska (D.C., 5/1/29)	86.60	126.50
❏ 677	8¢	Nebraska (D.C., 5/1/29)	82.50	93.45
❏ 678	9¢	Nebraska (D.C., 5/1/29)	82.50	93.45
❏ 679	10¢	Nebraska (D.C., 5/1/29)	88.70	—
❏ 659–669		Nebraska set on one cover (D.C., 5/1/29)	1338.75	—
❏ 680	2¢	Fallen Timbers (5 cities 9/14/29)	5.45	11.25
❏ 681	2¢	Ohio River (7 cities 10/19/29)	5.45	11.25
❏ 682	2¢	Massachusetts Bay Colony (2 cities 4/8/30)	4.30	10.05
❏ 683	2¢	Carolina-Charleston (4/10/30)	4.30	10.05
❏ 684	1½¢	Harding Marion, OH(12/1/30)	7.75	10.05
❏ 685	4¢	Taft Cinncinnati, OH (6/4/30)	7.75	10.05
❏ 686	1½¢	Harding Marion, OH (coil, 12/1/30)	7.75	10.05
❏ 687	4¢	Taft (coil, D.C., 9/18/30)	33.05	—
❏ 688	2¢	Braddock (7/9/30)	10.05	10.05
❏ 689	2¢	Von Steuben	10.05	10.05
❏ 690	2¢	Pulaski (12 cities, 1/16/31)	10.05	10.05
❏ 692	11¢	Hayes (D.C., 9/4/31)	6.55	162.20
❏ 693	12¢	Cleveland (D.C., 8/25/31)	6.55	162.20
❏ 694	13¢	Harrison (D.C., 9/4/31)	6.55	162.20
❏ 695	14¢	Indian (D.C., 9/8/31)	6.55	162.20
❏ 696	15¢	Liberty (D.C., 8/27/31)	6.55	162.20
❏ 697	17¢	Wilson (D.C., 7/27/31)	164.30	162.20
❏ 698	20¢	Golden Gate (D.C., 9/8/31)	164.30	162.20
❏ 699	25¢	Niagara Falls (D.C., 7/27/31)	191.10	164.30
❏ 700	30¢	Bison (D.C., 9/8/31)	175.35	164.30
❏ 701	50¢	Arlington (D.C., 9/4/31)	275.10	333.90
❏ 702	2¢	Red Cross (2 cities 5/21/31)	6.70	10.10
❏ 703	2¢	Yorktown (2 cities, 10/19/31)	6.70	10.10
❏ 704	½¢	Olive Brown (D.C., 1/1/32)	—	10.10
❏ 705	1¢	Green (D.C., 1/1/32)	6.70	10.10

Scott No.			Single	Block of 4
❑ 706	1½¢	Brown (D.C., 1/1/32)	4.45	6.75
❑ 707	2¢	Carmine Rose (D.C., 1/1/32)	4.45	6.75
❑ 708	3¢	Deep Violet (D.C., 1/1/32)	4.45	6.75
❑ 709	4¢	Light Brown (D.C., 1/1/32)	4.45	6.75
❑ 710	5¢	Blue (D.C., 1/1/32)	4.45	6.75
❑ 711	6¢	Red Orange (D.C., 1/1/32)	4.45	6.75
❑ 712	7¢	Black (D.C., 1/1/32)	4.45	6.75
❑ 713	8¢	Olive Bistre (D.C., 1/1/32)	4.45	6.75
❑ 714	9¢	Pale Red (D.C., 1/1/32)	4.45	6.75
❑ 715	10¢	Orange Yellow (D.C., 1/1/32)	4.45	6.75
❑ 704–715		set on one cover	44.60	—
❑ 716	2¢	Olympic Winter Games (1/25/32)	4.40	5.85
❑ 717	2¢	Arbor Day (4/22/32)	4.40	5.85
❑ 718	3¢	Olympic Summer Games (6/15/32)	3.30	4.45
❑ 719	5¢	Olympic Summer Games (6/15/32)	5.60	6.30
❑ 718–719		Olympic Summer Games set on one cover	5.60	6.70
❑ 720	3¢	Washington (D.C., 6/16/32)	5.35	5.75
❑ 720b	3¢	Washington (booklet of 6, D.C., 7/25/32)	56.70	—
❑ 721	3¢	Washington (coil, D.C., 6/24/32)	6.00	—
❑ 722	3¢	Washington (coil, D.C., 10/12/32)	6.00	—
❑ 723	6¢	Garfield (coil, 8/18/32)	6.00	—
❑ 724	3¢	William Penn (3 cities, 10/24/32)	5.25	6.70
❑ 725	3¢	Daniel Webster (3 cities, 10/24/32)	5.25	6.70
❑ 726	3¢	Gen. Oglethorpe (2/12/32)	5.25	6.70
❑ 727	3¢	Peace Proclamation (4/19/32)	5.25	6.70
❑ 728	1¢	Century of Progress (5/25/32)	3.35	6.10
❑ 729	3¢	Century of Progress (5/25/32)	3.35	6.10
❑ 728–729		Century of Progress set on one cover	4.40	6.10
❑ 730	1¢	American Philatelic Society (full sheet)	89.25	—
❑ 730a	1¢	American Philatelic Society (8/25/33)	4.40	6.80
❑ 731	3¢	American Philatelic Society (full sheet)	94.50	—
❑ 731a	3¢	American Philatelic Society (8/25/33)	3.15	4.70
❑ 732	3¢	National Recovery Administration (D.C., 8/15/33)	3.15	4.70
❑ 733	3¢	Byrd Antarctic (D.C., 10/9/33)	5.75	9.00
❑ 734	5¢	Kosciuszko (6 cities, 10/13/33)	5.75	9.00
❑ 734	5¢	Kosciuszko (Pittsburg, PA)	5.75	6.80
❑ 735	3¢	National Exhibition (full sheet)	5.75	—

Scott No.			Single	Block of 4
❏ 735a	3¢	National Exhibition (2/10/34)	5.65	6.75
❏ 736	3¢	Maryland Tercentenary (3/23/34)	5.65	6.75
❏ 737	3¢	Mothers of America (D.C., 5/2/34)	5.65	6.75
❏ 738	3¢	Mothers of America (D.C., 5/2/34)	5.65	6.75
❏ 739	3¢	Wisconsin (7/9/34)	5.65	6.75
❏ 740	1¢	Parks, Yosemite (2 cities, 7/16/34)	5.65	6.75
❏ 741	2¢	Parks, Grand Canyon (2 cities, 7/24/34)	5.65	6.75
❏ 742	3¢	Parks, Mt. Rainier (2 cities, 8/3/34)	5.65	6.75
❏ 743	4¢	Parks, Mesa Verde (2 cities, 9/25/34)	5.65	6.75
❏ 744	5¢	Parks, Yellowstone (2 cities, 7/30/34)	5.65	6.75
❏ 745	6¢	Parks, Crater Lake (2 cities, 9/5/34)	5.65	6.75
❏ 746	7¢	Parks, Acadia (2 cities, 10/2/34)	5.65	6.75
❏ 747	8¢	Parks, Zion (2 cities, 9/18/34)	5.65	6.75
❏ 748	9¢	Parks, Glacier Park (2 cities, 8/27/34)	5.65	6.75
❏ 749	10¢	Parks, Smoky Mountains (2 cities, 10/8/34)	5.67	7.75
❏ 750	3¢	American Philatelic Society (full sheet)	42.00	—
❏ 750a	3¢	American Philatelic Society (8/28/34)	5.50	—
❏ 751	1¢	Trans-Mississippi Philatelic Expo, (full sheet)	27.80	—
❏ 751a	1¢	Trans-Mississippi Philatelic Expo. (10/10/34)	4.70	—
❏ 752	3¢	Peace Commemoration (D.C., 3/15/35)	7.85	9.15
❏ 753	3¢	Byrd (D.C., 3/15/35)	7.85	9.15
❏ 754	3¢	Mothers of America (D.C., 3/15/35)	7.85	9.15
❏ 755	3¢	Wisconsin (D.C., 3/15/35)	7.85	9.15
❏ 756	1¢	Parks, Yosemite (D.C., 3/15/35)	7.85	9.15
❏ 757	2¢	Parks, Grand Canyon (D.C., 3/15/35)	7.85	9.15
❏ 758	3¢	Parks, Mount Ranier (D.C., 3/15/35)	7.85	9.15
❏ 759	4¢	Parks, Mesa Verde (D.C., 3/15/35)	7.85	9.15
❏ 760	5¢	Parks, Yellowstone (D.C., 3/15/35)	7.85	9.15
❏ 761	6¢	Parks, Crater Lake (D.C., 3/15/35)	9.00	13.40
❏ 762	7¢	Parks, Acadia (D.C., 3/15/35)	9.00	13.40
❏ 763	8¢	Parks, Zion (D.C., 3/15/35)	9.00	13.40
❏ 764	9¢	Parks, Glacier Park (D.C., 3/15/35)	9.00	13.40
❏ 765	10¢	Parks, Smoky Mountains (D.C., 3/15/35)	9.00	13.40
❏ 766a	1¢	Century of Progress (D.C., 3/15/35)	9.00	13.40
❏ 767a	3¢	Century of Progress (D.C., 3/15/35)	9.00	13.40
❏ 768a	3¢	Byrd (D.C., 3/15/35)	9.00	13.40
❏ 769a	1¢	Parks, Yosemite (D.C., 3/15/35)	9.00	13.40

Scott No.			Single	Block of 4
❏ 770a	3¢	Parks, Mount Ranier (D.C., 3/15/35)	6.70	11.30
❏ 771	16¢	Airmail, special delivery (D.C., 3/15/35)	6.70	11.30

Cacheted Covers.

NOTE: For dates of issue, see **Uncacheted Covers** above.

❏ 610	2¢	Harding	892.50	—
❏ 617	1¢	Lexington-Concord	153.30	—
❏ 618	2¢	Lexington-Concord	153.30	—
❏ 619	5¢	Lexington-Concord	252.00	—
❏ 620–621		Norse American set on one cover	252.00	
❏ 623	17¢	Wilson	336.00	—
❏ 627	2¢	Sesquicentennial	88.45	—
❏ 628	5¢	Erikson	446.25	—
❏ 629	2¢	White Plains	82.00	—
❏ 630	2¢	White Plains (souvenir sheet) single	82.00	—
❏ 635a	3¢	Bright Violet	55.15	—
❏ 643	2¢	Vermont	55.15	115.50
❏ 644	2¢	Burgoyne	59.30	92.90
❏ 645	2¢	Valley Forge	55.10	82.40
❏ 646	2¢	Molly Pitcher	111.30	—
❏ 647	2¢	Hawaii	71.90	92.90
❏ 648	5¢	Hawaii	82.15	105.25
❏ 647–648		Hawaii set on one cover	136.50	—
❏ 649	2¢	Aero Conf.	65.60	91.85
❏ 650	5¢	Aero Conf.	65.60	65.60
❏ 649–650		Aero Conf. set on one cover	71.90	—
❏ 651	2¢	Clark	38.30	54.60
❏ 654	2¢	Electric Light	38.30	54.60
❏ 655	2¢	Electric Light	153.80	—
❏ 656	2¢	Electric Light (coil)	262.50	—
❏ 657	2¢	Sullivan, Auburn N.Y.	57.20	65.60
❏ 680	2¢	Fallen Timbers	57.20	65.60
❏ 681	2¢	Ohio River	57.20	65.60
❏ 682	2¢	Massachusetts Bay Colony	57.20	65.60
❏ 683	2¢	California-Charleston	57.20	65.60
❏ 684	1½¢	Harding	57.20	65.60
❏ 685	4¢	Taft	59.30	89.25
❏ 686	1½¢	Harding (coil)	59.30	89.25
❏ 687	4¢	Taft (coil)	94.50	111.80

Scott No.			Single	Block of 4
❑ 688	2¢	Braddock	48.55	54.60
❑ 689	2¢	Von Steuben	48.55	54.60
❑ 690	2¢	Pulaski	48.55	54.60
❑ 702	2¢	Red Cross	48.55	54.60
❑ 703	2¢	Yorktown	48.55	54.60
❑ 704	½¢	Olive Brown	25.70	34.10
❑ 705	1¢	Green	25.70	34.10
❑ 706	1½¢	Brown	25.70	34.10
❑ 707	2¢	Carmine Rose	25.70	34.10
❑ 708	3¢	Deep Violet	25.70	34.10
❑ 709	4¢	Light Brown	25.70	34.10
❑ 710	5¢	Blue	25.70	34.10
❑ 711	6¢	Red Orange	25.70	34.10
❑ 712	7¢	Black	25.70	34.10
❑ 713	8¢	Olive Bistre	25.70	34.10
❑ 714	9¢	Pale Red	25.70	34.10
❑ 715	10¢	Orange Yellow	25.70	34.10
❑ 704–715		Set on one cover	181.10	—
❑ 716	2¢	Olympic Winter Games	36.20	71.60
❑ 717	2¢	Arbor Day	36.20	71.60
❑ 718	3¢	Olympic Summer Games	36.20	71.60
❑ 719	5¢	Olympic Summer Games	36.20	71.60
❑ 718–719		Set on one cover	36.20	71.60
❑ 720	3¢	Washington	36.75	71.60
❑ 720b	3¢	Booklet pane of 6	199.50	—
❑ 721	3¢	Washington (coil)	48.80	—
❑ 722	3¢	Washington (coil)	48.80	—
❑ 723	6¢	Garfield (coil)	54.05	—
❑ 724	3¢	William Penn	30.95	38.30
❑ 725	3¢	Daniel Webster	30.95	38.30
❑ 726	3¢	Gen. Oglethorpe	30.95	38.30
❑ 727	3¢	Peace Proclamation	30.95	38.30
❑ 728	1¢	Century of Progress	30.95	38.30
❑ 729	3¢	Century of Progress	17.30	23.60
❑ 730	1¢	American Philatelic Society (full sheet)	163.80	—
❑ 730a	1¢	American Philatelic Society (single)	27.30	38.05
❑ 731	3¢	American Philatelic Society (full sheet)	173.25	—
❑ 731a	3¢	American Philatelic Society (single)	22.55	22.55
❑ 732	3¢	National Recovery Administration	22.55	38.30
❑ 733	3¢	Byrd Antarctic	32.55	38.30

Scott No.			Single	Block of 4
❑ 734	5¢	Kosciuszko	22.55	33.60
❑ 734b	5¢	Kosciuszko (Pittsburgh, PA)	53.65	65.60
❑ 735	3¢	National Exhibition (full sheet)	53.65	—
❑ 735a	3¢	National Exhibition (single)	20.00	—
❑ 736	3¢	Maryland Tercentenary	22.80	34.10
❑ 737	3¢	Mothers of America	22.80	34.10
❑ 738	3¢	Mothers of America	22.80	34.10
❑ 739	2¢	Wisconsin	22.80	34.10
❑ 740	1¢	Parks, Yosemite	22.80	34.10
❑ 741	2¢	Parks, Grand Canyon	22.80	34.10
❑ 742	3¢	Parks, Mt. Ranier	22.80	34.10
❑ 743	4¢	Parks, Mesa Verde	22.80	34.10
❑ 744	5¢	Parks, Yellowstone	22.80	34.10
❑ 745	6¢	Parks, Crater Lake	19.65	27.80
❑ 746	7¢	Parks, Acadia	19.65	27.80
❑ 747	8¢	Parks, Zion	19.65	27.80
❑ 748	9¢	Parks, Glacier Park	19.65	27.80
❑ 749	10¢	Parks, Smoky Mountains	19.65	27.80
❑ 750	3¢	American Philatelic Society (full sheet)	54.60	—
❑ 750a	3¢	American Philatelic Society (single)	19.15	27.80
❑ 751	1¢	Trans-Mississippi Expo. (full sheet)	43.55	—
❑ 751a	1¢	Trans-Mississippi Expo. (single)	13.10	17.30
❑ 752	3¢	Peace Commemoration	38.30	49.45
❑ 753	3¢	Byrd	38.30	49.45
❑ 754	3¢	Mothers of America	38.30	49.45
❑ 755	3¢	Wisconsin Tercentenary	38.30	49.45
❑ 756	1¢	Parks, Yosemite	38.30	49.45
❑ 757	2¢	Parks, Grand Canyon	38.30	49.45
❑ 758	3¢	Parks, Mount Rainier	38.30	49.45
❑ 759	4¢	Parks, Mesa Verde	38.30	49.45
❑ 760	5¢	Parks, Yellowstone	38.30	49.45
❑ 761	6¢	Parks, Crater Lake	38.30	49.45
❑ 762	7¢	Parks, Acadia	38.30	49.45
❑ 763	8¢	Parks, Zion	38.30	49.45
❑ 764	9¢	Parks, Glacier Park	38.30	49.45
❑ 765	10¢	Parks, Smoky Mountains	38.30	49.45
❑ 766a	1¢	Century of Progress	49.45	66.90
❑ 767a	3¢	Century of Progress	49.45	66.90
❑ 768a	3¢	Byrd	49.45	66.90
❑ 769a	1¢	Parks, Yosemite	49.45	66.90

Scott No.			Single	Block of 4
❏ 770a	3¢	Parks, Mount Rainier	46.20	71.90
❏ 771	16¢	Airmail, special delivery	46.20	71.90

Scott No.			Single	Block	Plate Block
❏ 772	3¢	Connecticut Tercentenary	8.95	16.55	26.60
❏ 773	3¢	California Exposition	8.95	16.55	26.60
❏ 774	3¢	Boulder Dam	9.75	16.55	26.60
❏ 775	3¢	Michigan Centenary	9.75	16.55	26.60
❏ 776	3¢	Texas Centennial	11.05	16.55	26.60
❏ 777	3¢	Rhode Island Tercentenary	8.95	16.55	26.60
❏ 778	3¢	TIPEX	6.55	16.55	—
❏ 782	3¢	Arkansas Centennial	8.70	16.55	26.60
❏ 783	3¢	Oregon Territory	8.70	16.55	26.60
❏ 784	3¢	Susan B. Anthony	8.70	16.55	26.60
❏ 785	1¢	Army	5.35	13.15	24.70
❏ 786	2¢	Army	9.20	13.15	24.70
❏ 787	3¢	Army	9.20	13.15	24.70
❏ 788	4¢	Army	9.20	13.15	24.70
❏ 789	5¢	Army	9.20	13.15	24.70
❏ 790	1¢	Navy	9.20	13.15	24.70
❏ 791	2¢	Navy	9.20	13.15	24.70
❏ 792	3¢	Navy	9.20	13.15	24.70
❏ 793	4¢	Navy	9.20	13.15	24.70
❏ 794	5¢	Navy	9.20	13.15	24.70
❏ 795	3¢	Ordinance of 1787	9.20	9.50	15.80
❏ 796	5¢	Virginia Dare	9.20	9.50	15.80
❏ 797	10¢	Souvenir Sheet	9.20	—	—
❏ 798	3¢	Constitution	9.20	11.30	17.60
❏ 799	3¢	Hawaii	9.20	11.30	17.60
❏ 800	3¢	Alaska	9.20	11.30	17.60
❏ 801	3¢	Puerto Rico	9.20	11.30	17.60
❏ 802	3¢	Virgin Islands	9.20	11.30	17.60
❏ 803	½¢	Franklin	6.85	8.70	15.50
❏ 804	1¢	Washington	6.85	8.70	15.50
❏ 805	1½¢	Martha Washington	6.85	8.70	15.50
❏ 806	2¢	Adams	6.85	8.70	15.50
❏ 807	3¢	Jefferson	6.85	8.70	15.50

NOTE: Beginning with No. 795, first day covers bear the slogan cancellation "First Day Issue."

Scott No.			Single	Block	Plate Block
❑ 808	4¢	Madison	5.75	7.85	13.40
❑ 809	4½¢	White House	5.75	7.85	13.40
❑ 810	5¢	Monroe	5.75	7.85	13.40
❑ 811	6¢	Adams	5.75	7.85	13.40
❑ 812	7¢	Jackson	5.75	7.85	13.40
❑ 813	8¢	VanBuren	5.75	7.85	13.40
❑ 814	9¢	Harrison	5.75	7.85	13.40
❑ 815	10¢	Tyler	5.75	7.85	16.30
❑ 816	11¢	Polk	5.75	8.70	16.30
❑ 817	12¢	Taylor	5.75	8.70	16.30
❑ 818	13¢	Fillmore	5.75	8.70	16.30
❑ 819	14¢	Pierce	5.75	8.70	16.30
❑ 820	15¢	Buchanan	5.75	8.70	16.30
❑ 821	16¢	Lincoln	5.75	8.70	16.30
❑ 822	17¢	Johnson	6.55	8.70	15.25
❑ 823	18¢	Grant	6.55	8.70	15.25
❑ 824	19¢	Hayes	6.55	8.70	15.25
❑ 825	20¢	Garfield	6.55	8.70	15.25
❑ 826	21¢	Arthur	6.55	8.70	15.25
❑ 827	22¢	Cleveland	6.55	8.70	15.25
❑ 828	24¢	Harrison	6.55	8.70	15.25
❑ 829	25¢	McKinley	6.55	8.70	15.25
❑ 830	30¢	Roosevelt	6.55	10.80	15.25
❑ 831	50¢	Taft	13.10	19.45	27.30
❑ 832	$1	Wilson	43.55	86.60	136.50
❑ 832c	$1	Wilson	23.10	32.80	54.60
❑ 833	$2	Harding	124.00	163.80	252.00
❑ 834	$5	Coolidge	232.05	327.60	546.00
❑ 835	3¢	Constitution	8.95	16.55	22.35
❑ 836	3¢	Swedes and Finns	8.95	16.55	22.35
❑ 837	3¢	Northwest Sesquicentennial	8.95	16.55	22.35
❑ 838	3¢	Iowa	8.95	16.55	22.35
❑ 852	3¢	Golden Gate Expo	8.95	16.55	22.35
❑ 853	3¢	N.Y. World's Fair	8.95	16.55	22.35
❑ 854	3¢	Washington Inauguration	8.95	16.55	22.35
❑ 855	3¢	Baseball Centennial	22.55	32.55	49.35
❑ 856	3¢	Panama Canal	6.55	23.10	16.30
❑ 857	3¢	Printing Tercentenary	6.55	23.10	16.30
❑ 858	3¢	50th Statehood Anniversary	6.55	8.50	16.30
❑ 859	1¢	Washington Irving	4.45	6.85	8.95

Scott No.			Single	Block	Plate Block
❑ 860	2¢	James Fenimore Cooper	6.75	7.70	13.15
❑ 861	3¢	Ralph Waldo Emerson	6.75	7.70	13.15
❑ 862	5¢	Louisa May Alcott	6.75	7.70	13.15
❑ 863	10¢	Samuel L. Clemens	7.60	10.80	24.15
❑ 864	1¢	Henry W. Longfellow	4.50	5.80	15.50
❑ 865	2¢	John Greenleaf Whittier	4.50	5.80	15.50
❑ 866	3¢	James Russell Lowell	4.50	5.80	15.50
❑ 867	5¢	Walt Whitman	4.50	6.85	15.50
❑ 868	10¢	James Whitcomb Riley	6.60	6.85	23.65
❑ 869	1¢	Horace Mann	5.50	7.90	13.40
❑ 870	2¢	Mark Hopkins	5.50	7.90	13.40
❑ 871	3¢	Charles W. Eliot	5.50	7.90	13.40
❑ 872	5¢	Frances E. Willard	4.50	8.95	13.40
❑ 873	10¢	Booker T. Washington	8.95	12.95	27.50
❑ 874	1¢	John James Audubon	4.50	6.75	15.30
❑ 875	2¢	Dr. Crawford W. Long	4.50	6.75	15.30
❑ 876	3¢	Luther Burbank	4.50	6.75	15.30
❑ 877	5¢	Dr. Walter Reed	4.50	6.75	13.20
❑ 878	10¢	Jane Addams	5.75	10.80	23.10
❑ 879	1¢	Stephen Collins Foster	5.75	8.90	13.20
❑ 880	2¢	John Philip Sousa	5.75	8.90	13.20
❑ 881	3¢	Victor Herbert	5.75	8.90	13.20
❑ 882	5¢	Edward A. MacDowell	4.20	6.50	13.20
❑ 883	10¢	Ethelbert Nevin	7.90	10.80	23.70
❑ 884	1¢	Gilbert Charles Stuart	4.75	5.50	11.30
❑ 885	2¢	James A. McNeill Whistler	4.75	5.50	11.30
❑ 886	3¢	Augustus Saint-Gaudens	4.75	5.50	11.30
❑ 887	5¢	Daniel Chester French	4.75	5.50	15.75
❑ 888	10¢	Frederic Remington	6.75	9.00	22.60
❑ 889	1¢	Eli Whitney	5.80	9.00	16.60
❑ 890	2¢	Samuel F.B. Morse	5.80	9.00	16.60
❑ 891	3¢	Cyrus Hall McCormick	5.80	9.00	16.60
❑ 892	5¢	Elias Howe	4.40	9.00	22.60
❑ 893	10¢	Alexander Graham Bell	7.55	11.30	38.00
❑ 894	3¢	Pony Express	7.10	11.30	16.60
❑ 895	3¢	Pan American Union	7.10	11.30	16.60
❑ 896	3¢	Idaho Statehood	7.10	11.30	16.60
❑ 897	3¢	Wyoming Statehood	7.10	11.30	16.60
❑ 898	3¢	Coronado Expedition	7.10	11.30	16.60
❑ 899	1¢	Defense	7.10	11.30	16.60

Scott No.			Single	Block	Plate Block
❑ 900	2¢	Defense	7.70	9.00	17.60
❑ 901	3¢	Defense	7.70	9.00	17.60
❑ 899–901		Defense set on one cover	8.95	11.30	—
❑ 902	3¢	Thirteenth Amendment	8.95	11.30	17.60
❑ 903	3¢	Vermont Statehood	8.95	11.30	17.60
❑ 904	3¢	Kentucky Statehood	5.80	6.60	13.15
❑ 905	3¢	"Win the War"	5.80	9.20	13.15
❑ 906	5¢	Chinese Commemorative	8.95	13.15	20.00
❑ 907	2¢	United Nations	5.80	7.85	10.75
❑ 908	1¢	Four Freedoms	7.85	11.80	15.50
❑ 909	5¢	Poland	7.85	11.80	15.50
❑ 910	5¢	Czechoslovakia	7.85	11.80	15.50
❑ 911	5¢	Norway	7.85	11.80	15.50
❑ 912	5¢	Luxembourg	7.85	11.80	15.50
❑ 913	5¢	Netherlands	7.85	11.80	15.50
❑ 914	5¢	Belgium	7.85	11.80	15.50
❑ 915	5¢	France	7.85	11.80	15.50
❑ 916	5¢	Greece	7.35	11.80	15.50
❑ 917	5¢	Yugoslavia	7.85	11.80	15.50
❑ 918	5¢	Albania	7.85	11.80	15.50
❑ 919	5¢	Austria	7.85	11.80	15.50
❑ 920	5¢	Denmark	7.85	11.80	15.50
❑ 921	5¢	Korea	7.85	11.80	15.50
❑ 922	3¢	Railroad	7.85	11.80	10.50
❑ 923	3¢	Steamship	7.85	11.80	15.50
❑ 924	3¢	Telegraph	7.85	11.80	15.50
❑ 925	3¢	Philippines	7.85	11.80	13.15
❑ 926	3¢	Motion Picture	7.85	11.80	13.15
❑ 927	3¢	Florida	7.85	11.80	13.15
❑ 928	5¢	United Nations Conference	7.85	11.80	13.15
❑ 929	3¢	Iwo Jima	12.20	16.60	22.60
❑ 929, 934–936		Set on one cover	10.00	—	—
❑ 930	1¢	Roosevelt	5.65	8.95	13.15
❑ 931	2¢	Roosevelt	5.65	8.95	13.15
❑ 932	3¢	Roosevelt	5.65	8.95	13.15
❑ 933	5¢	Roosevelt	5.65	8.95	13.15
❑ 930–933		Roosevelt set on one cover	5.65	8.95	9.20
❑ 934	3¢	Army	5.65	8.95	9.20
❑ 935	3¢	Navy	5.65	8.95	9.20
❑ 936	3¢	Coast Guard	5.65	8.95	9.20

Scott No.			Single	Block	Plate Block
❏ 937	3¢	Alfred E. Smith	4.60	5.70	8.95
❏ 938	3¢	Texas	5.70	7.90	13.15
❏ 939	3¢	Merchant Marine	5.70	7.90	13.15
❏ 940	3¢	Honorable Discharge	5.70	7.90	13.15
❏ 941	3¢	Tennessee	5.70	7.90	12.20
❏ 942	3¢	Iowa	5.70	7.90	12.20
❏ 943	3¢	Smithsonian	5.70	7.90	12.20
❏ 944	3¢	Santa Fe	5.70	7.90	12.20
❏ 945	3¢	Thomas A. Edison	5.70	7.90	12.20
❏ 946	3¢	Joseph Pulitzer	5.70	7.90	12.20
❏ 947	3¢	Stamp Centenary	5.70	7.90	12.20
❏ 948	5¢,10¢	Centenary Exhibition Sheet	5.70	7.90	12.20
❏ 949	3¢	Doctors	5.70	7.90	12.20
❏ 950	3¢	Utah	5.70	7.90	12.20
❏ 951	3¢	"Constitution"	5.70	7.90	12.20
❏ 952	3¢	Everglades Park	5.70	7.90	12.20
❏ 953	3¢	Carver	5.70	7.90	12.20
❏ 954	3¢	California Gold	4.50	6.75	8.95
❏ 955	3¢	Mississippi Territory	4.50	6.75	8.95
❏ 956	3¢	Four Chaplains	4.50	6.75	8.95
❏ 957	3¢	Wisconsin Centennial	4.50	6.75	8.95
❏ 958	5¢	Swedish Pioneers	4.50	6.75	8.95
❏ 959	3¢	Women's Progress	4.50	6.75	8.95
❏ 960	3¢	William Allen White	4.50	6.75	8.95
❏ 961	3¢	U.S.-Canada Friendship	4.50	6.75	8.95
❏ 962	3¢	Francis Scott Key	4.50	6.75	8.95
❏ 963	3¢	Salute to Youth	4.50	6.75	8.95
❏ 964	3¢	Oregon Territory	4.50	6.75	8.95
❏ 965	3¢	Harlan Fiske Stone	4.50	6.75	8.95
❏ 966	3¢	Palomar Observatory	4.50	6.75	8.95
❏ 967	3¢	Clara Barton	4.50	6.75	8.95
❏ 968	3¢	Poultry Industry	4.50	6.75	8.95
❏ 969	3¢	Gold Star Mothers	4.50	6.75	8.95
❏ 970	3¢	Volunteer Fireman	4.50	6.75	13.25
❏ 971	3¢	Ft. Kearney, Nebraska	4.50	6.75	9.00
❏ 972	3¢	Indian Centennial	4.50	6.75	9.00
❏ 973	3¢	Rough Riders	4.50	6.75	9.00
❏ 974	3¢	Juliette Low	4.50	6.75	10.75
❏ 975	3¢	Will Rogers	4.50	6.75	9.00
❏ 976	3¢	Fort Bliss	4.50	6.75	9.00

Scott No.			Single	Block	Plate Block
❏ 977	3¢	Moina Michael	4.50	5.70	8.70
❏ 978	3¢	Gettysburg Address	4.50	5.70	8.70
❏ 979	3¢	American Turners Society	4.50	5.70	8.70
❏ 980	3¢	Joel Chandler Harris	4.50	5.70	8.70
❏ 981	3¢	Minnesota Territory	4.50	5.70	8.70
❏ 982	3¢	Washington and Lee University	4.50	5.70	8.70
❏ 983	3¢	Puerto Rico Election	4.50	5.70	8.70
❏ 984	3¢	Annapolis, Md.	4.50	5.70	8.70
❏ 985	3¢	G.A.R.	4.50	5.70	8.70
❏ 986	3¢	Edgar Allan Poe	4.50	5.70	8.70
❏ 987	3¢	American Bankers Association	4.50	5.70	8.70
❏ 988	3¢	Samuel Gompers	4.50	5.70	8.70
❏ 989	3¢	Freedom Statue	4.50	5.70	8.70
❏ 990	3¢	Executive	4.50	5.70	8.70
❏ 991	3¢	Judicial	4.50	5.70	8.70
❏ 992	3¢	Legislative	4.50	5.70	8.70
❏ 989–992		Capital set on one cover	4.50	5.70	8.70
❏ 993	3¢	Railroad Engineers	4.50	5.70	8.70
❏ 994	3¢	Kansas City Centenary	4.50	5.70	8.70
❏ 995	3¢	Boy Scout	4.50	8.95	13.15
❏ 996	3¢	Indiana Ter. Sesquicentennial	4.50	6.60	8.85
❏ 997	3¢	California Statehood	4.50	6.60	8.85
❏ 998	3¢	United Confederate Veterans	4.50	6.60	8.85
❏ 999	3¢	Nevada Centennial	4.50	6.60	8.85
❏ 1000	3¢	Landing of Cadillac	4.50	6.60	8.85
❏ 1001	3¢	Colorado Statehood	4.50	6.60	8.85
❏ 1002	3¢	American Chemical Society	4.50	6.60	8.85
❏ 1003	3¢	Battle of Brooklyn	4.50	6.60	8.85
❏ 1004	3¢	Betsy Ross	4.50	6.60	8.85
❏ 1005	3¢	4-H Clubs	4.50	6.60	8.85
❏ 1006	3¢	B & O Railroad	4.50	6.60	8.85
❏ 1007	3¢	American Automobile Assoc.	4.50	6.60	8.85
❏ 1008	3¢	NATO	4.50	6.60	8.85
❏ 1009	3¢	Grand Coulee Dam	4.50	6.60	8.85
❏ 1010	3¢	Lafayette	4.50	6.60	8.85
❏ 1011	3¢	Mt. Rushmore Memorial	4.50	6.60	8.85
❏ 1012	3¢	Civil Engineers	4.50	6.60	8.85
❏ 1013	3¢	Service Women	4.50	6.60	8.85
❏ 1014	3¢	Gutenberg Bible	4.50	6.60	8.85
❏ 1015	3¢	Newspaper Boys	4.50	6.60	8.85

Scott No.			Single	Block	Plate Block
❏ 1016	3¢	Red Cross	4.60	6.70	8.95
❏ 1017	3¢	National Guard	4.60	6.70	8.95
❏ 1018	3¢	Ohio Sesquicentennial	4.60	6.70	8.95
❏ 1019	3¢	Washington Territory	4.60	6.70	8.95
❏ 1020	3¢	Louisiana Purchase	4.60	6.70	8.95
❏ 1021	5¢	Opening of Japan	4.60	6.70	8.95
❏ 1022	3¢	American Bar Association	4.60	6.70	8.95
❏ 1023	3¢	Sagamore Hill	4.60	6.70	8.95
❏ 1024	3¢	Future Farmers	4.60	6.70	8.95
❏ 1025	3¢	Trucking Industry	4.60	6.70	8.95
❏ 1026	3¢	Gen. George S. Patton, Jr.	4.60	6.70	8.95
❏ 1027	3¢	New York City	4.60	6.70	8.95
❏ 1028	3¢	Gadsden Purchase	4.60	6.70	8.95
❏ 1029	3¢	Columbia University	4.60	6.70	8.95
❏ 1030	½¢	Franklin	—	3.95	5.40
❏ 1031	1¢	Washington	—	3.95	5.40
❏ 1031a	1¼¢	Palace of Governors	—	3.95	5.40
❏ 1032	1½¢	Mount Vernon	—	3.95	5.40
❏ 1033	2¢	Jefferson	—	3.95	5.40
❏ 1034	2½¢	Bunker Hill	—	3.95	5.40
❏ 1035	3¢	Statue of Liberty	4.60	5.50	7.90
❏ 1036	4¢	Lincoln	4.60	5.50	7.90
❏ 1037	4½¢	Hermitage	4.60	5.50	7.90
❏ 1038	5¢	Monroe	4.60	5.50	7.90
❏ 1039	6¢	Roosevelt	4.60	5.50	7.90
❏ 1040	7¢	Wilson	4.60	5.50	7.90
❏ 1041	8¢	Statue of Liberty	4.60	5.50	7.90
❏ 1042	8¢	Statue of Liberty	4.60	5.50	7.90
❏ 1042a	8¢	Pershing	4.60	5.70	8.70
❏ 1043	9¢	The Alamo	4.60	6.70	7.90
❏ 1044	10¢	Independence Hall	4.60	6.70	7.90
❏ 1045	12¢	Harrison	4.60	6.70	7.90
❏ 1046	15¢	John Jay	4.60	6.70	7.90
❏ 1047	20¢	Monticello	4.60	6.70	7.90
❏ 1048	25¢	Paul Revere	4.60	6.70	7.90
❏ 1049	30¢	Robert E. Lee	5.40	7.90	8.95
❏ 1050	40¢	John Marshall	5.40	8.95	10.80
❏ 1051	50¢	Susan Anthony	7.90	13.15	24.15
❏ 1052	$1	Patrick Henry	13.15	19.50	24.15
❏ 1053	$5	Alexander Hamilton	54.60	107.10	136.50

Scott No.			Single	Block	Plate Block
❑ 1054	1¢	Washington (coil)	3.30	—	—
❑ 1055	2¢	Jefferson (coil)	3.30	—	—
❑ 1056	2½¢	Bunker Hill (coil)	3.30	—	—
❑ 1057	3¢	Statue of Liberty (coil)	3.30	—	—
❑ 1058	4¢	Lincoln (coil)	3.30	—	—
❑ 1059	4½¢	The Hermitage (coil)	3.30	—	—
❑ 1059a	25¢	Paul Revere (coil)	3.30	—	—
❑ 1060	3¢	Nebraska Territory	3.30	5.55	6.60
❑ 1061	3¢	Kansas Territory	3.30	5.55	6.60
❑ 1062	3¢	George Eastman	3.30	5.55	6.60
❑ 1063	3¢	Lewis & Clark	3.30	5.55	6.60
❑ 1064	3¢	Pennsylvania Academy	3.30	5.55	6.60
❑ 1065	3¢	Land Grant Colleges	3.30	5.55	7.90
❑ 1066	8¢	Rotary International	3.40	5.55	7.90
❑ 1067	3¢	Armed Forces Reserve	2.90	5.55	7.90
❑ 1068	3¢	New Hampshire	2.90	6.05	7.90
❑ 1069	3¢	Soo Locks	2.90	6.05	7.90
❑ 1070	3¢	Atoms for Peace	2.90	6.05	7.90
❑ 1071	3¢	Fort Ticonderoga	2.90	6.05	7.90
❑ 1072	3¢	Andrew W. Mellon	2.90	6.05	7.90
❑ 1073	3¢	Benjamin Franklin	2.90	6.05	7.90
❑ 1074	3¢	Booker T. Washington	2.90	6.05	7.90
❑ 1075	3¢, 8¢	FIPEX Souvenir Sheet	11.05	—	—
❑ 1076	3¢	FIPEX	2.90	5.55	6.80
❑ 1077	3¢	Wildlife (Turkey)	2.90	5.55	6.80
❑ 1078	3¢	Wildlife (Antelope)	2.90	5.55	6.80
❑ 1079	3¢	Wildlife (Salmon)	2.90	5.55	6.80
❑ 1080	3¢	Pure Food and Drug Laws	2.90	5.55	6.80
❑ 1081	3¢	Wheatland	2.90	5.55	6.80
❑ 1082	3¢	Labor Day	2.90	5.55	6.80
❑ 1083	3¢	Nassau Hall	2.90	5.55	6.80
❑ 1084	3¢	Devil's Tower	2.90	5.55	6.80
❑ 1085	3¢	Children	2.90	5.55	6.80
❑ 1086	3¢	Alexander Hamilton	2.90	5.55	6.80
❑ 1087	3¢	Polio	2.90	5.55	7.90
❑ 1088	3¢	Coast & Geodetic Survey	2.90	4.50	7.90
❑ 1089	3¢	Architects	2.90	4.50	7.90
❑ 1090	3¢	Steel Industry	2.90	4.50	7.90
❑ 1091	3¢	Naval Review	2.90	4.50	7.90
❑ 1092	3¢	Oklahoma Statehood	2.90	4.50	7.90

Scott No.			Single	Block	Plate Block
❑ 1093	3¢	School Teachers	3.15	5.00	8.50
❑ 1094	4¢	Flag	3.15	5.00	8.50
❑ 1095	3¢	Shipbuilding	3.15	5.00	8.50
❑ 1096	8¢	Ramon Magsaysay	3.15	5.00	8.50
❑ 1097	3¢	Lafayette Bicentenary	3.15	5.00	8.50
❑ 1098	3¢	Wildlife (Whooping Crane)	3.15	5.00	8.50
❑ 1099	3¢	Religious Freedom	3.15	5.00	8.50
❑ 1100	3¢	Gardening Horticulture	3.15	5.00	8.50
❑ 1104	3¢	Brussels Exhibition	3.15	5.00	8.50
❑ 1105	3¢	James Monroe	3.15	5.00	8.50
❑ 1106	3¢	Minnesota Statehood	3.15	5.00	8.50
❑ 1107	3¢	International Geophysical Year	3.15	5.00	8.50
❑ 1108	3¢	Gunston Hall	3.15	5.00	8.50
❑ 1109	3¢	Mackinac Bridge	3.15	5.00	8.50
❑ 1110	4¢	Simon Bolivar	3.15	5.00	8.50
❑ 1111	8¢	Simon Bolivar	3.15	5.00	8.50
❑ 1110–1111		Bolivar set on one cover	3.15	5.00	8.50
❑ 1112	4¢	Atlantic Cable	2.55	5.00	8.50
❑ 1113	1¢	Lincoln Sesquicentennial	2.55	5.00	8.50
❑ 1114	3¢	Lincoln Sesquicentennial	2.55	5.00	8.50
❑ 1115	4¢	Lincoln-Douglas Debates	2.55	5.00	6.85
❑ 1116	4¢	Lincoln Sesquicentennial	2.55	5.00	6.85
❑ 1113–1116		Lincoln set on one cover	8.50	5.00	—
❑ 1117	4¢	Lajos Kossuth	2.75	5.00	6.85
❑ 1118	8¢	Lajos Kossuth	2.75	5.00	6.85
❑ 1117–1118		Kossuth set on one cover	2.75	—	—
❑ 1119	4¢	Freedom of Press	2.55	4.75	6.85
❑ 1120	4¢	Overland Mail	2.55	4.75	6.85
❑ 1121	4¢	Noah Webster	2.55	4.75	6.85
❑ 1122	4¢	Forest Conservation	2.55	4.75	6.85
❑ 1123	4¢	Fort Duquesne	2.55	4.75	6.85
❑ 1124	4¢	Oregon Statehood	2.55	4.75	6.85
❑ 1125	4¢	San Martin	2.55	4.75	6.85
❑ 1126	8¢	San Martin	2.55	4.75	6.85
❑ 1125–1126		San Martin set on one cover	2.55	4.75	6.85
❑ 1127	4¢	NATO	2.55	4.75	6.85
❑ 1128	4¢	Arctic Explorations	2.55	4.75	6.85
❑ 1129	8¢	World Trade	2.55	4.75	6.85
❑ 1130	4¢	Silver Centennial	2.55	4.75	6.85
❑ 1131	4¢	St. Lawrence Seaway	2.55	4.75	6.85

Scott No.			Single	Block	Plate Block
❏ 1132	4¢	Flag	2.55	4.75	5.55
❏ 1133	4¢	Soil Conservation	2.55	4.75	5.55
❏ 1134	4¢	Petroleum Industry	3.15	5.10	6.55
❏ 1135	4¢	Dental Health	3.15	5.10	6.55
❏ 1136	4¢	Reuter	3.15	5.10	6.05
❏ 1137	8¢	Reuter	3.15	5.10	6.05
❏ 1136–1137		Reuter set on one cover	4.20	5.10	6.05
❏ 1138	4¢	Dr. Ephraim McDowell	2.75	5.10	6.05
❏ 1139	4¢	Washington "Credo"	2.75	5.10	6.05
❏ 1140	4¢	Franklin "Credo"	2.75	5.10	6.05
❏ 1141	4¢	Jefferson "Credo"	2.75	5.10	6.30
❏ 1142	4¢	Francis Scott Key "Credo"	2.75	5.10	6.30
❏ 1143	4¢	Lincoln "Credo"	2.75	5.10	6.30
❏ 1144	4¢	Patrick Henry "Credo"	2.75	5.10	6.30
❏ 1145	4¢	Boy Scouts	2.90	5.10	6.30
❏ 1146	4¢	Olympic Winter Games	2.55	5.10	6.25
❏ 1147	4¢	Masaryk	2.55	5.10	6.25
❏ 1148	8¢	Masaryk	2.55	5.10	6.25
❏ 1147–1148		Masaryk set on one cover	3.15	5.10	—
❏ 1149	4¢	World Refugee Year	2.55	5.10	7.10
❏ 1150	4¢	Water Conservation	2.55	5.10	7.10
❏ 1151	4¢	SEATO	2.55	5.10	7.10
❏ 1152	4¢	American Woman	2.55	5.10	7.10
❏ 1153	4¢	50-Star Flag	2.55	5.10	7.10
❏ 1154	4¢	Pony Express Centennial	2.55	5.10	7.10
❏ 1155	4¢	Employ the Handicapped	2.55	5.10	7.10
❏ 1156	4¢	World Forestry Congress	2.55	5.10	7.10
❏ 1157	4¢	Mexican Independence	2.55	5.10	7.10
❏ 1158	4¢	U.S. Japan Treaty	2.55	5.10	7.10
❏ 1159	4¢	Paderewski	2.55	5.10	7.10
❏ 1160	8¢	Paderewski	2.55	5.10	7.10
❏ 1159–1160		Paderewski set on one cover	3.15	5.10	7.10
❏ 1161	4¢	Robert A. Taft	2.55	5.10	7.10
❏ 1162	4¢	Wheels of Freedom	2.55	5.10	7.10
❏ 1163	4¢	Boys' Clubs	2.55	5.10	7.10
❏ 1164	4¢	Automated P.O.	2.55	5.10	7.10
❏ 1165	4¢	Mannerheim	2.55	5.10	7.10
❏ 1166	8¢	Mannerheim	2.55	5.10	7.10
❏ 1165–1166		Mannerheim set on one cover	3.15	5.10	7.10
❏ 1167	4¢	Camp Fire Girls	2.55	5.10	7.10

Scott No.			Single	Block	Plate Block
❏ 1168	4¢	Garibaldi	2.55	4.65	6.70
❏ 1169	8¢	Garibaldi	2.55	4.65	6.70
❏ 1168–1169		Garibaldi set on one cover	3.15	4.65	6.70
❏ 1170	4¢	Senator George	2.55	4.65	6.70
❏ 1171	4¢	Andrew Carnegie	2.55	4.65	6.70
❏ 1172	4¢	John Foster Dulles	2.55	4.65	6.70
❏ 1173	4¢	Echo I	2.55	4.65	6.70
❏ 1174	4¢	Gandhi	2.55	4.65	6.70
❏ 1175	8¢	Gandhi	2.55	4.65	6.70
❏ 1174–1175		Gandhi set on one cover	4.50	—	6.70
❏ 1176	4¢	Range Conservation	2.55	4.50	6.70
❏ 1177	4¢	Horace Greeley	2.55	4.50	6.70
❏ 1178	4¢	Fort Sumter	4.20	5.60	6.70
❏ 1179	4¢	Battle of Shiloh	4.20	5.60	6.70
❏ 1180	5¢	Battle of Gettysburg	4.20	5.60	6.70
❏ 1181	5¢	Battle of Wilderness	4.20	5.60	6.70
❏ 1182	5¢	Appomattox	4.20	5.60	6.70
❏ 1179–1182		Set on one cover	13.15	—	6.70
❏ 1183	4¢	Kansas Statehood	3.05	5.60	6.70
❏ 1184	4¢	Senator Norris	3.40	4.45	6.70
❏ 1185	4¢	Naval Aviation	3.40	3.80	6.70
❏ 1186	4¢	Workmen's Compensation	3.40	3.80	6.70
❏ 1187	4¢	Frederic Remington	3.40	3.80	6.70
❏ 1188	4¢	China Republic	4.95	6.50	8.95
❏ 1189	4¢	Naismith	8.95	11.05	13.40
❏ 1190	4¢	Nursing	9.45	13.40	20.00
❏ 1191	4¢	New Mexico Statehood	2.75	4.50	5.55
❏ 1192	4¢	Arizona Statehood	2.75	4.50	5.55
❏ 1193	4¢	Project Mercury	2.90	5.90	8.15
❏ 1194	4¢	Malaria Eradication	2.90	4.75	6.85
❏ 1195	4¢	Charles Evans Hughes	2.90	4.75	6.85
❏ 1196	4¢	Seattle World's Fair	2.90	4.75	6.85
❏ 1197	4¢	Louisiana Statehood	2.90	4.75	6.85
❏ 1198	4¢	Homestead Act	2.90	4.75	6.85
❏ 1199	4¢	Girl Scouts	3.80	5.55	7.65
❏ 1200	4¢	Brien McMahon	2.55	4.60	6.70
❏ 1201	4¢	Apprenticeship	2.55	4.60	6.70
❏ 1202	4¢	Sam Rayburn	2.55	4.60	6.70
❏ 1203	4¢	Dag Hammarskjold	2.55	4.60	6.70
❏ 1204	4¢	Hammarskjold "Error"	5.35	8.95	11.30

Scott No.			Single	Block	Plate Block
❏ 1205	4¢	Christmas	2.55	4.75	6.40
❏ 1206	4¢	Higher Education	2.55	4.75	6.40
❏ 1207	4¢	Winslow Homer	2.55	4.75	6.40
❏ 1208	4¢	Flag	2.55	4.75	6.40
❏ 1209	1¢	Jackson	2.55	4.75	6.40
❏ 1213	5¢	Washington	2.55	4.75	6.40
❏ 1225	1¢	Jackson (coil)	2.55	—	—
❏ 1229	5¢	Washington (coil)	2.55	—	—
❏ 1230	5¢	Carolina Charter	2.55	4.75	6.60
❏ 1231	5¢	Food for Peace	2.55	4.75	6.60
❏ 1232	5¢	West Virginia Statehood	2.55	4.75	6.60
❏ 1233	5¢	Emancipation Proclamation	2.55	4.75	6.60
❏ 1234	5¢	Alliance for Progress	2.55	4.75	6.60
❏ 1235	5¢	Cordell Hull	2.55	4.75	6.60
❏ 1236	5¢	Eleanor Roosevelt	2.55	4.75	6.60
❏ 1237	5¢	Science	2.55	4.75	6.60
❏ 1238	5¢	City Mail Delivery	2.55	4.75	6.60
❏ 1239	5¢	Red Cross	2.55	4.75	6.60
❏ 1240	5¢	Christmas	2.55	4.75	6.60
❏ 1241	5¢	Audubon	2.55	4.75	6.60
❏ 1242	5¢	Sam Houston	2.55	4.75	6.60
❏ 1243	5¢	Charles Russell	2.55	4.75	6.60
❏ 1244	5¢	N.Y. World's Fair	2.55	4.75	6.60
❏ 1245	5¢	John Muir	2.55	4.75	6.60
❏ 1246	5¢	John F. Kennedy	2.55	4.75	6.60
❏ 1247	5¢	New Jersey Tercentenary	2.55	4.75	6.60
❏ 1248	5¢	Nevada Statehood	2.55	4.75	6.60
❏ 1249	5¢	Register & Vote	2.55	4.75	6.60
❏ 1250	5¢	Shakespeare	2.55	4.75	6.60
❏ 1251	5¢	Drs. Mayo	5.35	6.60	8.90
❏ 1252	5¢	American Music	3.45	4.60	6.45
❏ 1253	5¢	Homemakers	2.55	3.80	6.05
❏ 1254–57	5¢	Christmas	2.55	5.45	10.50
❏ 1258	5¢	Verrazano Narrows Bridge	2.55	5.45	7.00
❏ 1259	5¢	Fine Arts	2.55	5.45	7.00
❏ 1260	5¢	Amateur Radio	2.55	5.45	7.00
❏ 1261	5¢	Battle of New Orleans	2.55	5.45	7.00
❏ 1262	5¢	Physical Fitness	2.55	5.45	7.00
❏ 1263	5¢	Cancer Crusade	2.55	5.45	7.65
❏ 1264	5¢	Churchill	2.55	4.30	5.90

Scott No.			Single	Block	Plate Block
❑ 1265	5¢	Magna Carta	2.55	4.75	6.50
❑ 1266	5¢	Int'l. Cooperation Year	2.55	4.75	6.50
❑ 1267	5¢	Salvation Army	2.55	4.75	6.50
❑ 1268	5¢	Dante	2.55	4.75	6.50
❑ 1269	5¢	Herbert Hoover	2.55	4.75	6.50
❑ 1270	5¢	Robert Fulton	2.55	4.75	6.50
❑ 1271	5¢	Florida Settlement	2.55	4.75	6.50
❑ 1272	5¢	Traffic Safety	2.55	4.75	6.50
❑ 1273	5¢	Copley	2.55	4.75	6.50
❑ 1274	11¢	Int'l. Telecommunication Union	2.55	3.80	7.10
❑ 1275	5¢	Adlai Stevenson	2.55	3.80	7.10
❑ 1276	5¢	Christmas	2.55	3.80	7.10
❑ 1278	1¢	Jefferson	2.55	3.80	7.10
❑ 1279	1¼¢	Gallatin	2.55	3.80	7.10
❑ 1280	2¢	Wright	2.55	3.80	7.10
❑ 1281	3¢	Parkman	2.55	3.80	7.10
❑ 1282	4¢	Lincoln	2.55	3.80	7.10
❑ 1283	5¢	Washington	2.55	3.80	7.10
❑ 1283b	5¢	Washington	2.55	3.80	7.10
❑ 1284	6¢	Roosevelt	2.55	3.80	7.10
❑ 1285	8¢	Einstein	2.55	3.80	7.10
❑ 1286	10¢	Jackson	2.55	4.45	7.10
❑ 1286a	12¢	Ford	2.55	4.45	7.10
❑ 1287	13¢	Kennedy	2.55	5.55	8.70
❑ 1288	15¢	Holmes	2.75	4.05	5.60
❑ 1289	20¢	Marshall	2.75	4.50	7.75
❑ 1290	25¢	Douglas	2.75	4.50	7.75
❑ 1291	30¢	Dewey	2.95	4.85	7.75
❑ 1292	40¢	Paine	4.50	7.45	10.75
❑ 1293	50¢	Stone	4.50	11.05	15.25
❑ 1294	$1	O'Neill	5.00	11.05	15.25
❑ 1295	$5	Moore	54.50	94.50	159.50
❑ 1304	5¢	Washington (coil)	—	2.10 (pr)	5.65 (lp)
❑ 1305	6¢	Roosevelt (coil)	—	2.10 (pr)	5.65 (lp)
❑ 1305c	$1	O'Neill (coil)	—	2.10 (pr)	5.65 (lp)
❑ 1306	5¢	Migratory Bird Treaty	4.50	5.65	6.95
❑ 1307	5¢	Humane Treatment of Animals	4.50	5.65	6.95
❑ 1308	5¢	Indiana Statehood	2.20	4.50	6.95
❑ 1309	5¢	Circus	4.50	5.75	6.95
❑ 1310	5¢	SIPEX	2.20	4.50	5.80

Scott No.			Single	Block	Plate Block
❏ 1311	5¢	SIPEX (sheet)	3.60	4.60	5.90
❏ 1312	5¢	Bill of Rights	3.60	4.60	5.90
❏ 1313	5¢	Polish Millennium	3.60	4.60	5.90
❏ 1314	5¢	National Park Service	3.60	4.60	5.90
❏ 1315	5¢	Marine Corps Reserve	2.55	3.90	5.90
❏ 1316	5¢	Gen'l. Fed. of Women's Clubs	2.55	3.90	5.90
❏ 1317	5¢	Johnny Appleseed	2.55	3.90	5.90
❏ 1318	5¢	Beautification of America	2.55	3.90	5.90
❏ 1319	5¢	Great River Road	2.55	3.90	5.90
❏ 1320	5¢	Savings Bonds	2.55	3.90	5.90
❏ 1321	5¢	Christmas	2.55	3.90	5.90
❏ 1322	5¢	Mary Cassatt	2.55	3.90	5.90
❏ 1323	5¢	National Grange	2.55	3.90	5.90
❏ 1324	5¢	Canada Centenary	2.55	3.90	5.90
❏ 1325	5¢	Erie Canal	2.55	3.90	5.90
❏ 1326	5¢	Search for Peace	2.55	3.90	5.90
❏ 1327	5¢	Thoreau	2.55	3.90	5.90
❏ 1328	5¢	Nebraska Statehood	2.55	3.90	5.90
❏ 1329	5¢	Voice of America	2.55	3.90	5.90
❏ 1330	5¢	Davy Crockett	2.55	3.90	5.90
❏ 1331–32	5¢	Space Accomplishments	13.15	26.25 (pr)	30.65
❏ 1333	5¢	Urban Planning	2.55	3.90	5.90
❏ 1334	5¢	Finland Independence	2.55	3.90	5.90
❏ 1335	5¢	Thomas Eakins	2.55	3.90	5.90
❏ 1336	5¢	Christmas	2.55	3.90	5.90
❏ 1337	5¢	Mississippi Statehood	2.55	3.90	5.90
❏ 1338	6¢	Flag	2.55	3.90	5.90
❏ 1339	6¢	Illinois Statehood	2.55	3.90	5.90
❏ 1340	6¢	Hemis Fair '68	2.55	3.90	5.90
❏ 1341	$1	Airlift	8.50	16.20	22.05
❏ 1342	6¢	Youth-Elks	2.35	4.45	5.55
❏ 1343	6¢	Law and Order	3.80	5.55	9.15
❏ 1344	6¢	Register and Vote	3.80	5.55	9.15
❏ 1345–54	6¢	Historic Flags (on one cover)	11.05	—	17.65
❏ 1345–54		Set on 10 covers	37.80	—	—
❏ 1355	6¢	Disney	13.15	15.60	28.50
❏ 1356	6¢	Marquette	3.40	4.75	6.70
❏ 1357	6¢	Daniel Boone	3.40	4.75	6.70
❏ 1358	6¢	Arkansas River	3.40	4.75	6.70

Scott No.			Single	Block	Plate Block
❑ 1359	6¢	Leif Erikson	2.95	4.40	6.60
❑ 1360	6¢	Cherokee Strip	2.95	4.40	6.60
❑ 1361	6¢	John Trumbull	2.95	4.40	6.60
❑ 1362	6¢	Waterfowl Conservation	2.95	5.50	5.80
❑ 1363	6¢	Christmas	2.95	5.50	5.80
❑ 1364	6¢	American Indian	2.95	5.50	6.30
❑ 1365–68	6¢	Beautification of America	2.95	8.60	13.15
❑ 1369	6¢	American Legion	2.95	6.60	7.55
❑ 1370	6¢	Grandma Moses	2.95	6.60	7.55
❑ 1371	6¢	Apollo 8	4.40	7.70	13.15

NOTE: From No. 1372 to date, most first day covers have a value of $2.10 to $2.65 for single stamps, $3.15 to $4.75 for blocks of four and $4.75 to $5.80 for plate blocks of four.

STAMP COLLECTORS' TERMINOLOGY

Adhesives—A term given to stamps that have gummed backs and are intended to be pasted on articles and items that are to be mailed.

Aerophilately—The collecting of airmail or any form of stamps related to mail carried by air.

Airmail—Any mail carried by air.

Albino—An uncolored embossed impression of a stamp generally found on envelopes.

Approvals—Stamps sent to collectors. They are examined by the collector, who selects stamps to purchase and returns balance with payment for the stamps he retained.

Arrow Block—An arrow-like mark found on blocks of stamps in the selvage. This mark is used as a guide for cutting or perforating stamps.

As-is—A term used when selling a stamp. It means no representation is given as to its condition or authenticity. Buyers should beware.

Backprint—Any printing that may appear on reverse of stamp.

Backstamp—The postmark on the back of a letter indicating what time or date the letter arrived at the post office.

Bantams—A miniature stamp given to a war economy issue of stamps from South Africa.

Batonne—Watermarked paper used in printing stamps.

Bicolored—A two-color printed stamp.

Bisect—A stamp that could be used by cutting in half and at half the face value.

Block—A term used for a series of four or more stamps attached at least two high and two across.

Bourse—A meeting or convention of stamp collectors and dealers where stamps are bought, sold, and traded.

Cachet—A design printed on the face of an envelope, generally celebrating the commemoration of a new postage stamp issue. Generally called a first-day cover.

Cancellation—A marking placed on the face of a stamp to show that it has been used.

Cancelled to Order—A stamp cancelled by the government without being used. Generally remainder stamps or special issues. Common practice of Russian nations.

Centering—The manner in which the design of a stamp is printed and centered upon the stamp blank. A perfectly centered stamp would have equal margins on all sides.

Classic—A popular, unique, highly desired, or very artistic stamp. Not necessarily a rare stamp, but one sought after by the collector. Generally used only for nineteenth-century issues.

Coils—Stamps sold in rolls for use in vending machines.

Commemorative—A stamp issued to commemorate or celebrate a special event.

Crease—A fold or wrinkle in a stamp.

Cut Square—An embossed staple removed from the envelope by cutting.

Dead Country—A country no longer issuing stamps.

Demonetized—A stamp no longer valid for use.

Error—A stamp printed or produced with a major design or color defect.

Essay—Preliminary design for a postage stamp.

Face Value—The value of a stamp indicated on the face or surface of the stamp.

Frank—A marking on the face of an envelope indicating the free and legal use of postage. Generally for government use.

Fugitive Inks—A special ink used to print stamps, which can be rubbed or washed off easily, to eliminate erasures and forgeries.

General Collector—One who collects all kinds of issues and all types of stamps from different countries.

Granite Paper—A type of paper containing colored fibers to prevent forgery.

Gum—The adhesive coating on the back of a stamp.

Handstamped—A stamp that has been handcancelled.

Hinge—A specially gummed piece of glassine paper used to attach a stamp to the album page.

Imperforate—A stamp without perforations.

Inverted—Where one portion of a stamp's design is inverted or upside down from the remainder of the design.

Local Stamps—Stamps that are only valid in a limited area.

Margin—The unprinted area around a stamp.

Miniature Sheet—A smaller-than-usual sheet of stamps.

Mint Condition—A stamp in original condition as it left the postal printing office.

Mirror Print—A stamp error printed in reverse as though looking at a regular stamp reflected in a mirror.

Multicolored—A stamp printed in three or more colors.

Never Hinged—A stamp in original mint condition never hinged in an album.

Off Paper—A used stamp that has been removed from the envelope to which it was attached.

On Paper—A used stamp still attached to the envelope.

Original Gum—A stamp with the same or original adhesive that was applied in the manufacturing process.

Pair—Two stamps unseparated.

Pen Cancellation—A stamp cancelled by pen or pencil.

Perforation Gauge—A printed chart containing various sizes of perforation holes used in determining the type or size of perforation of a stamp.

Perforations—Holes punched along stamp designs allowing stamps to be easily separated.

Philatelist—One who collects stamps.

Pictorial Stamps—Stamps that bear large pictures of animals, birds, flowers, etc.

Plate Block Number—The printing plate number used to identify a block of four or more stamps taken from a sheet of stamps.

Postally Used—A stamp that has been properly used and cancelled.

Precancels—A stamp that has been cancelled in advance. Generally used on bulk mail.

Reissue—A new printing of an old stamp that has been out of circulation.

Revenue Stamp—A label or stamp affixed to an item as evidence of tax payment.

Seals—An adhesive label that looks like a stamp, used for various fund-raising campaigns.

Se-tenant—Two or more stamps joined together, each having a different design or value.

Sheet—A page of stamps as they are printed, usually separated before distribution to post offices.

Soaking—Removing used stamps from paper to which they are attached by soaking in water. (NOTE: Colored cancels may cause staining to other stamps.)

Souvenir Sheet—One or more specially designed stamps printed by the government in celebration of a special stamp.

Splice—The splice made between rolls of paper in the printing operation. Stamps printed on this splice are generally discarded.

Tete-Beche—A pair of stamps printed together so that the images point in opposite vertical directions.

Transit Mark—A mark made by an intermediate post office between the originating and final destination post office.

Typeset Stamp—A stamp printed with regular printer's type, as opposed to engraved, lithographed, etc.

Ungummed—Stamps printed without an adhesive back.

Unhinged—A stamp that has never been mounted with the use of a hinge.

Unperforated—A stamp produced without perforations.

Vignette—The central design portion of a stamp.

Want List—A list of stamps a collector needs to fill gaps in his collection.

Watermark—A mark put into paper by the manufacturer, not readily seen by the naked eye.

Wrapper—A strip of paper with adhesive on one end, used for wrapping bundles of mail. Especially in Great Britain, it refers to any bit of paper to which a used stamp is still attached.

EQUIPMENT

To collect stamps properly a collector will need some "tools of the trade." These need not be expensive and need not all be bought at the very outset. That might, in fact, be the worst thing to do. Many a beginning collector has spent his budget on equipment, only to have little or nothing left for stamps and then loses interest in the hobby.

It may be economical in the long run to buy the finest quality accessories, but few collectors, just starting out, have a clear idea of what they will and will not be needing. It is just as easy to make impulse purchases of accessories as of stamps and just as unwise. Equipment must be purchased on the basis of what sort of collection is being built now, rather than on what the collection may be in the future. There is no shame in working up from an elementary album.

Starter Kits. Starter or beginner outfits are sold in just about every variety shop, drugstore, etc. These come in attractive boxes and contain a juvenile or beginner's album; some stamps, which may be on paper and in need of removal; a packet of gummed hinges; tongs; a pocket stockbook or file; and often other items such as a perforation gauge, booklet on stamp collecting, magnifier, and watermark detector. These kits are specially suited to young collectors and can provide a good philatelic education.

Albums. When the hobby began, more than a century ago, collectors mounted their stamps in whatever albums were at hand. Scrapbooks, school exercise tablets, and diaries all were used, as well as homemade albums. Today a number of firms specialize in printing albums of all kinds for philatelists, ranging from softbounds for the cautious type to huge multi-volume sets that cost hundreds of dollars. There are general worldwide albums, country albums, U.N. albums, and albums for mint sheets, covers, and every other conceivable variety of philatelic material. Choose your album according to the specialty you intend to pursue. It is not necessary, however, to buy a printed album at all. Many collectors feel there is not enough room for creativity in a printed album and prefer to use a binder with unprinted sheets. This allows items to be arranged at will on the page, rather than following the publisher's format, and for a personal write-up to be added. Rod-type binders will prove more durable and satisfactory than ring binders for heavy collections. The pages of an album should not be too thin, unless only one side is used. The presence of tiny crisscrossing lines (quadrilled sheets) is intended as an aid to correct alignment. Once items have been mounted and written up, these lines are scarcely visible and do not interfere with the attractiveness of the page.

Hinges. These are small rectangular pieces of lightweight paper, usually clear or semiopaque, gummed and folded. One side is moistened and affixed to the back of the stamp and the other to the album page. Hinges are sold in packets of 1,000 and are very inexpensive. Though they are by far the most popular device for mounting stamps, the hobbyist has his choice of a number of other products if hinges are not satisfactory to him. These include cello mounts, which encase the stamp in clear sheeting and have a black background to provide a kind of frame. These are self-sticking. Their cost is much higher than hinges. The chief advantage of cello mounts is that they prevent injuries to the stamp and eliminate the moistening necessary in using hinges; however, they add considerably to the weight of each page, making flipping through an album less convenient, and become detached from the page more readily than hinges.

Glassine Interleaving. These are sheets made of thin semitransparent glassine paper, the same used to make envelopes in which stamps are stored. They come punched to fit albums of standard size and are designed to be placed between each set of sheets, to prevent stamps on one page from becoming entangled with those on the facing page. Glassine interleaving is not necessary if cello mounts are used, but any collection mounted with conventional hinges should be interleaved. The cost is small. Glassine interleaving is sold in packets of 100 sheets.

Magnifier. A magnifier is a necessary tool for most stamp collectors, excepting those who specialize in first-day covers or other items that would not likely require study by magnification. There are numerous types and grades on the market, ranging in price from about $1 to more than $20. The quality of magnifier to buy should be governed by the extent to which it is likely to be used, and the collector's dependence upon it for identification and study. A collector of plate varieties ought to have the best magnifier he can afford and carry it whenever visiting dealers, shows, or anywhere that he may wish to examine specimens. A good magnifier is also necessary for a specialist in grilled stamps and for collectors of Civil War and other nineteenth-century covers. Those with built-in illumination are best in these circumstances.

Tongs. Beginners have a habit of picking up stamps with their fingers, which can cause injuries, smudges, and grease stains. Efficient handling of tongs is not difficult to learn, and the sooner the better. Do not resort to ordinary tweezers, but get a pair of philatelic tongs which are specially shaped and of sufficiently large size to be easily manipulated.

Perforation Gauge. A very necessary, inexpensive article, as the identification of many stamps depends upon a correct measuring of their perforations.

TEN LOW-COST WAYS TO START COLLECTING STAMPS

Courtesy of the
American Philatelic Society.

If you have recently started collecting stamps, or are thinking about starting, you may be wondering if the hobby is expensive. Can you enjoy it with limited financial resources? What if you have no money at all for the hobby?

One of the biggest questions any stamp collector faces is where to find stamps inexpensively. If you intend to save stamps of the United States or the world and want to save used as well as unused stamps, the opportunities are really great. Not all collections consist mainly of unused stamps that you buy in the post office. Used stamps are worth saving, have value, and they may cost you nothing.

Many stamp collectors save only used stamps. Others save both used and unused ones. Others save stamps only from one country or one part of the world. Some collectors save stamps by "topic," for example, stamps that depict horses or trains or birds. There are any number of different types of collections.

1. All postally used stamps started out being received in someone's mailbox, at no cost to the person receiving them. The first place to search for stamps, then, is your own mailbox. Don't be discouraged when you notice that many senders use postage meters or the imprint "Bulk Rate Postage Paid" on their envelopes to enjoy a better postal rate or to keep from affixing stamps. Also, when people do use real stamps, they often use the same common small ones.

You can begin to change this by asking people who write to you to use commemorative stamps on their mail. These are normally the larger stamps issued to honor famous people, places, or events. These stamps are printed in lesser quantities than the common smaller (definitive) stamps and usually are of much more interest to collectors. Many people will remember to ask for commemorative stamps at the post office when mailing letters to you or your family if you let them know you are a stamp collector. Also, if you write away for offers that require postage or a self-addressed, stamped envelope, you can put commemoratives on your return envelope, knowing that they will come back to you later.

2. Neighbors, friends, and relatives are another good source of stamps. The majority of people just throw away stamps when they receive them on mail and are only too happy to save them for someone who appreciates them. You may even know someone who gets letters from other countries who can save these stamps, too. Always be on the lookout for potentially good stamp contacts, and don't be afraid to ask them to go through their mail for you before they throw away all the envelopes.

3. Office mail may be even better. You may know someone who works in an office that gets a lot of mail. Out of 100 letters a day, there may be ten or twenty good stamps that are being thrown away. Many businesses get a lot of foreign mail and regularly throw away stamps that have interest and/or value to a collector.

4. Ask friends and coworkers to save envelopes with stamps for you. Youngsters can ask parents if they have any old letters, which may have stamps on the envelopes. When taking stamps off envelopes, always tear off the corner so that there is paper all around the stamp, and the stamp and all its perforations are undamaged. Anyone who is saving stamps for you should be told that this is the way to do it; otherwise, he/she may try to peel the stamp off the envelope. This will cause thin spots or tears, both of which ruin a stamp's appearance and lessen its value to collectors. If you run across envelopes that are very old or have postal markings that may be of particular interest, it is best to save the entire envelope until you can find out if the stamp is worth more attached to the cover.

Now that you have stamps on paper, what do you do with them? The most common way to get stamps off paper is to soak them in cool water, then dry them on paper. To understand more about soaking stamps, refer to the following section, beginning on p. 621.

There is a lot to learn about stamps as you get more and more of them. For example, different shades of color may exist on stamps with the same design, or they may have different perforation measurements (number of holes per side). Major varieties of stamps and "catalog values" are listed in stamp catalogs, which are available in most libraries. The most common one, the Scott Standard Postage Stamp Catalogue, has a very good section in front that explains how stamps are made and how to tell varieties apart, as well as how to use the catalog. Having access to a catalog in a nearby library is very useful until you decide if you want one of your own.

5. Longtime collectors may be another source of stamps. Usually a person who has been a collector for a number of years has developed many sources for stamps. The collector may have thousands of duplicates, some of which may be very inexpensive while others may have more value. Often older collectors are willing to help new philatelists get started by giving them stamps, or at least providing packets of stamps much more cheaply than can be purchased in stores or by mail.

6. Many stamp companies advertise free stamps. However, these ads must be read carefully before you send away for anything. Usually these ads offer "approvals," which means they will send you the free stamps advertised, plus an assortment of other stamps which you may either buy or return. By sending for the free stamps, you have already agreed that you will return the other stamps within a reasonable period of time if you do not buy anything. Usually you must pay the return postage. This is a convenient way to buy stamps from your own home.

7. Stamp clubs are another place to get stamps. A club may offer stamps as prizes, or have inexpensive stamps you can afford to buy.

Some stamp clubs sponsor junior clubs that meet at schools or the local YMCA or community center. If you are fortunate enough to have one of these in your area, it can be a great source of both stamps and advice.

8. One way to increase your sources for stamps and also have a lot of fun is to help start a local club, if one does not already exist. All it takes are four or five other stamp collectors who are interested in getting together to learn about and trade stamps and ideas.

9. Obtaining a pen pal in another country is a very good way to get stamps from that country. His or her extra stamps may seem really common in that country, but over here they are much scarcer. Your own stamps may look fairly common to you, but he or she is sure to appreciate them.

10. Trading off your duplicate stamps can be a lot of fun. Even if you don't know many collectors where you live, stamps are so lightweight that they can easily be traded by mail. Check out the stamp newspapers and magazines available at your local library for classified ads that list stamp trades. You may find, for example, that another collector will send you 100 large foreign stamps if you send 100 U.S. commemoratives. Usually schools do not subscribe to any of the periodical stamp publications, so you will have to go to your public library. (Many stamp publications also offer to send one free sample issue if you request it, because they are always looking for potential new subscribers.)

Collecting stamps need not be an expensive hobby. Thousands of stamps are issued every year, and while some of them cost many dollars, others cost just a few cents each. Nobody expects you to try to save every stamp that exists, and the key to enjoying philately is to save whatever you enjoy the most! With free stamps and a few inexpensive accessories, such as a small album and a package of stamp hinges, even collectors with little money can have a great time. Don't forget to mention stamps, stamp albums, and hinges before your birthday or Christmas! Also remember that a great many inexpensive stamps in the past have turned into more valuable stamps over the years.

THREE TIPS FOR STAMP COLLECTORS:

Soaking Stamps,
Choosing an Album, and Using Tongs.
Courtesy of the American Philatelic Society.

• TIP 1: SOAKING STAMPS

BEFORE SOAKING

Set aside any stamps on colored paper, or on paper with a colored backing. Pick out any stamps with colored cancellations, especially with red or purple ink.

Set aside any dark-colored stamps, stamps on poor-quality paper, or with strange-looking inks that might dissolve in the water and stain other stamps being soaked, etc. Any "problem" stamps must be handled carefully later, one at a time.

Trim the envelope paper close to the stamp, being careful not to cut the perforated edges or otherwise damage the stamp.

SOAKING THE STAMPS

Use a shallow bowl and fill it with several inches of cool-to-lukewarm water. (Never use hot water.) Float the stamps with the picture side up. Make sure the stamps have room to float and do not stick to one another. Don't soak too many at one time.

Let the stamps float until the glue dissolves and the stamps slide easily off the paper. Paper is very weak when it is wet and it's easy to tear a wet stamp if you handle it roughly. Be patient, and let the water do its work!

Rinse the back of the stamp gently in fresh water to make sure all the glue is off. Change the water in the soaking bowl often to make sure it is clean.

Place the stamps to dry on paper towels or old newspapers. (Don't use the Sunday comics! The colored inks might stick to the wet stamps.) It's a good idea to use your stamp tongs (see p. 624) to lift the wet stamps, instead of using your fingers. Lay the stamps in a single layer, and so they are not touching one another.

Let the stamps dry on their own. They may curl a little or look wrinkled, but don't worry about that. When they are completely dry, lift them with your tongs and put them in a phone book or a dictionary or some other book. (Special "stamp drying books" also can be purchased.) It's important not to put the stamps in a book until they are completely dry. After a few days, they should be nice and flat, and you can put them in your collection.

STAMPS ON COLORED PAPER OR WITH COLORED-INK CANCELS

Cut away all the excess envelope paper without harming the edges of the stamp.

Fill a shallow dish with cool water (cooler than you would usually use for soaking) and float the stamp face up. If the water becomes stained before the stamp is free from the paper, empty it out and use clean water, to prevent the stamp from being stained.

Dry as before.

DIRTY OR STAINED STAMPS

These can be soaked carefully in a small amount of undiluted liquid dishwashing detergent (not dishwasher detergent), then rinsed in clean cool water.

Very badly stained stamps can be washed gently in a weak solution of water and a bit of enzyme laundry detergent. Careful! This can work too well and remove the printing ink!

SELF-ADHESIVE STAMPS

Some self-adhesive stamps have a special, water-soluble backing, and they can be soaked off envelopes. You just need extra patience, as they may have to soak for an hour or more before they will separate from the backing paper. In general, U.S. self-adhesive stamps from about 1990 and later can be soaked with water; earlier ones cannot. If you don't want to try soaking, just trim the paper closely around a self-adhesive stamp on cover, and then mount it in your collection with a stamp mount.

• TIP 2: CHOOSING AN ALBUM

You've raided the mailbox, rummaged in the wastebasket in the post office lobby, and pestered your friends to save their envelopes. Now that you have all these philatelic goodies, where will you put them?

True, an ordinary shoebox gives storage space, but you should want a nicer home for your treasures—a place to display your material, not just store it. And, on the practical side, stamps and covers (envelopes with stamps on them, used in the mail) kept in a shoebox or paper folder risk damage from dirt or creases, losing value as well as beauty.

Since the first known commercial stamp album was published in 1862, the stamp hobby has grown tremendously, and many types of albums have become available.

When buying a home for your collection, here are some things to think about:

It may be your first album, but it probably will not be your last or only one. Your first album may be a kind of experiment, unless you already have seen someone else's album and think that kind would be right for you too. You also may have tried homemade pages and got some ideas of what you would want in a standard album.

If you are buying an album in person, rather than by mail, listen to the seller's advice, but don't be fully convinced by claims that one or another album is "the best." An album may be by a famous maker, and expensive, but that doesn't make it "the best" one for you. Be a careful shopper; consider all the factors—appearance, price, format—and make the best choice. Good beginners' albums are available that are not too expensive, are fully illustrated to show which stamp goes where, and may even contain extra information, such as maps and facts about the countries.

Certain styles of albums can present problems. For example, if an album is designed for stamps to be mounted on the front and back of each page, when the book is closed, the stamps can become tangled with one another on the facing pages. Opening the book may tear the mounted stamps apart. If you are looking at an album with this page format and don't like that aspect, but do like other things about the album, buy some good-quality plastic sheets to insert between the pages, and prevent the tangles.

You may choose not to buy a top-of-the-line album because of cost, but do be willing to pay for some quality. An album with pages of flimsy paper will not stand up to the stress of increasing numbers of stamps as you fill the album. An album with torn, falling-out pages is not much better than the old shoebox.

Homemade pages can be experimented with before album-shopping or may even become your permanent storage choice. Some options include a notebook or looseleaf binder of plain paper, though longtime, safest storage of your stamps should be on acid-free paper. If you have an unusual specialty, or enjoy unique arrangements, no standard album may ever suit your needs, and homemade will be best.

Blank, acid-free album pages punched for three-hole binders are widely available. It is easy to assemble a safe, stable home for your personalized collection, if you don't need or want the kind of structured format that standard albums provide. Makers of custom pages and albums advertise regularly in the philatelic press.

Buying an album is not so different from buying anything else: Think before and during the purchase; buy as wisely as you can and not over your budget; and don't be too discouraged if your first acquisition turns out to be less than perfect. You will always need places for temporary storage as you continue in the hobby. Old albums never go to waste!

• TIP 3: USING TONGS

Philatelic tongs (not to be confused with the tweezers in the medicine cabinet) are must-have items for every stamp collector. Get into the habit early of using your tongs every time you work with your stamps. They will act as clean extensions of your fingers and keep dirt, skin oil, and other harmful things from getting on your philatelic paper.

It's important to use tongs correctly and carefully. As with knives, scissors, and other helpful tools, tongs used carelessly are harmful rather than helpful. Cut some plain paper into stamp-sized pieces and practice using your tongs, watching what happens as you change the angle, pressure, and method of using them.

Grip a bit of paper strongly with the pointy-end style of tongs and watch what happens. If that were a favorite stamp, would you have wanted that hole poked in the middle of it? Keep experimenting, and you will find that it's not difficult to hold a stamp firmly but gently with tongs.

There are several common styles of tongs to suit your preference and for special purposes.

Some have very pointed ends; they touch only a tiny part of the stamp, but there is the risk of poking holes through it. Working with extra-long tongs (five or six inches) with small pointed tips requires a lot of dexterity, and while experts may prefer them, they may not be comfortable or necessary for "everyday" stamp work.

The rounded, spatula-type style known as the "spade" are good, general-purpose tongs. A squared-off version of the spade also is commonly available, though the rather sharp corners present the same kind of risk as the thin, pointy tongs. One handy style is angled, with a bend near the tips that makes it easier to remove stamps from watermark or soaking trays, or to insert and remove stamps from stockbooks or mounts.

Tongs cost anywhere from a couple of dollars to quite a few for some of the imported, high-quality models. A special gift for a philatelist would be some gold-plated tongs, which are not hard to find, believe it or not! Tongs can be found anywhere stamp supplies are sold; check under "Accessories" in the philatelic press ads.

Tongs are among the least expensive and most essential stamp-hobby needs. You may even want to have several different kinds on hand—instead of your hands! Your stamps will appreciate it.

BUYING STAMPS

There are many ways to buy stamps: packets, poundage mixtures, approvals, new issue services, auctions, and a number of others. To buy wisely, a collector must get to know the language of philately and the techniques used by dealers and auctioneers in selling stamps.

Packets of all different worldwide stamps are sold in graduated sizes from 1,000 up to 50,000. True to their word, they contain no duplicates. The stamps come from all parts of the world and date from the 1800s to the present. Both mint and used are included. When you buy larger quantities of most things, a discount is offered; with stamp packets, it works in reverse. The larger the packet, the higher its price per stamp. This is because the smaller packets are filled almost exclusively with low-grade material.

Packets are suitable only as a collection base. A collector should never count on them to build his entire collection. The contents of one worldwide packet are much like that of another. Country jackets are sold in smaller sizes, but there are certain drawbacks with packets.

1. Most packets contain some cancelled-to-order stamps, which are not very desirable for a collection. These are stamps released with postmarks already on them, and are classified as used but have never gone through the mail. Eastern Europe and Russia are responsible for many C.T.O.s.

2. The advertised value of packets bears little relation to the actual value. Packet makers call attention to the catalog values of their stamps, based on prices listed in standard reference works. The lowest sum at which a stamp can be listed in these books is 2¢; therefore, a packet of 1,000 automatically has a minimum catalog value of $20. If the retail price is $3 this seems like a terrific buy when, in fact, most of those thousand stamps are so common they are almost worthless.

Poundage mixtures are very different than packets. Here the stamps are all postally used (no C.T.O.s) and still attached to small fragments of envelopes or parcel wrappings. Rather than sold by count, poundage mixtures are priced by the pound or ounce and quite often by kilos. Price varies depending on the grade, and the grade depends on where the mixture was assembled. Bank mixtures are considered the best, as banks receive a steady flow of foreign registered mail. Mission mixtures are also highly rated. Of course, the mixture should be sealed and unpicked. Unless a mixture is advertised as unpicked, the high values have been removed. The best poundage mixtures are sold only by mail. Those available in shops are of medium or low quality. Whatever the grade, poundage mixtures can be counted on to contain duplicates.

If you want to collect the stamps of a certain country, you can leave a standing order for its new releases with a new-issue service. Whenever that government puts out stamps, they will be sent to the collector along with a bill. Usually the service will supply only mint copies. The price charged is not the face value, but the face value with a surcharge added to meet the costs of importing, handling, and the like. New issue services are satisfactory only if the collector is positive he wants all the country's stamps, no matter what. Remember that its issues could include semipostals, long and maybe expensive sets, and extra high values.

By far the most popular way to buy stamps is via approvals. There is nothing new about approvals, as they go back to the Victorian era. Not all services are alike, though. Some offer sets, while others sell penny approvals. Then there are remainder approvals, advanced approvals, and seconds on approval. Penny approvals are really a thing of the past, though the term is still used. Before inflation, dealers would send a stockbook containing several thousand stamps, all priced at a penny each. If all the stamps were kept, the collector got a discount plus the book! Today the same sort of service can be found, but instead of 1¢ per stamp, the price is anywhere from 3¢ to 10¢. Remainder approvals are made up from collection remainders. Rather than dismount and sort stamps from incoming collections, the approval merchant saves himself time by sending them out right on the album pages. The collector receives leaves from someone else's collection with stamps mounted just as he arranged them. Seconds on approval are slightly defective specimens of scarce stamps, which would cost more if perfect. Advanced approvals are designed for specialized collectors who know exactly what they want and have a fairly substantial stamp budget.

In choosing an approval service you should know the ground rules of approval buying and not be unduly influenced by promotional offers. Most approval merchants allow the selections to be kept for ten days to two weeks. The unbought stamps are then returned along with payment for those kept. As soon as the selection is received back, another is mailed. This will go on, regardless of how much or how little is bought, until the company is notified to refrain from sending further selections. The reputable services will always stop when told.

Approval ads range from splashy full-pagers in the stamp publications to small three-line classified announcements in magazines and newspapers. Most firms catering to beginners offer loss leaders, or stamps on which they take a loss for the sake of getting new customers. If an approval dealer offers 100 pictorials for a dime, it is obvious he is losing money on that transaction, as 10¢ will not even pay the postage. It is very tempting to order these premiums. Remember that when ordering approvals. What sort of service is it? Will it offer the kind of stamps desired? Will prices be high to pay for the loss leaders? Be careful of confusing advertisements. Sometimes the premium offers seem to promise more than they actually do. A rare, early stamp may be pictured. Of course you do not receive the stamp, but merely a modern commemorative picturing it.

Auction Sales. Stamp auctions are held all over the country and account for millions of dollars in sales annually. Buying at auction is exciting and can be economical. Many sleepers turn up—stamps that can be bought at less than their actual value. To be a good auction buyer, the philatelist must know stamps and their prices pretty well, and know the ropes of auctions. An obvious drawback of auctions is that purchases are not returnable. A dealer will take back a stamp that proves not to a collector's liking, but an auctioneer will not. Also, auctioneers require immediate payment while a dealer may extend credit.

Stamps sold at auction come from private collections and the stocks of dealers; not necessarily defunct dealers, but those who want to get shelf space. Because they were brought together from a variety of sources, the nature and condition will vary. In catalog descriptions the full book value will be given for each stamp, but of course defective stamps will sell for much less than these figures. A bidder must calculate how much less. Other lots which can be difficult for the bidder to evaluate are those containing more than one stamp. Sometimes a superb specimen will be lotted along with a defective one. Then there are bulk lots which contain odds and ends from collections and such. It is usual in auctioning a collection for the better stamps to be removed and sold separately. The remainder is then offered in a single lot, which may consist of thousands or even tens of thousands of stamps. By all means examine lots before bidding. A period of inspection is always allowed before each sale, usually for several days. There may or may not be an inspection on sale day. If the bidder is not able to make a personal examination but must bid on strength of the catalog description, he should scale his bids for bulk lots much lower than for single stamp lots. He might bid $50 on a single stamp lot with a catalog value of $100, if the condition is listed as top-notch, but to bid one-half catalog value on a bulk lot would not be very wise. These lots are not scrutinized very carefully by the auctioneers and some stamps are bound to be disappointing. There may be some heavily canceled, creased, torn, etc. Also, there will very likely be duplication. A bid of one-fifth the catalog value on a bulk lot is considered high. Often a one-tenth bid is successful.

The mechanics of stamp auctions may strike the beginner as complicated. They are run no differently than other auctions. All material to be sold is lotted by the auctioneer; that is, broken down into lots or units and bidding is by lot. Everything in the lot must be bid on, even if just one of the stamps is desired. The motive of bulk lotting is to save time and give each lot a fair sales value.

Before the sale a catalog is published listing all the lots, describing the contents and sometimes picturing the better items. Catalogs are in the mail about thirty days before the sale date. If a bid is to be mailed, it must be sent early. Bids that arrive after the sale are disqualified, even if they would have been successful.

When the bid is received it is entered into a bidbook, along with the bidder's name and address. On sale day each lot opens on the floor at one level above the second-highest mail bid. Say the two highest mail bids are $30 and $20. The floor bidding would begin at $25. If the two highest bids are $100 and $500, the opening bid would probably be $150. The larger the amounts involved, the bigger will be the advances. The auctioneer will not accept an advance of $5 on a $500 lot; but on low-value lots even dollar advances are sometimes made. Then it becomes a contest of floor versus book. The auctioneer acts as an agent, bidding for the absentee until his limit is reached. If the floor tops him, he has lost. If the floor does not get as high as his bid, he wins the lot at one advance over the highest floor bid.

When a collector buys stamps by mail from a dealer, he should choose one who belongs to the American Stamp Dealers' Association or A.S.D.A. The emblem is carried in their ads.

HOW TO ORDER STAMPS "TOLL-FREE" FROM THE USPS

You can now order stamps, toll-free, from the USPS by calling the Philatelic Fulfillment Service Center located in Kansas City, Missouri, 1-800-782-6724. Listening to a computerized voice, you can choose from six options using a touch-tone phone: 1) ordering stamps, 2) catalog requests, subscription programs information, 3) customer assistance, 4) personalized envelopes, post offices and official mail agencies. This is a very useful service. It is recommended that you first order one of the catalogs, "Stamps, Etc." or "Not Just Stamps," in order to correctly place your order for stamps.

SELLING STAMPS

Almost every collector becomes a stamp seller sooner or later. Duplicates are inevitably accumulated, no matter how careful one may be in avoiding them. Then there are the G and VG stamps that have been replaced with F and VF specimens, and have become duplicates by intent. In addition to duplicates, a more advanced collector is likely to have stamps that are not duplicates but for which he has no further use. These will be odds and ends, sometimes quite valuable ones, that once suited the nature of his collection but are now out of place. Collectors' tastes change. The result is a stockpile of stamps that can be converted back to cash.

The alternative to selling the stamps you no longer need or want is trading them with a collector who does want them, and taking his unwanted stamps in return. All stamp clubs hold trading sessions. Larger national stamp societies operate trade-by-mail services for their members. The APS (American Philatelic Society) keeps $8,000,000 worth of stamps constantly circulating in its trading books or "circuit" books. Trading can be an excellent way of disposing of surplus stamps. In most cases it takes a bit longer than selling. Another potential drawback, especially if you are not a club member, is finding the right person with the right stamps.

The nature and value of the material involved may help in deciding whether to sell outright or trade. Also, there are your own personal considerations. If you're not going to continue in the stamp hobby, or need cash for some purpose other than stamp buying, trading is hardly suitable. Likewise, if you have developed an interest in some very exotic group of stamps or other philatelic items it may be impossible to find someone to trade with.

Once you have decided to sell, if indeed you do make that decision, the matter revolves upon how. To a stamp shop? To another collector? Through an auction house? Possibly by running your own advertisements and issuing price lists, if you have enough stamps and spare time to make this worthwhile?

While some individuals have an absolute horror at the prospect of selling anything, stamp collectors tend to enjoy selling. It is difficult to say why. Some enjoy it so much they keep right on selling stamps, as a business, long after their original objective is achieved. Nearly all professional stamp dealers were collectors before entering the trade.

Selling your stamps outright to a dealer, especially a local dealer whom you can personally visit, is not necessarily the most financially rewarding but it is quick and very problem-free. Of course it helps if the dealer knows you and it's even better if he knows some of your stamps. Dealers have no objection to repurchasing stamps they've sold to you. You will find that the dealers encourage their customers to sell to them just as much as they encourage them to buy. The dealers are really anxious to get your stamps if you have good salable material from popular countries. In fact most dealers would prefer buying from the public rather than any other source.

The collector selling stamps to a dealer has to be reasonable in his expectations. A dealer may not be able to use all the stamps you have. It is simply not smart business for a dealer to invest money in something he may not be able to sell. So, if you have esoteric or highly specialized items for sale, it might be necessary to find a specialist who deals in those particular areas rather than selling to a neighborhood stamp shop.

The local stamp shop will almost certainly want to buy anything you can offer in the way of medium-to-better-grade U.S. stamps of all kinds, including the so-called "back of the book" items. He may not want plate blocks or full sheets of commemoratives issued within the past twenty years. Most dealers are well supplied with material of this nature and have opportunities to buy more of it every day. The same is true of first-day covers, with a few exceptions, issued from the 1960s to the present. The dealers either have these items abundantly or can get them from a wholesaler at rock-bottom prices. They would rather buy stamps that are a bit harder to get from the wholesalers, or for which the wholesalers charge higher prices. On the whole you will meet with a favorable reception when offering U.S. stamps to a local dealer. With foreign stamps it becomes another matter: what do you have and how flexible are you in price? Nearly all the stamp shops in this country do stock foreign stamps to one extent or another. They do not, as a rule, attempt to carry comprehensive or specialized stocks of them. In the average shop you will discover that the selection of general foreign consists of a combination of modern mint sets, topicals, souvenir sheets, packets which come from the wholesaler, and a small sprinkling of older material, usually pre-1900. The price range of this older material will be $5 to $50. Non-specialist collectors of foreign stamps buy this type of item and that is essentially who the local shop caters to. When a local dealer buys rare foreign stamps or a large foreign collection, it is not for himself. He buys with the intent of passing them along to another dealer who has the right customers lined up. He acts only as a middleman or go-between. Therefore the price you receive for better-grade foreign stamps tends to be lower than for better-grade U.S., which the dealer buys for his own use.

What is a fair price to get for your stamps? This is always difficult to say, as many variable factors are involved. Consider their condition. Think in terms of what the dealer could reasonably hope to charge for them at retail and stand a good chance of selling them. Some of your stamps may have to be discounted because of no gum, poor centering, bent perfs, hinge remnants, repairs, or other problems. But even if your stamps are primarily F or VF, a dealer cannot pay book values for them. If you check his selling prices on his specimens of those same stamps, you can usually count on receiving from 40 to 50 percent of those prices. Considering the discount made from book values by the dealer in pricing his stock, your payment may work out to about 25 percent of book values. For rare U.S. stamps in top condition you can do better than 25 percent, but on most stamps sold to a dealer this is considered a fair offer. Keep in mind that the difference between a dealer's buying and selling prices is not just "profit margin." Most of the markup goes toward operating costs, for without this markup, there would be no stamp dealers.

WHAT IS AN ERROR, FREAK,
OR ODDITY?

In an attempt to answer the questions above, an article, "Listing of Existing EFO Variations According to Group," by Mr. John M. Hotchner, was published originally in the June 1982 issue of *The EFO Collector,* the quarterly journal of the Errors, Freaks, Oddities Collectors Club. Resulting correspondence and experience in the EFO field, plus selected portions of Mr. Hotchner's article, are contained herein to attempt to provide some guidance as to what constitutes an error, freak, or oddity.

Nothing makes a philatelist's head turn so fast as an obvious error in an issued stamp. Many of philately's true blue-chip errors are from the early days. The United States 1869 inverts on the fifteen-cent, twenty-four-cent and thirty-cent values, Spain's 1851 two-real value in a six-real blue sheet, New South Wales stamps of the 1850s and '60s with the wrong watermark, etc.

Why? Most stamps of this era had relatively small printings compared to today's. In addition, they were used with little thought given to looking for or saving errors or misprints of lesser significance. Most of the varieties that have been found were used, and exist in very small quantities. Incidentally, this is a very good reason for one to keep one's eye open, for there remains a possibility that classic errors can still be found in old albums or accumulations.

In the early days of philately, collectors gathered EFOs (errors, freaks, oddities) to dress up their country or topical collections. Many modern collectors continue to collect EFOs in that fashion. There has, however, been a recent increase in collecting and studying EFOs as a specialty area.

Modern-day specialization has been fostered by the greatly increased awareness of and search for EFO material. This is a search which is often rewarded because of the increasing complexity of modern production equipment and the continuing pressure to reduce cost.

The lack of commonly accepted definitions of EFO terms has been an impediment to the growth of EFO philately. In the absence of a clear sense of what EFOs include, philatelists, in large numbers, have found the area complex and difficult. It has been hard to understand how values developed, so collectors merely kept what they came across, but rarely sought out EFO material unless it was listed in a catalog.

Catalog listing is, of course, reserved for errors. Catalog-listed errors get space in albums. Thus, recognized errors tend to have an increased value because collectors search for them because they like to fill their empty album spaces. Without a catalog listing, the remainder of EFO material tended to wallow in a valley of conflicting and confusing opinion and wildly varying prices. Also, if an item lacks catalog recognition, one might call the item a "freak," "oddity," or "variety."

The answer to an often-asked question regarding EFOs—"Aren't they expensive?"—is that while some EFOs are valued in the thousands of dollars, others cost no more than a regular used stamp. In fact, it is quite possible for one to find a spectacular EFO item in one's own mailbox. You have probably heard of collectors who bought stamps or postal stationery at their local post office only to find something wrong with the purchase. Think of some of the people who used their find before they realized they had an EFO item. Knowledge is the key to recognizing EFO material when you find it.

The best possible source of information and education can be obtained by becoming a member of a philatelic organization such as the American Philatelic Society (APS), The American Topical Association (ATA), etc.; by joining specialty groups such as the Bureau Issues Association (BIA), The Errors, Freaks, Oddities Collectors Club (EFOCC), etc.; by subscribing to publications such as Linn's, Meekels, *Stamp Collector*, etc.; by joining libraries such as the Cardinal Spellman Museum, the Western Philatelic Library, etc. Through these organizations and publications, one will obtain knowledge so that one can differentiate between what a postal entity designs and what is the produced product.

The following is the best tool, to date, to attempt to type EFO material that is at variance from the intended design.

ERRORS

To be classed as such, an item must be completely missing a production step, i.e. the item must be completely missing a color, completely missing required perforations, contain an inverted design step, etc. Other examples might be:

- Perforations entirely missing between stamps—one or more sides.

- Perforations fully doubled or tripled.

- Perforations of wrong gauge applied.

- Items unintentionally printed on paper watermarked for another issue, or not watermarked at all.

FREAKS

To be classed as such, an item might have a lesser degree of production problem, or problems that are partial and not repeatable. Examples might be:

- Perforations shifted into the design portion of an issue.
- Overinking, underinking, smeared inking.
- Foldovers, foldunders, creases creating crazy perforations.
- Printer's waste (by definition, "Unlawfully Salvaged"). This category would include rejection markings that indicate material that should have been destroyed.
- Gutter snipes (less than a full stamp on one side).

ODDITIES

"Oddities" or, as European collectors seem to favor, "Varieties" include unusual issuances. Examples might be:

- Stamps printed on backs of stamps.
- Usages (bisects).
- Essays, proofs, specimens.
- Cancel/meter varieties.
- Unusual local overprints.
- Double transfers, layout lines, position dots.
- Pre–first-day-of-issue cancels.

The bottom line is any item, be it freak, error, oddity, or variety, can be collected as a specialty, or a collector can try to obtain an example of each. Some collectors will restrict their collecting to one country, or even one major issue within a country. Others simply accumulate and enjoy anything they come across with no particular rhyme-or-reasoned order.

The Errors, Freaks, Oddities Collectors Club has an international membership, quarterly publication and mail auction, heir's assistance program, study groups, etc. Annual dues are $17 USD North America, $34 elsewhere. Sample copy of The EFO Collector is $3 USD.

Contact David Hunt
45 Fairway Drive
Denver, PA 17517
Email: dhhunt@ptdprolog.net
Website: www.efocc.org

PUBLICATIONS—
LINN'S STAMP NEWS

Linn's Stamp News is a magazine-size full-color newspaper for stamp and postal history collectors. It has been published continuously as a weekly since 1928. *Linn's* is the largest weekly publication in the stamp hobby.

Linn's carries news stories about new stamp issues of the United States, Canada and other countries; outstanding auctions and realizations; new discoveries of errors and other valuable stamps and covers; and developments in the U.S. Postal Service. It also contains the regular columns Asia, Great Britain, World Classics, U.S. Notes, Modern First-Day Covers, Kitchen Table Philately, Stamp Market Tips, Topics and Themes, World of New Issues, Computers and Stamps, Latin America, Who's Who on U.S. Stamps, Modern U.S. Mail, Postmark Pursuit, Cradle of Civilization, The Insider, and Postal History.

Regular departments include the Collectors Forum (question and answer page), Readers' Opinions (letters page), Refresher Course (collecting workshops for new and not-so-new collectors), Stamp Events Calendar, U.S. Stamp Market Index, Auction Calendar, the Editor's Column, Collecting Made Easy, Puzzle and Trickies.

Linn's U.S. Stamp Program is published each week and includes a schedule of U.S. new issues for the year, with details and USPS ordering numbers for each issue.

Stamp programs for Canada and the United Nations are also published regularly.

Linn's editorial staff comprises the best journalistic talent, from professional reportage to knowledge of stamp collecting. *Linn's* columnists and freelancers are among the best informed and well-connected people in the hobby.

Linn's contains full-page, display and classified ads from all areas of the collecting community: from the most prestigious auction houses the world over to individual collectors who want to sell or trade their duplicates—and everyone in between.

Linn's averages 64 pages a week. An annual subscription is $59.99 for print and digital version. Collectors can take advantage of a special offer of just $19.99 for a one-year digital edition subscription. To view a sample of *Linn's* digital edition, visit *Linn's* web site at www.linns.com. The web site also offers a How-To feature, reference information, special features, weekly headlines, marketplace, stamp quiz, the new issue of the week, stamp wallpaper for computers, and more.

Linn's also operates the online retail database Linn's Zillions of Stamps (www.zillionsofstamps.com), which allows collectors the convenience of shopping for U.S. and worldwide stamps, covers, and supplies at one online address.

THE NATIONAL POSTAL MUSEUM

The National Postal Museum, part of the Smithsonian Institution, was established in 1990 through an agreement between the Smithsonian Institution and the United States Postal Service. The museum opened to the public on July 30, 1993 in the historic City Post Office building adjacent to Union Station near the U.S. Capitol in Washington, DC.

The museum presently occupies 75,000 square feet, with 23,000 square feet devoted to exhibition space. The museum also houses a 6,000 square foot research library, a United States Postal Service philatelic retail store, and a museum gift shop. In September 2013 the museum will be expanded by 12,000 square feet of new exhibit space housed in the William H. Gross Stamp Gallery.

The National Postal Museum has the oldest and largest philatelic and postal history collection of any museum in the world and the second largest collection within the Smithsonian. The National Philatelic Collection contains more than six million postage and revenue stamps, stamped envelopes and postal stationery, rare and unique philatelic proofs and essays. The Postal History Collection features a wide range of objects related to the history of the post, including mailboxes, mail sorting equipment, patent models, and historic postal vehicles.

The museum features highly interactive rotating and permanent exhibitions and is noted for providing a fun, family-friendly educational experience for visitors of all ages. In addition to its many exhibits, the museum also offers a full range of public programs, lectures, and workshops and hosts numerous special events. The museum also has a general website along with an award-winning collections website (Arago) that offers special online exhibits, access to the collections and resources and information about the museum, stamps and stamp collecting, and the history of the post.

MISSION

The Smithsonian National Postal Museum, through its collection and library, is dedicated to the preservation, study, and presentation of postal history and philately. The museum uses research, exhibits, education, and public programs to make this rich history available to a wide and diverse audience.

VISION

The Smithsonian National Postal Museum will be a leading innovator in the museum community and the world's premiere postal museum, home to creative and authoritative exhibits, publications, and programs. A leader in education and research in both the physical and virtual environments, the museum will contribute to advancing the scholarship and practice of museums in the 21st century.

HISTORY

The National Postal Museum was made possible by an agreement between the Smithsonian and the United States Postal Service. The museum was established after lengthy negotiations about relocating the Smithsonian's vast postal history and philatelic collection of more than 16 million stamps, covers and artifacts. Previously housed on the third and fourth floors of the National Museum of American History, the collections lacked adequate exhibit, storage and research space in that location.

On November 6, 1990, the Smithsonian Institution and the U.S. Postal Service signed an agreement in which the Postal Service would provide the site and approximately $15.4 million for start-up and construction costs and the Smithsonian would administer the museum and its staff.

The National Postal Museum is funded by both the Postal Service and the Smithsonian, as well as by money raised from endowments and ongoing fund-raising campaigns. The Smithsonian contribution to the new museum has been the same as that spent on the collection when it was at the Museum of American History. The more than $3 million raised from private organizations through March 1993 went toward the installation of the new and expanding exhibits. Private funds continue to be used to develop and expand exhibits.

MOVING THE MAIL (Permanent Exhibit)

Faced with the challenge of moving mail quickly, efficiently and securely, the postal service has always looked toward new forms of transportation to deliver the mail. Mail delivery must serve everyone, whether they live in the middle of Alaska or at the bottom of the Grand Canyon. Throughout American postal history, advances in transportation have altered and streamlined the way our mail is moved. The National Postal Museum showcases a variety of means of mail transportation throughout history; our atrium is a 90-foot ceiling home to three airmail planes—including a de Havilland DH-4, the "workhorse of airmail service"—as well as a 1931 Ford Model A parcel post mail truck, reconstructed mail train car, dog sled and an 1850s stagecoach.

Networking a Nation: the Star Route Service: A new mail service established in 1845 allowed mail to be contracted out to private carriers, who expanded the delivery range by moving mail through a variety of creative methods that worked the best to fit the route—from canoes to tugboats; skis to sled dogs; wagons to motorcycles. These delivery routes became known as Star Routes, and they connected everyone through a universal mandate to deliver the mail. An 1851 Concord stagecoach, which carried mail under the driver's seat, is a museum highlight. Today, over 10,000 Star Route contractors deliver mail.

Airmail in America: The U.S. Airmail service played the leading role in the development of commercial aviation in the early 1900s. Flying the mail was risky business as aviation was still young, and crashes were common. Hanging in the atrium are Stinson Reliant, Wiseman Cooke and de Havilland planes.

Mail by Rail: Could you sort 600 pieces of mail in an hour? This was the demanding test that Railway Post Office clerks had to pass—with 97% accuracy—to be among the elite of postal service employees. From the 1870s to the 1940s, trains moved most of America's mail. Railway Mail Service revolutionized the way mail was processed; the mode of transportation system itself was the spine of mail processing as mail was sorted by moving trains, rather than stationary centers. Step inside the mail train car found in the museum's atrium, which was recreated by the National Postal Museum using interior fixtures from a de-commissioned rail car. Check out the beloved Owney, a scruffy mutt who became the mascot of the Railway Mail Service. Watch a video that recounts the history of mail by rail, as told by four ex-Railway Post Office clerks.

On the Road: Creating the perfect postal vehicle from scratch was a challenge for the postal service. Durability through a variety of different conditions and the ability to carry a large volume of letters would be key to a truck's success. Automobile mail wagons were tested for the first time in 1899, and dramatically increased mail collection and delivery speed. Now, the postal service's vehicular fleet is the largest in the world. The postal service's trademark white delivery vehicles are easily recognizable; we watch and wait as they bring us our share of the over 600 million pieces of mail processed in the U.S. each day.

BINDING THE NATION (Permanent Exhibit)

Binding the Nation is a permanent exhibit of the Smithsonian National Postal Museum that depicts mail service through the 18th and 19th centuries, from the nation's birth through the legendary yet romanticized Pony Express. The exhibit builds an appreciation for the speed and reliability of today's postal service while illustrating how transportation innovations and human endeavors overcame the hurdles of America's vast and geographically diverse land to bind the country through communication.

Starting the System: George Washington envisioned a nation bound together by a system of post roads and post offices. Binding the Nation addresses America's increasing need for a mail system to ensure the free flow of information between citizens and their government. The exhibit documents the establishment of the U.S. postal system after the successes and failures of the British-run colonial post, and details how the post spread both mail and people across the continent as the government acquired new territory.

Early postal delivery bound Americans together via wooded paths, and eventually roads and waterways as new territories and states added on to the colonies. Exhibit visitors learn the origins of U.S. Route 1 as an early post road where taverns doubled as makeshift post offices. America's postal service was a revolutionary key that opened the door to an independent nation—one with a sense of common destiny that was united against European counterparts who ruled from afar. Notable elements of the exhibit include chronicles of Benjamin Franklin's strides as postmaster for the colonies, the role of newspapers for dissemination of information in early mail exchange, delivery during westward expansion and the gold rush, and the myths and realities of the Pony Express.

Exhibit highlights: Binding the Nation provides a multisensory museum experience as visitors travel through the woods, step on creaky tavern floors, and climb aboard a replica of a mud wagon. Visitors immerse themselves in American history while reading letters written by settlers in the 1800s, or by playing Post-Haste, an interactive surface table game that challenges visitors to deliver the mail quickly, cheaply and safely by choosing routes and transportation.

CUSTOMERS AND COMMUNITIES (Permanent Exhibit)

The Customers and Communities exhibit focuses on the innovations that altered mail delivery to vastly expanding urban and rural populations, including free delivery service and a multitude of transportation vehicles. The gallery highlights the challenges that postal workers faced at the turn of the 20th century to ensure letters were delivered to their recipients.

A cobblestone entryway and mail screen wagon transport exhibit visitors to the busting streets of early urban America. The postal service was challenged with a transition from delivering a few letters over thousands of miles, to thousands of letters over just a few miles. Motorcars, mail chutes, and mailboxes were just some of the key urban developments that made it possible for postal workers to handle new heights of mail volume as millions of newcomers surged into cities in the 1880s. A colorful diorama and displays highlighting letter carriers of the time demonstrate the inventive little ways postal workers solved big problems.

Visitors can listen to letters written by immigrants in their native language to develop a sense of the diversity of postal customers, who used international mail to overcome geographical distances between family members and friends.

Rural Free Delivery: In the country, long distances and harsh conditions created hurdles to regular mail service for rural America. Today, daily mail service is taken for granted. Rural Americans waited much longer than city dwellers before they were able to enjoy free home mail delivery. Beginning in 1896, free delivery service helped put isolated rural Americans in better touch with the world and instilled a sense of community in countryside locations that is found across America more than 100 years later.

Featured in the exhibit is a small-town post office that prevailed in Dillsburg, Pennsylvania from 1917 to 1971. For many rural Americans, the post office was the heart of the community. The role of the local post office is relevant for many Americans today as more and more post offices are closing their doors.

Object highlights in Customers and Communities include a wooden door knocker, pneumatic mail tube, and the Dillsburg post office.

MAIL CALL (Permanent Exhibit)

Mail Call is a permanent exhibit of the Smithsonian National Postal Museum that explores the history of America's military postal system. Visitors can discover how military mail communication has changed throughout history, learn about the armed forces postal system from the American Revolution to the present day, and experience military mail through artifacts and letters.

Mail has always played an important role in the lives of our troops and their families at home. Writing and receiving correspondence has a significant power in shaping morale; this relationship is expressed time and again in messages from deployed military personnel, and is a compelling reason behind the effort to maintain timely mail service. Mail Call offers an appreciation of the importance of military mail and the hard work that has gone into connecting service men and women to the world they have temporarily left behind.

The exhibit explores how the military postal system works as well as the innovations in technology, organization, and transportation methods that have changed the way military mail has been delivered over time. Adaptability has been key for military post offices in the field, which try to replicate the ones here at home. One constant remains—military mail is high priority because it provides members of the armed forces with a vital link to their communities. When members of the armed forces are sent overseas, the mail system allows them to continue their daily lives through communication, paying taxes, and voting.

Object highlights that bring the story of military mail to life include a camouflaged bag used to drop letters from helicopters during the Vietnam War and a postal handstamp recovered from the USS Oklahoma, which sank during the 1941 Pearl Harbor attack. Don't miss the souvenir coconut mailed from Hawaii to Massachusetts in 1944.

Mail Call shows how mail delivery to troops has overcome obstacles during times of adversity. The military mail service has required the coordinated efforts of the post office and the armed forces. In the current system, the Postal Service is responsible for moving the mail within the United States while the Department of Defense manages transportation abroad and the operation of overseas military post offices.

POSTAL INSPECTORS: THE SILENT SERVICE (Permanent Exhibit)

Postal Inspectors: the Silent Service highlights the crime lab aspects as well as the history of the postal inspection service while demonstrating the challenges surrounding the changes in what it takes to keep the U.S. mail safe, secure and private. The role of Postal Inspectors has evolved from protecting stagecoaches to preventing the spread of anthrax to ensure that postal customers can trust what's coming and going from their homes.

Over 40 percent of the world's mail passes through the United States mail system. With a structure that connects millions of people, including businesses to their customers and the government to its citizens, it's no wonder scam artists and criminals are tempted to use mail for illegal means.

U.S. Postal Inspectors protect the mail and the postal system and investigate crimes against mail including biohazards and financial, identity and security frauds. As one of the oldest federal law enforcement agencies in the country dating back to the postal surveyors of 1776, their role as evolved from ensuring successful and secure transportation of mail to playing a part in law enforcement and criminal investigations.

Vibrant stories of train robberies and mail thieves, mail bombers and anthrax mailings, and how the famous Hope Diamond was delivered to the Smithsonian Institution through registered mail are featured in the exhibit.

Can you solve the case? Postal inspectors and lab technicians use technology, skills and experience to help them solve postal crimes. In this exhibit, visitors can try their hand at identifying suspicious packages, reading fingerprints, analyzing handwriting, recognizing fugitives from wanted profiles, and more.

Learn how to protect yourself from mail crimes, including identity theft and consumer fraud, as well as how Postal Inspectors continue to serve the U.S. through their historic duties behind the scenes today.

Object highlights in Postal Inspectors: the Silent Service include handcuffs used on the infamous Unabomber, a knife made of human bone and a hidden camera.

SYSTEMS AT WORK (Permanent Exhibit)

While the very question of the postal service's survival is a hotly debated topic among Americans, few understand how the service operates. Systems at Work brings visitors into the core operating systems of the nation's postal service. What happens after a letter or package is handed over to the postal service? How does mail reach Americans both at home and at the office? The answers to these questions unfold in Systems at Work.

Exhibit highlights include a 270-degree film experience that puts visitors into the middle of the mammoth world of a mail-processing center, as well as ample opportunities to interact with postal history by tossing packages into mail pouches as clerks did in 1917, engaging handheld intelligent mail devices to scan barcodes, and more. Visitors also receive a postcard to gather cancellation marks from various eras to take away from the exhibit. Object highlights include first African-American postmaster John T. Jackson's distribution case, a Parcel Post crate for mailing eggs, a 19th century Peerless letter scale, and replica of a Wide Field of View camera that can read barcodes and even handwriting from four pieces of mail at a time.

Mail volume peaked at an annual rate of over 212 billion pieces in 2007. The U.S. Postal Service is working to position itself to continue its mandate to provide mail to everyone among a host of challenges. While mail volume drops, the number of delivery addresses grows, creating a financial Catch-22 for a service that relies on postage funds for financing. The Postal Service, as the nation's largest mail carrier, reaches all homes and businesses with the help of contracted private carriers who deliver items to millions of addresses outside of delivery zones.

Roughly 700 million pieces of mail are sorted and delivered to 150 million addresses each day. Delivery service depends on an astonishing network of people and technology that collects, carries, sorts, and delivers the mail. Visitors come to understand and appreciate the intricacy and efficiency of mail delivery by following the evolution of this system through America's history.

Systems at Work recreates the paths of letters, magazines, parcels, and other mail as they've traveled from sender to recipient over the last 200 years, while revealing the Postal Service's continuous history of implementing new technologies and processes. In 1808, a newspaper carries the latest news to people hundreds of miles away. Half a century later, a letter delivers news from a mother to her son stationed in the southwest. In the 1930s, a crate of eggs journeys from Seattle, Washington, to Alaska. These examples and many others offer a behind-the-scenes look at the inner workings of the postal system through time.

By the end of Systems at Work, visitors will have taken a journey through time and technologies—from post riders to airplanes; cubbyholes to computers—and may see the connections between mail, technology, engineering, the Internet, and their own lives in a new light.

WILLIAM H. GROSS STAMP GALLERY (Permanent Exhibit Opening September 22, 2013)

Named after its primary benefactor, the William H. Gross Stamp Gallery is the world's largest gallery dedicated to philately. It provides an experience available nowhere else and offers something for everyone, from casual visitors to experienced collectors.

As visitors move through six thematic areas, stunning displays and interactive moments reveal the amazing stories that unfold from the museum's unparalleled collection. Distributed throughout the thematic areas are hundreds of pullout frames containing more than 20,000 objects, providing ample opportunities to view noteworthy stamps that have never been on public display.

FIRE & ICE: HINDENBURG AND TITANIC (Temporary Exhibit: March 22, 2012 – January 6, 2014)

As the largest, fastest, and most glamorous ships of their eras, Hindenburg and Titanic share many similarities. As anniversaries of the disasters are marked in 2012—seventy-five years since Hindenburg burned and a century since Titanic sank—many questions remain unanswered. Original objects include mail, postcards, menus, photographs, keys from the Titanic post office, and the salvaged postmark device from the Hindenburg.

ALPHABETELATELY (Temporary Exhibit: September 26, 2008 – January 31, 2014)

This exhibition presents an alphabet of philately through twenty-six topics, in which each letter stands for some aspect of stamp collecting or the sending of mail.

CONNECT WITH THE NATIONAL POSTAL MUSEUM

Museum Main Website (www.npm.si.edu)

the main website provides access to information about the museum and all of the fascinating and wonderful things that it has to offer.

Arago Website (www.arago.si.edu)

Arago, the museum's award-winning collections website presents the collections in a context-rich setting with full color images and zoom-in capability.

Postmark e-Newsletter (www.npm.si.edu)

Subscribe to the National Postal Museum's FREE monthly e-newsletter—Postmark, highlighting the treasures of the museum.

Museum Blog (www.postalmuseumblog.si.edu)

The museum's Blog is dedicated to sharing behind-the-scenes stories, thoughts, and interesting discussion about our museum and our renowned collection.

Facebook (www.facebook.com/SmithsonianNationalPostalMuseum)

The museum's Facebook page shares the latest information from the museum and all things postal. Stay in the loop and join the conversation!

Twitter (www.twitter.com/PostalMuseum)

The Smithsonian National Postal Museum tweets about public programs and other cool stuff going on at the museum.

YouTube (www.youtube.com/user/SmithsonianNPM)

On the museum's YouTube channel you can enjoy a portfolio of the Museum's videos which include exhibit videos, historical footage, lectures and special features.

THE AMERICAN
PHILATELIC SOCIETY

Founded in 1886 the American Philatelic Society (APS) is a nonprofit association for stamp collectors, which seeks to promote the hobby and serve its members. The 34,000+ member organization is run by a full-time staff of thirty-three and is guided by a volunteer Board of Directors elected by the members.

Whether you are a beginning collector or have collected for years, the APS offers many services and educational opportunities to enhance your collecting enjoyment—including a subscription to *The American Philatelist.* The full-color one hundred page monthly magazine features articles written by members on all aspects of stamp collecting, information on U.S. news issues, hobby related websites, Society news, a calendar of upcoming stamp shows and exhibitions around the world.

The APS Sales Division provides an opportunity for collectors to buy or sell stamps from each other through the mail. Members may request "circuits" of stamps or covers from more than 160 categories of countries and topics. The items are priced by the submitting members, and most range from under $1 to $20. The APS also offers items for sale at our online StampsStore, www.stampstore.org. Anyone may browse the 300,000+ items, but buying and/or selling is a privilege of membership. The online store features some rarities and more expensive stamps in addition to the many modestly priced items.

Another popular service offered by the APS is the insurance program, which allows for the purchase of $8,500 in coverage for only $25 per year. Unlike most riders to homeowner policies, the standard Society insurance includes no deductible and requires no appraisal or inventory (except for individual items valued at $25,000 or more).

In addition to the APS, the American Philatelic Center, located in Bellefonte, Pennsylvania, also houses the American Philatelic Research Library (APRL). The APRL is the largest public philatelic library in the United States with more than two miles of books, catalogues, auction listings, journals, dealer price lists, indexes, research papers of famous collectors, and other materials. The materials in the library are supplemented by the Society's Reference Collection of genuine and fake postage stamps.

More than 6,000 items are submitted for authentication to the Society's Expertizing service each year. For as little as $25 an item, a member can receive a guaranteed opinion on the genuineness of their stamp or cover. This Society service has been a forerunner in the use of technological equipment employing the use of a Crimescope and other scientific analysis to assist personal expert evaluation.

Other APS services include estate advice, a translation service, an annual stamp show, a website at www.stamps.org to assist all collectors, even nonmembers, and much more!

MEMBERSHIP INFORMATION

Membership dues are just $48 per year. Our membership year runs from January 1 through December 31. New members applying will have their first year's dues prorated based on the quarter in which their application is received. A one-time $3 application fee is required.

More information on the American Philatelic Society is available from www.stamps.org, or by calling 814-933-3803 or writing to APS Dept. BB, 100 Match Factory Place, Bellefonte, PA 16823.

We Invite you to join in the fun!

LOCAL STAMP CLUBS

Numerous local stamp clubs exist all across the country, far too many to mention individually. Most hold regular meetings, often featuring presentations or slide programs by established collectors, and many permit trading sessions, an activity enjoyed by all. Newcomers, especially, find local stamp clubs useful in enriching their understanding and appreciation of the hobby. Some, either individually or in concert with other local clubs, sponsor annual stamp shows that feature exhibits as well as a dealer bourse.

Many local clubs are chapters of the American Philatelic Society. The APS Chapter Activities Committee serves as a focal point for services available to local stamp clubs. The committee publishes a quarterly newsletter, sponsors a publications contest, and conducts other programs for local clubs. APS chapters may schedule APS Sales Division circuits and philatelic slide programs produced by the Society exclusively for use by chapters for their meetings. Information about local APS chapters can be obtained from the APS, 100 Match Factory Place, Bellefonte, PA 16823; (814) 933-3803; or on the APS Web site www.stamps.org.

Information about local clubs that are not APS chapters often can be obtained by checking with a local stamp dealer or clerk in the nearest Postal Service philatelic center.

The Blackbooks!

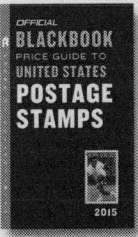